THE DEATH OF THE AMERICAN CORPORATION

THE PSYCHOLOGY OF GREED AND DESTRUCTIVENESS AMONG CEO'S AND BANKERS

*"The world holds enough to satisfy everyone's need but not everyone's **greed**." Mahatma Gandhi*

I would like to thank my loving wife Giovanna for her patience and thoughtfulness. Its good to be married to a theologian. And to my four Gen Y daughters I would like to thank them for their love and inspiration.

Copyright © 2012 by William Czander
All rights reserved.

ISBN: 0-615-41415-X
ISBN-13: 978-0-615-41415-7

Cover art by Dan shefelman

PRÉCIS

Just as one can destroy one's health, marriage, career, etc., CEOs and bankers can engage in behaviors and decisions that destroy the corporation they lead. For almost 25 years corporate America has resembled the Wild West. CEOs and their executives, Wall Street bankers, and others have been quietly engaged in terminating millions of jobs, stealing pensions, breaking up companies, committing fraud, outsourcing, and engaging in incomprehensible risk taking, all for the purpose of personal gain. It was blatant greed. And like most feeding frenzies it got out of control. Now, thanks to the greed demonstrated by executives at AIG, Merrill Lynch, Lehman and hundreds of other companies, Main Street America is finally outraged. It's as if Congress, journalists, pundits and even scholars have discovered that executives and bankers were cheating the system, and even in the midst of the present furor over pay, performance and bailouts, they cannot stop the greed, causing further outrage. We suggest that CEO greed has not only destroyed the American corporation, but it is responsible for the financial crises and a climate of mistrust that will take years if not decades to restore.

We begin by explaining the scope of the CEO pay problem and what business schools did for the past 20 years to create the type of thinking that facilitates a culture of greed. In addition, we explore how CEOs engaged in an array of decisions that destroyed the employee-employer compact, destroyed customer service, outsourced and made themselves and stockholders wealthy. We then explain the psychological motivation to engage in unthinkable greed and how the tremendous effort an executive makes climbing the corporate ladder and then staying there leads to a psychological state of entitlement, guilt, and depersonalization in which the CEO looses empathy and greed takes over as a defense. We then examine the nature of these problematic executive constellation cultures that become breeding grounds for greed, hubris and destruction. We discuss the psychology of the destruction of Lehman Brothers and then conduct an in-depth analysis of one of the most celebrated CEOs accused of greed and destructiveness, Bob Nardelli the former CEO of Home Depot. This follows with a discussion of the new generation of employees, the Gen Ys, who will contribute to the demise of the American Corporation as we know it. The book ends with a discussion of what needs to be done to end unemployment and the growing gap between the rich and the poor. An extensive appendix presents the actual misdeeds and greedy acts of hundreds of CEOs.

BIO

William Czander has taught in MBA programs for over 35 years and is a member of a unique group of scholars and practitioners called organizational psychoanalysts. He has consulted to organizations and treated executives since 1980. In 2002 he left full-time teaching to join Home Depot and spent almost 4 years observing a CEO destroy a once proud corporate culture. He witnessed firsthand how and why contemporary corporate leaders destroy commitment, how the life of becoming and then being an executive places an enormous psychological burden and often leads to decision making that to an outsider appears irrational but inside the executive constellation is normal and right. His years in business schools have given him insight into how young managers are trained and educated, and how faculty collude in creating the "bottom line" executive, where responsibility and empathy is replaced with entitlement and greed. He gives numerous examples of how executives are driven to destroy a company while enriching themselves.

He maintains that the enactment of laws, blaming, and yelling will not stop this executive behavior. At the rate they are going, these executives will destroy corporate America as we know it unless we engage in a radical transformation in how we select, govern, educate, and train our corporate leaders.

He is retired and occasionally teaches and has a private practice in Irvington, N.Y. He serves on the faculty at the following institutions: Fordham University Graduate School of Business, LIM College MBA Program, St. Thomas Aquinas Graduate School of Business, Thomas

Edison State and St. Mary's University College at the Mountbatten Institute.

He graduated Phi Beta Kappa from CCNY, holds a Ph.D. from NYU and completed two Postdoc's; at the Institute for Social and Policy Studies, Yale and the Postgraduate Center for Mental Health in Psychoanalysis. He has written three books and many articles on work, leadership and mental health.

THE DEATH OF THE AMERICAN CORPORATION

THE PSYCHOLOGY OF GREED AND DESTRUCTIVENESS AMONG CEO'S AND BANKERS

WILLIAM CZANDER, PH.D.

TABLE OF CONTENTS

Introduction i

Chapter 1 The Problem 1

Chapter 2 The Business Schools: The Evolution of Managerial Greed ... 51

Chapter 3 No Need for Employee Morale: Destroy the "Social Contract" Between Capital and Labor and CEOs Get Rich ... 119

Chapter 4 The Performance Review: Creating a Culture of Intimidation 153

Chapter 5 Lack of Commitment, the Quants and the Financial Crisis ... 203

Chapter 6 Development of the Executive Type: Becoming a CEO ... 219

Chapter 7 The CEO: Life at the Top 239

Chapter 8 The Power of Guilt: Entitlement, a Defense Against the Experience of Guilt and Shame 261

Chapter 9 Depersonalization: The Psychology of Entitlement 281

Chapter 10 Narcissism as a Cultural Phenomenon: Occupational Narcissism 297

Chapter 11 Why Wall Street and the Banks Failed: The Psychology of Self-Destruction 325

Chapter 12 Nardelli and Home Depot 365

Chapter 13 Gen Ys and the Future of the Corporation 409

Chapter 14 Conclusion: What We Need 479

Notes 527

APPENDICES

A. The Compensation Problem 531
B. The Stuff They Get 538
C. Women Join in 543
D. The Wall Street Gang 544
E. The Heath Care Gang 546
F. The Educators 561
G. The Charites and the Chosen Ones......................................565
H. The Long List-Performance Review for You Not for Me 568
I. Obscene Retirement Packages 606
J. Parachutes, Handshakes, Sendoffs, Hellos-:They're All Golden ..610
K. The Golden Boot 617
L. The Benefits of Mergers and Acquisitions 620
M. Terminate Your Employees and Get a Bonus 627
N. Fail and Get a Bonus 642
O. Kill the Unions and Get Rich 651
P. Pay Me More 654
Q. The Airline Industry-Stealing Pensions and More 655
R. Terminate Your Employees and Get a Raise 660
S. Terminate Employees and Run for Cover 680
T. Get Bailed Out and Get a Raise..683
U. The Boy Scouts and Other Nonprofit Agencies 685
V. The Golden Coffins 687
W. The Reason Food Prices Are Rising.....................................688
X. Want To Get Rich? Open a For-Profit School.......................699
Y. The Energy Boys 707
Z. Madness at HP..715
Z.1. Government Employees Become Multimillionaires 724
References 727

INTRODUCTION

Most CEOs have gone to business school and work closely with others who have taken classes in organizational and/or industrial psychology. They are familiar with the research exploring the negative consequences of salary inequity and the relationship between performance and pay. However, they continue to take entitlement to a level where they are accused collectively of gross insensitivity, greed, and culpability in the 2008 Wall Street meltdown, the financial crises, and loss of millions of jobs. While criticism abounds, there is very little understanding of CEO behavior, especially a deep understanding of the how the process of becoming a CEO and the work of leading a corporation can culminate into the motivation to reward oneself with apparent disregard to performance, employees, customers, or the corporation they lead.

According to Frydman and Molloy (2011) the decades following the second World War were high-growth decades and executive pay grew at a rate lower than the pace of corporate expansion. But after 1980 things changed and executive compensation expanded at the same rate as corporate expansion. In the beginning of 2000 executive pay continued to grow but it was not related to corporate expansion. Evidence began to turn up suggesting that executive pay was related to job terminations, that is, executives who terminated employees received greater compensation increases than those who did not terminate employees.

In this book, we will examine this phenomenon and explore the changes that have occurred in American corporations over the last 30 years, where CEOs have destroyed employee commitment and took risks seeking exorbitant short term profits to such a degree that they have put the American corporation and the American economy in dire straits.

The attempt to understand this phenomenal change in corporate leadership begins with an assessment of the education they gained in business schools, then explores the ambitious work of climbing the corporate ladder, and then analyzes of the culture in the executive suite, where some executives destroyed the very corporations they have been chose to lead.

The attempt to understand this phenomenal change in corporate leadership begins with an assessment of the education they gained in business schools, then explores the ambitious work of climbing the corporate ladder, and then analyzes of the culture in the executive suite, where some executives destroyed the very corporations they have been chose to lead.

In psychoanalytic circles greed and entitlement has been thoroughly explored. Many psychoanalysts maintain that intense ambition is associated with greed. In this book, we examine how greed evolves from the interplay of intense ambition, and how the processes of becoming an executive influences behaviors in the executive suite. We examine the phenomena of depersonalized entitlement which evolves as a defense against greed and the resulting feelings of shame associated with executive decisions and the need to "get more." We will then examine the destructive outcomes of corporate greed and how it triggers a type of thinking that undermines corporate success leading to corporate and personal failure. We will offer an in-depth study of a CEO who made several destructive decisions while becoming exceedingly wealthy. And, finally we will explore the changing nature of the corporation that will be brought about by a generation of employees now entering the workforce.

CHAPTER 1

The Problem

"A capitalist under penalty of his own destruction, *must strive to accumulate wealth*" (Fenichel 1938, p.37 italics in original)

Medieval theologian Thomas Aquinas said of greed: "It is a sin directly against one's neighbor, since one man cannot over-abound in external riches, without another man lacking them...." (2, 118, ad 1)

"There's class warfare, all right, but it's my class,

the rich class, that's making war, and we're winning."

Warren Buffett, CEO of Berkshire Hathaway

CORPORATE AMERICA

Let's look at what is occurring in America since 2008:

1. The consolidation of wealth in the hands of a few continues.

2. The prospect of continuous wars drains the economy and provides wealth to those who are connected to government.

3. Outsourcing of jobs and entire industries like manufacturing, service, and finance continue at an unprecedented pace.

4. Direct government support is continuing to grow as enormous numbers of baby boomers retire.

5. Climate change continues to wreak havoc with the coastal regions and parts of the Midwest.

6. The cost of health care continues to rise and the numbers of uninsured are dramatically increasing.

7. Higher education continues to decline as affordability causes families to stay away, at the same time as public institutions experience drastic cutbacks in government funding.

8. The cost of energy continues to increase the price of transportation and consumer products.

9. The price of goods made abroad continues to increase as developing countries become industrialized.

10. Government bailouts of industries continue amid an increase in antitrust regulation, licensing laws, environmental laws, subsidies to corporate farms and others, along with eminent domain.

11. Government continues to take an increasing role in employment, as the banks and financial service industries go the route of manufacturing and outsource and off shore their services.

12. Retail and manufacturing continues to cutback significantly as consumers reduce their spending.

13. Newsprint and books become obsolete as electronic communication grows.

14. The home building industry continues to collapse as home prices fall, credit tightens, and foreclosures increase.

15. Automotive and other transportation industries continue to struggle as the cost of energy continues to climb and consumers struggle to afford expensive, energy-efficient vehicles.

16. Foreign investment in America and its corporations will continue for the short run, but as profitability decreases, in the long run the pulling out of foreign investment will cripple the American currency, and destroy most corporations.

17. Banks and other financial institutions are closing.

18. The credit card, once called the vehicle of consumer debt is in trouble, as credit card companies wrote off $45 billion in bad debt in 2008, and $90 billion in 2009.

19. Towns and cities are filing for bankruptcy as the tax base declines, taxpayers revolt against rising property taxes and government employee pensions that eat up large amounts of tax revenue.

20. Corporations are continuing to decline to offer benefits, and are moving employees into part-time and contractor positions.

21. The gap between the rich and poor is continuing to grow.

These factors, and perhaps others, will push corporations as we know it towards extinction.

THE INCOME GAP IN AMERICA

Up until the 1980s the entire workforce in America experienced slow but equitable economic growth. Since 1919, the wage gap between the top 1 percent and the rest of the workforce basically remained stable. The gap that had been created during the Victorian era with entrepreneurial moguls at the top and the working poor at the bottom began to disappear as unions pushed for higher wages for the working class and the educated professionals grew in numbers. However, in the early 1980s, the gap between this richest 1 percent and the rest of the workforce grew significantly.

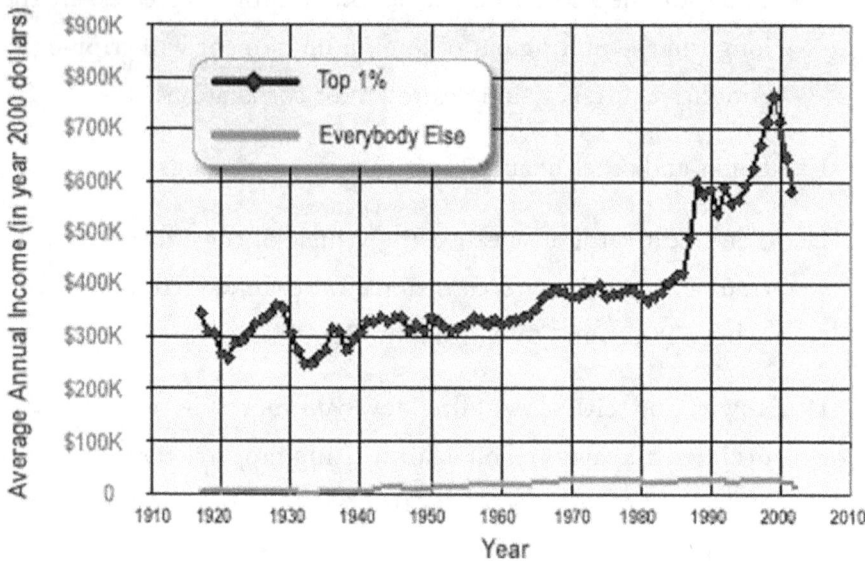

Source AFL-CIO – Emmanuel Saez, University of California, Berkeley, Department of Economics

The disparities between rich and middle and poor, ballooned accordingly. In 1979, the top 1 percent averaged eight times more in earnings than middle-income families and 23 times more than the poorest 20 percent. By 2005, this top 1 percent earned on average 21 times the income of middle-income families and 70 times the average income of the poorest 20 percent. In 2007 the 400 highest-earning households in America saw their income increase 31 percent from 2006, and since 2001 their income doubled and their tax contributions dropped. What was the annual income of this elite group? Some $345 million (Bloomberg News, 2010).

In the past 25 years the definition of wealth has undergone a significant change. In 1982, the first year of the Forbes wealthiest 400 list, it took about $159 million in today's dollars to make the list; in 2008, the minimum amount of wealth needed to make the list was $1.3 billion, (Arango & Creswell, 2008).

This meant that in the last 25 years, the average income of the top layer more than tripled, rising 228 percent from $319,000 to $1.1 million. During the same period, the average income of the poorest fifth grew only 6 percent and the average income of the middle fifth grew 21 percent, less than 1 percent a year. In recent years this gap has been growing at a faster pace. For example from 2003 to 2005, the average household in the top 1 percent enjoyed an increase of $465,700 in annual income; while the average household in the bottom 20 percent saw an increase of only $200, and those in the middle fifth saw a rise of just $2,400.

A Congressional Budget Office report provided other metrics for gauging the staggering growth of economic inequality. The total 2005 income of the top 3 million Americans was equivalent to the total income of the bottom 166 million.

CLASS WARFARE

As aggregate wealth in America increased, like a giant vacuum, or what Taibbi (2010), called the "Giant Vampire Squid," those at the top sucked money from those beneath them on the economic ladder. In 2010, the wealthiest 20 percent of the population now collected 55 percent of total annual national income, more than the total combined income of the bottom 80 percent. This is the highest such figure ever recorded in American history. Norton and Ariely, in Bookman (2010) maintained that the richest 20 percent controlled 84 percent of the nation's wealth, while the poorest 40 percent of households controlled a paltry 0.3 percent. This is another "gilded age." But unlike the gilded age at the turn of the 20th century this gilded age, 100 years later, does not mark the birth of modern America, but instead the opposite, it marks the beginning of the death of modern America. These barons of the second gilded age were very different than the barons of the earlier age. They did not accumulate their great wealth by building and industrializing this once great country. No. They have benefited by destroying it. This is why those in the bottom 80 percent are both frightened and outraged. Their outrage is manifested in the Occupy Wall Street movement in Manhattan, which has mushroomed into hundreds of towns and cities across America and in over 80 countries. The message is clear: Gilded Age II barons, do not practice what everyone should have learned in kindergarten- Share. These barons do not want to share. They want all the toys and their $36,000 per day income to go untaxed. These barons want the bottom 80 percent to pay the taxes, work for minimum wage and pay their own benefits. And smile.

In the last 30 years CEOs have come to believe employees work for outstanding CEOs, not outstanding companies. Executives saw their job as doing whatever it takes, cost-cutting, outsourcing, off shoring, to make lots of money for stockholders and Wall Street, and in the process become a wealthy celebrity CEO. Where did they learn these values? In business school, where they also learned the function of business is to make money and there is no profit in social responsibility. Employees and then Main Street came to see these executives as socially irresponsible and unethical. They saw their politicians as hacks for the corporate lobbyists, and trust vanished. Contemporary executives gained a Weltanschauung that's a mixture of positive thinking, ideological "right wing" conservatism, religious fundamentalism, Ayn Rand philosophy, and happiness psychologists. This promoted an attitude of blind optimism, entitlement and a demand that all their employees put on a happy-face and be thankful they have such a wonderful CEO.

IT'S THE GAP, STUPID.

What lay at the base of Main Street rage, both progressives and tea partyies? The income gap. A recent report by the International Monetary Fund suggests that the current economic crisis, the worst in almost a century, was caused by fancy financial instruments, government intervention in the housing market and Wall Street greed. They suggest that an even more significant contributor to the global brush with economic depression resulted from the colossal gap in incomes between rich, working Americans and the poor. This sadly obscure paper argues that a dramatic concentration in wealth at the top—at levels not seen anywhere else in the industrialized world—created a fundamental imbalance that brought the entire system down on itself. The document shows that the origins of America's last financial implosion, in 1929, were almost identical to those of 2008. In both cases, income inequality was the culprit. And even in the collapse's wake, the chasm between the top 10 percent and the remaining 90 percent appears to be widening further.

WHAT IS THIS GROWING GAP ATTRIBUTED TO? THE NEW MANAGERIAL CLASS

The gap is the result of the colossal growth in compensation among America's CEOs and financial executives and the tying of their compensation to stock awards. Bakija, Cole, and Heim (2010) confirm this through an exhaustive study of the occupations of the top 0.1 percent between 1979 and 2005. Based on information reported on U.S. individual income tax returns they discovered that executives, managers, supervisors, and financial professionals account for about 60 percent of the top 0.1 percent of income earners and can account for 70 percent of the increase in the share of national income going to the top

0.1 percent of the income distributed between 1979 and 2005. This has contributed to an inflated and volatile Wall Street and transformed American socio-economic structure. During this period, the share of national income taken by the top 0.1 percent has quadrupled, rising from 2.5 percent of national income in 1975 to 10.4 percent in 2008. The share commanded by the top 0.01 percent quintupled, soaring from 0.85 percent to 5.03 percent during that same period of time. In raw numbers, that means approximately 15,000 people, the richest of the rich, rake in an average annual income of $27 million. The study maintains that ever-rising pay and perks of corporate CEOs are the principal driver of this widening economic inequality. CEO pay quadrupled during the past 35 years, dovetailing with the increase in the incomes of the top 0.1 percent. While executives and managers comprised 60 percent of these top 140,000 taxpayers, they accounted for 70 percent of the income gain enjoyed by this super-rich stratum over the past 35 years.

What are the consequences of this growing gap between the rich and poor? Story (2010) suggests that income disparities before the crisis of 1929 and 2008 were strikingly similar and were the greatest in approximately the last 100 years. She says, "In 1928, the top 10 percent of earners received 49.29 percent of total income. In 2007, the top 10 percent earned a strikingly similar percentage: 49.74 percent. In 1928, the top 1 percent received 23.94 percent of income. In 2007, those earners received 23.5 percent." This suggests that when the rich are lining their pockets they may be doing so at the expense of the poor. In 2011 we witness ample evidence of executives and stockholders benefiting from outsourcing, off shoring and other cost-cutting activities as increasing numbers of the American workers lost their jobs and the ranks of the poor swelled. Income inequality in America is greater than Egypt's and closer to that of developing countries like Africa's Cote d'Ivoire and Central America's Nicaragua. The 2011 revolution in Egypt and the toppling of Hosni Mubarak's 30-year reign as president was the result of growing income inequality and rising prices for basic food.

GROWING SALARY INEQUITY – CEO PAY

In 1965 the difference between CEO earnings and the average American salary was a multiple of 24. On 1970 the average CEO compensation was 39 times what front-line workers were making annually. In 1989 it was 71 times: in 1995, 100 times, and in 2005 it rose to between 400 and 500 times the average front-line worker's pay. During the 1990s, CEO pay increased by 571 percent while the average worker's pay grew by 37 percent. A typical Fortune 500 CEO makes more in one day than what a rank and file worker makes in a year.

Consider banking CEOs. In 1989 their average total compensation of $2.8 million was 97 times the U.S. median household income ($28,906). By 2007 the top six bank holding company CEOs were earning an average of $26 million, which was 516 times the U.S. median household income ($50,233).

(To read more about the compensation problem go to Appendix A)

THE COMPENSATION PROBLEM IS AN AMERICAN PHENOMENON

The enormous gap in compensation between the average worker and CEO appears to be uniquely American phenomenon. For example in Japan in 2006, a typical executive made 11 times what a typical worker brought home. Hiroshi Okuda, the CEO of Toyota, earned $903,000 in 2006 and Mitsubishi CEO Shigemitsu Miki earned $360,000, while Rick Wagoner, CEO of General Motors, earned $10.19 million in 2006.

Like the United States, the Japanese government requires corporations to disclose compensation on executives but only those who earn Y100 million ($1.1 million) and above. In the year ending March 2009, only 8.3 percent of Japanese CEOs were paid above that mark. Toyota does not have to report executive compensation because it paid a total of $15.7 million to its top 38 executives, an average of $413,000. The sum total compensation for these 38 executives does not equal a single American auto CEO's annual compensation. In 2010 the CEO of Toyota received compensation worth $2.5 million while Ford Motor Company CEO Alan Mulally made more than $26.5 million in salary and stock options. In 2009 Japan Airlines CEO Haruka Nishimatsu's salary was less than his pilots', with no perks. He rode public transit to the office and ate in the employee cafeteria and stood in line like all his employees.

Consider the differences among petroleum CEOs. In 2005, the CEO of British Petroleum made a handsome $5.6 million, and the CEO of Royal Dutch Shell made $4.1 million. But in America the CEO of Exxon Mobil made $69.7 million and the average salary of American oil company top executives was $33 million. A study completed by Towers Perrin surveying CEOs' compensation from 2004-06, found that Japan's top 100 companies earned an average of around $1.5 million, while American CEOs earned $13.3 million and European CEOs earned $6.6 million. In addition when European and Asian companies faced losses their CEOs voluntarily took a significant cut in pay. For example, Japan Airlines lost $1 billion in the second quarter of 2009 and the CEO gave himself a salary of $90,000 a year (less than that of a pilot) and he took the bus to work. It is guaranteed that you will never find an American CEO engaging in similar behavior even in the face of bankruptcy. Jiang Jianqing, the CEO of the world's largest bank, Industrial and Commercial Bank of China, made $234,700 in 2008. His compensation was less than 2 percent of the $19.6 million awarded to Jamie Dimon, CEO of the world's fourth-largest bank, JP Morgan Chase.

In Germany the compensation ratio between the CEO and lowest paid worker is 12 times; France, 15 times; Britain, 22 times. In America it rises to between 400 and 500 times. The country that comes closest to the American ratio is Venezuela's CEOs at 50 times the average pay. Japan prides itself at having the smallest disparity in salary between executives and their employees. However, there is some evidence that CEOs of foreign corporations are beginning to emulate their U.S. counterparts and are slowly catching up. For example, research collated by the Centre for Corporate Governance at the University of Technology (2008) in Australia found that in 1992 a typical executive in Australia's top 50 companies earned 27 times the wage of an average worker. By 2002, this had risen to 98 times the wage of an average worker.

John Pierpont Morgan (1837-1913), the financier at what is today JPMorgan Chase, is turning over in his grave. Morgan believed the desirable top-to-bottom salary gap ratio in any company should be 20 to 1. In 2009, JP Morgan Chase CEO Jamie Dimon made more than $17 million and in 2010 he made $20.8 million. If he adhered to Mr. Morgan's rule of thumb the lowest salary at his bank would be $850,000. Tell that to some $10-per-hour teller. In March 2009, 14,000 Chase employees were terminated and in February 2011, 250 people were terminated while Dimon was getting a $17 million stock bonus. JP Morgan is turning over again.

WHO KILLED MANUFACTURING IN THE U.S.? THE HEDGE FUND BOYS

Since the 1980s the Wall Street banks, hedge funds and their investors virtually stopped doing what helped make the American economy strong. They stopped using their money to finance real business that created jobs. Instead Wall Street had become an asset-stripping machine focused exclusively on short-term profitability and making money betting that businesses will fail. They made the American economy derivative driven and discovered that the way to make easy profits are from outsourcing, offshoring, factory closings and bankruptcy. House-flipping a way to get rich during the housing boom is rank amatureism compared to company-flipping. The Simons Mattress Company is a classic case of how the so-called "buyout" firms can buy a company and flip it multiple times it and drive it into bankruptcy while making millions in profits. It is also a case of how these investment houses literally destroyed the America that once made things.

The Simmons Company was founded in 1870 by Zalmon Simmons and made significant contributions to the development of Kenosha Wisconsin. In 1916 Simmons began advertising nationally and rapidly grew as it acquired nine manufacturing plants in cities located in America and Canada.

The destruction of this once proud company began 1979. Shortly after they moved their headquarters to Atlanta they were purchased by Gulf & Western Industries at the time one of America's largest conglomerates and often referred to as Engulf & Devour. In 1985 Gulf & Western sold Simmons to the Wickes Corporation and in 1986 they sold it and Simmons moved through private equity firms like a foster care child with evil foster parents. The equity firms all got a turn raping the company and screwing its employees.

Not surprisingly the first to have its way with this company was a former Treasury Secretary under Nixon, William Simon, who bought Simmons in 1986 through his investment firm, Wesray Capital, along with 18 Simmons executives. Inviting the company's executives in on the deal is a way to ensure that the deal will go through. They were literally bought off. Wesray bought it for $120 million of borrowed money. In 1989 Wesray sold Simmons to the company's employee stock ownership plan for $241 million. A great deal for Wesray and Simon and the Simmons executives: in three years they doubled their investment. But according to Creswell (2009) the deal was a fiasco for Simmons employees, "As part of the buyout, Simmons stopped contributing to its pension plan, since the stock ownership plan shares were meant to pay for the employees' retirements. But then the bottom fell out of the housing market and Simmons, with its large debt, stumbled. Its pensions crumbled as the value of the stock plan shares plunged." Now the company was loaded with debt and pushed to the brink after paying Wesray and Simmons own executives $241 million. In 1991 Merrill Lynch Capital Partners got a turn. They offered to buy 60 percent of the company for the bargain price of $32 million, which was far less then Simon, Wesray and the executives paid for it in 1986. Simmons employees were screwed again as they were now left with only 30 percent of the company they once fully owned. In response Simmons employees filed a class-action suit against Wesray and Simmons executives, which was eventually settled out of court with a payment of about $15 million to the employee stock ownership plan (ESOP). Now we know something is radically wrong with a company when its employees have to bring their bosses and the company that they own to court to stop the pillaging.

In March 1996, with profits up, Merrill Lynch sold its stake in Simmons to a Bahrain-based investment group called Investcorp for $265 million. This amounted to a $231 million profit for Merrill Lynch. And guess who got screwed again. The employees were forced to sell part of their stake in the company, now leaving it with a paltry 15 percent. Investcorp now controlled 85 percent. By 1997, Simmons had sales of over $550 million, with a profit of about $50 million. In 1999, or two years later, Investcorp sold 75 percent of the company to Fenway Partners for $513 million. Fenway then sold all but 10 percent of its stake to the Thomas H. Lee group for $1.1 billion; this consisted of $327 million in new equity from Lee's firm and more than $745 million in bonds and bank loans that had to be raised from investors. This deal proved a bonanza for Fenway but also for Simmons executives. It turned out that the Simmons executives and Fenway partners were holding millions in options that were executed when the Lee Group bought the company. Simmons Chairman Charlie Eitel received a total compensation of $30.3 million, of that $29.2 million came from the exercise of stock options from the "old" Simmons. President Bob Hellyer had total compensation of $11.8 million, including $11.3 million from exercising options. Chief Financial Officer Bill Creekmuir's total was $11.5 million, including $11 million from his options. Over a 100 executives exercised options. What about the nonmanagerial employees? Screwed again.

What did the Lee Group do with Simmons? It was their piggy bank. By 2007 the Lee Group continued to bleed Simmons. They created a holding company to issue $300 million more in Simmons debt, which paid an additional $238 million dividend to the Lee gang. With that, they recouped its entire $327 million equity investment in Simmons and made a profit of over $48 million plus an additional $28.5 million in various fees. The Lee investment firm had pocketed around $77 million in profit from the Simmons purchase, even as the company's fortunes sank. The Lee gang also collected hundreds of millions of dollars from the company in the form of special dividends and it also paid itself millions in fees, first for buying the company, then for helping run it.

Wall Street investment banks also cashed in. They collected millions for helping to arrange the takeovers and for selling the bonds that made those deals possible. All told, the various private equity owners made around $750 million in profits from Simmons over a few years. They got rich and loaded Simmons with a giant amount of debt.

These private investors love their jobs. They are in the business to buy and sell businesses like Simmons with other people's money. They got a lot of money from the Ontario teacher's Pension Plan Fund. Teacher's pension funds are just a notch above Widows and Orphans Pension Funds. The investment bankers creed was "Don't bet with your money, you may lose." Get hold of retiree's pensions to bet. They operated like the housing bubble home-flippers who, with little or no money down, bought and sold property. The trick was to use the houses' assets as collateral so they could continue to borrow more with no money down. So they borrowed from retirement funds and in addition to risking other people's money they got the pension funds to pay fees and an array of additional charges. The Lee Group in a similar fashion took out two second mortgages against Simmons and kept $375 million for itself. It was the perfect shell game. But the Lee gang like many homeowners during the housing bust found themselves underwater. So what did the Lee gang do? Again, like many underwater homeowners, they walked away.

On Sept. 25, 2009, Simmons filed for Chapter 11 and signed a purchase agreement with an investor group led by Ares Management LLC and Ontario Teachers' Pension Plan (TPC). If approved by the bankruptcy court, the deal will reduce Simmons' total debt from about $1 billion to $450 million. While the Lee gang will profit, the investors (other people's money-the teachers retirement fund) stand to lose more than $450 million. Ares and TPC are also the owners of the Serta brand name under National Bedding Company LLC. They claim they plan to operate Serta and Simmons Bedding as independent entities that will continue to compete against each another. This is expected to fail, and it is certain that Serta mattresses will consume Simmons. Simmons, the once proud industry leader in bedding, will cease to exist and over a thousand employees will lose their jobs and thousands more will lose what little pension they have. But not the Lee Investment firm.

These so-called "buyout" firms that flip companies and ruin them for profit have destroyed manufacturing in America. For a company like Simmons to be flipped for a profit seven times in 20 years is outrageous.

On Jan. 7, 2010, a bankruptcy judge approved its restructuring plan Simmons and the $1 billion debt facilitated by the Lee Group will be reduced.

Is this case unique? According to Creswell (2009) Simmons is one of hundreds of companies swept up by private equity firms in the early part of this decade, during the greatest burst of corporate takeovers the world has ever seen. Many of these deals, cut in good times, left little or no margin for error — let alone for the Great Recession. She maintains that more than half the roughly 220 companies that have defaulted on their debt in some form in 2009 were either owned at one time or are still controlled by private equity firms, according to analysts at Standard & Poor's. How does this happen? Companies that borrow money from hedge funds often see a sharp rise in bets against their shares (short selling) before the loans or loan amendments are announced. These hedge fund scoundrels offer loans to struggling companies, when they finish paying off the loans they buy the company for a song. Then, having gained access to "insider information," they bet either for or against the company and they do so without any form of regulation. They are modern day robbers. In 2008 while S&P 500 CEOs earned average compensation that was 344 times the pay of a typical American worker, the top 50 hedge fund and private equity managers made an average of more than 19,000 times the average American worker. They also spent millions of dollars lobbying to stop Obama and Congress from passing regulations. So who is responsible for the death of manufacturing in America? It's these guys who got rich flipping companies or shutting them down then getting China to make the stuff that

American workers once made, and then putting the dead companies label on the product. Ten years ago 30 percent of the goods Americans bought were made by Americans, now it's down to 10 percent. Main Street has suddenly realizing that a country that manufactures nothing is doomed. Politicians, in the pocket of these hedge fund boys and their Wall Street friends, keep their heads in the sand. Consequently, these private equity firms continue to rape and pillage company after company, destroying millions of jobs. And they continue their reckless pursuit of profit, unchecked.

(To read more about the hedge fund boys and how they profit from destruction go to Section 14 in Chapter 13).

(For a more complete survey of these outrageous salaries go to Appendix A)

WHAT DO THESE EXECUTIVES GET? ANSWER: ALL KINDS OF STUFF

These executives get salary, bonuses, stock awards, option awards, non equity incentives, loans, retention awards, retention bonuses, compensation for retirement, life insurance, country club dues, golf club dues, disability, security systems, estate planning, legal advice vacations, tax preparations, financial planning, cars, and planes, drivers, coaches, shoppers, chefs, houses. And if you're Robert Keegan, CEO of Goodyear Tire, in addition to your outlandish compensation, you get two sets of tires. Take Eric Feldstein, CEO of GMAC. It doesn't matter if his company lost $2.33 billion in 2007, he got $14.6 million. This included a $1.2 million salary, a $900,000 bonus, and $3.63 million in other compensation. He also received a performance award valued at $2.95 million and incentive payments valued at $5.91 million also $2.35 million to cover taxes on a performance award, a $1 million retention payment, $66,703 for use of company aircraft, and $7,200 to pay for a rented parking space in New York City.

To park his car?

And, his company lost $2.33 billion and he got a bonus and performance reward.

(If you want to see some more lunacy you can see a list of outrageous perks in Appendix B)

THE WALL STREET GANG

Wall Street has always been known for its excesses and for promoting the mentality that relies exclusively on the profit motive and rewards. This way of thinking once the domain of Wall Street is now pervasive in corporate America. Wall Street executives became celebrities as their wealth and power was flaunted. However, their celebrity status quickly moved to greedy villains as they became the gang that significantly contributed to the financial meltdown in 2008. To witness the phenomenal growth of Wall Street compensation in 1986 the biggest Wall Street banker paycheck went to John Gutfreund, the Salomon Brothers CEO who made $3.2 million. If we fast-forward to 2006, compensation packages go beyond excessive.

In 2008, Lloyd Blankfein of Goldman Sacks made $58 million, followed by Stanley O'Neal of Merrill Lynch at $48 million, and John Mack of Morgan Stanley at $42.2 million. In 2007, Blankfein made over $53 million, and Mack made over $41 million. The CEO who took over for the ousted O'Neal, John Thain made over $83 million. Peter Kraus joined Merrill Lynch just before it collapsed and was bought by Bank of America; after three months on the job he got an exit package worth $25 million. He then was given $52 million to take a job at Alliance Bernstein. He gets rich going and coming.

THE WALL STREET BONUS

The famous bonuses are the so-called Christmas bonuses and are painful to observe from an average worker's perspective. In 2007, the four largest investment firms, Goldman Sachs, Morgan Stanley, Lehman Brothers and Bear Stearns, gave out year-end bonuses of nearly $30 billion.

Goldman Sachs bonuses increased 22 percent in 2007 as they awarded $12.1 billion in bonuses. CEO Lloyd Blankfein received $68 million, $14 million more than in 2006. Goldman co-presidents Gary Cohn and Jon Winkelried were each given bonuses worth $40.5 million, up from $26 million apiece in 2006.

Much of Goldman Sachs record profits in 2007 came from its successful financial manipulations in the subprime mortgage market. It essentially bet against its major Wall Street rivals, who plunged heavily into the business of repackaging home mortgages, into ever-more-complex financial securities whose value is now problematic, even unknowable. As a reward, in 2008 Goldman Sachs co-presidents each earned $67.5 million with Blankfein earning about $100 million. In 2008 Goldman's stock declined more than 60 percent. The firm had to obtain a $10 billion government bailout and Blankfein's compensation dropped to $42.9 million. In 2009, after two profitable quarters Goldman Sachs repaid the government its bailout money and set aside $11.36 billion for bonuses. Blankfein got a $9 million bonus. In 2010 as revenue dropped, $9.2 billion was set aside for bonuses and in July 2011 they set aside $8.44 billion for bonuses. As profits continue to fall and lawsuits mount (they paid an SEC fine of $550 million), Blankfein's total compensation continues to balloon. In 2010 he received $19 million, which included a $5.4 million cash bonus.

JPMorgan Chase also paid back taxpayer money and set aside $14.5 billion for bonuses in the first half of 2009, up 22 percent from 2008. Morgan Stanley recorded its third consecutive loss in the second quarter of 2009. Despite that, the bank has set aside $6 billion in 2010 for bonuses and $3.87 billion just in the second quarter, which represents 72 percent of its revenue. Morgan Chase CEO Jamie Dimon collected a $17 million bonus for 2009.

Sallie Krawcheck, once the highest-ranking woman on Wall Street, remarked, "It's better to be an employee of an investment bank than a shareholder." And she is certainly right. Shareholders in the securities industry lost $74 billion of their equity in 2009 but the Wall Street gang didn't suffer a bit. They got record bonuses, totaling almost $38 billion. That money, split among about 186,000 employees at the five biggest securities firms averaged $201,500 per person. Main Street is once again outraged. In December 2009 the NYPD reported that Goldman bankers had gun permits to essentially protect themselves from these angry Main Streeters. An in January 2010 police had to put up barriers around the Goldman building and brought in bomb sniffing dogs as employees became increasingly fearful. In the fall of 2011 hundreds protested on Wall Street. Many banking houses and hedge fund operations are taking their names off their buildings and employees go to work in jeans and sneakers out of fear they will be detected and harmed by some angry mob.

(To read more about the Wall Street gang go to Appendix D)

THE HEALTH CARE GANG

Corporate CEOs are not alone in this behavior. Consider this. A retired professor on Medicare reported the following: "The other day I received a mailing offering me a supplemental medical insurance plan for free from United Health. The next day I received a follow-up call from a friendly woman. I quickly discovered that this plan wasn't at all free. My co-pays would dramatically increase and things that are now covered like physical therapy, which are vital to me, would no longer be covered. She told me about the excellent hearing coverage but failed to mention a $500 deductible."

He told the woman the following: "You are mistaken, it is not free you can't tell old people it's free and then nickel and dime them into poverty."

She replied, "I'm doing my job that's all and it's free."

Professor, "But it's not, how can you do this?"

She "Sir I am doing my job"

Professor, "You are getting your bosses rich by lying. Do you know who your CEO is?"

She 'No"

Professor, "His name is Helmsley and he makes $57,000 per hour, not per day, not per year, per hour. Probably more than you make a year."

She, "You are too negative I like to be positive that's what they teach me here. Smile, be happy, positive and it's all good."

Professor, "OK you're right, let's be positive. Helmsley deserves his $57,000 an hour and you are thankful he has given you a job and maybe a career and he deserves every penny and you must applaud him for the good work he does for you and all the old people and if we can't read the fine print it's our fault."

She "Go f—k yourself." She hung up

Moral of the story—Sometimes it's just impossible to be happy, especially when you are working for some multimillionaire who gets rich sticking it to old people.

Why did the professor pick on Helmsley? He read in the Daily Planet (2007) that several organizations had demonstrated outside the annual shareholders meeting of United Health Group, the largest HMO in the United States to "decry the gap between need and greed." United's CEO Stephen Helmsley, as well as other Minnesota HMO executives, including former CEO William McGuire, took billions in stock options. McGuire was the highest-paid CEO in Minnesota history, with stock options totaling $2 billion. Helmsley, who replaced McGuire, has stock options in excess of $750 million. McGuire and other executives were ousted in October 2006, and are under criminal investigation due to stock option backdating fraud. When asked where all this money comes, from Herbert Sacks, past President of the American Psychiatric Association replied, "from the denial and interruption of ... patient care." In 2009 Helmsley's total compensation was $106 million. In 2010 Helmsley received compensation valued at some $10.8 million. In addition, he realized more than $43.5 million in value from exercising stock options

It is not just CEO salaries that are excessive, so are their Senior VPs', VPs', and board members. For example, in 2007, the top 6 health plan boards paid themselves a whopping $277,998,793 (Jodell, 2009).

Estimates of the compensation cost for health care CEOs and their executives total about $7 billion to 10 billion a year. If their pay were reduced by 80 percent it would cover health insurance for 500,000 families enrolled in a government insurance program at $10,000 per year per family. Also, if health care were nationalized the administrative savings alone would be enough to provide health care coverage for the 1 million uninsured in America. One third of every dollar spent on health care goes to administrative overhead and half of that goes to executives. According to the Security and Exchange Commission between 2000 and 2007 the 10 largest publicly traded health insurance corporations increased their profits 428 percent, from $2.8 billion to $12.9 billion, as premiums increased 87 percent.

Health care institutions have lost the confidence of a public that once valued their altruistic mission and many maintain that executive pay is a significant part of the health care problem in America. For example, Patrick Soon-Shiong the CEO of APP Pharmaceuticals stepped down as CEO in the spring of 2008, but the former surgeon still held 83 percent of the company's shares. In July, he agreed to sell APP to a German firm. The sale was finalized two months later for an initial $3.7 billion cash payment. As a result Soon-Shiong's personal fortune gain was $3 billion in 2008, (Brunwasser, 2008).

In 2011 Republicans in Congress planned to dismantle Medicare and Medicaid and use a voucher system to enroll this population in the cost-inefficient private health care system. This will put a smile on the faces of health care "fat cats" and their stockholders and will deny health care to even more millions.

(To read more about the health care gang see Appendix E)

THE INSURANCE GANG

We also find evidence of high salaries among insurance companies. In 2007 these CEOs made the following: Allstate - Thomas Wilson's $10.7 million; UNUM - Thomas Watjen's $7.3 million; AIG – former CEO, Robert Willumstad's 14.3 million; State Farm - Edward Rust's $11.7 million; CONSECO - C. James Prieur's $2.6 million.

THE UNIVERSITY GANG

We are now beginning to see colleges and universities embracing the corporate mentality that handsomely rewards their chiefs. In 2006, the highest paid president of a private university was Northwestern's Richard Freeland who was paid approximately $2.9 million. James Gallagher, President of Philadelphia University, is next at $2.6 million, followed by William Brody of Johns Hopkins at $1.9 million. The Northwestern University president who makes $2.9 million a year receives 42.6 times the salary of his faculty who average $68,000 per annum (Burger, 2007).

In 2007, the highest paid president was David Sargent of Suffolk University. He received a $2.8 million pay package, including a $436,000 longevity bonus. In 2009 Sargent received $1.5 million as he froze faculty salaries and raised student fees and caused an outrage. Salaries of university executives, not just presidents, have increased dramatically. For example, the University of Texas increased its budget for administrative jobs that paid more than $200,000 by 40 percent during the period 2004 to 2008, at the same time tuition rose 57 percent (Root, 2009). In 2011 Texas announced another tuition increase of 10 percent. In addition aid and grants to students has dropped dramatically in all states across America.

Presidents making more than $1 million increased to twelve in 2007, up from seven the year before (Glater, 2007). In 2010, thirty university presidents topped a million dollars annually.

The nonprofits pale in comparison to the for-profit educational executives. For example, the Apollo Group Inc., parent of the University of Phoenix, paid its co-CEOs Charles Edelstein $11.3 million and Greg Cappelli $7.3 million and its president and chief operating officer Joe D'Amico $6.5 million in 2009.

(To read more about these for-profit salaries and how they make their money go to Appendix X)
(To read more about University salaries go to Appendix F)

THE RELIGIOUS GANG TOO?

Not surprisingly, we find that religious leaders are also in line for their unfair share. Senator Chuck Grassley of Iowa is questioning religious leaders of some of the 200,000 mega churches who live in multi-million-dollar homes, own private jets and Rolls Royce's, and receive CEO-like salaries, perks and expense allowances. He is focusing on six of the most popular televangelists in the country. All are Pentecostals who preach the "prosperity gospel," which teaches that God will grant financial and spiritual wealth to the faithful. Their ministries include hundreds of thousands of worshipers who watch their TV shows, buy their products and donate to their churches. Perhaps the leader of this gang is evangelist Franklin Graham who is the CEO of the charitable organizations Billy Graham Evangelistic Association (BGEA) and Samaritan's Purse. BGEA paid him $669,000 and Samaritan's Purse paid him $535,000 in 2008. Wait, that's not all, he also gets two retirement packages. Graham has proven (1) that he is the greatest CEO in the world or, (2) that running a major organization is so easy one can lead two. By the way BGEA terminated 10 percent of its workforce months before Graham's compensation was announced.

To be fair this apparent greed in the church is not pervasive. For example in 2010 the "Church Investors Group" in the UK and Ireland, which managers $18.31 billion in pension funds for several Christian churches published a 30,000-word report, "The Ethics of Executive Remuneration: A Guide for Christian Investors," written by theologians Richard Higginson and David Clough. The report offers guidelines for executive pay and maintains that excessive executive pay will negatively influence where they will invest.

(To read more about who these people are, go to Appendix G)

Not the Boy Scouts

Roy Williams was Boy Scouts CEO from 2000 to 2007. Over that period his salary almost doubled, topping $580,000 in 2006 (Bensman, 2009). When he retired in September 2007, Williams received more than $1.5 million, including $912,000 from incentives for longevity of service. He qualified for a "retirement restoration" plan on top of the usual retirement offered employees. For Williams, that was worth $2.4 million, paid out over time (Bensman, 2009). By the way the CEO of the Girl Scouts Kathy Cloninger, only makes $349,912.

(To read more about these nonprofit "do good" nonprofits agencies see Appendix U)

EVEN THE CIO'S

You do not have to be a CEO to hit the jackpot. Let's consider chief information officers (CIOs). What do they do? Give out information and often protect their bosses, their CEOs, by giving out misleading, skewed, or inaccurate information to the press and stockholders. According to King (2009) in 2008, Randall Mott, CIO of Hewlett-Packard received a total compensation package of $24.65 million: Robert Willett, CIO of Best Buy, $9.88 million: Joseph Antonellis, CIO of State Street, $8.82 million: Stephen Squeri, CIO of American Express, $4.69 million: and Thomas Nealon, CIO of JC Penny, $3.6 million

A FEW WOMEN JOIN IN

Although men overwhelmingly occupy the ranks of the top salaried CEOs we also see evidence of women entering those lofty ranks of highly paid CEOs. Andrea Jung, CEO of Avon, headed the list in 2008 with total compensation of $13,697,232. As company's shares fell by 14.3 percent in 2008 and she terminated 3,000, she managed to get a 75 percent salary increase. In 2009 Avon announced that it would eliminate about 1,200 positions, or about 2.8 percent of its overall work force, by 2013. Meanwhile Jung received a 41 percent increase in compensation to $9.9 million up from her 2009 compensation. Her 2010 package included a $5.4 million performance bonus.

Also joining the ranks of CEOs who terminate employees and get a salary increase is Susan Ivey, CEO of Reynolds tobacco. She received a 12 percent salary increase in 2008, after a 2 percent decline in sales and 570 job cuts. While continuing to cut jobs through 2010 Ivey was given a compensation package valued at $16.8 million in fiscal 2010, up 4 percent from fiscal 2009. Her compensation package included a $7.8 million bonus. In February 2011 she resigned.

(For more on women CEOs see the list in Appendix C).

"THE GANG OF INCOMPETENTS": HOW CEOS GET BIG REWARDS FOR BAD PERFORMANCE (THIS LIST IS LONG)

Corporations and their boards find all sorts of ways to make certain their executives get rich; they lower the performance bar, change the rules and shorten the periods during which they measure performance, only award short-term profits, disguise the bonus, call it something else, or just disregard pay for performance and pay executives handsomely no matter what happens.

In corporate America pay for performance is in vogue. Most corporations, perhaps every nonunion company, has in place some type of performance review process that is supposed to reward employees based on performance. Performance review time is the dreaded time of the year for most employees. It is when employees get their annual assessment from their boss that determines raise, bonuses, and other rewards. But this is for employees, not the chiefs. It seems what CEOs get has very little to do with performance. As a matter of fact for many CEOs there is an inverse relationship between pay and performance. As performance drops, pay increases. Audit Integrity found a close correlation between excessive executive compensation, overall poor corporate governance and inferior market returns across a wide range of industries (Kaplan, 2008). Audit Integrity's analysis of the 80 firms found that all but 14 had excessive executive compensation (defined as exceeding the compensation of 80 percent of industry competitors). In other words, the executives who were delivering the worst performance were collecting the highest compensation. This was confirmed by Cooper, Gulen and Rau (2009). Also Bebchuk, Cremer and Peyer (2006) concluded that CEOs' pay slice, the share the CEO gets among the top five executives, had increased to 35 percent. They concluded as pay slice increases, profitability goes down. When a company designs its bonus in advance of performance as AIG did, the message is clear. Performance and pay may in fact have an inverse relationship.

If performance review does not work for CEOs then how is their compensation determined? A study of executive compensation by O'Reilly, Main, and Crystal (1988) tracked 105 large firms and compared numerous predictors to determine CEO pay. After controlling for traditional size and performance measures, they found that the amount of money made by outside directors, especially those on the compensation committee, had the greatest effect on CEO pay. They reported that for every $100,000 a member of the compensation committee was paid, the CEOs pay went up another $51,000 per year. They suggested that members of the compensation committee used their own pay as a guide to help determine how much to pay the CEO. Therefore CEOs get paid well if they carefully select a well paid or perhaps rich group to determine their compensation. It does not matter how well a CEO performs. If they put together a good compensation committee they will get paid well. Of course these compensation committees hire so-called "compensation consultants" who are paid well for making certain the CEO continues to be enriched. These consultants stay on by establishing programs to provide tax-advantaged benefits programs designed to protect the CEO's income and assets, and, of course, preserve their wealth.

(To read more about this long list the "Gang of Incompetents" go to Appendix H.)

TERMINATE EMPLOYEES AND GET A RAISE

Several research studies have discovered that CEOs who terminate employees receive more compensation and greater increases than those who do not. Consider Sepracor Corp. In 2008 they started announcing the terminations of about 940 employees then the top management team saw had their total compensation rise an average of 20 percent. CEO Adrian Adams compensation increased 44 percent from $4.5 million to $6.5 million. Terminating employees is hard work.

According to Anderson, et. al. (2009), since January 1, 2008, the top 20 financial industry recipients of bailout aid from the U.S.

government have together laid off more than 160,000 employees. In 2008, the 20 CEOs at these firms each averaged $13.8 million, for a collective total of over a quarter-billion dollars in compensation.

(To read more about these guys see Appendix R)

LOSE MILLIONS AND GET A BONUS

We tried to understand the concept of performance bonus. Of all employees, the CEO's performance is the easiest to quantify. The company has a profit or a loss, its stock goes up or down. If a company merges or acquires another company, logic would dictate that one would wait and see if it is successful and then compensate. But this is far from the case. We find that CEOs and their compensation consultants design compensation packages that intentionally focus only on those factors that contribute to a bonus. For example, in some cases a bonus will be given for the "intention to improve profits" or "longevity," or even the "double bonus" the bonus to pay the taxes on the bonus.

Consider Edgar Bronfman Jr. who received a $3 million bonus in 2008 even though his company, Warner Music Group, lost $56 million and the stock dropped 25 percent. According to the Wall Street Journal, the board awarded him the bonus because he did a "good job in a tough environment" (Satow, 2009).

In 2008, Varian Semiconductor Equipment saw its income drop 31 percent and stock fall 53 percent and its CEO Gary Dickerson was awarded a $1.1 million bonus (Satow, 2009).

(To read a lot more about the CEOs getting bonuses as their company fails see Appendix N)

LOSE MILLIONS AND GET A PAY RAISE

Sun Microsystems CEO Jonathan Schwartz received an $11.1 million pay package in 2008, a 44 percent increase from 2007. Sun's profit plunged 73 percent in the fourth quarter and it also forecast a decline in sales for the first quarter and indicated it likely wouldn't turn a profit (Robertson, 2008).

ValueClick suffered a loss of $256 million in the fourth quarter of 2008, however its five top executives received $19.8 million in compensation between them, a $14.2 million pay raise from 2007 (Edwards, 2009a).

(This is a small sampling. If you want to read the entire list go to Appendix H).

Merge or Buy a Company and Get Rich

Why do CEOs seek acquisitions and mergers? They seek to build their empire, to achieve wealth or both. Jarrad and Kia (2007) explored how CEO compensation was impacted following mergers and acquisitions. Namely, they wanted to answer the question: Did financial incentives motivate CEOs to pursue a merger? They discovered that immediately following an acquisition, company performance suffered; market to book value, return on assets and stock return all dropped, and leverage increased. However, the acquiring CEO's compensation and wealth increased substantially. Also, acquiring CEOs are not penalized in the post-merger period for poor performance.

A good example of this is the merger of Caremark a mail order pharmacy with CVS. Caremark's CEO Edwin Crawford was appointed to serve as chairman of the merged companies. Crawford negotiated a golden parachute from Caremark by claiming that he had departed from the merged Caremark. This parachute ranged from $36 million to $40 million. Crawford then agreed to limit his cash severance to $26 million; however, he benefited from an accelerated vesting of his stock options. This amounted to $22 million. In total, it is estimated that Crawford received $56 million from the merger. This estimate does not include the full value of an insurance policy that will transfer to Crawford's ownership. The policy's actual value is $17 million. Additionally, this estimate does not include the $248 million in stock options that Crawford owns that are exercisable. According to The Corporate Library, Crawford could walk away with a total of $287 million, not including the health and welfare benefits he will receive for the remaining eight years of his employment agreement. Crawford has maintained that no other Caremark employee will be allowed to benefit from its merger with CVS.

A 2007 study of 137 large companies by Equilar Inc. found that 72 percent of the CEOs had severance agreements and 82 percent were promised exit packages if they lost their jobs following a corporate takeover, or "change in control." In Equilar's study, the median CEO would receive $21 million for being ousted and $29 million following a change in control (Dvorak, 2008).

(To read about other merger and acquisition examples read Appendix L)

DECLARE BANKRUPTCY AND TAKE THE MONEY AND RUN

We found that when corporations are on their death bed and getting ready to file for bankruptcy their CEOs make it out the door with bags of money. In September 2009, Charter Communications hired a law firm to handle a bankruptcy filing while the company's board of directors increased CEO Neil Smit's pay $300,000 for the year. In January 2009, the company's Executive Cash Award Plan, which had been scheduled to vest on Dec. 31, 2009, was partially distributed to top executives. Under that plan, Smit received $1.19 million.

Consider Spansion computer chip makers. Two days before defaulting on $266 million worth of debt in February 2009, Spansion gave CEO John Kispert a four-month advance on his annual salary and he will not be required to pay it back if he should quit. He was also guaranteed a $1.75 million bonus contingent upon the company merging with another chip maker, or selling off its assets (Davis, 2009). Spansion filed for bankruptcy in March 2009.

It is rare that the details of pay packages for privately held companies are made public, but Crain's Detroit (2008) discovered the pay of the executives of the bankrupt Plastech Engineered Products. Julie Brown the CEO, earned $3.23 million in the 12 months before the financially troubled company's Chapter 11 petition on Feb. 1, 2008. Her compensation package included a base salary and life insurance benefits worth $957,724, company-paid aircraft use totaling $379,464.88, dues for Brown's membership at the Fairlane Country Club in Dearborn worth $22,263.36, a company car use valued at $30,750 and a $1.84 million bonus. Jim Brown, Julie Brown's husband and Plastech's COO, received a $2.25 million compensation package. It included a base salary and life insurance benefits worth $2.21 million and company car use worth $39,541.25. Ms. Brown's three brothers, two sisters-in-law, sister, cousin and nephew were also on Plastech's payroll, for a total of $6.4 million for the 2007 fiscal year

CEO PENSIONS

Equilar (2007) studied accumulated wealth among CEOs at Fortune 500 companies, and found that in 2006, the median value of total retirement benefits, including accumulated pensions and deferred compensation plan balances, was approximately $7 million. In addition, the median value of total accumulated wealth for Fortune 500 CEOs was approximately $48.2 million. This includes pension benefits, deferred compensation, outstanding option awards, unvested stock awards, and shares owned outright (Equilar, 2007).

Consider CEO of Gannett, Doug McCorkindale who retired in June 2006. In addition to his retirement bonus of $1.25 million, Gannett gave him the following:

- Health insurance for him and his spouse at no cost. This includes a Medicare supplement, and reimbursement for the cost of Medicare Part B coverage.

- Travel accident insurance. Estimated annual cost: $81,390.

- Legal and financial counseling services. Estimated annual cost: $25,000.

- $150,000, in annual $50,000 installments, to buy life insurance or other benefits .

- Home security system allowance.

- Country club membership fees.

- Computer and other home office equipment.

- An automobile.

- Use of company aircraft "at times not inconveniencing the company," the cost of which will be reimbursed by McCorkindale.

- Access to company offices, facilities and services -- including the use of an office and executive assistant.

There is no better example of out of control CEO pensions then Exxon Mobil's Lee Raymond, the highest paid pensioner, who receives $8,187,200 annually. He is followed by Henry A. McKinnell, who retired from Pfizer at $6,518,459 per year.

(To read more about these obscene retirement packages go to Appendix I)

RUN A GOVERNMENT AGENCY INTO THE GROUND AND GET RICH

While members of Congress decry the greed among CEOs in corporate America they cannot see the problem in their own backyard, as government agency chiefs get rich while their mismanaged agencies lose billions. Consider these examples. In 2008 as the U.S. Postal Service was considering cutting delivery service in the face of dwindling mail volume and rising costs its postmaster general received a big pay raise and a performance bonus. Postmaster General John Potter's base salary climbed to $265,000 in 2008 from $186,000 in 2007. He also received a performance bonus of $135,000. In his total compensation package -- salary, bonuses, retirement benefits and other perks -- topped $850,000 in 2008. Meanwhile the Postal Service lost $2.8 billion in 2008. In December 2008 Potter told a Senate committee that if current trends continue, the agency could lose $6 billion or more in 2009 (Clark, 2009). Potter's compensation has increased 40 percent since 2006, while the service lost billions. He told Congress in 2009 that he will cut costs by $2 billion, cut work hours by 50 million, perhaps cut mail delivery and of course increase the price of stamps. In 2010 after Potter earned nearly a quarter-million dollars in incentive pay on top of a $273,000 salary, he announced that in 2011 bonuses and salary increases would be tied to the agency's financial condition.

The USPS lost $8.5 billion in 2010 and terminated 30,000 employees. In March 2011 Potter announced he would terminate 7,500 positions, close seven district offices and 3,700 post offices. USPS expects to lose $8 billion in 2011. Plans are to cut 120,000 jobs by 2015 in addition to cutting employees' federal health and retirement plans. They underestimated the loss: at the end of the fiscal year in September 2011 the actual loss was $10 billion. They then upped the numbers to be terminated to 220,000 by 2015. He is planning to leave in late 2011.

(To read more about these government employees who become multimillionaires go to Appendix ZA.)

GET A GOVERNMENT BAILOUT AND GET A BONUS

In July 2009 the New York State Attorney General reported that Goldman Sachs, Morgan Stanley, Citigroup, Bank of America, and other banks gave bonuses to 5,000 employees while receiving $165 billion in bailout (TARP) money from the government. In total nine banks lost $81 billion in 2008 and gave out over $5 billion in bonuses.

GMAC paid CEO Eric Feldstein $14.6 million in 2007 while the finance company lost $2.33 billion. He was replaced by Alvaro de Molina, and despite continued operating losses his compensation doubled in 2008 to $11.62 million (Zin 2008). GMAC received a $6 billion bailout from the government. In November 2009 de Molina was fired. In December 2009 they received an additional $3.8 billion from the government bringing the total bailout funds to $16.3 billion. The newest CEO to swing in through the revolving door is Michael Carpenter and the government has decided he will receive $9.5 million in compensation in 2010.

Fortune magazine conducts an annual ranking of CEO salaries and found the highest paid CEO in the United States for 2006 was Richard

Fairbank of Capital One, who made $249 million. In 2007 Fairbank was awarded about $17.07 million in compensation and realized $73.1 million from the exercise of stock options and vesting of stock while shares of Capital One fell 38 percent, and profit dropped 35 percent. Fairbank was awarded $9.82 million of compensation in 2008, down 52 percent from a year earlier, but he gained $19.24 million from exercising stock options. Meanwhile Capital One lost $46 million in 2008 and needed about $3.55 billion from the government's Troubled Asset Relief Program (TARP) to avoid bankruptcy. In 2010 Fairbank banked a compensation package worth nearly $14.9 million more than double what he received in 2009. Meanwhile Fairbank has been terminating employees in droves. In April and May 2009, 386 were gone and in May 2010, 223 were terminated. On 2011, 2,000 employees were terminated.

State Street CEO Ronald Logue's compensation rose to $28.7 million in 2008 as the bank's shares plunged it disclosed billions in unrealized losses. In October, 2008 it received a $2 billion bailout (Levitz, 2009). In July 2011 State Street terminated 850 technology jobs, the second round of layoffs in one year. And where will these IT jobs go? Where data can be processed cheaply.

(For more on Government bailouts and pay see Appendix T)

YOUR COMPANY GETS SUED AND YOU GET RICH

When corporations face securities class-action lawsuits, CEOs actually increase their compensation. A study by Corporate Library looked at CEO compensation from 2003 to 2006 among 54 public companies, and found that 40 CEOs saw their salaries, bonuses, and benefits increase over the period in which their companies were sued. Bonuses, in particular, did not dip after class-action suits, and actually increased among 30 of the surveyed companies (Rummell, 2008). The study suggests that the financial impact of securities class-action lawsuits impacts share holders, and the CEO actually benefits.

Merck is a prime example. In 2007, Merck took a $4.85 billion charge to settle litigation over its former painkiller Vioxx, and the company's income fell 26 percent, yet CEO Richard T. Clark received an 80 percent raise. In 2008, the top five executives at Merck took home $36 million in compensation. They all received cash bonuses of between $563,767 and $2.2 million even though two of them had "below-target performance." They also got to use the corporate jet, and so did their wives. Merck's sales declined 3 percent and the stock fell 50 percent in 2008, and they terminated 8,400 (Edwards, 2009). In 2010 Clark retired but will continue to be paid $1.5 million and a cash bonus of 125 percent of his base salary. How does one get a bonus if one is retired? It is simple: Just join the board. Clark was replaced by Kenneth Frazier who will get $1.5 million an annual cash incentive award (bonus) of 150 percent of his annual base salary and a long term incentive (bonus) grant of $7.5 million. So he gets a short and long bonus called an incentive, and it's guaranteed. In July 2010 Merck announced it would terminate 15,000 employees and one year later in July 2011, another 13,000 were terminated.

MOVE MY COMPENSATION PACKAGE AROUND SO I STILL GET REWARDS

American Eagle Outfitters Inc. announced that its CEO James V. O'Donnell cut his bonus in half because its stock lost one third of its value in 2007, but to offset the loss, his salary was increased 32 percent and stock option awards increased 4 percent. He also received $15,250 to offset car expenses and $5,222 in club membership fees. In March 2009 its fourth-quarter profit dropped 77 percent. In 2010 O'Donnell given $17.9 million in salary, bonuses and stock options. In March 2011 O'Donnell announced his resignation. His replacement was Robert Hanson who was given the following:

- A signing bonus (Golden handshake) of $3.3 million
- A base salary of $1 million.
- The possibility of an annual cash bonus of 130 percent of his base salary
- After two years his bonus jumps to between 130 percent and 260 percent of his base salary.
- Long-term equity compensation of at least $3.2 million.
- A luxury automobile.
- $330,000 in deferred compensation.
- $2.5 million restricted stock award
- $2.5 million stock option
- Relocation costs
- And $15,000 in legal fees to pay the guys who got him the deal.

RETENTION BONUSES: IF I DON'T GET MORE I WILL LEAVE.

A growing phenomenon in executive circles is the retention bonuses. These are given out to secure the services of executives for an extra year or two and at times protect the executives from job loss due to mergers, or acquisitions. For example, Genentech was to spend up to $371 million in 2008 on retention bonuses to keep its executives from leaving because of a possible acquisition of the company by its majority shareowner, Roche (Pollack, 2008). Genentech's then CEO, Arthur D. Levinson, was entitled to a bonus of $8.7 million. But no retention bonuses for its employees: just the opposite, as 4800 were terminated in November, 2010.

August 2009 was the two-year anniversary mark when private equity firm Cerberus Capital Management bought an 80.1 percent stake in Chrysler. Since early 2007 Chrysler had cut 32,000 jobs (Bunkley and Vlasic, 2008). In November Chrysler, along with GM and Ford, asked the government for a bailout. As of March 2009, Chrysler had received $9 billion bailout money, but it was not enough. As its new CEO Bob Nardelli pleads for more federal money and terminates thousands of employees, he is paying about $30 million in bonuses to his top executives. They call these bonus "retention bonuses."

According to Walsh and Higgins, (2008), those promised the largest retention bonuses at Chrysler were:

- Frank Ewasyshyn, executive vice president, manufacturing, $1.89 million.

- Frank Klegon, executive vice president, product development, $1.8 million.

- Rae, $1.66 million.

- Simon Boag, president, Mopar/global service and parts, $1.65 million.

- Steven Landry, executive vice president, North American sales, $1.63 million.

- Michael Manley, executive vice president, international sales, marketing and business development, $1.53 million.

(To read more about retention bonuses, see Appendix P)

GET FIRED AND GET THE GOLDEN BOOT

What happens when these CEOs get fired for poor performance? They get what is called the golden parachute, golden handshake, golden boot, or golden sendoff. In either case what they get is golden. It is good to get the boot when one sits in the catbird seat. Most CEOs have a termination clause in the contracts. If they get fired, they get millions.

Consider the newly hired CEO of E*Trade Financial Corp., Donald Layton. He will receive a $5 million severance package if he is terminated.

(To read more about how it pays to be fired when you're a CEO, see Appendix K).

THE KING OF THE GOLDEN PARACHUTES: HE GOT THREE

Yes, Alan Fishman got three, and here is how he did it. In 2001, he became CEO of Independence Community Bank. In 2006, Sovereign Bancorp acquired Independence and Fishman received an $8.6 million golden parachute from Independence and a new contract with Sovereign Bancorp to become its CEO. In 2007, Sovereign's board then passed over Fishman and he collected his second golden parachute, worth $4.56 million in cash and another $12.58 million in other compensation. In September, 2008, Washington Mutual CEO Kerry Killinger was fired over mounting losses and a 65 percent drop in stock value. His exit package is valued at as much as $23.5 million. As of September 2008, its stock dipped below $42 a share. He was replaced by Fishman who was to receive a salary and incentive package worth more than $20 million through 2009. Fishman,

62, will receive an annual base salary of $1 million, a sign-on bonus of $7.5 million and an annual bonus of 365 percent of his base salary, or of $3.65 million. If he stays for the full year, he'll receive a long-term incentive award of no less than $8 million (Yes, one year equals a long term incentive award). He also will receive options to purchase 5 million shares of the company and 612,500 restricted shares, which will vest at an annual rate of 33.3 percent over three years if he's still employed. If Fishman gets fired or resigns as a result of "constructive termination," he'll receive a golden parachute within 10 days worth 2.5 times his current base salary and his annual bonus of the preceding year. Now what the hell is "constructive termination"? (A constructive termination means that the employer has acted in such a way as to let you know you're fired without actually formally terminating you. We are not making this up). Washington Mutual lost $4.5 billion in the third quarter of 2008. In September, 2008, the bank filed for bankruptcy (the largest bank failure in America history) and was taken over by JP Morgan Chase. And guess what, Alan Fishman was "constructively terminated". After three weeks on the job he was presented with $18 million, making Mr. Fishman the "The KING of Golden Parachutes." Rumor has it he's working on his fourth.

WHAT HAPPENS WHEN YOU RESIGN: THE GOLDEN RESIGNATION

Between 1985 and 2007, Wachovia CEO G. Kennedy Thompson engineered over 100 mergers and acquisitions. Among the biggest: the $25.5 billion purchase of subprime mortgage lender Golden West Financial in 2006, just before the subprime market started nose-diving.

Thompson lost his job in June 2008. He "retired" with a $34.5 million exit package after earning over $44.3 million in his eight years as Wachovia's CEO. In October 2008, near bankruptcy Wachovia was purchased by Wells Fargo.

One of Thompson's acquisitions was SouthTrust in a takeover deal that guaranteed SouthTrust CEO Wallace Malone Jr. $59 million in retirement awards, stock awards and options, if he left the newly merged bank within five years beginning 2004. And guess what? Malone left, with a retirement package worth $135 million, including a $3.8 million annual pension.

The record for exit packages would have been Richard Fuld if his company had not gone bankrupt. He was scheduled to receive $299 million when he exited.

(To read about the rich ex-CEOs go to Appendix J)

PADDING THE PENSIONS – PHANTOM EMPLOYMENT

George W. Bush's Treasury Secretary John Snow who wanted to privatize social security (now that would have decreased the gap between the rich and the poor), told a congressional committee in February 2004: "I think we need to be concerned about pensions and the security that employees have in their pensions. And I think we need to encourage people to save and become part of an ownership society, which is very much a part of the President's vision for America." But Snow did not have to worry about losing his 401K. When Snow stepped down as CEO of CSX Corp., to take over Treasury, he was given a lump-sum pension of $33.2 million. It was based on 44 years of employment at CSX he actually worked at CSX for 26 years. Not exactly the type of behavior we want from a Treasury Secretary. Or is it a requirement to get the job?

Adding years of service that do not exist is referred to as "the phantom employment record," and this form of lying to get more is becoming increasingly popular among CEOs. For example, Drew Lewis received a $1.5 million annual pension when he retired in 1996 as chairman and CEO of Union Pacific Corp. His pension was based on 30 years of service to the company, but he actually worked there only 11 years. Another is Leo Mullin, the former chairman and CEO of Delta Air Lines, who received a $16 million retirement package, based on 28.5 years of employment with Delta. He only worked 7.5 years at Delta (Time, 2008).

We also discover that air-lines pad their executive phantom employment years to pad their pensions at the same time they eliminate the pensions of their employees. For example, Delta/Northwest's 2005 proxy statement indicated that former CEO Douglas Steenland will receive $947,417 a year if he retires at 65 and guess what he did. Delta's "supplemental plan" adds multipliers to boost the pensions of the company's four top executives, crediting Steenland with 15 years of service for every five he works and paying him pension credits at twice the rate applied to regular salaried workers (Isaacs, 2005).

GOLDEN COFFIN: CEO LUNACY-STAY ON THE PAYROLL WHILE IN A COFFIN

Adding to this absurdity is the deal struck by Comcast's founder Ralph Roberts. He will receive a salary for five years after his death. In 2006 he received 1.8 million (Yao, 2007). These are called "golden coffins." The CEO of Nabors Industries, Eugene Isenberg got one. He will receive a "severance" payment of $263.6 million when he dies. The board at Nabors then made him reduce it to $100 million.

Robert Iger of Disney will receive $62.4 million when he kicks the bucket. Ivan Seidenberg of Verizon will receive $43.4 million. The CEO of the Shaw Group James Bernhard will be paid $17 million for not competing with the engineering and construction company after he dies. One of the earliest golden coffins was given to Armand Hammer of Occidental Corp. His contract called for his salary to be paid until his 99th year, whether he was alive or dead. He died at 92 in 1990. Another beneficiary was Steven J. Ross, the late chairman and co-CEO of Time Warner, who died in 1992 at age 65. His contract called for the company to pay his salary and bonus for three years after his death. It also gave his heirs nine years to exercise stock options on 7.2 million shares, a package estimated at the time of death to be worth between $75 million and $300 million (Maremont, 2008).

A recent study of 93 big companies, by Equilar, found that 17 percent offered severance-style death benefits to their chief executives in 2006, while 40 percent provided corporate-funded life insurance (Maremont, 2008). At Occidental Petroleum, the successor to Mr. Hammer, Ray R. Irani, would get immediate vesting of all of his options, restricted stock and performance-related awards if he died on the job. It is a benefit worth $101.9 million as of Dec. 31, 2007 (Maremont, 2008). In 2008 Irani cashed in $184.4 million in options.

(For more on Golden Coffins, go to Appendix V)

THE ULTIMATE GREEDY GANG: GETTING RICH WHILE PEOPLE STARVE

We are beginning to see a direct link between the impact of CEO greed and the pain suffering it is causing around the world. It is not just job loss, stealing billions from retirement funds and the growing gap between the rich and poor. Now we have CEOs who exploit the poor by stealing their food. For example, the Potash Corporation, CEO William Doyle has stock options worth $600 million, up from $7 million at the end of 2003. Doyle's windfall reflects soaring potash fertilizer prices, up from $100 to $600 per ton. On Oct. 23, 2008, the Potash Corporation of Saskatchewan reported that it earned more in its third quarter of 2008 ($1.24 billion) than it did in the entire record setting year of 2007 ($1.1 billion). According to Potash Corp records, Doyle's total compensation in 2007 was $17,188,621 (up from $8,943,757 in 2006), including a $2.19-million bonus based on the company's performance. This works out to $47,092.11 a day. According to Ebner (2008) "The soaring price of potash has made the top three executives who run Potash Corp. of Saskatchewan Inc. fantastically wealthy, with stock options worth a total of $846 million." To make this even more absurd if Potash is taken over by another company Doyle will get a $400 million golden parachute and Potash will pay his taxes.

The actions of Doyle and his executives may be contributing to the mounting worldwide food crisis by keeping fertilizer expensive. We see significantly higher prices for all Potash Corp products, including potash, nitrogen and phosphate fertilizers. This has contributed to the massive increase in food prices from the beginning of 2007 to early 2008. The prices of some of the most basic international food commodities increased dramatically on international markets. For example, the international market price of wheat doubled from February 2007 to February 2008, hitting a record high of over $10 a bushel. In some nations milk and meat prices more than doubled, and soy hit a 34-year high in December 2007.

Another contributor to the high price of food is Jim Prokopanko, CEO of MOSAIC. He earned $3,263,890 for the year ended May 31,

2008. Benefiting from increased global demand for agricultural commodities and fertilizer to grow them, Prokopanko got a non-equity incentive bump 96 percent higher than in fiscal 2007 (Kennedy, 2008). In 2009 Prokopanko received a 40 percent increase in compensation. In 2010 he received total compensation of $8,625,052 which included a bonus of $1 million.

Agricultural biotech giant Monsanto expects to see its profits double by 2012. Monsanto has been buying agriculture companies expecting the world wide food shortage to continue. In 2008 Monsanto raised CEO Hugh Grant's compensation 22 percent (Hiralal, 2008).

(To read more about the food crisis and the millions being made while people starve, see Appendix W)

CEOS' NEW STRATEGY TO GET RICH: STEALING EMPLOYEE PENSIONS

Since the early 1980s American corporations included in their business strategies ways to reduce and eliminate their employees' pensions plans. CEOs have frozen pension plans, terminated other plans and converted real pension plans to 410(k)'s. The 401(k) originally created to supplement corporate pensions and Social Security, eventually became for many employees the only corporate pension plan. The Bureau of Labor Statistics estimates that only 21 percent of workers in the private sector have defined-benefit pensions. In 2005, only 55 percent of full-time and part-time private sector workers worked at firms that sponsored a retirement plan. Of those, only 45 percent participated in an employer-sponsored plan. This compares with a 60 percent employer sponsorship rate and 50 percent employee participation rate in 2000 (Schultz and Francis, 2008). With the fiscal crisis of 2008-09, most corporations have decided to stop contributing to pension plans, or contributing to 401(k)'s. In a 10 month period following September 2008, 25 percent of American corporations have ceased contributing to their employees 401(k)'s, including AARP (American Association of Retired Persons). Given this trend, by the end of 2010, employer contribution to 401(k) plans along with defined-benefit pensions would end leaving employees alone as the only contributor to their 401(k) pension.

Wall Street has virtually taken over all 401(k) programs, putting most money in mutual funds, but they also served as Wall Street's cookie jar as they skimmed money in the form of real and hidden fees. There are legal fees, trustee fees, transactional fees, stewardship fees, bookkeeping fees, finder's fees, etc. and they eat up half the income of a typical 401(k) account. Once again, if it is good for Wall Street it is bad for Main Street. Also, since the financial crises of 2008, most of the 60 million American 401(k) pensioners have seen their retirement income drop around 50 percent.

CEOs have destroyed the so-called three-legged stool of Social Security, funded corporate pensions and matching 401(k) savings. All that is now left for most employees is a non-matching 401(k) plan and Social Security that keeps increasing the retirement age at which one can collect. It is horrifying to think what would have happened if George W. Bush had gotten his way when he proposed putting Social Security in the hands of the Wall Street gang. In 2009 instead of 40,000 homeless living on the streets of Los Angeles it would be more like 400,000.

While employee pension plans are in the dumpster, the pension plans of CEOs and their executives are thriving. Many CEOs are so concerned with creating ample pension plans for themselves they spend significant amounts of time and energy trying to find creative ways to get more, often at the expense of their employees.

Bankruptcy, like downsizing and outsourcing, has become a popular CEO strategy to cheat their employees and get rich. The airlines have proven to business consultants, pension attorneys and CEOs that it is a viable wealth strategy and other industries are following suit.

(To read about a case of executive stealing pensions in the Airline industry. go to Appendix Q)

Once again. It is easy to condemn these pirates who use their expertise to exploit their companies and employees. It's another thing, to try to understand the evolution of the type of contemporary managerial thinking and behavior and how it has been turned into acceptable business practice in America. For example, how did it come about that it is an acceptable business strategy to terminate employees to get stockholders and executives rich? These are the questions we will explore in the next chapter.

CHAPTER 2

Business Schools: The Evolution of Managerial Greed

The "worst excesses of recent management practices have their roots in a set of ideas that have emerged from business-school academics over the last 30 years." S. Ghoshal

"Business schools are partly to blame for the global recession and must change the way business is taught." B. Sheppard, former dean Duke University's Fuqua School of Business

Question: Who killed the shareholder-management-employee triangle?

Answer: Business schools

To understand how this culture of greed came about requires an understanding of the education and training these executives received, namely their education in American business schools.

The prevalence of gross compensation inequities in the corporation not only demoralized the workforce, it has literally destroyed the corporate compact between management and employees. This compact once allowed an employee to get a good job, and an opportunity to own a home in a community that was nurtured by the corporation, and have a defined pension and life-time health care. In return, employees gave to their corporations and generations went off to work for a company that was considered an extended family. This dramatically changed in the late 1970s as corporate acquisitions, global competition and capital mobility brought forth financiers, hedge fund managers and the infamous corporate raiders, orchestrating hostile takeovers where they generated enormous wealth by breaking up the corporations and selling off their assets.

The question is —how did this happen?

In the late 1970s seven important strategies were promoted by professors in business schools and business writers.

1. The integration of layoffs as a strategy to boost earnings. In many cases, the use of terminations as a strategy went from being a CEO decision of last resort to one of first resort (Uchitelle, 2006). It was given wording that neatly fit into the managerial glossary, with the popularization of words and phrases like downsizing, restructuring, reorganizing, transformation, reengineering, redesign, cost-cutting, rightsizing, staff cuts, early retirement, cost reduction, managed redundancy, and lean and mean. It was in early 1980s that downsizing first appeared in business schools' strategy textbooks and accepted as sound business practice. MBAs of the 1980s moved into executive suites at the turn of the century and ruined the lives of millions of hard working Americans.

2. In the late 1980s human resource departments accepted the concept of "human capital accounting" where employees were now treated as a "resource" and HR began to look more like finance departments.

3. The employer/employee compact ended. No longer could an employee expect the security of staying with a company for his or her career and to be taken care of after retirement. CEOs bought into the "lean and mean" metaphor, promoted by consultants and business writers. Strategies were put forth that suggested it was optimal to have a flexible workforce, expanding in good times, contracting in bad. Essentially, it meant one could reduce the work force and get those who remained behind to work harder, longer hours.

4. The reduction of the work force led to change in the hours of work. It was during the 1970s that a trend toward a decline in work hours ended. From the early 1900s to the 1970s (except during the Second World War), hours of work declined for most Americans. But around 1970, the share of employees working more than 50 hours per week began to increase. The increase in hours an employee worked began a steady increase: 25-to-64-year-olds who worked 50 or more hours per week rose from 14.7 percent in 1980 to 18.5 percent in 2001, and continued to climb. We now have a situation where employees work longer hours than any time since the industrial revolution. In 2007, employees worked a half a day more each week than they did in 2002, and a day more than they did a decade ago. In addition, one-third of American employees do not take their 10 days of paid vacation offered by their company, leading to a vacation-deprived workforce (HR.com, 2006). According to Bauerlein and Jaffferc (2011) Americans now put in an average of 122 more hours per year than Brits, and 378 hours (nearly 10 weeks!) more than Germans. The differential isn't solely accounted for by longer hours. Almost all countries maintain that weekends off, paid vacation time and paid maternity leave are a right. (The only other countries that don't mandate paid

time off for new moms are Papua New Guinea, Sierra Leone, Liberia, Samoa, and Swaziland). While American corporations give maternity leave, many do not offer paid leave. The amount of time working excludes working at home at night, on weekends or during vacation time on a BlackBerry or iPhone.

5. It was no longer considered good management practice to balance the interests of the shareholder-management-employee triangle. Executives were taught to focus on a single objective, the shareholder. They were motivated to maximize profit, and the "bottom line" became a popular metaphor. According to CEO Thomas Wilson, Allstate's corporate mission is clear: "Our obligation is to earn a return for our shareholders" (DiCello, 2008). Employees and the insured (customers) are not mentioned. Allstate lost $620 billion in the second quarter 2011.

6. An increased emphasis on mathematical and statistical modeling entered business school curriculum. During the early 1970's, business school deans, in their zeal to build their schools and seek favor among the science community, rushed to hire Nobel Laureates and in doing so added applied mathematical modeling to an ever-increasing array of financial and business problems. Decision analysis and decision modeling became widespread, assisted by sophisticated computer technology.

7. Critical thought and diagnosis was virtually removed from the curriculum in favor of an approach that emphasized formulation and implementation in the so-called decision sciences, which found a strong place in business school curriculum.

8. Professors of economics and finance climbed to central positions in business schools and substituted the words of "self interest" and "incentive to profit" for "greed." The Ronald Reagan con-

cept of "trickle-down" economics prevailed, and promoted the belief that allowing the wealthy to "have more" would be good for the economy, and if the rich got richer, their wealth would benefit the lower classes. In the face of such odds, more of the nation's pool of talented students decided there was no point in becoming a doctor or an engineer, when one could be a banker. During the heyday of business school growth, 1970 to 1990, Harvard graduates who entered finance career jumped from 5 to 15 percent, while those going into law and medicine fell from 39 to 30 percent (Goldin and Katz, 1999). These students entered corporate caverns in droves and we all know what happened.

9. Increasingly, university presidents were turning over their business schools to millionaire equity investment executives. Kenneth Freeman was offered the deanship of Boston University's B-School. He is from KKR, and his job was to oversee all of the firm's private equity investments around the world, including serving as director of hospital operator HCA, medical device maker Accellent, and building products manufacturer Masonite. In addition to his deanship Freeman will continue his affiliation with KKR as a senior advisor. Speaking of Kohlberg, Kravis and Roberts, in October 2010 Henry Kravis, called the Buy-Out king, pledged $100 million to his alma mater the Columbia Business School to help construct new facilities in Harlem and the building will be named after him. In another example Pace University's president appointed Neil Braun as their dean effective July 1, 2010. Braun, a lawyer, has 30 years experience in media management positions most recently as president of the NBC Television Network and CEO of Viacom Entertainment. B-schools seek these celebrity finance moguls to increase the school's visibility and of course

bring in "big bucks," like David Booth with his $300 million gift in 2008 creating the Chicago Booth School of Business or Philip Knight (of Nike) who gave who gave $105 million to Stanford creating the Knight Management Center. They want produce a David Tepper, who made $4 billion in 2009, or a multimillionaire celebrity politician like Mitt Romney.

B-school deans and their presidents have no idea of the negative consequences of such actions, especially on B-school faculty and students. To offer moguls positions and have buildings named after guys who destroyed much of the manufacturing in America and terminated millions of employees is brazenly unethical. They should all be given an ethics background check by outside ethicists before any university embraces them. But this will never happen. Instead a new generation of MBA students will dream of how to increase the "bottom line" and get rich.

BOTTOM LINE THINKING

The phrase "The bottom line is..." can be heard many times daily and is now pervasive in American contemporary language. It functions as an interesting metaphor. The purpose of the metaphor is to get people to focus on one thing, and that one thing is couched as the last thing; the most important thing, the bottom line. By using this metaphor one avoids discovering how one gets to the bottom line. The road to discovery is short-circuited as one races to the bottom line. It reduces speculation, doubt, and the possibility that many answers or perhaps no definitive answer can be found. When one makes a bottom line inference, one is stating that one has the answer. End of discussion. In polite discussion, one typically discusses the data used to support a theory or hypothesis. But often-times, the discussion is thwarted or data flow comes to a stop, as the discussant states, "the bottom line here is..." or "let's get to the bottom line." We have taken corporate thinking and applied it to everyday life.

FOCUS ON THE BOTTOM LINE

According to Mintzberg (2004), the obsessive focus on shareholder value at the expense of stakeholder value developed in the early 1990s as CEOs and business school academics linked shareholder value with bottom line thinking. Since 2000 more than half of all American CEOs compensation packages consisted of bonuses and stock options. These CEOs saw their only objective as "maximizing short-term shareholder value" and then they "get the hell out of Dodge." What these CEOs did not learn in B-school were the consequences of this behavior and the hurt they could inflict on men, women and children throughout the country. Even when economists suggested that the obsession with shareholder return caused the 2008 financial crisis, B-schools paid no heed. MBA students have drummed into them by professor after professor that business owners, managers, CEOs, and Boards of Directors are in business to add value to the shareholders – whether the shareholder is them or thousands of investors. And the bottom line for shareholders is the money a corporation can make for them: return on investment. They are told by professors "This is what capitalism is all about," and they read case after case about CEOs who have made shareholders and themselves rich. How can one properly educate a student when he/she enters a building or classroom honoring someone who got rich through the exploitation of workers?

This type of thinking coincides with the rise of the celebrity CEO, and the creation of the second "gilded age" where the rich got richer and the gap between the average employee and CEOs ballooned. There is no better example of this type of thinking then the bizarre contract (filed with SEC) that Yahoo had given to Carol Bartz, its CEO hired in January 2009.

The Agreement provides that Bartz will receive an annual base salary of $1,000,000, subject to annual review for increases, and will be eligible to receive an annual bonus with a target amount of 200% of base salary and a maximum amount of two times the target amount. The actual amount of the annual bonus will be determined by the Compensation Committee of the Board (the "Compensation Committee") based upon both the Company's and Bartz's performance for the relevant year.

In addition, Bartz will receive stock options (the "Inducement Options") for 5,000,000 shares of the Company's common stock ("Common Stock"), with a per share exercise price equal to the closing price of the Common Stock on the grant date (expected to be January 30, 2009) and a maximum term of seven years.

Vesting of the option will be dependent upon the attainment of average closing prices for the Common Stock for twenty consecutive trading days prior to January 1, 2013 (or, if a Change in Control occurs prior to January 1, 2013 or after that date if it is pursuant to an agreement signed before that date, the price immediately preceding the closing of the Change in Control) as follows: (i) 1/3 (1,666,667 shares) will vest at 150% of the exercise price; (ii) 1/6 (833,333 shares) will vest at 175% of the exercise price; (iii) 1/6 (833,334 shares) will vest at 200% of the exercise price; (iv) 1/12 (416,666 shares) will vest at 225% of the exercise price; (v) 1/12 (416,666 shares) will vest at 250% of the exercise price; and (vi) 1/6 (833,334 shares) will vest at 300% of the exercise price (the "Vesting Levels"). Any shares acquired upon exercise of the Inducement Options must be held until January 1, 2013, except in the event of death or a Change in Control.

Bartz will also be granted annual equity grants at the time grants are generally made to senior executives as determined by the Compensation Commit-

tee. She will receive an annual grant for 2009 with a value of approximately $8,000,000 which is expected to be granted in February 2009.

Bartz will be eligible to participate in the benefit programs generally available to senior executives of the Company, including health insurance, life and disability insurance, the Employee Stock Purchase Plan, 401(k) plan, and a Flexible Spending Plan. She will be entitled to four weeks of vacation per year. The Company will also pay or reimburse her for reasonable expenses incurred in connection with her employment, including up to $150,000 for advisory fees incurred in connection with entering into the Agreement.

In addition, to compensate Bartz for the forfeiture of the value of equity grants and post-employment medical coverage from her previous employer, the Agreement provides for an equity grant with a grant-date value of $10,000,000, payable 25% in cash and 75% in restricted stock, which will vest and be settled in equal and proportionate quarterly installments in 2009 (the "Make-Up Grant"). The Make-Up Grant will be subject to certain clawback provisions in the event of a termination for Cause or without Good Reason during the Term. The Company will also provide post employment medical coverage under its plans to Bartz, her spouse and eligible dependants as necessary, with Bartz paying the full premiums (Herscher, 2009).

The contract Bartz signed was all about the stock, and enriching stockholders and herself in the process. If the stock jumped she could earn up to $39 million in total compensation in 2009. Long-term planning, and taking care of Yahoo's workforce, are not tied into any rewards and are completely absent and apparently meaningless. A big mistake. It is possible, even probable, that Bartz could destroy Yahoo's workforce to enrich the bottom line and her compensation. And she has done just that. In December 2008, she terminated 1,500 employees, bringing the total terminations in 2008 to 2,400. In January 2009, Bartz announced a salary freeze for all employees, and in April 2009 she terminated 5 percent of Yahoo's workforce. Her stockholders and portfolio managers applauded, as the stock immediately went up almost 9 percent. In November 2010 it was announced that she would terminate 20 percent of the workforce, or 2,800 employees. Bartz, like many CEOs rationalized these mass terminations as "attacking the cost level," and not putting people out of work to get rich. There was a time when the press and media would find an appropriate nickname for such a CEO, perhaps calling them "chainsaw" or "neutron" and they would justifiably attack and embarrass the CEO. But in 2009, this type of behavior has become so accepted by the business-school-trained reporters that she is praised. Consider what Letzing (2009), writing in the Wall Street Journal, states: "Bartz's candid style and decisiveness have lifted morale and added clarity to the company's mission. She's unveiled a dramatic home-page revamp, and jettisoned moribund aspects of the company's online network." A dramatic home-page revamp? Letzing goes on: "For these reasons and more, Bartz has been named a finalist for MarketWatch's CEO of the Year award for 2009." This is expected from the WSJ but not the New York Times. She is called "tough-minded" by Times reporter Helft (2009). On October 21, 2009, Helft praised Bartz announcing that she had tripled profits and the stock jumped 244 percent in the third quarter of 09. How did she do it? She terminated employees and cut salaries. Neither of these reporters mentioned this fact, but they did mention that revenue fell 12 percent. The problem reporters have with CEOs, especially celebrity CEOs, is if they engage in a negative analysis or *muckraking*, they will quickly discover no CEO will talk to them. So they engage in positive reporting, often appearing to be the CEO's cheerleader, and they obtain lots of interviews. We know there is a relationship between the CEOs compensation and favorable reporting, and there may be a strong relationship between favorable CEO reporting and stock rise. One news report was not so favorable: On October 12, 2010, the New York Post called Bartz the most overpaid CEO in America when performance was compared with her $39 million pay package. As the 2010 holidays approached, droves of employees were observed carrying boxes of their belongings as they exited "The Bartz Debacle." In September 2011 Bartz received a phone call from the board chair and she was told she was out. She then sent an email to all Yahoos employees stating, "I am fired." and there was dancing in the streets. "When will they ever learn" you cannot treat employees badly and expect a company to survive? The work of the CEO is not to enrich the stockholders or oneself, it is to treat employees with respect and dignity and then everyone benefits. But Bartz did not care, she got her "golden boot." If she uses her "fired without cause" clause in her contract, does incompetence count? She may get $3 million cash: a pro-rated bonus (Who thinks these things up?) will add $1 million to $2 million and stock grants could total $5 million.

BOTTOM LINE THINKING AND DESTRUCTION OF THE EMPLOYER-EMPLOYEE COMPACT

Prior to the 1980s, layoffs were rare because corporations and employees both recognized they were bad for both. Prior to the 1980s generations of workers retired with defined pensions and lifelong benefits. When the focus shifted to the bottom line, the social compact between employer and employee was suddenly considered unprofitable and not in the interest of shareholder value. Gone was an appreciation of the complexity associated with thinking of the corporation as a "good citizen" or capable of "doing good" in the broader sense. The complexities associated with the social compact required critical thought and long-term planning with all its nuances and competing benefits. But executives were taught this was a waste of time and money. In the late 1970s business schools started moving away from critical thinking, and the move away rapidly escalated in the 1980s as business professors and consultants told real and potential CEOs they could use layoff's and outsourcing as a main management method for pumping up stock prices. Executives taking a "bottom line" approach quickly abdicated their responsibilities associated with commitment to employees and life-time benefits. They dumped a value system that emphasized responsibility over profitability, and they rejected a belief that their success was based on obtaining satisfaction among all stakeholders. They were taught and accepted the idea that corporate stockholders had a higher moral claim on the corporation. CEO success shifted and was now exclusively measured by share price, dividends, and economic profit. This trend continues. According to Conference Board (2008), almost all industries show a reallocation of compensation toward stock and away from cash compensation. Furthermore, in an assessment of the largest 10 percent of companies in their sample, the median CEO holds about 100 times his or her salary in total stock and stock options in the company.

A good example of this occurred in 1991, when defense contractor General Dynamics brought in new management team with the bottom line mentality. The new team adopted an explicit corporate objective of creating shareholder value. The company tied executive compensation to shareholder wealth creation, and subsequently implemented a strategy that included downsizing and restructuring. Paying large executive cash bonuses amid layoffs ignited controversy. By 1993 shareholders realized gains approaching $4.5 billion, representing a dividend-reinvested return of 553 percent (Dial and Murphy, 1995).

Dial and Murphy (1995) demonstrated how these types of financial incentives given to executives were a key motivation for shaping strategy. Their study also illustrates that the economic benefits of bottom line thinking for firms in declining industries can have substantial opportunities for value creation for the executives and stockholders.

CEOs also found another way to reduce costs and their responsibility to their employees. Corporations shifted their responsibilities for training employees to government funded vocational technical schools, community colleges and universities. When the company no longer needed an employee's particular attribute or skill there was no longer a recognized basis for the worker's employment in the company. The idea of the corporation training and retraining was no longer practiced. Obsolete employees were quickly discharged and sent off to public institutions to acquire the required skills necessary to return to find a job.

BUSINESS SCHOOLS BECOME VOCATIONAL INSTITUTES

The newly appointed MBA head of the Kelly B-school at Indiana University states in his first interview in August 2009 that "our sole goal in the MBA program this year is to confront the job market. This economy is unprecedented, and we will be implementing new ways to help students engage the job market effectively" (IU News Room, 2009). This type of thinking has permeated B-schools and has turned them in vocational training institutes for corporate America.

There is considerable controversy in America's business schools today concerning the best method to educate budding executives. There are the demands made by corporations and their CEOs who want MBAs ready to jump into executive roles and make significant contributions. They see the B-school as a training ground, and they donate large sums of money and send their executives to expensive executive programs where they expect schools to prepare them for leadership roles. The corporation has a direct investment in selected B-schools and they have turned them into "voctech" corporate training programs. CEOs do not want to establish their own training programs because they find it much easier to donate a few million to their favorite B-school, offer their faculty consulting gigs, sit on B-school boards, and send their executives to a customized training program. B-school deans eagerly pursue these arrangements and offer CEOs celebrity status on their campus. But there was a downside. In the process, B-schools have sold their souls, given up academic choice and freedoms, and pushed serious scholars aside in favor of "how to do it" motivational speakers and celebrity professors. A serious conflict has evolved. There are deans, corporate leaders and professors who want to push forth the "corporate/practice model" of education and others who reject the voctech approach and believe the "theoretician/practitioner or scholar/practitioner model" of education is the correct way to educate MBAs, and produce scholarly Ph.D.s. Both sides of this conflict claim the other side is destroying business schools, and some even claim the other side is responsible for corrupt and unethical CEO behavior. This battle is evenly split along ideological lines, with those pushing forth the "corporate/practice" calling "theoretical/scholars" longhair leftists. In many B-schools open warfare between the two groups exists. At the McMaster B-school, the president had to step in after an internal audit raised "grave concerns" describing a vicious conflict that has split the school into two camps - those from an academic background and those from a business background. The academics wanted the dean out and the corporate faculties want him to stay. According to Hemsworth (2010) "Even those who don't belong to either camp say it has become difficult to work in a toxic atmosphere where many have been driven to seek prescription medicine for stress, anxiety and depression… Each accuses the other of subverting the work of the school by blocking appointments and promotions in a form of "academic mobbing" that has brought the school to an impasse. The business school has become a dysfunctional work environment." The report maintains that this problem goes back 20 years between successive deans and faculty. Is this unique? Of course not. Dig deep pass the niceties of the collegial climate and one would find a cesspool of nastiness and envy. In B-schools that have an open tenure process where liberal arts faculty members have a say in the promotion and tenure process, the corporate faculty are often doomed exacerbating conflicts between the corporate dean and the entire faculty. This causes many deans to get a building away from the academics with their own promotion and tenure process. In some cases deans create a special track for these corporate faculties called the "clinical professorships", and they stay on forever never having to seek tenure and serving at the pleasure of the dean. In December 2010 the controversial Dean Paul Bates stepped down, and now they will begin the process of finding a new leader. This raises the question: How can they teach business management and leadership when they cannot even run their own B-School?

Across America deans of business schools have aligned themselves with the corporate/practice model. Why? The answer is simple. Deans run their schools with two objectives in mind: obtain corporate money, and increase their ranking status in the various magazines. And they are not unrelated.

On the theoretician or scholar/practitioner side of the argument is Zimmerman (2001), who maintains American business schools are on the decline. He claims that these institutions have moved away from their scholarly work of generating and disseminating new knowledge and instead are locked into a dysfunctional competition for rankings. On the other side, is Donald C. Hambrick, the former president of the Academy of Management, who wants to move away from the theory model to the practice model. He claims the field of management "... suffers from a 'theory fetish' that makes its research inaccessible and alienates the business community" (Gill, 2008). Hambrick may be correct. The theoretical/scholar model may alienate the business community. He seems confused about the goals of the educational community.

EDUCATING EXECUTIVES: THE MBA EDUCATION

There is a push afoot to professionalize B-schools and offer some form of licensure where one would be required to seek permission to practice management. Hambrick and others want MBA schools to follow the teaching model found in professional schools like medicine, law, clinical psychology, etc. He claims these schools succeed because they have rejected the academic the theoretician or scholar/practitioner model of education. This is not correct. These professional schools clearly utilize the scholar/practioner model. Consider the lunacy of relying exclusively on the corporate/practitioner model: A student completes his or her course of studies using the case study teaching method, without any background in theory and basics, and then goes off to join the corporate world. Would one let a medical, architecture, law, clinical psychology student go off to practice with a course of study devoid of a solid grounding in theory or basics? The medical student undertakes a long course of study on the basics of anatomy, physiology, pharmacology, and clinical disease states. Only when the student has a solid knowledge of the basics are they ready to start seeing patients. The medical student does not rely exclusively on written cases and textbook situations as the business school student does. Medical students learn from working with real people and with all the variability that patients offer, under close supervision from experienced physicians. Each patient encounter is rigorously critiqued by senior physicians. If there is any deficiency in history-taking or examination skills, they are addressed immediately, and the experienced physician then demonstrates the correct history-taking procedure and what physical findings the student missed or misinterpreted. In addition, the medical student formulates diagnoses and the treatment plans associated with each of the possible diagnoses. If there are five possible diagnoses, then students must come up with five different treatment plans. This includes what students will do to work up the diagnostic possibilities;

how they will confirm or deny each possibility, and what therapeutic regiment the student will prescribe for each of those diagnostic possibilities. The focus is on the student's critical thinking, analysis, and reasoning skills. If there are deficiencies, these are corrected and then honed, hopefully to razor sharpness.

If we contrast this with the education of an average MBA, we understand why they have a high failure rate and why senior executives do not value them and why we still have a preponderance of CEOs who do not have MBAs and why our corporations are in major trouble. According to Fortune magazine in April, 2001, the leading CEOs of the Fortune 200 had these degrees:

79 MBAs

15 JDs/LLBs

12 Ph.D.s

2 M.D.s

18 others had non-MBA graduate degree

74 had no graduate degree

There are four major questions facing MBA programs:

1. Is an MBA's training necessary to run a major corporation? Obviously not. In 2006 only a paltry 38 percent of Fortune 500 corporation CEOs had MBAs. In the retail industry only 26 percent of the 50 largest corporations have MBAs.

2. Do MBA holding CEOs perform better on the job than other CEOs? Again, the answer is no. As a matter of fact CEOs with no advanced degree did better with median total return to shareholders, followed by CEOs with a doctorate and then CEOs with a master's

degree. MBA CEOs came in forth, only capable of beating out CEOs with law degrees.

3. Who does a better job of maintaining the employer-employee compact? Anecdotal data suggests that MBAs do the poorest job of protecting their employees and are more prone to terminate employees to increase stock value

4. But what about those CEOs who commit crimes, lay off employees and get bonuses and compensation increases, or lose millions and get a raise or bonus? The survey suggests that MBA CEOs score high in these categories representing between 60 to 70 percent of the scoundrels. This is consistent with the research suggesting that MBA students not only cheat more than other graduate students in other disciplines, but they also cheat more on entry tests like the GMAT, the test that is typically required to gain entry into MBA programs. Students not only cheat on the test to gain entry, they cheat on interview questions where students pay between $5,000 to $9,000 for MBA admissions consultants to write their admission essays and prep them for interviews by stealing the interview questions. Who are these consultants? They are alumni or former admission officers at elite MBA schools.

Reiss (2010) claims that cheating on exams and term papers are at epidemic levels. Many universities are forced to put all term papers through Turnitin, software to detect cheating. But these clever students can get around any detection system. Also there is another phenomenon at play. Reiss (2010) states, "The universities have reacted by accommodating the cheats. When I was an undergraduate, my college expelled students caught cheating or plagiarizing. When I was an assistant professor, students caught cheating automatically flunked the course. When I was an associate professor, students caught cheating flunked the test. When I became a full professor, students caught cheating threatened to sue me for false accusation. Nobody wanted to deal with cheating; everybody wanted to look the other way." If MBAs make up only 38 percent of CEOs but 60 to 70 percent of the greedy CEOs, this implies that business schools are indeed failing. Where do these executives get their cheating lessons? In B-schools.

Think about this. As the result to the financial crisis and compensation scandals, many deans and educators know there is something rotten in their B-schools. They realize that the problems of greed and entitlement are associated with a curriculum that teaches MBAs to see employees as a commodity and corporate life as a Darwinian struggle. They know they are accepting for admission students who will readily lie, cheat and connive to pass courses they hold in contempt, and will do so in corporate life to climb the ladder and get rich. What are the deans going to do to change this corrupt educational system? They will offer oaths. Consider the Thunderbird School of Global Management's oath of honor:

I will strive to act with honesty and integrity. I will respect the rights and dignity of all people. I will strive to create sustainable prosperity worldwide. I will oppose all forms of corruption and exploitation. And I will take responsibility for my actions. As I hold true to these principles, it is my hope that I enjoy an honorable reputation and peace of conscience.

Here are the problems with this. First, it is an easy cover for the underlying problems with MBA programs and the covert ideology found in textbooks, teachers and curriculum that support the attainment of wealth for executives and corporate stockholders. And of course B-schools professors like Theo Vermaelen see the Oath's commitment to the social good at odds with the fiduciary duty of business executives towards shareholders. This leads right back to the type of thinking that created this crisis of 2008 and created the gap between the rich and everyone else and the loss of millions of jobs. The type of thinking that maintains the following position: "Isn't the point to maximize shareholder wealth no matter what?" (Parramore, 2011).

Second, what one says in B-school and what ones does when they get into the corporate world many years later has little or no relationship. The oath assumes that it will subsist overtime, like a marriage oath. We all know about that one. And, finally if one really wants to be clear about what one must do to oppose corruption and exploitation, this oath should include the following; *"When I see corruption or exploitation I will blow the whistle and willingly take the risk that I will spend years in court, become financially ruined, and increase the likelihood that I will be forever unemployable."*

Will this happen. Of course not. Instead we will witness B-schools claiming to teach ethical behavior while they run in an unethical race to look good, get bigger, and climb the rankings ladder. All it takes is fat cat donors who give money and lots of it. Administrators do not seem to care where the money comes from. Consider the University of Utah's school of business. The C.R. England trucking company gave the school a $3.5 million gift and they will get a new pavilion named after C. R. England. The building also has a lecture hall named after Eugene K. and June D. England, C.R. England's son and son's wife (Leonard, 2010). The B-school dean stated "This is a company that embodies the spirit of what we are trying to instill in our students." Unfortunately the dean did not conduct a background check on Mr. England and his company (all he needed to do was to Google- "CR England scam"). Or maybe he did. The company is notorious for cheating and abusing truckers and those unemployed and poor who are seeking employment. Recently a federal judge ruled against C.R. England in an OOIDA case:

In his ruling, U.S. District Judge Ted Stewart found that the company's independent contractor operating agreement is "unconscionable." The judge ruled that the operating agreements are so one-sided as to unfairly surprise an innocent party. He found that there is an overall imbalance in favor of C.R. England

and against the drivers in the rights and obligations of the parties under the agreements.

In particular, the judge noted that during any dispute between C.R. England and a driver, the company has control over the driver's money. The agreements allow C.R. England to choose whether to go to court or to bring a claim in arbitration. Also, C.R. England has the right to sell its claims to a collection agency and avoid the cost of either arbitration or a lawsuit.

The important issue here is the message the dean gave to his students. Can the dean justify his statement that England trucking embodies the spirit of what we are trying to instill in our students? Of course he cannot. What he does is to join the ranks of the many business leaders, bankers, hedge fund managers and others who set their number one priority: the accumulation of money. Business Week now ranks undergraduate B-schools on business ethics. This school should be ranked last.

Another movement by deans and B-school administrators to get money and grow big is to professionalize corporate leadership and have the MBA degree become the equivalent of a professional license to lead a corporation. Consider what "MBAoath.org." suggests: "Our long-term goal is to transform the field of management into a true profession..." This is delusional thinking. It was their MBA training that created these "let's get rich" corporate titans. If deans and celebrity business professors want to respond to the fiscal mess and change their training, the way to do it is simple. Do not teach your students how to manage from the top down. Teach them to understand the corporation from the bottom up. Have them read Studs Terkel instead of Michael Porter. Teach them to understand the lives of working people, not Jack Welch. Teach them the history of the industrial revolution and have them read Dickens. Teach them about the huge change in the human condition this industrial-corporate-global revolution has brought us, both positive and negative. Have students think about the nature of work and how a CEO can contribute to making a better life for their employees, their families, and communities. Teach them the value of the once dominant employee-employer compact. Do this and you do not have to teach a course in ethics, values, or how to be fiscally responsible, and you will not need to have them sign a "let's all be ethical" oath. And, one final thing, please, keep out of B-schools: celebrity CEOs, motivational gurus, and shameless consultants. And please do not give tenure to any professor who so arrogantly writes a "how to do it" book.

Will they do this? Never. Instead they will do what Harvard MBA does. Bring in multimillionaire celebrities (the 1 percenters) so students can tell them what they can do to increase their wealth. Harvard brought in Lebron James and his business partners and they were given access to research studies in branding and marketing strategy neatly packaged into a case study from students and professors. Other case studies were devoted to Lady Gaga, Real Madrid, Maria Sharapova, the NFL, Tom Cruise, and Radiohead. And what did the students get? They met the stars and got virtual backstage passes to Hollywood, to the highest levels of European soccer, to arena concert tours, to all the important places where the cult of celebrity multimillionaires reign. Why? To instill into the students minds an infatuation with wealth, status and celebrity. Why not bring in the unemployed, those foreclosed on, those declared surplus employees living in cars (the 99 percenters). Consider this, if B-school deans and professors put their efforts into helping those in need, they would not need to teach a course on ethics or make their students take an oath.

MBA PROGRAMS ARE FAILING

Most, if not all, MBA programs teach leadership. The truth of the matter is no one knows how to teach leadership, no one knows how to run a corporation, and no one knows how to properly train a manager. Why? Every manager is different; different personalities and different ways of seeing the world. Also, leadership is not generic, every corporation is different, and they all call for different leadership styles. What is the best we can do? Teach our students to know themselves, to know where they may function well and where they may not. This requires that we also teach them diagnostic skills: how to understand the depth of organizational difficulties. But instead we see a continuing trend toward decreasing educational quality and offering quickie, practice-oriented degree programs. Canisius B-school created one of these quickie MBA programs emphasizing the business decision process. In one year a student can complete 51 graduate credits and obtain an MBA. They claim the student will learn formulation and implementation, and the student will learn to *"...identify a problem, recognize the key issues involved and develop solutions."* No diagnosis. We need to teach them that trying to fix problems or bring about change (like a fiscal crisis) is fruitless unless they can develop a deep understanding of why the system is broken. However, given the money driven culture of B-schools and the fact they have not changed their basic curriculum in 50 years, the fact that deans see their job "looking good," and the quality of the faculty that occupy tenured positions, it is doubtful we will witness any genuine change, just window dressing.

We are now beginning to see why MBA applications have been dropping in America. The heyday of the 1990s is over and the value of the MBA is decreasing. Also, in 2008 with high unemployment, the fiscal crises at hand, and a glut of MBA job seekers, it is difficult to expect enrollment to increase. In 2009 applications at the top B-schools dropped and in 2010 they dropped further (Tracer, 2010). As applications drop in America, we witnessed the opposite in Europe, China and India. In Europe the numbers of applicants to their B-Schools increased 90 percent from 2006 to 2010, with a third of the applicants from

India and China. In the United States, 57 percent of the applicant pool was from Asian countries.

Also, according to The Financial Times, the 2010 global ranking had only 11 of the top 25 business schools located in America a drop from 1999, when 20 of the top 25 were located in America. This suggests that the quality of American business schools is dropping. In the top 10 alone, half of the schools are outside the United States: from England (No. 1 London Business School), France (No. 4 INSEAD), Spain (No. 8 IE Business School and No. 9 IESE Business School) and Hong Kong (No. 6 Hong Kong University of Science and Technology). In 2011 there are eight schools that feature in the top 100 business school rankings of the Financial Times, up from only three schools four years ago. The likes of Hong Kong University of Science and Technology (HKUST), the Indian School of Business (ISB), China Europe International Business School (CEIBS) and Singapore's Nanyang and National University of Singapore (NUS) are reaping the benefits of the global economic shift and will precipitate the demise of American B-schools. We will no longer see Asians making up the majority of students in two-year American MBA programs.

So what will American business school deans do? They will increase their marketing efforts to win the competition for status and students. And bring in Lebron James and other celebrities.

THE MARKETING OF THE B-SCHOOL

What is being suggested by Hambrick and business school deans is that business schools are professional schools and, therefore, research needs to focus more on practice. They want their faculty to link practice with scholarship, and they claim this has not happened. Zimmerman (2001), suggests that what underlies this push towards practice is the competition for rankings and MBA students, especially the newest generation (Gen Ys), who clearly want to get their money's worth. This new generation values rankings and accreditation. They want their school to be high in the rankings and have the "triple crown" of accreditations: AMBA (Association of MBAs), EQUIS (European Fund for Management Development) and AACSB (The Association to Advance Collegiate Schools of Business). In addition they believe that a faculty that focuses on teaching, rather than research, will have more time for them (the students). Students carefully study the rankings as they appear in BusinessWeek, the Wall Street Journal, Forbes, Financial Times, Princeton Review, The Economist, GMAT, Eduniversal, U.S. News and World Report and probably a few others. Hispanic Business magazine also is in the rankings game: they rank business graduate schools for Hispanics. Even G.I. Jobs Magazine has joined the rankings lunacy and the Mason School of Business at the College of William and Mary was named to G.I. Jobs Magazine's 2011 top 15 percent list of "Military Friendly Schools". BusinessWeek even ranks B-schools on their Return on Investment (ROI). Of course, the fact that one may or may not have received an enlightening education does not matter, just how long it takes to make up the education cost and then some. In 2011 the Aspen Institute got into the rankings game and chose the ethics niche. They created a list of socially responsible business schools ranked by their course material and research on ethics and environmental topics. How examining course material and research translates into educating an MBA in ethics is a stretch.

Making the list reaches the point of absurdity when the dean of the College of Business and Public Administration at Cal State San Bernardino announces that her school is ranked among the top 18 most innovative business schools in the world by none other than a European CEO magazine (Hughes, 2010). Also, those who do the ranking have found it's good for business. Eduniversal a Paris-based educational consulting organization is in the ranking business, and they ranked Chico State's Business School No. 10 because they have a strong national reputation. They do? Even the blogs have gotten into the ranking business. Findthebest http://www.findthebest.com/blog/2011/09/07/top-10-expert-rated-business-schools/ claims to have the best expert-rated B-schools. If one drives through Cape Cod one will notice a plethora of "Best Chowder on the Cape" signs. This is what B-schools have become.

In Europe in 2010 we witnessed major changes as universities are merging not only to survive shrinking budgets but to move up the "global" university rankings. This has significantly reduced the number of universities. In Finland, the number of universities has decreased from 20 to 15 in just a few years. In Denmark, 25 universities and research institutions have been reduced to eight universities and three research institutions since 2007. In France, the University of Strasbourg—the country's largest institution—was formed in 2009 through the merger of three universities (Labi, 2011). Merging has also occurred in Wales, Belgium, Germany and Sweden and will most likely occur in Spain. In Italy, universities already facing a funding shortfall of 1.35 billion Euros in 2011 will plan cuts and alter priorities that will weaken the higher education system. We also see this in Greece and England where dwindling public financial support has caused dramatic tuition increases. University executives publicly state that mergers increase the likelihood that they will survive, because their status and prestige will increase. They are attempting to differentiate themselves in the quest for public funds, but they are also seeking semi-private status and they are moving away from the model that treats all universities with a sense of equality toward the American model where universities compete to move up the rankings and appear in magazines' "Best of…" lists. France plans for all universities to become officially free from government control and funding by 2012. in addition the government endorses merging institutions as a way of driving some of the country's institutions up the international rankings. For example, the Saclay Campus project, on the outskirts of Paris, envisions a grouping of some two dozen universities, *grandes écoles* (as France's elite schools of higher education are known), clusters, and research institutes. Its director has said that the explicit goal of the $6-billion project, which is due for completion by 2015, is to rank among the top 10 universities in the world (Labi, 2010). The most influential ranking is produced by Shanghai Jiaotong University called the "Academic Ranking of World Universities" (ARWU) commonly known as the Shanghai Ranking. In ARWU's rankings of 1200 institutions: institutional size, distinguished professors and Nobel winners count. So in 2010 universities merge to get bigger and put top professors under one roof to move up the rankings while students riot in the streets protesting tuition increases and changes that diminish their educational opportunities. In some ranking methods, the cost of obtaining a degree is a factor, assuming an expensive education is somehow related to quality. You can guess what this has done?

How are schools ranked? Generally two ways: First, the rankers send surveys to the dean's office and they are given to students and/or alums. then they either collect the data or they ask the students to mail the surveys directly to the company engaged in ranking. This methodology is far from scientific, and it can be open to fraud. Students' surveys can account for between 10 AND 50 percent of the total ranking score. What are students asked? They are asked to rate their professors, the quality of education, the facilities and service and of course internship and/or job placement. academic quality can account for another 30 to 50 percent of the ranking score. Here is where it can be problematic; often the quality score included in the rankings is the students' scores on entry tests like the GMAT for MBA or SAT for undergraduates. They turn a blind eye to the fact that testing has become a major industry and people pay thousands of dollars to be prepped and given the answers to these tests. For administrators to assume that there is a relationship between high entry-test scores and the quality of education provided is nonsense. They also look at student-faculty ratio and sometimes ask head-hunters what school produced the most employable students. Is this arbitrary? Of course. In addition these ranking companies hide the fact that survey returns rarely exceed 25 percent. This spurious process is further reinforced by the fact that over the years these rating companies rarely agreed on each other's rankings. For example, in the 2009 MBA rankings, BusinessWeek claimed the University of Chicago was No/ 1, U.S. News claimed Harvard, The Economist claimed Spain's IESE.

Yet deans fight to get good comparative data, and a successful year occurs when they report they moved up a notch in the rankings. According to Zimmerman (2001):

"Business school deans rise and fall with the media ratings of their schools, even though they admit that such ratings are at best imperfect measures of school quality. A decline in a schools ranking generates angry calls from influential alumni, trustees, university administrators, potential donors, and, of course, current students who fear the devaluation of their soon-to-be-granted MBA degrees. Deans…stress their importance as a student recruiting device-especially for foreign applicants, who account for upwards of 40 percent of many schools' entering MBA classes."

THE COMPETITION TO LOOK GOOD

Corley and Gioia (2000), maintain that focusing on these rankings causes schools to focus on "looking good" rather than "being good." Virginia Commonwealth University is an example of the "looking good" approach. They recruited their new B-school dean from Disneyland Resort in Anaheim. That's right, the former president of a Disneyland Resort will bring his skills running operations at theme parks, his "looking good" skills, to the B-School. They have their priorities straight. In his career at Disney he served as the manager of marketing development at Disneyland Paris, general manager of operations at Disney's Hollywood Studios in Orlando, Fla., and vice president and representative of Walt Disney Attractions Japan in Tokyo, all the necessary ingredients to run a B-school. The University of New Haven is following suit when it named marketing executive Lawrence Flanagan as executive dean of the College of Business and Professional Studies on June 1, 2011. He is credited with launching the MasterCard advertising campaign with the punch line "Priceless."

These deans are in a fight to win the competition for students, And the competition is fierce and getting worse as the economy falters, American students consider alternatives, and globalization means schools are going to India and China to increase enrollment. Since the 1980s, growth of B-schools has been meteoric throughout the world. In India, MBA programs have grown from 80 university-based departments and schools of management in 1990 to an astounding 1,800 full-fledged MBA schools in 2008. In a six-year period beginning in 2003, business schools in China doubled in number. As American schools compete to get a foothold in China, the Chinese schools are also going abroad. In September 2011, the Cheung Kong Graduate School of Business (CKGSB), established an overseas branch, in London.

Beginning in 2000 in the United States, the MBA program, at one time the university's "cash cows," started to slip. In the growth period of MBAs from 1980 to 2008, every college and university had to have one. It did not matter where, on campus, off-campus, in hotels and corporations, and on-line, often without any regard to the quality of the education they were offering. Business Schools were popping up everywhere. In San Francisco there were over 25 MBA schools including Babson, Hult International, Cornell-Queens, Berkeley-Columbia and the Wharton School. Consider the affluent County of Westchester, a bedroom community 20 miles north of New York City. There are 14 MBA programs within a 25-mile radius of the Tappan Zee Bridge over the Hudson River, and this does not include nationwide online or for-profit programs. To compete for students, they try every gimmick: from strategic location, convenience of courses- online and face-to-face, blended, evening and weekend courses, "highly relevant" courses, specializations, high-tech classrooms, intensive marketing campaigns and of course, status in the rankings. Quickie MBAs are prevalent. Nyack College advertises an MBA in 16 months by attending two evenings a week. With the sudden drop in applications in 2010, the competition for students increased while quality of the MBA decreased. Loyola University B-school in Maryland is a good example; they will establish several new programs in 2010. The first, called "Life After Loyola," is a two-day crash course for seniors in business etiquette, how to behave at a business dinner, the art of interviewing, how to choose health insurance and other things post-college, including how to buy a suit. All this for a fee of $150. In August 2010 they will offer a 12-month "Emerging Leaders MBA" designed for recent graduates with little or no work experience but with "ambitions to become a corporate leader." They are engaged in the shameful process of educating students to be leaders when they have never led anything and some of them have never worked. That's like preparing the paperboy to perform surgery. Because applications are dropping B-schools are aggressively pursuing the young recent graduates with little or no work experience. These students younger, than 24, are the fastest-growing group among those who take the Graduate Management Admission Test, according to the Graduate Management Admission Council. From 2004 to 2009, their numbers grew an average of 24 percent a year and in 2010, roughly 40 percent of applicants to full-time MBA programs had less than three years of work experience (Garone, 2010). The question emerges: Why give a quickie graduate business degree to young and inexperienced recent grads and send them into the marketplace with a watered-down MBA? The answer is simple: To keep the cash cow flowing. This is embarrassing and perhaps unethical. Mintzberg along with other scholars who maintain you cannot teach management to inexperienced students are paid no heed. There are others who maintain you cannot teach leadership when we do not know what leadership is. These B-Schools are committing borderline fraud by making false claims.

We have a situation where private agencies loosely assess the quality of a B-school after a one-day visit where the school puts on a well rehearsed a "dog and pony show" to three well paid professors who determine if the school will be allowed into the club. AACSB is a prime example. We have no government agency to sanction educational mills that offer next to nothing in the way of a thoughtful management education. Canada is the only country that gives MBA programs a license to operate, and in 2010 Lansbridge University was ordered to stop offering an MBA or Executive MBA because it was considered "substandard." Lansbridge will no longer be able to call its MBA program "Canada's premiere online business university."

HYBRID DEGREES

Another method to keep the MBA programs from slipping is the so-called hybrid degree programs where the student attends some face-to-face classes and does the rest of the course work online. Another method is to offer dual degrees; the MBA/JD degree is popular, but we witness the growth of MBA/MPA, MBA/MPH, MBA/MD, etc. Trying to win the popularity contest for students, most schools advertise that they use the Harvard case study approach, or they find a "big name" to name their schools after, or they seek corporate sponsorship. Jack Welch has two business schools named after himself. According to Glader (2009), Welch paid more than $2 million for a 12 percent stake in Chancellor University, which bought bankrupt Myers University for $5.25 million. It offers an MBA online at The Jack Welch Institute. Welch's other school is the Welch School of Business at Sacred Heart University. Some schools name their B-school after two people. The Claremont B-school is named after Peter F. Drucker and Masatoshi Ito. On their web page, Drucker is named the "founder of modern management" and Ito is called "a doer." Whatever is a doer? In addition to the MBA, Claremont offers a Masters in Arts Management (AM), an Executive Management Program (EMBA), a Master of Science in Financial Engineering (MSFE), a Master in Politics, and Business and Economics (MAPEB), a variety of certificate programs and "customized" corporate executive education offerings. Deans work hard to establish niches to attract students. For example, New England College of Business is offering a master's in business ethics, and it's online. And of course they all claim they are accredited by one or more of the regional, national or international agencies and associations.

In addition, B-schools have linked up with any academic department to make a few bucks. The number of joint MD/MBA programs has grown from about 6 in the late 1990s to 65 in 2011. Consider what Dartmouth's Tuck B-school has done. For an extra year's tuition you can get:

- **MBA/MALD** with The Fletcher School at Tufts University

- **MBA/MPA** with the John F. Kennedy School of Government at Harvard University

- **MBA/MELP** with Vermont Law School Environmental Law program

- **MBA/MA** with the Paul H. Nitze School of Advanced International Studies at Johns Hopkins University

- An **MD/MBA**, is offered with Dartmouth Medical School.

- An **MPH/MBA** is offered in Dartmouth's three-year program in public health management.

In 2009 Dartmouth continued the shameless display of giving away their MBA when the Tuck School announced that for one year of additional work, and of course tuition, they will give an MBA to any Ph.D. from its 16 scientific departments of biology, biochemistry, chemistry, computer science, earth sciences, engineering, experimental and molecular medicine, genetics, health policy and clinical practice, immunology, microbiology, mathematics, molecular and cellular biology, pharmacology and toxicology, physics and astronomy, physiology, and psychological and brain sciences. Just another of the many ways an MBA is devalued, and it's a demonstration of the type of thinking these administrators follow. Their aim is short-term, bottom-line financial success with little or no interest in the impact this has on the quality of the education they are offering or the larger academic community they operate within. B-Schools are rapidly becoming an embarrassment to the entire academic community.

THE END OF GROWTH

The end of B-school growth in America began in the early 2000s. A drop-off in applications seems to be in a mounting freefall since the 2008 financial crisis, as the economic downturn has brought a major change in the number of students who reported that they would pursue either majors or careers in business. According Marchand (2010) the proportion of students planning to major in business dropped in 2009 to a 35-year low of 14.4 percent, and those with "business career aspirations" fell 2 percentage points from 2008. While B-school deans put on a happy face, privately they are scurrying about trying to develop new ways to attract students. The graduate management council reported in 2004 that 78 percent of all full-time MBA programs reported a drop in admissions and in 2008, except for the so-called elite programs, almost every MBA program has reported a drop in applications. In 2010 the Wall Street Journal reported an overall decline of 2 percent for two-year MBA programs, a 4 percent decline in online programs and a 7 percent drop in part-time applications. Deans are busy denying this fact and some are bragging that their applications are up. It has been reported that in 2009, Executive MBA programs had an application volume decline of 25 percent and this is expected to increase over the next few years. In addition, very few companies are willing to send their junior managers to these programs at a clip of $100,000 to $150,000.

So students must go into deep debt (the average is over $100,000) to obtain their MBAs especially from the so-called elites who may be pricing themselves out of the market:

	Total Cost	Tuition
Columbia	$168,307	$106,416
Wharton	$168,000	$108,018
Stanford	$166,812	$106,236
Chicago	$165,190	$101,400
Tuck	$162,750	$101,400
MIT	$160,378	$100,706
Harvard	$158,800	$97,200

Kellogg	$156,990	$102,990
Haas	$144,746	$95,274
Duke	$105,944	$ 95,920

Source: http://poetsandquants.com/

5/31/11

There are several other factors driving this drop-off:

1. A new generation of students are approaching the MBA age range, and they carefully study the ROI of investing thousands of dollars in a degree that may have little return. They know the major consulting firms are hiring non-MBAs and may actually prefer the liberal arts people. Among B-school applicants in 2009, conducting an ROI is the number one reason for applying: it's not only using an ROI comparing B-schools, it is also conducting an ROI among different professions. Consequently, the potential graduate student will do an ROI on medicine, law, MBA, etc. Also many will apply to schools in all of these disciplines and will decide to go to the one that accepts them and/or offers the most aid. What a way to choose an occupation.

2. The rankings game has left the smaller schools in the dust, gathering the crumbs of the shrinking applicant pool. Every applicant believes that gaining entry into a Top 10 elite school is the only certain way of making the so-called big bucks.

3. The financial crisis has taken a heavy toll on the banking and hedge fund industry and has caused potential MBA students to move in other career directions.

4. B-school deans have dropped the ball, demonstrating more interest in "looking good" while pushing a segmented curriculum that has changed little in 50 years.

5. MBA program endowments have taken a big hit in the fiscal crisis. Elite schools have responded by terminating staff, increasing the size of their classes, and taking in more paying customers. This hurts the non-elite programs the most, and we will see the closing of many programs.

6. Since 9/11 it has been difficult for foreign students to gain entry to do their MBA in America. And MBA programs abroad have grown tremendously. Many job banks for MBA faculty only advertise for faculty in Asia and the Middle East. Most MBA programs are seeking a base in these geographical areas, however only the elite programs will survive.

7. We have a glut of MBAs in America. Since 1990 over 1.6 million MBA degrees have been awarded, more than any other graduate degree except education and law.

8. The chief utility of the MBA experience is networking, which will continue to lose its value as the Facebook-era GenYs, who are at MBA age level, have already established thousands of friends and contacts from kindergarten on.

9. The growth of MBA programs has shifted from America to the gulf, India and China. INSEAD, the ubiquitous French B-school, will offer an Global Executive MBA in Abu Dhabi in 2010. This is consistent with the Emirate's plan to make Abu Dhabi the hub, not only for business education, but all graduate education. Harvard, Tuck, and INSEAD are already operating and SAID of Oxford and Duke are planning to establish MBA and executive programs in India. Many more foreign universities are lined up on Indian shores, and this has caused the Indian Parliament to establish a law, the "Foreign Educational Institutions Regulation of Entry and Operations" bill, passed in March 2010. The bill will regulate entry, operation and restriction of foreign universities in India. This is in response to a Western-style MBA edu-

cation that Asians see as promoting greed, and the type of management skills that are not good for the country as a whole.

And finally, many blame the business schools, their professors and MBAs for the Enron's, greed, and the type of thinking that has created the financial mess and the loss of millions of jobs. In some cases announcing that one is planning to get an MBA is the equivalent of announcing one is joining the Army to fight in Vietnam in the 1960s. We do not have an accurate accounting of the percentage of MBAs who had key roles in the financial crisis of 2008, but here of some of the Harvard MBAs involved;

- Christopher Cox (former U.S. Securities and Exchange Commission chairman)

- Former Treasury Secretary Hank Paulson (ex-Goldman Sachs chief)

- Former Merrill Lynch CEOs Stan O'Neal and John Thain

- Rick Wagoner, the ousted General Motors CEO.

- Andrew Hedley Hornby, failed former CEO of what used to be one of the U.K.'s largest bank group, HBOS, which had to merge with Lloyds in the face of bad mortgage loans.

- Let's not forget George W. Bush, who proudly stated when running for president that he would be the first MBA president and he would run the government as a business. He then proceeded to lead America into the greatest financial meltdown since the Great Depression, as the tsunami of unregulated Wall Street derivatives collided with the bursting of the housing bubble.

There are three other Harvard boys who made significant contributions to the crisis. Not MBAs but close enough:

- Lawrence Summers former president of Harvard University and a Harvard Ph.D. in economics. He was former deputy secretary of the Treasury under Bill Clinton, where he helped prevent government employee Brooksley Born from imposing government oversight of derivatives, those toxic Wall Street investments now believed to be at the root of much of the current crisis.

- Franklin Raines, Harvard Law: Former CEO of Fannie Mae who took "early retirement" amid an accounting investigation.

- Daniel Mudd, MPA, Harvard Kennedy School of Government: Took over Fannie Mae from Raines and increased the number of subprime mortgages it guaranteed until the government dismissed him in 2008, when the feds had to put Fannie into conservatorship to keep it afloat.

In addition, another Harvard MBA, Rajiv Gupta was charged with giving insider information to three other MBAs who were charged by the SEC for making millions using insider information. All three: Raj Rajaratnam, Rajiv Goel, and Anil Kumar, graduated in 1983, not from Harvard but from the Wharton School.

According to van Valkenburg (2011) about half of the 30 bankers summoned to the New York Federal Reserve in September 2008 to devise a rescue plan for Lehman Brothers were Harvard Business School graduates.

The deans at Harvard are counting their blessings that Bernie Madoff did not attend. He studied business at Hofstra.

The Harvard B-School embarrassment does not go away. They claim to teach ethics while their faculty, led by their faculty star Michael Porter, engaged in receiving millions from Muammar Qaddafi, the former dictator of Libya to polish his image. It didn't work.

In addition, most of these elite B-schools have little or no conflict-of-interest policies, and professors run free engaging in activities to fatten their wallets. They teach courses and write reports and cases while accepting consulting fees and sitting of the boards of the very same industry, associations, or corporations where they supposedly apply their objective academic scholarship. Deans actually encourage these incestuous relationships, believing they are good for their schools' reputation. This climate of deception teaches our young business leaders a new morality, and we see ample evidence of this new morality played out daily in our corporate caverns.

COMPETING FOR STUDENTS

Other ethical lapses come into play as schools try to win the competition for students. We are seeing a dramatic rise in exaggerated claims and messages B-schools are posting about the quality of their education, the salaries of their graduates and their faculty with "real world" corporate experience and connections.

This is a quote from a student that appeared on one the MBA program's web page:

The best thing about .... is the people I've met. I've made great connections. And the professors have been out in the world...so you make connections there as well."

Another MBA program claims it has a *"Real-world application"* and is *"...famous for its practical, hands-on approach to business education. The creative synergy between ... and business ensures that classroom learning is grounded in the real world..."*

Consequently, to gain a competitive edge, deans promote their links with corporations. The subtle and not-so-subtle message is, "if you attend our school you will land a top paying job with a top corporation" or "we promise a great return on your investment." This is a spurious ROI that often has little relationship to reality and is nothing more than a marketing gimmick. After all, what is a Return on Investment? Is it the salary one gets immediately after obtaining an MBA? Is it the salary one is making upon retirement? Or is it somewhere in-between? Or, is it the sum total of the contributions one makes to society? Now that's a good one. It seems the MBA programs want their students to think of their $100,000 investment that will offer high returns and it make education or more the obtaining a MBA as all about the money and is far removed from the wish to be a successful and enlightened businessman or woman who builds a company that will provide jobs to folk in the community and improve the human condition and build a flourishing society.

The Terry School of Business at the University of Georgia is a prime example of B-schools making shamelessly bold claims to attract students. This is a quote from their website:

"The Terry Advantage is based on the distinct set of leadership skills and behaviors you will acquire in the Terry MBA Program. It is an advantage our graduates carry with them throughout their lives and careers, as they work in teams, solve problems, contribute to the success of their companies, and collaborate with others around the world to cure the global ills that threaten our children's survival."

Wow! Give them skills to cure global ills that threaten the lives of our children, and they can teach you this in their 11 month "quickie" MBA program. What a school.

But the height of all shame in winning the recruitment battle is directly linking the attainment of an MBA from their institution to the dollars one will make. In 2010 MBA students saw Google, McKinsey,

Bain & Co., and Goldman Sachs as the best places to work (What does that tell you?). We are beginning to see MBA programs advertising the number of their graduates recruited by these firms and of course their starting salaries. The Sloan school states on its website that its 2009 graduates who entered investment banking started at $100,000 and Goldman Sachs hired five. On Harvard's website the 2009 median investment-banking salary was $95,000, plus a whooping median signing bonus of $40,000. For their graduates who took jobs in the consulting field, they started with a median salary of $125,000, plus a $20,000 median bonus. Talk about ethics. What type of values does a student have who is motivated to pursue an MBA at these institutions? They carry these values as they climb the corporate ladder and they eventually become one of those corporate titans who fire employees, outsource, get stinking rich and hire guards to protect them from angry Main Streeters.

WHY AN MBA EDUCATION FAILS

It seems fair to conclude that B-schools contribute very little to the development of the ethical skills needed to function effectively for the benefit of society. This will continue as long as B-schools rely on marketing, rankings, celebrity professors and CEOs and have dean's who push their professors to write hastily written cases designed to promote executive decision making, emphasize problem solving, and teach the economics of shareholder primacy. While there is ample criticism of the excessive reliance on teaching financial models, theorems and theories and an abundance of financial professors publicly state that this financial bottom-line focus is too simplistic and led to the financial crisis of 2008, in 2011 B-schools are still teaching this was even though they are convinced they such approaches are based on false mathematical assumptions that create a sense of security even as failure approaches (Cossin, 2011).

It is also fair to conclude that when compared to traditional professional education, business schools come up woefully short. They have little or no idea of the inner workings of the world of business.

Here is the problem. The corporation and its executive constellation represent an exceedingly difficult phenomenon to study. It is not like the patient in psychotherapy, or the patient on the operating table, or the design and construction of a house. Studying the corporate community is similar to an anthropological study of a lost culture. This requires not a weekend in the field, completion of a questionnaire, a consultation, or an analysis of a case, but a full immersion. Margaret Mead spent almost 10 years living in New Guinea to complete her studies, a relatively simple society when compared to a major international corporation. Therefore, it is not a fetish with theory that trouble business schools, it is the lack of theory and this is the result of the difficulty gaining entry and becoming fully immersed in a corporation. Schools suffer from the lack of trained scholars who can test hypothesis in practice and they are given the time and luxury of living and work in the corporate world.

Several scholars report that their work as consultants to corporations gives them the opportunity to gain hands-on knowledge. But this does not work very well. Paid consultation merely gives a glimpse of the company. Rarely does a consultation offer an in-depth understand of the company as an interpersonal ecological system. In addition, most faculty at non-elite schools find it difficult to obtain consultations (they certainly could use the money) and most have never set foot in a corporation except as a customer. Those few academics who do take time off to live and study a corporation report being so overwhelmed by the pace, intensity, and anxiety of the workplace that it makes objective assessment difficult. In addition, in a corporation a participant-observer can often influence events to a significant degree and can also be influenced by what is referred to as biases and countertansference reactions (Czander and Eisold, 2001). However, those academics who do spend significant amounts of time working in the corporate world report that the experience changed their lives and the way they thought about organizations, leadership, employees, the way they teach and what they teach.

Given the requirements necessary to provide practice-oriented research, and with limited in-depth knowledge of the complexities of the corporation, we have an abundance of literature that narrowly focuses on a small aspect of corporate life. What we have is the blind man with the elephant. It is like trying to find a study of family life, by looking at a receipt for an evening's dinner out. What would happen if a faculty member went to his/her dean and asked permission to take a few years off to conduct a participation-observation study of a corporation? The dean would reply that the job of a faculty member is to teach and do research, not go off for a few years to learn about corporate life. So what is the primary source of information for business school faculty? Perhaps some consulting work, research publications, newspapers and magazines, textbooks, speeches (war stories) by CEOs: if lucky, they can learn from students who attend their evening class after working all day in the corporation. But the truth of the matter is that many teach in business schools with limited or no actual corporate experience. This is like teaching surgery without ever performing surgery or teaching psychotherapy without ever seeing a patient. To do this would be considered lunacy in professional schools, but it goes on in B-schools. Consequently it makes business education a travesty. If AACSB were serious about the quality of B-school education it would require its schools to have faculty take a sabbatical every five years and spend a year working 9 to 5 in a corporation. Instead of taking a sabbatical to write a "how-to-do-it" book.

The fields of law, medicine, anthropology, sociology, psychology, etc. would not have survived under the business school model of education.

They grew and became vehicles of quality education because they were devoted to field study, participant observation, controlled experimentation, and actual practice with students and teachers/mentors working together on internships and residencies.

FORGET THEORY, GET IT FIXED: THE FIX-IT MENTALITY

Business school deans desperate to move up in the rankings push their faculty to write professional trade books. They want their faculty to be on the business best-seller lists. Many elite B-schools have public relations and marketing experts to promote faculty members' books, consultations and speeches. Deans value the publication of trade books as opposed to research or theory based articles and books. A professor commented, that on his walk through the lobby of the Wharton School, he observed copies of books written by Wharton professors on display. He noticed that almost half were "How to do it" books devoid of theory or critical thought and analysis. Here are a few examples.

H. Bouchikhi and J. R. Kimberly. *The Soul of the Corporation: How to Manage the Identity of Your Company*, Wharton School Publishing, 2008.

V. Fung, W. Fung and Y. Wind. *Competing in a Flat World: Building Enterprises for a Borderless World*, Wharton School Publishing, 2008.

P. Cappelli. *Talent on Demand: Managing Talent in an Age of Uncertainty*, Harvard Business Press, 2008.

S. Friedman. *Total Leadership: Be A Better Leader, Have A Richer Life*, Harvard Business Press, 2008.

G. R. Shell and **M. Moussa**. *The Art of Woo: Using Strategic Persuasion to Sell Your Ideas*, Penguin Books, 2007.

J. Waldfogel. *The Tyranny of the Market: Why You Can't Always Get What You Want*, Harvard University Press, 2007.

L. M. Lodish, **H. Morgan** and **S. Archambeau**. *Marketing That Works: How Entrepreneurial Marketing Can Add Sustainable Value To Any Size Company*, Wharton School Publishing, 2007.

H. Wainer, E.T. Bradlow and **X. Wang**. *Testlet Response Theory and Its Applications*, Cambridge University Press, 2007.

D. Reibstein. *Marketing Metrics: 50+ Metrics Every Marketer Should Master*, Wharton School Publishing, 2006.

These "How to…," or "What every manager should do" or "What every manager should know" books would be considered "pop psychology" books in the world of academic psychology. They would never be allowed for consideration in the tenure process. We also make these "how to do it" professors deans. In 2010, Harvard appointed Nitin Nohria its dean. He is the co-author or co-editor of 16 books, almost all of them how-to books. One of his latest which he co-authored is *"What Really Works: The 4 + 2 Formula for Sustained Business Success."* Nohria's other claim to fame was his involvement in the "ethical oath movement" for B-school students.

What are professors teaching their MBAs? They are teaching: How to…, What to do…, What to know…, and lots of "Should do's" (like the latest take an oath to be ethical fad). These professors make the presumption they know how complex corporations function. These tend to be the most popular and well attended classes like: How to be an Entrepreneur, How to do Business with China, or How to Manage in Turbulent Times. As if anyone knows how to do these things. It is clear they are failing to teach an appreciation of the complexities of organizational life and the necessary critical analysis one must engage in to understand the consequences of executive decisions on their employees, their families and communities. Equally absent is their failure to teach the realities of climbing the corporate ladder and the toll it takes, as well as the experience of being an executive and working in the culture of an executive constellation. Instead they teach how to outsource and offshore.

As a result of the 2008 financial crisis and outrage over CEO greed, the blame has been placed on the MBA executives. B-schools have responded by engaging in curriculum reform. Zimmerman (2002) maintains that "…curriculum reforms lead to less rigorous, trendier, vocational style courses that students believe will help them obtain their first job."

In addition, Mintzberg (2004) doubts business schools can train a student to be a manager if the student never had an opportunity to manage. He maintains that business schools are making a mistake when they believe they can train people to be top managers with the present curriculum. He refers to David Ewing's 1990 book, *Inside the Harvard Business School*, which lists 19 of Harvard Business School's best alumni, the superstars of that time. Mintzberg (2004) then tracked these alumni from 1990 to 2003. Ten were total failures, four were very questionable in their performance, and only five had clean records. On the list was Frank Lorenzo, who had major failures with three airlines and major problems with employees. Mintzberg maintains Lorenzo should not have been allowed to run anything because he didn't have managerial skills. All he had was good manipulative financial skills. According to Bhagat, Bolton, and Subramanian (2010) there is no significant systematic relationship between CEO education and long-term company performance. They found that the education a CEO obtains has no relationship to his or her ability to manage. Mintzberg's findings suggest there may be an inverse relationship between an MBA elite education and long-term corporate performance.

B-schools hop from trend to trend, looking toward Harvard Business for guidance. In the process they have given up the creativity and experimentation that goes into making a quality graduate program. For example, trendsetter Harvard has decided to step up the teaching of leadership skills, personal values and cases analyzing the crises, and sure enough, the other B-schools followed along. A professor with 35 years of teaching in MBA programs stated, "Here we go again, after Enron it was all about teaching ethics and now it's all about greed, so they will teach leadership values and character building when there is a substantial lobby that maintains we do not know how to do this. How in the world can a professor teach values or character building when he doesn't know what he's doing and how can we teach leadership when we don't know what the hell leadership is?" However, we do know that rewards, bonuses and the promise of a high-paying job can undermine self-perceived altruism and decrease intrinsic motivation to help others (Batson, 1978). Plus we know that positive reinforcement will reduce a person's sense of responsibility, fairness, sharing, and kindness. We can teach these MBAs the problems they will face when they move into the corporate world, and we can tell students there is a strong possibility that they will be changed by the competition for rewards, advancement, and success, and there is a good chance they will become one of those greedy characters they read about. But this will not happen. Instead students will read case studies of how the corporate princes got us into the financial mess and what we "should do" to get out of it.

EMPHASIS ON THE CASE STUDY

The chief learning instrument used in most business schools is the case study method, developed by none other than Harvard. Almost every textbook contains an abundance of cases. For example, Gareth Jones' Sixth Edition of Organizational Theory, Design, and Change contains 29 cases. Some of these cases are outdated, some are fictional, and some are simply wrong. The case study method is a classroom discussion of a story; in some cases a vignette and in others a complex lengthy description of a problem. The major issue traditional academics have with cases is that they are limited tools for establishing reliability or generality of findings. In addition, these cases have a top-down view of corporate issues. The assumption is the case will get the student to begin to think like an executive. This is nonsense. Students have little or no corporate experience, and certainly no executive experience.

Some dismiss the case study method as useful only as an exploratory tool. Others claim that teaching, patterned on the Harvard Business School model, deprives students of an authentic learning experience. As a result, students fail to develop important entry-level skills that they need for success in their business careers. Consequently, students become less active and more dependent on the professor in class, make decisions about the unreal world of business with little understanding of theory, and engage in group projects that are far removed from the tasks they are expected to perform on the job.

When using the case approach the professor becomes a genius, a star and at the same time students become passive, in awe of the brilliance of their professor. This is a critical factor in determining why professors embrace the method and it requires little effort or knowledge. It's important to remember most business professors never worked in a formal corporation and most never occupied a managerial position. That is why they need and rely on answer keys. Most students are not aware that every teacher receives the equivalent of the answer key or trot. It works this way: After student's struggle discussing the case, the professor chimes in with the "bottom line." Students prepare for class by reading the case. They then select a strategy and prepare to defend it. If time permits, they discuss their work with a few classmates before coming to class. The real action is in the classroom. The professor, who is expected to be a skilled discussion leader, asks provocative questions, pits one student against another, compares alternative solutions and goads the class into reaching significant conclusions (Bonoma, 1989). Students must read the case and then with little information they must make quick decisions. According to Harvard B-school graduate van Valkenburgh (2011), through two years of case method learning MBA, candidates make and defend over 500 decisions and "Plans-of-Action." She goes on, "The goal is to train leaders with confidence to take bold action despite intense time pressure and incomplete information. Valuing the decision above all, however, without careful examination of its ramifications, denigrates deeper reflection and trains managers to leap to shaky conclusions."

Given typically large class sizes, the individual student's participation consists of perhaps one or two verbal contributions and a lot of watching and listening. Furthermore, even if the instructor wants to shift the focus of the learning experience from him/herself to the students and organizes them into small groups to make a presentation on the case, the learning is limited. Consider the layout of contemporary business school "smart rooms." According to Atlas (1996), the classroom layout makes group study and preparation very difficult. In many business schools students sit at tables fixed to the floor and arranged in five levels, colloquially identified (in rising order) as Worm Deck, Garden Deck, Power Deck, Warning Track and Sky Deck.

Newly-hired MBAs quickly discover that what they learned in business school has little applicability to the corporate world. First, they do not participate in meetings of 90 people, arranged in decks and tracks conducted by expert case study discussion leaders. Typical business meetings consist of three to six people. In these meetings it is expected that MBAs will be able to function effectively as members of small teams, sometimes working under tight time pressures. In addition, in real-world business settings MBAs are not given case studies written by expert writers to analyze. If the newly-hired MBA is assigned to make a recommendation about a business situation, a substantial part of the assignment is to gather information and prepare an unbiased analysis of the situation.

In addition, cases are rarely studied from the perspective of lower-level employees. Typically, the student studies the decision-making of the executive constellation, a collection of people who are very far from any relevant experience of the typical student. It is like teaching someone about human behavior who has never met a human being.

Also, focusing on a case as an instrument of learning without a strong background in theory and practice avoids standard scholarly research that is historically valued in academia. For example, we see no evidence of the use of any thoughtful and rigorous methodology required to assess and evaluate variables. Plus we see little evidence of rigorous participant or observational research. The best we can say about a case is that it offers the student an opportunity to analyze a story. Even worse, students and professors avoid conducting an analysis and spend their time offering solutions. Critical thinking, a vital part of managerial thought, is often absent and the student approaches each case with a "fix-it" mentality. Unfortunately, this type of thinking is pervasive in American corporation. It is reasonable to assume that the teachers do not have the necessary information, skills or background to analyze a case and they rely on the "cheat sheet" that comes with each case.

We have seen the use of case studies increase while the production of research and theory has decreased. In many schools, case studies are used as the single teaching method. We also witness many who tout the value of the case method with little or no research to support their claims. Consider what Davis and Wilcox (2008) claim: "Teaching and learning styles are, by their very nature, changing and in recent years there has been a noticeable move from lecture-based activities towards more student-centered activities." They continue: "Case studies are an increasingly popular form of teaching and have an important role in developing skills and knowledge in students." While this unsupported claim may be true, does it have any relevancy to the creation of thoughtful and caring executives?

WHY USE THE CASE METHOD?

Case studies are easy to write, and academics from elite institutions are welcomed into corporations and are provided with data by the corporations' marketing and public relations personnel. In some cases the faculty member is paid by the corporation he or she are writing about. Deans like case studies because it fosters a link between the school and the corporation under study. Some case studies are published, and most are packaged and are either contained in textbooks or supplement textbooks or are free-standing cases.

In addition, it does not matter how accurate or responsible these cases are. They are given to naive students to read and discuss. Students are sometimes given 10 to 20 cases to analyze in a given course. In some instances cases select are taken from consultations professors engaged in and were paid by the very CEOs they are exemplifying. For example, during the heyday of Enron, according to McLean and Elkind (2003):

"Harvard Business School professors were practically swarming over the premises, working up case studies about the company's triumphs. (There were at least five touting the Enron model.) Management gurus like Gary Hamel made the pilgrimage as well: a half-dozen management books published beginning in the late 1990s contained admiring discussions about Enron.

Even a collection of so-called celebrity leadership experts who put together a book of readings supposedly for MBA students (tomorrow's leaders) contains a section devoted to Enron's CEO as the prototype of CEO who reinvents the company (Schurr, 2002).

The "Dell model" case was developed by Harvard and in the past 25 years dozens of cases about the Dell computer company have been written. There is even an article in the Harvard Business Review assessing the value of the numerous Dell cases. Dell may be the corporation with the most case studies. They are ubiquitous in MBA teaching, and they became synonymous with efficiency, outsourcing and tight inventories, and like Enron, widely praised as creating the one of the smartest business models. However, since 2003 the company has been plagued by serious problems, including misreading the desires of its customers, poor customer service, suspect product quality and improper accounting. Reports maintain that thousands of Dell computers purchased in large quantities by universities and corporations break down, and the problems are caused by internal chemical leakages. It is expected the company will spend years in litigation as customers sue. Since 2000 Dell's failure to renew value has wiped out $68 billion in stock market value. In July 2010 the company paid $100 million to the SEC for questionable financial reports and discrepancies in financial reporting between 2001 and 2006. Soon we may see cases telling students how Dell failed. However, this is doubtful. Rarely are cases written about failure or bad decision-making or incompetence in the executive constellation or dynamics that promote psychopathological or delusional thinking in the boardroom or the executive suite. Business students are led to believe that CEOs are special people without issues or personal problems or psychopathology. This is far from reality.

What we have in Americans B-schools is reckless behavior that is similar to the recklessness among Wall Street traders, bankers and many corporate executives. And it's all about greed. These celebrity professors and consultants believe they need to get out their written cases quickly before the competition beats them. They do so for the purpose of obtaining status and money, and in the process, caution is "thrown to the wind" and critical thought and scholarly pursuits are considered wasteful, slow, and counterproductive. Who gets shortchanged in this process? The young MBA.

Most business schools require their students to take one courses in each of the following areas: Management, International Management, Marketing, Operations, Finance, and Information Systems. Then they take what is referred to as the "capstone" course, typically called strategy or business policy. Cases are used in all courses, and depending on the professor, the "capstone" course is designed around cases that encompass the discipline the professor is most comfortable with. For example, you will rarely find a professor trained in organizational psychology to focus on the financial matters of a case, or a finance professor to focus on psychology. And again the student is cheated. Multidisciplinary analysis is rare, and each department lives in isolation with their own meetings, curriculum, faculty and in some cases their own building or wing.

In the case analysis, the best one can hope for is that the student develops an awareness of the interrelatedness of the various disciplines, something they should have learned as an undergraduate.

Cases rarely offer what can be considered an anthropological, sociopolitical, psychodynamic, or in-depth view of the corporation under study. Instead the case is broken into the business school disciplines (Management, International Management, Marketing, Operations, Finance, and Information Systems). When case presentations are given by students in teams, each member of the team will present the case from the perspective of each of the school's disciplines. The major failure associated with the case approach is its inability to strive towards a holistic or ecological understanding of the corporation as a social system. Instead they learn about disconnected parts. The marketing major will study the case from the perspective of marketing, the finance major from that perspective, and so on.

Cases can be divided into two types Some cases present problems, and most present successes. Both present dangerous learning issues for the student. Consider the first: A company is experiencing problems, sales have dropped, turnover is high and there is conflict between the various departments as they blame each other for failure. Too often the students take a tactical approach to case analysis, and like hedge hogs, they attack the case and immediately prepare their presentations. They are aware of the professor's biases and focus heavily in those areas of the case that will bring the best grade. They answer the question, "Why did the failure occur?" by identifying superficial causes, with a limited understanding of the complex dynamics that may have contributed to the failure. Sometimes they avoid understanding this question and go straight to discussing what needs to be corrected. This is similar to comments made by President George W. Bush and Treasury Secretary Bernanke when commenting on the $700 billion bailout of banks and Wall Street. Bush commented "We need to fix the problem now, we can discuss the cause of the problem later." Bernanke stated, "The root cause of the problem is a lack of confidence in the markets." Such shallow understanding is typical. Lack of confidence is a symptom, not a cause and certainly not a root cause.

Studying corporate successes is even more dangerous. The underlying assumption is wrong, that the ingredients for success in one corporation can be applied in a similar fashion to another corporation. One professor reported getting an irate phone call from the CEO of a small company. It seemed that two of his part-time MBA students had just read a case about implementing a program to motivate employees, and they attempted to apply it. It backfired and precipitated so much conflict that they were immediately terminated.

Ideally, an analysis of a case should put the student in the role of an analyst. The student should analyze all the data available: memoranda, emails, agendas, administrative documents, newspaper articles, financial records, resumes, organizational chart, history, existing strategic plans, information on the web, etc. Documents should corroborate the evidence from other sources and should be useful for making inferences about events. However, documents often lead to false conclusions, especially when left to the analysis of inexperienced students, that is, students with little or no managerial experience and/or weak knowledge of theory. One professor reported that when he gives his students a case, he tells them to bring the case up to date and research the corporation on the web. The students report that the case has little relationship to what is reported on the web, or the issues discussed in the case no longer exist or have changed. Another professor reports never using off-the-shelf cases and instead has students write cases of companies they would like to study. He uses local companies and brings the top executives in to hear the students' presentations. He reports that in most cases the executives are thrilled, and learn a great deal. And the students learn how to collect data, analyze it, and give a report.

The major complaint is that case analysis has proven to have little relationship to preparation for a managerial role and later on leader effectiveness. However, if we look at programs that utilize the case approach effectively, we find a major departure from business schools. For example, a discipline that utilizes the case analysis is clinical psychology. Unlike business school cases, these cases have theoretical underpinnings and students are first schooled in theory and are expected to apply multiple theories to an understanding of the case. This does not occur in business schools. To say that the case approach leads to the education of the manager is questionable, to say that it contributes to the development of a corporate leader is close to promoting a lie.

BOTTOM-LINE THINKING

When executives were asked why they do not appreciate the complexities of their decisions or why they do not engage in critical thought, the most often-used excuse is that they are overwhelmed by change and pressed for time, therefore they seek "quick-fix" solutions. However, they engage in a "fix-it" mentality because this is what they are taught in business schools with the case approach. The case method teaches students to engage in excessive simplification of complex problems. This leads to simple "solutions" typically referred to as "bottom-line thinking". They are not taught that complex organizational problems seldom present themselves as neat packages that can be isolated and systematically solved through a series of action steps.

The type of thinking that is promoted in business schools is sequential. As business students, executive were taught that problems isolated in cases could be solved by following steps. This absurdity is exemplified by professors who claim they can teach critical thinking by using five steps:

1. Define the problem.

2. Assess the information related to the problem.

3. Draw conclusions and solutions.

4. Develop and implement an action plan.

5. Review results and assess.

This view is remarkably similar to the steps one uses in the case study method:

- Determine the facts of the case.
- Understand the dynamics of the situation.
- Define the presenting problem. Determine the problem to be solved.
- Generate a possible course of action or generate, assess, and propose a number of possible solutions.
- Evaluate the strengths, weaknesses, opportunities, and threats to each course of action.
- Make a decision regarding a satisfactory or a workable plan of action.

Critical thinking is an oxymoron in the corporate world. A trainer schooled in learning theory once asked a VP if he could develop a training program to teach critical thinking for his young managers. The VP replied, "No, we have enough critical people around here." While the VP's comment is a misreading of the concept of critical thinking, it represented a wish to keep or preserve the belief system embedded in the culture of his organization, an aversion towards critical thought.

A key element in critical thinking is confronting and perhaps changing prevailing beliefs. This is especially problematic in the corporation, where Janus' "group think" is prevalent, and a hierarchical structure and a performance review process that stifles creativity and risk.

We all have cognitive biases and blind spots that corrupt our thinking and contaminate beliefs. However, to the critical thinker it is vital to be aware of, and to confront these biases. This rarely happens in the executive suite. According to van Gelder (2003) one of the most profound biases in corporate America is belief preservation He claims that "...belief preservation is the tendency to make evidence subservient to belief, rather than the other way around."

The bottom line orientation suggests that only results matter. Diagnosis, reflection, deep understanding, and certainly critical thinking are left out. Any ideas or thoughts that may go against bottom line thinking are quickly dismissed as foolish and ill-fated. Thinking about the consequences of focusing on bottom line profits is quickly dismissed. An example of this occurred at Home Depot, America's largest home improvement retail corporation, which was started in 1978 with a reputation for quality customer service. Bob Nardelli became CEO in 2000 and immediately instituted cost-cutting measures. He cut full-time jobs, capped wages, and recruited former military officers to run the stores. Staff morale and customer service began to collapse under his new regime. The number of part-time employees skyrocketed from 26 percent to a high of 50 percent in 2002. In addition, he replaced many experienced store associates who made high hourly wages with inexperienced part-timers (Alic, 2007). The executive constellation, using data from Six Sigma, discovered that there were many senior and experienced store associates making upwards to $28 per hour. A cost analysis pointed to the cost of these salaries and the savings the company could obtain if the high priced sales associates were replaced by $10 per hour part-timers. Home Depot veterans were horrified of the consequences of the plan; understanding the brain drain, the impact of the loss of experienced sales people, and how their absence would negatively impact customer service. But they remained quiet and only shared their thoughts with trusted colleagues. Some did suggest doing a pilot study. However, this type of thinking was rejected. In the face of overwhelming evidence, Nardelli's executive constellation held onto their beliefs that profitability and share-holder value would increase if they fired the high-priced, full time hourly associates. The move was made, and in the first two months the bottom line improved and profits rose then disaster occurred as customer service rapidly dropped and the stocks began to slide. In 2005 Home Depot slipped to last place among major U.S. retailers in the University of Michigan's annual American Consumer Satisfaction Index. It is doubtful the company will ever return to its former days of quality customer service (An in depth analysis of Nardelli is offered in Chapter 11)

In 2003, the executive constellation of Circuit City did something similar. On the advice of their Six Sigma people, the second-largest electronics store in the United States switched employees from commission-based pay to hourly pay, then fired 3,400 of its highest-paid hourly and most experienced sales employees and hired inexperienced replacements willing to work for less. Like Home Depot, quality customer service turned from good to bad overnight. In November, 2008, Circuit City announced that it was closing 155 stores and terminating 7,300 employees, and declared bankruptcy. CEO Philip Schoonover, who resigned in September 2008, was paid $8.52 million in fiscal 2006, including a salary of $975,000. His severance package is estimated at $1.8 million. In January 2009, Circuit City announced it was closing all of its stores and going out of business. Then the executives who remained asked the bankruptcy judge for permission to pay up to $4.65 million to "incentivize" them to stay and help shut down the company (Iosco, 2009).

What accounts for this type of foolish decision making? These corporations have a Six Sigma, data-driven "bottom line" belief system. They embrace a decision-making process that evolved from the case study approach used in business schools where decisions are made after reading a case. The data-driven, quick-read decision process is filled with a combination of naiveté and grandiosity. The time-tested processes of caution, hypothesis testing, critical thought, analysis and experience are dispensed with as being slow and bothersome. In the cases above, experienced employees are dismissed because the data suggests that these employees are failing to enrich the bottom line. The bottom line approach cannot consider "brain drain" or the loss of experience or its consequences for customer service because they are too psychological. These executives who are distanced from the work on the store floor have no idea of the necessity of quality customer service, and how important this is to the "bottom line," and they fail to connect the association of pay and morale with customer service.

They are taught in business school that "good" executives make quick, decisive decisions based on "the numbers" or metrics. They were taught that executives are powerful, aggressive and have a level of confidence that borders on arrogance. To be thoughtful or cautious is the equivalent of "choking." To ask for help, is a sign of weakness.

BUSINESS SCHOOLS AND TRAINING TO BE AGGRESSIVE

Consider what a professor described as the qualities of students, he believes will be successful in the executive role. He said.

"In the corporate world they will be seen as reliable, dependable and responsible. They have a powerful sense of duty to their company and colleagues. They are expansive, something of a perfectionist and a "doer." They have a hedgehog attitude toward work, they get the present job finished and move on to the next task, demonstrating "workaholic" behavior, with time constantly filled with real activities. They intensely dislike ambiguous situations, incomplete information, work half-finished, or any feeling of "loose strings hanging" and they will be impatient with those who demonstrate those behaviors. If someone does not uphold their high standards of perfection, they become indignant. They can demonstrate charming behavior along with an air of self-importance. In social situations, they may be at their best. They are the classic after-dinner speaker,

funny, relaxed and informative demonstrating a type of inverted modesty in speaking and eliciting responses from the audience that they are wonderful."

In a class of MBA students in New York City who were making presentations, their dress was indicative of the Wall Street tycoons depicted in Hollywood movies. The young men wore bold striped shirts with loud red ties and red or yellow suspenders holding up their dark pleated pants. The young women wore dress suits, and a dark skirt with matching jacket, bold striped shirt with a loud colored ascot and black high heel shoes. They were preparing for their simulated executive class presentations in Business Strategy.

For these students, it was, as Goffman (1959) states, "a performance." They exuded the required self-confidence, maintained an air of polished and excessively friendly smiles, and demonstrated a capacity to spout off data and business clichés to support their number-crunching results. They worked at communicating to their observers that it was just a matter of time, with their MBA in hand, that they would be living in the penthouse. Many shoot for the hot Wall Street job and they tell each other stories of graduates obtaining million-dollar bonuses two years out of graduate school. The students were rehearsing for their role as an actor would. While all professionals learn the requirements of the role, for business professionals the training is highly intense and structured to promote certain behaviors. Business professionals, more than any other profession, have less room for the demonstration of variant behaviors, even less than a West Point graduate. [3]

Business schools love tough, aggressive, polished students. Professors stage debating activities to promote aggressiveness and they claim aggressiveness is required to succeed in what they maintain is the "barracuda" corporate world. Presentations are gladiator events where students attempt to defeat others by convincing them and their professors they are right and the others are wrong. Students, exposed to Hollywood's version of the tough "Gordon Gekko" stereotype believe this is what they must become. They also attend lectures from celebrity CEOs and they see how tough they are. They hear the nicknames: Neutron Jack, Chainsaw Al, Iron Man Barrett, Skillful Scalpel, and Gorilla Fuld. They are taught to be aggressive, quick, to the point, and to "ooze confidence." To be cautious, thoughtful, and engage in critical thought, and value analysis and diagnosis is too feminine and removed from the machismo world of "Get the quant's" to "run the data" and make the decision." According to Dattner, "The real value of an Ivy League business degree is arguably not the education itself, but the screening of intelligence, drive and accomplishment that the schools do. Just like with undergraduate degrees, if you are smart enough to get into a top-tier school, you are likely to inspire confidence" (Ellin, 2006). What he is suggesting is that these top tier MBAs inspire such confidence, that those around them will assume they know what they're doing, even when they don't have a clue.

Belmont University's MBA web page claims success by quoting several alums: "Her MBA training equipped her for combat in the business arena." "It helped me be more aggressive and gave me more confidence." In a popular book "How to Get an MBA," discussing aggression during presentations, Witzel (2000) gives this advice, "Rudeness, interrupting others or talking people down is not good." He goes on to suggest that if you try this in the workplace, senior executives will not like it. But Witzel suggests that being able to get a hearing and getting a view across, "...requires fairly forceful actions and speech" and there is "...a fine line between energy and outright aggression." What is this aggressive zeal he is focusing on? Moving ahead, climbing the ladder, beating the competition and getting rich. It is as if the most aggressive barracuda will get the most to eat.

A critical question is: Why do professors see the corporate world as a Darwinian struggle for survival and prepare their students to survive? They believe this type of behavior is necessary to win the corporate steeplechase or obtain the multi-million dollar bonus. But what they have done is to contribute to the creation of a hostile work environment, where the promise of promotions and riches are beyond the grasp of most, leaving them with disappointment, racked with debt and depressed. Several studies suggest that workplace aggression has dramatically increased since the rise of business schools. In 2007, nearly half of all U.S. workers were victims of workplace aggression. Workplace aggression includes incivility; rudeness, glaring and staring, interrupting, talking over someone else, and displaying an array of discourteous verbal and non-verbal behaviors. Bullying is also apparent and includes excessively criticizing employees' work; yelling; repeatedly reminding an employee of mistakes; spreading gossip or lies; ignoring or excluding workers; and insulting employees' habits, attitudes or private life. Interpersonal conflict included behaviors that involved hostility, verbal aggression, and threats. Professors claim that they are preparing their students for the inevitable workplace struggle. It is unclear if business school preparation contributes to the increasing problem of aggression in the workplace, but it is certain schools are not sending thoughtful, empathic and supportive team players to the corporate caverns.

Professors and business students watch the popular TV show "The Office" a comedy that demonstrates the meanness and the blatant insensitivity of life in the workplace. Workers are cynical and aware that no one cares about them and they work in an environment with a "lifeboat" mentality. Cynicism is embedded in the culture of the workplace and is established in the executive suite. These attitudes are often acted out in aggressive and insensitive rites of passage as junior executives attempt to fit in. According to Hickok (2008):

"In a Newsweek cover story, Sloan (1996: 44) argues that "Firing people has gotten to be trendy in corporate America, in the same way that building new

plants and being considered a good corporate citizen gave you bragging rights 25 years ago. Now you fire workers — especially white-collar workers — to make your corporate 'bones'"."

Thus we see an executive culture that has an established "right of passage," perhaps a culture of machismo where one must prove their toughness to the "executive gang" to be a member. This type of CEO is spawned in business schools where they learned the "bottom line" belief system and came to believe their job is to restructure and/or streamline the corporation for the sole purpose of the bottom line enrichment, i.e., making money for shareholders and themselves. In achieving this goal they are trained to be strong, aggressive and tough, a practice that helps them defend against the inhumanity of their decisions to do whatever it takes to make a profit.

The metaphors "bottom line" and "dashboard management" are an attempt by CEOs to simplify the work of leading a corporation and are connected to the CEO's motivation to become the wealthy and a celebrity who receives accolades by the press, business writers and business school officials. To reach their goal, they surround themselves with CIOs, CFOs, IT Officers, Six Sigma experts, "quant's" and other "numbers crunchers", who provide "bottom line" services. They also hire consultants who provide the mathematical models to assist CEOs in making their "bottom line" decisions. In addition, they hire coaches, consultants, and public relations to help them engage in the work of self-promotion. Human Resources have even jumped into this way of thinking by using computer calculations to put values on employees to determine their worth to the company.

REENGINEERING A METAPHOR FOR TERMINATIONS

The book that had the greatest impact on promoting the celebrity CEO, and making layoffs and terminations legitimate are found in bestselling book by Hammer and Champy (1993), who put forth the idea of "reengineering the corporation." They urged CEOs to rethink the very processes by which organizations functioned and to be courageous about replacing any processes that get in the way of organizational efficiency.

What is efficiency? Profitability.

The reengineering process became a buzzword in the 1990's, and CEOs came to believe they could dramatically increase profitability by changing current processes, information systems, business strategies, and the overall corporate structure. However, what was underneath these innocuous terms were terminations and downsizing. According to Neidhart (2005)

"Hammer admitted later to paying little attention to the human element when first defining reengineering. He used such expressions as, "In reengineering, we carry the wounded and shoot the stragglers," and "It's basically taking an ax and a machine gun to your existing organization." This terminology resulted in massive layoffs for some companies that were quick to "fix" their business via reengineering. Reengineering became synonymous with downsizing when Pacific Bell announced the reduction of 10,000 employees as a result of "reengineering" in 1995. Apple Computer publicized a cutback of comparable proportions shortly after Pacific Bell, again due to the "reengineering" of the company (Davenport 2003). 2.6 million jobs were cut by 500 of the largest firms in the U.S. between 1984 and 1993 by one estimate owing to massive overhauls under the label of "reengineering" (Sheridan, 1997). "

In an economic slowdown or when profitability or sales slowdown CEOs embraced reengineering, as a metaphor of choice. They gleefully cut their workforce and then placed the burden for profitability on those who remain employed, the so-called survivors. According to Neidhart (2005), American Expresses did just that in 2001, when the company's earnings dropped 76 percent from the previous year. CEO Kenneth Chenault said that the company was "making substantial progress in the reengineering efforts announced earlier this year... We're moving some stuff to the Internet to reduce support staff. We'll also be moving more rapidly to scale back American Express Bank's infrastructure in overseas markets" (Ring, 2001). Shortly afterward, American Express cut 6,000 jobs. In September 2010, 11 deans from leading business schools would meet with corporate leaders at a symposium hosted by American Express and the Penn State Smeal College at American Express headquarters in New York to forge a new partnership in promoting business ethics in academia and corporate America. Business deans are at it again, turning a blind eye to corporate greed. Furthermore getting together with Chenault and AMEX to promote ethics is outrageous and in and of itself an unethical act.

With the fiscal crises of 2008-09, CEOs are running to the termination guillotine with a vengeance as they collectively terminate millions of employees. To do what? Make their share-holder's content and their jobs and compensation intact.

CEOs have created a work climate that is wrought with anger, paranoia, and conflict. If the CEOs do not see the conflict they have created, it is because they have created such an intimidating environment that their employees are fearful of displaying any form of emotional displays. Employees work to convince their managers they are happy, hardworking, and committed, and they seek every opportunity to publicly praise their chiefs as the greatest managers in the world. These CEOs have created nothing more than a culture of "ass kissers." CEOs rarely understand that all these employees are trying to do is to hold onto their jobs, and even worse they fail to understand the feelings that underlie these public displays. CEOs have created delusional systems;

CEOs believe they are wonderful: employees, publicly praise and privately hate.

How can executives continuously display such apparent greed while their subordinates and others become disillusioned and bitter?

CHAPTER 3

No Need for Employee Morale: Destroy the "social contract" between capital and labor and CEOs Get Rich

"Greed does funny things to us. It paints a picture of a reality that is just beyond our reach. As long as we are experiencing greed we are projected into the future, and able to miss the enjoyment and appreciation of what we have now. This wanting keeps us on the run, on the search for more, and prevents us from stopping and smelling the roses..." (Boswell, 2008)

McLean and Elkind, (2003), claimed that the collapse of Enron was a "...human drama of people drunk on their own success. People so ambitious, so certain of their own brilliance, so fueled by greed and hubris that they believed they could fool the world." Jeffrey Skilling, former CEO of Enron, a Harvard Business School graduate, did not set out to cheat investors, employees, or his company. Over time he found himself doing and saying things that at earlier point in his life would have given him pause.

The Psychology of Greed and Destructiveness among CEOs and Bankers

What happens when one gets to the top? What goes on when justifications for wrong doing are internalized and become the norm? What we will explore in this chapter is the dramatic shift in commitment, a shift from commitment to the corporation and its employees and community to a commitment directed at enhancing one's own self-interests. For Skilling, and others at Enron, the commitment was not to the company, the company's customers and employees, but to obtaining wealth for themselves. If others also benefited, that was fine. As we have observed, the executives at Enron in this sense were not unique. They, like many, if not most, of today's CEOs, consider their job as serving the financial interests of those who hired them; their shareholders, and these shareholders have made it clear that if they gain, their CEOs will also gain.

This has propelled a management movement that will lead to the death of the American corporation.

According to Cassidy (2002), Financial Times published a series of articles on what it termed the "barons of bankruptcy - a privileged group of top business people who made extraordinary personal fortunes even as their companies were heading for disaster." Financial Times examined the 25 biggest business collapses beginning at the start of 1999, to the end of 2001. Senior executives and directors of these doomed companies walked away with some $33 billion in salary, bonuses, and the proceeds from sales of stock and stock options.

In an ideal world, we would have CEOs who are knowledgeable and who understand the meaning of their actions; who are moral people that embrace the great responsibility given to them with altruism. But in the last 30 years we have witnessed CEO behavior that is in some cases outrageous, destructive, immoral and criminal. It seems that CEOs are not very different from the rest of the population. Just as some people destroy their marriages, ruin their health, make bizarre and destructive decisions, we find CEOs behaving unethically, engaging in irresponsible greed, and destroying the corporations they were chosen to lead. Americans are outraged at the spectacle of CEOs legally looting their companies with enormous pay and pensions, while their employees struggle with wages that fail to keep pace with inflation, and live with fear that decent health care will be lost and pensions will be taken.

The furor over CEO compensation began in March 7, 2008. The House of Representatives Oversight and Government Operations Committee held hearings in Washington, D.C. They invited Angelo Mozilo, CEO of nearly bankrupt Countrywide Financial who gained $120 million in options in 2007 and $400 million in compensation during his tenure. He pledged to give back $37.5 million. Also invited was Stan O'Neal, former chief executive of Merrill Lynch & Co. He received $161 million in stock, options and retirement benefits after leaving the brokerage with its biggest-ever quarterly loss, Charles Prince, the former CEO of Citigroup received a $10 million bonus, $28 million in stock and options and $1.5 million in other perks when he left the bank after its stocks lost 58 percent of their worth. Combined, these three companies had lost $20 billion in 2007. It was not a pretty sight watching these elitist multimillionaires squirm in their seats as they were grilled. But in the end it was just a show, they suffered some public embarrassment and returned to their mansions relatively unscathed.

The outrage became intensely pervasive when banks and investment houses collapsed in September, 2008 and the federal government offered bailouts. The metaphor "Main Street bails out Wall Street" became popular, but when "Main Street" realized they were bearing the burden for the bailouts as they were losing their retirement funds, jobs, and homes they were outraged. When the media, press and blogs began publishing CEO and banker salaries and bonuses the outrage grew so loud that Congress began holding hearings and CEOs began to put gates around their homes, hire security guards, and withdraw from employees and customers while seeking refuge in their fenced in country clubs. The outrage is not uniquely American. In France, 3 million workers took to the streets to protest both the widening gap between the rich and workers and their President Sarkozy, who like Bush, favored the wealthy and the so-called "trickle down" theory.

"Main Street" is livid at executives who took wild risks and made incredibly bad decisions, and never apologized, or even tried to explain their actions, but instead remained aloof, entitled, and full of excuses and finger-pointing as they continued to line their pockets

CEO SALARY AND EMPLOYEE MORALE

Most employees of publicly traded companies may not know the salary of the guy in the cubicle next to them, but they all know what their CEO makes. According to Dietsch (2006), "There are few secrets people guard more anxiously than their pay details. Even among work colleagues, open discussion about the size of their paycheques is the exception." But, since 2002 all publicly traded corporations are required by law to publish the salaries of their officers.

Does knowledge of a CEO's salary have an impact on an employee's attitude about the company, their morale and motivation? It would be difficult to find an organizational psychologist who would say knowledge of their CEOs salary does not have an impact on employees. Most CEOs have gone to business school and they are typically surrounded by executives who have taken classes in organizational psychology. They are familiar with the research exploring the negative consequences of salary inequity, but they continue to take entitlement to new levels where they are accused collectively of gross insensitivity and greed. We occasionally see some CEOs publicly announcing an intention to keep their compensation low, not because they want their employees to see them in a favorable light, but because they are facing massive losses, or approaching bankruptcy.

Research concerning the impact of high CEO wages has been dubious. On one side are those who maintain that high CEO pay contributes to high subordinate turnover, lower job satisfaction, and lower product quality. Levine (1992) maintains that: "The idea, that a single person can be worth 531 times the average worker salary must be demoralizing." He goes on, "The overwhelming evidence supports the effects of high CEO salary effects on morale and turnover." Anderson and Batemen (1997), suggest that high CEO compensation leads to high levels of cynicism among lower level employees. Cowherd and Levine (1992) discovered that perceptions of pay inequity result in lower product quality. Crosby (1984) maintains that the feeling of relative deprivation in the workplace may lead to strikes, vandalism, and violence. Qantas Airline is a good example of this. In May 2008, Qantas engineers walked off their jobs when they were offered a 3 percent raise. They had asked for a 5 percent increase. They angrily protested against the company's CEO Geoff Dixon, who is being paid $6 million a year.

Another example is Google. In January 2011, Sergey Brin, a co-founder of Google had to return to his former CEO position to focus on strategic products. He stated, "I would like to work more on my personal passions, including several new significant products that I hope to tell you about in the future." There are also claims that Google has become too bureaucratic and creative engineers are leaving in droves. In order to keep employees from leaving in December 2010 former CEO Eric Schmidt gave Googles 23,000 employees a 10 percent raise and a $1,000 Christmas bonus. Then Schmidt publicly fired an engineer who leaked the raises and bonuses to the press. He then proceeded to give his executives major increases. For example CFO Patrick Pichette, president of global sales and business development Nikesh Arora, senior vice president of engineering and research Alan Eustace, and Jonathan Rosenberg, senior vice president of product management, will see their annual base salaries increase from $500,000 to $650,000 in 2011. In addition, they will be eligible for bonuses of up to 250 percent of their base salaries, an increase from 150 percent from 2010, for a total take home of up to $2.28 million. If anyone wanted to design a program to kill employee morale, hire Schmidt.

It is surprising that these executives do not see how this type of largess is perceived by the 23,000 Google employees who "get a bone while the big guys get fat." It is these types of actions that resemble bureaucratic companies where gross inequity is pervasive. Executives who engage in these behaviors create a "we they" culture and lower morale and destroy creativity.

Why can't they see the damage compensation inequity causes? Perhaps Upton Sinclair said it best: "It is difficult to get a man to understand something when his salary depends on his not understanding it" (Berenson, 2003).

By the way, Google will give Schmidt $100 million for giving up the CEO post. He owns 9.2 million shares of Google stock which were valued in January 2011 at $5.8 billion. Yes that's right billions is not a misprint.

Feelings associated with pay inequity have profound consequences for a company. Greenberg (1990) demonstrated that anger with pay inequity was related to increased employee theft. And, as one would suspect pay inequity influences motivation, job satisfaction, and behavior in a negative manner (Cowherd and Levine, 1992).

Verneulen (2008) reports on a study of pay inequity and team performance conducted by Matt Bloom on Major League Baseball teams.

Baseball teams performed better if the salaries of the players were not too different from each other. *"The larger the payment differences, the lower the individual players' performance; mostly so – perhaps not surprisingly – for the players receiving the lowest payment. But – perhaps more surprisingly – also the players who found themselves pretty high in the payment pecking order, receiving an above-average salary package, saw their individual performance being negatively affected by the pay dispersion within the team. Those teams with high pay differences among players had markedly poorer performance. It seems substantial differences in pay are more of a de-motivator than an incentive, even for the majority of people who end up in the high payment bracket!"*

On the other side are those who suggest positive reactions to salary inequity by claiming that lower-level managers are motivated by high executive salaries, and employees are more satisfied when they see others at work making more money. They base their research on the Hirschmanian tournament theory, which maintains that knowledge of higher wages provides information about one's future prospects, and will increase the motivation to get more. While this may be true when the gap between wage differences is relatively small, it is doubtful this theory holds up when the gap is very wide.

Another argument evolves out of the outrage over CEO compensation and the movement to cap compensation. In response to the movement to reduce executive pay, they claim that if these high salaries are not paid then noone will want to be a CEO. According to Frank (2009), the problem with capping pay "…is that although every company wants a talented chief executive, there are only so many to go around. Relative salaries guide job choices. If salaries were capped at say, $2 million annually, then most talented candidates would have less reason to seek the positions that make best use of their talents." He goes on, "More troubling, if CEO pay were capped and pay for other jobs was not, the most talented potential managers would more likely to become lawyers or hedge fund operators." This argument suggests CEOs are only in the business for the money and casts their motivation to become a CEO in a negative light. Furthermore, if Frank is correct, could it be that the only managers who make the Herculean effort to attain the top position are greedy, self-centered narcissists, who would never consider the occupations of social work, teaching, or primary care physicians? It may also be true that the CEO's quest for riches evolves over time. and making the long trek up the corporate ladder changes a CEO, and entitlement evolves as they settle into the executive suite. It may also be true that the culture of entitlement exists before the CEO arrives and the newly appointed chief fears suggesting change and accepts the riches.

When every publicly traded corporation was required to make public the amount of compensation given to all corporate officers/executives it was expected to put sanctions on those executives who violated the morality of distributive justice. Dietsch (2006) had argued that transparency would compel those who make enormous amounts of money to perceive the income gap as an unjust distribution of income and they would take action to reduce the gap. But this has not occurred. CEOs and their executives do not seem to care if the public knows their compensation and they do not seem to care if the public or their own employees are outraged. Dietsch (2006) goes on to describe under what conditions transparency will not work. He says, "If ties of civil society are weak, then transparency [of salary] will not have an impact on distributive justice." What are these weak ties of a civil society? The weakening of ties is similar to Emile Durkheim's "anomie," a condition where social and/or moral norms become unclear. But we are not talking about a society here, we are discussing CEOs. In their corporate culture it is safe to say these CEOs have lost their ethical moorings, and in the process the compass that guides a just person is lost, as well as empathy for others. We maintain that their training, preparation, and the actual climb up the corporate ladder creates a condition of anomie. A culture is established in the executive constellation where norms and regulations break down. It is as if a social deregulation occurs and in the process they no longer care about the less fortunate or the impact gross inequity has on their employees. Salary transparency has not worked and has no impact on reducing the gap between CEOs and their employees. The only thing it has done is gotten a lot of people angry.

ONE WAY TO GET RICH- TERMINATE EMPLOYEES AND DESTROY COMMITMENT

Employees are readily aware of the gross inequities in the workplace. They are well aware of their CEOs' opulent salaries and retirement packages that guarantee a life of security and wealth. At the same time, CEOs are well aware of their employee's struggles; their need for two family incomes, the demands for working longer hours and pension systems that are precarious.

CEOs have created a workplace that employees experience as: intimidating, devoid of commitment and motivation, filled with mistrust, contempt, and cheating. Some corporations resemble armed camps where management engages in continuous surveillance of employees. They have created corporations that have evolved into a costly and never-ending struggle, as employees spend increasing amounts of time attempting to outwit their employer's attempts to increase control.

For example, at Home Depot, the CEO had surveillance cameras strategically placed in all of its 1,800 stores. Employees were told the cameras were installed to catch thieves, but they were also used to monitor their work behavior and employee theft. The CEO and several

VPs had the capability of focusing anyone of the 36,000 cameras from their offices to observe employee behavior in the stores. Employees had to be on the floor, selling; breaks and meals required punching in and out, even if the employees went to the company "break room" which also had cameras. Chatting with fellow employees on the floor was discouraged, and called "pumpkin patches" by management (a group of employees wearing orange aprons talking). If there were no customers to be served, employees were expected to keep busy stocking the shelves or cleaning up.

No wonder many stores experienced 70 percent annual turnover. This turnover rate increased when store employees received an average 10 cents-an-hour salary increase the same year, Bob Nardelli, their CEO, made $32 million.

CEOs show an incredible lack of sensitivity to the experience of their underlings and pay little attention to the ways in which they destroy employee motivation. In addition, conflicts in the workplace between management and their employees have increased to the point where all-out war exists in many corporations.

Consider this example. The CEO of a large electronic retail company that is now bankrupt called in a consultant because of employee theft in a warehouse. The consultant was shown a video-tape of a terminated employee in his mid 40s crawling on his stomach with a box under his arm. It turned out he was stealing something and was crawling to avoid being detected on the surveillance cameras. The consultant was told cameras were not very effective: only two workers were caught and an 18 percent shrink remained. Management then bought package sensor detectors which were placed at two entrances. They did not work. Then management hired security guards. The security guards did not work: the guards were also stealing. One day the consultant observed an employee loading an expensive computer system into the trunk of an expensive car. The employee said he was instructed to do so by his boss. When the consultant queried the boss, he replied, "Oh it's for my daughter." It seemed management had two standards for theft: For management to steal it was called a perk; for employees it was theft. The consultant called a meeting of the company's executives and told them if they were serious about reducing theft they would have to eliminate all company perks. The consultant also suggested their high shrink may be the result of their so-called "perks." The consultant was immediately dismissed.

The employees knew about management's perks, their company credit cards, meetings in the Caribbean, company cars and outrageous salaries and bonuses. One employee stated, "The Company is management's cookie jar." Employees maintained that management cared only about profitability and personal gain, and had an attitude that demonstrated little concern about them. Employees were bitter; they enjoyed stealing as an act of revenge, and were in constant conflict with their bosses.

OUTSOURCING: A WAY TO GET RID OF A PROBLEM AND GET RICH

In the late 1980s executives discovered a new method to remove themselves from these types of conflicts with their employees. It was outsourcing. As a CEO said, "I get rid of a major headache by outsourcing." Executives discovered they could solve the never-ending struggles with their employees; all they had to do was terminate them, embrace outsourcing, increase profitability and increase their personal wealth. According to Associated Press (2004), executives of U.S. companies that outsourced the greatest number of jobs reaped bigger pay and benefits. The average CEO compensation at the 50 companies that outsourced the most jobs rose by 46 percent in 2003, from a year earlier, compared with a 9 percent increase for CEOs of 365 companies that did not outsource (Anderson, 2004).

The outsourcing trend started in the 1980s and exploded as we entered 2000. Manufacturing was the first to go. Between 2001 and 2008, about 40,000 US manufacturing plants closed. Six million manufacturing jobs -- one out of every three -- disappeared in a dozen years (Clark, 2010). In 1970 one in four jobs were in manufacturing in America, and in 2010 it dropped to one in 10. Soon after, Wall Street, banking and IT companies joined in. Wall Street firms outsourced 80,000 finance jobs globally (Story, 2008). In July of 2008, Citigroup employed 22,000 and Deutsche Bank 6,000 in India. Before bankruptcy, Wachovia expected to save $1.1 billion by terminating 4,000 American employees and shifting their jobs to India where the average annual salary is $6,000. Credit Suisse had 6,500 employees in lower-cost locations like India, Poland and Singapore. In addition, it was expected that U.S. banks would cut 200,000 employees by 2009 (Timmons, 2008). This trend is expected to grow. According to Drezner, (2004),

"The McKinsey Global Institute estimates that the volume of offshore outsourcing will increase by 30 to 40 percent a year for the next five years. Forrester Research estimates that 3.3 million white-collar jobs will move overseas by 2015. According to projections, the hardest hit sectors will be financial services and information technology (IT). In one May 2003 survey of chief information officers, 68 percent of IT executives said that their offshore contracts would grow in the subsequent year. The Gartner research firm has estimated that by the end of this year, 1 out of every 10 IT jobs will be outsourced overseas. Deloitte Research predicts the outsourcing of 2 million financial-sector jobs by 2009." (1)

The second-biggest bank in America, JP Morgan Chase, which acquired Washington Mutual and Bear Stearns in 2008, was to increase the money spent outsourcing to India by 25 percent in 2009 to nearly $400 million. The newly acquired companies will have their information technology integrated exclusively in India. In 2008, JP Morgan outsourced $250 million to $300 million worth of IT and back-office projects to Indian companies like Cognizant, TCS and Accenture, apart from to its own captive center in Mumbai (Mishra, 2009). American bank employees tremble at the sight of Indian trainees in their departments. As one Citibank employee said, "When you see them in your department on Monday morning you know the end is near, your department will soon be outsourced to India. It infuriates me, it's one thing to close your department down and send it to India, but it is another thing to have to spend months training them to do your job in India for peanuts. It is humiliating, they (management) just don't care, they'll make millions and we will have to sell our condos and lose everything we worked so hard for." An Indian MBA graduate will start at 450,000 rupees or $9,736 U.S., a tenth of what American MBAs from top schools are demanding.

With the global bank mergers of Lloyds TSB and HBOS, and Bank of America & Merrill Lynch, India's top tech firms, including Infosys, TCS and Cognizant, are bidding for contracts worth hundreds of millions. In 2008 it was estimated that 400,000 American jobs were lost to outsourcing. Wall Street is now benefiting from these Indian companies as their stocks are soaring. It becomes another way to get rich while Americans lose their jobs. And the gap between the rich and poor increases, as Wall Street now claims outsourcing is great.

Here we see the lunacy of the outsourcing phenomena: An American company wants to cut costs so it terminates its employees and outsources to an Indian company. The Indian company discovers it needs to be physically near the American company. Therefore they bring their Indian employees to America house them in squalor and pay them

Indian wages. Who benefits? Surprise: Wall Street that invested in both the American company and the Indian company and of course, their executives. Who loses? The workers from both countries. Exploitation at its best. Several states are tightening visa requirements for Indian workers as a way to force these companies to hire American workers.

Of course the health care industry is in it. In 2011 Omega, a health care business process outsourcing company is planning to increase its staff strength by recruiting 1,000 Indian employees and investing $18 million to $20 million in India. More jobs for India and less for Americans.

Believe it or not there is an association for outsourcers, "The International Association of Outsourcing Professionals" or IAOP. They claim to have over 110,000 members and affiliates worldwide, and they help companies increase their outsourcing success rate, improve their outsourcing ROI, and expand the opportunities for outsourcing across their businesses. And they have the audacity to have an annual outsource Top 100 where they rank the top outsourcers. That's like giving an award to the company that steals the most American jobs.

While outsourcing increases short-term profitability and CEOs compensation, CEOs have discovered that even the threat of outsourcing will have positive results on their compensation. Consider this example: In the winter of 2008, about 3,600 UAW members went on strike at the American Axle plant when Richard Dauch, chairman and CEO, pushed to cut union worker's salaries, reducing them to $11 to $14 per hour. Dauch received a 9.5 percent salary and bonus increase in 2007, a package of $10.2 million. Since 2003, Dauch has reaped nearly $70 million in compensation. Under the pay package approved by the company's board of directors, Dauch will make about $196,154 a week.

If he cuts wages in half, workers will see their pay reduced to $580 a week. His employees are angry: However if they do not comply with Dauch's demands he has threatened to close plants and move operations to Mexico or some other Latin American country. Over the last several years he has done just that. Dauch has cut the workforce at his original American-based plants by nearly half. He closed the Buffalo, N.Y. plant and expanded American Axle's low-cost factories to Mexico and other countries. After 87 days of striking the UAW agreed to a contract in which union members will receive a $10 per hour cut in pay, or if they resign, they will receive three annual "buydown" payments totaling as much as $105,000 (Bunkley, 2008). In addition, Dauch will close two more plants.

After a settlement, in June, 2008, Dauch was awarded a bonus of $8.5 million for leading his company through the bitter strikes and weakening the UAW union. Dauch recently named one of his sons, David, president and COO of the company.

(To read more about how CEOs kill the unions and get rich see Appendix O)

Another sign of the times is pharmaceutical drug manufacturing. Drug making is outsourced and factories in America are being closed. The Food and Drug Administration estimates that of the 1,154 drug manufacturing plants only 13 percent remained in America in 2007 (Harris, 2009). Forty-three percent have located to China and 39 percent to India. Again, cheap labor, low construction costs and low regulatory and environmental costs lead to increased profitability. CEOs rarely see or do not want to see the chain reaction that occurs with outsourcing. New Jersey once had the largest number of pharmaceutical drug manufacturing plants and companies. Outsourcing and offshoring has turned New Jersey into the home foreclosure capital of the world, with local communities bankrupt, state and local pensions decimated, and millions unemployed. But CEOs and their stockholders get barrels of cash and the gap between the rich and poor widens.

PLAYING THE OUTSOURCING GAME

Even when companies outsource to one country, stability can be short-lived. Global companies, especially manufacturing, will move from one country to another locating the cheapest labor and the weakest environmental laws. For example, Adidas discovered that the Chinese government set employees' salaries too high, so they are leaving China to open factories in India, Laos, Cambodia and Vietnam, and they are looking down the road to the former Soviet republics and eastern European countries.

It is estimated that a corporation saves between 30 to 40 percent annually by outsourcing. In the retail business every company relies on outsourcing. For example it is estimated that 80 percent of all apparel sold in America is made in China, and it is estimated that 40 percent of the goods sold at Wal-Mart come from China. Why do we only have estimates? We do not know where many products are made. For example, Wal-Mart and many corporations respond to "Buy America" campaigns by setting up shell companies with American-sounding names where they claim they buy goods. Many of these shell companies are run by ex-executives who make millions by buying Chinese-made goods and then put American labels on them.

The same issue applies to food. Americans rarely know where the food they eat comes from. In the United States 98 percent of all restaurants are owned by chains. They get their food from all over the world. Profitability is a function of purchasing large quantities of inexpensive food and then making it taste good. Of course bioengineered food is included. American farms cannot compete with the cost of outsourcing food production. Neither can the automobile manufacturers. While American automobile makers are on their deathbed, Wal-Mart may put the nail in their coffin when they start importing Chinese-made vehicles with a $5,500 price tag. The big boxes will make certain that the United States manufactures nothing. Americans will sell, and buy, and eat bad food, drive Chinese made autos, own some worthless stocks, and end up working for foreign-owned companies. And it is happening.

IKEA a Swedish company that sells furniture all over the world in its big box stores, set up a furniture-making plant in Danville, Va. The poorly paid and overworked employees are seeking to unionize, and IKEA has hired a union-busting company. Sweden is a heavily union organized country, and all of Ikea's workers in Sweden are union members. Ikeas code of conduct, known as IWAY, guarantees workers the right to organize and even stipulates that all overtime be voluntary. IKEA workers in Sweden make $19 per hour and they work a seven-hour day and at 35 hours a week they take home $35000 a year. Not true in "third world" America. IKEA pays its Danville employees $8 an hour with 12 vacation days, of which six are determined by the company. American workers get paid on average $16,000 per year less than half of what their counterparts make in Sweden. In addition, one-third of the employees in Danville are temp workers and get even lower wages. The company acknowledged the pay gap between factories in Europe and the U.S. and stated "That is related to the standard of living and general conditions in the different countries." This is exactly the same line one heard years ago when American CEOs tried to justified the low wages they paid to employees on the assembly line in China or Mexico or Vietnam (Leonard, 2011). What goes around comes around. To confirm the fact that B-schools consistently support worker exploitation, Columbia University Business School presented Ikeas CEO Mikael Ohlsson its 2011 Botwinick Prize in Business Ethics.

In the month of April 2010, the trade deficit was over $40 billion and almost half a million lost their jobs. At this rate, Americans will make nothing and not be able to buy anything.

OUTSOURCE CUSTOMER SERVICE

If you want to kill customer service outsource it. Why do CEOs do it? To get rich. Call center workers make less than $11 net per hour in India or the Philippines while it costs over $30 net per hour to hire call center employees in-house in America. But there is a real down side to outsourcing customer service. Customer service drops dramatically due to language and cultural difficulties. American customers are angry when they buy their item made in China, and they call an 800 number and get a person from India they cannot understand. If they ask for an American-trained representative, they are put on hold until they hang up in frustration. It is expected that customer service outsourcing will dramatically increase with American corporations using destinations like South Africa, Pakistan, Sri Lanka, Mauritius, Kenya, Romania and Ghana. And, we will soon see America outsourcing to India and India outsourcing to "where-ever," perhaps outsourcing those call center jobs back to Americans for $10 net per hour. Believe it or not, in 2008 it started to happen when India quietly set up a call center in Idaho.

Who will use these services? Retail, utilities, insurance, banks, and all sorts of manufacturers, and thousands of Indians will be trained as stock analysts ending Wall Street as we know it. Do CEOs care about the impact of long term destruction of customer service? Probably not. They want short-term profitability and enrichment of their stock holdings. They are hoping they can train their customers to accept less and less. They want to model their business after Costco or Sam's Club, where the customer pays an annual fee for the privilege to shop in their store. In a store with no floor help and where customers bring their items to self-checkout, where they are expected to unload and reload their wagon with no bags. As one manager said "If we could only train the customer to unload the trucks and stack the shelves it would be great, we wouldn't need employees." Maybe he is on to something. Just as Tom Sawyer convinced Ben and other boys that whitewashing Aunt Polly's fence was great fun and got them to pay him for the privilege, a type of reverse psychology could work for these self-service, big box retailers. For these CEOs the eternal search is for the ideal business model; where the customer becomes the employee and pays for the privilege of working and shopping for items made by robots. MBAs are taught in management, strategic planning and marketing classes across America that this is a way to maximize profitability. Professors do not teach the dark side of what Ivan Illich called "shadow work." Just as customers now must pump their own gas, check their own oil and tire pressure, managers are devising new ways to get customers to "paint the fence" for them. Professors do not teach about the pain and suffering this has caused by the jobs that were lost. According to Lambert (2011), in 1998 the IRS estimated that Americans spent 6 billion hours-per-year on "tax compliance" activities, the equivalent of 3 million full-time jobs. In 2011, it is certain that the job loss continues, with an estimated 20 million jobs that are now being performed by customers.

ANOTHER WAY TO GET RICH- KILL THE UNIONS

In the early 1950s, more than one-third of American workers belonged to unions. Bargaining between these workers and their employers helped raise wages, provide health care and pensions for workers. It kept the employer-employee compact firm. It also kept executive rewards reasonable, and during this period the gap between the CEO and their lowest level employee was approximately a multiple of 20.

Research has demonstrated that a union presence can have a significant impact on executive pay. One survey, published in the Journal of Labor Research, found that CEOs at nonunion companies take home nearly 20 percent more than executives in unionized firms. Workers in union companies, meanwhile, make $200 more a week than their non-union counterparts.

In 2008, only 7.4 percent of employees in the corporate world belonged to unions and 37 percent in the public sector belonged to unions making government employees the majority of union workers in America for the first time. This absence of a union check on executive pay leaves Wall Street and their CEOs free of sanctions. CEOs are now free to lower wages, lay off workers at will, reduce health care benefits, eliminate pensions and reward themselves and their stockholders handsomely.

The gap between CEO and employee pay is significantly wide in the service industries, where only a small percentage of employees belong to unions. For example, in food services, employees average about $18,877 a year. The CEOs of the top 10 firms in this industry, corporations like McDonald's, YUM Brands, KFC and Pizza Hut, took home 354 times that much in 2007 (Pizzigati and Anderson, 2008).

(To read more about killing the unions, see Appendix O)

THE DEATH OF COMMITMENT: TERMINATE EMPLOYEES AND GET RICH

We maintain that a significant motivation for terminating employees and engaging in outsourcing is that it increases the CEO's wealth but reckless destruction of a company also brings riches. Consider the following examples.

Bill Weldon CEO of Johnson & Johnson gained a 22 percent hike in compensation in 2007, raising his compensation to $25.1 million. Restructuring lowered profits by 4 percent, as he cut 4,820 jobs. In November 2009 he produced another restructuring with plans to eliminate about 8,100 jobs globally and freeze salaries that are above pay grade and offer lump sums instead of salary increases. These tactics made it possible for Weldon to reward stockholders as shares rose 41 cents to $64.39, and also make Weldon rich. His 2009 compensation package is about $29.3 million, containing lots of bonus money, $1.8 million in salary and a whopping $8 million for his pension. In 2010 he got a 3 percent salary increase after two years of revenue declines and an unprecedented string of recalls involving Tylenol and other household medicines (Perrone, 2011).

It was a very bad year for Nortel in 2007, which included a stock slump and the termination of over 2,000 employees. However, CEO Mike Zafirovski received a 21.5 percent raise in compensation. Again, in November, 2008 they announced the termination of 1,300 more jobs, including key management positions, and freezing salary increases after posting a $3.4 billion third-quarter loss. Eight years ago, Nortel had 100,000 employees. In November, 2008 that number was down to 31,000 and expected to continue to drop. In January 2009, Nortel filed for bankruptcy and Zafirovski refused to take a pay cut. In February 2009, as more employees were laid off, its stock was selling for .08 a share. In August 2009, Zafirovski was terminated. In October 2009, the ousted Zafirovski sought $12 million in bankruptcy court. He demanded the equivalent of 24 months' base pay, or $2.4 million; $3.8 million in bonuses under the company's SUCCESS Incentive Award Plan; $50,000 in insurance benefits, and at least $6 million in pension benefits. The SUCCESS INCENTIVE AWARD? It was discovered in December 2009 that 72 Nortel executives will divide up $7.5 in bonuses. This follows the awarding of $45 million in retention bonuses in March 2009 for some 100 executives. It seems that the bankruptcy filing had as its main objective to steal pensions from retired employees and make executives rich (Marlow, 2009).

Michael Lockhart, CEO of Armstrong, received a 57.8 percent pay increase in 2007, while putting its employees on a three week-per-month work schedule because of weak demand for their products. This meant that employees would see a loss of $400 in their weekly paychecks. Lockhart's executives received substantial raises. His CFO, F. Nicholas Grasberger, received a 39.8 percent increase in pay, and President Stephen Senkowski, a 31.7 percent increase.

(To read more about these CEOs, go to Appendix M)

CEOs have systematically rejected the ideas of contemporary management writers who suggest that organizations should have organic structures and a culture of collaboration and be less hierarchical. CEOs turn a blind eye to the research suggesting that high commitment is positively related to job satisfaction. CEOs accept the research that suggests when commitment is low, turnover will increase. Why? Because this is what they want: high turnover. CEOs do not care if low commitment increases resistance to change, increases employee stress and has a negative impact on employee health. CEOs seek to destroy the very essence of an employee's work ethic by destroying organizational commitment. A committed employee believes in what the organization is trying to achieve and is motivated to contribute to the company's objectives, and is a satisfied team member, but they are too costly, too demanding and bothersome. Look at the history of the committed employee.

The prototype of the committed employee evolved after World War II, as returning veterans sought employment in the evolving corporations, many of which grew in size and shape to resemble the enormous military machines created during the war. Writers and sociologists gave these post-war employees names like; the company man, the corporate man, the organizational man, the man in the grey flannel suit and the bureaucratic personality. Witness Whyte's (1956) view of this employee:

They are not the workers, nor are they the white-collar people in the usual, clerk sense of the word. These people only work for The Organization. The ones I am talking about belong to it as well. They are the ones of our middle class who have left home, spiritually as well as physically, to take the vows of organizational life, and it is they who are the mind and soul of our great self-perpetuating institutions. Only a few are top managers or ever will be. In a system that makes such hazy terminology as "junior executive" psychologically necessary, they are the staff as much as the line, and most are destined to live poised in the middle area that still waits a satisfactory euphemism. But they are dominant members of our society nonetheless. They have not joined together into a recognizable elite-our country does not stand still long enough for that-but it is from their ranks that are coming most of the first and second echelons of our leadership, and it is their values which will set the American temper.

These employees brought loyalty to the corporation, and they expected the same from the corporation. The employer-employee compact was formed. According to Maccoby (1976), "...they equated their personal interests with the corporation's long-term development and success, but their belief in the company may transcend self-interest." Like the good soldiers they were, they brought these values to the corporation. What did they expect from the corporation? They expected an identity, membership in a social community, responsibility, security for life and an opportunity to be committed. This demand or what was called the employee-employer compact eventually came to be seen by CEOs, stockholders and their consultants from business schools as unreasonable, bothersome and cost-inefficient.

DESTROY THE EMPLOYER-EMPLOYEE COMPACT

The employee-employer relationship, based on mutual commitment and loyalty, began to wane in the 1970s with the writings of Milton Friedman and others, who suggested a new model for America, with a greater emphasis on corporate wealth and profits, using the label "free market economy" as a code word for giving sway to corporatist ideology. This was taken up by business writers/professors, in the early 1980s, with textbooks in the area of business strategy now recommending large-scale terminations as a viable cost-cutting strategy. Academic writers and their students offered terminations as a strategy with little or no details concerning the negative consequences of such acts. The downsizing phenomenon was born in these textbooks and students were taught it and practicing managers quickly embraced it. Soon legions of MBAs entered into corporate caverns with a new way of managing. Managers began to think of their personnel (en masse) as accordions, expanding in times of growth and contracting in bad times. Downsizing meant maximizing profits, minimizing payroll costs. It quickly became the darling of Wall Street. Corporate boards were now looking for CEOs' who could push around the workforce. This became increasingly apparent following President Reagan's 1981 tough stance against striking Air Traffic Controllers, when he terminated 11,500 employees. Also, the fact that union enrollment was dropping precipitously, and millions of undocumented workers were now in the U.S., made toughness easy. The workforce could no longer fight back. The American worker was now disposable.

In the Unites States, in the month of April 2003, 223,000 jobs were terminated, the largest loss of jobs in more than ten years. These job losses were called variable costs, and it was suggested that CEOs could cut their variable costs much easier than their fixed costs. This was a major rationalization by CEOs. Consider the following. A professor addressed a group of corporate executives in the early 1980s, he was an expert in organizational commitment. He said to the group, "if you really want to study organizational commitment you can start by studying cults, they know how to create commitment." As he began his lecture he was interrupted. An executive said "commitment is outmoded," the audience agreed. The professor said, "What about the Japanese, they have become the fastest growing industrial economy and they have a powerfully committed workforce." The executives argued, "That's a function of their culture, you will not find commitment in our culture". The professor responded, "In Japan they can get employees to work 16 hour days and never complain, would you like to hear how they do it?" The group said, "It's a waste of time." Another member said, "Today's employees are narcissistic corporate vagabonds out to get all they can for themselves." The group concurred.

WHY NO OUTRAGE?

A critical question to examine is when these large-scale dismissals became an acceptable strategy in the 1980s, why were there were no protests or investigations. It is reasonable to assume that if these large-scale terminations occurred in the 1950s, 60s and perhaps the 70s, it would have precipitated public outrage. But since the 1980s through the turn-of-the-century, we witnessed not only the flourishing practice of large scale terminations, but CEOs who committed such acts treated by stockholders, B-school deans and their corporate boards as heroes. In addition, consultants, scholars and popular corporate writers and gurus praised them as corporate winners in their speeches, stories and cases to be studied in business schools.

There is another significant factor that contributed to this phenomenon of terminating employees and destroying commitment. This is the tying of stock grants to CEO compensation. When boards and stockholders gave CEOs significant stock options and grants, CEOs and their stockholders reaped the short-term bonanzas associated with terminations. In the early 1990s, Wall Street and institutional investors'; pension funds, mutual funds and trusts started insisting that corporations return more money to shareholders. CEOs who did not respond to these demands were quickly fired. Soon stocks and stock options made up the bulk of CEO pay. Jacoby (2008) uses GM as an example. In the early 1990s executive compensation was heavily tied to stock ownership and options and between 1996 to 2000 GM delivered more than $20 billion to shareholders, $13 billion in multiple repurchases and $7 billion in dividends. He maintains that if GM had used that money for research and development it would not have been in bankruptcy in 2009. Another example is Motorola. In 2008, Co-Chief Executive Gregory Brown received a base salary of at least $1.2 million. He was promised an annual bonus of not less than 220 percent of his base salary and a 2008 special bonus of not less than 130 percent of his base salary, based on meeting performance goals. His long-range incentive plan had a target of not less than 350 percent of his base salary for 2008, and not less than 250 percent of his base salary for each following fiscal year. Brown also could receive 583,123 shares of restricted stock as well as an option to purchase 2.32 million shares of common stock (Dow Jones Newswire, 2008).

Consequently, these new incentive systems meant that executives got rich while employees got axed. In the process executives created corporate cultures where no one could feel safe or secure. Fear of termination and losing everything kept one on the treadmill. Consider this example: A young wife of a high power Wall Street executive entered therapy. Her chief complaint was against her neglectful husband. He left the house daily at 5 a.m. and returned often at 11 p.m. On some nights, after spending the evening at high-priced strip clubs with his colleagues, where they would spend upwards to $50,000 on alcohol and strippers in private club rooms, he would arrive home at 4 a.m.. After a few hours of sleep he would wake to start the day. On weekends, he worked Saturday until 2 p.m., and if he didn't play golf he sometimes worked Sunday until noon. She hadn't had sex in three years. She would take vacations with their children to their summer house. Her husband would join them on weekends and he would sit on the beach with his laptop, blackberry and two cell phones. Summer parties would always be with colleagues from work. He made millions and he promised his wife that as soon as they accumulated enough money he would quit. It's been almost 15 years and many millions later. She believes he is so driven he will never give it up, and will drop dead from exhaustion. What drives this man? Fear, that if he stops or even slows down, all will be lost. He accumulates wealth, fearing that the market will drop, he will lose his job and his tenuous position will be destroyed. He was right. In 2008 he lost his job and half his savings.

CORPORATIONS AND THE ECONOMY-INSTILL FEAR

Contrast employment in America with France. In France, hours worked per week are fixed at 35 by law. Overtime payments are usually fixed by collective agreement, but also by law employees had to be paid with at least an extra 10 percent an hour. In the case of no other collective agreement, overtime was paid at an extra 25 percent an hour for the first eight hours and then at an extra 50 percent an hour. The 35-hour week has led many companies to be a lot more flexible about working hours. Some have implemented an 8 hour per day schedule with Friday afternoon off, whereas others make 10:00 a.m. to 4:00 p.m. required time at work and leave individuals to organize the rest of their time. Managerial jobs have always tended to be more flexible, with people often starting later in the day (10 or later), longer lunches and then finishing 8:00 p.m. All employees are entitled to two and a half days of paid leave per month worked. This gives five full weeks of vacation a year. Italians get more, 45 days, but not Americans. They rank woefully last of all industrialized nations with an average of seven days, as few employees take their entitled vacation time of 10 days. If American workers are given a day off, they are so intimidated that they would most likely show up for work. Saulny and Brown, (2009) report that employees who are "furloughed" during the 2008 financial crisis come to work even when they were forced to have days off with no pay "…because they fear for the long-term safety of their position and hope self-sacrifice impresses the management." Unlike Americans, French employees fight for their work week and time off. French President Sarkozy and other politicians know that corporate CEOs in Europe work between 48 and 68 hours a week, and it infuriates them that their employees work a 35-hour week. When Sarkozy wanted to increase the work week and made it clear he favored the American approach, over a million of France's workers took to the streets in protest. But not in America; the workforce is so intimidated that they suffer quietly, put in their 60 to 70 hours a week and often are willing to give up their vacation or even work for free. It is not devotion to work that keeps Americans glued to the workplace, it is downright fear. CEOs love the American way. They almost get two employees for the price of one. Think about what would happen if America adopted the European 35 hours per week. It would lead to a significant reduction in the numbers of millions unemployed. But this would lead to one unpopular side effect, it would dramatically increase labor costs and lower CEO wealth. But there is another side that CEOs rarely think of: the cost of having an overworked stressed out work force that experiences little joy in their work and drudgingly shows up day in and day out no matter what. This anomaly of an intimidated and fearful workforce is not found exclusively in the corporate world. We are beginning to see it in the public sector. In the past federal employees enjoyed liberal amounts of paid time off: 13 days of sick leave per year, 10 paid federal holidays, and depending on years of service, 13 to 26 days each year. This can amount to 52 days off a year, and in the past they took them. But as the recession deepened, federal, state and local governments discovered they were mired in a deep financial crisis and things began to dramatically change. In the summer of 2010, 51 percent of American cities said they had to either cut or freeze employee salaries and 22 percent said they had to revise union contracts to reduce pay and benefits and 19 percent introduced furloughs (Greenhouse, 2010). At the publically funded universities professors began to accept pay cuts and tenure quickly became obsolete and the academic adjunct became the norm. Employees throughout America are being told they will be out of a job unless they accept less and work more.

Employee protest against the demise of the employer-employee compact and abuse by corporate executives will not happen until this docile generation of employees is either pushed out of the work, enters into voluntary or involuntary retirement or dies off, and at the rate they are going, this may occur soon, perhaps within the next 15 to 20 years. They will be followed by a new generation of workers the Gen Ys who will not be docile corporate androids content to spend a life on the assembly line or in a cubicle

(You can read about this generation in Chapter 11).

STRESS AT WORK

Studies of stress-related work began to appear as the work week began to increase. We have no statistics concerning the consequences of working such long hours under stress. The Japanese do. They even have a word for this, working oneself to death, called "Karoshi". Japan even has a secretary general of the Karoshi Bengo Dan Zenkoki Renraku Ki-ghee, or National Liaison Council of Lawyers on Death from Overwork. The Labor Bureau of Japan claims that 147 people died in Japan in 2007, due to overwork. The evidence used in determining death due to work included; working over 100 hours of overtime in a month over a six month period, many times working overnight and excessive compulsive attendance to the job, that is excessive worry. This leads to stress and cardiac failure. In France workers are capable of protesting the increased stress on the job. At France Telecom over a 20 month period beginning in February 2008, 24 employees committed suicide. Foxconn a China technology manufacturing company witnessed 10 suicides at their company's base in Longhua, southern China this year. They were all young migrant workers, among the millions of people who left the poor hinterlands of China for the boom towns of the south and east coastal areas. Young workers being overworked, living in crowded conditions (over 800,000 employees) away from family and friends experience dramatic increases in stress. How common is this in America?

In a study by Galinsky, et.al. (2004) they reported that 44 percent of American employees feel overworked often or very often and 98 percent of employees said their job requires them to work very hard and they do not have enough time in the day to complete their work. Overwork is defined as simply working too many hours. In 1999 the National Institute of Occupational Safety and Health said that job stress is a threat to the health of workers. Of particular concern is the degree to which these overworked employees show symptoms of clinical depression. These symptoms include a preoccupation or rumination over thoughts and feelings of inadequacy or worthlessness, hopelessness and self-hatred. They also suffer from insomnia, poor eating habits, low sex drive and an inability to take care of themselves and an array of physical symptoms such as fatigue, headaches, or digestive problems. When we consider the impact associated with so-called occupational stress, we can see its pervasiveness. Consider alcohol and drug abuse, the high divorce rate, latchkey children, smoking, obesity, and especially violence in the workplace. Estimates suggest that more than 2 million employees suffer physical attacks at work each year and more than 6 million are threatened in some way. Threats can range from rumor spreading, to sexual harassment, to death threats sent to executives through untraceable electronic mail, to workers talking of mass murder. The most common form of violence are outbursts of anger and rage resulting from the building up of stress overtime.

In a survey of 500 human resource managers conducted by the American Management Association in 1994, one out of 13 respondents indicated one violent workplace death had occurred at their organization in the last four years. More than one-half (51.2 percent) of the managers reported some kind of violent incident since the beginning of 1990, and they expected the trend to continue. When asked to provide details regarding the most recent violent incident at their workplace, managers stated that the victim's relationship to the attacker was most commonly that of a co-worker (27.2 percent), followed by direct supervisor (15.3 percent). Employees were attacked by strangers in 12.3 percent of the cases, while superiors who were not the attacker's direct supervisors were the victims in 10 percent of the incidents. Only 1.1 percent of the cases involved attacks on employees by direct supervisors. Clients or customers were attacked in 5.7 percent of the incidents. Among managers reporting violent incidents, 29.1 percent said the organization had ignored early warning signs displayed by the attacker, and 25.7 percent said the victim had ignored early signs of the potential violence (Neuman and Baron, 1996).

What we have is a workplace filled with stress and in response executives have turned workplaces into armed camps, with security cameras, guards and an array of electronic security devices, where points of entry are carefully guarded.

The stress that employees experience is associated with intimidation, fear, competition, and termination. Employees use an array of defenses to protect themselves from being overwhelmed with stress. They become overwhelmingly cynical and detached. The cynicism allows them to defend against feeling, anxiety and pain. For many of these employees the cynicism may become malignant, and like the Wall Street executive described above, he cannot feel for his wife and children. This leaves the executive alone in the world, except for work. At work, he feels alive, work provides him a "rush," especially when he has a good day. Work has the potential to provide the narcissistic supplies that makes him feel special and grandiose, when they are not available, he remembers the "good times," and seeks colleagues to reminisce. The talk, laughter and memories protect him from anxiety, loneliness and feelings of dread. This executive works; not for the accumulation of wealth, not for achievement, or a sense of gratification, but to avoid the deadness in his life, work is his oasis.

On the train to and from work these worried and stressed employees can be found reading reports, talking on their cell phones and using their Blackberry's. They begin work when they wake, and stop working when they go to sleep. In addition to working longer hours, 81 percent of employees say they work harder than five years ago, and 85 percent feel compelled to be on their BlackBerry 24/7 (McNamara and Goldiner, 2008). You see these employees taking the train home to their bedroom communities, asleep from exhaustion, clutching their blackberry. Just as a toddler needs their teddy to go to sleep, to protect them from the fear and anxiety of darkness, these overworked and frightened employees face their own darkness. The darkness is the same type of loneliness that the toddler feels when the parents leave and the lights go out. The employee sees termination, as the toddler sees bedtime and their BlackBerry functions as their teddy bear, a classic transitional object.

There is still another phenomenon that executives, consultants and business writers have created to put the nail in the commitment coffin. This is the performance review. It is an instrument that was created in direct response to the destruction of commitment. When commitment was destroyed, the question that followed was: How would the corporation keep the employee glued to their jobs? How could the corporation keep reins on these so-called non-committed vagabond employees? It was the performance review.

CHAPTER 4

The Performance Review: Creating a Culture of Intimidation

"Performance appraisal is that occasion when once a year you find out who claims sovereignty over you." Peter Block

Another way to get Rich- the Performance Review: An Instrument to Destroy Commitment but Keep the Employee Working

In addition to large-scale terminations, CEOs discovered that they could use performance reviews to quietly reduce their workforce and at the same time create a climate that would dramatically increase productivity. In addition, corporate leadership discovered that commitment was not necessary to have an engaged workforce. All one needed to do was use a performance appraisal system to create a culture of intimidation to induce performance.

Consider this example. General Electric maintained that it was good business to stop trying to gain commitment from so-called "unmotivated" employees, going a step further they maintained it is wise to "give up" on these uncommitted employees. GE's retired CEO, Jack Welch writes; "a company that bets its future on its people must remove that lower 10 percent and keep removing it every year."

Welch is among the most vocal advocates of the performance appraisal system that "forced ranked" employees in every department and fired the lowest-performing employees every year.

According to Lawler (2002), *"At GE, it's the bottom 10 percent of employees who are supposed to be eliminated. Mr. Welch feels so strongly about this practice that he highlighted it in his 1999 letter to GE shareholders and advocated it again in his book,* Jack: Straight from the Gut *(Warner Books, 2001). In addition to arguing that a forced ranking or distribution system is good for organizations, he reasons, it is good for individuals because it takes people who are failing out of situations that are bad for them and the company. GE is not alone in using this system. Similar policies have been adopted by Ford Motor, Conoco, Sun Microsystems, Cisco Systems, EDS, Enron, and a host of other U.S. corporations.* "

In February 2010 the newly appointed CEO of AIG Robert Benmoshe announced he was rolling out the Welch "forced distribution" performance review system. AIG employees will be ranked on a scale of 1 to 4 based on their performance relative to their peers. Low performers will be sacked. Annual compensation, including bonuses, will be based on one's ranking. Only employees ranked in the top 10 percent will be the winners. Benmosche claims he implemented Welch's system when he was CEO of Met Life with great success. This is nothing more than a CEO implementing a program that will play havoc with his employees. American taxpayers will never see the $90 billion bailout they gave to AIG.

It seems, as CEOs embraced these types of review systems, they failed to look at a more covert motivation for using them. These performance-based evaluation systems gave management a sense of power, and a chance to humiliate, and get those people identified as disloyal. At the same time it created an environment of fear, subordination and the appearance of hard work (called face-time). These "disposable workers", who received bad reviews and were either terminated, experienced humiliation and blamed themselves and would often think; "If I just worked harder, this would not be happening." And, the workforce worked harder, longer hours. According to Bowman (2010) incentive compensation may perversely:

- focus on the short term at the expense of the long term,
- encourage mediocrity by setting limits on expectations,
- reduce creativity and risk-taking,
- promote self-interest above other interests,
- destroy teamwork because it increases dependence on individual accomplishment,
- generate counterproductive, win-lose competition for merit monies,
- encourage sycophancy ("do-as-I-say performance pay"), and/or
- generally politicize the compensation system

Edward Deming, writing, about 14 points needed to transform management and the corporation, believed performance appraisals were counterproductive and simply bad management. In his point #3 called– Evaluation of Performance, Merit Rating, or Annual Review, he proposed their eradication. Deming writes, "The performance appraisal nourishes short-term performance, annihilates long-term planning, builds fear, demolishes teamwork, nourishes rivalry and politics… it leaves people bitter, crushed, bruised, battered, desolate, despondent, dejected, feeling inferior, some even depressed, unfit for work for weeks after receipt of rating, unable to comprehend why they are inferior. It is unfair, as it ascribes to the people in a group differences that may be caused totally by the system that they work in." In other words, commitment is destroyed.

It is commonly understood that performance reviews, pay for performance, and incentive systems have little to do with the motivation, but they are successful in punishing employees and rupturing relationships. Going further, Kohn (1993) maintains that many studies point out that rewards actually undermine the very process they are intended to enhance. In agreement, Deming believed that extrinsic motivators were a fallacy. When asked the question, "Is money a motivator?" he replied, "It is not!" He believed the same applies to all forms of extrinsic motivators: they do not motivate. Money is a complex and deeply held psychological artifact that varies from employee to employee. In the American culture people are more apt to freely discuss their sex life than their income. Employees are not only unwilling to discuss their salary with colleagues, but rarely will they tell their closest friends and some research suggests that 15 percent of employees do not even tell their family what they earn.

When it comes to intrinsic motivation the relationship between reward and motivation is even more complex. For example, offering rewards for easy tasks or just completing a task may lower intrinsic motivation. It is a mistake to assume that employees are motivated in predictable ways by differential rewards and punishments.

Many human resource managers believe that rewards and punishments, the key element in the performance review, are motivators. They base their thinking on the work of B.F. Skinner who could get animals to do extraordinary things through a carefully controlled system of positive and negative reinforcements. Unfortunately most HR managers, like many scholars, misread Skinner. Most agree that positive reinforcement leads to the strengthening of behaviors by the application of some event (e.g., praise after some behavior is performed); however negative reinforcements are not punishments. Negative reinforcement is the strengthening of behavior by the removal or avoidance of some aversive event (e.g., Opening and raising an umbrella over your head on a rainy day is reinforced by the cessation of rain falling on you). Do positive and negative reinforcement strengthen behavior? No, and here is the problem with Skinner's approach; He worked almost exclusively with animals, and while he had ample evidence it worked with animals there is little evidence that this approached worked effectively on adults. Despite this, the so-called "carrot and the stick" approach, which forms the basis for the performance reviews, is still believed. Harry Levinson a leading organizational psychologist maintains that the carrot and stick approach not only does not work but it is demeaning. Levinson asked executives what was the dominant philosophy underlying theories of motivation. They collectively agreed it was the carrot and stick or punishment and reward. He then asked the executives to close their eyes and envision a carrot and stick and he asked them to identify the central figure in their mental image. It was usually a jackass. He calls this the "Great Jackass Fallacy" the title of his book. The jackass becomes a metaphor for the image CEOs and their HR managers have of employees and this underlies the use of performance reviews. This image is held consciously or unconsciously or both. The image clearly is attached to the "theory X" view of the employee as lazy, work avoiding, stupid, and unwilling to do work unless driven, controlled, watched and punished. This is straight out of the work by F.W. Taylor, who believed that immigrant laborers were dumb and/or retarded. What are the consequences of the "carrot and stick" ideology? It means subordinates need to be continuously driven by their superiors; they must be electronically watched and punished for any infraction. If the employee is dutiful, obedient and works diligently with success then they get a carrot; a bonus, pin, or public praise all done with the assumption that it will inspire the other "mules". But it fails to inspire and only creates a grumbling, cynical, bitter group who would like to pummel the "asskisser." These HR managers and performance gurus do not know what every kindergarten teacher knows. You never tell a class: "Why can't the rest of you be like good little Johnny?" It's the "kiss of death" for little Johnny. The ultimate outcome of the carrot and stick approach is it becomes a self-fulfilling prophecy; the employee becomes unmotivated and disengaged and inefficient.

Returning to "forced rankings." Lawler (2002) says, "Mr. Welch notes in his CEO memoir that by the third year of forced firings, "it's war." It creates a culture of stress. What manager wants to face an annual or semiannual process where he/she must identify the lowest-ranking subordinates and recommend which ones should be fired? Sometimes managers just lack the courage to fire someone, and they turn over the data to human resources which take on the work of termination. In many companies HR handles all performance assessments, reviews and terminations, this is especially apparent when legal issues prevail.

Terminations are only one reason managers don't like forced distribution systems. Managers worry about what will happen to the survivors, especially survivors who had close relationships with those terminated. In addition, they're concerned about firings disrupting the work of other employees and increasing their workload.

Welch did anything but establish a system of motivation. What he did accomplish was to create a culture of fear, competition, depersonalization and repressed anger. Like Welch, CEOs embraced performance reviews and incentives (or bribes) because reviews did to their employees exactly what they wanted them to do. They secured temporary compliance.

Over the years American corporations have become fixated with variable pay and the performance review process and human resource managers became obsessed with finding the perfect/objective assessment instrument. HR managers and their consultants now push for what they call "performance driven cultures" and they announce spurious research claiming that corporations that invest in these talent management practices will outperform their competitors. What is a performance-driven culture? It is nothing more than a recreation of Welch's evaluation system, these HR managers and consultants are "putting lipstick on the pig".

CEOs, with their HR managers, developed a variety of contingent or variable pay schemes to be used for rewarding performance. They maintained that variable pay is the best method to recognize achievement and they believed that pay should be related to contributions, and that those who contributed more, should get more.

Smith (2008), maintains the following arguments are commonly used by executives and HR managers to support rewarding performance and giving performance rewards:

- They act as a motivator

- They encourage and support desired behaviors

- They deliver the message that performance, competence, contribution and skill are important

- They provide a means for defining and agreeing on performance and competence expectations

- They reinforce the organization's value system

- Finally, they help to achieve a culture of change

- The problem with these claims is the fact that none are supported by research.

THE PROBLEM WITH PERFORMANCE REVIEW

Levy & Williams (2005) report that studies that described performance review as a negative clearly outweigh studies suggesting positive qualities. The ratio of negative studies versus positive studies may be as high as 2 to 1. The question is what is it about performance review that scholars find so overwhelmingly negative? They found that rater bias or rater influence is the major culprit in the negative studies, also rater characteristics such as likeability, similar personalities, background, education, and family will influence rater judgment. Consider this question: Would raters assess their employee higher if they had hired the employee as opposed to a manager who did not hire the employee? Common sense would suggest that the manager who hired the employee would have a greater investment in seeing their employee do well and opposed to a manager who inherited the employee. This would translate into rater bias. In addition research studies question whether raters are even motivated to rate accurately (Levy & Williams, 2005). This raises the question of the interplay between conscious and unconscious motivations that color the rater's judgment when giving a rating to an employee. In the psychoanalytic world, this type of reaction is referred to as a countertransference reaction where a characteristic of the person being rated (the ratee) triggers off feelings and emotions in the rater. The ratee may bring up some forbidden feelings or emotions (hatred, sex, maternal longing, envy, etc.), and while these feelings may be beyond the awareness they nonetheless will motivate the rater to move in one direction as oppose to another when rating employees. Also the mood and emotions contained in the rater can influence the entire process. Most ratee's would cringe at the prospect of being rated by a boss who learned the night before their spouse was filing for divorce. Researchers have used scales to assess rater's emotional states and depending on the nature of their emotional state the rating was influenced. For example raters who experienced the performance review

(PR) process as discomforting tended to give higher ratings (Villanova, Bernardin, Dahmus, & Sims, 1993). It may well be that raters who are nervous or fearful of the consequences of a negative rating would give higher ratings. Consider this example a young Caucasian manager in a company located in the Bronx N.Y. who gave a very negative rating and the equivalent of a performance improvement process (PIP) warning to an African-American woman. Outraged, she obtained an attorney and proceeded to file a lawsuit. The young man's career at the company was finished as several executives had to give depositions. To avoid going to court in the Bronx, where 80 to 90 percent of all cases go against the "Hated Corporation" she was given her old job back and they settled out of court. The young man knowing his career had ended, left. Other managers aware of this case tended to give positive reviews especially to members of minority groups.

A study released in August, 2011 by Georgetown University's McDonough School of Business indicates that connections and relationships play a significant role in employee promotions, despite policies and procedures at most companies designed to lower the impact of non-objective assessment and despite general acknowledgment that such favoritism leads to bad decision making, they found that 92 percent of senior business executives surveyed said that they have seen favoritism at play in employee promotions, including 84 percent at their own companies (Gardner, 2011). Favoritism is often the key factor in not only getting a good review but also in getting promoted. This suggests that the variable pay processes are no more than a screen for a corrupt system loaded with bias.

Cultural values have a powerful influence on the performance review process. By cultural values, we are referring to the performance review process as a cultural artifact. Rarely has a performance review process been accepted as an integral part of an organization's culture. It is most often a cultural artifact ranging from considerable suspicion to an outright evil and is either rejected or remained on the periphery of the larger culture and begrudgingly performed. One manager reported that the performance review process was not well integrated into the company and managers found it overwhelming. When this occurs the process tends to become politicized and raters will quickly dispense with the process and complete the necessary forms guided by their impressions. Consider what this company did: Wanting to jump on the performance review bandwagon after hearing the exaggerated benefits it would bring by consultants they hired a Ph.D., recommended by the consultants, and created the position of VP of Performance. After a year the VP rolled out a 500-page instruction manual and sent managers off for a five-day training program where everything was covered, from the language use to legal ramifications. The managers were delighted when they were told they would be given three days off each year to work in the privacy of their home completing their evaluations. Managers quickly turned this into a mini-vacation and combined the three days with a weekend where they spent five days in the Caribbean with their spouses. Needless to say the evaluations were meaningless. A "boiler plate" was created for high, medium, and low evaluations which allowed the managers to quickly expedite the process to get on with their vacations. It is estimated that 90 percent of all performance review processes are politicized and managers experience it a burden and react with cynicism.

AN EXAMPLE OF A FAILURE TO CONSIDER SYSTEM DYNAMICS IN THE PERFORMANCE REVIEW

As we can see, a major problem with performance evaluations is that they fail to consider how interpersonal and system dynamics influence the evaluation both positively and negatively. Consider this example. An OD psychologist took a position as an internal consultant to a major corporation. A VP asked him to consult to a manager of a department and help the manager with leadership skills. After two weeks, the VP fired the manager. Shortly after, the VP asked the psychologist to consult to another manager. The psychologist made it very clear that the manager should remain in position during the consultation and if the VP wanted to fire the manager, he should first talk with the psychologist. After a few weeks the VP, detecting what he saw as gross incompetence, impulsively fired the manager. The psychologist was now in a difficult position. Whenever he would meet with a manager, the manager would break out in a "cold sweat." Managers avoided the psychologist, who was now feared and referred to as the terminator, as the person responsible for the firings. The psychologist told the VP that it would be a long time before he could obtain the trust of the VP's managers.

At the annual performance review, the psychologist was told by the HR director that it was widely believed that he had problems working with managers and that his failure to work with managers was a liability, and if he continued to neglect his consulting duties he would be put on probation. The psychologist, outraged, tried to explain what the VP's actions did to his reputation and trust. The HR director failed to understand the dynamics at play between the VP, psychologist and managers.

The psychologist also explained that in his role of internal consultant; consulting to managers was not even in his job description. He then sent off a lengthy letter of resignation to the VP of HR and left the company. He received no response.

What occurs here are three things that the performance review failed to consider: (1) Decisions were made by a superior (VP) that created a series of dynamics that made it impossible for the psychologist to succeed. (2) It is often impossible to operationalize an employee's job description and then neatly place it in a category, let alone quantify it. (3) It often happens that a manger engages in an assessment of an employee on work that is not in the employee's job description. In this case, consulting to managers was not in the psychologist's initial job description, it was added later on, after the VP's actions severely compromised any potential consulting relationships.

These types of problems are especially apparent in the office where an employee works on many tasks during the year, some within his/her realm of expertise and others considered a stretch assignment. A manager with several employees would find it impossible to keep track of all his or her activities and could possibly focus on those activities that confirm or support his or her preconceived ideas of the employee's performance. Also, at the time of review, if an employee brings in a well documented list of the duties performed and presents a case, the reviewer may take offense.

CEOS AND PERFORMANCE REVIEWS

We find widespread acceptance of performance reviews among corporate executives. They are so well accepted that 80 percent of all CEOs have a performance review bonus written into their contract, and when hired, 56 percent of new CEOs will have a performance review within their first six months (Execunet, 2008). However, as we observe, performance assessments for executives have little or no relationship to reality. There is no better example of this then the reactions Wall Street executives and their compensation consultants had when the government, in the process of bailing out banks and Wall Street, decided that they would tie compensation to performance, and if corporations received bailout money no executive could earn more than $500,000. All of a sudden executives and their compensation consultants determined that performance reviews were only valid when times were good. When times were bad, performance reviews were devalued. Consider this "Performance is not the end-all, be-all," said Jamie Dimon, CEO of JPMorgan Chase. As he was attempting to justify Wall Street giving billions in bonuses as the stock market and economy tanked and millions of jobs were lost, in 2009. Compensation consultants stated that it was outrageous to pay a top executive $500,000 when they were used to living off millions. As one consultant stated, "It's not fair to ask an executive to adjust their life-style so drastically." As millions lose their jobs, retirement money and homes, CEOs are outraged that their pay may be reduced. They are rushing to give the bailout money back, not because it is patriotic or the right thing to do, but they want their million-dollar salaries back. Goldman Sachs received a government bailout of $10 billion in 2008 and received $13 billion from AIG after the government bailed them out and in 2009 Goldman's CEO Lloyd Blankfein reaped a $6.1 million gain by cashing in more than 90,000 stock options before they expired. It is not surprising Goldman is the most vilified company in America by Main Streeters. In 2010 Goldman had to pay the SEC $550 billion to settle civil fraud charges and a $600 million charge for trying to cheat the British government by not paying employee bonus tax.

The Harvard Business Review published a list of the Top 50 CEOs in 2009. They maintained that this group of 50 created 32 percent average gains every year and over $48.2 billion of value for investors. Comparatively, the bottom 50 CEOs had a negative 20 percent annual return, and lost over $18.3 billion. However, only 5 of the top best performers were on the list of top 50 highest paid CEOs. This clearly demonstrates that CEO pay is not really tied to performance (Hartung, 2009).

In 2005, the Securities and Exchange Commission began requiring companies to explain the review process for executives and identify performance targets used to calculate incentive pay, such as bonuses. Under the rule, companies were supposed to divulge performance benchmarks — for example, growth in earnings per share — and why they were chosen. Companies were also supposed to detail the range of performance under which incentive payouts would be made, and the corresponding payout percentages. However, this did not happen. Many companies simply did not bother to comply with the rules, and outright rejected making public pay for performance. According to 2007 proxy filings, only 47 percent of corporations made the required disclosures concerning short-term incentive pay for their executives (Morgenson, 2008a). Corporations continue to fight disclosure, and offer a wide range of excuses as to why pay for performance should not apply to their executives. With the fiscal crises of 2008-09, the percentage of corporations refusing to file disclosures dramatically increased. Executives maintained that the performance review is only for their underlings, not for them, that to assess their work is impossible and failure is a result of unseen forces in the marketplace. This is sheer folly. Of all employees, the performance that is the easiest to assess is the CEO. A similar phenomenon is found in England, where the High Pay Commission stated there was rarely a link between directors' incentives and the way a company performs. In the past 10 years, the average annual bonus for FTSE 350 directors went up by 187 per cent, and the average year-end share price declined by 71 per cent.

CEOs prefer to live in a perfect world where they not only review themselves, but also reward themselves. How do they do it? They hire consultants to write glowing accounts of their exploits, and it doesn't matter if profits are up or down, they find someone to report that they have done a "heck of a job." For example in 2008, the stock price for Cell Therapeutics dropped 99.25 percent. But on December 31, 2008, the top five executives received wonderful reviews and were awarded year-end bonuses totaling more than $1 million. CEO James Bianco was awarded a $487,500 bonus in 2008 and in March 2009, he terminated 34 employees. The company continues to suffer financially.

CEOs and their top executives who always get great reviews, along with raises and bonuses are immune to the suffering of their demoralized and bitter employees who are thoroughly scrutinized, evaluated, inspected, judged and humiliated. Employees see the system as unfair, and the corporate culture is charged with attitudes of cynicism and rage. Hewlett-Packard is a prime example of how CEO pay and behavior ruined the culture of a once great company.

(To Read more about HP go to Appendix Z).

We will discuss the motivations of top management to conduct these reviews, but before we do it is helpful to assess what many consider the most problematic and destructive of all performance reviews: the infamous 360 Feedback, a process that is rapidly growing among American corporations with little concern over the consequences.

360 DEGREE FEEDBACK- THE WORSE REVIEW

Many corporations (estimates are 65 percent) are adopting what they call 360 degree feedback evaluations or reviews. The so-called 360 degree feedback is designed to provide each employee in the corporation performance feedback. The stated purpose of this feedback is to assist each individual to understand his or her strengths and weaknesses, and identify what needs to improve and perhaps suggest how to go about improving. There is considerable variation among corporations concerning 360 methodology. There is disagreement about how to select the feedback tool, the process to follow, selection of raters, what to review and how to give feedback, and how to integrate the process into the corporation's goals and mission. The general assumption is that the employees "key constituents" should include supervisors, peers, subordinates, suppliers and customers and these people will be part of the performance review process.

In many corporations employees conduct an "anonymous" review of everyone they work with. This includes an upward review of their boss (as if that could be done in an honest way). The process typically begins by having employees complete self-evaluation forms and then compare the self evaluation with evaluations from others. In some corporations the self evaluation begins after the employee receives his or her peer review. Then the employee will evaluate his or her immediate superior and in some instances select cross discipline employees to evaluate. It's as if everyone is evaluating everyone. And chaos results.

If employees get a negative review they may have to meet with their key constituents. If a manager gets a negative review a meeting is called by the company's OD or HR staff. Facilitators encourage employees to engage in an open discussion of the issues they have had with their manager. They are sometimes written on boards. Once these discussions are completed the boss is invited in. The stress and tension is often "thick." Managers who have been given a negative review and must appear in front of their subordinates under public review and will have one of three reactions; they can be open to hearing their subordinates' complaints, they can be defensive, or they can make it clear they will seek revenge against anyone who is critical. In most cases the manager is defensive and feels humiliated and helpless. In addition the manager knows that OD/HR facilitators will make recommendations to their superior.

When a manager gets a negative 360 from their subordinates it usually means the end of their managerial career with that company. Negative 360s are particularly problematic for managers hired from outside the company. Those who did not get the position will seek support from their colleagues to "nail" the new manager and will use the 360 review as a vehicle to get the new manager.

In most cases, these negative feedback sessions are humiliating experiences for all; employees and raters. Some report that they feel like children in grade school and they can never feel secure with their colleagues again. Some managers report that they are set up by revengeful subordinates who are getting back at them for the previous year's evaluation.

When face-to-face meetings are absent and the review process concludes with an anonymous written review from superiors and subordinates, the entire process is poisoned. The reviewed wonders who is writing things about them, and they spend countless hours trying to figure out who is out to get them. It promotes a paranoid culture. In addition, the system does not give managers a chance to meet discuss and correct whatever issues they may have with their subordinates, superiors, the corporation, fellow workers, etc.

Any evaluation system that is anonymous and has as its aim protection against deceit and retribution is a failed system and can end up doing the opposite of what it is trying to do. These reviews resemble the old "suggestion box," and symbolize a corporate culture that cannot allow managers and employees to sit down and have open and honest discussions as adults who care about each other. These reviews damage relationships and promote distrust, anger and revenge. It stimulates a system that is anything but honest, open or helpful.

Problems with review systems are compounded when the corporation brings in outside consultants or 360 appraisal vendors. Despite the paucity of research showing the usefulness and validity or reliability of these systems, vendors promote their effectiveness and cite case after case of success. They tell executives they must adopt the system because everyone else is doing so, the latest fad. The major problem with vendors is that they are interested in selling their systems. They enter from the outside, do not know the corporation or its members, and all they really have is a generic performance assessment system that asks an array of typical questions. In addition, these firms and consultants use their assessments to promote further training and leadership development for those who do poorly on the review. Of course the consulting firm professes that it can do the necessary training. As one manager put it, "I got a bad review, I didn't know what they were going to do to me; they didn't fire me they sent me off to this awful program that was going to make me sensitive. I felt humiliated." In another case, a manager's assistant had a particularly close relationship with the boss. They often talked for hours in the boss's glass-enclosed office. When review time came, the envious employees gave the assistant a scathing review. She had to attend empowerment classes based on the consultant's assumption she was too dependent on her boss. Consulting firms will typically increase the numbers of negative reviews to increase the number of employees that they can put through their expensive training programs.

In many organizations, review time is the most stressful time, not only for those being reviewed and those conducting reviews but also those tabulating the results and connecting them to rewards and punishments. HR and performance review employees function like accountants at tax time. Under stressful conditions, an array of mistakes are made. In addition, during 360 reviews, managers who have a reputation of giving good reviews can get deluged with requests for evaluations. As one popular VP reported, "I get between 100 and 200 evaluation requests, many from people I don't know." He avoids doing them.

According to Pfau and Kay (2002), "...research shows that 360-degree feedback programs may hurt more than they help. Watson Wyatt's 2001 Human Capital Index (HCI), an ongoing study of the linkages between specific HR practices and shareholder value at 750 large, publicly traded companies found that 360-degree feedback programs were associated with a 10.6 percent decrease in shareholder value." And yet they continue to be used by corporations large and small.

Pfau and Kay (2002) continue, "Watson Wyatt's 2001 HCI report revealed that companies using 360-degree feedback have lower market value. According to the study, companies that use peer review have a market value that is 4.9 percent lower than similarly situated companies that don't use peer review. Likewise, companies that allow employees to evaluate their managers are valued 5.7 percent lower than similar firms that don't. Taken together, these practices are associated with a 10.6 percent decline in shareholder value."

In essence, a company literally shuts down for a period of time to conduct these reviews and then it takes months for the dust to settle and for employees to engage in competent work. Is it any wonder why companies that use them perform poorly? In addition, these performance reviews kill morale and increase turnover.

Finally, there is no proof or data showing that any performance review or appraisal systems, including 360 feedback, improve productivity, increase job satisfaction, promote teamwork, increases retention or decrease grievances. In addition, Ariely (2008) studied the impact of bonuses on performance and discovered that the greater the bonus, the lower the performance. That is, the greater the bonus, the greater the negative impact on work performance. Even HR managers are increasingly opposed. In a 2011 survey by People Management, nearly half (45 per cent) of the 579 HR respondents said that their organization is either "ineffective" or "very ineffective" at linking pay and performance, compared to 38 percent who said it was effective. http://www.peoplemanagement.co.uk/pm/articles/2011/09/hr-professionals-unhappy-with-pay-performance-link.htm

So why do CEOs want to use them?

Lawler (2003) offers an answer:

"One thing I find interesting is the issue of employment stability. That change took place over the last 20 years and has accelerated in the last 10 years. Many companies once made statements about the importance of employment stability, their commitment to employees, and their desire for employees to be loyal. This has changed to a relationship that is based on the employee's performance and the need the organization has for that employee's skills. Companies are saying to the employee that you have a job here as long as you perform well and we need you and you shouldn't expect anything more than that. Employees are recognizing this and saying, "I am here as long as you are the best alternative and you shouldn't expect anything more than that."

This was Lawler's view in 2003. In 2011, loyalty and commitment to a company are officially dead, and this is precisely what CEOs want. They want an employee who has limited alternatives. They want an employee who cannot say, "Take this job and shove it." So what does an employee do to survive the harsh reality of a review system that does not work? They learn to play the game of survival.

FALSE COMMITMENT - PLAYING THE GAME

Performance evaluation systems not only destroy genuine commitment, they create a false or gamesmanship culture where the game of "survivor" is played out daily. The game of survivor is an art form. This game is played by engaging in a game of sociability, where one can sell oneself as if his/her bubbling, likeable personality were a commodity. It's called "branding oneself" as if the person is a brand like Colgate or Toyota. One must constantly be on guard and be calculating. Employees do not show feelings. No longer are they allowed to show anger or the occasional grouchiness. The "pleasing personality" gets the good review. It is as if the corporation is now filled with ever-smiling, super-friendly neighbors who feel rage and contempt toward others underneath the surface. They put in their face time and work hard to convince others they are a team player. What does it do to employees? It kills the capacity for spontaneity.

This game is heightened when the employee is stuck and cannot leave a bad situation. Employees often try to beat the system because they think it is dysfunctional, or because they find the whole process distasteful or corrupt. When faced with forced ranking and the elimination of the lower ranked employees, according to Lawler (2002), " ... to meet their reduction number(s), managers may keep bad employees around until the performance-rating period, instead of firing them earlier in the year, so that they will have people to select when it is time to make the cuts. Also, if managers have more candidates than they need to meet their quota one year, they may retain the "extras" as targets for the next round of appraisals. There are also examples of managers creating false employee performance records so they can justify firing them."

GOLF AND THE PERFORMANCE REVIEW

Performance appraisal systems influence every aspect of an employee's working life, both in the corporation and outside. A young executive was invited to a golf match. He knew his promotion counted on attending the match and being liked by those who would be determining his future training and development. His problem was he had never set foot on a golf course. Before the match he spent his weekends at the driving range, practicing until his hands blistered. He found himself deeply troubled, believing he was in a career where his future depended on golf and his capacity to impress on the course. The week before, overwhelmed with ambivalence, he attended the match, played poorly and was not very impressive. Realizing he did not fit in, he resigned himself to becoming a middle manager and gave up his pursuit of a top position.

One of the most significant experiences in business school is learning how to play the game. Students take classes in interviewing, resume writing, toastmasters and golf. Almost every course requires a standup presentation and the student is often graded on the quality of their presentation. Almost every MBA program in America has a golf association. The function of these programs is to prepare the candidate to play the sport of corporate executives: golf. Golf Digest even publishes the rankings of the top CEO golfers. These MBAs not only learn how to play the game, but how to use the time on the golf course to network and promote oneself. The importance of golf is so critical that there are papers and scholarly studies exploring the necessity of golf and its relationship to advancement. One prevailing belief is that superiors can view an employee's leadership style on the golf course. Kenworthy (2008) equates six styles of playing golf with six corresponding leadership styles, suggesting that the candidate who knows the favorite leadership style of their superior should demonstrate that style on the golf course. This is truly playing the game. Golf is so important to executives that Northern Trust bank, a recipient of $1.6 billion in federal bailout funds, outraged the public and members of Congress by continuing its sponsorship of a professional golf tournament called the Northern Trust Open. At other golf tournaments, bailout corporations pay upwards of $100,000 for tent tables where their executives can attend and hob knob with other executives, but to avoid public scrutiny they have no identification markings like company logos. Why do it if the corporation gains no benefit? It's to keep alive the fantasy that being in the golf world will maintain the necessary networking that will enhance their executive status and careers

IMPRESSING THE BOSS TO GET THAT GREAT REVIEW

Corporate training can also contribute to an employee playing the game, especially if it is part of the employee's performance assessment. Employees use training arenas to show their brilliance and cast their reputation. If higher level executives are involved, employees seek opportunities to deliver their well rehearsed "elevator speech." Wheeling, dealing, and engaging in the politics of visibility and impression making are critical to obtaining a favorable evaluation. At a five-day training program, an executive VP sat down at the dinner table occupied by a group of young managers. They were thrilled. One young manager went on about his knowledge and desperately tried to impress the EVP. When he left the table for a few minutes, the EVP said, "Wow, he is some self-promoter." Afterwards the group told the young manager what the EVP said. They had a lengthy discussion and agreed that the young manager tried too hard, and he missed the real skill needed to move up the ladder, promoting oneself without the boss knowing that you are "gaming."

On the other side of the coin, employees go to great lengths to praise their bosses. At training events, top managers typically receive applause and congratulations, even when they give poorly prepared and ill-informed presentations to neophyte managers. These executives, and the performance review systems they put in place, create a culture of "apple polishers." Employees work hard to convince their bosses they are "world class managers." The sad part of this game is that the bosses actually believe the accolades they receive.

Gaming is also played when CEOs try to "pump up" their demoralized, cynical, overworked, and angry workforce that will continuously seek better jobs elsewhere. They hold large-scale "motivational" meetings and events. They bring in celebrities, motivational speakers and play quick-fix business games. These events are geared to get employees to show an outpouring of emotion and commitment. As one employee said, "I spend five days here; I use it to network and promote myself, I yell, laugh, hear the speeches from everyone, but the reality is, I go back to the same dismal place on Monday and after a few days back at the job I'm even more depressed." Some suggest that these motivational events are more for the well being of executives, then for their employees.

Consider the following example of the superficial nature of these events. Medtronic, a medical electronic company resorts to gimmicks to create commitment to customer care and service. At their holiday events customers are invited in to speak, and they tell tearful tales about how the Medtronic equipment saved their lives. Heartfelt stories are in continuous use at Medtronic. Management believes that these stories create genuine commitment. What they really create is a superficial environment where employees maneuver to advance their careers. In many cases these well orchestrated "motivational events" are nothing more than opportunities for the corporation's executives to show off and deliver PowerPoint addresses aggrandizing their past, present and future accomplishments. Most corporate event consultants see these events as marketing events, where the employee is the customer and the executives is the seller. They say the problem with these events is that most executives do not know what to sell, or how to sell. At these events HR managers are seen observing the behavior of employees, not only at the event, but at breakfast, lunch and dinner. They have a watchful eye for cynicisms, unruly behavior and negativity. If a manager should ask the CEO a question that is considered embarrassing or too negative HR will make a note and the employee's career is ended.

HUMAN RESOURCE MANAGERS - THE CEO'S POLICE

There has been a dramatic shift in the nature of the work of corporate Human Resource managers. Over the past 15 years HR managers have moved from being employee advocates to corporate police. By embracing the performance review process they have become the legal go-between for management and employees, typically siding with management and carrying out their orders. Consider the lunacy of this HR type of trainer when referring to negative reviews. "It's important to see bad reviews as wonderful gifts" said Wendy Kaufman, CEO of Balancing Life's Issues, "At the very least, they are going to make you stronger and give you a road map of strategies to do your job better down the road." This self-serving HR consultant is clearly distorting reality to get corporate contracts and unfortunately this way of doing business is increasingly popular in the Human Resource world. One would be hard-pressed to find a single employee who received a bad review agreeing with her that the review is a "wonderful gift," but it is certain many executives would find her a worthy consultant. Corporate executives think so little of the HR function that presently the HR function is the leading outsourced department surpassing IT functions. Also, the field of HR consultation as grown considerably in the last 15 years, and this has led to a significant change in the work of HR professionals and especially in how are perceived by fellow employees.

The work of HR managers in today's corporations resembles Henry Ford's "Social Relations Department," which was established in 1922 with a staff of 50 to investigate and spy on Ford's employees. Consider what a contemporary HR manager does:

- Conduct background investigations –Criminal, Credit and Computer
- Require drug tests
- Assess company computer and telephone use
- Assess employee theft, including stealing time
- Develop, implement performance review processes
- Intervene when conflict arises
- Develop human capital strategy
- Develop IT/personnel systems
- Promote hiring and firing strategies
- Conduct video surveillance
- Conduct personality assessment, including honesty and loyalty evaluation
- And spy on employees who are perceived as cheating the company: sick days, long lunches, misuse of time clocks or work logs

According to Spitznagel (2011), 57 percent of American workers take sick days when they are not sick. Rather than try to understand this phenomenon which may be associated with job stress, HR instead investigates and in some cases hires detective agencies and engages in playing a game of "gotcha" to fire these employees.

William Czander

A NEW ROLE FOR HR: JUSTIFYING THEIR BOSSES GREED

Executive compensation has grown to such a large and complex process that many companies have full-time specialists in "executive compensation." Some have teams who focus exclusively on compensation for executives. They are typically housed within human resource departments, and many are officers of the corporation rising to the level of Executive VP.

What do they do?

Their job is to make certain the CEO and executives not only get the greatest compensation, but avoid paying taxes on it. JP Morgan Chase advertised for a VP of Executive Compensation for its London office and the duties of this position were identified:

- Overseeing the feasibility phase of the Dual Contracts project, in partnership with the relevant tax advisors and working with key internal stakeholders where appropriate. Continuing responsibility for the implementation of the project and then ongoing auditing and review where necessary.

- Coordination of internal and external legal, accounting and tax advice on a range of Compensation and Benefit policies within EMEA. Drafting formal proposal documents for review by senior management and drafting of employee communications.

- Management of existing Bonus delivery plans, including review of documentation, fund transfers, liaison with trustees etc

- Assessing the impact of legislative changes upon existing bonus plans and LTIPs.

- Management of the annual Incentive Compensation Preference process, coordinating cross functional teams to ensure correct delivery

- Management of the annual Average Rate Election process and collation of data required for hedging purposes

- Determining global tax withholding obligations for annual LTIP stock distributions

- Reviewing beneficial tax regimes globally to determine whether stock plans could qualify for beneficial treatment, work with local advisors to draft required documentation for review by NY

- Providing technical input to drafting of award terms and conditions with reference to cross region variations in legislation.

- Providing technical support to our regional offices, adding a regional perspective to global Compensation and Benefits discussions.

- Assisting Business Partners in both the recruitment and exit of employees e.g. contract wording, structure of termination agreements

- Maintaining proactive relationships and working on projects with other internal groups such as legal, accounting policies, corporate tax and the New York Compensation team.

- Developing effective relationships with bulge bracket competitors

- Advising on cross border issues to structure employments in the most cost effective and compliant way

- Providing compensation-related input into the due diligence process for acquisitions and divestitures.

- Designing and delivering strategic subject area solutions that meet the critical needs of the business

- Collaborating with US to produce integrated global subject area initiatives

- Inter-acting with global counterpart(s) to ensure consistency

- Managing policy exceptions

- Relationship management with subject area vendors

Taken from: http://www.linkedin.com/jobs?viewJob=&jobId=1708864

Notice: There is no performance review or assessment of the quality of the executive's effort, there is no mention of compensation being tied to corporate performance or developing metrics and tying compensation to meeting any type of metric. It's all about designing a legal, tax-free, and opulent pay package. One could bet that the work of HR for lower-level employees is all about assessment and reviewing performance. Here is the lunacy, and it's just as problematic as hiring compensation consultants to determine the compensation of the CEO who hired them. The question is: How does one design a compensation package for one's boss?

SURVIVING THE PERFORMANCE REVIEW

The question that arises is: Who is most likely to survive the performance review process? The thousands of self-help books and articles written on the subject collectively suggest that to survive, one must market oneself, develop a strategy for convincing one's boss that they are invaluable by selling the great accomplishments and contributions made and above all else creating a "personal brand." What is this? It is the latest fad of the, "how to sell yourself" snake oil salespeople. Essentially, they believe that to succeed, one must take on narcissistic characteristics: Flamboyance, self-confidence, and always winning, never losing. Donald Trump is the poster boy for this fad. Consider this: A young manager was given the opportunity to advance her career by the company's president. She was told to get all the employees up to speed on a new software package, and do it in one month. She thought she succeeded and at a manager's meeting, the president asked her if she accomplished the task. She proudly said "yes, 97 percent were trained." The president angrily responded; "I wanted 100 percent." After the meeting two senior HR managers approached the young manager and told her it was not the correct way to sell herself. One senior manager told her: "97 percent is wrong, you say 100 percent. Never say you fell short of the boss's goal." She responded that it was impossible to get 100 percent: people are absent, out sick, on vacation. She wanted to tell the truth, she was advised that to get ahead she had to distort, exaggerate and lie. She was disturbed at what she was hearing, and worse, what she was learning to do.

It seems certain that the performance review process is designed to favor those who not only "perform" best, or put forth their "brand" as above-average or close to perfect, even if it takes making up things, exaggerating and lying. It also seems that some people can do this better than others and that it takes certain type of personality to do well in these systems. We will discuss this in depth later on in the book.

THE PSYCHODYNAMICS OF PERFORMANCE REVIEWS: THE CASE OF A NEWSPAPER

The Gannett newspaper chain presents a valuable case study of the psychodynamics that underlie performance review systems. Gannett saw its revenue and income tumble 35 percent in 2007, but its CEO Craig Dubow got a $1.8 million bonus on top of his $1.2 million in base salary. Stock options and other perks boosted his pay even higher, to an estimated $5.8 million.

In 2007, Dubow's compensation included a $1,750,000 bonus, $1,067,980 in stock awards, $3,351,000 in option awards, $57,101 in nonqualified deferred compensation earnings, and $120,629 in "all other compensation." As part of his employment agreement received the following:

*Paid life insurance

*Supplemental medical benefits

*A security system allowance

*Company provided lunch during working hours

*Unspecified legal and financial services

*Tickets to sporting events

*Use of company automobile

*Use of company aircraft

The proxy statement indicates Gannett would no longer pay activity and membership fees for its CEO. If Dubow were to be fired today, based on his most recent annual compensation, since he just turned 54 in October, his severance package would be somewhere in the neighborhood of $12 million (Turner, 2008).

Remarkably very little is known about Mr. Dubow. Profiles that appear about him on the web are all "executive profiles" with one paragraph of information. He graduated from the University of Texas at Austin in 1977 with BS in TV, Film and Radio. At 25 years old he joined Gannett in 1981, working in advertising sales for KUSA TV in Denver, Colorado. He then held various positions at another Gannett-owned TV station, this time in Austin, Texas at KVUE TV, and in 1990 he became its president and general manager. In 1992, he became the president and general manager of Gannett-owned WXIA TV in Atlanta, Georgia, and from 1996 to 2000, he served as executive vice president of Gannett TV. In 2000 he became President of Gannett Broadcastings and became its CEO in 2001. He became president and CEO and director of Gannett in July 2005, and chairman of Gannett in July 2006. In 2010, at 56 years old he served as chairman, president and CEO. He was the first top executive at Gannett without experience in the newspaper industry

Rumor has it that Dubow is hated by his employees, and it's easy to see why. In August 2008, Dubow terminated 1,000 employees. In November, Gannett announced that 10 percent of 3,000 workers would be terminated before Christmas, as its stock dropped 71 percent. Dubow also froze its defined pension plan in August 2008, with participants no longer accruing benefits. In its place he offered a 401(k) plan by matching employees' salary deferrals up to the first 5 percent of pay, with company stock. Gannett would now match 50 percent of employees' salary deferrals up to the first 6 percent of pay, also in company stock. We know what Gannett's stock is worth. Dubow responded to these hardships inflicted on employees by reducing his pay 3 percent (Krangel, 2008).

In January of 2009, Dubow announced that thousands of workers must take a week off without pay (Perez-Pena, 2009). In July 2009 another 4,500 employees were terminated. So did Dubow do? He gave up a week's pay, or $18,960, which is one week of his base salary. What a CEO. As Dubow was proudly announcing he was giving up a week's pay in 2009, he actually received an overall 41 percent increase in compensation. Since early 2008 Dubow has terminated 11,000 employees and in January 2011 the process continued as he terminated 99 employees in New Jersey's three Gannett-owned newspapers. In June 2011 he announced another 700 employees would be terminated.

In 2010 Dubow continued to terminate employees and for his hard work he received an 80 percent increase in compensation to $7.9 million. In January 2011 Dubow told employees who worked in the community news division that they would be required to take another furlough week and they announced that Dubow and his COO Gracia Martore would also take a reduction in pay that was the equivalent of a week's furlough. Not so fast. Carr (2011) discovered that Dubow had agreed to lower his salary 17 percent but he then received a cash bonus of $1.75 million from 2010. It turns out that while employees took furloughs Dubow and his top six executives received bonuses of more than $28 million. So let's see, employees give back $33 million of their salaries and executives take $28 million. In his five years at the helm, he terminated 20,000 employees, reducing Gannett's workforce to 32,000. In 2010 Dubow's total compensation was $9.4 million, twice what he earned in 2009; his pay included a $1.75 million cash bonus " ...based partly on his success in reducing costs through layoffs, furloughs and other austerity measures, according to Gannett Blog (2011). http://gannettblog.blogspot.com/2011/06/urgent-gannett-announces-700-newspaper.html

GANNETT EXECUTIVES GET TOUGH

In August 2009, Dubow fired all 288 of its news and advertising sales employees at its Journal News paper, located in the northern suburbs of New York City, and told them they had one week to apply for the 218 jobs the paper would keep. Overall, 20 jobs were being cut in ad sales, and 50 in the newsroom.

Michael Fisch, then the newspaper's publisher and president, said, "We could have used the traditional layoff approach but we really felt that we needed to restructure in order to prepare ourselves for the longer term and redefine the skill sets we need to be successful." So he fired everyone and created enormous stress by putting every employee in a humiliating position and requiring each employee to appear in front of consultants and HR managers to plead their case to get their old job back, or find some other position in the company. Fisch said columnists, editors and managers all must reapply, except for "a small handful of senior management positions." Fisch exempted himself and a few of his pals. No humiliation for the executives, the ones who caused the newspaper to lose readership and advertisers.

DEFENDING AGAINST THE FEELING OF SHAME BY SHAMING OTHERS

By exempting themselves, Fisch and his executives were able to use this process as defense against their deep experience of shame and humiliation associated with having failed to find ways get their newspaper out of its fiscal slump. It also was a defense against the shame and guilt associated with "getting more" as they employees were "getting less."

A question needs to be explored, and doing so will shed light on the unconscious motivation executives have for conducting performance reviews and putting their employees through these awful experiences. Put another way, why the need to humiliate grown men and women, and in this case of Gannett, many men and women with major reputations in the newspaper industry?

It is common for people occupying superior positions and who feel humiliated, threatened or weak to engage in two types of behavior. The first is to increase demands for more and increase their sense of entitlement. The second is to find scapegoats and act out in a violent and sadistic manner.

The case of Gannett, where executives fail, then terminate employees and then receive major compensation increases, is not an isolated case. This is confirmed in a study be Bebchuck and Fried (2006) where they researched 500 firms and found an inverse relationship between compensation and company performance. That is CEOs of failed companies demanded and obtained greater compensation increases than successful companies. Why? The first response to failure is for the CEO to need and demand more total compensation than successful CEOs. This allows them to feel on top and once again successful. At the country club, they can hold their heads high and proclaim it is not their fault the company is performing poorly: it's their employees' and a restructuring is needed.

One response to failure and insecurity is to act out in a sadistic manner to prop up feelings of power and strength by making others feel weak, insecure, and frightened. In psychoanalytic terms this is referred to as projection, where the person rids the self of unwanted feelings and projects them onto other objects or persons. It is similar to saying, "I am not weak and powerless, you are." This is also consistent with the research of Rennie (2006) who discovered that CEOs who terminated employees received higher compensation than CEOs who did not terminate employees.

In this case, Fisch and his boss Dubow project their failure and all the feeling that result into the fired employees who would now contain these unwanted feelings. Now these ex-employees will experience shame, humiliation, insecurity and fear. We can think of this in terms of the 9/11 attacks on the powerful nation of America. In response to the experience of weakness, threat, and violation, Bush and his generals needed to parade strength and power and to invade Iraq (shock and awe) and humiliate Muslims around the world. It is as if they unconsciously said "I am not weak, you are weak and I have power to make certain you feel weak and humiliated." We refer to this as a level two defense mechanism, most often used by adolescents as a way to reduce stress and anxiety that is precipitated by people who they perceive as threatening or capable of making them feel uncomfortable. They are also referred to as immature defenses. Their use of projection is paranoia in its primitive state. Their fear and worries are only allayed when they can put their unwanted feelings onto the other and then bully or crush the other. At work they will use their position of authority to create situations where their employees become receptacles and are made to feel what their bosses are feeling, so that those same thoughts, feelings, beliefs and motivations are perceived as being possessed by the other.

This is also a form of acting out aggression toward employees. In this case, the structuring of firing and hiring is a passive-aggressive expression of anger toward the employees, a wish to make them suffer. Also connected to the experience of failure are feelings of envy. This is especially apparent in organizations where creativity is of high value. Managers often look on people who occupy creative positions, in this case reporters and writers, with feelings of envy. Conversely, the creative people see the managers as "bean counters." When these organizations fail management blames the "undisciplined" creative employees. We see envy, considered the great spoiler, acted out as these Gannett executives devalued their creative and competent reporters and writers.

In the corporate world, leaders frequently experience fear, insecurity and humiliation. Often they will attempt to rid themselves of these feelings through excessive compensation and the fantasies of power that are connected socially and culturally to the accumulation of wealth. Or they may surround themselves with "yes" people. Or they may use the performance review to ensure that their subordinates experience insecurity and powerlessness. In the Gannett case Mr. Fisch responds to his own insecurities and humiliation as his newspaper fails by structuring the fire and hire situation and placing himself into a god-like position. Fisch now has the power to terminate the workforce and the power to decide who shall symbolically live and die. He no longer feels weak, insecure, or humiliated. His employees are on their knees begging for a job. In Dubow's case he needs excessive compensation and he needs to terminate employees who are filled with collective hate and proclaim the SS Gannett is sinking.

We now see the psychodynamic function of the performance review and terminations. Just as during the financial meltdown businesses that surround Wall Street were empty except one---the strip clubs---when executives fail, they find ways to feel powerful and in many cases hardworking employees are run over by the CEO, who drive the bus that reads, "I am powerful and entitled."

PERFORMANCE REVIEWS AND THE GAINS ASSOCIATED WITH LEAVING THE COMPANY

In many corporations, the lack of commitment coupled with archaic performance appraisal systems promote astonishing turnover rates. Employees know the value of not being committed to the corporation. Employees have no problem jumping from one job to another, and they clearly recognize the benefits of job change. They use the web constantly to search for jobs. According to Greenberg (2008), 77 percent of all employees are actively looking for new employment, and of this number, 91 percent spend three hours each week searching while at work. In addition, they can quite readily access job compensation in their respective industry. If they find a job that pays better, the resume is off with the press of a computer button. It is reasonable to assume in 2010, with full-blown use of Internet job posting and chronic fear of being terminated, that those employees who are on a constant lookout for a better paying and more secure job was most likely in the 95 percent range.

Employees are clearly are aware of the rewards of frequent job-changing. There is ample data suggesting that job-changing is a critical factor in increasing an employee's income. In the U.S., with every job change, the average compensation increase is 12 percent, while the average per annum increase is only 3 or 4 percent. Typically employees who stay soon discover that newly hired employees are starting at higher salaries. For example, a nurse who is hired in 2006 with a $45,000 starting salary and $3,000 bonus will discover that in 2007, nurses are hired at $48,000 with a $5,000 bonus. In some industries, newly hired employees start at salaries 30 to 40 percent higher than those who remain with the company.

These uncommitted employees clearly understand salary compression. Plus, they are aware that corporate leaders pay little attention to turnover rates and the expense their corporation endures, especially the "brain drain," as well-qualified employees defect to better paying jobs.

A major growth industry has evolved from the job-hopping phenomenon. These are employment agencies, so-called head-hunters, and online recruiters. They are thriving, and this suggests that more and more employees are on the move. This is reinforced by the trends in corporations that value and hire contract or temporary employees, and use: outsourcing, consulting, downsizing. Depending on one's occupation, the number of job changes an employee will have during their life time now varies from 11 to 25, and this number is expected to increase.

Performance reviews take the joy out of corporate life. Consider the use of teams. While many corporations embrace the concept of teams and executives continuously tell their managers they are a team, they fail to explore the contradictions apparent when promoting teamwork in a system where commitment does not exist and employees are reviewed and rewarded based on individual performance.

USING PERFORMANCE EVALUATION TO DESTROY TEAMS

Sometimes work groups, departments and teams find that their capacity to function well starts to build over a period of months. They are beginning to jell to form a team as members begin to experience a degree of trust. Then it's performance review time. The review drives wedges between team members, because the poorly-rated are jealous of the highly-rated, in a process that DeMarco and Lester (1999) refer to as *teamicide*: the inadvertent destruction of jelled teams. Why would an executive wish to destroy a jelled team? This may be a somewhat absurd question to most people, but if one thinks about it from a psychoanalytic perspective it seems to make sense. The problem is everyone wants to be in a "jelled" team. Those who are not, are like children not invited to a wonderful birthday party that is being held in the yard next door. Let's begin by looking at the ingredients of a "jelled" team. They have a heightened sense of cooperation and collaboration, they support each other, they have a high degree of trust, they give each other support, and they have fun. Those who work in a corporation rarely, if ever, have this type of experience. Consequently, they are filled with envy. From a psychoanalytic perspective envy is a great spoiler and envy occupies a major place as arbiter of the motivation for evaluation, as well as a consequence of the process of evaluation. The end result is to destroy, teams, collaboration, trust, and cooperation. Czander (1993) claims:

> *"The organization is an arena in which the experience of envy is played out in a continuous fashion. Conflict is inevitable given the inequitable nature of the organization, its reward system, various levels of capacity to use discretion, status, and power differentials, and the allocation of scarce resources. Underlying conflicts are the affects associated with envy. Whether conscious or unconscious, envy may lay at the base of all organizational conflict."*

As one management consultant stated, "When a team jells or develops into a high performing team, I tell them to watch out." Teams, with all the attributes described above, will experience impingements and sundry attempts to destroy them. Evaluating individuals, who work in a genuine team, is one way to destroy a team. Consider this example of a team member who received his annual performance review. On the team he was a cheerful catalyst, and had the capacity to motivate the team when the going got tough. He was also the glue that held the team together when conflict arose. But he tended to get negative reviews, because his manager didn't understand his contributions. Another team member was incredibly insightful; his conversations with other people about how things should be done allowed everyone else to do much better work. He tended to spend more time than average trying out new technologies and he introduced them to team members. He made the presentations given by the team artful and fun. In this area he was invaluable to the rest of the team. His manager failed to notice all his contributions, so he received negative reviews.

While negative reviews destroy a team, so does a review that is positive, but not as positive as the person expected. From a psychological perspective, this is where performance reviews get exceedingly complex for a manager. Performance reviews cannot integrate into their assessments the fact that it is quite common for people to believe they are better than they really are. That is, they tend to overestimate their contributions, talents, skills and how well they are liked, etc.. Consequently, most employees become disappointed by their reviews and most managers become angered when what they considered to be a positive is received with distained.

Performance reviews impact the culture of the organization and influence behavior, decision-making and what teams and meetings the corporation will value.

It would be difficult to find a scholar and writer on teams who would not find trust to be a key ingredient in effective teams. We have been discussing performance review as inducing mistrust, suspicion and even paranoia. Under these conditions it is not possible to develop a team. Nonetheless, many companies maintain that teams are important and they maintain that employees need and should work collaboratively in teams. Many corporate leaders even claim they have high-powered teams. But they create a false illusion. They have no teams. What they have are groups of employees behaving "as if" they are a fully functioning team. They do give a performance, but it is performing to obtain the favorable review. A consultant reported the following: He was asked to consult to what the CEO described as a dysfunctional team. The CEO told the consultant it was a shame, he has several executive teams that function great and he could not understand why one team could not function as the others. The consultant said he would like to observe one of these high functioning teams. The CEO immediately contacted the team leader and they arranged for him to sit in. The consultant observed the following behavior: a heightened sense of cooperation and niceness. Members entered with smiles, jokes and lots of laughter. They spoke about an elevator being stuck with a low level "nerd" trapped with a beautiful blond. There were two women in the group who laughed along. About 20 minutes after the meeting started the team leader began by describing the progress they made in discussing a relocation of the company's back office. They had discussed this issue for several weeks. Posted on the wall were many large post-it pads, listing the pros and cons associated with the relocation. The list they generated was long, with 45 pros and 25 cons. During the 60 minute meeting they went off topic 27 times, and the consultant determined they spent 10 minutes on the task, generating three more pros and one con. At this rate they would create an astounding "laundry list," but no decision. After the meeting, the consultant asked the team leader how he thought the team was functioning. The leader replied that it was the best team he'd been on. The consultant asked what he thought was the work of the team. He replied, to create a list of pros and cons and give them to the executive committee. The consultant then met with the CEO and asked him what the task of the team was, and he said to make a recommendation. The consultant told him what the team leader said, and the CEO replied, "Oh maybe, I don't remember, I'll talk to him."

The consultant then observed the dysfunctional team. They were working hard on a controversial issue and had to find a solution. They knew what their task was. They argued and took their work seriously. The group was clearly not dysfunctional. It was clear, in this corporation, the teams that were described as successful did little work, they all got along and received good-to-excellent performance reviews. They knew quite well, that if they disagreed and engaged in conflict they would be considered dysfunctional.

This corporation had the type of culture Bill George, the former CEO of Medtronic, described as "Minnesota nice" (George, 2004). It is a culture where everyone was expected to "get along" where conflict was prohibited. Those who disagreed, or were comfortable with conflict, were often viewed as "personal attacking" and worse. During their reviews they were identified as "not a team player." Prominently displayed on everyone's performance review, was a category labeled "team player," with several criteria that required ranking from excellent to poor: "team player," "interpersonal skills," "likeability," "open to new ideas," "helps others," "gets along with others." Team player is perhaps the most interesting metaphor used to evaluate an employee. It is clearly from the sports world and is generally embraced by those executives who like sports. It is consistently used by executives who tend to think that life in the corporation is similar to a sporting event. It's a culture where executives congratulate each other by giving high-fives and announcing, "You hit a home run."

KEEPING WOMEN OFF THE TEAM

Consider these metaphors:

- "What we need is a level playing field"
- "He dropped the ball"
- "Keep your eye on the ball"
- "You're a crowd pleaser"
- "You need a coach"
- "The a soft pitch"
- "Let's play hard ball"
- "You're a team leader"
- "The game is about to begin"
- "Where loosing the game"
- "It's a slam dunk"
- "That's out of bounds"

- "Play fair"
- "You did an end run"
- "Are you on the team or off?"
- "You have two sticks"
- "That's a curve ball"
- "Let's not be losers, let's be winners."

Palmatier and Ray (1989) have identified 1,700 sports metaphors and they maintain language in America is permeated with these terms. At work we just assume that everyone understands them, but this is not true

The use of sports language has the effect of discriminating against those who are not schooled in the subject, and the group most often pushed out by sports metaphors are women. Sallie Krawcheck probably the highest-ranking woman on Wall Street was pushed out of Citigroup in October 2008, because she was not considered a "team player." This metaphor implies that she was not willing to "drink the Kool-Aid" and become a team player. The team player metaphor implies that if one disagrees with others, maintains autonomous thinking, or is different, they may receive the infamous; "not a team player" evaluation. If teams are to serve a protective function then male bonding is a powerful method: here the boys meet to work, have fun and feel free from assessment and criticism.

One can clearly see the performance review determines behavior, but not necessarily desired behavior. To avoid the "not a team player" review, an employee will work to "fit in," be agreeable and friendly, and go along unarguably with group decisions. In this type of review system, members in a genuine team, a team capable of critical thinking and disagreement would be labeled dysfunctional, and would most likely receive negative reviews.

SNAKE OIL SALESPEOPLE

Why do these review programs keep growing when research suggests they cannot measure accurately, employees hate them and they create cultures of stress? It's the consultants. The performance review industry convinces executives reviews are the panacea for extracting the greatest degree of labor from employees with minimal managerial effort.

Variable pay review plans and performance-based compensation keeps gaining in popularity. In 2011, 92 percent of non-union corporations had implemented some type of program. This is a significant increase compared to 2005, when 78 percent of employers offered variable pay. . There are thousands of human resource consultants and consulting companies offering performance measurement assistance and hundreds of software programs. They are used in government, education, financial services, manufacturing, retail, non-profit, and food and beverage. It is difficult to find a non-union, for-profit or nonprofit company that does not have a performance appraisal system. They promise an array of positive outcomes and do not mention any negative possibilities, except to suggest that if you do not follow their program problems could occur. Consider what the Society for Human Resource Management offers in their SHRM Foundation a program called "Performance Management: A Roadmap for Developing, Implementing and Evaluating Performance Management Systems." They claim the following outcomes will occur if one follows their guidelines and of course hires their consultants. Their program will:

- Clarify job responsibilities and expectations
- Enhance individual and group productivity
- Develop employee capabilities to their fullest extent through effective feedback and coaching
- Drive behavior to align with the organization's core values, goals and strategy
- Provide a basis for making operational human capital disclosures (e.g., pay)
- Improve communication between employees and managers.

They go on to say that performance management is an essential tool for high performing organizations and it's one of a manager's most important responsibilities if not the most important responsibility. Wow.

These are exaggerated claims, and they are embarrassingly outrageous in the face of the research that maintains performance review systems are inaccurate, political, corrupt, and promote widespread cheating. According to McLean Parks and Carpenter Taylor (2010), "If you pay someone contingent on their performance, you have motivated them to perform. However, if they are unable to perform well because the task is hard because of economic conditions you have also given them an incentive to cook the books!" In school districts that tie merit pay to test scores what did they discover? The teachers and their administrators cheated: "...Educators Tamper With The Test Scores" (Gabriel, 2010). When the state of Colorado passed a law making tenure dependent on test results, they may have passed a new law requiring cheating. These are "target-based compensation systems," also called "performance based systems," where managers identify a goal or outcome or target, and the employee must reach it. When "No Child

Left Behind" failed, President Obama decided to forget about assessing school performance and instead focus on teacher performance. If one thought "No Child..." fostered cheating, then just wait until you see this one. Politicians have done nothing except to create a system of cheaters, and this includes teachers, administrators and of course their students

None the less executives, HR managers, politicians and consultants push these programs despite the fact that it is common knowledge we cannot measure performance and we do not know how to reward. What do we know? We know these systems precipitate conflict between employees and their managers, and put managers in the position to evaluate, judge, punish and reward each and every employee. In other words, all these programs do is decrease the employee's power and increase the manager's power. But it also increases the employee's capacity to "cheat and beat the system" and collectively they are much smarter than their managers.

The worded measurements used in these review instruments require a series of judgments which are impossible for the manager to justify. Consider this performance review instrument. It uses four major categories, each having 35 subcategories and a written program for improvement. The manager is required to assess: Self Management, Teamwork, Work Results, and Innovation and Change. In the last category, these questions were asked: "Does employee accept change?" and "Does the employee help others overcome their resistance to change?" These questions cannot be answered and if answered, they are clouded with such subjectivity that it boggles the mind. The manager must not only pass judgment, but is often prohibited from considering system factors that may contribute to his/her observations. Performance results are further complicated by taking corporate goals and the company mission and turning them into actionable and measurable tasks.

The major problem with performance appraisal is in trying to establish attribution. Consider this example: What does a manager do when two employees achieved the same sales objectives, but only one can be given the number one award, and one employee is a friend and other is disliked? Also, how does a manager measure who is more hard-working, ethical, responsible, etc? Can a measurement be fully attributed to the actor, or are there some other intervening factors that will have greater influence? Little consideration is given to the fact that in most cases, performance evaluation results have less to do with the employee and more to do with intervening factors.

Consider a manager with 15 subordinates. Typically the manager is given a two week period to conduct their reviews. If each review takes two hours, with 15 employees it will take 30 hours, and the manager still has the normal work to complete. In addition, what is the sense of taking 30 hours to review, when they are all going to get the same wage increase? One manager complained that HR purchased new software that made it impossible to cut and paste the same comments for all his subordinates. Plus he complained it had no spell check. Now he had to spend longer hours writing reviews, and when he sat down with subordinates they complained about his poor spelling.

HR and Organizational Development (OD) personnel approach the review process with so much caution and fear of legal ramifications that they instruct reviewers to give the review within the confines of carefully selected phrases and defined skill areas. Managers receive training and step-by-step procedures to conduct face-to-face reviews and write an appraisal. This controls the process and depersonalizes the review. It also fosters humiliation, as managers and employees, who spend up to eight hours a day, five days a week with each other, now must pass an impersonal judgment about each other. The bizarre nature of the review process is further magnified when one considers that managers spend more time with their employees than they do with their spouses and children. Consider this lunacy: What would be the consequences if a husband decided to give his wife and children an annual review?

The fact that performance reviews have no relationship to reality is most likely true for all employees. Salaries are predetermined long before the review process begins and what we typically have for most employees is a reward system where the good review gets 2 percent and the average performer gets 1.8 percent. Of course this does not apply to executives.

Why don't employees complain? There are two reasons. To complain about salary unfairness would lead to dismissal, especially if one became troublesome and threatened lawsuits. The second reason is even more hideous: employees are kept in the dark. Why do companies try to keep knowledge of employee compensation secret? Every HR manager knows why: To avoid envy, conflicts, and demands for more. This has been practiced for years and HR and payroll departments typically have policies and rules to maintain confidentiality. In some corporations discussing compensation can be grounds for immediate dismissal. On the other, hand managers know what all of their people make and they have a distinct advantage when review time and annual salary discussions occur. How can an employee negotiate compensation when he/she has no comparison, that is, they do not know anyone's compensation? Management wants it this way. This may be changing. In a study by CROP, 70 percent of employees admitted to discussing salaries with co-workers. In fact, a significant percentage of respondents (58 percent) feel that the ban on talking about salaries should be lifted, with more women (65 percent) than men being in favor of this type of transparency. What is the result of discussing salaries? Employees find out they are being cheated. Half those interviewed (51 to 59 percent) do not think that their salary was determined in a fair or equitable manner.

These results suggest that employees are angry and their motivational level is exceedingly low. Another interesting finding is that when they asked GenYs the percent of those who discuss salaries jumps to 84 percent.

(Read more about Gen Y's in Chapter 12).

CHAPTER 5

Lack of Commitment, the Quants and the Financial Crisis

A Wall Street Trader reported how he was recruited during the 2008 crisis when millions were losing their jobs. "This bigshot guy from {Big Wall Street Firm} walks into the room of 25 expectant recruits, and says, 'Who here is motivated by fear and greed?' Me and another guy raised our hands timidly. 'The rest of you can go home,' he says, 'I'm only interested in these two."
C. Green (2008)

Many executives, analysts, academics, and economists have stated that they saw the housing bubble, the enormous debt, and risk coming. They claimed they could have predicted the financial crises. The question is- where were they? Where was dissent, the naysayers, and those who questioned the CEOs, experts, "quants"and authority? One explanation is they were pushed aside or too intimidated to speak up. They kept silent because they wanted to be "team players." The most common metaphor associated with the sudden rise of teams in corporate America is to be a team player. This means one must go along and not raise doubt. Psychologists and the consultants who pushed the concept of team-work in the corporate world failed to properly teach executives that if they wanted to create genuine teams, dissent, disagreement, and conflict was necessary. Consequently, those who saw the financial train wreck coming said nothing and went along functioning as "team players," to the approval of their CEOs and other executives.

According to Morgenson, (2009b), "Executives at seven major financial institutions that have collapsed, were sold at distressed prices or are in deep to the taxpayer received $464 million in performance pay since 2005…" She goes on, "Yet these firms have reported losses of $107 billion since 2007, a result of their own missteps and the ensuing economic downturn. And $740 billion in stock market value has been lost…"How can this phenomenon be explained? What we have witnessed since the 1970s is a shift away from a mentality that took the notion of being a member of the firm as the equivalent of being a team member in the genuine sense. In the past, loyalty was to the firm and bonuses tied to the firm's profitability were invested back into the firm and paid out at retirement. This insured a view towards long-term profitability and a fear of short-term reckless investing. According to Nocera (2009), "Today's bonus system is a warped legacy of these old partnerships." When the Wall Street firms began going public in the 1970s a dramatic shift occurred, a partner's capital was replaced by shareholder equity.

The experience of loyalty and commitment to the firm began to wane as traders dominated. They made millions for their firms and they demanded a share of the profit in bonuses or they were gone. The trader who made a million dollars one year out of college facilitated a stampede of ambitious traders to the caverns of Wall Street. Pushed by their executives they made extraordinary short-term profits in high risk situations. Traders were paid by the number of transactions, not the quality. Quality and thoughtfulness disappeared as blatant greed took over. What contributed to the Wall Street crises was a performance review system that was focused exclusively on short-term profitability and commitment, not to the firm, but to enriching oneself as quickly as possible so they could get away from the toxic workplace environment. One could not find a trader who would reject the idea that "I will bust my ass and make tons of money and get out." Under these conditions, disaster is around the corner.

ENTER THE QUANTS

In the late 1990s the question was asked; Where are all the Ph.D., Engineers, Mathematicians, Physicists, and Computer Scientist? They went to Wall Street and created the financial crisis of 2008. Warren Buffet stated to Charlie Rose, "Beware of Geeks bearing formulas." What did he mean by this? Simply stated, a system that is metrics-driven and relies on metrics to assess performance of either people or stocks will eventually crash. These systems cannot account for the array of variables that impact a system over time. We certainly witness this in October 2008. Consider Lehman Brothers, the collapsed holding company, Lehman had Ph.D.s writing programs designed to sift through billions of trades and spot subtle patterns in world markets. These Ph.D.s, mathematicians and other computer-loving disciples of quantitative analysis challenged traditional traders and money managers. They set out to build the ultimate money machine. Quants, as they are called, sought to create investing programs to eliminate human emotions such as fear and greed from investing. However, the motivation of these money makers who designed the models was just that: greed with the absence of fear. Greed with the absence of fear is a toxic combination. A third of all American stock trades in 2006 were driven by automatic programs, or algorithms, according to Boston-based consulting firm Aite Group LLC. In 2008 that figure reached 50 percent. At Lehman and other investment institutions, an excessive reliance on these models created the problems that led to the financial meltdowns witnessed in the fall of 2008 and the demise of Lehman. Fanny and Freddie Mac, the government sponsored loan agency that needed a $200 billion bailout in September 2008, relied on a "vast network of computer programs and mathematical models that analyzed its millions of daily transactions...." (Duhigg, 2008). (read more about Fanny and Freddie go to Appendix cz)

METRICS- CREATE AN INTIMIDATING CULTURE AND A FINANCIAL CRISIS

Many corporations rely heavily on metrics and create so-called "dashboards" to measure performance. These dashboards can be used weekly, monthly or yearly to assess an employee's performance, or more likely their "worth to the company." A dashboard as a metaphor is particularly relevant. It assumes that the employee's performance can be measured in a manner similar to assessing the functioning of an automobile. As a driver assesses the oil pressure, RPM, battery, speed, gas level and consumption, etc., an employee can assess his or her performance metrics by looking at the gauges on a dashboard. It is an attempt to reduce complex work and responsibilities to a few gauges. When using the dashboard for performance review, human factors, and all that cannot be quantified to a gauge, are left out. In addition, the gauge presents little data about long-term performance. For example, a manager had great metrics and was the envy of the managerial team. However, it took two years to discover he had created such a poisonous and data-driven culture that his staff left in droves, and the replacements he found had limited skills. His third-year metrics were a disaster, and he was fired. The metrics could not assess the negative dynamics he had created in his department. In many cases these metrics are combined into formulas where a rating is established and so-called comparative data is presented. Thos at the bottom start typing their resumes.

In retail and manufacturing the so-called quant's created dashboards, and these are used to give scores and rankings for managers based on mathematical models. Non-quant managers hate dashboards and believe these models measure the wrong data and even when accurate, merely describe a "desired" end result that is time limited. These gauges and their underlying models rarely have the capability to quantify the long-term outcome of the present effort. Consequently, like the financial collapses in the fall of 2008, models were designed to reap in money on a daily and weekly basis, only to fail to assess the damage and collapse they would cause over the long haul. In addition, dashboards and the mathematical models that underlie them are too simplistic and cannot assess environmental changes that negatively impact outcomes. They are motivated by a guessing game that goes like this: "These metrics will drive performance." One must pick and chose the appropriate metrics and it completely disregards any qualitative process that drives results that cannot be measured. Plus, they cannot determine whether a negative reading at present may be necessary for a positive reading down the road.

Returning to the use of dashboards to review performance, we find that vendors and software consultants exaggerate their value. They claim that corporations succeed or fail, based on their ability to identify, define, track, and act upon key performance indicators (KPIs) contained in dashboards.

It is reasonable to assume that the broader a person's responsibilities, the more complex and subjective an evaluation of their performance would be. Most mangers interact with and are required to please a variety of stakeholders with a wide range of needs. We also know that assessments are completed at specific points in time, and there are always short-term versus long-term tradeoffs. When we rely on metrics and dashboards in the face of such complexities, we run the risk of destroying morale, motivation and commitment. In addition, over the long haul we create a corporation that is short sighted and doomed to failure. The major reason for failure is found in its inability to appreciate the complexities of the corporation, to understand and diagnose problems and make the necessary sacrifices to ensure long-term survival.

In meetings where data-driven analysis prevails, managers compete for the best metrics. The meeting chair, generally a boss, reads off a dizzying array of numbers and presents each manager's metrics in rank order. To be at the bottom in several categories of metrics leads to doom. There is little discussion of the reasons for high or low metrics, and little help is offered to the manager who is consistently low. The low scorer becomes an outcast, beset with anxiety that termination is looming. Team-work and collaboration is destroyed, and if intimate discussions are held, they occur in private, among two or three colleagues who trust each other. An OD psychologist was invited to a managers meeting by a VP. After admonishing a manager for scoring the lowest among several measures the VP asked the OD psychologist what he thought, he said, "Yeah, as I understand it many think he is your best manager, first you set his metrics too high and second he's got the worse clients." The psychologist was not invited back.

What do these reviews and constant emphasis on evaluation do to employees? They create a climate of fear. In Joseph Heller's novel "Something Happened," the protagonist's boss makes it clear what he wants from his subordinates: not "good work," but "spastic colitis and nervous exhaustion" (Lasch, 1979). Heller's boss says: "God dammit, I want the people working for me to be worse off than I am, not better. That's the reason I pay you so well. I want to see you right on the verge, I want it right out in the open. I want to be able to hear it in a stuttering, flustered, tongue-tied voice.... Don't trust me. I don't trust flattery, loyalty, sociability. I don't trust deference, respect, and cooperation. I trust fear." While this suggests a somewhat bizarre, sadomasochistic relationship, we suggest that elements of this exist in the contemporary corporation where employees work long hours, take little time off, play the non-complaining, positive team-player game, and experience constant paranoia.

These corporations relied on dashboards and underlying mathematical models that just did not work. According to Wilmott (2008), "I spend a great deal of time speaking to people in banks about their mathematical models. I know which are using good models (a very few banks) and which are using bad models (most banks)." Of course the universities are jumping on the quant's bandwagon. Most major universities have graduate programs in financial engineering, and we are beginning to see undergraduate programs in Quantitative Finance. But here is the problem: Anyone who has taught business students knows that quant's and non-quant's have trouble communicating with each other. In many instances they do not communicate at all. In business-class group projects, quant's will be in one group and non-quant's in another. Business schools have neglected this problem for years and it has moved onto the corporate world, where non-quant's, who are often executives, work in their world and quant's are off in their world of mathematical models, sometimes physically removed from executive offices. This problem has a long history in corporate America; it was the engineers and the non-engineers, the techies and non-techies, and the geeks and non-geeks. The biggest problem between these two groups is the use of a language that non-geeks fail to understand.

When we look at this shift away from commitment in the workplace, it goes against psychological theory that suggests commitment is necessary for one's mental health and an important part of human nature. Organizational psychologists and psychoanalysts maintain that the wish to be committed to work and to an organization is universal, except in cases of psychological dysfunction or psychopathology. However, this may no longer be true. We now have a generation of employees who no longer see commitment to work and organization as a psychological need. How can we understand and this shift?

We have established that the real problem with Wall Street and other corporations that went financially awry was the absence of commitment and the wish to get rich and get out. The quant's are a prime example of this, they view themselves as hired guns and they are "in it" to get rich and get out. These banks and Wall Street firms were very far removed from a cooperative, "team" oriented culture where decisions are carefully discussed. In fact they became stressful nightmares. Where employees take extraordinary risks to make the big hit, win the corporate lottery, and get the hell out.

THE ABSENCE OF COMMITMENT: STRESS

Commitment and loyalty has long been a buttress to employment stress. The employee could work long hard hours without stress if they felt the company would take care of them and their family. This was the employer-employee compact.

In a psychological sense, commitment is related to the drive to master, create, and accomplish. However, when commitment is reduced or eliminated, stress increases, involvement is reduced and creativity drops. Without commitment the employee goes through the motions, work becomes an alienated endeavor and stress skyrockets.

Consider this. In the mid 1980s the downsizing phenomena was in full swing and thousands of middle managers were being terminated. In response, the board of trustees of a major university wanted to establish a training program for laid-off managers and executives during the summer months. A professor responded: "We better not house these people above the ground floor, they will be jumping out the window." It never happened. The program was established, but only a handful of laid-off managers showed up. Much to the surprise of many business professors, unemployed managers did not fall apart when the corporate compact ended. Instead the terminated employees found a new toughness and a major attitudinal shift. Now loyalty was out and employment was exclusively for money, benefits, and perks. Stress was certainly apparent and was the result of the fear of losing one's job, becoming obsolete, feeling alienated on the job, and having no money to live a life style one had grown accustomed to. But to buttress the stress employees came to believe that they better be out for themselves and not trust any corporate leader.

We also have several factors unique to American culture that pushes against the idea of commitment. Consider the following:

1. Over the years the psychological sense of community in America has weakened. The days when one would: grow up, marry, raise children and live into old age in a neighborhood are gone and with it the shared emotional support system. The lack of stability, heightened mobility and the weakness of "attachments" within the family and community leaves one "on their own," alienated, alone and without roots. Employees go where the jobs are, seeking opportunities and income. In many instances we witness a population that is committed to nothing; not to community, church, employment or family.

2. Embedded in American culture is the idea that suggests it's good to "question authority." There exists a value system that maintains the individual has the right and power to push against authority. The history of the American corporation contains a struggle of the worker against paternal authority. This struggle is valued, even celebrated. It is paternal authority that is perceived with mistrust. This mistrust is especially apparent for employees beginning in the 1980s, as the income gap between the top and bottom dramatically increased, the middle-class began to shrink, and the employee was considered a resource. These employees, who rejected the value of commitment, were students of the Vietnam era, the hippies who fought against authority and injustice, the baby boomers. The boomers and their offspring, the Gen Ys responded to corporate insensitivity by rejecting the very idea of a corporate life. They saw submissiveness and deference to authority as demeaning, and self-respect was attained through competition with or against the larger "system." They value and expect employers to emphasize their uniqueness or separateness (Morgan, 1985).

3. A value that works against commitment is the value of the pioneer spirit that has permeated all aspects of American life. Beginning with the rugged individualism of the early settlers, the glorification of the entrepreneur and the value American society holds for its "stars" or heroes', pushes against commitment to an organization. This is a culture that promotes individualism. This also promotes a form of conservatism, especially against the expectation that one needs to be taken care of by a larger system, like the government or corporation. It is a value system that symbolically sees the family as maternal and the corporation as paternal (paternal authority).

4. The need to appear to be successful pushes against commitment. Several years ago a social critic commented, "Instead of manufacturers neatly tucking their label inside our apparel, they somehow have convinced us that its necessary to boldly display it on the outside. It seems that every American is now a walking billboard." Americans were convinced that they could present themselves as independent, if they could portray themselves as having wealth. Proudly displaying the logo of very expensive apparel is one small way of demonstrating to others that one has wealth. If wealthy people could flaunt their wealth, poor people could also flaunt the appearance of wealth, even if it meant sewing an expensive label on a cheap piece of clothing or buying a knockoff made in China. These displays are the great equalizer. It was similar to the 1950's, when a man living in a tenement could drive his expensive Cadillac and pretend he was something, he was not. What we have is a powerful element of pretense at play within American culture, where one is primarily concerned about "me" and the presentation of "me," even if it is deceptive. It is as if everyone is on the "promenade," showing off. This promenade is not limited to the streets, it is also found in the corporation and among executives at the country club.

What we may have is a new form of commitment based on a different psychic attachment to the corporation. This is called "narcissistic commitment." To begin this exploration, it may be helpful to explore the traditional view of commitment.

THE TRADITIONAL VIEW OF COMMITMENT

Beginning in the 1920's the traditional thinking about commitment to a company shifted from an economic position to a human relations and then to a socio-cultural position. This created a plethora of studies and publications suggesting that management must pay attention to the social and psychological needs of their employees i.e., a happy workforce is a productive and commitment workforce. [1.]

Consider committed employees. When they were terminated, received negative performance reviews, or saw their CEOs getting sinful compensation, they experienced psychological abused. Loyalty, commitment or attachment to their corporation was gradually destroyed. Consider the responses committed and non-committed employees have when they are terminated. First, is acceptance and resiliency. The committed employee believes; "it's my fault, if I only worked harder this would not have happened." This is a depressive response, where the person feels a sense of loss, humiliation and shame. If terminated they accept the termination speeches of human resource managers who say; "your termination is an opportunity." Or if their boss tells them they are not cutting it, and they react by working harder, longer hours, giving up their vacation, coming to work sick. Overtime these employees accept the fact that layoffs and job hopping is the new reality. Their attitude changes and the feelings of commitment disappear and they become the noncommittal employee. The non-committed employee's reaction to termination also has an aim of functioning as a defense against the depression. But the reaction is quite different. These employees respond with self righteousness and outrage. They go to great lengths to condemn the corporation. This may be why many corporations bring security guards in to escort the terminated employee out the door.

A real problem occurs when a formerly committed employee who once trusted the company and management becomes a disillusioned non-committed employee and then returns to being committed again. This employee experienced a profound sense of ambivalence. This occurred to a top level manager had just returned from a three day training session pumped up and his commitment renewed. He told his staff about the new product line and said sales were going to go sky-high. In the afternoon he was called into his VP's office and told he was being put on a PIP (Performance Improvement Program). He was outraged and exploded. The VP called in the HR director and after an hour of ranting, the director told him he was fired and to leave the premises. When he refused to leave, two security guards were called in. He quietly left under the threat of arrest and a lawsuit. The manager blamed the VP and an array of "higher-ups" of being petty and filled with envy at his high quality work. He failed to realize that the company had plans to reduce the payroll. He was replaced by a much younger and cheaper manager.

In a remarkable way we witness a similar pattern of weak commitment among the children of these intimidated and frequently laid-off employees; the Gen Ys. They believe frequent job change is vital to career development, and staying in one job for several years is a sign of failure. As one college student stated, "Yeah, I'm committed to the corporation, the corporation of one, me."

(Chapter 12 is devoted to this new generation of employees)

What we may have is not the idea of commitment, in the traditional sense, but a new type of commitment, called narcissistic commitment. Narcissistic commitment the evolutionary response by employees to the type of corporation created by consultants, business school professors and executives.

NARCISSISTIC ATTACHMENTS: THE NEW FORM OF COMMITMENT TO THE CORPORATION

Attachment theory is an attempt to make sense of the basic need for human connectedness: it is the end point of a developmental process involving the interplay of predefined and acquired behaviors. Attachment is typically used in the psychological sense as having an investment in, and having an affective emotional component to an object (such as a corporation or one's occupation or profession). However, in these troubled corporations a culture evolves where it is impossible for healthy attachments to thrive. Researchers on attachment theory suggest that breaks or disruptions in attachments lead to a reduced capacity to form future attachments. In a similar way these breaks or disruptions occur with such frequency in corporations that, like an orphaned child who experiences continual rejections and abuse, the employee not only loses the capacity to form attachments, but they become numb and mistrustful.

However, there are some employees who seem to flourish in these cultures. They have no need for attachments of loyalty, and they seem to flourish in corporate cultures where terminations occur and greed prevails. In addition they seem to prefer corporations that have excessive reliance on performance reviews that reward achievement, success and visibility. Why seek the performance review? Two reasons: One, they do not have the capacity to judge their efforts themselves therefore they need the other, some authority to tell them how they are doing. Second they see themselves as driven, high performers and they need others to see them in this favorable light. In business schools they are taught how to perform in the corporation, just as an actor is taught to perform in acting school. They actively seek reviews. If they get a good-to-great review they stay, if not they leave and go onto another stage (company). They excel in seeking self-enhancement opportunities. They seek corporations where the only attachment one can have is a narcissistic attachment. These attachments are never deep and are often free-floating and confounded by manipulations. In addition, they are "insecure attachments" that require significant levels of strategy. Strategy takes the form of plotting, and planning. It is as if the employee is engaged in continuous survival strategy. Survival is based on performance, and successful performance is based on manipulation and deception to gain the favor of those above them.

THE DEATH OF THE AMERICAN CORPORATION

In these narcissistic communities employees are expected to extract gratification quickly, to fill oneself up (have their needs met). If this is not apparent then one moves on. These corporations have created a "culture of narcissism", typified by a "me first" attitude where one will work hard to be observed by significant others in a glorious light, for the purpose of "getting more" for oneself, even it is at the expense of others. This work hard, play hard, me first attitude is prevalent in these cultures, and CEOs want employees who are ambitious, mobile, and have an exceedingly low tolerance for delaying gratification. American CEOs have learned to exploit this attitude. For example, in American corporations a young, just-out-of-college employee will change jobs three times in the first five years of employment. American corporations encourage job-changing, and it is rewarded. This as indicated by the data above suggesting that job-changing is a critical factor in increasing an employee's income. Employment agencies, so-called head-hunters, and recruiters have approached the status of a major industry, suggesting that more and more employees are on the move. This is reinforced by the trend among CEOs to hire temps or contract employees and offer no benefits. If America ever gets around to offering universal health care, the numbers of contract employees could grow to 70 percent of the workforce.

These cultural shifts are the direct result of destruction of the employer-employee compact. This is what American CEOs sought: the demise of commitment, a "bottom line" approach to management that saw employees as a resource, and commitment as an expensive waste. This allowed the CEOs and their executive constellation to dramatically maximize control, and over the short haul, increase their compensation. However, the failure to assess the long-term costs associated with their greed and behavior, and their failure to assess cultural shifts, is leading to the "Death of the American Corporation" as we know it.

It is easy to condemn these behaviors, and journalists, bloggers, unions, politicians and others have done so. But it is quite another thing to try and understand it. We begin this journey of understanding by examining the road one travels on the way up the corporate ladder. We have established that it begins in business school. Next we will examine the process of climbing the corporate ladder and the psychic toll it takes.

CHAPTER 6

Development of the Executive Type: Becoming a CEO

(O)ur cultural emphasis on technology, competition, individualism, temporariness, and mobility has resulted in a population that has frequently experienced the terror of loneliness and seldom the satisfaction of engagement.

Jerry Harvey (1988, p.25)

Who are these people who climb the corporate ladder and reach the pinnacle? If one looks at the corporate pyramid, many start out at the bottom and only one reaches the top. We begin this study with the development of the "executive type." The word "type" is used here because we maintain that a certain type of person with certain characteristics, beliefs, attitudes, and even personality will make it to the top.

As with most professional occupations, executive types learn the required executive behaviors early on in life through friends and family, through stories about bosses at the dinner table, through the mass media, and later on in the university, especially in graduate school. Consider the professional training of lawyers, physicians, engineers, professors, psychiatrists, psychoanalysts, etc. Some observers of human behavior maintain they can identify one's profession after a few minutes of conversation, while others maintain they can identify one's profession by their appearance, their mannerisms, and language. The same holds true for the executive population. They are shaped by family, business school curriculum and culture, as well as professors, mentors, and corporate training programs. As a matter of fact, there are some who suggest that it is precisely the type of training and education one receives from these venues that are responsible for, the Enron's of the world, corporate greed, the collapse of Wall Street, the housing debacle, outsourcing, massive layoffs, the death of manufacturing in the U.S., and ultimately the death of the American corporation.

BECOMING A CEO: MOVING THROUGH STAGES

There are eight stages or social mechanisms associated with joining, entering the role of an executive, and becoming a CEO:

Stage 1. Becoming a manager. The characteristics of most executive constellations demonstrate distinctive qualities. Many MBAs quickly discover the importance of socio-demographic characteristics like gender, age, and race are significant at this first stage of development. Many young MBAs discovering they do not share the characteristics of the top executive will move on to another career or knowingly tone down their ambition. However, some refuse to accept the fact that bias or prejudice will keep them out of the executive suite and they push ahead. Clearly it helps one move into a rudimentary junior executive role if they are physically similar to the corporation's executives. Consider the fact that CEOs are overwhelmingly white, male and in their 50s and early 60s. This establishes them as a distinct social grouping. While an executive training program may contain a variety of people with diverse backgrounds, they quickly learn that the executives they meet in training are a specific type: white males in their 50s. They may also be of a certain height, weight, complexion, educational background and discipline, giving the message to the trainees that those who do not fit the type may not be welcome.

Stage 2. Obtaining the right stuff. There may be discriminatory effects related to formal job requirements. Degrees and specific education or training may be required. This important socialization requirement is not only related to skills, but to the way in which executives think, make decisions and respond to crisis. It also may be directly related to issues associated with beliefs about executive compensation and the employer-employee compact.

Stage 3. Self selection: Deciding to stay or leave. Young managers enter the occupation with specific goals in mind. In the case of becoming an executive it may be the pursuit of power, the wish to be admired, be on top or become "king of the mountain." They select an occupation based on an array of wishes and fantasies, some accurate, some associated with distorted wishes and needs. Gratification of these wishes and needs propels the young manager to continue the pursuit of that occupational choice. Many discover that the time commitment and the effort required is too much. Many become disillusioned and exit the competition.

Stage 4. Indirect self-selection: Screwing up. The screw-up occurs when the manager unconsciously makes choices or decisions that prohibit or ruin the chances for advancement. It could be a major mistake, a conflict or fight, an embarrassing situation either at work or outside, a messy divorce, legal trouble or a lapse in judgment that precipitates a negative evaluation. On the other hand indirect selection is also related to these very same issues. Marrying the boss's daughter a popular conception cynically associated with movement up the ladder, would be associated with indirect self-selection.

Stage 5. Making the leap. At this stage the executive is motivated by the wish to contribute to an economic interest. Here one continues to advance in the executive position to contribute to an economic grouping. It may be to increase the likelihood of curing a disease, helping the sick, educating the masses, bringing wealth to stockholders. A banker may see accumulating wealth as a way to contribute to philanthropy, or in some cases to increase personal wealth.

Stage 6. Entry into the executive constellation. This process occurs when the manager seeks entry into executive's suite. Those seeking entry into the constellation are screened for their aptitudes, attitudes and values. The question takes on serious importance for those in the constellation: Does the candidate have executive qualities? Those selected are further encouraged to assume the executive identity, and entry into this stage promotes a concretization of this identity.

Stage 7. I've made it. At the stage the manager moves into the executive constellation. Here the executive accepts the type and degree of occupational socialization and finds congruity between the attitudes and values of the "occupational community" and their own. For example, corporate executives tend to be more conservative then the non-executive population. Consequently the executive now publicly demonstrates the appropriate ideological or political leading and will engage in supporting candidates for political office. In addition the executive is now a member of the "executive family" and must be able to spend significant amount of time in this family without demonstrating conflict. Failure to do so will result in ejection.

Stage 8. **The mobilization stage** Here the executive can become mobile. This occurs when the executive reaches maturity and fully becomes the executive type. Their name becomes familiar, "a household name," in the business world, and they may reach celebrity status. As a result they are afforded the opportunity to move across various industries while maintaining the executive role. They become the generic CEO.

Many researchers of corporate behavior maintain that it is not the accuracy of executive decisions, brilliance or hard work that leads to success. Instead, they claim, it's the ability to speak sharply, align with powerful patrons, engage in shameless self-promotion, hide intentions, have a powerful competitive spirit, and possess an ability to avoid or hide mistakes. And, of course, some luck. What is this luck? It may be being in the right-place at the right-time, aligning oneself with a powerful patron, or standing out in some fortunate event. They need to be able to put on a show and obtain the focus of the company's leaders, especially their superiors. Getting superiors to pay attention is a major skill that few possess. After getting noticed, they are capable of keeping the spotlight on oneself by making certain that all involved in observing them see that it's their contribution that makes the difference. They make certain their superiors understand how much money they can save or make for the corporation. The art is making their superior feel that if they ignore their contributions they may lose potential revenue. When they accomplish this task, they receive significant attention.

A young manager did just this. He was always present when a project was being completed, especially when the project made a significant contribution. He would seek out VPs and make certain they knew about the project and its worth to the company, even when he had little to do with it. His colleagues both feared and hated him, but they remained silent, believing he had a special connection to the VPs. He was able to fool everyone and was shortly promoted to a VP position.

Consider what happens when one is not skilled in the art of presentation and self-promotion. Several years ago a professor told this story. He took a sabbatical from academe to work full time for a major corporation that was experiencing a problematic turnover among employees. The professor worked for two months writing up a strategic plan to correct the problem. He sent off his 63page plan to corporate headquarters, and waited for a response. He heard nothing. He told a neighbor about his concern. An experienced corporate executive, she said, "No one in corporate America reads a 63-page proposal." He quickly went to work, and sent off a 32-page proposal. Again, he heard nothing. After three weeks he called headquarters to find out what was wrong. A VP told him he could come to headquarters and deliver a presentation but it could be no more than five PowerPoint slides. The VP laughed and said, "Welcome to corporate America." The professor, quite unfamiliar with corporate presentations, prepared his slide show and gave his presentation. After 15 minutes he was cut off and told he could leave. He never heard from headquarters again. His planned one-year sabbatical lasted four months. If he had gone to business school and spent years giving presentations to professors he may have succeeded. He was not skilled in the art of any type of promotion. He mistakenly thought his proposal was rich and thoughtful and after careful reading would be embraced by the company's leaders. He failed to understand it was not the proposal that would sell the plan, it was he.

Consider another example. The director of Six Sigma at a major corporation announced she hired a corporate makeover specialist and an executive coach. She was preparing to make a push up the ladder. She had a graduate degree in statistics from a foreign university and felt she was not properly prepared for an executive role. Her newly hired makeover team took her shopping, shaped and colored her hair to make her look more "executive." She then proceeded to learn how to talk, think, and behave like an executive. After a year she was fired. She made the mistake of alienating her Six Sigma colleagues who gave her a negative 360 performance evaluation. She failed to consider the disdain her "number crunching" colleagues had for "executive types" and called her a phony.

Clearly, not everyone can pull off this move up the corporate ladder. It takes a special type, with the right type of training, background and some luck. Had she received an MBA education she would have known the value of what it takes to become the "executive type." She would have prepared herself for entry into the corporate world; prepped for the interview, carefully polished and added to her resume, made the necessary contacts, and honed her appearance, language and self-presentation skills. She would have entered the right MBA program, taken the right courses, with the right professors and prepared herself for entry into the right corporation. She would have started at $95,000 a year, instead of $50,000 working with the nerds in Six Sigma. She would have moved ahead rapidly, instead of floundering in "Siberia" for six years. She was bitter. She felt the corporate ship of advancement had left the dock and she was not on it. How many are there like her? One professor of management, with 30 years of experience, suggested that only 10 percent end up satisfied with the corporate life they had chosen.

Legions of business school graduates set their sights on the CEO's seat and gleefully join the race to the top. However, only a select few make it, and those who fail look on with envy, despair and feelings that range from depressed resignation to rage. In a survey (Czander,

2002) of 200 part-time employed MBA students with an average age of 29 years, 68 percent of the men and 79 percent of the women stated they were not going to get to the top of their industry. Obtaining a MBA was just to keep their foot in the game or perhaps help them get promoted or make a lateral move to a higher-paying job. In addition, 52 percent of the men and 25 percent of the women stated they were unhappy with their lives. The major reason was being stuck in a career, overwhelmed with debt and family obligations. These responsibilities made it impossible to change careers.

It was not surprising to discover that 63 percent of these students came from working class families with parents who had no college degrees, and of the remaining 37 percent, 26 percent had college degrees and 11 percent held graduate degrees. This put the unhappy manager's frustrations into perspective; they were losing the competition with those managers with higher social and economic status (SES), who have a much greater chance of moving ahead. This is confirmed by Lee (1981) who conducted open-ended interviews with 166 top executives and found that they came from a "birth elite." Birth elites are defined as coming from a family with a high SES, important family contacts, money and professional socialization. This is further supported by a Pew study by Eckholm (2008), who maintains that economic mobility: the chance that children of the poor or middle class will climb the income ladder has not changed over the past three decades, and that children born into the top fifth income families will tend to remain in this category as adults. This is supported by a recent study suggesting that graduates of elite undergraduate institutions make significantly more in mid-career than those who graduate from non-elite schools. Yale graduates have the highest mid-career incomes (Gopal, 2008), and Yale students come from exceptionally high SES families.

From a social stratification perspective, the best predictor of occupational success, like moving to the top corporate position, is a function of a cluster of variables such as SES, selective education, good advice and capacity to present oneself as "executive material." The part-time MBA students who were surveyed and who experienced the despair associated with the lack of career mobility early on in their careers were from an SES cluster that would make moving to a top position exceedingly remote.

Let's look at those from the "birth elite," who stand a much better chance of making it into an elite MBA program and to the executive suite. A report in The Economist in 1994 suggested that there is almost no economic gain from obtaining an MBA, except for those who graduated from top-tiered programs. This is confirmed by a Forbes study of the common attributes of the super-wealthy, where nearly 90 per cent of billionaires who derived their fortunes from finance obtained MBAs from one of three Ivy League schools: Harvard, Columbia, or University of Pennsylvania's Wharton School of Business (Lee, 2009).

It is also clear that the sons and daughters from "birth elite" families stand a better chance of gaining entry into elite business schools. Therefore, it is unclear if the economic gains are from graduating from a top tiered program or being a "birth elite." Also, we do not know if non-birth elites benefit as much from being in an elite business school. If we follow the assumptions made by several consultants and observers of business schools that these elite schools function as a networking instrument, and offer a pedigree, then it makes sense that top-tier schools offer the best and perhaps only chance for non-birth elites to "move up the corporate ladder." We do know that elite MBA programs serve a filtering function.

Those "birth elite" managers who came from families with college educated parents and executive backgrounds not only had a better statistical chance of becoming a top executive, they also had the pressures associated with high expectations. For them, having a so-called "decent" job was not good enough. Expectations to climb the corporate ladder were placed upon them at an early age, and over time, the pressure to succeed increased.

Consider this example of two young managers; one manager comes from a "birth elite" family, and the other from a "working class" family. The "birth elite" manager, a Harvard MBA, received pressure from family members to immediately enroll in MIT after graduation to obtain his masters in metallurgical engineering. He did. Upon graduation he joined a major corporation, at the age of 26, and was offered the directorship of a nonproductive foundry. This was his first formal job. He took two recent Ph.D.'s from MIT with him. After six months, he carefully assessed his potential with his father and relatives, and decided to leave. They advised him to leave because staying could potentially harm his movement up the corporate ladder. He was directing a foundry that was losing money, he faced union problems, and he discovered the parent company would most likely merge with another company. He took their advice and left, and immediately took a job with another foundry, with a better chance of success.

Why did he choose to work in the foundry industry in the first place? His father and two uncles carefully laid out the industries that would offer the least competition for promotions and solid opportunities for success. He and his family maintained that the foundry industry in America was a dying industry. Foundry plants were old and beset with inefficiencies and employee problems. He said his family told him to put his career on the fast track: he needed to join an industry that was either in its infancy or near death. This young executive would not make a career move without dutiful and thoughtful family counsel. His father had an MBA, and a successful career as an executive and consultant. His uncles were also successful in business.

After he left, he was immediately replaced by a young man who recently received his MBA from a below average, part-time program.

When offered the position his working class family celebrated his success. They were exceedingly proud. But that was all. His family had no idea of what the young man was getting into. After two years of extreme hardship the foundry closed, and he was out of a job, with little prospects and a negative reputation.

To have family members who have experienced life in the "executive suite" is clearly an advantage to an aspiring executive. They have ready and able coaches who help the young executive navigate his/her way through the politics and pot-holes in the corporate maze. Just as we see young actors enter the same business as their celebrity parents, being connected makes entry into an industry and the attainment of significant roles more accessible. However, the pressure to succeed as their parents had can also be a significant source of stress.

This was the case of the young Harvard graduate described above. He married an artist who had little value for her husband's life in the corporate fast lane. This marriage was not approved by his family. They saw her as someone who would not support her husband's effort to climb the corporate ladder. They were right. What his family did not observe was the ambivalence the young executive was experiencing. His ambivalence was symbolized by his choice of a marriage partner, an intellectual and an artist. After the young executive left the foundry and quickly obtained another position, he and his wife made certain this new job would take them far away from his family. He lasted six months at this new job. He quit and decided to devote himself to furniture making. He reported that the pressure to succeed was overwhelming. He said the years he spent with his family; discussing how to succeed had taught him that he would have to pay a major price to make it to the executive suite. His marriage, the wish to have a family, and his realization that he and his wife were on a long road to unhappiness, made his choice easy.

The young MBA from a working class family, who took over the foundry thought he was being given the opportunity of a life time. He was young and confident, handsome and articulate. He was recently married and had a young child. Shortly after he was offered the opportunity, he heard through the grapevine the foundry was to be closed down by its parent company. Union issues, obsolescence and energy costs were contributing to the foundry's doom. He reported the following: "On my first day on the job I was surprised; my upper and middle level managers marched into my office and instead of offering congratulations they wanted to know if their jobs were intact. I had to act confident, when deep down I wasn't. This is not like me. I lied. I told them if I detected a hint that I was being asked to close the foundry, I would not have taken the position." He publicly promised his managers he would work with them to make the foundry productive. But privately he reported that his mind was now clouded with doubt. He had suspicions the foundry was not going to survive, and that's why the Harvard guy left. He thought, if his managers were worried maybe they had more information than he had. He then began to feel angry at himself for not digging more and finding out if this was the type of job that would advance his career or hinder it. After all, he thought, he had just obtained his MBA and to fail at his first big job would be a disaster. He discussed this with his wife who advised him to get out fast. Tormented, he could not sleep. He was entwined in what he described as a potentially disastrous career move. He reported that four days after settling into to his new position he had called the parent company and spoke to the person who hired him and he was assured things were OK. He was not convinced. He had a history of authority figures lying to him. As a teenager his father assured him that in spite of the problematic relationship with his mother, he would not leave. Shortly after, he discovered that his father was having an affair and would soon leave his wife and three children. At work, reassuring his managers that things were OK, and lying to them made him angry, he was experiencing himself as his father, a liar. Additionally, he found himself in a turbulent corporate environment. He was presented with an array of union demands, and he was advised by the parent company that he would receive no assistance from corporate lawyers and no financial offerings. Managers told him they were planning to leave. He pleaded with them to stay, and convinced them they could collectively turn things around. He also knew he was faced with a major operational problem. He could not complete a major order. The production was too complicated. He was now working 15 hour days feeling overwhelmed, in what seemed like an impossible situation. His wife began to aggressively push him to quit. He promised her he would, but secretly he knew he would not quit. He was driven to keep the foundry going and he did not know why.

He was overwhelmed with guilt associated with lying to employees. He experienced himself as his despised father, the liar and the failure. After a year, it was announced by the parent company the foundry would close in six months. He decided to seek a head hunter to find another job. He explained to the head hunter the situation he had gotten himself into. The head hunter said she could not help him. She said the foundry industry was difficult, and said unless he successfully turned around the foundry he would be tainted. The headhunter said, "For me to tell clients that in your only managerial job you were the directorship of a foundry that closed is not good." He was devastated. Emotionally distraught, he entered therapy with his wife. They discussed what to do.

The young CEO was enraged. In therapy he realized that psychologically he was in the same familiar situation; the parent company was nothing more than another authority (father) lying to him, and leaving him with an angry wife (mother), enraged managers and union workers (siblings). He discovered that his compulsion to stay was a repeat to save the family his father destroyed. He was once again stuck in the middle. At a meeting with his managers, as they angrily discussed how to deal with the union, he suddenly stood up and announced he had it, and immediately walked out. He declared to his wife and family he would never aspire to be a manager again. After much thought and counsel, he decided that he wanted to be an engineer (his undergrad degree). He returned to school and received his master's in engineering and went on to work in a position that had very little to do with management. Many years later he was asked what do he thought would have happened had he stayed in management. He responded," I would not be married to my wife, and I would probably be lying and feeling OK about it. I could not take that. If I stayed, it would have made me a different person, a person that is not me."

The young Harvard manager had a choice. He knew the consequences of staying in the corporate world and climbing the ladder. The non-birth elite manager would later state, "I was lucky." The choice to leave was made for him.

The story is not complete. The plant manager position was then given to a very young technician who was completing his undergraduate degree in chemical engineering at night school. An important message fits in here: If your want to move up the ladder quickly, take over a dying company. He operated the foundry by the "seat of his pants." He knew nothing and was distraught, and became thoroughly intrigued with management psychology. He left and went back to school. He became the author of this book and spent the rest of his professional life studying management. What happened to the foundry? It closed.

The MBA education failed both of these young managers. Their education failed to give them the skills to diagnose the corporate environment and know not only what they were getting into, but how they would fit in the executive role. Most students go through their MBA education without learning the complexities of careerism, adult development or the psychological necessities of work-life balance.

As stated above, succeeding and moving up the ladder requires considerable knowledge and perhaps some luck. This knowledge is rarely taught in graduate school, that is, the capacity to diagnose the environment one is moving into and then the self-knowledge to assess whether one has the skill set and personality to function well in the environment. Here we can see why "birth elites" stand a better chance of surviving the long push up the ladder. They have the support network that has the necessary experience and knowledge that can advise them on their career movement. They also have the financial support that functions as a safety net should they fall. This goes a long way towards building self-confidence and lessening anxiety associated with failure or career change.

What we observe among these young managers is a high degree of self-confidence, a capacity to be less than honest with those around them and fear of making a blunder. Mintzberg (2004) maintains that elite MBA programs attract large numbers of people whom he characterizes as impatient, aggressive, and self-serving. It may be that these students display narcissistic characteristics. It may not take many to create this impression that there are many narcissists in these programs because they are the ones who are stand out and grab all the attention. These are the characters that grab the attention in business school, do the same on the job, and over time these characteristics are reflected in their management style.

Once the budding executive enters the corporate world, his or her work is to not only be successful, but also to be recognized; to stand out and remain on the "fast track." Almost everyone who has worked in a corporation has heard the phrase "he/she is executive material." What does this mean? To a psychologist, this means that the person demonstrates certain characteristics, attitude, and the types of behaviors, thinking and maybe even appearance of someone who will someday occupy the executive suite. It also means that the young recruit may have the personality characteristics and values that will fit into a social grouping called the "executive constellation". It also may mean that the recruit is viewed as someone who will support the efforts of the executive team, and add to team's cohesion, at the same time demonstrating appropriate subordinate behavior.

THE RIGHT STUFF

What are the characteristics a young recruit must demonstrate to become "executive material?" These characteristics may vary from culture to corporate culture, but to be selected requires three modal characteristics: (1) The recruit must display a weltanschauung that is similar to the executive team, (2) The recruit must have intense ambition, and (3) The recruit must have a type of self-system that promotes identification with corporate executives. That is, a wish to be like them.

There are a number of ways of characterizing these candidates. They can be what Lifton (1968) refers to as having a "protean self" or what Riesman's et. al. (1950) refer to as "other directed" personality, or what Winnicott (1960) calls the false self, or what Bollas (1987) calls the normotic personality, or what Solomon (2004) calls the "as if" personality. It's as if the candidate "to be" is a blank slate eager to be molded, and is ready to accept the expected identity, as one would put on a suit of clothes.

This malleable self or flexible personality emerges not from some structural defect in the personality, but from two factors: (1) intense ambition and desire, and (2) real confusion about what type of person one is. Lifton (1968) claims this confusion comes from without and lay in the very culture the person tries to survive or thrive within. One can readily observe that in this volatile ever changing environment where the highly mobile, culturally confused, but intensely ambitious young person, is without a "mooring", and is exceedingly ambivalent and dependent. As the young person embraces careerism, he/she is ambivalent about ties to the past or future. Whether these ties will hinder or propel their movement forward is questioned. Consider this example, a student was admitted to an elite MBA program. He was from a poor family and went to a state university. He was thoroughly intimidated by the impressive credentials of the students in his class. At an informal wine and cheese gathering he told a professor that his background may be a liability. The wise professor commented, "Your background is how you look at it, it can be your strength." The student was no longer intimidated.

Overtime, the young candidate, who carefully watches and imitates the behaviors of executives identifies with the executives and comes to accept the behaviors as real. These behaviors become part of the young candidate's professional identity..

THE YOUNG EXECUTIVE AND THE DEVELOPMENT OF THE EGO IDEAL

The young executive's ambition is nurtured through identifications with key objects; be they mentors or executives or even the corporation itself. Sometimes, being selected and then undergoing the company's management training program nurtures this ambition, by having trainers, guest lecturers and consultants, and executive speakers give them what they perceive as the "keys to the kingdom." In addition to management training programs, executives place considerable pressure and demands on the young candidate; the candidate is mentored and molded into the required type. The selection process is thorough, and only the person who displays the right "executive behaviors" will be allowed to continue. The process is complete when there is a fusion of what Schwartz (1990) calls the "organizational ideal" with the self. The young recruit comes to see himself or herself as competent member and on the road to great success.

Those who question the "realness", or fail to internalize these expected behavioral displays are quickly rejected and labeled as cynics, non-team players, loose cannons, disrespectful, or even having problems with authority. When young recruits are rejected or experience failure, as the MBA foundry director did, it is a powerful narcissistic injury. They react by displaying contempt towards those executives they once identified with as well as the company that rejected them. In the young candidate's mind the organization moves from being perfect (that which gave him a wonderful opportunity) to imperfect. (that which deceived him and made him fail). This is a defense aimed at protecting the ego ideal. If this defense fails, the young recruit moves into a depressive position.

As the young candidate moves up the ladder, he or she may be bombarded with impingements associated with doubt, rejection, fear, and failure. The capacity to keep ambition alive allows one to continue to function at work despite numerous narcissistic injuries. As we shall see, the young executive who makes it to the executive suite develops an interpersonal style that serves to protect and promotes depersonalized entitlement ("I am great, I deserve more") as a functional defense.

The young Harvard graduate who gave up the climb to the executive suite was able to maintain ambition through withdrawal: He seeks both sanctuary and perfection in a new form, by making furniture. He becomes a perfect craftsman and is capable of satisfying obsessive cravings of perfection by crafting the most admired objects of furniture. In the process he rejects his family of origins' approving parental ideal and accepts his wife's ideal and becomes the ideal husband. The engineer/MBA in a similar fashion maintains ambition by leaving the world of management and the fear he would become his father an imperfect object. He is able to maintain ambition by moving into a new occupation and like his counterpart, the Harvard graduate, he is able to see himself in a favorable light. These two young MBAs do not need to maintain false ambitions by using the defense of entitlement ("I deserve more"), which is commonly used to protect ambition from narcissistic injuries. The question worthy of analysis is: What happens to those who stay in the corporation?

CHAPTER 7

The CEO: Life at the Top

"The definition of a good CEO is not someone who leads a profitable corporation in good economic times, but one who leads a profitable corporation in bad economic times."

(Czander)

Through its (the corporation's) primary concern for increased effectiveness, economic growth, rationalization, automation, and worldwide competition this seems to be devoted exclusively to the principles of the Olympic games: faster, higher, and wider!

Burkard Sievers (1990, p.89)

Considerable effort goes into climbing the corporate ladder. However, no matter how hard one thinks they worked to get to the top, CEOs report the effort climbing was nothing compared to the effort necessary to stay on top. A typical CEO works 14 to 16 hours a day, and many work seven days a week. They attend several meetings a day, often traveling from meeting to meeting. Travel times that once were considered "down time," where CEOs could get away from the office, is now spent electronically connected, via laptop, phone or BlackBerry. They often have breakfast, lunch, and dinner meetings. They get to bed late and wake up early.

The CEO must not only have the capacity to be a workaholic but must also have the unique capacity to spend 16 hours a day multi-tasking. These multiple tasks often have little relationship to each other. Multi-tasking is especially apparent when the CEO is leading a conglomerate or global business. In these businesses, multi-tasking may involve several different industries, languages and cultures. Unlike scientists, scholars, surgeons and other professionals who must concentrate for long periods of time on a single task or goal, CEOs must move quickly from situation to situation, handling scores of disconnected events each day. In addition, with world financial markets running 24 hours a day, the CEO must continuously pay attention to the impact these markets may have of his/her corporation, and this often includes even the most remote corners of the globe.

How long can they do it? Not long. The average length of stay at the top has been decreasing, from 11.4 years in 1980 to 8.6 years in 2000 (Klein, 2007) and 3.2 years in 2007 (New York Times, 2008b). Lubin (2010) found only 28 CEOs of companies in the Standard & Poor's 500 have held office more than 15 years, and she maintains that the average for S&P 500 CEO was about 6.6 years. While we see the length of stay drop significantly, so has the age. The CEO "class of 2004" was the youngest on record, with an average age of 57.8 years. With a young age and short stay these CEOs have been called "the most prominent young temp workers" who retire at an early age. Where do they go after their term has ended? The most difficult CEOs to retread are those with high compensation, bad press coming from either a scandal or grossly unhappy stockholders, and of course those who attained celebrity status. It is not that no board wants to hire a celebrity CEO. They are in hot demand. It's because once CEOs attains such lofty status, they do not want to return to the trenches. They prefer to write books or give after dinner-speeches, and appear on talk shows telling all who will listen "how they did it." They also become instant experts, giving advice and criticism on a wide variety of subjects. If one did research on "What are they doing now?" One would find that they join venture capital or hedge fund firms or sit on corporate or nonprofit boards or become dean or professor at some B-school. Few return to the corporate ranks, and most retire to the corporate CEO "graveyard" the golf course.

Some of the reasons for such a short stay at the top are attributed to burnout, retirements, resignations and forced terminations. With the average length of stay at 3.2 years, these CEOs barely have time to affect the corporation before they leave. What we have is instability at the top caused by this revolving door. The brief length of stay strongly suggests we have weakly committed CEOs, preoccupied with "filling their personal coffers," with little concern for their employees, who they do not know or care about. Long gone are the days when a beloved CEO personally knew all their employees and symbolically "bled" when his company "bled"

What we may have is the equivalent of athletes who have devoted themselves to becoming a professional, and making "it to the big leagues." They have worked hard, practiced countless hours for many years with clear awareness that others may come along who are more talented, or they may suffer an injury (failure) that will dash their dreams. If they make it, their insecurity increases with the realization that they have a few years before injury, loss of skills or better athletes come along. In addition, they dread the failure associated with being a member of a losing team. They take illegal drugs, doctor their equipment, and hire trainers to keep them fit or mask their injuries. In their professional position, they want to make as much as they can in their short-lived occupation. They want to have a "Career Year," especially the year before their contract ends. They welcome the off-season to refresh and prepare to face another year. Here is where the analogy ends.

The season does not end for a CEO. They get no time off to refresh, no sabbatical, and for many no vacation.

However, these CEOs want to have a career year. They want their picture on a news magazine they want to become a celebrity CEO.

THE CELEBRITY CEOS- THEY WILL SCREW UP YOUR COMPANY

The numbers of CEOs hired from the outside as opposed to hiring from within increases every year. In 2010 estimates are that over 28 to 30 percent of all CEOs hired were brought in from outside the company. In the 1970s 15 percent of CEOs were external hires and in the 1990s the number grew to 26 percent, according to Conyon (2008). The increase in the numbers of external CEO hires results from corporate boards' infatuation with powerful corporate stars, the so-called celebrity CEOs.

Often these celebrity CEOs are brought in with considerable fanfare and they typically bring their entourage with them. Their entry shakes up the executive constellation and those who have been with the corporation leave in droves. The best example of this is Bob Nardelli, who took over the top position Home Depot in December 2000. He brought with him many former GE executives, none of whom had retail experience. Needless to say they attempted to apply the only methodology and managerial style they knew, the GE way. And they failed miserably. During Nardelli's short stay, every executive who had been in position before he arrived left the company. We will explore Nardelli and his stay at Home Depot in depth in chapter 9.

The idea of the celebrity CEOs came into prominence with the publication in 1982 of the world's largest selling business book, *In Search of*

Excellence by Thomas Peters and Robert Waterman. In their book, they identified 43 corporations as "excellent" along with their "top performing" CEOs. However, as early as five years after publication, one-third of the corporations identified as "excellent" were in financial difficulties. According to Schurr (2002), many of yesterday's magazine-cover CEOs now grace Most Wanted posters. Of the 92 CEOs on the cover of *BusinessWeek* from 1997 to 2001, 49 were gone in 2005.

However, this did not stop the growth of awards given to: "Excellent Companies," "Visionary CEOs," "Successful Corporations" and "Best Corporations." Business publications, and then consulting firms, jumped on board the "award giving" circuit, where CEOs could gain the spotlight. In addition, they eagerly sought photo opportunities and publications attesting to their leadership skills. Business schools loved them, they wanted them for their boards and guest lectures. If they were alums their school would shamelessly post their pictures, photos, and accomplishments. Like the business schools they graduated from, CEOs placed public relations and marketing experts on their payroll for the purpose of winning these awards and moving up in the "best of..." rankings. This spurred on evolution of the so-called imperial CEO. It is not surprising that the start of the CEO celebrity culture coincides with the exceedingly popular television show "Lifestyles of the Rich and Famous" where Americans got to observe how the rich and famous lived. Following *In Search of Excellence,* in 1984, this show featured the extravagant lifestyles of wealthy business moguls and others. The show's host Robin Leach ended each episode with the phrase, *"May you have champagne wishes and caviar dreams."*

Often awards given to these celebrity CEOs had little relationship to reality. For example McLean and Elkind (2003), found that Fortune named the scandalous Enron corporation the "Most Innovative Company" six years in a row. CEO magazine selected Enron's board as one of the top five corporate boards in America. This was before the collapse and the discovery that the board engaged in little or no oversight.

The key for the contemporary CEO is to quickly build the corporation's profitability, make the shareholders happy, obtain millions in compensation, become a celebrity CEO, write a book, and go on the lecture circuit telling others how they did it. To accomplish this they embrace bottom line thinking, where the focus is on shareholder value.

There is no better example of this than Jack Welch, the CEO of General Electric from 1981 to 2001. During his tenure he shut down factories, reduced payrolls and cut unprofitable old-line units. Welch's philosophy was that a company should be either No. 1 or No.2 in a particular industry, or else leave it completely. He also adopted an annual performance review process in which every year he would fire the bottom 10 percent of his managers and reward the top 20 percent with bonuses and stock options. Welch's strategy was adopted by other CEOs across corporate America.

Welch was called "Neutron Jack" for eliminating employees while leaving buildings intact. In his book *Jack: Straight From The Gut*, Welch states that GE had 411,000 employees at the end of 1980, and 299,000 at the end of 1985. Of the 112,000 who left the payroll, 37,000 were in sold businesses, and 81,000 were terminated in continuing businesses. In return, GE had increased its market capital tremendously. In 1999 he was named "Manager of the Century" by Fortune magazine. Welch was the only ex-CEO to have his name on two B-schools, Sacred Heart University and the for-profit Chancellor University. However, Welch's $30,000 online MBA at Chancellor did not do well and in November 2011 he took his program to another for-profit, Strayer. He claimed the Welch Institute at Strayer will become the "number one online business school in the world," enrolling over 5,000 students.

Welch was a champion of paying executives well and was not concerned with the growing gap between executives and their employees. He believed CEO compensation should be dictated by the free market. Welch made over a billion dollars during his tenure at GE (Heller, 2005).

It turns out the "manager of the century" left a mess behind. Since 2001, when Welch left, the company has spiraled down, selling off many parts to sustain itself. In 2008 the Federal Reserve had to lend GE $16.1 billion to keep it from going bankrupt, and in December 2009 GE had to sell its popular jewel, NBC universal to Comcast for $30 billion. If that was not enough, in December 2010 GE sold its Mexican mortgage unit to Santander of Spain for $162 million. Jack's replacement, Jeffrey Immelt received a Forbes pay/performance efficiency score of 188, the worse score a CEO could get is 188. This suggests the depth of the mess the "manager of the century" left behind. The shares of General Electric have plunged in value by 60.8 per cent during the tenure of CEO Jeffrey Immelt, who was rewarded for this performance with $37.2 million in free stock in 2010 (Olive, 2011).

Another famous example of "the celebrity CEO" is Al Dunlap. In the late 90s, he become a popular "turnaround" CEO and was given nicknames like, "Chainsaw Al," "Rambo in Pinstripes" and "Al the shredder." He made a career terminating employees. In his book *"Mean Business"* he laid out four principles: 1) get the right management team, 2) cut back to the lowest costs, 3) focus on the core business, and 4) get a real strategy. Dunlap ran Sterling, American Can, Lily Tulip, Crown-Zellerbach, Diamond International, and Consolidated Press Holdings. In his last four years in the "catbird seat." he made more than $100 million, ran Scott Paper and Sunbeam corporations, wrote a best-selling vainglorious autobiography exaggerating everything from his upbringing to corporate leadership, and fired some 18,000 employees.

According to Business Week (1998)

"Dunlap, ... was hardly the only chieftain to order hefty workforce cuts or to say that the only stakeholders in a public corporation are its investors. But by eagerly seeking publicity to expound his simple philosophy, he emerged as the poster boy for "shareholder wealth." To investors who made millions by following him, Dunlap was, if not a god, certainly a savior. He parachuted into poorly performing companies and made tough decisions that quickly brought shareholders sizable profits."

Another example is Sanford Sigoloff, who in the late 1970s and 1980s was called "Mr. Chapter 11," "Ming the Merciless" and "the Skillful Scalpel." Like Dunlap, this so-called turn-around artist would fire employees by the thousands (Walsh, 2011). In addition, like Lee Iacocca, the former CEO of Chrysler, he would appear in many of his company's commercials in the Mid-west and West. He sat on the board of UCLA's Anderson School of Business for 18 years and actually taught a course call Corporate Renewal, creating a Professorship Chair in Corporate Renewal.

Perhaps the most popular celebrity CEO was Richard Fuld, of bankrupted Lehman Brothers, who appeared in magazines and newspapers on a regular basis, and was called "Gorilla" Fuld. Over a period of 12 years, he converted Lehman into a financial high roller that earned more than $15 billion in profits from 2003 through 2007. In 2006, *Institutional Investor* magazine named Fuld America's top chief executive. The "gorilla" nickname was given because of his aggressiveness, which brought his company considerable success. However, success and accolades may have had two problematic consequences. It may have encouraged Mr. Fuld to take more and bigger risks, in particular, aggressively piling into high-risk mortgages, and to find it difficult to acknowledge that his company was in difficulty despite frequent warnings from leading analysts. For example, even as Lehman's stock dropped from

$85 to $22, Fuld was persuading investors that the bank remained on solid ground. After, 30 years with the company, he came to believe he was invincible and rejected reports that the bank was in serious trouble. Consequently, his failure to admit failure and sell at prices he rejected as too low led Lehman to the brink.

In September 2008, Lehman filed for bankruptcy. Lehman, "... did this to themselves with their own greed," according to A. M. Sabino, a St. John's University business professor who specializes in bankruptcy. "People just got crazy and in their endless obsession to squeeze every penny of profit, they forgot about the perils of taking on too much risk." Consequently 28,600 employees lost their jobs and life savings. Between 1993 and 2007, Fuld received about $466 million in compensation, according to executive pay research firm Equilar (Associated Press, 2008b).

Celebrity CEOs create a narcissistic climate in the executive suite where they feel invincible, and in order to convince their employees and others they are "special," they take risks.

In 2008 when AIG failed, the federal regulators seeking a new leader found a celebrity CEO. In September, 2008, the U.S. government gave AIG a loan of $85 billion to save it from doom. They installed Edward Liddy, the former CEO of Allstate. Liddy was credited with shaking up Allstate's rigid, conservative culture, and expanded it into new businesses like banking. Shortly before he became CEO in 1999, he told a roomful of the company's 200 top managers that a number of them would be gone within the year. About 6,400 Allstate agents sued the insurer the next year, after Mr. Liddy reclassified them as independent contractors, ending their health and pension benefits. The lawsuit eventually collapsed (Walsh, 2008). Liddy retired from Allstate in the spring of 2008, leaving the company on top of the list as the worse insurance company in America in a report published by American

Association for Justice (AAJ). According to DiCello (2008), the AAJ's report states, "there is no greater poster child for insurance industry greed than Allstate." He states, *"AAJ's investigation revealed that when Allstate policyholders file a claim, they are often offered an unreasonably low payment for their injuries. This offer is generated by a secretive claim-evaluation computer program called Colossus. Those who refuse the low offer usually get the "boxing gloves" treatment; an aggressive litigation strategy aimed at denying the insured's claim at any cost. Allstate implemented this unconscionable practice while Edward Liddy was at the helm from 1999 to 2006 when he retired, receiving more than $25 million in benefits. Liddy was paid almost $19 million in salary for 2006."* (DiCello, 2008)." For his efforts to terminate employees, take away benefits and enrich the bottom line, federal regulations appointed him CEO of AIG in September 2008.

What do these celebrity CEOs have in common? They enrich their shareholders and themselves during their tenure, they demand immediate results. Because of their focus on immediate profitability, they see no need to engage in long-term planning, especially if the planning requires negative profitability in the present for the purpose of long-term profitability. As a consequence, their employees suffer as stockholders gain. These CEOs see themselves as Thomas Wolf's "masters of the universe" and they are a one man show making critical decisions by themselves. They drive their employees and create aggressive, often hostile cultures where thoughtfulness or critical thought is outlawed in favor of a "ready, fire, aim" attitude. However, most significantly they do not "stick around" long enough to see the consequences of their actions. When they reach celebrity status they move from company to company welding the axe and making their shareholders happy. However, there is another consequence, returning to the comparison of the CEOs and the professional athlete. The comparison of CEO to the athlete breaks down when we consider the enormous responsibilities of trying to successfully lead a company, with the absence of an off-season, or sabbatical. This enormous effort often precipitates conflicts and impacts the support systems necessary to maintain a level constant level of ego functioning. This is why we witness celebrity CEOs breaking down, often in public displays of greed, corruption, and crime.

THE INTENSITY OF AMBITION AND THE LOSS OF FEELING

Given intense ambition and the absence of time to relax, contemplate or engage in the important work of self-reflection, the CEO's ego runs the risk of being overwhelmed. Thus, the ego cannot engage in the work of finer differentiation between vital and pleasurable acts and activities. It's as if war is waged against the pursuit of pleasure; now money and the pursuit of wealth step forth as the arbiter of psychic salvation. From a psychoanalytic perspective, the required endurance leads to a blunting of basic impulses and fights against the impulses, preoedipal, oedipal, sex and love, often extending to the point where the CEO denies fulfillment of basic physical needs such as sleep and bodily comfort.

Of critical importance is the inability to engage in the work of self-reflection or the work of introspection. A psychologist reported he hated the work of self-reflection. It was often painful, especially when the work required examination of parts of himself that he did not admire, and left him feeling humiliated. He said, "Why did I have to become a therapist, why didn't I choose an occupation that did not require that I look at myself?" He then laughed at himself and said, "I guess all occupations required self-reflection, perhaps some more than others." This is most apparent in those occupations that have the potential to greatly impact others; employees, families, and even entire communities. This would certainly include CEOs.

The work of self-reflection, introspection, or even what Irving Janus called "the work of worry," requires a degree of self-knowledge that consists of understanding traits or characteristics that the person knows can be troublesome. These traits may be repressed anger, self-humiliation, self-destruction, or a "blind spot" where the person is unable to think or see things clearly. Most psychoanalysts suggest that the work of self-reflection is a requirement when major decisions are being made. The fear is that the decision-maker may be motivated by some aspect of the personality beyond their awareness, and this will increase the risk that the decision will have a negative impact. A critical factor associated with the process of engaging in self-reflection is to take the time to allow oneself to feel and to examine the quality and intensity of these feelings. An example of the contrast between someone engaging in self-reflection and someone fearful of the process is in a report from a organizational development consultant. The consultant bought a car with no radio. He claimed he had no use for a radio. He used his time in his car to engage in self-reflection especially driving to and from consultations. One day a neighbor, hearing about his car with no radio, came to his house and asked why he did such a foolish thing. His neighbor had a BMW loaded with speakers, his house was wired with speakers and he even had outdoor speakers on his backyard deck. When asked, the consultant told the neighbor he uses time in the car to engage in self-reflection and the radio would be a distraction. The neighbor puzzled asked about self-reflection, the consultant replied, I listen to the voices in my head, at which point the neighbor took a step back and replied, "whoa." The neighbor could not listen to the voices in his head. He surrounded himself with "noise" to avoid the work of self-reflection. He did not or could not listen to his voices in his head. The neighbor may suffer from what Kets de Vries (1989) refers to as Alexithymia. This disorder is often used in clinical descriptions. It is not a mental disorder but is considered a personality trait, and some researchers even consider it a stable personality trait. It is marked by difficulty identifying and describing feelings. This person has a personality style that is super-adjusted to reality. The person works to adjust to the situation. However, for the CEO what we may be witnessing is not so much a personality trait but an interpersonal style closely associated with a combination of requirements of the role of being a CEO, and the status attained within the role, or perhaps a combination of the two. If we return to the neighbor who was appalled that the consultant listens to the voices in his head, he is a successful corporate attorney specializing in employee litigation. He defends his company against lawsuits brought by former employees who sue for wrongful termination. He was in an unhappy marriage and boasted he took a one-week vacation every year away from his wife and children to "have lots of great sex." In his job he focused exclusively on the facts, no emotions, and no doubt. The same was true with his annual sex vacation, a bodily experience devoid of emotionality.

Another way of looking at the CEO and why they cannot feel or cannot identify their feelings is to see them as being members of elite group of high social and economic status (SES) people. Therapists report that exceedingly high SES patients have a great deal of difficulty exhibiting an emotional life in therapy. Therapists claim that it is often difficult for high SES patients to show vulnerability. According to Krystal (1988), in psychotherapy they tend to recount trivial, chronologically ordered actions, reactions and events of daily life with monotonous detail. What we may be witnessing in the therapy office is a continuation of their life outside, where they are in complete control and are surrounded by dutiful employees who cater to them and if necessary prop up their status and ego with displays of praise and adoration. Dr. Karasu, a psychiatrist who treats successful Wall Street executives, states, "It's not the priority of people who are successful...to be intimate." "It is their priority to be aggressive. Many will not open themselves up to intimacy even in love affairs. They are slow to trust anyone-even the therapist" (Konigsberg, 2008).

In corporations, the expression of permitted emotions and moods are defined and embedded in the culture. This includes what types of emotions can be expressed and what is forbidden. Many of the expressed emotions are learned, including what type of mood one must display. CEOs like teenagers working at McDonald's, are required to smile, make eye contact and say, "Have a nice day." Learning these emotions can have a significant impact on ones outlook and even personality. Consider this example. A young Jamaican male was brought into a retail store manager's office and given a warning about his failure to greet customers and be friendly. He told the manager he grew up in a crime-ridden neighborhood where one never made eye contact with strangers and never talked to them. He was having a hard time at the retail store. With help and coaching, he began to overcome his fears and he began to enjoy greeting and helping customers (strangers). He became so good at it, he was asked to be a trainer for new employees in customer service. At one class he proudly told the story of his fear and how he overcame it. He said, "My mother was wrong, it's good to say hello to strangers, it's good to help people, and when I go back to the neighborhood and walk down the street I say hello to everybody and they smile back. It may be hard at first, but it will change your life." Of course, this is not the first shy and fearful person to learn new behavior. At work, over time the role will impact the occupant's personality and personality characteristics like self-perception, confidence, interpersonal style and an array of other characteristics and attitudes. Like this young man and the McDonald's server, CEOs learn the type of expressive mood to demonstrate, and the necessary consistency of mood which is an integral part of the role of being an executive.

This begs the question: What type of emotional life does the role of being a CEO in a corporation require? The emotional life may vary. People smile, show friendly faces and offer greetings. These are typically superficial. However, from time to time genuine feelings are expressed. Gabriel (1998) maintains that organizations are filled with a powerful emotional life. He says, just "scratch the surface" and you will see this life. But, in many corporations emotional life is stilted and defended against. One thing is certain: The CEO rarely if ever shows emotions associated with vulnerability, and is constantly on call to show optimism, determination, and confidence. This may be why many see narcissistic personality types as over-represented in the CEO population. They may they appear to be narcissistic types.

What we may be witnessing is not alexithymia, but defensive process to avoid mental thoughts and feelings that are unacceptable within the context of the executive role. For example, the emotional life of the corporation may reignite deep emotional attachment feelings, or longing for paternal or maternal connections, or perhaps fears and vulnerabilities. All of these emotions precipitate defenses that may include detachment and entitlement. But whatever type of emotion the CEO experiences, he/she is not allowed to show it. This is why CEOs prefer to see "coaches" rather than psychologists or psychiatrists. Many coaches report they feel like psychologists when they work with CEOs, and many professionals trained in mental health hide their profession and call themselves "coaches" in order to get work. What is the work of a coach? Stated simply they are used to shore up an executive's defenses. When a CEO is in a vulnerable situation, is frustrated or burned out and feels a sense of helplessness, the coach enters, not to diagnose or work through the underlying causes of the problem, but to instill a sense of confidence, to essentially tell the CEO how great he/she is, or what the CEO must do to stay on top.

CEOs come to believe that they must stifle their emotions if they are to survive. Consider this. A CEO was hired from outside the company. His first day on the job, he called a meeting with his VPs to introduce himself. On his way to the meeting he stopped at the bathroom and was using the urinal. The person next to him said, "You don't have to be here, you have your own private bathroom." He left the bathroom thinking what an idiot he was and how the word would spread and all would have a good laugh. He went into the meeting with his VPs no longer in a relaxed mood. He came across as distant and aloof, an image he did not want to communicate. On his way home he was distraught. His first day had been a disaster. The point is that the CEO could not show his emotional life. He had to construct defenses. Rather than be honest and laugh about his newness and lack of experience in his new role, he wound up using poorly constructed defenses. Fitting in and being successful requires joining in the corporation's emotional life and demonstrating the expected emotions and mood. This CEO knew from experience that he had to hide his emotions until he knew what type of emotions where permitted. The point here is when we see CEOs making decisions that negatively impact workers, families, and communities, like terminating employees, these CEOs may not blink an eye, that is show no emotion. It may be that the culture of the corporation requires this no show of emotion. However, this does not mean it doesn't impact the CEO. A therapist reported the following. "Many CEOs come to me depressed, their personal lives in ruins. Sometimes if I ask them, during your lifetime in this position how many employees have you terminated? One CEO thought for a minute and said, "Oh maybe 10,000-20,000." What this therapist is saying that while they can send thousands to a symbolic death and appear to think nothing of it, "Its business, not personal" it eats them up inside and overtime destroys their life.

Consequently, the CEO engages in behaviors to defend against emotions associated with their decisions, especially bad or regretful decisions. In Chapter 1, we identified a lengthy list of CEOs who received salary increases as they terminated their employees. These acts are not isolated cases. They seem to be more the rule then exception, and perhaps there is an explanation for this troubling behavior.

TERMINATE EMPLOYEES AND GET A RAISE- TAKING BAD MANAGEMENT TO NEW HEIGHTS

What are the attitudes and feelings that prevail in the executive constellation of the modern corporation? We can begin to understand this by looking at the behaviors of CEOs and their underlying motivations.

The Corporate Library (2006) studied 11 major corporations, and found that over a five-year period the CEOs gained $865 million in compensation while the corporations they led had an aggregate loss of $640 billion in shareholder value. Companies included were- AT&T, Hewlett-Packard, Home Depot, Lucent Technologies, Merck, Pfizer, Safeway, Procter and Gamble, Time Warner, Verizon and Wal-Mart. Over a period from 2005 to 2010 these companies collectively terminated over 90,000 employees. We suggest that since 2007, over half of all corporations that lost money or terminated employees or did both- gave their CEOs raises and/or bonuses.

Consider this. In the early 1980s we witnessed two significant changes in attitudes and values among those who ran America's major corporations. Terminations moved from becoming a decision of "last resort" to a decision of "first resort" (Kochan, 2006), and at the same time CEO pay packages began to dramatically increase. In agreement Hickok, (2008) maintains that during the period between 1980 and 1995 record layoffs occurred. For example, during 1980s layoffs accounted for 9 percent of the adult population in the U.S. At the same time senior executive salaries increased more than 1,000 times.

Rennie (2006) confirms this phenomenon. She compared CEOs who terminated employees and those who did not. She discovered CEOs who terminated employees obtained greater increases in compensation then those who did not terminate employees. She studied 229 firms that terminated employees at least once between 1993 and 1999, and found that in the year after layoffs occurred CEOs of these firms received 22.8 percent more in total pay than CEOs of firms that did not have layoffs. Rennie (2006) also discovered that the year layoffs occurred CEOs of layoff firms received 19.6 percent more stock-based compensation than CEOs of non-layoff firms. This stock-based enrichment increased significantly over the years following layoffs. One year after layoffs, CEOs of firms that terminated employees received 42.6 percent more stock-based compensation than CEOs of non-layoff firms. Two years after layoffs, that percentage rose to only 44.9, but jumped to 77.4 percent after three years. Research by the Policy Studies Institute confirms this, suggesting in 1996, the CEOs who laid off between 2,800 and 49,000 employees received an average salary increase of 67 percent (Leondar-Wright & Cavanaugh, 1997). The average increase for all CEOs in 1996 was 39 percent (the average increase for all workers was 3 percent). They identified the *Downsizer Dozen* those CEOs who gained the most from the pain of terminating their own employees.

HIGHLIGHTS FROM THE DOWNSIZER DOZEN

- American Express Company announced the termination of 3,300 employees in 1997. CEO at the time, Harvey Golub earned 229 percent increase in his take-home pay over 1996, including $27 million in options gains. His annual compensation of $33.2 million equals the total annual pay of 1,500 employees earning the average 1997 weekly wage of $424.

- Eastman Kodak terminated over 20,100 workers in 1997. They have made additional lay-off announcements in 1998. CEO George Fisher didn't get a bonus in 1997, but he exercised stock option gains worth $8.7 million, increasing his total 1997 compensation by 96 percent. Fisher's total compensation of $10.7 million is equal to the pay of 487 average U.S. workers.

- International Paper Company announced plans to terminate 9,215 employees in 1997. They rewarded their CEO John T. Dillon with a 140 percent increase in salary and bonuses.

- Barbie-maker Mattel announced over 3,174 terminations. CEO Jill Barad received a 29 percent increase in salary and bonuses from 1996, and her $9.1 million in long-term compensation gave her a 126 percent total pay hike. Robert Eckert, who took over for Barad, will continue terminations and outsourcing to China and in 2010 he received a salary increase to $11.4 million.

The 30 US corporations with the most lay-offs in 1997 eliminated a total of 169,484 jobs. Additional companies include: Boeing (12,000), Citicorp (9,000) and Nationsbank (6,450).

In 2008 America entered an economic recession, with some referring to it as the worse since the Great Depression and 1.9 million Americans lost their jobs. However, this did not stop CEOs from lining their pockets. According to Trivedi (2008) who studied 24 corporations that reduced their workforce in 2008, he found that only three of the 24 CEOs took a pay cut. H. Lawrence Culp, CEO of Danaher, has been terminating thousands of employees since 2008, and in 2009 he was the highest paid executive in the Forbes 500 CEO compensation rankings at $141,360,000. His CEO/Average-Pay Multiple was 4,411 times the average employee (DeFeo, 2010).

A study by the Institute for Policy Studies (2010) found that the CEOs who terminated the most employees during the recession are also the CEOs who took home the biggest pay checks. They found that the CEOs of the 50 U.S. firms that slashed the most jobs between November 2008 and April 2010 took in 42 percent more than the average CEO at an S&P 500 firm. They also found that 36 of the 50 layoff leaders "announced their mass layoffs at a time of positive earnings reports," suggesting a trend of "squeezing workers to boost profits and maintain high CEO pay." It's a shift in attitude where CEOs adopt the language and image learned in B-Schools and their textbooks to justify their compensation increases. Consider this: As most CEOs in 2010 adopted the language of "cost cutting," almost a euphemism for job terminations, in that same year the average CEO compensation increase was 27 percent. In the same year millions of employees lost their jobs, and the average employee compensation increase was a little over 2 percent. Connected to this is the "tough guy, macho" image and behavior that is expected and is part of the role of being a modern CEO. It is as if within the culture of CEOs, giving in or taking a pay cut is a sign of weakness. CEOs in the financial meltdown, watching stocks dropping and companies losing millions if not billions, responded with toughness. Also there are some cynics who say there is an unwritten rule among CEOs that one is not allowed entry into the circle (country club) of high-powered executives unless one demonstrates this type of macho behavior, and the best way to do it is to terminate employees while demanding greater compensation.

Look at the 10 "highest-paid CEO layoff (cost cutting) leaders" ranked in 2009:

1. Ivan Seidenberg, CEO, Verizon Total Compensation 2009: $17,485,796

2. Announced Annual Layoffs (11/1/08-4/1/10): 21,308

3. Louis Chenevert, CEO, United Technologies. Total Compensation 2009: $17,897,666, 2010 $24 million

4. Announced Annual Layoffs (11/1/08-4/1/10): 13,290

5. Alan Mulally, CEO, Ford. Total Compensation 2009: $17,916,654

6. Announced Annual Layoffs (11/1/08-4/1/10): 4,700

7. Michael Duke, CEO, Wal-Mart. Total Compensation 2009: $19,234,269

8. Announced Annual Layoffs (11/1/08-4/1/10): 13,350

9. Randall Stephenson, CEO, AT&T. Total Compensation 2009: $20,244,312

10. Announced Annual Layoffs (11/1/08-4/1/10): 12,300

11. Sam Palmisano, CEO, IBM. Total Compensation 2009: $21,159,289

12. Announced Annual Layoffs (11/1/08-4/1/10): 7,800

13. Roger Iger, CEO, Disney. Total Compensation 2009: $$21,578,471

14. Announced Annual Layoffs (11/1/08-4/1/10): 3,400

15. Michael Hurd, CEO, HP. Total Compensation 2009: $24,201,448

16. Announced Annual Layoffs (11/1/08-4/1/10): 6,400 (A sex scandal and abusive expense reporting led to a $40 million Golden Boot)

17. William Weldon, CEO, Johnson and Johnson. Total Compensation 2009: $25,569,844

18. Announced Annual Layoffs (11/1/08-4/1/10): 8,900

19. Fred Hassan, CEO, Schering-Plough. Total Compensation 2009: $49,653,063

20. Announced Annual Layoffs (11/1/08-4/1/10): 16,000*

21. *Includes all layoffs announced by the firm resulting from merger between Schering-Plough and Merck

This book would be incomplete if we failed to provide a deeper psychological understand of the motivation and the need CEOs have to terminate their employees and receive handsome increases in compensation.

Consequently, the next three chapters will do just that. Each chapter will offer and explanation: (1) Guilt and entitlement, (2) Depersonalization, and (3) Narcissism.

CHAPTER 8

The Power of Guilt: Entitlement, a Defense Against the Experience of Guilt and Shame

"Are we going to once again be a community of people who feel obligated to take care of one another, or are we going to continue as a collection of individuals, each one increasingly concerned only with his/her well-being?" (Uchitelle, 2003, p.205)

The classical psychological position maintains that if a CEO must terminate employees, he/she would experience guilt. Furthermore, when experiencing guilt, they would seek resolution or reparations. Therefore, we would expect that a CEO would attempt to resolve guilt by accepting an unjust distribution of income position and would reduce the income gap they helped create. But this does not occur. The opposite occurs. Why?

Consider this case. A middle-aged executive was recruited to become the CEO of a medium-size company. For the first 8 months, he flew by private jet several hundred miles each weekend to be with his family. He quickly discovered that he needed to devote more time to work on weekends, and he demanded that his family relocate to be near the office. It was their third move in seven years. His two teenage children, feeling the absence of an opportunity to settle in and make friends, began to act out rage. He and his family had a feeble social structure; no friends, relatives far away, and both he and his wife had grown distant and angry.

Increasingly, he tried to use work as a refuge. However, it became increasingly difficult to use work to defend against guilt and paranoid ideations, and he became an angry person. His anger was a defense, and he would fly into bouts of rage when feeling guilt or fear. Entering his new position from the outside, he joined a company that had a tight-knit culture and two powerful VPs who made no secret of their angry feelings about being passed over for the CEO position. They clearly disliked the new CEO, "the outsider". The CEO found no social structure at work, and it became a fearful place. After months of negotiating with the Board, he convinced members that the two VPs were blocking his ability to bring change and he received permission to fire them. After firing the VPs, he then renegotiated his contract and obtained a major salary increase with millions in stock options for himself. He was now in control. Or was he? The firing of the VPs precipitated guilt: he attempted in vain to defend against the guilt feelings by renegotiating his contract. The millions he received reinforced the illusion that he was good, deserving and entitled. But the new wealth on top of the firings created a new set of feelings: shame. However, these feelings of shame lay deeper in his unconscious, beyond his awareness. He struggled to communicate to others, his wife and co-workers that he was OK and on top of things. He tried to convince himself that all he needed to do was throw himself into his work and he would feel potent, strong and admired by others.

Guilt and shame are closely connected. Lynd (1968) claims that guilt is usually specific and close to the surface of awareness and it involves specific acts done or not done. Guilt is about what one did. Shame is about the self, who one is, an identity. In addition, guilt involves feelings that one is strong: one is powerful enough to injure another, and one is also powerful enough to make amends. By contrast, shame feels like weakness. Guilt is a highly individualist emotion, reaffirming the centrality of the isolated person; shame is a social emotion, reaffirming the emotional interdependency of people.

The experience of shame is directly related to ones sense of self. By contrast, guilt is the thing done or not done. According to Lewis (1971), the difference between shame and guilt is found in how the person reports it. We say, "I am ashamed of myself." And we say "I am guilty of having done or not done something." We see that shame is about the self and is directly tied to one's identity. It's connected to the imagery of who ones is and who one is in the eyes of the other. Shame involves the experience of the other, and the other is important in the eyes of the CEO. It may be colleagues at work, those the CEO mentored, stockholders, or one's board of directors. Or it may be the CEOs friends at the club. This is why CEOs are exceedingly vulnerable to the experience of shame. In these communities there is no forgiveness, no unconditional love. They face the real potential of being rejected and kicked, out leaving them alone and filled with shame. A study by Wright, O'Leary and Balkin (1989), examined the relationship between shame, guilt, narcissism and depression. They discovered that shame is a more powerful contributor to both narcissism and depression than guilt. They maintain that unconscious shame plays an important role in narcissism in men and depression in women.

NEVER APOLOGIZE: DEALING WITH GUILT AND SHAME AMONG CEOS

In March, 2008, Alan Schwartz, CEO of Bear Sterns was interviewed on CNBC, he said "Bear Sterns' balance sheet, liquidity and capital remain strong." Two days later the corporation effectively went bankrupt. He has not apologized. CEOs lie, exaggerate, and twist the truth, not only to the public, but to their boards, their employees and their customers. Consider the most often used statements CEOs make, a list compiled by Guy Kawasaki, (2006). These comments are often made without any thought given to accuracy or truth.

1. **"Working together, we've established our goals."** In other words, these are the goals that the CEO decided will make him look good. Few managers believe that these goals are doable, and yet they are the ones who are going to have to accomplish them. But that's what working together means: the CEO decides, and the workers do.

2. **"It's like a startup around here."** This could mean that the place lacks adult supervision; capital is running out; the product is behind schedule; investors have given up, and employees are paid below market rates. Sure, it could alternatively mean that the company is energized, entrepreneurial, making meaning, and kicking butt, but just be sure to double check.

3. **"Your project will be a skunk works reporting directly to me."** This means that no one else at the management level buys into the idea. The CEO might protect you—as this lie implies. Or, you may be fighting for your life against the naysayers when the CEO moves on to the next brilliant idea *du jour*.

4. **"I wanted to do this, but the board wouldn't let me."** This is a cop-out. A good CEO tells the board what she wants to do. She doesn't seek permission—forgiveness maybe, but never permission. So this statement means one of two things: the CEO didn't really try her best to get something approved or the board is losing confidence in the CEO.

5. **"I expect you to figure this out."** This is a loaded, supposed backhanded compliment. It's supposed to mean, "I have such confidence in you that I know you can do this." Sometimes it does mean this. Most times, though, it means that the CEO has no clue and is praying that you can save his butt.

6. **"Our sales pipeline looks good."** This means that the vice president of sales leaned on the regional sales manager who leaned on the regional sales rep to pump up the forecast because the CEO doesn't want to look bad to the board of directors.

7. **"We will be profitable soon."** After leaning on the sales organization and it "came through with a great pipeline," the CEO could then "reliably" predict profitability. He never did check with the CFO, though. If the company isn't profitable, then it's the fault of the vice president of sales or CFO anyway.

8. **"The stock price is not important; what's important is building a great company."** There are handfuls of visionary CEOs who mean this when they say it. However, you don't work for one of them. If one could get an honest answer out of CEOs, most would tell you that they'd rather have a rising stock price than a great company. Very few have the courage to build a great company and trust that a rising stock price is a natural outcome of this accomplishment.

9. **"I've never worked with a better group of people."** The career limiting comeback to this is, "Well, I have—starting at the top." This can be a legitimate morale boosting statement when it is infrequently made. However, if a CEO spouts this off more than once every five to 10 years, and you know there are clearly bozos on the team (often protected by the CEO), then you know that he's playing you.

10. **"I'm open to new ideas."** The CEO must have recently read a book by a management guru. She's probably open to new ideas from the consultants that she hired at $10,000 a day. Maybe she read a new idea in a blog, God help us. The relevant question is whether she's open to new ideas from the rank-and-file employees who really know how to fix the company.

11. **"I want to hear the truth; I don't want yes-men around me."** Maybe this is the truth: he doesn't want yes men around—he wants yes women. But I doubt it. It could be that he's so arrogant that he believes that he's always right so there's nothing to disagree with. But I doubt that too. The most likely situation is that he's just lying, and he wants people to always agree with him.

12. **"I will gladly step aside when the time comes."** Sure, with a $10 million severance package, who wouldn't be glad to step aside?

13. **"This is how we did it at (name of previous company he was fired from), and it worked."** And that's why the company let him go. And that's why the employees at the previous company rejoiced when the news spread. And, unfortunately, that's why the directors of this company hired him: because he was a senior-level packaged goods guy who was available, and the board thought that your tech products should be sold like laundry detergent.

14. **"I don't need to understand all that whiz-bang stuff to be a good CEO."** Absolutely. Your customers aren't that smart. Neither are your employees, vendors, and partners. The CEO just needs to stand there: tall, white, and gray haired, and let everyone kisses his ring.

15. **"I don't need to rehearse my speech."** This is because he's not to going to gauge audience reaction since his limo is waiting to whisk him away. He'll simply ask his handlers, Trixie and Biff, how they think he did. And they will tell him that the emperor has very fine clothes indeed.

16. **"We are a customer-focused'.** If only the CEO had appended two additional words: "this quarter." Because next quarter the company will be an innovation-driven company. And the quarter after that a Six Sigma driven company.

WE CAN ADD A FEW MORE

17. **What we have here is a "world class" team.** This is frequently used to describe the CEO's management team or some other team in the organization that may need a boost.

18. **"We have some 'low hanging fruit' with this action plan."** This is a term used to describe the easy part of the work. No one talks about the "high hanging fruit" Managers discuss these "low hanging fruit" as opportunities with a sense of urgency when promoting their plans. It's as if you don't pick the fruit quickly it will fall from the tree and lie on the ground and rot, therefore act quickly.

19. **"We have a great team."** Maybe the team has accomplished something and is getting verbal praise. However, most CEOs do not know what a great team is and have never been on a great team, because at the base of every team is a powerful sense of trust. They most often work on teams surrounded by "yes" people

20. **"I expect that most of you will be working in stretch assignments where you will learn new skills."** The CEO

tells this to survivors after mass layoffs. It means that the survivors will do the jobs of the laid off employees and work 8 to 8.

21. **"We are now a 24/7 company."** Given the global economy the CEO expects all employees to be working around the clock, but it is also a way to once again get the survivors to do the work of those laid off. This was actually stated by the CEO of UBS six months before he announced plans to terminate 8,700 employees before the end of 2010. Those who remained got a brand new BlackBerry.

Why do they lie and say things to their employees that will not only be unbelievable, but will produce cynicism?

It's because within the culture of executives and especially among CEOs, there is continuous worry and even obsession with their image. They have a profound need to put themselves in a favorable light and they hire people; coaches, public relations, etc., to make certain their image is not tarnished. CEOs will not accept blame and make major efforts to avoid embarrassment, shame, or "loss of face." "Losing face" is from a Chinese phrase for losing one's dignity before others. "Tiu lien" translates into "to lose face." This is a powerful cultural phenomenon.

"Losing face" is a cultural artifact that is pervasive in Asian cultures. When one suffers an indignity one is required to make amends. This is especially apparent among Japanese executives who frequently cut their own pay as punishment for their company's bad performance or wrongdoing. For example, Elpida Memory, a Japanese computer chip maker suffered a net loss of 46 percent in September 2008. Elpida's CEO, Yukio Sakamoto, would accept no salary in November and December of 2008, and would reduce his salary by at least half until the company started making a profit. Mr. Sakamoto, experienced "loss of face" in front of his workers. The experience of shame motivated him to make amends, to seek public punishment. Not to do so would increase the experience of shame, that is, to continue to reap rewards would increase his loss of face and precipitate considerable anger and backlash among employees.

This contrasts sharply with American CEOs who receive multimillion dollar severance packages and salary increases as their corporations fail. American CEOs do not accept blame even when they are sent to jail for crimes. They find fault elsewhere, and defend against any accusations that they are at fault. For example, AIG, near bankruptcy in September 2008, needed a $85 billion bailout from the federal government. AIG's ex-CEOs, Robert Willumstad and Martin Sullivan, refused to accept responsibility, and blamed accounting rules and market conditions for the problems that led to the crisis. In another example, Treasury Sectary Henry Paulson, who is largely responsible for doling out $700 billion during the fall 2008 Wall Street meltdown and recession, initially wanted to offer loans to banks and financial corporations that were suffering from bad home mortgage loans under a bill he demanded that Congress pass in September 2008. In November, a month later, he demanded that the government change course and offer loans to ease credit pressure on consumer credit by making direct investments and bailouts to banks and by giving money to non-bank lenders like credit card companies and student loan and auto-financing companies. He said, "When we went to Congress, (buying) liquid assets looked like the way to go. But the situation worsened, the facts changed." He went on," I will never apologize for changing a strategy or an approach if the facts change." Paulson never disclosed what facts had changed, and he would not admit he was just wrong, or that his initial plan was a mistake.

Executives can not admit they may have misread the situation, acted too rash, or heaven forbid, were wrong. Executives adopt an unwritten rule, "never apologize and never explain." The closest they come to accepting blame is to offer a detached apology like "I'm sorry it happened" or "I have deep regret..." or "I'm sorry if I offended you." You will rarely hear a CEO say, "I'm sorry I did it." One could say American executives "show no shame." Executives believe that to apologize or accept responsibility is a sign of weakness. They create the impression they are above ordinary laws or social norms and they are indeed privileged.

We maintain that the same psychological processes are at play when a CEO shows no shame and when they reward themselves and deny responsibility as they terminate employees or the company becomes unprofitable. They defend themselves and utilize the defenses of denial and projection. It is not their fault (denial), it is those out there; the rules or regulations, laws, unions, employees and some CEOs have even blamed their customers (projection).

When CEOs fail, their reaction is a function of the interplay of their narcissist characterological style within the context of the corporate culture that cannot accept personal failure. In most corporate cultures, "failure is not an option." What does this often-used phrase mean? It means personal failure does not exist, it is not allowed to exist, one does not discuss it, and it is not an option as one strives toward perfection. Consider the long climb up the corporate ladder. Can one make it to the pinnacle and experience failure? Perhaps, but if one fails or admits they fail and continuously moves up, this is indeed rare. One could never move up the ladder by behaving like CEO Sakamoto. American CEOs would never lose face, and they can never experience shame (personal failure). Instead they hide their failure, blame others and work hard to deny it was their fault. The experience of guilt is OK. In this sense guilt is a collective experience where a CEO can say "I feel sorry for your pain and suffering" or "I am sorry things did not work out."

but never say "I am sorry I did this to you." This is close to the experience of shame, and this need to avoid shame is so great that CEOs will prove to themselves and others around them that they not only had anything to do with the failure, but they too are victims of a series of identifiable forces, or unforeseen events. Then they carry this defensive need further, by giving themselves a reward. This can be considered a type of reaction formation, a defense where the person experiencing the wrath of "badness" would come to the conclusion that he/she is "good" and then identify with the victims by announcing that they feel their pain, a common phrase of Bill Clinton.

When in a potential or embarrassing situation associated with terminating employees, it will precipitate a reaction where CEOs will convince themselves, as well as others within the executive constellation that they are suffering as well and they are sharing the pain of those who lost their jobs, but also that they have cut costs and made their stockholders some money: that they had to do it and it was the toughest decision they ever had to make and therefore they are indeed good, exceptional, powerful, and deserving of a reward.

YOU LOSE-I WIN

As we have claimed, guilt is also associated with the experience of doing something to another and shame is associated with the experience that "I am no good." Czander (1993) suggests guilt is a pervasive experience in the corporate world. If we consider the nature of competition, the pyramid-shaped structure, and secretive and harmful evaluation systems which imply that if one succeeds, it is because someone else has failed. This "I win-you lose" attitude is accepted practice. The CEO who has spent years in this type of competition will carry this attitude into the executive suite and continue it with terminations (you lose) and hefty salary increases (I win). It is as if the experience of guilt is tolerated, but the experience of shame is intolerable and not allowed. But why? Because guilt is associated with power and us associated with the experience that "I have the power to do something to you. I have power to hurt you, I am strong and you are weak." Like bullying, hurting someone confirms the experience that one is bigger, stronger and more powerful.

One would expect a CEO to accept the reality of failure and guilt if he/she had to terminate employees. But as we maintain, public knowledge of failure cannot occur because it is associated with shame. It's as if the CEO is immune to the experience of shame but not guilt. The CEO can report that they feel bad for their terminated employees and their families and will make public announcements, but the CEO, surrounded by like-minded executives, will join in defending against the experience of guilt. To say one feels bad is OK, but to announce publicly that he/she failed is taboo. To say one feels bad will bring forth a chorus of responses from executives, their colleagues that they are being "too hard on themselves," "it's not their fault" or they seek a scapegoat or someone or something to blame. There have even been situations where those who were terminated were forgiving and told the CEO that it was not their fault.

We can now understand the behavior of the newly hired CEO at the beginning of this chapter. He projected his guilt onto the VPs, and their symbolic killing allowed the CEO to unconsciously disavow some of his "bad" feelings. The VPs were a split-off part of the CEO's self that contained his "bad" rage at himself for crimes against his family and others. By projecting his rage into the VPs and claiming they were responsible for his failures and then terminating (killing) them allowed the CEO to be freed from guilt. The terminations freed the CEO to then feast and reinforce his wish to be the "successful CEO."

After the terminations and an increase in compensation he joined an exclusive country club where he would spend his weekends engaged in fundraisers, dinners, and social events designed to offer a sense of power and make reparations, to reduce guilt. His disgruntled wife joined a society that she considered "garish and showy." These activities served an important function for the CEO; they served as a showplace where he could validate his power and defend against the guilt and shame associated neglect of his family and the termination of his VPs. He further reinforced the wish to be the "successful CEO" by engaging in country club activities. Work, money, and the country club provided much needed narcissistic supplies. When feasting on narcissistic supplies, the CEO was elated, omnipotent, omniscient, handsome, sexy, adventurous, invincible, and irresistible. When in this excited state, he was particularly fond of meeting new people. He would remember everyone's name and conversations. When he was "on top," he was in a manic state; he was bubbly, generous, the life of the party

GREED AND VITALITY

The gratification associated with the act of greed and entitlement allowed the CEO to experience vitality. He was now the clean, handsome, successful boy of his mother's dreams, not the dirty, angry, revengeful kid who was disliked (those VPs). The question is, how? By linking greed with vitality. Vitality defined as being alive in the physical and psychical sense. But for the CEO, the vitality obtained from the money and the accoutrements it bought, as well as his celebrity status, was short-lived. The CEO shifted back and forth between the brooding, angry man flooded with guilt, and the happy, gratified CEO. His greed had to continue, it was a need, and like the obese person he had to continue to feed himself. The vitality was like a rush, an addiction, when he experienced the vitality it was as if he were whole, and omnipotent.

We see this inside and outside the corporation, where the CEO seeks celebrity status, and surrounds himself or herself with admiring people whose job it is to heap praise upon their "king" when they feel he/she needs it.

The newly appointed CEO described above, racked with guilt, worked very hard to avoid the other side of the coin, the failure associated with the inability to replenish. In the meantime the company suffered from the loss of the two experienced VPs. Sales dropped and turnover increased. He increased his hours, and terminated several hundred employees, and was pushing the board for a significant bonus. In the past two years he has worked to bring the company back to the level it was at when he joined. It is not clear if he will succeed. The only thing for certain is he will be a wealthy man.

We now see the function wealth provides. For this CEO, and other CEOs, who feel helpless, impotent and over-their heads in the face of often complex and multiple dangers, the more they need wealth. Wealth provides the feeling of power and success. This is the meaning of greed. Greed is a method to defend against angry, frustrated, bad, and destructive feelings that evolve under these conditions where they feel helpless and impotent. Paul Wachtel (2003), in his paper "Full Pockets, Empty Lives," agrees, and sees greed as a defense against fragile self-esteem. Reich (1960) sees a fragile self-esteem system, marked grandiose fantasies, inflated self-esteem, that shifts to bouts of helplessness, rage and anxiety when faced with threats. Do CEOs suffer from a real or potential loss of self-esteem? Given the nature of the work, constant pressure to succeed, their self-esteem is certainly under attack. While most people feel a sense of helplessness from time to time, the typical reaction is to feel depressed and seek help and support to overcome the emotional state. However, with this CEO population, the reaction to helplessness is a type of panic that motivates them to quickly extricate themselves from this experience. Consider this, a CEO came into treatment, and during the initial session he proudly announced that he was a proponent of "managing by walking around." Later on in treatment it became clear that during a typical workday, when he would experience a bout of helplessness, he would immediately bolt from his desk and take a walk around his company and greet his employees. The walks were his method of replenishing his self when he felt depleted, that is, when he experienced helplessness and impotence.

CEOs, who obtain wealth as they terminate their employees, do so as an act of replenishment to defend against the feelings of shame associated with failure. They also suffer from a type of paranoia typically associated with intense ambition, and compounded by feeling they are surrounded by angry people. An analysis of the famous quote from Gordon Gekko, a symbol of greed, in the movie "Wall Street" may help explain this somewhat problematic relationship- symbolically killing employees to accumulate wealth. In the movie, with the help of a young executive (Bud Fox), who has insider information about a company, Gekko plans to sell off this company and terminate many jobs, and make millions. Included in the terminations is Bud's father. A speech by Gekko may help explain the relationship between guilt and greed. Gekko says, "Greed is good, greed works, greed clarifies, cuts through and captures the essence of the evolutionary spirit." For Gekko, greed serves an important function, and like the executive described above, his feelings of "being on top" are continuously sustained through the fantasy that things will get better once enough wealth is accumulated. This fantasy serves a defensive function by protecting him from overwhelming guilt and the paranoia associated with the fear of loss and termination, a symbolic death. Consequently, the experience of dissatisfaction and helplessness is avoided, not in the sense of creativity and accomplishment, but by being driven to terminate others and accumulate wealth. According to Levine (2000), the end result of greed is not a gain in satisfaction, but as a method to avoid frustrations associated with feeling helpless. Gekko, like many CEOs, consumes, but is never filled. Like Gekko, they cannot engage in the finer differentiation between the needed, vital, or pleasurable acts. Gekko, surrounds himself with beauty, but cannot see it. All he sees is value. When showing off a work of art, Gekko states: "This painting here, I bought it 10 years ago for $60,000, I can sell it today for 600 ($600,000); the illusion has become real, and the more real it becomes, the more desperate they want it—capitalism at its finest." For Gekko the illusion is not the beauty in the painting, the illusion is himself as an admired, successful, and lovable man. For Gekko, this only becomes real when it's worth is articulated. His greed creates a rupture between the pursuit and consumption of the object, and the pleasure and satisfaction it is supposed to bring.

Gekko says, "… greed clarifies…" What is clarified is his view of himself as a success. Wealth and continuous involvement in attaining wealth keeps feeding this view of himself as admirable, handsome, and wealthy, and avoids the overwhelming experience of frustration which is unconscious guilt, shame, and fear. Gekko goes on to say, "…greed… captures the essence of the evolutionary spirit." According to Shefelman (2008), the essence that is captured is social Darwinism. Gekko has survived, he feels on top. An evolutionary winner, an oedipal winner, filled with a powerful sense of vitality. He feels special and entitled. He has gone out into the world and not only has survived, he is the winner, the boy Mother admires.

However, he fails, like many CEOs. The need to succeed is so great and the wish to accumulate wealth is so powerful and their need to be invincible so overwhelming that risk taking increases. Increased risk-taking is motivated by the unconscious need to end it all, to get out of the pathological race, to self destruct. Upon discovering of Gekko's plans to symbolically kill his father, Bud sets out to destroy Gekko.

Bud, unlike Gekko cannot defend against the guilt and shame with a heightened sense of entitlement. He needs to seek what may be considered a normal reaction, and he seeks reparations. Motivated by guilt and the wish to seek reparations an angry Bud destroys Gekko. It's as if Gekko knows the day will come. It's what all who have intense ambition fear, the end.

ENTITLEMENT AND EMPTINESS-A FALSE SELF WORLD

In another way of understanding greed, Klein and Riviere (1964) suggest that the act of entitlement associated with greed may be a response to the experience of an internal deadness, as the executive operates and succeeds in an impersonal and emotionally distant corporate world. This is referred to as a "False Self World." The concept of false self developed by Winnicott (1960), maintains that the personality structure of an individual may be built on a false self foundation-that is, a conformist self in which creativity, genuineness, and originality is sacrificed for security, image, and adoration. Overtime the executive comes to see career advancement as a game. They believe everyone plays the game, all the time (Simeon and Abugel, 2006). It is similar to a Machiavellian game, devoid of spontaneity and emotions and filled with calculations and strategy.

In the corporate world, the false-self personality organization is not always unwanted, that is, it may be useful. A certain amount of false-self organization is present in everyone, and is necessary for survival especially in the corporate world. Fromm (1955) sees this false self organization in the executive constellation where executives must hide vulnerabilities; continuously promote themselves, and put forth an image of being impressive, brilliant, and confident. To maintain this image is difficult and stressful work.

Consider this example. Several psychoanalysts were engaged in a program to help them move into the practice of organizational consulting. After several months of training, the work focused on the activities associated with advertising and practice building. The anxiety level in the group increased, and one analyst made everyone in the class laugh when he stated, "I know what we need to do, engage in the act of shameless self-promotion." Several of the psychoanalysts dropped out. They could not "market" themselves. The question that arises: Can one succeed in a chosen career without engaging in the work self-promotion? Writing about the tenure process Lang (2003) suggests that to obtain tenure requires self-promotion. This may be true in all professions, especially those high status professions like acting, or sitting in the corporate "cat-bird" seat.

THE COUNTRY CLUB

Another way of defending against guilt is through collective action. It's as if the CEO seeks others, typically fellow officers, to engage in these "acts of entitlement." If these "others" are not found in the organization, the CEO will find them outside the organization, typically the country club. Just as the executive constellation provides an important psychic function for the CEO so can the country club. According to Lochkar (1992), executives will use the country club to find others to confirm their feelings of entitlement and approval. This results in the creation of a "we/they" environment, where they can see themselves as the entitled, clean, handsome "goodfellers" and their employees as a "bothersome" group. Also, in the process they distance themselves from their employees.

Executives embrace entitlement, because it also protects against shameful feelings like feelings of vulnerability and longing. The need for emotional interdependency is defended against by the illusion of control that is associated with the accumulation of wealth. At the country club, or for that matter, being with "likeminded" executives creates a structure where they can give each other constant assurances that they are unique, talented, and entitled.

On the other hand, there are successful CEOs who demonstrate empathy and genuinely care about their employees' welfare. These CEOs have established relationships with their colleagues, and use the executive constellation to function as confidants, and to provide the necessary support and strength to function effectively. When these relationships are open and honest, they help protect the CEO from fearful paranoid ideations. When the executive constellation abandons the CEO, and does not offer support, then money and the symbols associated with wealth and power become important ways to regulate self-esteem. Thus, the weakened CEO is in a constant state of hunger; substituting money and status for intimacy and meaningful relationships.

Another way to understand greed and entitlement is to see the CEO who will use employees as a means to an end. This requires that the CEO see employees as objects, as a resource or capital investment. This allows CEO to distance themselves from feelings of guilt and shame as they terminate them. In these executive constellations feelings of guilt and shame are not permitted, the only feelings permitted are dread, anger, and hate. And they often use the defense of projection to disown these feelings. For example, when an executive was asked about outsourcing, he said, "I don't want to deal with these demanding, angry, self-righteous employees anymore. When I outsource they become a problem for someone else." These executives cannot feel empathy for their employees, they are objects and when they terminate them they may verbalize sadness, but not feel it. To feel empathy would precipitate overwhelming and intolerable feelings of guilt and shame. We now turn to the second factor that contributes to CEO greed, insensitivity and a desire to enrich themselves as they "downsize." This is depersonalization.

CHAPTER 9

Depersonalization: The Psychology of Entitlement

IBM does not to use the word "layoff" when they release employees. They believe it will personalize its victims. IBM uses the term "resource action". If you were to read the IBM dictionary, you would see that the company does not have employees, only resources. Everyone and everything is a resource.

We have established that entitlement serves two purposes: First, it reduces the experience of guilt associated with terminations and getting too much. Secondly, it is a way to escape the narcissistic injury associated with the fear of persecution and shame. However, entitlement serves a third purpose. It is a restorative defense against depersonalization. That is, entitlement means, "I will be real again".

The depersonalization process develops over a period of time as the CEO struggles to climb the corporate ladder and this process is also found within the culture of the executive suite.

First, when we are discussing depersonalization we are not referring to it in the clinical sense, or what is sometimes called chronic depersonalization. Also, we do not see it as a symptom that may occur in panic disorder, borderline personality disorder, and post-traumatic stress disorder (PTSD), acute stress disorder, or a dissociative disorder. What we are discussing is a depersonalization process that evolves over time, and may be associated with the requirements of a role, in this case the role of being a CEO.

There are two factors that contribute to depersonalization among executives; first it is the result of the continuous and intense demands placed on the CEO, and secondly, it is associated with termination of employees.

According to Simeon and Abugel (2006), "the symptom of depersonalization can occur in normal individuals under such circumstances as sleep deprivation, the use of certain anesthetics, experimental conditions in a laboratory (experiments involving weightlessness, for example), and emotionally stressful situations (such as taking an important academic examination or being in a traffic accident)." As discussed previously, CEOs experience significant stress, over long periods of time. According to Maslach, et. al., (1996) this type of stress is similar to burnout. They see burnout as a type of emotional exhaustion that can occur among individuals who work extensively with others under considerable time pressures. Furthermore, burnout is particularly relevant in individuals working in emotionally charged situations. Therefore, depersonalization evolves over time where executives, overworked and overstressed, no longer feel. They make calculated decisions devoid of feelings about those impacted by their decision, This is a form of executive distancing. In addition, Cameron, et. al. (1993) maintain that executives distance themselves to avoid criticism and blame.

Consider the following methods executives use to distance themselves from their actions. According to Rogers (2006), Radio Shack was planning to terminate many employees. They called their employees to a large meeting hall. Upon entry, they were given either a pink slip or a blue slip. Those receiving a pink slip went into one auditorium and were instructed about the termination process by an HR consultant. Those receiving a blue slip entered another auditorium to hear from the CEO about how the company was moving forward. The question is raised: How could the CEO discuss the future of the company in glowing terms to an audience of survivors, at the same time their colleagues were being symbolically killed in the room next to them? This can only be accomplished though distancing, which is further accomplished by using outsiders, consultants hired to send the terminated employees on their way. Consistent with the overwhelming number of CEOs who engage in the psychological process of distancing themselves from the pain they inflict, and feelings of failure, they also use their time in the catbird seat to fill their coffers. Julian Day, Radio Shack's CEO who entered in the summer of 2006, saw its stock decline from $35 a share to about $16 a share as he prepared to depart in May, 2011. He will depart with a compensation package of $24.4 million.

In another example, a small engineering firm developed this unique depersonalization process to terminate their engineers. On Monday morning, when arriving at work, if one found their personal belongings outside their office entrance in a cardboard box, it meant they were fired. They were expected to pick up the box and immediately depart. If they did not immediately depart, a security guard would be called. As expected Monday morning, arrival at work was particularly stressful. Employees would peer down the hall and breathe a sigh of relief if they saw no box. While the executive constellation employed this depersonalization process, it also had the effect of projecting their stress, anxiety and humiliation onto their employees. It was the employees who now contained the anxiety and humiliation every Monday morning. The executives established this structure to defend against anxiety, guilt and shame. Furthermore, if someone was "laid off," the decision was made on a 3:30 p.m. at the Friday HR meeting. The timing of this meeting ensured that lengthy discussions and emotionally charged conflicts would be minimized. The executives would wrap up their decisions within an hour so they could get a head start on the weekend.

These terminations symbolically resemble the powerful feelings of loss. It leaves a void, an emptiness where survivors are left angry, fearful and overwhelmed that they must carry the load of their departed colleagues.

PUNITIVE STRUCTURES: A WAY TO DEPERSONALIZE TERMINATIONS

To survive the rage of their employees and the powerful guilt associated with terminations, those who conduct the terminations, the executive constellation, develop a defensive structure where, according to Schwartz (1990), they collectively substitute the organization for the ego ideal. The corporation is psychically catapulted to the status of utopia, a place that is "all good." To carry out this functional fantasy, the executive constellation establishes a punitive structure to punish those who are seen in reality or fantasy as threats to this ideal. What evolves is an executive constellation that develops a type of punitive culture that corresponds to the personality of the executives. Also, entry into this executive culture requires members with a certain type of personality. In agreement Kellerman (1981) maintains that, "the most powerful affiliative element attracting any member to a group will depend upon the extent to which the group's punitive structure corresponds to the punitive ... structure in the personality of that particular member."

The punitive structure is developed in the corporation to contain the executive constellation's view of how to and how not to punish others, be they fellow employees, vendors, customers, competitors, nonbelievers, outsiders, etc. Kellerman (1981) describes three types of punitive structures:

Extrapunitive structures where the executive constellation seeks to fix blame and searches for scapegoats, or those who are considered dangerous outsiders. In the corporation these groups could be unions, competitors, employees or even departments that the executive constellation will publicly or privately blame. They could also be individuals, where the CEO will isolate an employee through demotion and then blame that employee for an array of problems.

Intrapunitive structures are where the executive constellation believes they are all powerful, creative, and brilliant and are a wonderful team. They look for no one to be blamed or punished because this constellation does not make mistakes. This group develops a powerful sense of cohesion as it seeks justice and uses self-righteousness as a type of "groupthink."

Impunitive structures occur where self-examination is at the core of the executive constellation's culture.

Consider the following example: An extrapunitive structure was apparent in the executive constellation of a retail company. The regional VP and his district managers would meet weekly and discuss sales and future events. Blame was projected onto the store managers who were constantly criticized at the executive meetings. On the average of once a month, a store manager would be terminated. They were the classic scapegoats. The problems were always "out there," and never in the group. When a consultant was called in by an executive VP from the home office, the group immediately established defenses. The group refused to discuss any internal issues. The consultant was seen as a threat because he represented self-examination (impunitive structure). This was experienced as a threat to the executive constellation. For anyone to be affectively expressive, or engage in self-reflection, precipitated conflict. The executive constellation fused its extrapunitive structure with an intrapunitive structure. The more threatened, the more they intensified a macho/tough guy culture and worked hard to create an image of "New York tough guys." When they would meet with executive teams from other parts of the country, they would aggressively put forth this image of what they called "street smart managers". Needless to say, candidates were selected to join this "elite team" based on having these extrapunitive characteristics. Over a period of time this New York team began to dress the same, had frequent parties and even vacationed together. They bonded together with such strength that they forced out two VPs who did not fit the "image". When a third VP entered, sensing that he was next, he fired half the team and broke their bond. Still feeling a threat, he proceeded to terminate the entire team.

Many executive teams vacillate back and forth between extrapunitive and intrapunitive structures. It is often a function of the behavior of the CEO, who leads the executive team in one direction, as opposed to another. However, the team can also recruit a new member who will be unconsciously called upon to move the team to a new structure. An example of this occurred at a college that was having difficulty with their student population. The executive team at a university brought in a consultant to give a keynote address at their annual retreat for administrators. The consultant proceeded to make the executive team feel good by blaming all their woes on students and faculty. Shortly after the event, the president of the college hired the consultant as a dean. At a "meet the new dean" event the dean explained why he had chosen to join the college and said it was because of the superb administration that he called "World Class." The executive constellation moved from an extrapunitive structure to intrapunitive.

Extra and intra-punitive executive structures present an interesting way to understand problematic executive constellations where depersonalized entitlement is apparent. These are seductive structures. They are extraordinarily cohesive, they promote a rich grandiose fantasy life, and because of this, they can be a compelling and attractive. Being a member of this type of executive team can validate one's identity or even create an identity.

In extrapunitive structures, consider the following example of how a management constellation made excessive use of projective identification both within the team and without. The management team fostered a collusive system between junior managers and senior managers. The senior members split off their self-doubts and incompetence, and projected these feelings onto the juniors. Now, the junior members could be seen as less experienced and incompetent, and the senior members could hold onto the illusion that they were brilliant and wise. Along with this attitude, the executives now were "entitled." They deserved more. In turn, the junior members split off and projected their competent and brilliant self's onto the seniors. This allowed the junior members to avoid responsibility, anxiety and failure. The senior members were now free to engage in performance reviews of the junior members and punish those who became too "uppity," that is, showed competence. For the junior members, they could hide behind their lower status. All they needed to do was make the senior executives feel competent and from time to time show incompetence.

THE ILLUSION OF SUCCESS AND ENTITLEMENT

It's the creation of these illusions that feed the CEO, and one of these illusions is "I'm entitled." Chasseguet-Smirgel (1985) states the illusion of entitlement has greater relevancy for group cohesion. Freud

(1921) argued that the authority of the group, in this case the executive constellation, can allow forbidden greed. This occurs when the executive constellation creates an illusion of their self-importance and power. Obtaining large amounts of money, terminating employees, and engaging in immoral acts can reinforce this illusion. The internal controls like guilt is lost and conscience are externalized: control is "out there," and an attitude prevails in the executive suite that greed is permitted, and no one will be punished because they are too brilliant, too perfect, too important, and have too many friends in high places to be punished by any authority. Furthermore, it is they, the executive team that does the punishing.

Now we can see the motivation to engage in high-risk situations. It is the high-risk situation where the executives celebrate their prowess. These situations are antidotes to the fear of failure. Consider what occurred in September 2008 when Wall Street was collapsing and thousands of executives were losing their jobs, and restaurants, retail and limousine services were all noticeably empty except for one industry, the strip clubs. According to Arango and Creswell (2008), during this period the strip clubs were filled with stock brokers, bankers and foreign businessmen. At these clubs, executives could continue to flaunt their power, paying thousands of dollars for champagne in private rooms. As Wall Street looses billions, and executives experience fear and humiliation, they flock to the clubs where they can maintain the illusion of superiority. They do this in the manner that is consistent with depersonalization, anonymity, no emotional attachment, or empathy. Like the lawyer who takes his sex vacation to engage in anonymous sex. Also, in a remarkable way this activity offers the vitality the executive needs to experience at work. He may engage in high-risk activity and run a risk of destroying things; his company, investments of clients, his marriage and family. The risk is the high. The greater the risk the greater the experience of vitality.

Entitlement can be embedded in the culture of executive constellation. When this occur, executives either direct blame outward for their predicament, or engage in self idealization, or both. We have established that when entitlement becomes the primary task it brings about a heightened sense of trust and security within the constellation group. In an extrapunitive structure, they get more by pushing against the larger corporate culture and unconsciously creating a "we-they" climate. In most of these cases, the executive constellation forms a tight bond centered on a self-righteous delusion that they are collectively entitled, they shift from an extrapunitive structure to an intrapunitive structure.

In the intrapunitive structure, they deserve more. Again, getting more is symbolic. It could be love, admiration, blessings, or buying a stripper a $500 class of champagne.

Following Klein (1957), entitlement becomes a way of escaping injustice. That is, entitlement allows one to escape persecutory feelings, and defend against internal fears. This is accomplished by creating external conflict, that is, externalizing fears. Seven brief cases will illustrate this. In first six cases, executive constellations, in a chronic state of fear, utilize the defense of depersonalized entitlement by exhibiting appalling greed and a gross loss of empathy. In the seventh case, a CEO demonstrates guilt, shame and empathy, only to be symbolically killed by his executive constellation.

Case 1: There is no better example of a culture of entitlement then the behavior of Wall Street at bonus time in January 2009. The country was in a financial crisis, millions of employees lost their jobs, and banks and brokerage houses lost billions and needed government bailouts. However, according to White (2009) these troubled financial institutions (lost $35 billion in 2008), awash in "red ink," gave out an estimated $18.4 billion in bonuses, the sixth largest bonus compensation on record. A young broker discussing the stock market wanted everyone to know why he needed a bonus. He said, "We need bonuses, it would be smart for the government to give us the bonus money directly. If we don't get bonuses we will quit and the country will fall apart." Such hubris. While eight out of 10 Wall Street employees got bonuses, 46 percent thought they deserved more (White, 2009).

Case 2: Two weeks before Christmas, the executive constellation of a large technology firm terminated 20,000 employees. The CEO and his close circle of executives were so fearful they asked the police to close a nearby gun shop. On the day before Christmas, the CEO gave himself and his executive constellation a handsome Christmas bonus. Here, we see the connection persecution and entitlement. The executives feared retaliation, that the entire executive constellation would be shot by angry employees, (persecution). For this group the money was a symbolic protector against the fear associated with harm. Their feelings of entitlement were an attempt to get out of the CEO's predicament that they were indeed guilty, and should be punished for sending off 20,000 employees. The entitlement is also supported by the idea that they struggled with difficult decisions worked long hours, and asked their families to make significant sacrifices during the holiday season. This is not an isolated case. Many CEOs seek tightened security after terminating employees.

(See Appendix S for a more complete list of these CEOs.)

Case 3: In 2006, Paul Otellini, CEO of the Intel Corporation, terminated 10,500 employees but received a 15 percent salary boost, bringing his compensation to $6.18 million (Robertson, 2007). In 2007, Otellini's pay almost doubled, to $12.1 million. In 2008 he imposed a salary freeze for his employees and his compensation increased to $12.4 million. In 2009 he shut four plants and terminated 6,000 employees, and in 2010 Otellini received an 8 percent raise from 2009, a pay package worth $15.5 million, which included a bonus of $6.8 million. These are not isolated instances.

Case 4: On October 24, 2007 Merrill Lynch announced a write-down of $8.4 billion (New York Times, 11/4/07). Six days later its CEO, E. Stanley O'Neal, was fired. He was given $161.5 million in stock options and retirement benefits on top of his $70 million annual salary. Then John Thain took over the top spot. He received more than $83 million in 2007, which included a $15 million bonus, while shareholder return dropped 41 percent, and 4,000 employees were terminated. On January 1, 2009, on the verge of bankruptcy, Merrill Lynch was purchased by Bank of America for $50 billion. Thain could receive a payout of $9.7 million if he stays with the combined company (Graybow, 2008). Merrill Lynch expects to terminate 30,000 employees in 2009. Three days before Bank of America was to purchase Merrill Lynch to save it from bankruptcy, Thain gave out $3 billion to $4 billion in bonuses to his executives. This was done despite a fourth quarter loss of $21.5 billion (Giannone, 2009). Knowing that his new boss at Bank of America would forbid bonuses under such dire conditions, Thain quickly gave out the bonus payments in December, just before the purchase. Bonus payouts are generally given out in January. Shortly after this debacle, reports leaked that Thain had spent $1.2 million to redecorate his office, with furnishings including an $87,000 rug and $68,000 credenza (Creswell and Story, 2009). In a short period of time Thain went from a major Wall Street player with an impeccable reputation to a man with questionable judgment. On January 24, 2009, Ken Lewis, CEO of Bank of America, Thain's new boss, fired him. In 2008 as the company lost billions almost 700 Merrill Lynch employees each obtained a bonus for more than a million dollars while terminating 35,000 employees. In March 2009, it was discovered that while Merrill's net loss reached $27.6 billion in 2008 its top eleven executives were each paid more than $10 million in cash and stock and 149 employees received $3 million or more (Hightower, 2009). Thain has more CEO lives than Bob Nardelli. In 2010 he became CEO of the CIT group. He will get a base salary of $6 million and a bonus up to $1.5 million. In 2008 CIT got a $2.3 billion bailout from the government TARP program, then filed for bankruptcy, and guess what, the obligation was wiped out in bankruptcy court.

Case 5: Ken Lewis CEO of Bank of America, has spent $129 billion since 2001 buying financial companies, including regional lenders, FleetBoston Financial Corp., LaSalle Bank, U.S. Trust and credit-card issuer MBNA. He was often praised and given awards for building a powerful bank and staying away from the subprime mortgage crisis. Then Lewis made two decisions that disturbed stock holders and outraged analysts. In September 2007 he purchased Countrywide for $2.5 billion, which suddenly gave Bank of America a role in about one out of every four U.S. home sales. Lewis plunged his bank into the mortgage crises. Then shortly afterward he paid $19.4 billion for Merrill Lynch in a rushed transaction over a weekend.

After buying one toxic company it was clear that another purchase, Merrill Lynch was also filled of toxic waste and needed a government bail out to survive. In January 2009, a deal was struck. The government would pay $20 billion for a capital injection (after a $25 billion bailout in fall 2007) and cover $100 billion in potential losses. Bank of America lost billions and under the deal with the government, the bank would be responsible for the first $10 billion in losses; the government would take on the next $10 billion in losses and then the government would absorb 90 percent of the next $98 billion. In turn, the government would own $45 billion worth of Bank of America.

Has Lewis suffered from these mistakes and failures? From 2001 to 2007, he received $213 million. This included salary, bonus, restricted stock, exercised options and other compensation. His biggest payday came in 2006, when he made $96 million, most of it from exercising stock options he had accumulated over the years. Of course this payday came before Lewis' buying spree where his angry investors saw their stock go from $45.08 in 2008 to $8.32 on January 7, 2009. While Bank of America's profits fell 30 percent as it lost $15 billion in 2007, Lewis received a $4.25 million bonus, bringing his total compensation to $17 million. Lewis was the given the "Banker of the Year" award in 2008 as profits declined 29 percent and he terminated 3,200 employees. At the same time he announced an 11 percent decrease in his compensation to $20.4 million. Lewis' reputation was badly damaged by decisions clouded by excessive displays of optimism, a belief that he deserved such wealth and all would be wonderful in the long run. In April 2009 at a stock-holders meeting, the title of chairman was taken from Lewis as punishment. He now only holds the title of CEO. In late 2008 Lewis announced plans to terminate 35,000 employees over a three-year period. At the end of 2009 Lewis retired, and his retirement package had caused an outrage. According to the bank's 2009 proxy, Lewis' retirement package included a pension of $53.2 million; deferred compensation of $10.6 million, and 305,000 restricted shares valued at about $5 million. In 2011 government pay czar Ken Feinberg forced Lewis to pay back $1 million for getting a $1.5 million bonus while receiving TARP money.

In January 2009 the bank needed $20 billion in government aid and $118 billion in guarantees against bad assets. The government spent almost a year looking for a replacement for Lewis. Why so long? No one wanted the job. In December 2009 they finally settled on Brian Moynihan, who had been with the bank for several years. Moynihan promptly gave Thomas Montag a $29.9 million compensation package in 2009 for being president of its global banking and markets units and to fulfill promises made when Merrill Lynch & Co. hired him in 2008. In 2010, Moynihan's total compensation reached $10 million, a 67 percent increase from 2009 despite a $2.2 billion loss for the year. In April 2011, 1,500 employees were terminated with many more to follow. In 2010 the bank paid its Chief Risk Officer Bruce Thompson $11.4 million in compensation and then promoted to him CFO. In August 2011 the bank announced 3,500 employees would be terminated. It has been suggested that between 30,000 and 40,000 employees will be terminated by the time the bank is finished hemorrhaging. Incredibly BofA held a job fair a week later at its Rancho Cordova branch. It seems they were hiring 30 new employees. Why did no one think of offering the jobs to a few of the thousands expected to be fired? It may have been because the salaries now being offered are near the poverty level. Or maybe these 30 new hires will be shortly fired.

Case 6: After a significant stock decline, and the laying off of hundreds of what the CEO considered to be overpaid retail store associates, the CEO presented all his senior VPs with high priced automobiles for Christmas. The gifts were presented in the most ostentatious fashion: Several automobile haulers arrived at the headquarters. The VPs then went into the company's parking lot and jumped with joy as their new cars were unloaded. They failed to pay attention to the hundreds of employees looking out the glass windows at the display.

Case 7: Consider what happens when the CEO moves in the opposite direction: Shows empathy, and responds to layoffs by reducing his and his manager's compensation. The CEO of a small privately held, non-ferrous foundry lost multiple contracts, and had to lay off most of his production workforce. At an employee meeting, he shared his upset and promised he would bring them back as soon as he obtained more work. The workers wanted to know why he did not layoff his managers, who were responsible for procurement of contracts. The CEO said he needed them to procure contracts, but he would significantly reduce their compensation during this period. Shortly after, the CEO met with his managers and announced a significant pay reduction. They were outraged and demanded that the CEO tell the laidoff workers to leave the premises immediately, and if they did not, to call in the police. The CEO responded with outrage at his managers lack of empathy. He was caught in the middle. The managers refused a pay cut and said they would leave the company. The CEO gave in to his managers, knowing that his company would fail if they left. His HR manager escorted the laidoff employees to the parking lot. The employees wanted their managers to share the pain of the layoffs; the managers responded with outrage and forced the CEO to their side. If the managers had allowed themselves to exhibit empathy it would have intensified their feelings of guilt, shame, and the narcissistic injury associated with the lost contracts. Their intrapunitive structure allowed the managers to join together in engaging in self-righteous entitlement which served as a defense against feelings of guilt, shame, and persecution.

Attempting to answer the question. Why do people in leadership positions engage in greedy behavior? is problematic without exploring the third factor, the construct of narcissism. Narcissistic behavior is apparent when CEOs continuously display greed and little empathy and become desensitized to the outrage from their employees, stockholders and others. We will refer to this as occupational narcissism.

CHAPTER 10

Narcissism as a Cultural Phenomenon- Occupational Narcissism

...every social organization produces those character structures which it needs to exist.

Wilhelm Reich (1928, p.122)

According to Post (1993), the upper levels of government and corporations are filled with "successful narcissists," or what Maccoby (2000) calls "productive narcissists." How can we understand this phenomenon?

Before we attempt to answer this question we need to answer the following questions.

When reviewing the literature on narcissism the question that typically arises is: Are these behaviors that appear to be narcissistic a function of a characterological disorder. or are they behaviors that are part of a role requirement? Put another way: Is what we observe as narcissistic behaviors of CEOs inherent in the role of CEO, and are learned? That is, are narcissistic behaviors a function of the role of being an executive?

Or is narcissism a precondition to move into the executive role? Or is it a combination of the two?

Organizational psychologists who study psychopathology typically segment the organization when engaging in an investigation. For example, some investigate psychopathology of the individual in the organization, primarily the organization's leadership or its CEO. Others study the executive constellation and the types of delusional collectivities that evolve from a psychopathological system. Still others study the culture or the organization, and they see culture as a psychological system capable of demonstrating characteristics resembling those often associated with individual psychopathology.

These three types of investigations rarely bear fruit when segmented and studied in isolation. These views, the person, the person in system, and the system are deeply and thoroughly interconnected. They influence each other, play out success and failure, precipitate conflict and harmony, create impersonal environments and nurturing and supportive cultures, and they evolve and shift over time. To explore this interplay between the psychopathology of the individual, the executive constellation and the organization's culture, along with the delusional system of the executive constellation, we can understand how organizations can contain psychopathological structures, functions, roles, and cultures that can be de-habilitating for its members and the overall functioning of the system. These pathological structures are not related to factors typically associated with unproductive organizations. At times these pathological structures can be quite functional, at other times they underlie low morale, high turnover, bizarre and destructive decision-making and severe lapses in rational thought and action. Pathological structures can only be understood from a psychoanalytic perspective, which is the only methodology capable of explaining the deep-rooted and repressed attitudes, values and wishes that are protected in the pathological system. Most organizational psychologists can identify a pathological system as leading to organizational stress, decay, and death. But none of these surface analyses explain why these systems exist, their conscious and unconscious motivation and their functional nature. It is only after a thorough psychoanalytic diagnosis of the system is fully completed can an investigator hope to reduce the pathology of the system and make it more effective and efficient.

From a systemic perspective, we understand organizational roles as being at the intersection between the individual's biography on the one side, and on the other, the organization, with its tasks, structures, history, culture, and role requirements. Therefore, it may very well be that what we witness as narcissism in the executive is a function of characteristics of the person and the demands of the role. It may also be that if the role requires the demonstration of narcissistic behaviors, this would have a significantly stronger pull for the executive who possesses narcissistic traits than would any other cluster of personality characteristics. Two factors are relevant. First, if the executive has narcissistic proclivities he/she may fit into the executive role with relative ease. Secondly, if the executive has a characterological structure that is malleable, or "other directed" (Reisman, Glazer and Denney, 1957), or protean (Lifton, 1968), they may be able to adopt and internalize the role requirements that appear to be narcissistic.

Another view suggests that narcissism may develop as a function of being in the role of a corporate "king," a form of what Robert Millman refers to as 'acquired situational narcissism' (ASN). ASN is a form of narcissism that is brought on by wealth, status, fame and the other trappings associated with elite status. ASN differs from conventional narcissism in that it evolves from interactions with celebrity-obsessed fans, assistants, employees and even tabloid and business press and media. In the corporate world, employees' play into the idea that the top executive is vastly more important than other people, and this can trigger a narcissistic condition that at one time might have been a latent tendency. Being in the 'catbird seat' means one is surrounded by conditions that can precipitate latent narcissistic tendencies that overtime may evolve into a full-blown personality disorder. A CEO like Richard Fuld of Lehman sat in the top seat for 16 years, long enough to be transformed into a narcissistic type.

The more these narcissistic characteristics increase or become pathological, the greater will be the need for celebrity status and the more the CEO will demand bigger compensation packages to show off to colleagues, friends, family and those at the country club. In addition, the narcissistic CEO becomes devoted to the bottom line, and profitability is all that matters.

To understand these behaviors it may be helpful to examine the narcissistic elements described by Kohut (1968) and Kernberg (1970). They both suggest the following characteristics or elements are associated with narcissism: excessive self-absorption, intense ambition, fantasies of grandeur, a need to be admired and a lack of empathy. They defined narcissistic exhibitionism as a function of the desire or need for attention or admiration, and a tendency to present oneself as unique or exclusive. Narcissists direct their activities mainly toward obtaining maximum appreciation and acclaim. This need for continual approval demands great effort, and this part of the self system called the "grandiose me"' has an insatiable desire and need to consume positive external experiences. No detail can be forgotten. From being concerned for physical appearance, to reading the most recent fashionable author, they are constantly prepared.

Therapists report that narcissistic patients have a great deal of difficulty exhibiting an emotional life in therapy because to do so is associated with allowing oneself to feel and show vulnerability. According to Krystal (1988), in psychotherapy they tend to recount trivial, chronologically ordered actions, reactions and events of daily life with monotonous detail. There is ample evidence among psychoanalysts that narcissists are afraid of their interior. Self-reflection is not practiced, and their time is spent offering an appearance that all is good even when it is not. Many will not open themselves up to intimacy even in love affairs. They are slow to trust anyone - even their own therapist (Konigsberg, 2008). What we may be witnessing in the therapy office is a continuation of their life outside where they are in complete control and are surrounded by dutiful employees who cater to them and, if necessary, prop up their status and ego with displays of praise and adoration. According to Czander (2010):

The strong need to present themselves and maintain a type of image that prepares them for the struggle to survive and thrive in the interpersonal "Machiavellian" corporate world where the objective is not to "be" but to "seem to be," is to seem to be comfortable with their emotional self when they are not. In their interpersonal relations they detach themselves from their emotions and carefully calculate and plot. In their relations with other people, they like to function as if they have a "remote control." This is why they prefer to manage by the numbers, it allows them to maintain a high degree of control and at the same time keep a safe distance from any feelings or emotions. They prefer to surround themselves with numbers crunchers and financial engineers who feed them the data about a world of winners and losers, black and white. Those who get rewards and those who get punished. In the process they become the invincible prince and those in their employ are in a constant state of fear that they will not meet the numbers. P. 3

We can now begin this investigation with a definition of narcissism.

A DEFINITION OF NARCISSISM

Narcissism is a relative newcomer to the list of clinical diagnosis, not fully defined until the late 80s. It is perhaps the most overused and misunderstood diagnosis, and for that reason it was dropped from the DSM 5 as a personality disorder in December 2010. Variants on the word "narcissistic" are frequently used in everyday life and will often take the form of "name-calling." For example, if one is rude one is called a narcissist; if one is selfish, one is called a narcissist; if one attains celebrity status one is called a narcissist. People frequently misjudge others by observing a narcissistic trait, often a trait or behavior they do not like, see as selfish and then respond by calling the person a narcissist.

People who have narcissistic disorders have difficulty regulating self-esteem needs. As a result self-regard is accomplished through merging or distancing, and self-esteem regulation requires the use of external object relations. One view of narcissism suggests that contrary to the myth of narcissus, narcissism is not self-love but a defense against aggressive impulses. Another view suggests that it is a response to maternal deprivation that results in a tendency toward precocity, with a constant movement forward toward achievement, to be ahead of others. Another view maintains that at its base is an inflated, grandiose self, and this is a defense against devalued images of the self and a view of others as real or potential persecutors. In addition, this view maintains that the inflated self is a defense against the lack of genuine intimate relationships. Consequently they seek and gain inflated gratification from superficial and weak interpersonal relations, the type of relations typically found in the corporate world.

There is not much research suggesting the pervasiveness of narcissism in America, or whether narcissists would be more likely to be found in one occupation as opposed to another. Estimates suggest that between 3 and 15 percent of the population is narcissistic. However, many organizational psychologists/psychoanalysts would agree that narcissists are overrepresented in the executive suites in corporate

America. It is difficult to say if this impression of overrepresentation is a function of a high number of narcissists in the executive suite or more a function of seeing them stand out, as narcissists tend to do.

NARCISSISTIC TYPES

Bursten (1973) identifies four narcissistic personality types: craving, paranoid, manipulative, and phallic-narcissistic.

Craving narcissist-Consider this example. A CEO proudly claimed that he used the concept of "management by walking around" very effectively. He would walk around gathering hellos and good mornings from his staff. It was clear that he was using these walks as a way to fill his self-esteem cup, that is, obtain narcissistic supplies. One day a few managers decided that they would ignore him. He was observed running after these sadistic managers trying to obtain the much-needed greeting. While most would consider such a greeting as informal and lacking significance, for this manager it is a powerful form of gratification. The greeting was a defense against the intense feelings of emptiness and unauthenticity. Being ignored meant that he could no longer receive the self-confirming smile and greeting which was so necessary for his self-esteem regulation. When ignored, panic resulted. He chased after his employees. With no greeting, these feelings of emptiness began to emerge.

We also observe a schizoid or isolated aspect to this CEO's narcissism. The CEO spent a large a quantity of time in his office going over numbers. His managers joked about the fantasies they had about what he was doing in his office all day. A few times a week, while on one of his walks, he would call a meeting by yelling at the top of his lungs "2 o'clock" and getting his managers attention, he would point to his watch and continue his walk. He held what his managers called "dashboard" meetings, where he would go through reams of numbers, citing who was up and who was down. As these meetings went on managers would be text-messaging on their Blackberry's or perhaps playing video games. He was impervious, and rarely looked up from the data he was presenting. This CEO gets along in the world with little or no feelings at all, he keeps detached from human relations, while keeping his frightened sense of isolation repressed or unconscious. He quickly moves in and out of relationships. When the impulse strikes him he bolts from his office to wander the halls seeking friendly faces to engage in brief conversations. His rage at those who do not value him is acted out when he can ferret out negative information from his brief contacts in the halls or at his frequently held "data dump" meetings. The walks through the halls provide him with the material to maintain a delusion. The greeting means he is OK, and as long as he is receiving greetings he is giving the appearance that he is OK. Similar to Bollas' (1987) concept of normative personality, he comes to use the appearance of normality as a defense against the inner life in much the same way an obsessive compulsive uses external order to control inner chaos. If he is seen as normal, he will obtain the supplies he craves.

Manipulative narcissist: This is a large, overweight director who was described as larger than life, a college dropout who worked his way up the corporate ladder. He was always on stage and had a blustery personality, who would physically blow himself up when anxious or threatened. He would give his superiors the impression that he was eager to please and dutiful, but he was really engaging in self-promotion. To his managers and subordinates he demanded obedience. When a problem occurred he would take over, or as one manager stated, "ride in on his white horse." He loved to be in the roles of teaching, especially in front of a large group, the larger the better. However, he used teaching as a stage, where he could feel superior and obtain narcissist supplies. In order to maintain his feelings of superiority he would seek, and at times create, a crisis. On one occasion he called an emergency meeting, and reported that headquarters was concerned about operations in the field. He proceeded to suggest major structural changes that had his managers giving up increased amounts of autonomy. He was lying. No such report from headquarters existed. He is a manipulative narcissist. He has a need to "put something over" on others, and in doing so is able to sustain feelings of superiority by manipulating them. He engages in shameless self-promotion. He can be charismatic, articulate, and times humorous, but will often disrespect boundaries and the privacy of others. He can be patronizing and critical of others, but unwilling or unable to accept criticism or disagreement.

If he feels disrespected or "wronged," he relentlessly seeks revenge. He works to set others up for failure or pit co-workers against one another. He can be cruel and abusive, often targeting one person at a time until he quits. He may need an ongoing "narcissist supply" of people who he can easily manipulate and who will do whatever he suggest—including targeting a co-worker—without question. But in front of his superiors he is charming and innocent.

As you might imagine, narcissists can be highly disruptive to a workplace, creating a traumatic environment with high turnover. Eventually the narcissist is caught in action enough times that he is fired, but this does nothing to change his behavior (Hoffman, 2008).

There is a tendency to find manipulative narcissists in the consulting business. They may lie or exaggerate their consultations and successes. They feel its "OK to lie" to their consultees and work hard to avoid any form of behavior that hints of failure or incompetence. Despite the fact that, given the nature of organizational consulting, one is frequently "over one's head", they cannot admit it, or ask for help. When these narcissistic consultants get together, they try to "outdo" each other by overstating the degree and the importance of their work. It's as if they are always "drumming up business," despite their claims that they are very busy.

Paranoid narcissist-This VP is a frail 55 year old male who prided himself as a great humanitarian. He proudly put forth a very fair and all encompassing employee benefit program that he called the pride of the industry. He worked six and sometimes seven days a week. He was recently married for the third time, to a woman who was clearly a trophy wife. He surrounded himself with young, energetic employees and roughly 75 percent were women. He loved their energy, and he was especially fond of after-hours work time where they would eat and drink together. He started an affair with one of the employees, and things turned sour. After threatening to sue the company, she was amply paid off. The VP was scolded by the CEO and told he would try to keep it quiet. The VP was outraged and began to feel all his staff was against him. They turned on him and mocked his age and physical size. He felt that they knew all of his defects, his inadequate love-making and even penis size. His paranoid delusions were all-enveloping and consumed his waking hours, causing sleepless nights. He also suspected his wife knew about the affair and was plotting to leave him with all his money. At a major meeting he began to feel all would know about him and they would be laughing at him. He stopped the late work hours, fearing his employees were after him and out to exploit his expertise and special traits, or to force him to abstain and refrain from certain actions.

He began to feel that he was at the center of intrigues and conspiracies of colossal magnitudes. Alternatively, he began to feel victimized by what he considered mediocre underlings and intellectual dwarves who consistently failed to appreciate his outstanding, unparalleled talents, skills, and accomplishments. He was haunted by these inferiors, who were challenging his superiority. He felt utter contempt towards all he worked with. He felt they were driven by envy and they were colluding to defraud him, badger him, deny him his due. Of course these were his projections. He projected onto his employees his own defects, hatred and seething jealousy. This is the paranoid narcissist. The paranoia erupts when the image of himself is tarnished and his self-worth is denied. Like all narcissists, there is limited introspection. He cannot look inward and assess how he might have contributed to the mess he created. As a matter of fact, trying to convince him he had the slightest involvement in creating the mess is problematic. This is why so many therapists believe narcissists are hell in treatment, and some say they are incurable.

Phallic narcissism: A CEO lived what can be described as a charmed existence. He was the envy of his colleagues and friends. He grew up in wealth, the son of a successful corporate executive and doting "blueblood" mother. He went to an elite boarding school and then to an Ivy League university. He played football and was admired by many girls. He was considered by his chums a generous and brilliant budding star, who cannot miss being successful. After college he obtained his MBA in finance from an elite program and quickly entered into a finance career. Through family connections and his Ivy network he quickly rose up the hierarchy and was exceedingly successful in his late 20s. He met and married a beautiful debutant type and lived in a fabulous NYC apartment where they frequently entertained and enjoyed the New York nightlife with friends. Now as a couple, they were the envy of all. He is described by his wife, who entered therapy, as a perfectionist and exceedingly concerned about his self-image. She claimed that she frequently felt as if her life were a performance, and her role was to ensure that his image was continuously propped up to a level she found difficult to sustain. She also felt that she would be divorced as soon as she failed to maintain the performance. She felt he would dump her and acquire a trophy wife when she grew old, and be not as youthful and attractive, or she would give up the pretense. She also wanted children, however he insisted they wait and enjoy their present life where he was the "prince."

What she was describing is a phallic narcissist. These types are often driven to succeed and are often seen as successful. Sexuality for these individuals is based on proving their own sexual attractiveness and their power is derived from physical skill and mental prowess. This young man found it difficult to relax and find joy in a loving relationship. His image of himself was that of a lover and sexual conqueror, but not as one who loves. People relating to him, as his wife describes, do not feel loved, and often feel judged and inadequate.

As long as he remains in his world of aloofness and avoids intimacy, he can keep his image intact. Intimacy offers the possibility of being tarnished and vulnerable, where his needs, which were great, would pour out.

Narcissists can be exceedingly charming. They remember names and are masters of small talk. They can discuss any topic and they believe they are capable of discussing topics with experts. They are not shy, they love to travel and they see travel as a way to meet new friends and become valued. They are "well packaged" and have a wonderful veneer which allows them to succeed in the corporate world. Intense discussions, intimate relations are shunned: they could lead to disagreement or worse, they could be vulnerable and fail. They seek, and flourish in, an interpersonal world that is quite suited for the contemporary CEO. If Mintzberg (1975) is correct that the typical CEO spends most of his day in a series two to five minute conversations and half of all activities lasted less than nine minutes and only 10 percent lasted more than one hour, then one can see how they fit into the culture or how the culture is suited to them. The culture of the executive suite is fast-paced and characterized by brevity, variety and discontinuity, with limited or no time for self-reflection or reflective activities.

THE NARCISSISTIC EXECUTIVE

A narcissistic patient reported:

"Being an executive means you live in the world of executives, we attend the gin and tonic parties, eat at the country club, play golf and tennis, and make sure our wives and kids hangout together. I get my support there, in these circles. We all know we can't establish intense personal relations in our world, you get paranoid after a while, when you're in these high powered positions everybody is nice to you- they kiss ass, they all want something from you, like gold diggers. In my executive circle, with people like me, I know they don't want anything from me, sure they admire me, but they know I could fall. If I do, they pick me up, but if they can't, then I have to leave the circle, no room for losers here."

We get a picture of a tenuous existence that is transitory in nature and devoid of genuine friendship. Another executive came for treatment because he was grossly unhappy. "I keep having the recurrent thought, like I want to go back to my old neighborhood in the Bronx and hang out, play stickball with my friends," he said This executive found the superficial life in the executive world alienating, he longed for something of substance, the ethnic bonds of the neighborhood, his extended family, and the secure institutions.

Another view of narcissism is to see it as a metaphor of the contemporary personality or what Christopher Lasch (1979) calls the personality of our time. Maccoby (2000) uses social narcissism in a manner similar to Fromm (1970) he removes it from its clinical meaning and expands it to cover vanity, self admiration and self glorification as a synonym for the "social" individualism or the antithesis of love for others in the community. This view uses the psychiatric label of narcissism loosely, and its description or narcissistic behavior has a moralistic tone. For example, when a selfish person is called narcissistic.

The social narcissist, like the clinical narcissist, lacks empathy. In many ways this social narcissist resembles Richard Christie's (1970) Machiavellian type. According to Christie, Machiavellians are able to be successful, or be what Maccoby call "productive narcissists" because they are able to emotionally detach themselves from interpersonal situations, they have a keenly developed sense of how to win in interpersonal contests, they can "size up the opposition" without emotionality. In these win-lose situations they are guided by guile and strategy as opposed to empathy. Like these Machiavellians the social narcissist may be a productive leader if they are able to "put their feelings into or onto their subordinates," that is, utilize projections and consequently induce others (subordinates) into behaving in ways that lead to success. This may explain why certain CEOs are seen as idealized, charismatic figures. They surround themselves with subordinates who are low Machiavellians characterized by a strong need to be liked and a high degree of empathy.

OCCUPATIONAL NARCISSISM- BEING IN THE EXECUTIVE ROLE

An executive came into treatment outraged at a therapist that he had seen a week before:

"Do you know what the SOB said to me? When you enter my office I hear chapel bells, when I get close to you I hear nothing."

It may very well be that the "nothing" is an internal deadness, a lack of feeling. This CEO feels empty. He has spent his life on the run, in an array of work and non-work relationships devoid of intimacy. As one CEO claimed in therapy, "Yeah I have lots of friends, don't all us big shots, sure, as long as I'm a big shot." In addition, these CEOs have lived a politically correct corporate life. No chance of rebelling. It may very well be that to make it in the corporate world, one has to give up that inner voice. It can create doubts and trouble.

Being a CEO requires that one must take on the behaviors of the CEO role. Let's examine this in the context of role acquisition. It has long been established that for one to move successfully through the various roles we occupy, being a son, daughter, patient, parent, uncle, aunt, teacher, policewoman, husband, friend, wife, lover, customer, employee, etc., requires taking on the behaviors associated with that role. Writing about "patient hood," Levinson and Gallagher (1965) maintain that in order to function successfully in the role of being a patient one must learn the required behaviors of that role. For example, attempting to gain entry into a mental health center requires careful study of those who gained entry, and an avoidance of those behaviors that did not lead to entry. Often the waiting room is where patients learn to demonstrate the appropriate behaviors to the intake worker and gain entry (Levinson and Astrachan, 1974).

Harry Stack Sullivan writing in 1931, says:

"A study of 'social recovery's' in one of our large mental hospitals some years ago, taught me that patients were often released from care because they had learned not to manifest symptoms to the environing persons; in other words, they had integrated enough of the personal environment to realize the prejudice opposed to their delusions. It seemed almost as if they grew wise enough to be tolerant of the imbecility surrounding them, having finally discovered that it was stupidity and not malice. They could then secure satisfaction from contact with others, while discharging a part of their cravings by psychotic means." P. 982

It has also been established that to function successfully in a professional role not only requires learning the required behaviors associated with the role, it also requires abstaining from demonstrating behaviors considered inappropriate.

We can see the relationship between those who seek the MBA degree as a ticket to the executive suite, and how MBA and corporate training and mentoring may reinforce certain role behaviors that we would consider narcissistic. If the role requires the demonstration of narcissistic type behaviors, then this would mean that the person who already has narcissistic characteristics would stand a better chance to succeed in the corporate world than other personality types. This appears to be borne out in a study by Westerman, Bergman, Bergman, and Daly, found in Lavelle (2010) B-school students scored higher on the Narcissistic Personality Inventory than psychology students, suggesting there is indeed a tendency for those with narcissistic traits to go into business. Westerman blames business schools, who he says are either attracting narcissists, creating them from scratch, or a little of both. And that, he says, is a big problem for business, where he says the personality trait can cause all manner of mayhem. "Increasing narcissism has been linked to risky decision-making, alcohol abuse, and toxic work environments," Westerman says. "The fact that business schools are creating narcissists and sending them out into the workplace is not a good thing" Lavelle, (2010). This is especially troubling considering that most corporate cultures require the executive role occupant to demonstrate narcissistic behaviors. This is called "occupational narcissism" and it is found in most professions. We also have data suggesting that there is a link between narcissism and cheating. According to Bartlett (2010) researchers asked 199 college students from a "regional Midwestern college" to take the Narcissistic Personality Inventory and a questionnaire that evaluated their academic dishonesty and how guilty (or not) they felt about what they'd done. They found that students who tested high for a particular dimension of narcissism — exhibitionism — were more likely to be cheaters. Also these students were less likely to feel remorse when cheating. As stated earlier, business school students cheat more than students in other disciplines and considering their scores on narcissism it is clear that the business schools are continuing to be engaged in producing another generation of executives that will continue the "me first" climate that presently exists in corporate America.

The pervasiveness of narcissism is not unique to business students and corporate executives. John Banja (2004) coined the term "medical narcissism" as the need of health professionals to preserve their self-esteem leading to the compromise of error disclosure to patients. Also, Banja (2004) used the term "deification projections," where patients literally deify their doctors. He maintains that the adulation and respect the physician gets from so many patients is a narcissistic aphrodisiac. Barnes (2008) suggests that lawyers, as an occupational group, suffer from narcissism, and he calls it the "narcissistic entitlement syndrome."

Occupational narcissism evolves from the interaction between the corporate culture, role, training, mentoring and the personality types that are drawn to the profession. Occupational narcissism is generally marked by a pervasive pattern of grandiosity, a lack of empathy, a strong desire to be noticed (singled out as being special), a powerful sense of entitlement, and a need for constant attention.

Glowinski (2008) adds to our understanding of occupational narcissism, countering those that believed narcissism was primarily a female disorder. He maintains it is found primarily in men, and he maintains that 75 percent of those diagnosed as narcissists are men. He also claims there is considerable difference between female and male narcissists with respect to how they behave. He claims male narcissists often seek attention and control through employment, publicity, and short-term sexual relationships. They seek the accoutrements associated with wealth and to be on top, holding power in terms of social and economic status is required. In the corporate world, these men gravitate toward extrapunitive and intrapunitative cultures which allow them to utilize blame and scapegoating. They embrace an image that it is aggressive and manipulating in order to gain power, status, or money.

NARCISSISM AND WEALTH

These narcissistic CEOs seek celebrity status, and believe that achieving this status will increase their managerial prowess and wealth. It is apparent that as long as a narcissistic culture is dominant in the corporation, and CEOs seek celebrity status, the compensation gap between the top and the bottom will continue to grow. In a study of 1,500 companies from 1997 to 2005, Fritz, Hayward and Larsen (2008) looked at how often CEOs appeared in the press and popular magazines. They found that every time a CEO's name appeared in a major publication their salary increased $650,000. Getting one's picture on the cover was worth an extra $1.1million. It did not matter if the company was failing or succeeding.

According to the Hotchliss (2002), "our culture is full of narcissistic influences that numb us to the reality of the problems we face." Their distortions of reality can cause others to question themselves and doubt their own perceptions. Narcissists will go to great lengths to promote fantasies that sustain their grandiosity, omnipotence, and self-worth. Occupational narcissists are found in high numbers among prominent elected officials, sports idols, entertainment figures, and other celebrity or image-based occupations where the accumulation of wealth is used as a measure of one's self-worth. Campbell, Bush, Brunell and Shelton (2005) set up a series of experiments and discovered that narcissistic types worked to provide a benefit to the self at the expense of long-term costs to both individuals and society. In addition, Campbell and Bonacci (2004) in their discussion of the traits or dimensions of narcissism maintained that entitlement is a significant trait or feature of narcissism.

THE ORGANIZATION AS A SELF-REGULATOR

Many writers maintain that narcissists have trouble with internalization, which leads to problems with self-regulation. If this is the case, then how do narcissistic CEOs function successfully in highly public and responsible positions of authority? They do so by using the organization, the role of CEO, and its executive constellation to maintain self-regulation. Self-regulation is maintained in two ways: (1) control of mood and feelings are paramount in the executive role. One is expected to behave in a particular manner to show or demonstrate appropriate executive behaviors and to abstain from demonstrating inappropriate behaviors. The metaphor "he is management material" is appropriate here. This phrase suggests the candidate for a managerial position is capable of demonstrating the appropriate affects. If executives cannot demonstrate appropriate affects and contain unwanted emotional displays they cannot move up the ladder and some are labeled "loose cannons" (2) Control of emotions are maintained when the organization can serve as an attachment figure for the executive. Everyone has a different style of attachment, and executives typically shift back and forth between avoidant-dismissive to avoidant-fearful styles. They rarely feel securely attached, they worry their career could quickly end and they could be demoted or sent to another country. While their career is their mooring, it is quite vulnerable to impingements.

We believe that those who are securely attached are more stable, secure, and competent in their emotional interactions and are more "happy, friendly, and trusting." However, many executives, especially narcissistic types, tend to show attachment distinguished by emotional distance, control of relationships, and a compulsive self-reliance (avoidant- attachment). For example, a style of interaction of many narcissistic CEOs is to tell those seeking an audience or meeting with them that they only have a certain amount of time to meet and at the end of the allotted time they must leave. Hanging out or schmoozing is not permitted, it may bring forth feelings of intimacy. The phrase "It is lonely at the top" is appropriate here. What is the nature of the loneliness? It is the executive who is unable to form intimate relations. It is the executive who fails to form genuine attachments and instead controls objects, especially those people he works with.

As stated before, avoidant attachment is closely associated with the narcissistic character. Under conditions when their need to control is frustrated or threatened or they experience vulnerability, they typically enter into paranoid rage. Consider this example. An executive was given an assignment that caused considerable anxiety. He was expected to work closely with a group of friendly strongly attached executives from another company to explore a possible merger. He and his wife were invited by one of the executives to his home for a dinner. He said he could not recall being invited to dinner at someone's home outside the family. While he frequently had dinner with friends and colleagues they were always at restaurants or the country club. It was the intimacy that terrified him. He could not control the needed distancing he required, He would be giving up control to the host. This never would have occurred if he were at a restaurant or club.

When the executive constellation fails to offer the needed degree of regulation and control there is an increase in attachment anxieties, fears, and rage. When this occurs the CEO will typically go outside the company and find a consultant, life-coach, or "positive thinking" guru to stabilize their internal state.

SUCCESS AS A SELF-REGULATORY MECHANISM

It is commonly understood that being a CEO inflates self-esteem. The narcissist is able to control an array of unwanted feelings and emotions by achieving power and control. Success is a self-regulatory mechanism. Consider this. When a neighbor entered a successful narcissist's house he was overwhelmed with his need to show off his things; perhaps his collections, art work, and the trappings of his success. It is as if he is saying; "look at me," "admire me," "see how successful I am, now do you love me?"

Regulation is also maintained in their complementary relationships with closely aligned associates. In many corporations narcissistic CEOs surround themselves with masochistic executive assistants. They occupy roles similar to the role of Panza, Don Quixote's faithful servant who supports his fantasized ideal world which he believes to be real. In their relationships with their "chief," these masochistic executive assistants enact humiliation through painful attachments. Each identifies with the other,s experience. The narcissist identifies with the assistant's dependency and vulnerability, and the assistant identifies with the narcissist's control and power. If one looks carefully at the relationships developed by these powerful narcissistic CEOs, one may find several of these assistants in orbit. These assistants could be a VP, a friend from college or the "old neighborhood," drinking buddies, a spouse, or even a paramour. These assistants may complain in private, but they joyfully suffer while idealizing this powerful object.

The down-side occurs when the narcissistic CEO, as an idealized figure, promotes a psychic connection and the staff has the powerful wish to fuse. This fusion takes the form of, "You are perfect and I am part of you." Just as one "hangs out" with celebrities in the hope that one will be recognized as a celebrity, these colleagues "hang on" hoping that they will ride the coat-tails of the star and become a celebrity themselves. But in order to realize their dream these subordinates must continuously praise and serve their chief. Failure to do so, or having a slip, could mean the termination and in some cases the end of a career. This creates a culture where no one questions the CEO's decisions. Questioning the chief is the equivalent of criticizing, and it is not permitted. Many Wall Street executives have come forth after the financial meltdown and stated they knew their CEO was going in the wrong direction but could not challenge them. These executives can be referred to as the classic "yes men." These employees are often required to feed the CEOs and his constellation narcissistic supplies through idealizing. CEOs create anxiety-producing situations where their "yes men" constantly worry about their careers and survival. The CEO benefits from the excessive fear and the projected idealization. It feeds their narcissism. When these "yes men" are not available, the CEO may demonstrate increased rigidity and the narcissistic pursuit of perfection takes on a more compulsive form that may be more isolating and maladaptive.

We are suggesting that the narcissist has many traits that make for success as well as failure in organizations. The narcissist has an extraordinary capacity to manipulate interpersonal relations, maintain a smooth interpersonal style with anxiety- free confidence, and form many attachments that give approval and support their image.

Rothstein (1979,1982,1984) studied six male narcissists and concluded that executives with narcissistic personalities were first-born sons adulated by mothers who denigrated and humiliated their fathers whom they considered failures. They were described by Rothstein as Oedipal winners, who are required by the powerful mother and defeated father to be perfect. For these executives, failure is considered to bring excessive humiliation. Their fear is, if they fail, they will be symbolically castrated like their father. This almost pathological fear of failure lends a paranoid quality to their relationships and the defenses of denial and projections.

NO PERFORMANCE REVIEW FOR THESE CEOS

King (2007) suggests the following to organizations concerning how to deal with narcissists.

"Organizations might also consider implementing a 360-degree feedback survey to employees within the company (DuBrin, 2004). Narcissists are unlikely to contain their problematic behaviors when communicating with employees within the organization, especially in the event of a crisis. Surveys could be administered to employees after each rehearsal and actual crisis. All members would be expected to provide anonymous, confidential information on their superiors' performance (Lubit, 2002). Information collected from the survey may be shared with the crisis leader, and assist upper-management in reexamining their choice as the crisis management leader."

The author fails to demonstrate a real understanding of the narcissistic type. It is precisely these types of situations where a narcissistic will flourish. For example, a newly hired VP was given a horrendous 360 review by his subordinates. A team of 3 HR/OD specialists were called in to conduct a meeting with his staff. After an hour-long discussion, the OD consultant called in the VP. The VP addressed his subordinates and proceeded to admonish them for their inability to work collaboratively, he then quizzed the HR/OD specialists on the accuracy of their data and the time they were wasting, as the organization had more urgent needs which he articulated. After placing everyone on the defensive, he then proceeded to ease up and accept their viewpoints if they offered a renewed commitment to work with him and "not against" him. They happily agreed. The VP was "on his game" and he spent the next six months on a "search and destroy" mission to ferret out and fire those who wrote the anonymous negative reviews. The message to his subordinates was, "admire me and I will take care of you, cross me and you're dead."

We have established that for the narcissist, the experience of guilt precipitates entitlement. The feeling of guilt evolves from the experience of power; "I have hurt someone." However, for this VP the negative 360 review precipitated the experience of shame. When narcissists experience shame, they strike back with outrage and revenge. At the very least, they engage in intimidating those who are responsible for creating this feeling state of shame. Shame is a much deeper psychological experience associated with the deeply buried and troubling feelings: "I am no good. I am defected, worthless and unlovable." The tarnished narcissist must lash out and destroy those who in his or her experience are trying to kill him/her.

NARCISSISTIC CULTURES

We maintain that while the bureaucratic organization of the 1950s and 1960s tends to promote the type of executive called by Whyte (1956) the "company or organizational man," the contemporary organization promotes the "narcissistic man." What has changed since the 1950s and 1960s is a shift from Whyte's stereotype of the "organization man" to Maccoby's "gamesman." What we may be talking about is not a narcissist or any clear personality type but merely an employee successfully fitting into the narcissistic culture of the executive constellation and taking on the behaviors required to be successful in this culture.

How are these cultures created? Management and business textbooks state that if corporations are to survive in this turbulent environment, they must be entrepreneurial. These entrepreneurial firms are characterized as flexible, organic, innovative, risk-taking, and flamboyant CEOs. The CEOs of these firms claim that in their organization, "the only constant is change." According to Morgan (1988) CEOs of these corporations work in a culture driven by conquests, acquisition, and an array of exhibitionistic behaviors. The "me-oriented" culture of these organizations lavishes attention on its chief. In these aggressive, star oriented cultures Morgan (1988) suggests they resemble what Wilhelm Reich would describe as a phallic-narcissistic ethos, and to derive gratification in this culture one must be visible, adored, and most important "a winner." These contemporary organizations encourage egocentricism and demands narcissistic behavior. Just as Whyte's bureaucratic organization demanded rigidity, conformity, and anality, these contemporary knowledge-based institutions make the chief sacrosanct (Krantz & Gilmore, 1990). In addition, American culture values celebrity. We give awards for almost everything: knowledge, dancing, singing, strength, hitting home runs, etc. We create shows called "survivor," "top chef," and "the apprentice," hosted by stars, like the real estate mogul Donald Trump, and they are based on winning and losing. These shows are used in MBA programs as demonstrations of how to succeed in the business world.

If these narcissistic cultures do not exist, these MBA-trained CEOs will create them, especially within their executive constellation. In many corporations the culture of the executive constellation is a discrete entity, a community separate from their corporate environment. This is part of the motivation for off-shoring and outsourcing. They assume a narcissistic stand that requires enemies "out there" in their corporate environment, but they also see opportunities as well. They maintain that if they are "gifted and talented, then they can be "winners." This is accomplished when they take advantage of opportunities and take risks, sometimes extraordinary risks, as we see with Wall Street and banks in 2007-08. In these contemporary organizations, when they win, they engage in unabashed celebrations about their capacities, they hoist their leaders up and heap adulation on them.

We have established that these tycoons of industry live in a special world and they rarely interact with the population they depend on to keep their industries afloat. This may be why they appear insensitive to their employees as they treat them like cannon fodder to win the war on obtaining wealth. Equally important is what these insulated communities provide the CEO. Rather than offering opportunities for genuine encounters and real friendship, these insular communities merely reinforce the CEO's sense of entitlement and hubris. Often the only communities the CEO moves through are their work and the club (golf, country, boat, etc.). CEOs rarely live in a neighborhood community they often live in a gated house or in a remote mansion not even a trick-or-treater would visit. They typically have staff whose job is to shop and take care of the things that would ordinarily promote meeting others in their community. It may very well be that they spend their time with fellow narcissists each supporting the other and convincing each other they are special.

NARCISSISTIC CULTURE AND THE USE OF WOMEN

When the CEO devalues, criticizes, or psychically exploits the executive staff, as narcissist characters will eventually do, the important idealizing connection is severed. When this occurs, the CEO's staff will experience confusion and will vacillate between the wish for return of the idealized object or denigration and hate. Thus, we see that excessive idealization increases the vulnerability of relationships in the executive constellation (Czander, 1993). When these relationships are no longer idealizing, the CEO and subordinates seek a crisis or a scapegoat to return to the blissful state. When executive constellations are hunting for scapegoats, women become exceedingly vulnerable. Women are likely to be devalued, undermined, challenged, and overtly criticized. According to Lang (1984), idealizing needs are more pronounced in men than women, and he suggests that for women to be part of these cultures can be problematic.

We may see a differentiating psychic difference between men and women, where men are prone to creating idealized relationships and women are prone toward establishing mirroring relationships. If this is the case, it may help to explain the paucity of women in these narcissistic corporate cultures, despite the fact that women make up more than 50 percent of the workforce.

Women are most likely to be given the top position when the organization is on its death bed. They are the symbolic equivalent of the "big nurse" who is brought in to heal the company and bring it back to life. However, what typically happens is, if successful, she is terminated and a handsome narcissistic male enters.

We have been hinting that the road these narcissistic CEOs travel is short-lived. Tenure in the catbird seat was 3.2 years in 2007. In 2008 a record 1,484 CEOs left their jobs, and in 2009 that number was expected to increase. We may be able to understand this as a crisis of leadership, where CEOs self-destruct, burnout, or just take the money and run.

CHAPTER 11

Why Wall Street and the Banks Failed: The Psychology of Self-Destruction

"Guilt aims at self-destruction, and pride aims at the destruction of others."

Bill Wilson, founder of AA

"Banking establishments are more dangerous than standing armies."
Thomas Jefferson

We have established that the attainment of enormous wealth precipitates guilt. The question we will explore in this chapter is what the CEO does when overwhelmed with guilt. The classic response to feelings of guilt is to make reparations. Typically, reparations made to reduce guilt are accomplished through the establishment of foundations or institutions to give away wealth, and many wealthy CEOs have engaged in this activity. Many institutions, especially academic institutions, count on these wealthy CEOs who need to make reparations for their greed and resulting guilt. Examples are Jack Welch having his name on the Business School of Sacred Heart University or

George Peterson who gave $1 billion to establish his George Peterson Foundation. Peterson says, "Its fun giving money away. I never had a better time in my life." What joy there is when one can feel guilt-free and still remain a billionaire? Successful moguls racked with guilt may retire and live a life of opulence and reap narcissistic supplies by giving away some of the wealth. They have buildings named after themselves and establish foundations in their names, they have their pictures in newspapers and magazines; The New York Times even offers an annual 18-page section devoted to the top 40 who gave away half their wealth.

We maintain that when a CEO/multimillionaire does not engage in the work of making reparations they will be overwhelmed with guilt. Unable to defend against the guilt, they will be motivated to make reparations unconsciously. How does this work? The person makes reparations through the unconscious motivation to lose wealth, to fail, and/or engage in self-destructive behaviors. This has happened throughout history as people make what is generally considered foolish decisions and they lose everything. Politicians are notorious for engaging in behaviors, often sexual, to destroy their political careers. To a psychoanalyst these so-called foolish decisions are unconsciously motivated. The need to fail or lose everything is a problematic response guilt feelings; here the person turns aggressive rage and destructive impulses against the self, taking the form of an unconscious need for punishment (Nunberg, 1934).

We have observed three potential psychological consequences associated with leading contemporary corporations: entitlement, depersonalization and the creation of a narcissistic culture. However, there is another psychic reaction, and this is associated with destruction. Just as people are capable of destroying their health, marriages and families, they are also capable of destroying the corporations they lead.

NARCISSISM AND DEPRESSION

We have established that in many cases, a narcissistic veneer serves as a cover for covert depression. One can also consider narcissistic displays, like the accumulation of wealth at the same time demonstrating gross insensitivity, a defense against depression. It is this buried depression which motivates unconscious self-destruction, as suggested by Freud in Mourning and Melancholia, depression (which underlies narcissism) is a form of inner violence, a form of hatred against self.

These executives avoid depressive ideation by having limited self-awareness. They not only do not know themselves, they do not want to know themselves. Looking inward one finds depressive ideations. Overtime this evolves into a personality with concrete prohibitions against self-reflection and anything that proposes self-reflection. This is why many consultants with psychological backgrounds report experiencing major resistances and conflicts when working with these executives. In addition, they need to engage in hyped-up, fast-paced activities to avoid inner feelings. Multitasking, working long hours, intense involvement, and intense ambition is necessary. Vacations and time off to relax is avoided. Work, power and accumulation of wealth are ways to conceal their depression. According to Real (1999), the common defense against the painful experience of deflated value (depressive worthlessness) is inflated value; and a common compensation for the experience of shame is a flagrant flight into grandiosity.

Several writers maintain that being in the CEO position is perhaps the most stressful role one could occupy. As we have established, CEOs work long hours, six days a week, continuously muti-tasking, and must satisfy the demands of their employees, customers, suppliers, board of directors, as well as Wall Street, the media and an array of critics. They have little time to escape from this frenzied state of continuous activity. They are constantly bombarded to explain their behaviors by stockbrokers, post-adolescent hedge fund analysts, business writers, stockholders, and now the public and Congress if their salary is too high and their corporate stock is too low. They are deluged for interviews by writers who see them as psychopaths and others who see them as crooks. Barnard (2008), a lawyer, is a prime example of these writers who engage in accusatory pop psychology and name-calling. She attempts to study CEOs by focusing what she describes as five "pathologies"; narcissism, over-optimism, fear, anger and depression. In her study she seems to mix clinical diagnostic assessments such as narcissism and depression with behavioral observations, such as over-optimism, fear and anger. What she does, however, is to uniquely connect the clinical assessment of narcissism and its underlying depression, (the most troubling type of CEO) and describes the resulting behavior over-optimism, fear and anger.

According to Scelfo (2007), 6 million American men will be diagnosed with depression this year, but millions more suffer silently unaware or unwilling to seek treatment...because men are reluctant to own up to emotional difficulties. Instead of talking about their feelings, men may mask them with alcohol and/or drug abuse, gambling, anger, or workaholism. Men often view asking for help as an admission of weakness. These men quickly learn that they must appear to be positive, on top of things and in control of their emotions. They seek others like themselves and unconsciously create a support group; golf buddies, drinking partners, sports buddies, never quite realizing that their "friends" offer the necessary support to prevent a spiral into depression. For these men, work offers the same function, a place where they can appear to be a high-powered, polished and successful. Their depression is safely tucked away, never discussed or witnessed. These Wall Street men finish up at 6 PM, go out with their "buddies" to the local bar to eat and drink. Take the 9 p.m. train home, having more drinks en route, get home and space-out with a beer in one hand and the remote in the other. Stagger to bed at midnight only to rise five hours later to do it over again. No smelling of the roses here, no time for self-examination, just work and self-anesthetizing.

THE DECAYING PROCESS

Schwartz (1989) describes organizational decay is a condition of systemic ineffectiveness marked by flawed decision making. The decaying process is also marked by an illusion of perfection. The decay process is typically located in the organization's executive constellation, although it can be located in other corporate units, including its Board of Directors. Employees who are recruited into the executive constellation do so because they "march lockstep," they unquestioningly accept this illusion of perfection. However, we find this decaying constellation is marked high turnover and conflict, as executives compete in "turf wars" as they try to increase their power and status hoping to get the next shot at the top position. Managers who maintain their connection to reality and question risks (the constellation's illusion of perfection) will be isolated and rejected. They are typically referred to as "non-team players."

Employees who do survive engage on a continuous struggle to maintain the illusion of perfection. They search for statistics, and nuances in procedures and policies to reinforce their positions, if none are available they will freely make them up and communicate to subordinates and customers that the organization is "doing well," or that "we have data suggesting that we're on the road to making the necessary corrections to environmental changes." They never admit they made a mistake, or may be in trouble and they proudly put forth the image of perfection because they have the capacity to change with the changing facts, a sign of great management. Illusions of perfection are also maintained by utilizing the defenses of denial or scapegoating. In particular, subordinates, stakeholders, government policies or customers are denigrated as being responsible, and dismissed as troublemakers. It is never their foolish decisions that are responsible for failure; the problem is out there, some type of "unstoppable," "unforeseen force."

They utilize a narcissistic defense to protect what is underneath the illusion of perfection: low self-esteem, depression, a deep sense of uncared-for worthlessness and rejection, and a hunger for response and reassurance (Masterson, 1981). But this defense may fail if overwhelmed with guilt. When the defense fails, the passion which motivated the CEO to make the Herculean effort to climb the ladder is turned away towards failure. This is "tragic man." The CEO is unconsciously motivated to fail, to destroy the corporation and career. This CEO is now left with regret, despair, guilt and shame. There is no better example of this than the fall of Lehman Brothers, a once proud Wall Street firm.

LEHMAN BROTHERS

Wall Street bankers have been condemned, vilified and called names such as "narcissists" filled with hubris and greed. However, we rarely get a deep social and psychological understanding of the conscious and unconscious motivations of why an executive constellation engages in high risk behaviors and denies realities associated with potential failure.

We do not know how a culture for greed evolves. Whether it can be viewed as a distinct corporate culture or if greed is a unique cultural artifact is still in question. Also, we do not have a deep understanding of the motivations these bankers must have had to recklessly engage in destructive behaviors for the seeming sole purpose of wealth accumulation. We will offer a psychodynamic discussion of the evolution of the executive constellation of Lehman Brothers, a culture of marked entitlement, depersonalization and occupational narcissism. This psychodynamic analysis centers on Richard (Dick) "Gorilla" Fuld and his motivation for destroying the fourth largest investment bank in the world, with 25,000 employees. According to Onaran and Helyar (2008), "Fuld's failure to save Lehman ... is a story about how the most indomitable man on Wall Street became addicted to leverage and intoxicated with the power it brought. ...Isolated, surrounded by acolytes and unaware of the rivalries tearing his firm apart, Fuld was too prideful to accept the fast-eroding value of the empire he had built, too slow to cut a deal.

The extraordinary collapse of Lehman Brothers, the largest bankruptcy in history, offers a glimpse into a Wall Street filled with celebrity multimillionaires and thousands of 'wanna-bes'. Lehman's CEO Richard Fuld is the point of analysis. According to Onaran and Helyar (2008), "Fuld .... spent his entire career there, so his saga is also a story of Wall Street over the past four decades." Several books have been written about Lehman: Ken Auletta's 1985 *Greed and Glory on Wall Street;* William Cohan's 2008 *House of Cards*; Lawrence McDonald and Patrick Robinson's 2009 *A Colossal Failure of Common Sense;* Peter Chapman's 2010 *The Last of the Imperious Rich: Lehman Brothers 1844-2008, and* Vicky Wade's 2010 *The Devils Casino.* They collectively suggest that a culture of greed and arrogance existed, and maintain that Lehman's CEO was the prototype of bankers responsible for the financial crisis of 2008 and the loss of millions of jobs. Some suggest Fuld was proud, rageful, and a control freak. Some writers over-simplify by suggesting that CEOs like Fuld suffer from the 'Lake Wobegon Syndrome' in which all children are deemed above average. These current statements do not offer an in-depth or psychoanalytic inquiry into the type of culture that not only supported Fuld but may have created him.

The largest bankruptcy in American history, Lehman Brothers filed for bankruptcy in fall, 2008. The story of this failure centers on Richard Fuld, Lehman's CEO. Fuld joined Lehman as a college intern in 1969. He was appointed CEO in 1993 and became the longest serving CEO on Wall Street. In his 16 years he was considered one of the industry's most skilled chief executives, boosting the firm's profit from $113 million in 1994 to $4.2 billion in 2007, and multiplying its share price 20 times. According to Onaran and Helyar (2008), "Fuld lived for and identified with his firm. It was his oxygen .... He had spent his entire career there, so his saga is also a story of Wall Street over the past four decades." Over the past eight years his compensation totaled about $300 million.

FULD THE 'GORILLA'

Fuld was called "The Gorilla" by his employees and business writers. He did not like the name and preferred to be called Dick. Viewing his nickname "gorilla" as a metaphor for a personality type offers a graphic description of a larger-than-life man. We tend to see the gorilla, the largest living primate with a DNA 98 percent identical to humans as the powerful troop leader. He is protective of his troop and is the exclusive decision-maker, capable of killing all those who threaten the troop. Fuld was known as a competitive squash player and weightlifter, and had a long history of losing his temper in bouts of violence. He was a "brawler, known as the scariest man on Wall Street" (Times of London, 2008).

Fuld fully took on the stereotypic characteristics associated with Wall Street bankers: He was tough, combative, hard driving, and confident- though also an exceedingly private man. He would have his limo pick him six days a week and drive him from his Greenwich home into the garage of the Lehman building in Manhattan. He would take his private elevator to the top floor, which only he and a few assistants occupied. He would rarely leave the floor and his private chef would prepare his lunch and dinner meals. Most employees had never met him or seen him, including several vice presidents and directors. He was incommunicative and at meetings he would often grunt and groan and stare to show displeasure. Managers who had a negative report to submit would often send up a young man to be sacrificed knowing that he would be immediately fired (Tibman, 2009). Fuld's commitment, control, and optimism were legendary on Wall Street. Weinstein (1980) suggests that excessive optimism is most apparent when CEOs believe they can exert control and have a high level of commitment. It may be that that excessive optimism is found in CEOs who believe they can exert control and have what on the surface appears to be a high level of commitment, but closer scrutiny indicates they are surrounded by "yes men" filled with fear, anger and contempt. In either case it was Fuld's excessive need to see only the positive and maintain the image of perfection that would eventually contribute to his downfall.

Fuld was deeply attached to Lehman. It was his life and apparently replaced his family of origin, a New York Jewish family that Fuld refused to discuss. His choice of attending college in Colorado suggests that he perhaps needed to get far away from his family. In college he enrolled in the Navy Reserve. His stay in the Navy comes as no surprise: corporate Boards prefer executives with some form of military background. While students were protesting the ethics of the Vietnam War these budding executives were marching lock step in uniform.

It can be hypothesized that Fuld was searching for a different kind of family; one that he could control and where he could someday become the "General." In Lehman he found it. He repeatedly stated how proud he was of the family atmosphere he created at Lehman. The culture he created may have been a family in his eyes, but it was clearly not functional. An analysis of his motivation for his problematic and destructive decisions can be conducted in the context of the dysfunctional family culture he created at Lehman where interrelationships served to detract from, rather than promote, the emotional and psychical health and well-being necessary to keep the company functioning.

FULD'S DYSFUNCTIONAL FAMILY

Fuld had created the illusion that Lehman was a close-knit family, but examining characteristics of dysfunctional families (Kaslow, 1996), and how the executive constellation at Lehman resembled them suggest that it was anything but functional (Tibman, 2009; Ward, 2010; Fishman, 2008).

- *In dysfunctional families speech is stifled and there is emotional intolerance to the expression of feelings or opinions.* Lehman was a culture of fear and intimidation where bad news was not allowed. Fuld's interactions were brief to the point of bluntness. Monosyllables and at times grunting was an often-used mode of communication. When Fuld was angry he would give his underling his intimidating stare. This meant one had better depart.

- *Dysfunctional families have addiction problems. Alcohol and drugs are most prevalent.* At Lehman the addiction was money. Fuld hired what he considered the 'best brains' on Wall Street, often at the highest salaries, with the highest bonuses.

- *In dysfunctional families there may exist a perfectionist attitude where there is a fixation on prestige, power, and putting up a good front to impress others.* According to Fuld he never let managers who disagreed 'square off' directly. The most dissension he tolerated was an agreement to disagree. Fuld stated, 'What I need is peace in the family.' (Wharton, 2007).

- *In dysfunctional families, isolation is often an issue.* According to Onaran and Helyar (2008), Fuld became increasing isolated, turning more of the operations over to his officers. However, the authoritarian climate he created cut him off from dissenting opinion.

- *In dysfunctional families the lack of impulse control is often a problem.* Fuld was feared because of his temper and outbursts.

- *In dysfunctional families there is little show of feelings and denial of an inner life.* 'In public at least, Fuld has never seemed to react with emotion to anything. When times were bad, he just said they would get better. When times were good, he said the same,' (Onaran and Helyar, 2008, p.1).

- *In dysfunctional families conflict is apparent.* Lehman had a reputation for turf wars, personality clashes, and power grabs.

- *Dysfunctional families avoid change or doing things differently.* In a discussion about leadership at the Wharton school in 2004, giving leadership advice, Fuld said, "Pick a strategy and stick with it...unless of course, you're wrong."

- *Dysfunctional families have an aura of self-righteousness about them.* Fuld recalled that in 1998 the financial press was filled with false rumors about the firm. Fuld's policy had always been to ignore the press and let false rumors die. He would follow that strategy when Lehman's stock fell. However, if things became really bad, he would be forced to go out on the road and talk to analysts and pre-release earnings to explain away rumors (Wharton 2004). This strategy failed in 2008.

What Fuld created was a culture that was a toxic mixture of resistance to and a fear of him, associated with ever increasing risk. This was most apparent when Fuld spoke at the Wharton school of business in 2004, where he cautioned that "the global financial system remains awash in liquidity that could dry up suddenly. If that were to happen, I do not want Lehman to be overextended" (Wharton, 2008). He did the opposite he embraced risk and overextended his company.

THE DELUSIONAL CEO

Fuld, while considered by many to be a private man, was also a celebrity CEO appearing in magazines and newspapers on a regular basis. However, his celebrity status and accolades may have had two problematic consequences. It may have encouraged Mr. Fuld to take more and bigger risks - in particular, aggressively piling into high-risk mortgages - and it caused him to find it difficult to acknowledge that his company was in difficulty. Despite frequent warnings from leading analysts outside the firm (even as its stock dropped from $85 to $22) Fuld was persuading investors that the bank remained on solid ground. After 30 years with the company, he came to believe he was invincible and rejected reports that the bank was in serious trouble. Consequently, his inability to admit failure and sell at prices he rejected as too low, led Lehman to the brink. This grandiose delusion was a function of Fuld's over-inflated sense of worth, power, and knowledge. This type of delusion is considered a motivated or defensive delusion which occurs when trying to cope with threats to self-esteem. In addition when failure results this delusional person blames others as the cause of their personal difficulties in order to preserve this positive self-view. This was clearly evident when Fuld was called to testify before Congress after the Lehman collapse, where he accepted no responsibility and blamed others.

Fuld created such an intimidating and demoralizing environment that his staff came to believe that he was not the problem, just the opposite, that he was in fact quite superior, and they, the employees, were the problem. The way employees survived in Fuld's culture was to target him with projections associated with fantasies of perfection. This phenomenon occurs in cult-like cultures and fear-driven environments. Employees, especially those in management positions continuously struggle with the fear of being devalued and unappreciated. Consequently a paranoid delusional system is created. The paranoid construction is maintained among employees when an aggressive wish is fused with idealization of the object and the hidden wish that the object (Fuld) will be all giving. This phenomenon is apparent in situations where a once idealized leader is destroyed. The idealized leader is now hated because during the employees' struggles with ambivalent representations of their leader as an ideal they also experienced him as persecuting. Thus, when the leader is destroyed employees regress toward the negative pole. This was carried out when Fuld was physically attacked after Lehman's collapse and Fuld had to flee to a retreat in Idaho.

Those employees, cognizant of reality, rejected an idealization of Fuld and observed him as being out of touch. Such employees were recipients of his rage, and they were then attacked as being troublemakers and not 'team players'. In reality they are bubble-bursting cynics and they pointed out how the CEO and his constellation used distortions to protect their delusions. To point out the emperor had 'no clothes' meant a symbolic death (Ward, 2010).

Over time, and spurred on by looming failure, Fuld became increasingly insulated. He was called the "Invisible CEO," withdrawing from reality and engaging in behaviors that appeared to outsiders as bizarre and contradictory. He created an exclusive club within the executive constellation called the "31 gang." This type of bonding within the executive constellation evolved almost exclusively from scapegoating activities where non-believers were labeled, blamed, and attacked. Fuld's 'gang' became exceedingly conservative, politically correct, and judgmental. Their primary activity was to support the illusion of perfection. As Fuld fired the nonbelievers, he reached downward, selecting more and more managers and potential managers who supported his delusion or pretended to do so. Reality became increasingly distorted as the deterioration continued, but no one saw it. Insulation is one method CEOs used to protect the fantasy of perfection. Another way is to dismiss statistics or "the metrics," suggesting the organization is failing and to increasingly rely on testimonials and anecdotal data to maintain the fantasy that things are very well. Another way the CEO maintains delusions is by increasing ceremonies where they congratulate each other and share stories about their perfections. Often the recipients of these testimonials are low-level employees or interns. The others, those who are scapegoated and labeled, are left out of these functions because often they are the ones who were verbally criticized either formally of informally in speeches. Another way is by following Richard Nixon's paranoid methodology and creating an 'enemies list'– and Fuld had his list (McDonald, 2009).

RISK TAKING – AN ARTIFACT OF A NARCISSISTIC CULTURE IN THE EXECUTIVE CONSTELLATION

Babiak and Hare (2006) see these CEOs as white-collar psychopaths, but in their description of the behaviors they appear to resemble narcissistic types. They describe them as: smooth-talking, energetic individuals who easily charm their way into jobs and promotions but who are also exceedingly manipulative, and ruthless. Herein lies the problem: The need to maintain an illusion.

Several authors identify organization decay as a narcissistic process; Diamond,01989; Schwartz, 1990; Morgan, 1988. They maintain that in these narcissistic executive constellations, rational engagement is subordinated to the need to maintain the illusion of perfection. Overtime the process of decay and the loss of reality increases. Each time failure occurs it is experienced as a narcissistic assault and requires the establishment of defenses to deny or avoid the experience. The executive constellation moves further and further away from reality, into high-risk situations.

Fuld has been widely criticized as the major reason for Lehman's demise and he has been ridiculed as an example of the high-risk Wall Street practices that sent the American economy into turmoil in the fall of 2008. According to New York State Comptroller Thomas DiNapoli, "Mr. Fuld's decisions drove the company toward ruin ...." (Tong, 2008). What was the motivation for these decisions?

Fuld was always a risk-taker. He began his work at Lehman on the commercial-paper desk, and was considered a formidable fixed-income trader. According to Onaran and Helyar (2008), "Fuld took a franchise he'd built from almost nothing, brick by brick, and then trashed it in less than two years," said Sean Egan, president and founder of Egan-Jones Ratings Co. in Haverford, Pennsylvania. "His biggest mistake was in not understanding the risks that had evolved since he was last active in debt markets. And he relied on the support of others whose interests were aligned with him." Who were the others? It did not matter, what mattered was that he surrounded himself with the infamous "yes men." One can easily come to the conclusion that any CEO who has the need to be surrounded by "yes men" is on the road to self-destruction, because these subordinates are filled with conscious and unconscious hostility that evolves out of the function of serving their master. They function as intimidated, obliging and thoughtless underlings, who may occupy prestigious positions but do so because they always say "yes." The hostility evolves from their feelings of being a fraud and their contempt towards their boss. Consequently, they withheld important information from Fuld and worst, they lied to him. Have "yes men" been known to lie to their bosses. Of course.

What Lehman had was a toxic mixture of resistance to and a fear of change, associated with ever increasing risk. This was most apparent when Fuld spoke at the Wharton school of business in 2004. "Fuld was asked how Lehman would be able to compete against much larger investment firms and international banks such as Citigroup. He responded that the size of a firm is not as important as its understanding of risk tolerance. While Lehman could support six or seven major deals a year, it will instead focus on three or four that can most benefit from Lehman's expertise," said Fuld, who cautioned that "the global financial system remains awash in liquidity that could dry up suddenly. If that were to happen, Fuld does not want Lehman to be overextended" (Wharton, 2008). The real tragedy was he allowed or perhaps encouraged Lehman to do the opposite. He avoided change and embraced risk and overextended his company.

The high-risk situation serves two purposes. One, it allows the executive constellation to maintain the fantasy of omnipotence, (they are winners). Two, it maintains the illusion of "perfection." (Only they, the executive constellation, have the skill to achieve in these situations: lesser executives would surely fail.) We have witnessed ample evidence of this in the Wall Street and banking meltdown.

The risk-taking also allows the executive constellation to engage in another wish, the unconscious wish to fail. As we have established failure, is reparation for the feelings of guilt associated with decisions they made that have injured others while benefiting themselves.

Examining the Wall Street financial crisis of 2008, Cohan (2008) states, "Bankers and traders get paid more for doing larger and riskier deals with other people's money. They're encouraged to take short-term risks with shareholders' investments. Praise and pay are based on size, not safety." While Wall Street executives work in a high-risk climate, the degree of risk may be a function of the intrapsychic life of the executives, as well as a function of the psychodynamics within the culture of the executive constellation.

THE DECAYING PROCESS AND GUILT: WHY FULD LET LEHMAN DIE

As mentioned before in these narcissistic executive constellations, rational engagement is subordinated to the need to maintain the illusion of their own perfection. Overtime, the process of decay and the loss of reality increases. Each time failure occurs it is experienced as a narcissistic assault and requires the establishment of defenses to deny or avoid the experience. The executive constellation moves increasingly further away from reality, into high-risk situations. A high-risk situation serves two purposes. One, it allows the executive constellation to maintain the fantasy of omnipotence, (they are winners). Two, it maintains the illusion of 'perfection' (only they, the executive constellation, have the skill to achieve in these situations; lesser executives would surely fail). However, it also increases the probability of failure. As we have witnessed with Fuld and others during the Wall Street and banking meltdown, risk-taking increases the probability of failure.

Fuld's actions, like bullying, and the accumulation of enormous wealth, should have precipitated guilt. One would expect the classic response to feelings of guilt; the making of reparations. Fuld could have followed many wealthy executives and established foundations or institutions to "do good." Multibillionaire Peter George Peterson is the classic example of engaging in reparation behaviors. He gave $1 billion to establish his Peter George Peterson Foundation. He said, "It's fun giving money away. I never had a better time in my life" (Newsweek, 2009). What joy there is when one can feel guilt free and still remain a billionaire. Making reparations according to Klein can not only reduce guilt but also depressive anxiety which will allow one to negotiate destructive affects or feelings and increase the feeling of being connected to work and people (Czander, 1993).

Fuld missed his opportunity. He was beginning the reparation process, and he had informed Williams College he would donate $100 million, but had to withdraw his pledge as the fiscal crisis hit. Consequently, he was faced with the guilt associated with his failure to make reparations at the same time that his Lehman family was in a crisis. Guilt is a powerful motivator and (it might be hypothesized) Fuld, overwhelmed by unconscious guilt, was driven to make the only reparation permitted: self-destruction. He would do this by unconsciously making reparations through lost wealth, becoming a profound failure and experiencing abject humiliation and shame. This has happened throughout history, as such people make what is generally considered foolish decisions and they lose everything. To a psychoanalyst these so-called foolish decisions are unconsciously motivated. The need to fail or lose everything is a problematic response to feelings of guilt; here the person turns aggressive rage and destructive impulses against the self, taking the form of an unconscious need for punishment and humiliation (Nunberg, 1934). But for Fuld, his self system was so fused with Lehman that to turn the rage against the self was also to turn the rage against his family (Lehman).

Rage is contained in the depressive position which lies beneath the narcissistic character structure, and, as we have established, it is the depressive position that fosters self-destruction. In the past, it seems that Fuld had used exuberance and over-optimism as a defense against the unconscious wish to fail. For Fuld and others like him, having spent their lives defending against failure required that, if he continued to be fully optimistic, he would continue to be successful. The depressive position is avoided by maintaining this optimistic attitude, even in the face of a crisis. This is why Wall Street executives became enamored with positive thinkers and used them on a regular basis. Consider what Lovallo and Kahneman (2003) say:

When forecasting the outcomes of {these} projects, executives {often} fall victim to what psychologists call the planning fallacy. In its grip, managers make decisions based on delusional optimism rather than on a traditional weighting of gains, losses, and probabilities. They overestimate benefits and underestimate costs. They spin scenarios of success while overlooking the potential for mistakes and miscalculations. As a result, managers pursue initiatives that are unlikely to come in on budget or on time-or to ever deliver the expected returns. P.58

Narcissism is a defense to protect what is underneath: low self-esteem, depression, a deep sense of uncared-for worthlessness and rejection, and a hunger for response and reassurance (Masterson, 1981). Lehman gave Fuld all the narcissistic supplies he needed. But this defense most likely failed with a lethal combination of overwhelming guilt and a dying family. When the defense failed, the aggression which Fuld needed to make the Herculean effort to climb the ladder was turned inward against the self and outwards towards the object (his Lehman family). Consequently, Fuld became a "tragic man" motivated to fail, to destroy his family, his company, and his career. Lehman was the object of his own guilt and he tried to defend against it by seeking sadistic gratification and by humiliating the object just as the object humiliated him. Klein (1940) calls this the "manic position" which interferes with any attempts at reparation.

Fuld had several opportunities to save Lehman but he rejected them all. Warren Buffett's offer was considered too low, and banks from Japan, China, and Dubai were also rejected. If he had accepted offers, Lehman would have survived, but Fuld refused.

Why did Fuld reject these offers? We propose that unconsciously he needed to kill Lehman. Lehman failed him and he failed his family. His defensive structure was weakened, and in the process paranoid fears were revived. Narcissistic gratification associated with controlling the object of his love would be gone, and the prospect of having someone other than he controlling that object terrified him. My thoughts are that he reacted against the fantasy that he would be forever humiliated by Lehman and would forever be outside his family looking in. But the outcome of his refusal to accept an offer was not only tragic for Lehman and its employees, it was tragic for Fuld. He was now left with regret, despair, guilt and shame.

He now survives by selling off properties, art collections, and other possessions. He will spend the rest of his life in court responding to the many lawsuits against him.

Psychologists and psychoanalysts have studied the hidden motivations people have to destroy their health, marriages and families, and they have studied how faulty policy decisions can be made by seemingly well intentioned leaders. But we have very little understanding of what motivates CEOs and bankers to engage in behaviors and decision-making that destroys the corporations they lead. However, one thread seems to emerge among these executives: They tend to avoid any form of engagement in thoughtful critical examination by creating cultures that breed overconfidence and "positive thinking." After the fiscal crisis of 2008 many executives claimed they saw it coming but failed to speak up. To speak up, make negative pronouncements or express fears and doubts are not permitted in these cultures. The need to maintain the delusion is paramount.

THE NARCISSISTIC DELUSION

Consider the following case. A hospital management team at a university-based HMO had failed to obtain a critical clinic operational license. This meant that they had to refer almost all of their medical cases to the university-based teaching hospital. Their failure was a major embarrassment. Management's handling of the licensing process was criticized by the state review as exceedingly inept.

Before the licensing process the CEO communicated to the staff that it was "in the bag." He hired a consultant who reported that their application was "perfect." Consequently, the CEO and his team were "perfect."

The CEO was brimming with confidence and grandiosity. At a luncheon, a week before the licensing review he gave the following speech:

"I have just looked over the consultants report (*no such report ever existed, it was verbal*), and let me tell you that in spite of some real problems (*referring to the "bad" staff*) we have overcome them. We are in terrific shape and we will breeze through the applicancy process. Of course we have some issues, but with our top management team, we will make all the corrections necessary. Don't worry no one is going to be fired (*nervous laughter*). By this time next week we will be drinking champagne (*applause*)."

He then proceeded to introduce each member of his management team and they each stood up and were applauded. He then continued:

"You know when I first arrived here five years ago this place was in shambles. I put together this world class team and we went to work. Some thought it was not possible. But we did the impossible. You know when you have a great team you can do anything, you can accomplish any task. That's what you have here. (More applause)"

The review process was a disaster.

An executive meeting was quickly, called and scapegoats were located. A "spin" memo was written and sent out to the staff. The executive constellation bonded even more tightly. They were meeting daily to share stories and observations concerning those identified as responsible for the defeat. Resignations were asked for and conflicts escalated as the HMO staff began to fight back. The evaluation report and the reasons for the failure were hotly debated and these debates went on for several months. It was only after the university president sent in a consultant did the conflict wane. After the consultant made his report to the university president, the entire management team, including the CEO, resigned. A year later, with a new management team, the HMO obtained a license to operate as a free-standing HMO.

These types of executive constellations facilitate decay. Even in a flourishing environment they struggle to survive. When the environment makes survival difficult, they are among the first to suggest it was others who caused the failure. They hold onto this belief even as they are walking out the door.

THE PURPOSE OF THE ILLUSION OF PERFECTION

The illusion of perfection is a distortion of reality. In this type of constellation, critical thought, criticism, and second-guessing cannot be tolerated. So powerful is the wish to be perfect, all slights are viewed as a massive narcissistic injury, not so much as the loss of self-esteem, face, shame, and so forth, but as a blow against the search, a discouraging setback against their need, and an assault against the fear that they will never attain nirvana.

This is the depressive position that lies beneath the narcissistic character, and as we have established, it is the depressive position that fosters self-destruction. The exuberance and over-optimism is a defense against the unconscious need to fail. Having spent a life defending against failure, they are fully optimistic they will succeed. The depressive position is avoided by maintaining this optimistic attitude, even in the face of a crisis. Consider what Lovallo and Kahneman (2003) wrote:

"When forecasting the outcomes of (these) projects, executives (often) fall victim to what psychologists call the planning fallacy. In its grip, managers make decisions based on delusional optimism rather than on a traditional weighting of gains, losses, and probabilities. They overestimate benefits and underestimate costs. They spin scenarios of success while overlooking the potential for mistakes and miscalculations. As a result, managers pursue initiatives that are unlikely to come in on budget or on time-or to ever deliver the expected returns."

While we can single out Richard Fuld as a member of this delusional club, we know that he has company. Daniel H. Mudd, the former CEO of Fannie Mae, had seen his shares drop from $26.5 million to $476,000. James Cayne, the former CEO of Bear Stearns, saw his value drop from $1.06 billion to $61.2 million. "These executives ignore the warning signs because they sought to massage their own egos and gambled with their clients' money for the chance of building much larger fortunes" (Piekara, 2008). Promoting optimism, engaging in diversionary strategies, and locating scapegoats are defenses often used against pending failure. When hearing about the problems, they immediately begin a process that has worked so well in the past. The more negative information they receive, the more agitated they become, until no more negative information is sent their way. From a psychological perspective, when these CEOs face the prospect of failure, they vacillate back and forth between a type of mania where they are "on top", and then swing to feelings of embarrassment, shame, and rage.

We have witnessed another method CEOs and bankers use to maintain a delusional system in the executive constellation and at the same time create a happy, overworked workforce that idealizes them. They adopt a philosophy, a belief system perhaps an ideology that suits their narcissistic strivings and helps to defend against the guilt associated with the need to have more. This form of thinking that has been widely accepted by executives, and now military generals, is positive thinking, which not only helps the executives maintain their winning, on top attitude and defend against entitlement and its consequential guilt, but keeps their underlings in the trenches working without question in constant fear they will be terminated.

The Negative Influence of Positive Thinking: Enter the Gurus and Coaches

Ehrenreich (2008) suggests that the greed we see in America's corporations may be a function of the cultural phenomenon of "positive thinking," and she suggests this way of thinking is firmly embedded in American culture. This type of thinking entered corporate America in the early 1990s and is now a staple, permeating executive constellations and in most corporations all levels of management. It can be said that in the modern corporation one cannot gain entry into the executive constellation unless one can demonstrate that they are proponents of positive thinking. Simply defined, positive thinking is a dangerous mixture of ideological "right wing" conservatism, religious fundamentalism, Ayn Rand's philosophy, and happiness psychology.

Positive thinking has been around for some time, gaining wide popularity during the Great Depression and further popularized by a Protestant preacher Norman Vincent Peale in his 1952 book, "The Power of Positive Thinking." He preached that one is thinking positively when one has a mental attitude that expects good and favorable results. These were the steps he laid out in his book and sermons for developing personal strength; steps that, if followed would lead to a successful, healthy, and happy life. He claims to give:

- **Confidence-building words to live by**
- **Ways to overcome self-doubt**
- **Strategies for achieving good health**
- **A program to release the vast energies within you**
- **Accepting ourselves and our individual needs**
- **Embracing the spiritual forces that surround you**

In corporate America it is almost impossible for a manager to avoid those who sell the virtues of a positive mental attitude. The attitude and how to get it is contained in a barrage of books, business magazines, corporate literature, and newspapers, and forms the basic message at corporate "pep rallies," which range from large scale, cavernous meetings of several thousand employees to intimate, pseudo group therapy meetings and inspirational retreats. Managers returning from these events eschew all forms of negativism even to the point of isolating employees accused of spreading "negative energy or vibes" and in some cases terminating them. What is a negative employee? Typically they are those who cause trouble, give their manager a "headache," may seek to mobilize employees against management or some change initiative, but in most cases they are employees who point out flaws, suggest alternatives, and question assumptions. They enjoy critical thinking and they love to diagnose and solve problems. One could say they embrace what the positive/happiness people dread, the diagnostic medical model. As a matter of fact, the positive/happiness people don't refer to it as the medical model of diagnosis, they call it the disease model, and maintain that it promotes victimization, pathology, and of course, negativity. As a consultant stated in an address to several hundred managers, "We have to stop focusing on problems or what's wrong, we need to change our attitude and the attitudes of our employees and develop their strengths. Negativity and pessimism spreads like a cancer and the only way to combat it is to get on with what's good, what works, that's our strength." While condemning the medical model he conveniently uses it. Positive consultants aggressively report that negativity is a disease and must be defeated and only a positive attitude defeats this disease. This is indeed simplistic or magical thinking, but it has a powerful voice in universities and among an ever growing field of organizational consultants, coaches, gurus, speakers, and writers.

In many American universities there are "positive thinkers" who like to call themselves "happiness coaches." Executives and bankers subscribe to "positive thinking" ideology and they point to the happiness research that has been pouring out of these universities. Conceptually and perhaps in other ways connected to "positive thinking" ideology is the happiness researcher, a former American Psychological Association President and University of Pennsylvania scholar Martin Seligman, who has also been connected to the CIA and Bush's torture programs. He chairs the university's master program in Applied Positive psychology. Seligman is also the author of "Authentic Happiness: Using the New Positive Psychology to Realize Your Potential for Lasting Fulfillment." Positive thinkers led by Seligman claim they have "scientifically" discovered what truly makes people happy and they now offer programs where they claim they can teach people to overcome negative emotions (anger, fear, pessimism, and sadness) and replace them with positive thoughts and feelings, and help individuals identify and cultivate their character strengths and use them every day to achieve happiness in their work. Of course, included in this potpourri of magic is a motivation to change corporate America by putting a smile on every employee's face and to develop and strengthen employees' positive emotions so that they can work harder and longer hours like non-complaining robots. To further their claims of legitimacy, the happiness researchers and consultants have created the Journal of Happiness Studies and a World Data-base of Happiness. Others who lend credibility to this movement are Tal Ben-Shahar, who teaches a course on Positive Psychology and Psychology of Leadership, and Shawn Achor, who teaches Positive Psychology and the Science of Happiness. They claim these are the most popular courses in the history of Harvard. Ben-Shahar gives advice and self-help tips, writes books on how to be happy, has lists of what one must do to be happy, gives inspirational advice talks and is called "Dr. Prozac" by his students. Anecdotal data suggest that every university in America is either offering or planning to offer a "Happiness" course in 2011. There is very little evidence these advice courses focus on making others happy, it's "all about making me happy." **Ayn Rand and the positive thinkers**

What does this all mean for corporate employees? This is nothing more than a brainwashing movement supported and funded by corporate titans and bankers to keep employees happily working at the "grindstone" while filling the coffers of the elite. Consider this. We find the thinking of Ayn Rand intertwined with positive thinkers and happiness gurus. Followers of the late Ayn Rand are found in large numbers among bankers and corporate executives and this fits neatly into the positive thinkers and happiness ideology. These Randians, or objectivists, as they liked to be called, believe that any encroachment by government into the free market system is a recipe for disaster, except when they screw up. Then it's OK to get a bailout. It's a perfect world.

Their rationalizations boggle the mind. While accepting the federal bailout they go so far as to conclude that the 2008 financial crisis was the direct result of government interference and regulation. They also believe:

- Altruism is destructive
- Redistribution of wealth is bad
- Self-interest/selfishness is good

This philosophy (if one could call it that) is not only preached throughout the corporate world, it formed the basis for how the Federal Reserve and the American government operated for many years. This was recently borne out when Alan Greenspan, the Federal Reserve Chairman from 1987 to 2006 and a long time disciple of Rand, told members of the House Oversight and Government Reform Committee that past decisions and the lack of government regulations helped pave the way for the current financial crisis. He angered Randians when he acknowledged that his libertarian (he did not use the term Randian) view of markets and the financial world had not worked out so well. "You know," he told the legislators, "that's precisely the reason I was shocked, because I have been going for 40 years or more with very considerable evidence that it was working exceptionally well." While Greenspan did defend his various decisions, he admitted that his faith in the ability of free and loosely-regulated markets to produce the best outcomes had been shaken: "I made a mistake in presuming that the self-interests of organizations, specifically banks and others, were such as that they were best capable of protecting their own shareholders and their equity in the firms." After more than 40 years, an admission by one Randian that her philosophy not only does not work but was responsible for the financial crisis and the loss of millions of jobs. In spite of this, corporate titans still pitch the Randian belief system to their employees on the basis it will enhance their wealth. There is no better example of this than John Allison, CEO of BB&T, America's 11th largest bank, who gives all his new executives a copy of Rand's "Atlas Shrugged" and new employees a 30 page pamphlet based on the company's Randian philosophy and values (Martin, 2009). In 2009 he resigned his CEO position, (he remained as chairman) to travel the country condemning government interference and joined the faculty of the School of Business as distinguished professor of practice at Wake Forest University. BB&T's Charitable Foundation offers as much as $2 million to schools that agree to create a course on capitalism and make Rand's "Atlas Shrugged" required reading. Some 60 schools, including at least four campuses of the University of North Carolina, began teaching Rand's book after getting the foundation money (Levin, 2011). By the way, in 2008, his bank, BB&T, received a $3.1 billion bailout from the government (TARP) while spending $5 million to finance teaching positions and research on Rand. We now see the B-schools fighting for the opportunity to teach their undergraduates the wonders of an almost perfect immorality. And of course these Randians collectively deny any responsibility for the financial crisis and teach B-students it was all the fault of "big government" and their excessive regulations.

But all is not lost. The faculty at little Meredith College in Raleigh voted 54-34 to reject $420,000 grant from the BB&T Charitable Foundation for an honors program featuring, at the bank's insistence, such right-wing texts as Rand's *Atlas Shrugged* and Frederick Hayek's *The Road to Serfdom* (Geary, 2010). All thanks to the liberal arts faculty. Hey, what an idea: Require business students to take courses in ethics, leadership, and economics taught by faculty from liberal arts.

We not only see an underlying connection between the Randians, positivist thinkers and happiness gurus spreading their ideas in corporations, banks and government, but we also see a bizarre, unholy alliance between the Christian Free Enterprise evangelists and the Randian atheists. While the Christian Free Enterprisers would most likely not accept Rand's position that Jesus devoted his life in an erroneous attempt to help a bunch of losers, they would suggest something akin to Ronald Reagan's "trickle-down" theory that maintains one should be free to accumulate as much wealth as one wants and those so-called losers will somehow benefit. We see the religious roots in positive thinking beginning with its founder, the Rev. Norman V. Peale, and carried forth in the studies by Robert Emmons, the editor in chief of the Journal of Positive Psychology. Emmons includes religion in his happiness studies. He says that religious people are grateful and gratitude is found in religion, and religious people see God as the ultimate benefactor. This is spelled out in the title of a chapter in his latest book "Thanks be to God: Gratitude and the Human Spirit" (Emmons, 2007). It comes as no surprise that "right-wing" ideologist's have embraced positive thinking and used it to lambaste the "left" by accusing them of being negative, anti-Christian, socialists. The late William Safire, writing for Vice President Spiro Agnew, called Vietnam protesters "nattering nabobs of negativism." President Obama is condemned by the "right" as being negative when he points out the policy mistakes America has made in the past.

Positive/happiness/evangelical/Randian thinking forms the basis for those who believe the following: government should leave free enterprise alone, programs that give to the poor are evil, government-led health insurance is socialism, and the wealthy should have hefty tax relief. There are even some of these thinkers who occupy positions of authority in Washington and corporations who believe God has chosen them to lead America.

Believe it or not, there is another group, an offshoot of these positive/happiness/evangelical/right-wing/Randians. This is a growing group of so-called organizational development consultants who preach a model of consulting based on positive thinking. They call it "appreciative inquiry" or "AI". Following the positive thinkers, their approach focuses on what works, rather than trying to fix what doesn't work. It is the opposite of problem solving or critical thinking, and rejects diagnosis. Narcissistic CEOs and bankers love "AI" because it never considers inadequacies, blame, or the need for remedial skills or practice. They preach a "you can do it if you just believe you can" attitude that claims if one builds on successes, strengths, and focuses on how to create more exceptional performance, then one need not understand what is "broken" or dysfunctional. To focus on what is broken or is not working is not only too negative, it is consistent with the medical model of diagnosis and that is to be avoided.

These "AI" consultants, "positive thinking" preachers and "happiness" coaches entered the financial corporations in the early 1990s and told managers and executives just what they wanted to hear. They were told to be positive, dismiss trouble and critical analysis. They were selling blind optimism, and bankers were buying. Gurus and motivational speakers told executives, managers and bankers to be successful "go for it," "you deserve success." "negativity is for losers" and have a "yes attitude." This type of thinking feeds into the development and maintenance of narcissistic cultures and what Ehrenreich and others maintain led to the financial crisis of 2008. They claim that financial executives, influenced by these gurus and coaches, took extraordinary risks and avoided caution, and engaged in behaviors that went beyond the boundaries of good business practice. These "success gurus" sold a delusion that success comes when one wills it. The "go for it" mentality is the equivalent of saying it's OK to be greedy, you deserve it. Narcissistic corporate cultures brought in these gurus, consultants, and motivational speakers for three reasons. First, they needed to justify their behavior of greed, selfishness. Second they needed to have someone say it was not their fault that millions of employees were losing their jobs as their executives got rich. Just as the compensation consultants obtained fat fees for suggesting outrageous compensation for CEOs was deserved and justified, these consultants and coaches told executives they deserved to be rich, and they were handsomely paid for their advice. Thirdly, consultants, motivational speakers and coaches were used to pump up employees. Based on the flimsy notion put forth by Tal Ben-Shahar, the Harvard happiness professor, who maintained that if a traumatic experience could create a post-traumatic stress disorder (PTSD) than an exceedingly positive, euphoric event could create a happy joyful employee. We witnessed the meteoric growth of corporate "pep rallies," or what some called "brainwashing events." These positive thinking "AI" consultants are not only running amuck in the corporate world they infiltrated America's B-schools. For example, consider this course, *Appreciative Inquiry & The Discovery and Design of Positive Institutions* – this is the title of course that was to be offered at, of all places, the Peter Drucker School of Management in the spring of 2010. Drucker is rolling over in his grave. This is something new in the annals of organizational psychology- the course instructor claims he will introduce the concept of a *"positive organization,"* which he describes as an organization that elevates, magnifies and refracts the highest human strengths into the world. Wow! This course is being organized by the prolific David Copperrider who claims to be the father of "AI". He defines appreciative inquiry as a "co-constructive inquiry process that searches for everything that gives life to organizations, communities, and larger human systems when they are most effective, creative and healthy." How is that for exaggerated nonsense.

POSITIVE ORGANIZATIONAL BEHAVIOR

Another similar form of the "School of Smile or Your Fired" is Positive Organizational Behavior (POB) developed and defined by Luthans

(2003) as the "study and application of positively oriented human resource strengths and psychological capacities that can be measured, developed, and effectively managed for performance improvement in today's workplace." They claim that one can "validly" measure and develop positive psychological capacities: efficacy, hope, optimism, and resiliency. To develop these capacities all one has to do is stay far away from negativity and what may be wrong with employees, leadership or the organization. No whining or complaining. One cannot thrive or prosper because there is no joy in negativity. I wonder if the day will come when these positive thinkers are old and grumpy and they meet each day and sit on a park bench and thoroughly complain about young people, their ailments, how pollution and technology has destroyed the quality of life and how the rich are getting richer and the poor are getting poorer, and they thoroughly enjoy sitting on the bench complaining. Their applied negative psychology for these grumpy old men facilitates their good life and enables them to be happy.

Luthans and others maintain that an organization's success depends on employees' creativity, innovation and:

1. Friendly and supportive colleagues

2. Enjoyable work

3. Good boss/line manager

4. Good work/life balance

5. Varied work

6. Belief that we're doing something worthwhile

7. Feeling that what we do makes a difference

8. Being part of a successful team

9. Recognition for our achievements

10. Competitive salary

These factors are nothing new. They have been around since the 1930s beginning with the Rothlingsberger and Dickson studies and the HR movement. Anyone who has been in a contemporary organization these days would find little evidence that these factors exist. How about searching for the reasons these factors have disappeared and what contributes to the destruction of a good life in organizations, at work, in communities and the larger system? No, that's too negative. Maybe Luthans, Copperrider and the positive people should read this book. What would Copperrider and the happy people say to someone who taught a course that introduced the concept of the "negative organization," an organization that valued diagnosis and focused on problems, where all employees were open to discussing not only what was "good" about working for the company but what was "bad," where management had an open door and wanted to hear their employee's personal difficulties, where no one was terminated if the company was in trouble and the gap in salary between the top and bottom was 20 times not 400 times. A company where all workers were happy because everyone shared the joy of good times and the pain of bad times and were open to deep analysis of both good and bad, a true learning organization. Hey, this is what B-schools once taught.

Is it any wonder that the rise of these happiness gurus coincides with the financial crisis, the death of manufacturing, the loss of millions of jobs and a growing gap between the rich and poor? It appears the thrust of their work is to alleviate the guilt of the rich and put a smile on the faces of the poor.

William Czander

PUMPING UP EMPLOYEES- "SMILE OR YOU'RE FIRED"

What do Wall Street bankers and retail giants like Wal-Mart and Home Depot have in common? They embrace this mixture of Randian, "AI", positive thinking, happiness ideology as well as free enterprise fundamentalist philosophy that seeks to maintain traditional male and female sex roles where men are the conquerors and heroic hunters (in this case in wealth accumulation), and women, use your imagination. Executives stage major corporate events that become celebrations of Christian manliness by emphasizing power, correctness, and dominance over all things, especially women. The pep rally in and of itself is a masculine activity. Like a football pep rally, the warriors are celebrated as they go off to battle and women are turned into submissive cheerleaders in skimpy outfits. At these corporate rallies they hear inspirational speeches from military heroes, celebrity professors, gurus, positive consultants and retired billionaires. They use an array of techniques to foster a collective or mass psychology by putting employees through a variety of exercises or activities where they visualize themselves as successful, instill a passion to be successful, and tell them if they "will it," they will be wealthy. They complete happiness questionnaires and are told to memorize and follow certain steps that will make them happy. They sing, clap, cheer, laugh, yell and cry. They are told that being a happy and eager follower is "servant leadership" and a good Christian value. They rally around corporate slogans "You can do it," "We can do it," "You can have it your way," "It's up to you," "Just do it," "It's up to you," etc. Psychologically they are expected to merge their self system with the corporation and its leadership. They become children of the corporation, and if the event is successful they become children of a cult. Employees identify with their corporate executives and in the process want their leaders to have wealth and privilege. Under these conditions leaders can do no wrong. If the company falters it is not the system or leaders who are responsible, it is the employees because they are not working hard enough.

There is another side to this. There are those employees who attend these events and go through these brainwashing programs and maintain an intact self system by using the defense of cynicism. They go through the motions, play the game and hold on to their job. Just as the elf in McDonalds looks the customer in the eyes and says, "Have a nice day," if they are good actors, the customer believes it is genuine and not part of the requirements of the role. However, if the customer knows it is not genuine and the employee must smile and say nice things, then it is a game, and the customer either feels insulted or detaches from the interaction. However, there have been occasions where the employee fails to express the correct mood, and the customer may complain that his or her expectations have not been met.

Here the customer is drawn into a latent or real conflict between employee and management.

This brings us to the real function of these AI consultants, positive gurus, Randians, and fundamentalist with their happiness programs, celebrations and demands. Their aim is to eliminate employer-employee conflict and create an unquestioning workforce that will idealize its leadership by cherishing their power and wealth while never realizing they are being exploited and oppressed. Also, we can see why these corporations and their followers are so vehemently anti-union. Unions are not only a threat to the executive's power, masculinity, and all the accoutrements that go with it: wealth, private jets, limousines, etc. Unions form a collectivity that is capable of defeating elitism and restoring the middle class. Consequently the elites have spent millions convincing a segment of the population that union activities and values have destroyed America. Over the years unions have been reduced to a quarrelsome sort, making concession after concession to the new power elite and their threats. Meanwhile a workforce faced with the anxiety of being terminated and losing everything defend against an array of dreads, real and imagined, by conforming and "smiling."

Failing to smile or exhibit a positive attitude, no matter what horrors exist in the external reality, are considered maladjusted. They are either fired or sent to "positive adjustment" events or rallies where they are pumped up with positive emotions in a climate that resembles a religious revival. They are convinced that they must adopt an upbeat vision of reality they must eschew any form of negativity. The goal of positive thinkers and their gurus and executives are to create a belief system or state of mind where the employee must deny reality even when reality does not elicit positive feelings.

And of course they have their "bag of tricks." One nonsensical argument they put forth is that one is capable of attracting those things in life both positive and negative. It goes something like this "You can have anything you want and if you think about it you attract it." This is what they call the Law of Attraction, whether it is money, relationships or employment, both good and bad, if we focus on it we will get it. What does this mean? It means those who are abused and battered, employees, wives or children, the unemployed, the depressed and mentally ill, the illiterate, the lonely, those crushed by poverty, the terminally ill, those fighting with addictions, those suffering from trauma, those trapped in menial and poorly paid jobs, those who are terminated, those whose homes are in foreclosure or who are filing for bankruptcy because they cannot pay their medical bills, are to blame for their negativity. It's their fault because they are focusing too much on negativity. Hummm. I wonder what they would say about the writer of this book. The positive, happiness, right-wing, evangelical ideology justifies the cruelty of Rand's unfettered capitalism and absolves CEOs and bankers of guilt by shifting the blame to those they oppress: "If you are in a sorry state it's your fault, not mine." This is consistent William Ryans' 1971 book titled *Blaming the Victim*. He concluded that the civil rights and feminist movements have shed light on the utmost form of injustice, the holding of the poor, rape or incest victims, minorities, or the handicapped responsible for their misfortunes. In it he contends that blaming the victim is a method of maintaining the status quo in the interest of the group in power.

THE HOKUM PEOPLE- PROMISING NOT ONLY HAPPINESS BUT WEALTH

The groundswell of all groundswells, the hokum of positivism that promises wealth, success and happiness is officially embedded in American culture and is rapidly being carried throughout the world by gurus, New Age and alternative therapists and fast talkers who claim the title of motivational speakers. Positive thinking may have had its beginnings in America, but that is all. We find ample evidence of positive thinking embedded in cultures all over the world, even in Tehran. According to Fassihi (2009), Alireza Azmandian is Iran's most famous motivational speaker and positive thinking guru who attracts tens of thousands each week to his lectures. Happiness books and dozens of magazines can be found at every newsstand, and "Happiness" magazine is the most popular magazine. Every day, dozens of self-help seminars take place, some underground at people's homes and others in public venues, all around the sprawling capital and in some of Iran's bigger cities.

One of the most popular books being hawked by positive thinkers is "The Secret." This book written by Australian author Rhonda Byrne was featured on Oprah Winfrey and tops the best-seller lists in Australia. The Farsi translation is in its 10th printing. State-owned television Channel Four has broadcast the book's companion video, shot in documentary style and distributed world-wide on DVD, four times in the past six months.

Another Australian David Schirmer, one of the so-called experts in this DVD, maintains that anyone can have happiness, health and wealth and that the secret of success is positive thinking. He maintains that one can transform their lives through their thoughts and that positive thoughts work like magnets, attracting wealth, health and happiness. This "law of attraction" is also espoused by Bob Protor, who maintains he has discovered the truth and is willing to teach the "science of getting rich." As expected, the only one getting rich here is Bob. In Australia positive thinking is taught at many universities and psychiatrists have adopted it and teach it to teachers under the assumption it will improve everything from depression to body image to mental health to grades.

In England teachers are taught to use positive thinking to get 7,000 high school students out of the depths of depression. They received millions of government pounds to support the training program. This approach is so widely accepted that a positive thinking guru was brought in to motivate the British rugby team as it was taking on its rival Australia in preparation for the Rugby World Cup, they lost. Maybe the Australian positive thinking guru was better.

The problem with this type of thinking is that it creates an illusion that is not based on reality but on ideological belief that rejects facts, critical thinking and all forms of disagreeable thought. The question is, who is in charge of defining negative or positive thoughts? In the "real world" it is the person. In the hierarchical world of work, it is the people at the top. What these positive gurus aim at is the restructuring of reality and creating a hierarchical world where they define what is positive and how to achieve success. This type of hokum has existed through history and the positive people are just a continuation of the false promise.

Psychotherapists and psychoanalysts get to work with these people after the power elite and their positive happiness gurus, coaches and consultants have done their damage. When the person is burned out, rejected, failed, or accused of being responsible for all the failure in their lives, they then seek genuine help, if they can afford it. But beware, the happiness people are entering the field of psychotherapy with promises of how positive psychology or PP interventions can be used to alleviate depression, anxiety, ADHA, relationship problems, and all forms of emotional difficulties.

There is no better example of an executive who tried to apply an array of positive techniques and gimmicks and failed than Robert Nardelli who nearly destroyed remarkably successful company-Home Depot.

CHAPTER 12

Nardelli and Home Depot

"While nothing is easier than to denounce the evildoer, nothing is more difficult than to understand him."

— Fyodor Dostoevsky

"The customer is King" Marcus and Blank (founders)

"We believe in the 3 E's" Bob Nardelli (the replacement)

This is a question those who study human behavior at work want to answer: Can a CEO be so rigid, so obstinate, so arrogant or delusional in his beliefs that he destroys the company he was hired to lead? Just as one is capable of destroying one's marriage, health, and career, can a CEO motivated to destroy a corporation?

Despite the fact that we witness many CEOs presiding over the demise of their corporations, and we have evidence that their behaviors, strategies and decisions have contributed to downfall and bankruptcy, we have no evidence that the motivations that underlie these decisions are associated with the unconscious wish to be destructive. The reason why this is a difficult question to answer is because the motivation to engage in destructiveness is a function of deeply hidden psychodynamic processes. An investigation into these processes involves an assessment of the interplay between unconscious and conscious ideations that underlie human behavior. While we cannot place a CEO who engages in such destructive behaviors "on the couch," we can study a CEO's personal and work history and draw inferences of motivations both conscious and unconscious that lead to destructive decisions.

We will attempt to develop a psychodynamic understanding of the decisions, actions and strategies of the former CEO of Home Depot, Robert Nardelli. In particular we will investigate Nardelli's attempts to transform Home Depot's culture from a decentralized, entrepreneurial retail culture to a command and control bureaucratic culture with a military emphasis.

In a brief period, Nardelli managed to destroy the customer-oriented culture that Home Depot's founders Bernie Marcus and Arthur Blank built over 20 years. The question we will attempt to answer is, why did he do it?

With no retail experience, Nardelli took a high-flying retailer with an impeccable reputation for customer service and moved it to a place where it became known as having the worst customer service among retailers. A year after his entry (December 2000), Home Depot was quickly removed from the top ten list of best places to work and never returned. How did Nardelli destroy the once undisputed heavyweight champion of home improvement? And, why did Wall Street, customers, and employees view Nardelli as toxic to the company they had once admired and loved?

A SERIES OF FAILURES

In studies of CEOs, they rarely face failures in their lives. Some suggest they live charmed existences. But not Nardelli. He faced multiple failures, and he kept pushing forth picking himself up every time he failed only to fail again. Bob (as he liked to be called) grew up in the All-American town of Rockford, Ill., and as soon as he was able, he sought entry into the military world. In his freshman year of high school, while many were protesting the Vietnam War he joined ROTC, eventually becoming company commander. After high school he applied to the U.S. Military Academy at West Point. He was rejected. While this was a major disappointment, it was nothing compared to the disappointment he received when he graduated from college. He was drafted into the military, but, according to Nardelli he failed his physical (Sonnefeld, 2007). While at college he played football, and dreams of a professional football career were also dashed.

Perhaps Nardelli's most crushing defeat came while at GE. In the late 1990s, Jack Welch was planning to retire and Nardelli was in the running for the top spot, but Welch picked Jeff Immelt to succeed him as CEO. After 25 years, Nardelli was out: another major failure. He lost something he desperately wanted and thought he should have gotten.

He was immediately tapped by Ken Langone to take the CEO position at Home Depot, and took the job in December 2000. This established what is perhaps Nardelli's most infamous and well-publicized defeat.

While his failure at Home Depot is well documented, we do not have a psychodynamic understanding of his motivations for an array of decisions that created confusion, intimidation and later anger among his employees and led to his downfall. We will attempt to understand what led to these failures.

TAKING OVER FROM THE FOUNDERS

According to Sellers (2002), Nardelli was the first executive without retail experience ever to become CEO of a major retailer and the first to take over from the founders. According to Sellers (2002), minutes after Welch told him he lost the succession race at GE, he received a phone call and was offered the CEO position at Home Depot by Ken Langone. It is questionable whether Nardelli had time to think about what he was getting into. It is clear that he did not take the time to fully assess and digest the meaning of his loss at GE. Instead he jumped at the Home Depot job, as a jilted lover who quickly starts a new relationship "on the rebound."

Many professional managers would never step into the founder's shoes, especially those of two founders who were idealized and had a powerful winning record. In sports history it is impossible for a new coach to succeed or replace a so-called mythical coach. Consider John Wooden at UCLA or Bear Bryant at Alabama. Their replacements could have a good season but they were fired, no one could fill their shoes. It often takes several years and firings before a new coach can settle in, and in the meantime coaches who enter too soon are destroyed. Wooden is a prime example. His heir Gene Bartow had 28 wins and 5 losses and won 85.2 percent of his games compared to Wooden's 80.8 percent, yet he received death threats from UCLA fans. Four coaches left UCLA in the nine years following Wooden. This is why most professional managers avoid these situations. But what can we say about those who jump in? One could say they are thoughtless or perhaps they are megalomaniacs, or in the case of failure they behave like a jilted lover and they grab onto the first thing that comes along, or they thoughtlessly grab on trying to forget or perhaps seek revenge for their failures. Witness the jilted lover who proudly shows off his or her new love, trying to give off the message, "I don't need you," "Now are you sorry?" or "See, I found someone better." These games people play may be somewhat functional in the affairs of the heart but certainly not in the case of CEO succession. Nardelli failed, and he grabbed onto the first job offer.

An important question was, why didn't the board carefully investigate, hire headhunters, or conduct a careful search when hiring a replacement for Home Depot founder Arthur Blank, the CEO who preceded Nardelli? It is difficult to understand Langone's motivation for selecting Nardelli. However, we can make some assumptions.

- The board was so frightened of having Blank in control that they grabbed the first executive available. They believed that Home Depot was out of control and that Blank, who was not a hands-on manager, could not rein in his managers in the stores. This was especially true for board chair Langone, located in New York City where stores could not keep their shelves stocked and chaos was prevalent especially on a Saturday. As a store manager in Yonkers, N.Y. reported, "we could have the store Opening Day ready, neat and clean, but by 11 a.m. the store would be trashed." Langone had a biased picture of what stores needed from executives in Atlanta. He witnessed Home Depot stores that were in dire need of supply chain management. He thought that GE managers could bring about this type of change and also combat the growing threat of unionization.

- There is general fascination with GE executives. Written up in business magazines and attested to by celebrity business school professors, GE was considered the elite training arena for executives. Boards often sought GE alumni to lead their corporations. However, this was more myth than fact. A study of these GE alumni has found that just as many fail as succeed.

- Langone served on the board at GE: Welch may have told Langone to call Nardelli the evening he received the bad news and give him the Home Depot job to ease his pain.

- Langone was the founder of a capital investment firm. He had a reputation for stirring things up. With his choice of Nardelli, he clearly stirred things up.

- This may be a real stretch, with one Italian selecting another: an Italian bias. We are only talking about Langone, here not the board. Langone was a controlling, loud, and at times intimidating man. He controlled the board. They quickly approved whatever he wished. There is even some speculation that he hired Nardelli without consulting the board.

This succession problem was further compounded because Nardelli was a MBA trained, "professional manager," replacing not one, but two founders who were classic entrepreneurs. Research on founding entrepreneurs who make or cannot make the transition to lead their company into maturity is dubious. Classic thinking on the subject suggests that founders are motivated by the creative part of building an enterprise, and will move on once the company matures. Others suggest that entrepreneurs burn out over time and simply retire. Others suggest that overtime the founders become embittered, that their company resembles a bureaucracy and they engage in conflicts that eventually lead to their ouster. Others also maintain that these founders can stay on and successfully manage. However, there is general agreement that the real problem for founders occurs when a "professional manager" is brought in to take their place, and they hang around. This is a recipe for conflict. This was the case with Nardelli. Marcus left the company and Blank took over as CEO, and after a brief period at the helm the board took the position away from him, but he stayed. In a fashion similar to Scully's expulsion of Steve Jobs, the co-founder of Apple, Nardelli got Langone to get rid of an angry Arthur Blank. Rumor had it that Nardelli and Blank hated each other so much that they had a physical confrontation.

Nardelli became Langone's "professional manager," but it is difficult to call someone a professional manager who's spent almost their entire career with one company. Professional managers are generally people who have had successes at multiple companies and demonstrate a significant degree of adaptability. Not Nardelli. He may be the best example of why many of these GE alumni fail. They fail because they take over a company and then superimpose the "GE way" and they quickly discover the corporate culture that cannot accept the "GE way." Before we begin to investigate why the "GE way" failed at Home Depot it may be helpful to look at the culture Marcus and Blank created.

BERNIE'S AND ARTHUR'S CULTURE OF FAILED CAREERS

It would have been simple for Nardelli to state in his first address to several hundred district managers at a meeting in Atlanta that he was similar to Home Depot's founders. He had failed at GE and he came to Home Depot to resurrect his career. Home Depot would continue to be a place that prided itself as a company that could redeem failed careers. Marcus and Blank believe that this fact was an important part of the culture and would lecture their managers on the need to use Home Depot as a vehicle to overcome professional and even personal disappointments. In addition they would proudly discuss the fact that they started Home Depot after they were both fired by celebrity CEO Sanford Sigoloff. But Nardelli could not do this. Instead he carried the weight of his failures. Consequently, he missed this opportunity to join the existing culture. When Marcus and Blank would smile while stating, "Thank you Mr. Sigoloff," Nardelli could not join in by stating, "Thank you Jack Welch."

Public self-disclosure or sharing one's story, was an important part of the culture that existed at Home Depot before Nardelli's arrival; it was the underpinning of its entrepreneurial spirit as it permitted autonomy and the motivation to deliver quality customer service. As Marcus and Blank would tell their associates, "Go the extra mile, bust your butt. You have a career here and if you keep that customer happy you will have a nest egg." Executives who grew up at "The Depot" would love to tell stories of the lengths they would go to satisfy their customers; how they came from failed careers, and the opportunities that "The Depot" gave them.

The Marcus Blank culture was built on eight principles. They included:

- Excellent Customer Service

- Take Care of the Employees

- Galvanizing, Recognizing, and Promoting Entrepreneurial Spirit

- Respect for all People

- Do the Right Thing

- Giving Back

- Creating Shareholder Value

- Entrepreneurial Spirit

It is important to understand the delicate balance needed to maintain quality customer service especially at Home Depot. Stein (2007) suggests that the relationship between the front line worker and customer can be easily disrupted, and he refers to "system toxins" that can easily poison this relationship. When does a front line employee go from happy, cheerful and ready to serve, to a remote, disinterested employee with a scowl, is a question most retailers would like answered. The answer is simple, and it lies in the relationship the front line worker has with managers, and so on, up the ladder. If decisions made by these managers negatively influence the worker, they destroy morale and customer service. These decisions can be simple suggestions that "snowball" into major issues. Nardelli's decision to install cameras in all stores is a powerful example. Management said it was to catch thieves, but employees saw it as an attempt by management to keep an eye on them. It caused a furor and further reduced the quality of customer service that had been badly damaged by series of thoughtless decisions. Above all else, the front line worker needs to be valued, not only by the customer who is grateful for the help offered, but by management throughout the hierarchy. Think of it this way. When a customer enters a Home Depot store he/she is entering a theater. The customer has items in their mind and these items are often connected to fantasies associated with the most valuable thing they own, his or her home, referred to as "the American Dream." From a psychodynamic perspective, the associate must continuously put on a show, be helpful and possess a genuine "have nice day" attitude. It's a performance. However, if management fails to support, disappoints or upsets the employee, they can no longer perform. Consequently, the job of management is to serve the performers, give them everything they need to continue to perform. When this does not happen, or worse, when members of management believe they are the actors, then the customer service system breaks down. When Nardelli gets a bonus and makes $32 million, and the store employees get on the average 10 cent an hour increase, it's a recipe for disaster. Quality customer service is only attainable if management understands its role as servicing their front line employees. If management makes certain these employees are content and happy, then they can go out every day and deliver quality customer service. Unfortunately Nardelli and his GE friends, with no retail experience, could not understand this.

CULTURE CLASH: GE MEETS HOME DEPOT

It is important to understand how a culture can be destroyed by the entry of another culture. For example, considerable attention has been given to the impact in Europe of the entry of millions of Islamic immigrants who have a strong disinclination to assimilate into the European culture. Instead they form what Caldwell calls "a parallel society." This is especially problematic when the immigrants (Nardelli and his GE alumni) have authority and/or power (beliefs). And it happened at Home Depot. Nardelli spent 20 years under the perfectionist rule of (Neutron) Jack Welch, who could not tolerate failure of any form. Poor performance was considered failure and each year the bottom 10 percent (in GE's forced ranking system) were fired. Nardelli came from a culture that emphasized deal-making, cost-cutting and efficiency. At GE, competition ruled both internally and externally. Loyalty was determined by performance, communication was direct and confrontational, and it was believed that leadership came from individuals, not groups or teams. Welch was called "Neutron Jack" because he left buildings standing while employees were terminated. GE had 411,000 employees in 1980, and five years later, 299,000. Nardelli came from this harsh, competitive business environment, run with coldness and military precision. GE, like the military he embraced, saw people in terms of good guys and bad guys. When he entered Home Depot he entered into a soft, friendly culture, where work was play and everyone was a good guy If we look at the eight principles that lay at the base of a culture created by Marcus and Blank we see that they are in direct opposition to the Welch/GE culture that Nardelli admired:

- **Excellent Customer Service** – GE made products and offered services to corporations and manufacturers. No retail customers shopping at GE. At Home Depot, the focus was exclusively on the customer.

- **Take Care of the Employees** – GE valued competition and only rewarded top performers. If one did not meet the numbers they were out. Calling his executives in for weekend meetings, Nardelli reminded them that it was not a job but a life, while Marcus and Blank encouraged weekends off for their executives. Whereas Blank and Marcus had motivated employees with hugs and cheers, Nardelli motivated them by instilling fear (Alic, 2008).

- **Galvanizing, Recognizing, and Promoting Entrepreneurial Spirit** – GE valued deal-making, cost-cutting and efficiency. Plans and endeavors go through the pervasive Six Sigma process and the numbers are crunched. Under Marcus and Blank, they lead a decentralized, entrepreneurial company. Blank had 10 managers reporting to him and they were brought together for a quarterly business review. Nardelli had 21 individuals reporting directly to him and they met every Monday morning for a two-hour "market intelligence" conference call. He demanded their data and action plans (Alic, 2008), and created a command and control culture.

- **Respect for all People** – GE valued confrontation, and Six Sigma determined worth and value. According to Welch, the forced ranking performance review systems created intense competition and at times warfare among employees. One of the first things Nardelli did when he arrived at Home Depot was to instill the GE performance review system. He could not fire the lowest 10 percent. Unhappy employees were leaving in droves.

- **Do the Right Thing-** GE had a reputation of skirting the law to make profits. Shareholder wealth came first. GE had been in chronic legal trouble in the areas of environmental laws, government fraud, and workplace violations. At Home Depot, doing the right thing not only encompassed laws, but also doing right by the customer and employee.

- **Giving Back-**GE gave only to the high performers. One worked hard and got rewarded. Home Depot associates gave back to the community, customer and their company.

- **Creating Shareholder Value-**At Home Depot, the employees were shareholders and shareholder wealth increased employee wealth. At GE shareholder wealth meant Wall Street wealth.

- **Entrepreneurial Spirit-**At GE, all decisions had to go through deliberate statistical or quantitative processes. No hunches were allowed. At Home Depot, the decentralized, entrepreneurial "do the right thing" culture was incorrectly perceived by many outsiders as being out of control.

These differences can also be understood at a deeper, more social and psychological level. The Home Depot culture under Marcus and Blank consisted of uneducated men and some women who shared personal stories about their past, experiences in the stores, and how they went the "extra mile" in delivering customer service. They were "meat and potatoes" people who owned dogs, loved NASCAR and drove pickup trucks. The culture quickly changed under Nardelli. He and his GE followers created a parallel culture that excluded everything about the old culture, even employees with 20 years of experience. Nardelli's culture was "corporate" and his employees were "salad eating" people, owned cats, were well educated, never told personal stories, and used quick wit and corporate metaphors. It could be said that when he began his program for hiring military officers, a third culture was established. They were like the Swiss Guard protecting the Vatican, closely aligned and protective of the GE culture.

Of critical importance in understanding why Nardelli entered into an impossible situation and could only fail, is to understand the distinction Zaleznik (1977) makes between managers who promote efficiency through deals and an eye for detail (Nardelli), and leaders who stir emotion, provide vision and generate commitment (Marcus and Blank). Gabriel (1998) following Weber's thoughts, suggests that leadership and administration (professional management) are not merely different entities but diametrical opposites. These two companies were also diametrically opposed; culturally, philosophically, and structurally. Home Depot under Marcus and Blank was highly collaborative, which encouraged risk-taking, and it was organic, open, accepting of failure and intuitive (a model appropriate to retail). Ideas and problem-solving suggestions were accepted from all quarters, and everyone was encouraged to contribute to making customer service successful. GE was performance focused, competitive, numbers driven, mechanistic. Risk-taking was valued and rewarded only if successful, and status was a function of the role one occupied, and roles dictated expertise (a model more appropriate to manufacturing and financial services).

It seems evident that Nardelli may have misdiagnosed Home Depot, or more likely in a compulsively rigid manner could not flex or engage in the required thoughtful strategic work. His strategy represented his theory of the organization, and that theory was "the GE way". The board and those who hired Nardelli failed to see how his limited experience with a variety of organizations would place severe limitations on his capacity to be successful in a retail culture like Home Depot.

APPLING GE'S BUSINESS MODEL TO HOME DEPOT

Nardelli failed to assess the most critical aspect of strategic change, the organization's environment or culture. If Nardelli understood Home Depot's culture or even the general retail environment, he may not have attempted to implement the GE model. In most cases implementing a strategic direction is similar to the scientific experimentation used to test a theory, where the results will either support or dispose a proposed strategy. Nardelli failed to understand this, or apply the experimental paradigm. This suggests that he either was unconsciously terrified of the Home Depot culture and he had to destroy it, or he was so enamored with the "GE way" that any thought of going in a different direction was immediately dismissed. In addition, having spent his professional life at GE, that's all he knew. It may well be that his motivation was a combination of the three.

Nardelli quickly brought in GE managers and GE engineering practices such as "Six Sigma" quality improvement processes, and Home Depot quickly became a business run by the "numbers" by assessing key performance indicators (KPIs). It is astonishing that while he was immediately implementing the "GE way," he failed to run any of these changes through Six Sigma, the GE Change Acceleration Process (CAP) or any of the types of experimental model GE faithfully used.

The GE programs Nardelli and his cohorts brought from GE had never been tried in retail. They were clearly untested. Applying the GE efficiency model by centralizing authority and decision making, and promoting uniformity (along with his military command model) was a complete disaster.

Nardelli wanted complete control. Headquarters would now make all the decisions about almost everything, from where to locate product displays to controlling the temperature of every store. A store manager complained, "We're becoming like Target and Kohl's; If you put the blue socks where the brown socks are supposed to go, you're fired." Store managers complained he was destroying their entrepreneurial spirit, and subsequently, turnover dramatically increased.

It seems evident that the corporate mentality Nardelli created infantilized his employees in the field and created an intimidated, hyped-up workforce at headquarters, where the blame game was played out in full force. Workers in the stores were constantly watched and monitored, their boss and their boss's boss, the district managers, or DMs, were ordered to fire store managers by headquarters, and VPs were ordered to fire DMs who failed to meet their metrics by the corporate chiefs in Atlanta. All managerial selection, promotions and training were centralized in Atlanta and conformity was the mantra. To engage in what was considered "a one off" were grounds for termination. This killed the entrepreneurial spirit.

Probably the worse example of Nardelli's inept attempt to apply the GE efficiency model was his termination of scores of hourly workers with years of experience. Six Sigma decided that senior employees who possessed excellent home building knowledge and customer service skills were making too much money, some as much as $28 per hour. They decided they could save millions by getting rid of these "overpaid" full-time employees and replacing them with part-timers. During Nardelli's tenure, half the workforce became low-wage, part-timers (in contrast to their historic model, ironically followed successfully by leading competitor Lowe's). These part-timers were not the experienced plumbers, electricians, and paint salesmen and women that built Home Depot's reputation. These part timers were inexperienced and uncommitted; they did not see Home Depot as a career, and they could not be adequately trained because the extraordinary turnover rate made training inefficient and costly.

Employee behaviors that endeared Home Depot to customers disappeared, like the "handoff rule." This rule meant customer was to be brought directly to the spot where the merchandise was shelved.

Store managers were inundated with conference calls from Atlanta, and they spent less and less time training or understanding their store. Having them focus exclusively on the numbers killed the entrepreneurial spirit of the store managers, and customer service began to fall. Inexperienced store-based HR (put in place by Nardelli's close friend Dennis Donovan) took over the training of store associates as well as the hiring and firing. Stores now became "sick," saddled with extraordinary high turnover, conflicts, stealing and gross incompetence.

Despite significant evidence that retail customer satisfaction was dropping, Nardelli's managerial emphasis was on efficient process execution, cost-cutting and meeting the numbers. He demanded his managers show obedience to authority by unquestioningly following orders. Couple this with grueling seven-day-a-week engagement, and managers bailed. During his first 19 months he lost 24 of 30 senior officers (Sellers, 2002). The dissatisfaction and fear among managers in the field trickled down to the workforce on the sales floor. Senior retail managers know it is impossible to deliver quality customer service when motivation and morale is low. In addition, Nardelli's Six Sigma people continued to centralize training. Consistency of training was the rally-cry. He moved training from the hands of experienced store managers and salespeople in the field and had legions of college grads at headquarters, many with no retail experience, writing classes that had to be taught following a page-by-page guide. Hundreds of leadership and field trainers were demoralized. At the same time they dramatically increased computerized training. One could go into any back room of any store and see several newly hired part-time sales associates sitting at kiosks learning about products and how to sell. Unfortunately most of them were napping. Nardelli failed to see that this method of training went completely against the learning styles of the new associates, and it meant that associates were on the floor selling with absolutely no training. Of course at headquarters in Atlanta the learning staff was touting the wonderful results of the new training software. Nardelli believed them, and they kept their jobs. Any company that manages by the numbers will have managers that fudge the numbers. And at Home Depot there was a lot of fudging going on.

THE THREE E'S

Nardelli quickly moved away from the "customer is king" service model. He wanted Home Depot to resemble GE's commercial and manufacturing businesses. His strategy was to "enhance, extend and expand." He proudly called this his three E's, perhaps taken after Welch's 4 E's. Nardelli's E's were: enhance the core business, extend into new business (like installed sales and PRO) and expand into new businesses outside the core orange boxes. He began to acquire supply and service businesses. Using the only business model he knew, he began squeezing efficiencies out of Home Depot's core business (the retail stores), while buying up new businesses. Nardelli spent billions buying companies to bulk up Home Depot Supply, and it paid $3.5 billion to buy Orlando-based Hughes Supply Inc.

At the time Nardelli left GE in 2000, business school cases and magazines were touting GE as the finest-run company of its kind in the world. A careful look, however, exposed a company in trouble, with a problematic managerial culture. Immlet, Welch's replacement, quickly recognized this and began to shift away from the Jack Welch GE culture. Immelt was creating a new management culture that surprisingly had attributes of the Home Depot Marcus and Blank managerial culture. Nardelli, caught in a managerial style time warp. came into Home Depot with a style that had quickly become obsolete. His autocratic, top-down, command and control style that may have worked at GE in the 1990s was no longer in vogue, not even at GE in the 2000s. Perhaps the only place it was being used was in the military. When complex acronyms for GE manufacturing programs were coupled with military language, managers who served under Marcus and Blank reported they had to learn a whole new language, and they could not adapt.

Nardelli may have realized this model was not working, but he could not change or adapt his leadership style. Instead he shifted away from retail into businesses he could more easily control and measure. To expand into these new businesses, he cut costs and streamlined operations in the core business, the retail stores. He radically altered employee incentives for good customer service. In 2004 the profit-sharing pool for retail workers shrank to $44 million, down from $90 million the prior year (Grow, 2006). In addition, the GE alumni who took over Home Depot failed to differentiate between the end users at GE (other companies) and Home Depot's end users (store customers).

In addition, Nardelli mistakenly believed he could move Home Depot into a market twice the size of do-it-yourself retail, namely the construction business. He was planning to service those who maintained the mentality "time is money." These were the professional contractors and builders who demanded low prices, great quality, and instant service. This created two problems. First: Could Home Depot meet the demands of service professionals? And, second: Wall Street analysts came to believe he was giving up retail. The stock went nowhere.

Nardelli grew up with measurement and numbers at GE, so that's what he built —things he could easily measure. Because of this, retail prerequisites, morale, motivation, expertise and passion, suffered. Nardelli neglected these important characteristics because they could not be measured. In 2006, the year before Nardelli was fired, the University of Michigan's annual American Customer Satisfaction index reported that Home Depot slipped to dead last among major U.S. retailers (Grow, 2006). When Nardelli was hired, Home Depot was first, and over a few years it was dead last. Quite an accomplishment.

BRINGING HUMAN RESOURCE MANAGEMENT TO HOME DEPOT

The mechanistic school that Nardelli embraced viewed employees as resource-objects, and he brought in a friend and colleague, who shared this view, from GE Dennis Donovan. Donovan was to take over the HR department as executive vice president. Donovan was one of the many GE alumni to enter Home Depot. Donovan's job was to make certain there was a steady supply of raw materials-people, and he was an exceedingly influential contributor to the havoc the GE boys brought to Home Depot. Donovan was Nardelli's HR manager at GE Transportation and Power and spent 26 years at GE. Donovan was hired in 2001 and Nardelli made him the highest paid HR manager in America at over $21 million in total compensation his first year (Personnel Today, 2005). He probably is the highest paid HR manager in history. Nardelli is reported to have said of Donovan, "He's not a backroom, second-chair member of staff." Donovan was the third-highest-paid executive at Home Depot. He had topped the "Workforce Management" yearly list of highest-paid HR leaders in publicly traded companies. Nardelli turned Donovan loose, another GE executive with zero retail experience. It was a disaster.

Donovan's job was to revamp Home Depot's HR Department. Within his first few weeks on the job he began a thorough assessment of all the department's capabilities, from staffing to benefits to training and all of its processes. According to McIlvaine (2003), Donovan said, "Basically, I wanted to ensure that all of our human resource initiatives are world-class in design, process-focused, metrics-based, systems-capable and simple." He continued, "There are lots of brilliant plans and theories that end up sitting on a shelf in three-ring binders, collecting dust. Effective execution is the difference between plans that become reality, and those that go nowhere." Donovan devised an equation that summarizes his thinking on this matter, one he repeats like a mantra to his staff and during presentations to managers. It goes like this: "The value added of any HR initiative is the result of the quality of the effort, the acceptance of stakeholders and its execution or $VA = Q \times A \times E$."

Donovan and his HR team took on the Herculean task of promoting more than 300 HR initiatives. For example, they developed an annual HR Review process, created four "learning institutes" (focusing on leadership, Six Sigma, customer service and enterprise learning), deployed a Web-based e-learning platform (to deliver basic product knowledge and selling skills to employees in every store) and implemented a profit-sharing plan for non-bonus eligible employees (McIlvaine, 2003). He also brought in a 360 degree performance review program to assess every manager and make certain all had to meet performance metrics.

As the result of lawsuits against Home Depot alleging hostile work environments based on gender, race, and national origin, Donovan decided to place HR managers in every store. The company was also dealing with increased union activity, and Donovan rushed to have these HR managers schooled in union-busting activities like spying and imposing anti-union rules. According to Verschuren, president of Home Depot's Canadian division, "Introducing HR managers into the stores was a smart, gutsy move that's been extraordinarily key. ... The HR managers work with the store team on developing talent, conflict resolution, union avoidance, and government compliance--things that require professional attention" (McIlvaine 2003). Within three months, the HR department processed more than 37,000 applications for positions, conducted 97 full-day career forums, interviewed 3,000 candidates, and ultimately selected 1,500 new HR managers (800 of whom came from outside the company). The project also ushered in a new "mass hiring" model that Home Depot would use for other companywide positions (McIlvaine, 2003). This "mass hiring" model was utilized during "peak season" which occurred during the spring when the garden departments opened in the North, Northeast and Northwest. These hires were spring/summer positions and thousands were hired and trained over a five-day period. Before Nardelli, the hiring was at the store level, which gave store managers control over the timing of hiring according to the weather. When Atlanta took over the hiring they were often hiring garden employees when there was snow on the ground and below freezing temperatures, or sometimes faced with no employees hired in the garden department as spring weather broke. Things were so bad that snow shovels were stock piled in Florida while supplies ran out in New York. Nardelli and his supply chain experts from GE were lost, and never figured it out.

Donovan prided himself on the speed with which he pushed forth his initiatives. "We accomplished in eight hours what would take most companies months, if not years, to do," Donovan proudly stated. He failed to state that most of these initiatives were taken from GE: Six

Sigma, Leadership Institute, the Change Acceleration Process, and SOAR (strategic Initiatives). All he did was remove the GE name on the manuals and add Home Depot.

While company leaders stated publicly that having HR managers in the stores was a good idea, they privately complained it was a disaster.

- First, it took away the important work of the store manager. The store manager was no longer closely aligned with store associates (employees are called associates). Store HR managers (SHRM) did not help. As one store manager complained, "They (SHRMs) just muddy the waters."

- Second, when hired, these HR managers often had no idea what they were getting into. They often did not have an office, and privacy was not available. Many HR managers were women, joining a heavily male-dominated culture. Joining the store manager team was, for many, a trauma. Turnover was exceedingly high, and this meant a continuous flow of ill-prepared and naive HR managers.

- HR managers were now responsible for hiring hourly store associates. Store managers became frustrated that these ill-prepared HR managers were now doing what they once did. Hiring was put in the hands of HR managers who had limited knowledge of what to look for when hiring, like skills in home improvement, tools, repair and customer service. The stores were being flooded with part-time incompetents. Some store managers reported that HR managers were hiring their friends.

- Home Depot moved away from a culture where the slogan "each one teach one" was prominent. Education in the store was taken away from the store manager and experienced assistants and given over to a HR manager who checked the box after the associate spent several hours on web-based learning.

- Store managers witnessed their responsibility for running their stores erode. It was not only eroded by bringing in HR managers, but also by Nardelli's centralization plans. Decisions once made by store managers were now made by headquarters. Autonomy was gone, and so were many managers.

Donovan maintained he was getting the buy-in of all his HR initiatives from the company's leaders, and that "acceptance" was an important part of his equation. Donovan failed to understand that with an increased amount of firings, Home Depot quickly developed a culture of fear and intimidation. Executives and managers were trying to survive in this metric-based system. What Donovan witnessed was not collaboration, but the nodding of the "yes men's" heads.

Despite failing miserably to win over the managers in the field, Donovan maintained a close relationship with his long-time boss. According to McIlvainey (2003), "Dennis is a partner and a confidant," said Nardelli. "He's brought credibility and respect to a function that was in total disarray. His personal energy, his ability to energize others, and the professionalism by which he packages and gets acceptance of his ideas has been a credit to us in making this transformation." Neither Donovan nor Nardelli worked to create the type of climate where open and honest assessment could flow. Instead they created a delusional system where the "emperor was always wearing new clothes."

In February 2007, Donovan resigned. Under the terms of his 2001 employee agreement, Donovan was entitled to a multimillion-dollar severance package, which was triggered by the January 3 departure of Nardelli. Donovan structured a most unusual employment contract. According to Home Depot's April 15, 2006, proxy filing, "cessation of a direct reporting relationship with Mr. Nardelli" entitled Donovan to leave the company "for good reason" and receive "all cash compensation accrued but not paid as of the termination date and certain additional benefits, including salary and target bonus continuation for 24 months and immediate vesting of all unvested equity-based awards." Including Donovan's past compensation, it is estimated that Donovan may have received $15 million to $20 million, plus retirement benefits, stock options and compensation already earned.

In April, 2008, Home Depot finally recognized the failure of the Donovan's programs (Six Sigma was gone), and announced it was cutting its 2,200-person HR staff in the field by approximately 50 percent. Over 1,000 store human resource managers were given the option to leave or work in their store as a sales associate. In keeping with the centralization of authority, now store managers use a call center to handle administrative HR duties like department transfers. Districts which once had between 10 and 15 stores now had four HR managers to assist the stores. There was also a district HR manager who supervised the remaining HR managers, and three HR generalists who focused on the areas of associate relations, associate learning and development and talent management, and of course keeping out the unions.

While Donovan's HR experiments negatively impacted customer service, it is trivial when compared impact of Nardelli's attempts to militarize Home Depot.

APPLYING GE'S MILITARY RECRUITMENT PROGRAM: GENERAL NARDELLI

The biggest challenge Nardelli faced was how to fit into the Home Depot culture, which was "thick," vibrant, fun and friendly. Or put another way, how could an executive who spent a career at GE, and with no retail experience, fit into the Home Depot culture? The answer was quick and decisive: He did not. Not joining the culture that Marcus and Blank carefully developed over 20 years left Nardelli little choice but to destroy it and try to build his own. He quickly jumped on the work of culture transformation by bringing in a score of GE managers and creating his junior officer program.

This was not the first time Nardelli applied the idea of recruiting junior military officers. In the early 1980s, while at GE transportation (despite the high unemployment rate in Erie, Pa.), Nardelli reached out to military personnel. His boss Jack Welch liked the idea, and GE became a major recruiter of junior officers.

In 2002, after two years at the helm, his managers were leaving at an alarming rate. Nardelli saw this as an opportunity to launch his store leadership program (SLP), a two-year training regimen for future store managers. He maintained this would solve the leadership vacuum. Almost half of the recruits into this two year program were from the military. In 2002, of the 1,142 people hired into the Store Leadership Program, 528 were junior military officers and 125 were military academy graduates. In 2006, more than 100 of them advanced to store manager positions. In 2003, Home Depot, along with the Department of Defense (DOD), established Operation Career Front. Through this program, Home Depot hired 10,000 veterans in 2003, 16,000 in 2004, and 17,000 in 2005. Nardelli's plan was working: He would establish a centralized organization run with military precision. Home Depot would now have a command and control structure, and he would be in command.

Grow, et.al, (2006) confirms Nardelli's wish was to embrace all things military. He called his employees "troops," and when he mentioned markets and customers, he dropped words like "enemy," "war," "mission," and "command." He liked to be called "The General" (Sonnefeld, 2007).

Early on in Nardelli's tenure, the company had good earnings, but the stock did not move. Analyst's told him it was because Lowe's had "out-comped" him. He responded by announcing to his troops a "Call to Arms" initiative. Grow (2006) maintains, "The military, to a large extent, has become the management model for his entire enterprise."

Home Depot and Nardelli received a number of awards from the military and related organizations. For example, in 2005, he received the Most Distinguished American Award from the Marine Corps Law Enforcement Foundation. Home Depot received the MOAA Distinguished Service Award for its strong support of military people, especially the Home Depot associates in the Guard and Reserve who had been deployed to Iraq and Afghanistan. Nardelli accepted the award. He was proud to have 1,800 associates who were deployed in the National Guard and reserves. Nardelli responded by establishing another program that made up the difference between military and Home Depot salaries of these deployed associates. In addition, Home Depot volunteers were sent to their homes to do repair for military families in a program called Operation Home Front. In the main corridor of headquarters (Nardelli called it the store support center) 1,800 banners were displayed. Importing ideas, people, and platitudes from the military was a key part of Nardelli's sweeping move to reshape Home Depot. "The military," Nardelli said in an interview, "trains its recruits to be leaders and think on their feet" (Grow et.al., 2006).

Nardelli also established the Marine Corps Corporate Fellows program, to prepare military on the fast track to top positions. James E. Izen, a lieutenant colonel in the Marine Corps, "was stationed outside Nardelli's door." According to Grow et.al. (2006), "During one recent project to help Home Depot hone its motivational message to 317,000 store troops, Izen consulted the Marine Corps Doctrinal Publication 1 on "War-Fighting." MCDP 1, as it's called in the Marines, this included a chapter on "developing subordinate leaders," which Izen found a handy guide for Home Depot workers. "It's about how to out-think your enemy," says Izen. Who was the enemy? The customer.

In keeping with his design to militarize Home Depot, in 2004 Nardelli recruited Carl Liebert to take over all Home Depot's stores in the U.S. and Mexico. He was a perfect Nardelli leader: A graduate of the U.S. Naval Academy, and he ran Six Sigma Programs at GE.

At large training events, military leaders were brought in to tell hundreds of managers how to be a leader, integrating Christian values into their talks and on occasion speaking highly of Bush's invasion of Iraq. If one was Jewish or Muslim it had to be hidden, an affront to Home Depot's founders who were Jewish.

Nardelli's leadership team imposed a dashboard, a KPI management system that was exclusively numbers-based. It didn't matter what went on in the store as long as it "made plan," which was a combination of sales and profit targets. Monday was the most stressful day for managers in the field. If a store failed to make plan, the bad news emanated from Atlanta to the regional VP, then the regional VP would dump on the district manager, and the district manager would dump on the store manager, and the store manger would dump on the assistant store managers, who would dump on the department heads. Failure to make plan would lead to terminations, and thus a climate of fear was created. Since 2001, 98 percent of Home Depot's 170 top executives have been new to their positions. Every executive who was on board when Nardelli arrived were gone by the time he left. The brain drain was phenomenal.

But did Nardelli worry? No. He was proud that Home Depot was continuously in the top rankings in GI Jobs Magazine. In the meantime,

Home Depot was removed from the lists as "Best Companies to Work For" in Fortune, and from best in customer service in all polls.

AN ANALYSIS OF NARDELLI'S FAILURE AT HOME DEPOT

All CEOs have obsessions that make it possible to achieve, climb the corporate ladder, and have continuous passion despite setbacks and frustrations. Failure does not stop CEOs relentless climb. They are driven to succeed, and the key is continuously channeling their obsession into productive accomplishment with a limited capacity to engage in self-reflection, especially when the obsession does not function well or is counterproductive. CEOs are typically surrounded by enablers who encourage their executive's obsession with accomplishment and success even in the face of obvious disaster. Therefore it is reasonable to assume that just as these obsessions can drive an executive to be extraordinarily successful, they can also lead to failure and defeat.

Consider this example: A young psychiatrist aggressively pursued his passion, studying the prevalence of mental illness in communities. He obtained a faculty appointment at a major university and was on a tenure track. He received grants from federal and state governments and private foundations. In his zeal to conduct his research, he overstated the percent of time he was working on the grants he received. When the percent of time given to each grant was added up, it came to 140 percent. Federal agencies wanted to send a message to all researchers and threatened jail. To avoid jail he resigned and gave up the grants. He said, "I wanted so much to make a contribution, to be a top scholar and attain fame, that I lost control." Did he lose control? Or, were some intrapsychic forces at play that unconsciously motivated him to ruin his career. One would think that being a psychiatrist he would have a capacity to engage in self-reflection and to know he was engaging in behavior that was illegal and potentially self-destructive. But if this wish is deeply hidden and unconscious then no amount of self-reflection would ferret it out, make it conscious. Just as Elliot Spitzer the former Governor of New York, and so many before him, destroyed their careers. No one is immune from this unfortunate behavior, and we see the process unfold with many CEOs.

Bob Nardelli had an obsession, not only his drive and ambition, but an obsession with all things military. Like all obsessions, Nardelli's began in his family. Perhaps it began with his father, Raymond, an officer, who served in Europe during World War II with the Pennsylvania Keystone unit of the National Guard, the Army's oldest division. Nardelli's relationship with his father centered around his military success. "I have always been extremely proud of my father," said Nardelli. "He served as a captain in Europe during World War II. After he retired from GE, he served as a volunteer at a VA hospital" (Hudson, 2008). In July 2006, the Home Depot Board of Directors provided donations to support the Veterans Memories and Commemorative Gallery in the Wilkes-Barre, Pa. Veterans Administration. The gallery was dedicated to Bob's father.

Nardelli idolized and identified with his father's military career and his father's life-long career at GE. Nardelli tired to follow in his father's footsteps in the military but failed. He failed to gain entry into West Point and even failed to gain entry when drafted. His hopes for a military career dashed, he followed his father into GE, where his father had been a plant manager.

His father worked at a succession of GE plants, from Scranton, Pa., to Rockford, Ill., to Louisville, Ky. In 1975, Nardelli graduated from college, married his college sweetheart, and went to work for his father at GE. After attending night school at Louisville University, he obtained his MBA. Nardelli wanted to move up the GE ladder. However, believing his career was stuck, after 13 years he left. He took a position as general manager at Case Construction, but after 3 years, he returned to GE, where he came to believe that he would replace Jack Welch, who was retiring in 2000. After all, he was referred to as "little Jack." Following in Welch's footsteps was similar to trying to follow in his father's footsteps. But he failed. He could not follow in his father's or Welch's footsteps, he was not going to be GE's CEO, and he was crushed. Overwhelmed with a powerful sense of inadequacy as a result of these rejections, he became obsessed with the military. If he could not become his father's ideal or Welch's ideal in reality, he could do so in his fantasy, by creating a "corporate military." He would further this fantasy by winning the favor of military leaders and veterans. Winning favor would also attach him to his father, the successful military man, who would be proud. In addition, turning Home Depot into GE would make Welch proud, and he would regret not giving him the GE top position.

Nardelli moved Home Depot away from retail and quickly pushed it into what he called adjacent areas, primarily service. This is in opposition to what Peters and Waterman (1982) maintain "excellent corporations do, they stick to their knitting." That is, they stay focused on what they do best. At GE, they did just the opposite. GE was all over the place seeking profitable ventures and disposing of them as soon as they became unprofitable. At Home Depot Nardelli moved the company in an array of failed directions. In 2002 he started Landscape Supply, flooring stores, HD Supply and in 2006, he opened Mall Kiosks, purchased Chem-Dry franchises and proposed buying a bank. These all failed or went nowhere, as did many other ventures.

ANALYSIS OF THE OBSESSION WITH FAILURE

The concept that has received the most attention in psychoanalytic research and literature has been that of defense, particularly repression.

Repression is defined as the suppression of conflicted thoughts, anxiety-evoking ideas, impulses, and fears. The idea is that emotions are not passive responses to stimulation, but rather mental states that motivate the person to actively seek or avoid by means of thought and action. Repression results from the intention to suppress an unwanted thought or feeling, and will paradoxically produce a pre-occupation with that thought or feeling. For example, repressing the fear of failure will promote an obsession with failure. For Nardelli, repressing the emotions associated with his failures actually promoted obsessions with them. The critical tipping point in the analysis of Nardelli is not so much that he brought the GE way and military ideas into Home Depot; it was his inability to recognize that a change of course was necessary when his methodology was not working.

There was so much evidence that his GE/military approach was a dismal failure. Yet he kept on pushing it, and in the process he denied it was not working. Instead he deluded himself with the belief that it was successful and that it was others, like the Wall Street brokers and the old Marcus Blank Home Depotites, who were at fault, and they were undermining his methodology. This is the *modus operandi* of a CEO driven to unconsciously fail. They fail to recognize that change is necessary when their grand plans are failing. In the case of Nardelli and his GE alums they only knew one way of running a company, and to try another method was too anxiety-producing. In the case of Home Depot, accepting the Marcus Blank entrepreneurial culture was, in a psychological sense, impossible for the GE boys. Why?

Pride prevented Nardelli from joining the Home Depot culture. This culture was beneath Nardelli and well-educated GE alums who joined him, and beneath the idealized "GE way." When he began to experience failure at Home Depot he filled himself with delusions of success, power and hubris which not only caused him to engage in immoderate or risky behavior but led to imprudent and dangerous business decisions. These decisions inexorably led to failure.

PRIDE AND HUBRIS

CEOs in general have expansive tendencies and what they find appeals to them most is not love, but mastery. They abhor helplessness, are ashamed of suffering, and need to achieve success, prestige, or recognition. In *Neurosis and Human Growth* (1950), Horney divided these expansive people into three types -- narcissistic, perfectionist, and arrogant-vindictive.

Nardelli was clearly not a narcissistic type. While he did contain elements of self-admiration, he failed to demonstrate the major characteristics of the narcissistic personality; charm, attractiveness, or star quality. Nardelli most likely demonstrated a remarkable ability to shape his behavior and character to fit into the narcissistic executive constellation culture at GE. On the other hand, he was clearly perfectionist, arrogant and vindictive. Nardelli had extremely high standards, which allowed him to look down upon others. He took great pride in his attention to details and aimed for "flawless execution." He would insist that his managers live up to his standards of perfection, and if they could not, he would "flip-out." His expressions of anger and contempt were a way of externalizing his own self-condemnation. Perfectionists create a legalistic bargain in their mind which goes something like this: "I am dutiful and hard-working and strive to be the best, therefore this entitles me to be idealized and loved by others." This conviction of an infallible justice operating in life gives [them] a feeling of mastery (Horney, 1950). However, at Home Depot, pushing high standards and demands on overwhelmed and overworked managers brought about failure, and Nardelli responded to these failures with arrogant-vindictive behavior.

He needed vindictive triumphs, and the non-GE alums and left over Marcus and Blank managers were his victims. Consequently, Nardelli created a Darwinian culture at Home Depot where only the fittest survived and the strong annihilated the weak. Who were these weak people? The weak were those who loved to deliver customer service with a smile, they loved Home Depot, they were highly spirited and joyful and they were annihilated. Nardelli needed to re-create the hard and tough GE culture where all manifestations of feelings were regarded as signs of weakness. Nardelli's vision of life was that it was a battle. He created a battle-field and then brought in the military to win the war.

Over time as Nardelli faced failure he became increasingly tyrannical. Obsessed with the avoidance of failure and capable of becoming enraged, self-righteous and prideful, it was those around him who made mistakes, not he. When things were not going right he became aggressive, tenacious and relentless. In other words, when his decisions were questioned or when he felt he was wrong (failing), he became tyrannical.

His obsessional fear of failure also interfered with his ability to think strategically, to take a step back and engage in critical thought or self-reflection. Sellers (2002) in agreement states that the obsessive or perfectionist individual excessively focuses on details. "They cannot see the big picture and are not very strategic." Nardelli was tactical, not strategic, meaning that he could not engage in the work of assessing the long-term consequences of his actions (failure). In the case of Home Depot this deficiency was certainly in evidence.

When he joined Home Depot Nardelli met a unique culture, filled with excitement, recklessness, fun, and passion. This culture threatened what he idealized; the rigid military and the GE structure that he knew and loved. He was compelled to destroy Home Depot's culture and replace it with the world of structure, obedience, order, rules and command. This wish to destroy the culture was an internal saboteur, or similar to Carl G. Jung's "Shadow" or that part of the personality that acts like an inner tyrant. GE and the military also functioned as Nardelli's "shadow" because eventually they sabotaged his ability to succeed.

Why did Nardelli need to keep pushing and rigidly impose the GE/Military structure when early signs indicated it was not working? It was not only the only thing he knew, he fully believed it would work. Nardelli's pride and self system was clearly attached to this way of managing and his pride contributed to his rigidity. According to Bell (1999), pride that derives from self-respect has no need for enemies. However, pride based on arrogance requires enemies to denigrate and destroy. This explains why he terminated so many executives. He saw them as enemies, as sons and daughters of Marcus and Blank. They represented customer service and the warm, friendly, and caring relations needed to deliver "quality" customer service. Consider this example. A group of managers were on a store walk and they saw an elderly man trying to lift and place a 5-gallon can of paint in his wagon. A regional vice president (RVP) ran over and lifted the heavy can into the man's wagon and took him to the checkout counter and then to the man's car and loaded it in his trunk. The RVP had a wonderful time discussing how he was helping his son-in-law paint his house. After the paint was loaded, at the encouragement of the RVP, the man went back to the store and purchased an additional amount of paint supplies. The RVP came back to the group with a smiled and said "this is like the good old days and it makes me feel good. Why can't we get that back?" The RVP, who worked his way up the ladder from a lot-wagon attendant, soon left the company. Only a manager who worked at the store level on their trip to the top understood the realities associated with customer service. For an executive like Nardelli who had no retail or customer service experience, he was at a terrible disadvantage. Instead he followed what he learned at GE and went on a destructive acquisition spree.

The most critical period for any CEO entering a company from the outside is the first three months. Home Depot managers neither heard nor saw Nardelli during his first three months. The joke was that he was in Atlanta hiding under his desk. Success would have occurred if Nardelli did three things when he entered Home Depot: (1) Promised and sought to maintain the existing culture, namely customer service, and (2) Joined the culture and exhibited respect for the founding fathers, Marcus and Blank, and (3) Made it clear he was going to put on an apron and join the boys in the field. For Nardelli his idea of work would not allow play, spontaneity, and the passion. Nardelli perceived these activities as exposing vulnerability and would bring to the surface the increase possibility of failure. According to Lubit (2004), for some, the fear of failure or loss is so great and the solution so rigorous that they lose all flexibility and spontaneity. This explains why the Home Depot officers were terminated or forced out because they represented a culture of spontaneity, flexibility, playfulness, and people-orientated activity. Lubit (2004), also maintains that "expression of warm feelings toward people and engagement in playful activities require spontaneity and a loosening of controls." Again, this is threatening to Nardelli and his followers. It was often said he and his followers looked uncomfortable when they eventually donned the orange aprons. The apron represented the feelings of "let's go have some fun and sell stuff." For people who needed control and perfection, fun was out and it was replaced with a culture preoccupied with numbers, details, rules, lists, and order. The culture Nardelli wanted was a failure avoidance culture. It is similar to the U.S. military's invasion of Iraq, and Afghanistan. Now that we have landed in this strange country let's try to avoid failure.

THE DEFECTIVE CEO AND THE DRIVE TO SUCCEED

At GE, Nardelli was known as "Little Jack." In June 2002 he stated: "There was always this rap against me about being functionally proficient but not very strategic" (Sellers, 2002). Nardelli also had a reputation for being somewhat inarticulate, (Alic, 2008). This is the closest Nardelli comes to self-examination. He calls it a "rap against me," meaning it was true. If it were untrue, it would have been referred to as a "bum rap." Nardelli had to compensate for these perceived "defects". His size (too small) made him tenacious on the football field, his failure to be accepted into the military made him a tough military devotee, and his inability to come off as polished and "presidential" made him work harder and longer hours. The perception of being defective must have dramatically increased when Welch chose Immelt, the articulate, polished, Ivy Leaguer.

Following Adler (1956), Nardelli's drive to succeed was motivated by compensating or striving to overcome real or imagined defects. Adler maintains all people problems, short-comings, inferiorities of one sort or another, and personalities could be accounted for by the ways in which people do -- or don't -- compensate or overcome these problems. For Nardelli multiple defeats caused him to pursue success with great tenacity. His reaction was to be tougher, more in command and control.

MAKING THE HOME DEPOT CULTURE MACHO

Marcus and Blank had created a revolutionary model. They took men from typically male oriented occupations plumbers, electricians, carpenters, etc. and turned them into caring salespeople. From a psychological perspective, they integrated the animus/anima or masculine/feminine. How did Marcus and Blank do it? They created a safe environment for their employees. They were seen by employees as "good leaders and idealized father figures" who instilled passion, love and affection. Together they created a culture where it was valued to work hard, have fun, play, and smile. Showing emotions, from telling heart-felt stories, hearing stirring speeches, and "bleeding orange" was almost a constant. For many employees, Home Depot became a "cult-like" experience. This raises an important issue. Business writers, celebrity professors, Nardelli, and his GE alumni maintained that the Home Depot they took over was out of control; a decentralized, free-wheeling culture that had to be reined in. The truth of the matter was that this "cult-like" Home Depot had a great deal of discipline. Not discipline in the top-down corporate or military sense, but discipline based on emotional attachment, commitment, and charisma. Nardelli and his GE boys could not understand this, and more important, they were frightened by it. Nardelli had to install his model of management that followed a top-down, discipline based structure, fear and threat. In Nardelli's world showing emotions, sensitivity or empathy were considered signs of weakness. Being strong, tough and macho were accepted, therefore, in Nardelli's culture, the joy of serving the customer was out, it was too feminine.

Donovan's attempt to increase the role of human resources (HR) was an attempt to split Home Depot into a feminine side (HR) and a masculine side (operations). But it did not work. Donovan made a futile attempt to bring the GE way of order, numbers, rules and Six Sigma into HR. The HR hires, mostly women, were trained in classic HR work and rejected his attempts to turn their work into a masculine disciplinary model. They left in droves.

Just as Donovan failed to get his HR women onboard, it became clear that Nardelli was not going to get these Home Depot men onboard. He could not be passionate and inspirational. He could not get up on the stage and connect with his managers in the field. He could not "bleed orange." and over a short period of time neither did anyone else. He could not show vulnerability, he could not give up the "tough-guy," no nonsense, "my way or the highway" approach. All he could lead were the numbers crunchers from GE, military officers, and the college boys he hired into his Store Leadership Program. In the field there was a major gap between the military/college hires and store associates. Also the message was clear to store associates: if they worked hard and gave great customer service they would never be promoted. Management jobs in the field were given to his external hires with the promise that after some time in the stores they would be sent to headquarters. This was an unmitigated failure; military men hated working in the stores and knew nothing of customer service, fought with and fired experienced associates, demanded obedience, and became impatient with the lack of fast promotion to Atlanta headquarters. When one military recruit asked Nardelli how long it would take to get to headquarters, Nardelli responded by stating, "Son, this is a coaching moment, we do not call it headquarters, we call it the store support center." Nardelli failed to respond to the meaning of the young man's question which was read by some as, "How long will it take to get my ass out of this war zone, called the store, and get home to a desk job."

When Nardelli realized that things were not working and his board began to question his leadership and Wall Street began to call for his resignation, he grew increasingly distant and angry. He failed to show up at store manager's meetings, and at a stock-holders meeting he showed up by himself without his board of directors or officers, refused to answer questions and quickly departed. It was clear to all that the end was near.

In conclusion, we observe a troubling story of distorted needs and wishes that began early on in Nardelli's life. All he needed to do was to get rid of these Marcus loyalists and surround himself with his GE colleagues and junior officers and all would be well. Obviously, it did not work. While he successfully surrounded himself with his military people, he found himself alone with the Marcus gang demanding he leave. He left as the poster child of excess, greed (he received a $210 million exit package) and failure, with his reputation in shambles and his legacy being rapidly dismembered.

HOWEVER, THIS IS NOT THE END OF THE STORY

Nardelli gets to live another day. In August 2007, just days after private equity firm Cerberus Capital Finance closed its purchase of 80.1 percent of Chrysler from DaimlerChrysler AG, taking the automaker private, they shocked the business community by appointing Nardelli its CEO. In January 2008, Nardelli announced his three-year plan to make Chrysler profitable. He wouldn't say when this plan would be implemented, but he said: "We have a very clear vision on when we'll return to profitability." He said "We made progress in 2007 (Chrysler lost $1.6 billion in 2007) and we'll make more progress in 2008."

Since, early 2007 Chrysler had cut 32,000 jobs, (Bunkley and Vlasic,2008). Nardelli terminated 1,000 salaried employees in September 2008 and 4,333 in October. He called these terminations "voluntary retirements." In December 2008, Nardelli along with the CEOs from Ford and GM were in Washington seeking a bailout, to avoid bankruptcy. He closed all of its plants in December 2008 for at least four weeks, after receiving a pledge of a $4 billion "bridge loan" from the government. In May 2006, Chrysler filed for bankruptcy.

While accepting a federal bailout and terminating thousands of employees, Nardelli paid about $30 million in bonuses to top executives. Because Chrysler was now private, no one knew Nardelli's compensation. However, occasionally some information was leaked. Documents obtained by Walsh and Higgin, (2008) show that at least six Chrysler executives were due to receive bonuses of more than $1 million apiece to stay through 2010. They called these "retention bonuses." According to Walsh and Higgins, (2008), those promised the largest retention bonuses were:

- Frank Ewasyshyn, EVP, manufacturing, $1.89 million.

- Frank Klegon, EVP, product development, $1.8 million.

- Nancy Rae, HR and Communications VP$1.66 million.

- Simon Boag, President, Mopar/global service and parts, $1.65 million.

- Steven Landry, EVP, North American sales, $1.63 million.

- Michael Manley, EVP, international sales, marketing and business development, $1.53 million.

According to Sonnenfeld (2007), "In my studies on how leaders recover from adversity, I have found that leaders must acknowledge their setbacks and identify new heroic missions. Nardelli's formula for repeated failure was to deny setbacks and try to re-create lost battles, slipping into the quicksand of his past failures. Humorist Stephen Wright's complaint of suffering amnesia and déjà vu at once, "I think I've forgotten this before," might apply to many fallen leaders who failed to learn from failure.

Now that Nardelli is a CEO again, does he indicate any insight into his decisions that led to failures? In August 2009, Nardelli was asked if he would apply the plan he used for Home Depot at Chrysler. He replied, "Ab-so-lute-ly." "This is the third time this business model has been successful" (Marks, 2009). In April 2009 Chrysler filed for bankruptcy and in June of 2009 emerged under Automobile Workers Union, Fiat and government ownership. Under the leadership of Fiat, Nardelli resigned from Chrysler in June 2009. Nardelli's denial of reality was so profound he saw success in the face of gross failure. For example when exploring the fact that Steve Feinberg the founder of Cerberus who bought Chrysler for $7.4 billion and in July 2009 it was worth $1.4 billion, and needed a $22.6 billion federal government bailout to stay afloat, Nardelli stated "Steve saw this as a huge patriotic opportunity, in addition to a great investment." Feinberg looses $6 billion and Nardelli called it a great investment.

So what did Nardelli do at Chrysler? He restructured, fought with senior leaders, and imposed his business model, the same as he did at Home Depot. If he'd his way he would have lowered employee salaries, but unlike Home Depot, Chrysler was unionized. Instead he fired non-union, white collar employees, especially those who disagreed with him. In addition, he cut spending by taking away from research and development. Were fuel-efficient cars on the planning board? Probably not, his team planned to introduce only four new cars within the next five years And, to the surprise of no one he claimed he had a secret weapon to turn around Chrysler, " Military Talent" and of course Dennis "I will change everything" Donovan.

We will leave this analysis with this observation: Failure to acknowledge failure is the *modus operandi* of the "tragic man."

In July 2009 Fiat CEO Sergio Marchionne took over Chrysler operations upon its emergence from bankruptcy. What did he find? "A mess," said Marchionne. This is not surprising given what private equity firms typically do when they purchase a company: they cut everything. Cerberus was no different; they brought in Nardelli to do a poor imitation of "chainsaw" Al Dunlap. Nardelli indiscriminately gutted departments and literally destroyed Chrysler. It is highly doubtful that Marchionne will be able to keep this destroyed company alive let alone return to its glory days. Meanwhile Marchionne is having big problems across the Atlanta and he is threatening to terminate as many as 60,000 employees in 2010 unless the Italian government doesn't bail Fiat out. Marchionne is so enamored with being a CEO of an American auto company that he is behaving like one. In 2009 he earned $6.5 million (4.8 million euro), a 41 percent increase in compensation. In 2010 Marchionne received almost $5 million in total compensation. In 2011 as he was preparing to enter into contract negotiations with Chrysler unions he aligned himself with the tenants of the Occupy Wall Street movement and decried income inequality in the world and said he would be looking for concessions from the unions in 2012 to remain competitive. He also thanked the Canadian and Ontario governments for the $2.9 billion bailout package they gave Chrysler in 2009.

Let's see, he gets a bailout, wants to reduce the gap between the rich and the poor and he tells his employees to take wage reductions as he gets millions. Here we go again. Sounds like Nardelli in disguise.

DESTRUCTION OF THE AMERICAN CORPORATION

We have set out to prove that just as people can destroy their marriage, their health, children and careers, they are capable of destroying a corporation. With the Nardelli case we are able to get a glimpse into his history, background, and psychological motivations and how this may have contributed to the remarkably problematic decisions he made. He did not destroy Home Depot, but he certainly destroyed its culture. It is doubtful Home Depot will ever return to its glory days. Did he destroy Chrysler? We shall see if it can be saved.

Is this an isolated case? We believe not. We have found a wide array of CEOs engaged in selfish, money-grabbing acts devoid of any thought or concern for the corporations they are responsible to lead. We have found that when these CEOs discover that they are over their heads, unable to adapt to a set of organizational realities, they respond by forcing their own values and beliefs on the corporation and they rigidly hold onto that which they know best, even in the face of repeated failures. In addition they become inflexible and angry at those who propose alternative ways of thinking or acting and in the process cause great suffering. Many corporate boards discover too late that the inner turbulence of their CEOs leads to problematic decision-making. This seems to occur more often when CEOs are recruited from outside the firm.

HE'S BACK

After leading Chrysler into bankruptcy and then departing, Nardelli turns up again. In July 2009 he was appointed CEO of Cerberus Operating and Advisory Company LLC. the unit that oversees management and operations of companies that funds and accounts managed by Cerberus. And his partner Donovan will join him. Cerberus Chief Operating Officer Mark Neporent called Nardelli "one of the world's best operating executives and a proven leader" (Kingsbury, 2009). What will an employee say to hold onto a job?

In August 2009, investors in Cerberus began leaving in droves as the hedge fund lost 71 percent of its value. Did Nardelli have anything to do with this? He has the "golden managerial touch" every company he touches quickly takes a dive. Rumor has it that the mere mention of his name will lower a company's stock. There may be an opportunity here.

Nardelli, who has nine CEO lives, is at it again. In June 2010 Cerberus, which bought NewPage for $2.4 billion, appointed Nardelli non-executive chairman after its third CEO and third board chairman resigned in one year. Presumably they resigned because they refused to follow through on Cerberus's cost cutting efforts. So who do they bring in? "Mr. Cost Cutter" and 360 employees were terminated. Then they filed for bankruptcy in September 2011 after a year of negative cash flow. Who are these geniuses who buy a paper company as the world goes paperless?

In September 2010 Nardelli went into the seventh of his nine CEO lives when Cerberus which controls "Freedom Group," a group of eight gun and ammunition makers (Great name for a gun maker) appointed Nardelli temporary CEO while Cerberus looks for a permanent CEO. A month after he arrived, 25 employees were terminated. He has already closed down one factory. In April 2011, Freedom Group, after discovering there was no one better, named Nardelli permanent CEO. Freedom is now on the GE culture road show that worships the gods of forced employee rankings, synergy, rationalization and Six Sigma.

Meanwhile Nardelli maintains his celebrity status, if you believe there is no such thing as bad publicity. In 2010 he made Newsweek's top ten list of "CEOs Behaving Badly" http://www.newsweek.com/photo/2010/07/22/ceos-behaving-badly.html and he also made CNN's list of the "Worse American CEOs of All Time." http://www.cnbc.com/id/30502091?slide=5

What we have tried to explore with the Nardelli analysis is the notion that CEOs bring to the corporation an array of values, beliefs, and psychological issues that can impact the company in negative ways. So can a generation of employees.

We will now examine the generation of employees who will be entering the workplace, a group that is terrifying managers and has the potential to bring the corporation, as we know it, to its death.

CHAPTER 13

Gen Y's and the Future of the Corporation

Given the nature of the contemporary American corporation it is quite probable that the next generation of employees will either reject corporate life or present such an array of issues that the corporation as we know it, will no longer exist.

Shifts in economic development, ideology, and culture have rarely been studied as evolving from the populace or a particular generation. Even revolutions are not studied from the perspective of the culture and characteristics of the particular generation involved. For example, those who study the shift from an agrarian culture to an industrial culture study the industrial revolution's impact on a generation, as opposed to the generation's impact on creating the industrial revolution. Economists and social psychologists have maintained that a populace will revolt or create a particular type of culture in response to external characteristics like oppression, economic conditions, war or calamities. They fail to assume that every generation is different and the development of a generation's culture is typically in response to a previous generation, their parents, communities, schools and peers. Likewise a generational response to oppression, economic conditions, war or calamities will be different from generation to generation.

When studying the corporation we maintain that each generation has had and will have differing impacts. For example, beginning with the "Matures," (those born before 1943), also referred to as the "Silent Generation," or the "Veterans," returning World War II veterans, they built corporations based on the military model, for most, the only organizational model they had known. They returned from WW II and built top-down, hierarchical structures that required obedience, loyalty and commitment. They believed in life-time employment with one company and valued advancement based on seniority. They trusted institutions and leadership. In addition, they established bedroom communities, worked hard, followed rigid sex roles and raised children in large numbers, the baby boomers.

These matures were exceedingly loyal and they expected the corporation would offer pensions and take care of employees during their lifetime as a payoff for commitment. The employer-employee compact was strong and valued by both sides. In addition they were truly silent, rarely speaking up or against injustice. If we compare the complaints and needs demonstrated by the GenY soldiers returning from Iraq and Afghanistan in 2009 to those veterans returning from WW II they were indeed silent and stoic.

THE BOOMERS

Their children, the boomers, embraced the idealism of President Kennedy, and during their lifetime evolved from the counterculture movement that rejected consumerism to become the largest consumer demographic group in history (Heath and Potter, 2005). The boomers consumed the most food, land, fuel, and wealth than any previous generation. How did this happen? How did the boomers become what the late George Carlin described as "Whiny, narcissistic, self-indulgent people with a simple philosophy: *Gimme it, it's mine*!!" (LeBlanc, 2008). Most boomers grew up comfortable, living in suburbia, having their own bedroom, TV, car, and parents to support them. Free from the need to work they engaged in causes: Antiwar, racial equality, feminism, etc. At the same time they wanted to break away from their parent's life-style. They traveled, joined communes, took drugs and dropped out of the so-called "rat race." Many stayed in school (avoiding the draft) becoming the most credentialed group in history. The road they took toward being more affluent than their parents was easy. When they completed their education, activism, and play, they entered work, probably the oldest group to do so. Many were 30 when they got their first "real job". Some never did. Many went to business school and spent their life moving up the corporate ladder. How these choices are made are intriguing fodder for psychologists and psychoanalysts to ponder (but not here).

When they went to work and started making money these boomers leaped into the consumer world, or perhaps they never left it. Home ownership was quickly sought, whether a house, coop, or condo. They would not rent like many of their parents did. And, with the stampede to own a home, a housing boom grew, and grew, making many boomers house wealthy.

During their stays in corporate finance, banking, retail, service and even manufacturing, economic growth was meteoric. There was entrepreneurial growth and boomers made millions in technology, Hollywood, finance and the media.

But somehow the boomers took their idealism and turned it into greed. Or, perhaps it never was idealism in the sense of care, concern and devotion for the other. Perhaps it was idealism found in "it's all about me." Tom Wolfe coined the 1970s the "me decade," a status-driven period where the boomers came to believe that their own "well-being" was the number one priority in life. Tyler (2007) maintains the "me decade" of Wolfe is not a decade but a millennium and continues into 2000. She reinforces the idea of Christopher Lasch that we live in a "culture of narcissism" that is fed by consumerism, celebrity obsession, and new forms of media, and of course "15 minutes of fame."

What did these boomers accomplish? They built major institutions and bilked them, they polluted the environment, they stole retirement funds, disposed of hundreds of thousands of workers, took their parents' houses and stuck them in old age homes, reaped the benefits of over insured parents, created a growing gap between the rich and poor, and alienated a significant part of the world's population. And yes, they gave us the Gen Y's.

GEN Y'S

It is important to understand that throughout history young generations have been condemned by their older generation, suggesting a powerful bias. Consider some of the comments made by some of our greatest philosophers: "I have no hope in the future of our country if today's youth are going to be tomorrow's leaders. They are unbearable, foolish, and even frightening." The author of this sentence is Hesiod a Greek philosopher, in 740 B.C. A Babylonian tablet from 3000 B.C. reads: "Today's youth are deeply corrupt, evil, mean and unreliable. They will never be like the youth in the past, and will be unable to preserve our culture." In 400 B.C. Socrates said: "Our youth love luxury, they are rude, despise authority, have no respect for the elderly, have become tyrants, talk back to their parents, they are impossible to deal with." Finally, Aristotle says: "Youth have many desires, are volatile, readily lose interest. Youth desire with great enthusiasm but quickly get tired." As we move into the 21st century we may take the wisdom of these philosophers with a grain a salt and maintain that the one thing we can be certain of about our younger generation is that when they grow old they will observe the younger generation with the same disdain.

Before we explore the GenY's it may be helpful to assess the difficulty associated with developing a picture of any generation, including the boomers, as a modal personality. For example, how can we establish that there is a set of characteristics that are unique to such a large social grouping? To isolate characteristics raises the potential of stereotyping, a phenomenon that has plagued social groupings for generations. For example, to refer to this generation under study, Gen Y alludes to a succession from Gen X, a term that was originally coined as a pejorative label. On the other hand, attempting to understand a particular social group, in this case an age group, can help us understand our reactions and prejudices associated with this group. If one approaches the study of this group, as one would study a corporation, organization, family, it may increase our capacity to be more tolerant, and sensitive to their choices, decisions, conflicts, etc. Mind you, we are not judging, but merely understanding, and hopefully in doing so a more compassionate view will be obtained. We also need to know that much of what writers think they know about Gen Y's comes from anecdotal evidence. It is a group that has not received serious study. According to Hoover (2007), the only longitudinal study of Gen Y's was completed by the Cooperative Research Institute at UCLA. They took issue with the findings of Strauss and Howe, authors of *Millennial Rising* (Vintage Books, 2000). For example, they found today's students are spending more time studying than their predecessors, and that students were becoming more preoccupied with finding lucrative careers-not less so. However, several studies have contradicted the Cooperative Research Institute suggesting that engineering undergrads study about 19 hours a week with Business school students studying the least depending on what study one uses their study time ranges from 6 to 9 hours per week. This also suggests that Gen Y business students are the most poorly educated academic group in history.

GEN Y'S AND OTHER GENERATIONS

These generations are not defined by any formal process, but rather by demographers, the media, popular culture writers, market researchers, and by members of the generation themselves. Also, the birthdates applied to these generations vary greatly, especially the Gen Y's and the Gen Jones. As a matter of fact, many writers completely leave out Gen Jones. Gen Jones is left out because most writers and demographers claim the boomer population was born between 1943 and 1964, and would include the Gen Jones as part of the boomer population. For our purpose we will establish the baby boomers born between 1943 and 1964. Many put the boomer date at 1945, assuming that at the end of the European war, the baby boom began. However, the soldiers actually started to return home in 1943. The Gen X's, also known as the latch-key generation, were born between 1965 and 1979. In addition, we will expand the Gen Y's to a period from 1980 to 1994. This gives us the best idea of how one generation impacts another. For example, putting together a book of readings called the Feminist Papers, Alice Rossi discovered that the feminists movement actually skipped a generation. One generation would accept the feminist banner and push for equality, while the generation that followed would be less active, but would reap the gains made by the earlier generation. The next generation would embrace the feminist movement, and so on. We see this now with the Gen Y women and to some degree the Gen X's who are benefiting from the gains of the feminist baby boomers. We certainly see the effects one generation has on another when we examine the impact the baby boomer parents have on their children, the Gen Y's.

WHO ARE GEN Y'S?

The term Generation Y first appeared in an August 1993 magazine, Advertising Age, editorial to describe those children born between 1980 and 1995 (Melbourne, 1999). The U.S. Department of Commerce places Gen Y from 1980 to 1989. For our purpose we will use the demographics most demographers and writers on the subject agree upon. By maintaining that Gen Y's were born between 1980 to 1994 allows us to put the Gen Y population at approximately 75 million which approximates the number of baby boomers.

Based on year 2007	Age	% of US Population	Actual Numbers (millions)
Gen Z	1995-?	20%	60
Gen Y	1980-1994	25%	75
Gen X	1965-1979	8%	26
Baby boomers	1943-1964	27%	80
Matures	Before-1943	20%	60

A notable demographic shift was expected in 2008 when the oldest Baby Boomers hit the U.S. legal retirement age of 65. As boomers retire, more members of Generation X will be expected to take roles in middle and upper management, and the large membership of Generation Y will take up positions in the lower half of the workforce. This process has begun and a spurred on a multimillion-dollar consulting business where hoards of so-called experts are claiming that management must understand these young men and women, or suffer problematic consequences. This volatile shift, the constant flow of numbers exiting and entering the workplace, will occur well into 2030, and experts believe it will have a profound, if not revolutionary, impact on the workplace.

This means that between 2008 and 2030 two generations will leave the workforce, the matures and the baby boomers. It also means that 140 million people will be out of the work force and the work force will drop to 100 million with three-fourths, or 75 million from the GenY group.

IMPACT ON THE WORKPLACE

The biggest impact brought about by the Gen Y's will be the blurring of the traditional boundaries between work, home and play as well as the boundaries between; family, friends and workplace colleagues.

Let's look at some of the characteristics of the Gen Y's, which may explain why management and others in positions of authority are expecting significant change and perhaps conflict in the workplace.

THE ONLINE GENERATION

Consider these facts about GenY's from a survey of 7,705 U.S. college students by Junco and Mastrodicasa (2007):

- 97 percent own a computer
- 94 percent own a cell phone
- 76 percent use Instant Messaging (IM).
- 15 percent of IM users are logged on 24 hours a day, 7 days a week
- 34 percent use websites as their primary source of news
- 28 percent own a blog and 44 percent read blogs

- 49 percent download music using peer-to-peer file sharing
- 75 percent of college students have a Facebook account
- 60 percent own some type of portable music and/or video device such as an iPod

While we consider some baby boomers and definitely Gen X's a generation of multi-taskers, the Gen Y's are a generation of "continuous partial attention." According to Stone (2006), who coined the phrase, there is a given need to stay on top of all the real and potential information and data that passes by. In this mindset, the Gen Y continuously scans the environment for opportunities. It explains the apparent lack of attention Boomers experience when interacting with Gen Y's. Boomers complain "they are in another world". This is not true, according to Stone (2006): they have a method of cognitive functioning shaped by electronic communication. Don't forget, the oldest of the GenY's reached the age of 10 in 1990 when the price of computers began to drop precipitously. Consequently, they have developed their own unique style and method of gathering and disseminating information. For example in a restaurant three Gen Y's were eating dinner, all were on their cell phones talking while also talking to each other. This would drive some boomers "nuts."

From a psychological perspective, the Gen Y's are motivated to be "part of" or perhaps motivated by the fear of not being "part of." For Gen Y's not to be "part of" is experienced as catastrophic. Therefore, continuously searching for information and data is a search for a "feel good" piece of data; data that will make them feel alive, important, loved, and above all successful. As one Gen Y put on her cell phone answering service, "Give me something goooood."

This post-multi-tasker, "always on" generation can study for exams with all of their electronic devices operating simultaneously: the TV, laptop or iPhone for IM'ing, their cell close by, and an iPod in an ear, and multiple screens on their computer. At work, they can juggle e-mail on their BlackBerries while talking on cell phones and working on a project. At the university they prefer to tape their professors' lectures rather than sit and listen. At University of California, Berkeley, and other institutions, professors place webcams of their entire classes on the web. This allows students to avoid sitting in class, and to attend class on the web and, of course, do other things.

http://webcast.berkeley.edu/course details.php?seriesid=1906978253

The question that arises with "continuous partial attention" is whether one can one focus and devote full attention while jumping from subject to subject. Can a Gen Y study for an examination and answer face mails on their split-screen laptop? We are beginning to see some anecdotal evidence suggesting it cannot be done. However we have no definitive research on how or whether it impacts school performance. But according to Klass (2009) medical students study while engaging in what he calls "oscillating" back and forth between media devices. Perhaps the most troubling media device is Facebook. The relationship between grades and Facebook suggests that the more time on Facebook, the lower one's grades. We also see the development of a clinical diagnosis called Facebook addiction, to go alongside other types of computer addiction. In addition, some suggest that the Gen Ys are quickly becoming a generation with less face-to-face interaction than previous generations. One can raise the question: What will be the mental and physical consequences of spending the bulk of one's interpersonal interactions electronically? The jury is out, and we do not know. We do know that apps like four square increase the probability of face-to-face interaction, as members can note locations with a mobile phone and can find out where friends are located.

It does not matter where or when, they wire-up. As a consequence, they prefer not to have an office or set hours. They are just as comfortable working on a park bench, coffee shop, the office or home. In response some corporations have eliminated permanent offices and have structured opportunities where employees can work anywhere, have meetings anywhere and offer exercise rooms, nap and massage rooms and free health food. Google is a prime example of this new workplace. No personal offices, only work spaces, lots of toys, meeting rooms and spaces to sit, with decompression rooms and brightly colored airy space.

The Gen Y's handle work differently from others and have a sense of duty that clearly goes against the traditions of contemporary corporations. Mark Liston (2007) author of Valpaks' blog "Entry" gives an example of how a Gen Y sales rep would handle work differently than their Gen X and baby boomer counterparts:

It is 10 a.m. in an office with three sales people - a boomer, a Gen X'er and a Gen Y. The sales manager tells each of them that they need to get new sales and the sales manager wants them to go out prospecting and come back with four appointments. The following occurs:

- *The Gen Y is back by noon announcing he has four appointments, a lunch appointment with a friend and will be back in the office right after lunch. (Gen Y heroe's are "the nerds" and "geeks" who created and dominate their cyber world.)*

- *The Gen X'er starts to argue with the sales manager and asks why they must go out of the office to prospect. Why can't they just use the phone to set the appointments and save some gas? They then ask why new sales are so important and get into a philosophical debate on growing old customers versus having to get new customers. At the end of the argument everyone is frustrated. (Gen X heroe's are men and a few women who got their MBA's from prestigious universities and became celebrity CEOs)*

- *The boomer grabs a cup of coffee and tells the rest of the people in the office how he used to be able to get 10 appointments a day. He goes on ad nauseaum about how he knocked on doors, got around the gatekeeper, made huge sales to the president of the company, etc. By lunch-time he is still in the office pontificating. (Boomer heroes are men who proudly display their athletic accomplishments, the successful ex- jocks).*

A CEO (baby boomer), trying to motivate a Gen Y'er said, "You come in late and go home early; do you know how many hours I put in each week?" The Gen Y'er said, "No." The CEO said, "60 hours." The Gen Y responded, "Why does it take you so long?"

But there is a down-side. In a survey of business owners in Australia, Martin and Tulgan (2007) found Gen Y's to be "demanding, impatient and bad at communicating." The survey found that almost 70 percent of those surveyed found their Generation Y workers to be problematic; with poor spelling and grammar and no understanding of appropriate corporate behaviors. However, the survey also suggested most employers praised the energy and charisma of their Generation Y workers.

According to Martin and Tulgan (2007), nearly half (49 percent) of employers surveyed said the biggest gap in communication styles between Generation Y employees and others are Gen Y's capacity to communicate more through technology rather than in person. Older workers prefer face-to-face communication, while Gen Y's prefer on-line. It is common to have Gen Y's in cubical next to each other communicating via the computer. According to MBA Alliance (2006), two-thirds of all MBAs are now earned on-line. It is suggested that two-thirds of all graduate degrees (master's and doctorates) within the next 10 years will be earned on-line. Presently, colleges are scrambling to get into the business.

WHAT DO GEN Y'S WANT OR DEMAND ?

Martin and Tulgan (2007) surveyed job expectations and found that 87 percent of all hiring managers and HR professionals say some or most Gen Y workers feel more entitled in terms of compensation, benefits and career advancement than older generations.

The Society for HR Managers (2007) claimed the following:

- 74 percent of employers say Gen Y workers expect to be paid more
- 61 percent say Gen Y workers expect to have flexible work schedules
- 56 percent say Gen Y workers expect to be promoted within a year
- 50 percent say Gen Y workers expect to have more vacation or personal time
- 37 percent say Gen Y workers expect to have access to state-of-the-art technology

Over half (55 percent) of employers maintain Gen Y workers have a more difficult time taking direction or responding to authority than other generations of workers.

Fifteen percent of employers said they changed or implemented new policies or programs to accommodate Gen Y workers (Haefner, 2007). Examples include:

- More flexible work schedules (57 percent)
- More recognition programs (33 percent)
- More access to state-of-the-art technology (26 percent)

- Increased salaries and bonuses (26 percent)
- More ongoing education programs (24 percent)
- Paying for cell phones, BlackBerries, etc. (20 percent)
- More telecommuting options (18 percent)
- More vacation time (11 percent)

TENSION IN THE WORKPLACE

More than 60 percent of employers say they are experiencing tension between employees from different generations, according to a survey by Lee Hecht Harrison (2007). Conflicts will typically arise over intergenerational expectations. Gen Y entitlement and their wish to be treated fairly and equitably will clearly go against the grain of the traditional corporation that values obedience and hierarchical respect. If you couple the attitudes of the Gen Y's with their appearance, (tattoos, body piercing, casual dress, in some cases torn jeans and flip-flops) then tensions will be most apparent.

Corporations are already beginning to gear up and adapt to the Gen Y's and they are well aware that if they are unable to recruit and attract Gen Y's they will face significant problems.

At Abbott Laboratories in Chicago, recruiters are offering benefits such as flexible work schedules, telecommuting, full tuition reimbursement and an online mentoring tool.

Aflac, an insurer based in Columbus, Ga., is highlighting such perks as time off given as awards, flexible work schedules and recognition.

Sun Microsystems' telecommuting program, for example, has kicked into high gear in response to Generation Y's demands. Today more than half of Sun's employees work remotely.

Xerox is using the slogan "Express Yourself," a phrase popular in the 1970s, as a way to describe its culture to recruits. The hope is that the slogan will appeal to Gen Y's desire to be themselves, and develop solutions and work toward change. Recruiters also point out the importance of diversity at the company; Gen Y is one of the most diverse demographic groups — one out of three is a minority. In this sense it appears that Xerox may be responding to what would have happened if the hippy baby boomers had not rejected the corporate world but instead decided to enter at the same age as the Gen Y's. Xerox may be aware that generation Y's are primarily children of the baby boomers. Xerox may be aware of the Gen Y's tendency to share social views and culture with their boomer parents and the Gen X'ers, their "older cousins" or even older siblings.

In an interesting way Maccoby (2002) describes a shift in what he calls "Organizational Social Character." He summarizes changes in socio-economic base, the social character, and the ideals, ideology, or social self rooted in the bureaucratic and interactive social characters. In the Gen Y we see the full evolution of the interactive character. We also see the intergenerational shift described by Maccoby (2002), a shift brought about by boomer parenting.

Maccoby (2002) explains the relationship between the baby boomers and their children, but more importantly the reason the boomers maintain such a high degree of involvement in their children's lives. The boomers do not want their Gen Y children to become the bureaucratic characters that they have become, and the children do not want this either. Boomers do not want their children to become victims of the corporate treadmill. They want them to be successful, but they do not see the corporation as a vehicle for success.

This will have significant consequences for corporations that were essentially structured by the Matures and modified by the Boomers and to some degree the X's. We will discuss this in depth. However, it may be helpful to discuss the Gen Y parents first.

THE PARENTS

When the boomer generation went off to college they spoke very little to their parents. Typically, the only mode of communication was a letter or the pay phone on the wall in the dorm hall. Today's Gen Y's have cell phones (74 percent own a cell phone) and computers (94 percent own a computer). The Gen Y's are in constant contact with Mom and Dad via electronic devices. A psychologist reports that his son had started college about 300 miles from their home. Both parents speak to their son every day, and the communication continues through email. They know how well he sleeps, what he eats, when tests are given, etc. They know his dates, his friends, and his study partners. And, he loves the connection. In a 60 Minutes television show a vignette is given of a student complaining to his professor about a low grade. The student then hands him his cell phone and says, "Talk to my mother." This is an accurate portrayal of this new form of parenting; some psychologists call it pathological involvement. Just as his mother would go to his grade school to argue in favor of her son and try to convince his teachers that he was much better than the given grades, the process continues through high school, the university and even the Gen Y's workplace.

To fully understand the Gen Y's we must understand the relationships they have with their boomer parents. They have been called "helicopter parents." They hover above their children watching, coaching, mentoring, giving advice, demanding, threatening, and making certain they are achieving. These parents have the technological capacity to keep track of their children 24/7. Reports, assignments, tests and school progress are posted daily on the school web site beginning in middle school. Any aberrations are quickly confronted with a teacher-parent-guidance conference. No more end-of-the-semester report cards.

The former financial institution Merrill Lynch held "parents' day" for interns parents to tour the trading floor. KPMG invites parents to the Gen Y's first day of work. This is a rapidly growing phenomenon. The Collegiate Employee Research Institute (CERI) at Michigan State University claims that 23 percent of corporations in the U.S. report interacting with parents of Gen Y's. It seems the larger the company the greater the numbers of interactions with parents. In corporations with over 3,799 employees, the numbers reporting interaction with parents increases to 32 percent. In addition, this number increases when the Gen Y's are recruited internationally. HR managers are well aware of these dependency relationships and are eager to sell their company to the Gen Y parents. If the parents are impressed, it will improve recruitment and retention.

Where does this dependency begin? It is easy to understand the necessary dependency in the early ages (4 to 7 years) as children leave the nest for school, but now we see it continuing through high school, college and at work. In addition, we do not see the necessary autonomous development as the child gets older. Consider what a baby boomer parent recalled when contrasting his experience as a child with those of his children. He said, "We went to the park or vacant lot and we played by ourselves, no adults. If it was baseball, we chose sides and played a game. We argued and we settled the conflicts." He went on to say, "I never see kids playing games without adult supervision. The pickup game is dead, everything is organized and structured by parents, and if the parents are not around, then it's some hired professional." The Gen Y's have considerable difficulty functioning autonomously, and the reason is simple: They were never given the chance to succeed or fail on their own.

An example of this was offered by a psychologist watching mothers and their children in a pediatrician's office. Two mothers were watching their children on the floor building towers out of blocks. When one child placed the blocks in a precarious position, the mother quickly leaped to the rescue and adjusted the tower to keep it from falling. The other mother, witnessing the precarious tower, let it fall, and said "Try again." The child began to build the tower again. The child whose tower was rescued lost interest and went on to play something else. Which child has the better chance of functioning autonomously in the adult world?

Many psychologists, counselors, and advisors worry that this over-indulgence and ubiquitous safety net has stifled normal social development and the necessary steps required to move successfully into the adult world. These parents have promoted dependency, and they maintain it is necessary.

The parents appear to be in a race, and their children are in it. The finish line is success and financial security, and it also includes keeping up with the "Jonese's" and perhaps beating them. They wish to proudly display achievements that become fused with parental/child achievements. This is evidenced when they place their "my child is on the honor roll at …school" bumper sticker on their car. The competition begins in K-1, goes through college acceptance day and later onto their child's career. The young man, who handed his cell phone to his professor so his mother could fight for him, was most likely the same student whose mother arrived at his middle school 30 minutes after he received a grade of "C."

These parents are not only excessively involved in their children's grades, choice of teacher, selection into honors classes, but also their social life, and athletic activities. It would be hard to find a coach who has not been accosted by an irate parent over their child's treatment;

lack of playing time, poor use of their child, general coaching competence, etc.

Of particular notice is the degree to which these parents plan and prepare their children to be successful, whether in sports, education, playing an instrument, writing, acting, horse riding, language, etc. GenY's are prepared to excel, they are prepared by tutors, coaches, summer camps and, after-school programs. Given the financial investment it is understandable, when we witness outraged parents reacting when their investment fails to produce the expected results. They fight to get "their money's worth."

The Gen Y's are insulated from anything resembling failure. If they do fail, it is not their fault, it's the fault of the tutor, coach, camp, teacher, etc., and especially those who offered the assessment. In many cases parents offer warnings to teachers that they have made a significant investment in preparing their child for success and they will not tolerate failure.

We now see the function of over-scheduling and controlling the Gen Y's life. It's to avoid the possibility of failure. Gen Y's never use the term failure. If a Gen Y is fired from a job he or she is told by fellow Gen Y's and parents, "It's not for you." The word failure is omitted from the Gen Y's vocabulary. One middle school counselor reported a parent pleading for a higher grade, was told they should understand, math is not their child's "thing."

The Gen Y's parents are the equivalent of the so called "stage moms" who coach and manage their children's career and road to success. All parents want to feel a sense of pride in their children, however, for these parents, pride and success become an obsession. These parents, according to Rosenfeld and Wise (2000), are "in constant fear that their children will underperform in any area-academic, social or athletic."

GEN Y'S AND AUTHORITY

GenY's embrace the rapid socio-communicative change brought about by advancing technology. Consider this. Forever gone are the joys of getting lost and asking for directions (GPS). GenY's have not grown up understanding that those in positions of authority know more, demand respect and offer direction. They go straight to the source and have the technological capacity to avoid getting lost. They will never have to ask for directions.

They have the capacity to locate almost anyone. They know where all of their classmates are from K1 through college and if they wish they can be in contact with all of them and they have the technological capacity to focus in on their living quarters and even watch them. Every book ever written is being scanned, along with every film, newspaper and every email. There is no better observation of the speed of change occurring from one generation to another than to observe the 1982 teen movie "Fast Times at Ridgemont High". In the movie Jeff Spicoli a drugged out Gen X'er orders a pizza delivered to class. This is considered outrageous and extremely funny: only a druggie would do this, in 1982. However, in 2008 GenY's not only order their lunch on cell phones in class, they text message while the teacher lectures. Some teachers have given up trying to combat technological disruptions in class. The GenY's do not see this as disrespect they do not see this as an interruption. In their world many forms of communication go on simultaneously. This is expected and even cool behavior

A professor with 35 years of teaching experience entered the faculty lounge infuriated: "They want to call me by my first name and when I told them no, they looked at me as if I was nuts, is this the new world, my students will now call me Ed, who do they think they are." He went on, "I'm up there lecturing and they have their laptops out and they're typing away. I don't know what they're doing- surfing the net, watching porn, on Facebook I can't even see their faces. I feel like I'm talking to myself." At school and work, GenY's present an array of issues to those who occupy traditionally superior roles or positions of authority. The first difficulty is the Gen Y's wish to be treated as an equal. In their child-centered family they were not only treated as equals, they were often catered to, their indiscretions overlooked and punishment avoided under the assumption in would be psychologically damaging, or worse, it would precipitate rageful outbursts directed at their parents, or the parents may be labeled an abuser. Every child is taught in school to recognize parent abuse and knows how to report it. In some instances abuse takes on dimensions of wide latitude.

It is widely recognized that Gen Y's have an attitude of entitlement. In grade school and at home they were told they were entitled to their opinions and their opinions were valued. Teachers and parents believe that if they fail to value opinions it would hurt their self-esteem. A parent reported the following; "While discussing autos with my daughter when she was 10 years old, she commented that she liked Toyota's best, they were a good American company. Seeking to correct, the parent told her Toyota was a Japanese company. She said the parent was wrong. When the parent insisted that he was correct, she responded, "I'm entitled to my opinion." The parent responded "But… But… But… it's a fact." End of discussion. With her arms crossed, she looked straight ahead. She went on to graduate from the Gallatin School at NYU, a school made for Gen Y's. Students refer to their teachers by first name, they study what they want, and every student's opinion is considered. It's a relaxed environment with limited competition and lots of student talking and professors listening.

In the "60 Minutes" news show on GenY's trophies are being awarded to young children. Everyone gets a trophy, all the trophies are the same size the top team gets the same trophy as the bottom team.

GenY's grew up expecting a trophy for every sport they played. Not for winning but for merely showing up or showing spirit, team-work and an array of categories. One can go into a typical GenY bedroom and see more trophies than a boomer All-American. Here is the problem that is created. At school and later the workplace they expect the symbolic trophy for just playing, not excelling. At college they expect a B or better just for attending or perhaps "working hard" and they are quite insistent. Entitlement means just that, they wore the uniform, attended practice and played hard: "Now give me the trophy." In the workplace they expect the same: praise and rewards for showing up. GenY's grew up in a world where praise and positive reinforcement were constant. Any form of criticism was met with anger, not only from the child, but from the parents. Children were told they were special, not just by Mr. Rogers, but by their parents, teachers, coaches, relatives, and mass media.

WHY DID THE BOOMERS CREATE THESE CHILDREN?

A critical question is the motivation baby boomers had to produce this type of generation. The answer can be found by assessing the baby boomers' development. First, they were part of the first "child centered culture." An explosion of births after WW II, followed by the so-called "white flight" to the suburbs where children and later adolescents bonded together and collectively rejected parental values, authority, segregation, war, corporate and conventional life styles. The hippie generation accepted diversity, open sex, communalism, drugs, and music and went "back to the earth." Most baby boomers enjoyed their freedom in the late 60s through the 70s and then discovered an important fact of life, the need for a career and money. In their attempts to prolong adolescence they failed to plan for work, a career, children and middle age. Many then took jobs and quickly discovered they were not happy. A boomer along with his hippie wife in their 30s when they had their first child, discovered he needed a career, he decided to go to graduate school and study literature. They soon had another baby. He dropped out of graduate school and took a job in a bank. The boomer, ex-hippie, was now taking the 7:45 a.m. train into the city five days a week. He had become Whyte's "Organizational Man," "the man in the grey flannel suit," the corporate automaton he had maintained he would never become. To buy a home, his wife took a job. They hired a nanny and saved money. They both worked long hard hours, and returned home every night exhausted. They fed their children, ate, drank and went to sleep… and did the same thing the next day. The ex-hippie said, "We are going to make certain that our kids don't 'piss away' their childhood, teenage, and young adult years, like we did. We want them to have a plan, to be happy. I'll be dammed if I let my kinds to turn out like us."

The GenY's worry more about money than any previous generation, and their adult/parents, the baby boomers, join their Gen Y's in money worries. During their life time the boomers have seen the price of family homes grow from a median of $45,000 to $250,000 -$500,000, depending upon geographical location. They see college tuition increase every year, out of reach for many, with the competition for scholarships intensifying. In the United States, 43 percent of families spend more than they earn. Average households carry $8,000 in credit card debt. There are more than 159 million credit cards in America and families currently owe about $973 billion to card companies; their total indebtedness, not including mortgages, is $2.56 trillion. In 1960 the ratio of debt-to-personal-disposable income was 55 percent and in 2007 it has more than doubled to 133 percent. In 2004 the average family debt of baby boomers was close to $80,000. In England, the numbers declaring insolvency has risen 95 percent in a decade, and the average family debt, 30,000 pounds. In Canada it's $70,000. In the U.S. the bankruptcy rate increased 65 percent from March 2008 to March 2009. This rate will continue to rise as housing prices continue to fall and joblessness makes it problematic for Americans to pay off debt.

In addition the financial crisis of 2008-09 has reduced the boomers' retirement 401(k) by 40 to 50 percent along with the loss of jobs and homes. Consequently, the incentive to mold that child into a downsized non-consumer survivor has dramatically increased.

Another reason for money worries is that before they enter the workplace, the GenY's are overwhelmingly in debt. They face higher costs for higher education than any previous generation. Where a baby boomer could have paid tuition of $37 per semester at CCNY, that same boomer as a parent just finished paying $250,000 for his daughter's NYU degree.

The average student loan debt varies from $22,000 to $29,000 and is climbing fast. Three out of four GenY's obtained their own credit cards while in college, often pushed by overzealous banks and loan companies. As a consequence, Gen Y's leave college with between $3,000 and $4,500 in credit card debt. It is not surprising that 30 cents of every dollar earned will go to service their debt. In addition, one in nine high school students have credit cards co-signed by a parent.

Being in such debt at an early age contributes to considerable financial knowledge. GenY's work hard to get out of debt and worry about their credit scores. This may explain why so many, 50 percent to 60 percent, move home after graduation from college, why they cram into urban apartments, and why they depend upon parents for financial help. This also may explain why CEOs and managers maintain that all GenY's care about is money. They are like their parents, and now the general population, with their concern for money. The 2007 job satisfaction results from the Society for Human Resource Management states that compensation/pay is the number one factor in selecting a job. Following are benefits, job security, flexibility to balance work/life, and the ability to communicate effectively with management. In 2009 this will be replaced by job security. It may be that the GenY's are more vociferous in their desire for more pay. They are so electronically connected, that it's not unusual for them to know the salary and perks that companies in a given field are offering. According to Ketter (2006), 81 percent of 18- to 25-year-olds surveyed by the Pew Research Center for People and the Press said getting rich is their generation's most important or second-most-important life goal. Fifty-one percent said the same about being famous, probably with the assumption that if one is famous they will also be wealthy. They also plan for their retirement and believe retirement is an important factor in their choice of employer.

As we can see, when it comes to money the GenY's are a pragmatic group. They have learned from their boomer parents that wasting time, going into debt and not planning can lead to financial failure. They are told, "If you fail to plan you will never get that home, or that second vacation home, or the boat, etc." They must be pragmatic, they know the stark realities of owning a home, car, taking vacations, obtaining degrees, being unemployed and living on their own, and raising a family. This worry or anxiety is now even more apparent as the financial crunch and job loss that began in September 2008 continues.

Now with the fiscal crisis, millions losing their jobs, 401 (k) in the toilet, and home values falling, the Boomers must rethink retirement. Boomers cannot afford to retire, keeping the GenY's out of the workforce. In 2007, 51 percent of June college grads had jobs waiting for them. In 2009 only 20 percent had jobs. Replacing the boomers is now a slow process and they GenY's will need to be patient. In the meantime they can do their internships, take low paying part-time jobs, stay in school, move to other countries, especially countries without a fiscal crises. If they cannot live on their own they can move back home. If they cannot pay their loans they seek deferments or simply default

Despite their considerable financial knowledge and efforts to survive financially, after GenX's, they have the second highest bankruptcy rate of any generation. It is expected that the bankruptcy rate will dramatically increase as the Gen Y population ages.

The Gen Y's know about their parent's financial situations. They see the debt and the psychological issues it brings and they bond with them about money anxieties.

FEAR AND ANXIETY

For the baby boomer, stress and anxiety over money, healthcare, employment and general stability takes the form of dread. This fear of losing a foothold or perhaps losing everything is displaced onto the children, who are pressured into structured plans created and controlled by their parents to make them successful. If their GenY offspring are accomplished and competent; have a plan for career success, and are well coached, they can grow up avoiding the situation in which the baby boomers and many GenX's now find themselves.

However, these fears, while real in many cases, also function as a defense against the anxiety of moving into the adult world; a world painted by their parents as dangerous, because it contains failure and potential ruin. Again, the concept of autonomy is relevant to our understanding of the relationship between GenY and their parents. If the baby boomer parents withdraw closeness of supervision and the visibility of their authority it would allow for autonomous functioning. However, from a developmental perspective, one can only function autonomously if one has been able to separate and function without the need for attachment. For the GenY, attachment is necessary because if he/she separates or differentiates, anxiety and fear will be overwhelming. It is as if the GenY's are taught to say to themselves, "If I do this on my own I will be in danger. If I fail I will be blamed. If I stay attached and avoid separation, then I can be protected: I will be safe in the holding arms of mother." They are safe from uncertainties, the risks of unhappiness, misery and failure, all for which they unfortunately have not been prepared.

The Gen Y denies the reality of his/her separateness and the responsibility of fashioning a life of his or her own. Consequently, they rely on a wide variety of regressive and neurotic psychic structures that provide illusions and fantasies that enable them to avoid the actuality that he/she is separate, and support the pretense that he/she resides in the earliest state of blissful security. This illusion is a type of rapprochement. They feel the freedom to experiment, try new things-thus to take risks. They develop this illusion of being on their own. Also, because their parents can keep tabs on them they feel much more comfortable letting them go. So the GenY's go backpacking overseas, take a semester off in Spain, teach in Africa, sail the Atlantic, engage in research in Japan. Like the 3 year old who runs away and then turns to see if mom is chasing, the GenY is never fully detached. Technology makes this possible.

GEN Y FEMALES AND MALES

While many GenY's appear to be autonomous, they stay at home longer than any recent generation. In 1960, 65 percent of men and 77 percent of women under 30 years of age had attained what is called the five milestones to adulthood. In 2000, 31 percent of men and 46 percent of women had attained these milestones. Kimmel (2008) describes these milestones as: leaving home, completing one's education, starting work, getting married and becoming a parent.

While baby boomers liked to think of themselves as risk-takers, who went off on their own and left the nest, the complaint often heard by critics of the boomers was their propensity to prolong adolescence. However, compared to their parents, the GenY's have taken the extended adolescence to new heights. Staying at home and avoiding the adult world is considered a good thing among GenY's, and despite their dire warnings that career building is necessary, their parents welcome it. The nest is no longer empty. The nest may simply be that, a nest, a home base where the GenY can operate "out of." They can now afford to take their vacations, visit friends, leave unhappy employment, relationships, and jobs that are "not for them."

We also see noticeable differences between Gen Y males and females. Females seem to be more capable of leaving home, completing their education, finding and keeping employment or establishing a career, getting married and having children (Yang, 2008). How can we explain the consistent difference between men and women?

Some higher-education statistics do paint a rosy picture for women, who now are the majority of undergraduates (about 58 percent nationally), earn better college grades than men do, and are more likely than men to complete college. In 2002 females made up 46 percent of the workforce, and this percentage is increasing, in 2008, the percentage increased to 48 percent (Healthfield, 2008). In 2009 we have more women in the workplace than men. This has been facilitated by the financial crisis of 2008-09 in which many male occupations like construction, manufacturing, and financial services have witnessed the loss of hundreds of thousands of jobs while female occupations like teaching and nursing have remained stable. We also will witness African-

Americans, Latinas, and members of Asian communities entering the work force in record numbers.

White males are on the road to extinction as members of an elite socioeconomic group. Since the 1950's we have seen the numbers of white males drop as occupants of the positions in the professions and corporate leadership. As they move closer to becoming a minority versus women, it is expected that by 2025, ethnic and racial minorities will become the majority in American and white males will make up a paltry percentage in the work force. Will white males still dominate executive constellations? The answer is no.

ACCOMMODATING THE GEN Y'S: THE NEW CORPORATION

Wall Street is toxic to the GenY's. Money shuffling is out. Building something hands on, working together, and finding out what customers want is in. Finance is not the occupation of choice. Many even see Capitalism as obsolete. In addition, corporations will be hard-pressed to find a GenY willing to spend their career in a 9 to 5 cubicle.

ENTITLEMENT

GenY's have been mistakenly criticized and condemned by numerous writers as being "entitled." But they confuse the issue; wanting to be treated fairly and equitably or the same as everyone else at work is not entitlement. These writers see GenY behaviors through a bias associated with traditional views of authority structures. In hierarchical corporations, entitlement increases as one goes up the ladder. Lower level, and especially entry- level employees have little say and are expected to dutifully follow orders. This may have been true for the Boomers and GenXs. In a study of GenX business school students, Mitchell et. al. (1993) discovered they had little sensitivity to the overall fairness of high executive salaries; they were not bothered by gross salary inequity. However, if one assesses today's GenY's entering our business schools, attitudes have changed. GenYs believe in equity and do not like it when one gets more and behaves as if they are special or better than someone else. They were not brought up with the hierarchical authority tradition. It's not that they are unwilling to pay their dues or show deference or respect. It's just that they and those who want to call their professor Ed simply want to move away from the trappings of authority that are intended to make one feel superior at the expense of another. In their world technology is the great equalizer. Facebook just has friends, no place for a hierarchy driven world. In their world, everyone gets a trophy. Corporations will need to adapt, not to employees who feel entitled, but employees who want to fit in, offer contributions, and feel part of the decision-making process.

GenY's expect to be paid well, not because they are entitled, but because they have access to electronic communication which gives them access to salary differences among occupations, but also among corporations in the same industry. Gone are the days where one worked next to a colleague for 10 years and did not know that person's salary. Public and nonprofit organizations will have to openly acknowledge what they pay if they are to create a climate of trust and become appealing to GenY's. GenY's understand the value to job-hopping. It not only increases their salary but allows them to gain valuable experience. We know what they need and want; the question is will the corporation accommodate them? They are far removed from the type of loyalty demonstrated by earlier generations, especially their grandparents, the Matures. Yet they want their company to value them, train them and reward them. Once they get stale, bored and criticized, they are gone

BLOW UP THE OFFICE

We will not see GenY's lining up to work 9 to 5 in some cubicle. The punch clock, face time, and clock watching are dead. They are willing to work 60 hours a week but not in their cubicel, and only if the work interests them. They have an entrepreneurial spirit. To start one's own business is what they want and they don't care where it is; Australia, Germany or Iceland. They travel to assess the market possibilities and prepare a business plan. Hierarchical structures will need to be nonexistent or severely flat. There will be bosses, but in order to earn the respect of GenY's they will have to be experts or teachers, and above all else their friends. Merely having a title and being "the manager," popular among the Matures and tolerated among the boomers and GenX's, will be out among the GenY's. "Earn my respect" is in.

They will be educated, but brick and mortar universities will be out, brick and mortar corporations will also be out, brick and mortar shopping will be out. They are happy living in an Amazon world. These shoppers buy shoes online, and if the shoes don't fit or they don't like them they send them back. Over time, their computer will know their tastes, body dimensions, and how they move and walk and run, making the purchase of a comfortable pair of shoes on-line better than going to a store and trying them on.

GenY's and Creative Destruction: The demise of the brick and mortar university and the looming college debt bubble

Given the growth in the cost of obtaining an undergraduate degree in America and the current business model followed by college presidents along with mismanagement and misplaced priorities, the brick and mortar universities are on the road to becoming dinosaurs. Also GenY students seriously question the "Return on Investment" of the brick and mortar education. They represent the first generation of students who will embrace inexpensive online institutions, programs and courses, expediting the demise of the brick and mortar university.

Examining the ROI of a university education puts into question the wide variance in cost of an education. On one extreme of the spectrum, tuition at state and regional schools cost between $3,000 and $9,000 each year, while at the other end of the spectrum private universities cost between $21,000 and $42,000 each year. In 2011, 57 percent of adults said the higher education system in the United States failed to provide students with good value for the money (Stillman, 2011). To believe that the ROI of a $42,000 education is 14 times greater than a $3,000 education is simply wrong, and Gen Y's and their parents will not accept it.

When does one know things are out of control? Consider this. Since 1980 the cost of obtaining a degree at most universities and colleges has increased 100 percent every 10 years (Wells College increased their tuition 67 percent in two years). The National Center for Public Policy and Higher Education maintains that college tuition and fees increased 439 percent from 1982 to 2007.

In 2010 Sarah Lawrence College was the first to break the $60,000 a year threshold for an undergraduate education (tuition, room and board). Taylor (2010) suggests that "If recent trends continue, four years at a top-tier school will cost $330,000 in 2020, $525,000 in 2028 and $785,000 in 2035. " Believe it or not, Taylor's estimates may be too low. At 100 percent every 10 years, by 2020 Sarah Lawrence will cost $480,000 and will easily break the million-dollar barrier by 2035." If one follows the Lewin (2008) report, between 1982 and 2008, the costs of higher education increased over 430 percent which suggests that costs have increased 150 percent every 10 years. At that rate Sarah Lawrence will reach the million-dollar mark by 2025. This raises a question: Who will be the first to have their grandchild get the million-dollar diploma? In 2011 it is expected that Columbia, NYU and Bard will join the $60,000 club with many more to follow. The unthinkable million-dollar degree is around the corner. Of course this is only for four-year private, so-called elitist institutions, not the public institutions. However, the public universities are quickly catching up. In 1985, public education costs were a bit less than one-third of the private universities, and in 2006 they were a bit less than half. In 2011, with states strapped for cash, the gap will close at an even faster rate. Berkeley, a public institution, is charging out-of-state residents over $52,000 a year. Also, it's not only the puny undergraduate degree that is skyrocketing – just consider the cash cow's at most elitist institutions, the MBA programs. In 2010 Stanford had the distinction of offering the highest tuition for an MBA diploma in the country at $106,000 for a full-time two year MBA, and Harvard, right behind increased its MBA tuition from $54,000 in 1999 to over $97,000 in 2010 (this is tuition only and excludes fees, books, instructional supplies, insurance, housing, food, transportation, etc). McGill a publicly funded MBA program outraged Quebec officials when it increased tuition in 2010 from $3,400 a year to $29,500. So what will happen? In 1997, Peter Drucker predicted that in 30 years the brick and mortar university campuses would be driven out of existence by their inexorable tuition increases. We are beginning to see evidence that Drucker's prediction may occur earlier than he predicted.

THE ABSURD COST OF A DIPLOMA: GREED, MISMANAGEMENT AND THE GOVERNMENT

Higher education executives have no incentive to reduce expenses as long as admissions stay high and students and their families are willing to absorb the burden of years of college loan debt. These university executives are following a business model that is outmoded and increasingly cost-inefficient and certain to bring about the demise of many of these private and public institutions.

Consider the once-proud University of California, Berkeley: In 2010 it announced a 32 percent increase in tuition that followed a $150 million loss in state funds. Tuition for in-state residents is now more than $10,000 annually (a three-fold increase in the past 10 years). Berkeley is not unique. Public universities and private colleges and universities have seen their endowments slip, budgets cut, and they have had to follow the same path as Berkeley. Fire some faculty, close some departments, eliminate some degree offerings and hold down salaries, but keep on building high-tech campuses and above all else keep those games alive. Berkeley announced it will spend $150 million to build a high-performance center for athletes and $321 million to renovate its football stadium. In 2009 it paid football coach Jeff Tedford $2.8 million while facing a reduction of $150 million in state funding. While the football team was gettong more in 2010, the university was laying off faculty and staff, cutting enrollment, slashing course offerings and degree programs and raising tuition again. They have their priorities straight. In January 2011 the terminations began as 280 positions were eliminated and the following email went out to all employees:

"We are committed to treating all of our employees with dignity, respect and fairness while recognizing that in the end, we will have fewer administrative positions on campus," the e-mail said. *"In addition to crafting a somewhat smaller workforce, our goal is to rationalize policies and procedures such that many staff will find their jobs more rewarding and less frustrating."*

UC-Berkeley has undergone a number of major changes in recent months: In addition to increasing tuition and fees 32 percent, in September 2010 they announced that five sports programs would be eliminated, not football. They eliminated women's lacrosse and gymnastics and men's rugby, baseball and gymnastics about the equivalent of two football squads (Thomas, 2011).

So while the State of California deals with a major fiscal crisis and tuition zooms up and jobs are eliminated, Chancellor Mark Yudof made $591,000 in 2010 and was given $11,500-a-month for housing rental. That came to almost three-quarters of a million dollars. Meanwhile Yudof's university system struggled with $2.1 billion pension liabilities and a $1.4 billion budget cut in state contributions. To control the pension liability and deal with the state's fiscal crisis it was proposed that pensions be capped. This brought an angry response from 36 university executives who sent a letter to UC regents on Dec. 9, 2010 threatening to sue the state for violating their "legal, moral and ethical obligation." The state is trying to grapple with an excessively generous pension system that gives university administrators who make $400,000 a year and retire after 30 years an annual pension of $300,000. These top executives throughout the system insist on being well-paid despite the fiscal crisis. In January 2011 the vice chancellor for administration and finance at Berkeley was to earn a base salary of $375,000, 9 percent higher than the salary midpoint of $344,000 earned by colleagues at other universities. The chief financial officer of the UCLA hospital system was to receive a 10.5 percent raise, bringing his salary to $420,000 from $380,000. The campus called it a "preemptive retention salary adjustment." And University of California, San Francisco is providing a 10 percent increase of about $20,000 a year to three executives at the Oakland headquarters (Asimov, 2011). Another California school San Diego State University, in 2011 decided to pay $400,000 to its new president-about $100,000 more than to his predecessor. And on the same day trustees voted to increase tuition by 12 percent. In addition, most presidents in the California State University (CSU) system have their pay supplemented by using private funds that typically go to student scholarships. For example Cal

Poly, San Luis Obispo President Jeffrey Armstrong's $380,000 salary includes $30,000 from the Cal Poly Foundation. San Jose State University President Mohammad H. Qayoumi's $353,200 salary includes $25,000 from the SJSU Foundation, and CSU Chancellor Charles B. Reed's $451,500 salary includes $30,000 from the CSU Foundation. In addition these top executives' salaries are determined in a manner similar to those of corporate CEOs: compensation consultants compare one president's salary to that of others at similar universities. Of course they typically find that their president is below the market and demand a raise to keep the poor president from having his feelings hurt. This creates a rigged system where salaries continue to rise. If they find a president who makes $800,000 at a similar university then they can justify their claim for a hefty raise.

While raises and bonuses were being given to executives, Yudof told the regents that University of California system would need to close a $1 billion budget gap. Layoffs and course reductions are inevitable, and he expects to turn away 20,000 to 30,000 qualified students over the next decade because the university won't have the money to educate them (Asimov, 2011). It's already happening and Yudof's numbers are way off. In the fall of 2010 Cal State's Long Beach campus received 69,000 applications for 6,250 seats, meaning 62,750 students were turned away. In 2011 Yudof decided to give all employees who made less than $200,000 a whopping 3 percent raise provided they obtain a "good performance review."

These types of misplaced priorities and mismanagement will speed up the demise of the brick and mortar institutions.

Again Berkeley and CSU mismanagement is not unique. Consider Duke University, one of the $200,000-per-diploma institutions with a business model that would make an MBA cringe. Duke, as we discover with most of these expensive universities cannot turn a profit and must continue to increase tuition because management is both dysfunctional and greedy. In the summer of 2010 Duke released financial reports for the academic year that ended on June 30, 2009. The university reported that its endowment had dropped from $6.1 billion to $4.4 billion, and massive investments for the pension plan and health system reserves did as poorly. A new trustee reported Duke was in "dire financial strait." The president threatened job cuts and salary freezes for lower-level employees, the usual victims of university cutbacks. Janitorial staff, grounds keepers, clerks, cafeteria workers and of course adjuncts were hit hard by the so-called crisis. But not the Duke management team. They did "rather well." For example, the Duke Management Company, the investment arm that lost billions, awarded huge bonuses, and two managers got bonuses that were double their annual salaries. Richard Broadhead, Duke's president, is engaged in the type of management that can only fire up the forces of creative destruction. Here is some of what Fact Checker found out: many administrators and executives made over a million dollars or close to it, and raises and bonuses for the management team were rampant as Duke's employees lost jobs and suffered financial loss. Mike Krzyzewski was the highest paid Duke employee with salary and bonus totaling $4.1 million; he is the men's basketball coach. The football coach makes a paltry $1.5 million and the president of the university only makes $824,755. Embarrassed and fearing backlash for such largess the Athletic Department announced in April 2011 that $1 of every ticket sold for Duke sporting events will go to its library. Hey they have a library. Duke's bizarre managerial decisions don't stop. Seeking to make a "fast buck," the Duke executives decided to spend $37 million to open a Duke campus in China. How will they pay for this? Duke will charge Chinese students $41,000 a year. Reports out of China are that no one wants to attend. It seems the geniuses on the Duke executive management team forgot to consider the fact that Duke's tuition is 40 times higher than Chinese tuition.

Consider Nick Saban of Alabama University. He made $3.75 million in 2008, but after his football team won the national championship title the next year, coach Saban was given new a contract paying him an average of $5.5 million a year through 2018. Meanwhile Alabama's president Robert Witt, who makes over $600,000 a year, told his faculty the school was in a major financial crisis and forced its professors to take a salary reduction in 2009 of 1.5 percent. Since 2008 hundreds of jobs have been eliminated. So while Saban makes his millions the faculty average about $80,000 annually.

Auburn University, another example, won the 2010 national title and the win earned their coach Gene Chizik $600,000 in bonuses, giving him $1.1 million in performance- related compensation for the season. Meanwhile Auburn's budget has been sliced by a third since 2008 and faculty had not been given raises for three years.

In 2011 as the football powerhouses scrambled to join new conferences seeking fat television contracts, Oklahoma gave their coach Bob Stoops a new contract to pay him $34.5 million through 2018. Meanwhile, in-state tuition increased 5 percent in 2011. It is expected that tuition will increase 5 percent every year, as it has done since 2006. Politicians and others blame the increases on professors who they say get paid too much and do not teach enough.

Let's look at the University of Southern California coaches. In 2007 Pete Carroll was the highest paid coach receiving $4.4 Million. In 2009 athletic director Mike Garrett, Carroll's boss, took home more than $1 million, while Carroll made $4.1 million and Steve Sarkisian, Carroll's assistant, made nearly $1.2 million (Sander, 2010). Tim Floyd, the USC basketball coach made $1.6-million. Tuition, room and board is over $55,000 a year.

Giving coaches million-dollar salaries while their institutions sink in a financial quagmire is apparent at most universities. Bo Pelini coach of U of Nebraska football, was given a four-year deal in 2011 worth $2.775 million, a raise of $425,000 from his 2010 contract. Under his new five-year deal, Pelini's salary will increase $100,000 annually, reaching $3.175 million in 2015. Meanwhile in 2010 the school was in a financial crisis and was planning to terminate 56 employees and again increase tuition to deal with a $3.7 million budget shortfall.

TAKING MONEY FROM ACADEMICS

According to Zimbalist (2010) more than 100 college football coaches had annual compensation packages that surpassed $1 million and more than a dozen of them exceed $3 million. At least 42 of the 119 Division I-A coaches earned $1 million or more in 2006 (Upton and Wieberg, 2006) and in 2008 the average pay of major college football coaches was more than $1 million a year. From 2007 to 2009, head football coaches' salaries rose 46 percent to an average of $1.36 million in the Football Bowl Subdivision of Division I. Some coaches earn five to 10 times what university presidents do (Zimbalist, 2010).

So why have these sports programs and their high priced coaches? Some say because they bring in money. But do they? A recent report by the NCAA suggests that college sports lose money. Among the 120 schools with top Division I football teams, only 19 had athletic departments that generated a profit in 2006 (Winick, 2008) and in 2009 that number was down to 14. However in 2010, the NCAA reported 22 programs made money while the other 98 programs lost money with a median deficit of $11.6 million. According to Berkowitz and Upton (2011), between 2006 and 2010 Rutgers University needed more money to subsidize its athletic department than any college in the country. They needed more than $115 million in university funds and student fees to keep their programs alive. In 2009-10 the athletic department needed $26.9 million at the same time they announced a freeze on all employee salaries. Rutgers is not alone, in 2010 the University of Connecticut was $14.6 million in the red, the University of South Florida needed $14.2 million, the University of Maryland at College Park needed $13.7 million, and the University of Tennessee at Knoxville needed $13.6 million and Vanderbilt took $2,000 to $3,000 from every student enrolled to keep its games alive. Estimates are that the students' fees to support the Division I games total between $800 million to $1 trillion annually. It's the 12 football games played each year that causes the financial drain that TV contracts, ticket income and student fees cannot cover.

Almost all programs in the Football Championship Subdivision (formerly Division I-AA) operated in the red and the losses continue to grow each year (Sander, 2011), while all Division I athletic departments without football programs operated in the black. A study found nearly a third of the 125 college division 1-AA athletic departments increased their spending by more than 40 percent over 5 years and the median deficit at those programs had grown to more than $9 million (Sander and Fuller, 2011). Colleges are now beginning to drop a variety of athletic programs but only two schools saw fit to end their football programs. Hofstra University was able to save $4.5 million by dropping its football program and using the money for financial aid to students who cannot pay the more than $45,000 per year for tuition, room and board. Also Northeastern has announced it will end its 74-year old football program. But they are clearly in the minority. Believe it or not the National Football Foundation reported in 2011 that in a span of six years, 36 colleges and universities will field new football programs-eight of those in 2011. Why? Pushed by alums promising wheelbarrows filled with money, these presidents operate under the assumption that to build a university, a packed football stadium six Saturdays a year is the ticket. **The Bowls**

While the universities lose money, there are plenty of affiliated "not-for-profit" groups that make a lot of money. For example the CEO of the New Orleans-based Sugar Bowl, Paul Hoolahan, made $645,000 in 2009. In Tampa the CEO of the Outback Bowl Jim McVay made $808,000. The CEO of the Fiesta Bowl John Junker, also did well. He made $600,000 plus a $120,000 no-interest loan, and like the other bowl CEOs he is responsible for one game and one parade a year. Junker also has a COO, a VP, several executives and nine directors to run this one-game-a-year program.

In March 2011 Junker was exposed as running a corrupt organization and using the Fiesta Bowl funds as his personal piggy bank. He was immediately fired. Here is what turned up:

$13,000 for an assistant's wedding

$1,200 at a strip club

$33,000 for a birthday party (For Junker's 50th birthday celebration, he and his buddies went to Pebble Beach for a few days of golf, food and toasts)

$75 for flowers to suck up to the University of Texas' admissions office

$4,200 to John McCain's political campaign

That's not all. According to Thomas (2011a):

"The most serious revelations involve nearly a dozen employees who told investigators that the chief executive and others working for the bowl, the host of one of the nation's pre-eminent college football games, encouraged them to make political contributions, then reimbursed them with sham bonus payments. Some said they were then pressured to lie about the practice.

In May 2011 the Presidential Oversight Committee of the Bowl Championship Series (BCS) decided the "good old boys" at the Fiesta Bowl should pay $1 million fine. Now they have to raise ticket prices.

Junker was replaced by former University of Arizona President Robert Shelton who will be paid a $455,000 salary, plus about $30,000 for his retirement account, with other incentives of $135,000.

RUN THE COLLEGE LIKE A CORPORATION: PAY ME LIKE A CEO

While this madness is going on executives have embraced another characteristic associated with the corporate mentality; higher education chiefs want to be paid like their corporate brothers. In 2006, the highest paid president of a private university was Northwestern's Richard Freeland, who was paid approximately $2.9 million. James Gallagher President of Philadelphia University, was next at $2.6 million, followed by William Brody of Johns Hopkins at $1.9 million. In 2008, 30 college presidents passed the $1 million mark. In the 2009-10 academic year E. Gordon Gee president of Ohio State made $1.8 million. In 2006 Northwestern University President who made $2.9 million earned 42.6 times the salary of his faculty, who average $68,000 per annum (Burger, 2007). The number of presidents making more than $1 million increased to 12 in 2007, up from seven the year before (Glater, 2007).

The chancellor and the board of Minnesota's universities decided to give their college presidents performance bonuses in 2009 totaling over $300,000, while calling for 550 jobs in the university system to be left open or eliminated. They also raised tuition by about 3 percent. In 2011 they announced the termination of 6,000 employees and a 5 percent hike in tuition, the elimination of programs and a wage freeze. Do they teach ethics?

In 2011 The University of Minnesota's newly appointed president was paid $610,000, a $155,000 increase from the previous president's pay.

Michael McRobbie the president of Indiana University, will receive a 12 percent salary increase in 2011. In 2010 he received 10 percent, which amounts to a 22 percent increase over two years. Meanwhile tuition has been raised and faculty and staff received paltry salary increases. And what did the university's governing board say? It's a retention award.

According to Lewin (2008), in 2007 David Roselle of the University of Delaware received a package of $2.4 million. In 2007, the highest paid president was David Sargent of Suffolk University. He received a $2.8 million pay package, including a $436,000 longevity bonus. In 2009 Sargent received $1.5 million as he froze faculty salaries and raised student fees and caused an outrage. Following the corporate model these presidents and high ranking administrators and their well paid coaches fly around in private jets. For example the Southeastern Conference (SEC) has 12 university members and they own at least 22 jets (Fain, 2010).

In 2011 faculty in the Kentucky university system went without pay increases for a third year and state funds dropped about 1 percent in 2011 after dropping about 9 percent in 2009 and 2010. But Chancellor James Ramsey did OK. In 2011 he got a 5 percent raise to $313,818 and a bonus of $114,033. That's not all. The university's foundation increased his annual supplemental salary to $142,314 (Kiley, 2011).

The Ivies are right in the mix paying their presidents corporate style CEO salaries. Pennsylvania University President Amy Gutmann received $1,321,040 in total compensation in 2009. She was behind Yale's President Richard Levin, whose total compensation package was $1,627,649, and Columbia University President Lee Bollinger, who received $1,527,217.

It's not only the presidents who get rich. Salaries of university executives, not just presidents, have increased dramatically. In 2007, Michael Johns, Executive VP of Health Affairs at Emory University, made $3,753,759. Arthur Rubenstein Executive VP and Dean of the School of Medicine at the University of Pennsylvania, made $3,335,767 (Lewin, 2009).

Consider the University of Texas, it has increased its budget for administrative jobs that paid more than $200,000 by 40 percent during the period 2004 to 2008, at the same time tuition rose 57 percent (Root, 2009). For example, the University of Texas has not one but two athletic directors and in 2011 DeLoss Dodds the men's athletic director, will get a raise of $72,891, upping his base salary to $700,000 a year through Aug. 31, 2015. Dodds will be 76 years old when he will step down and then he will take a part time position at the school through Aug. 31, 2020, with a $100,000 yearly salary and benefits (Maher, 2011). In addition, Dodds would receive a $1 million annuity after taxes if he is still employed by UT in some capacity on Aug. 31, 2014. His current contract calls for a $750,000 annuity to be paid this year. Chris Plonsky, the other athletic director (women), will be paid be paid $265,848 a year through 2017. But her supplement for helping Dodds with his men's program will jump from $40,000 to $90,000 per year. Plonsky, will also get an annual $62,500 windfall if no major NCAA infractions are committed (Maher, 2011). And guess what? Another increase is scheduled for students and their families in fall 2011. In December 2010 the Tuition Policy Advisory Committee wrote that without the increases in tuition and fees, UT would have to cut at least $17.3 million from its budget during the 2010-11 school year and another $14.2 million in 2011-12 (Rosales, 2010). Meanwhile the university is sitting on a tax-free endowment of $7.2 billion and the guy who manages it is the CEO of UT Investment Management, Bruce Zimmerman, who got a raise of 4.3 percent bringing his base salary to $600,000 in 2011 and a bonus of $1.15 million awarded in November 2010.

What we have are university systems being run by corporate type executives who have never taught and are far removed from "academic life." Many spend their time in the "administrative building," with their own dinning room and chef, only associating with other executives and invited quests. The only time they mingle with students and faculty are at ceremonies and, of course, football games.

SUPPLEMENT SALARIES BY TAKING FROM ENDOWMENTS

On the same day the Board of Trustees at San Diego State approved to pay its new president $400,000 a year ($350,000 in state funds and an additional $50,000 from the schools foundation) along with $1,000 a month car allowance and free housing. They voted to increase student fees by 12 percent, the second tuition hike in less than a year. Since 2007 tuition and costs for students have doubled. The justification for the higher fees: The State university system lost $650 million in the new state budget, and could face another $100 million cut if state revenue falls short of projections. In 2011 the new president at Cal. Polytechnic State University at San Luis Obispo will make $350,000 in state-funded salary, plus a $30,000 supplement from the campus foundation.

In 2011 the University of South Carolina lost 21 percent of its state funding enacting a hiring freeze and a 6.9 percent tuition hike. Since

2008, 160 full time employees were terminated. Under these extraordinary "belt-tightening" circumstances what did the president do? Give out more than $2.7 million in what is called "salary supplements" to 146 of their managers and executives who already earn more than $100,000 (Kittle, 2011). For example Provost Michael Amiridis got a supplement of $50,000, in addition to his $260,000 salary. Business School Dean Hildy Teegen got a $50,000 supplement, which brought her salary to $277,250 (Kittle, 2011). And, that's not all. South Carolinas' football assistant coaches collectively received over $320,000 in salary increases in 2010 bringing their total salaries to $2.15, this excludes head coach Spurrier's compensation of $1.75 million.

TAX EXEMPT STATUS

The IRS is looking into the tax exempt status of these institutions that pay their executives corporate style compensation and perks, sit on billion dollar endowments (Harvard's endowment is over $27 billion and the CEO of Harvard Management Co. made $3.5 million in 2009) and offer students very little financial help while claiming they are non-profit educational charities and should pay no taxes. The IRS is looking at the revenue these institutions derive from advertising, including printed publications, internet advertising, billboards, television and radio broadcasting; corporate sponsorship, including printed materials, events, internet sponsorship, billboards, and television or radio broadcasting; the rental of property, including facilities, arenas, recreation centers, athletic facilities, personal property, and telecommunications; and a wide range of miscellaneous activities, including internet and catalog sales, royalties, mailing lists, affinity cards, scientific research and intellectual property, hotels and conference centers, catering and food services, parking lots, bookstores, golf courses, investments in partnerships and S corporations, and controlled entities (Cerny, M.; McKinnon, M.A.W., Capwell, J.R. and Hellmuth, K.L., 2010).

CUTTING COSTS- SHRINKING THE BEHEMOTHS

While sinking millions into sports and managerial compensation these public, nonprofit and private institutions face financial exigency. So what will they do? Fire tenured faculty by using financial exigency, close departments that do not attract paying customers (Classics and Language departments are dropping like flies), eliminate and combine degree offerings, hold down salaries and by all means get rid of those high-priced-full-time faculty and hire lots of adjuncts. As of 2010 poorly paid adjuncts with no benefits made up over 50 percent of the teaching faculty and only 30 percent of the faculty had tenure (20 years ago, 70 percent had tenure) and what about the other 20 percent, they are made up of non-tenured faculty, so-called clinical professors, teaching assistants and graduate students. The data is even worse among community colleges. Among Massachusetts community colleges, part-time faculty

outnumber full-timers 5,000 to 2,000. A professor reported bringing his daughter to visit the chair of the Classics Department during a college visit to NYU. After they left he told his daughter "This is the first and last time you will meet this full professor." He knew what he would get for $60,000 a year (tuition, room and board): she will be taught by teaching assistants (TA's) and adjuncts. Throughout the country, tenured professors are being offered "buy-outs" and resigning in large numbers. At University of Nevada, Las Vegas, 48 senior tenured professors left after receiving their "buy-outs." Junior, non-tenured and adjunct faculty remain.

Many predict not only tenure will be a thing of the past but full-time employment will be extinct, as conservative state and local politicians not only call for the end of tenure but also placing a cap on faculty salaries and the elimination of sabbaticals and an increase in teaching loads. Some are even calling for outsourcing of major degree programs by hiring private companies.

While cost-cutting decimates the ranks of full time teachers, administrators keep on building high-tech, student-friendly campuses named after billionaires.

WHAT ABOUT THE STUDENTS?

They become the victims of this mess. According to the National Center for Educational Statistics, the graduation rate after four years is: 51 percent at private nonprofit institutions, 31 percent at public institutions, and a criminal 13 percent at for-profit schools. According to Kiley (2010), the graduation rate after six years is 65 percent for private nonprofits and 50 percent for public universities and it will continue to drop as more and more students walk away from the outrageous price tag.

In addition, a study by Arum and Roksa (2011) suggests that at least 45 percent of undergraduates demonstrated "no improvement in critical thinking, complex reasoning, and writing skills in the first two years of college, and 36 percent showed no progress in four years." Students are now considered consumers of an "experience." Learning and engaging in complex, critical thought is considered as too burdensome and bad for business by administrators who embrace a business model of survival. Students' priorities are vocationalism, grades, financial benefits, and of course having a good time. Therefore 32 percent of students do not take a single course with more than 40 pages of reading per week, and 50 percent do not take any course requiring more than 20 pages of writing over a semester and only spend 12 to 13 hours a week studying (Arum and Roksa, 2011).

Faculty complain about grade inflation and the lack of quality education (40 to 45 percent of all grades given are A's), as administrators demand that seats be kept filled because it's an economic necessity. The business model embraced by administrators of these colleges and universities suggests their priorities are not focused on education but on keeping students happy, high-tech dorms filled, games alive and administrators well compensated.

HOW DID THIS HAPPEN?

It began in the early '50s when the GI Bill of Rights gave returning veterans a ticket to an education and the behemoth universities were created. Their growth continued into the '60s as the "boomer" generation flooded campuses. The percentage of the population having a degree grew and became an artifact of national pride. Many universities became large education factories and they were managed like factories. Students moved through the system as raw materials ready to be converted by a never-ending cadre of specialists offering lectures from yellow note pads turned brown. Overtime these institutions became vocational technical schools and the liberal arts, language and science departments were dwarfed by the so-called professional schools. People with sound financial and fund raising skills moved into top management positions. Boards of trustees, composed of industrialists and financiers, demanded their institutions be run by financially savvy managers. So they appointed ex-CEOs and lawyers to run their universities. Fifteen of the 19 executives who are running UC Berkeley into the ground while enriching themselves are ex-CEOs or lawyers (Nijhawan, 2011).

Presidents and deans were now judged on their business acumen, fund-raising skills, and ability to attract students who want the type of training that would land them a good job. Except at several small colleges, liberal learning and critical thinking were lost. In addition these educational factories had to move up the rankings, pass the regional, state and professional accrediting agencies by offering standardized training. Imposed on schools, departments and teachers were standard syllabi, degree requirements, curricula, textbooks, cases, technology and even grading rubrics. These institutions increasingly resembled high schools. All the student did was to declare a major and a minor and have a good time in the student-friendly campuses that resembled Disney-land for late adolescents, and of course have Mom and Dad pay for it.

Consider New York, the last state to establish a state university system. Since 1948 the state has created a university behemoth containing 64 campuses with 5,000 undergraduate programs and close to half a million students enrolled. This excludes New Youk City which has its own City University system. With enrollment and graduation rates dropping, a paucity of jobs waiting for those who leave, and state and local governments in fiscal crisis, executives of these institutions now manage by the numbers, and financial exigencies take precedence over educational quality as departments are closed, tenured and non-tenured faculty are terminated, courses are eliminated and class sizes balloon. An exception may be the prestigious City University of New York. While most schools charge tuition of between $20,000 a semester to $20,000 a year, one can complete an entire degree for $20,000, and it's face-to-face with full professors teaching undergraduates. However, if public support for these institutions dries up, the tuition will increase and administrators will do the same financial juggling act they witness at the state university level.

The brick and mortar institutions in America may be shrinking faster than Drucker suggested.

TECHNOLOGY AND DEMISE OF THE BRICK AND MORTAR UNIVERSITY

Besides the cost, another factor led Drucker to predict that brick and mortar universities would be driven to extinction. This was his assessment of the competition from alternative education systems made possible by technology.

Drucker predicted that these sprawling total institutions called university campuses with their multiple departments, research labs, dorms, athletic fields and stadiums and hordes of tenured faculty would become relics. The libraries would be the first to go. Then the laboratories would become separate corporate entities engaging in research and development for a profit. Then the sports teams would become what they truly are; minor league systems for professional teams. Then the classrooms would go, giving way to the online universities. Tuition would drop as "big name" professors would leave in droves, giving up their $100,000 to $200,000 labor intensive professorships, to give lectures electronically to thousands and make a lot of money. We might even witness "free universities" offering online degrees, sponsored by a combination of corporate advertising, donations and public funds similar to National Public Radio (NPR). We now have the technology for courses to be offered across universities and the potential for students around the world to freely engage in discussions and have free access to course materials, books, articles and video lectures. Student papers and test results would be read and graded by computer software, and sophisticated versions of "Turnitin."

Electronic education offers the potential to be on going, and unbounded by age or any socioeconomic group. Everyone would have access, all the time, at any time. Learned societies and professional associations would function similarly without the need to hold location based conferences. Like-minded scholars could freely meet, discuss and collaborate using information technology.

Brick and mortar universities are currently in a fight, not for prestige but for survival, and this is based in part on Joseph Schumpeter's description of the transformation process that follows radical innovation. In his book, *Capitalism, Socialism and Democracy*. Schumpeter, maintains that organizations like the university that were once dominant would lose out as technological advances improve delivery of goods and services, alter customer service and significantly cut costs.

We may even see a Wal-Mart type of university. Wal-Mart has become a retail giant in its short history through its use of innovative supply-chain and inventory-management processes, economy of scale, and personnel-management techniques – all resulting in significantly lower prices that allowed it to destroy older or smaller companies. Older behemoths once perceived as retail powers died (e.g., Montgomery Ward, A&S, Korvetts, S.S. Kresge, Fedmart, and Woolworth) because they could not compete with their nimbler and more innovative competitors. Not surprisingly it may turn out that Wal-Mart will also die as it faces threats brought about by globalization. Wal-Mart relies on China to produce the products they sell: some suggest as much as 80 percent of the products they sell are made in Asia. Will there come a day when the Chinese decide to eliminate the middleman (Wal-Mart)? It is happening: China has its own online store, 360buy.com, and Wal-Mart sensing the competition, has invested half a billion dollars in the company. In 2011 Wal-Mart purchased a 51 percent stake in Africa's largest big box, Massmart, for $2.4 billion.

As the Chinese and Wal-Mart compete, we witness Schumpeter's "creative destruction" in action. Just as the eight track replaced the vinyl record and the cassette tape replaced the eight track, only to be destroyed by the compact disc, and then the compact disc sent to scrapheap by the MP3 player and then the iPod followed by the iPhone and droid, and iPads, which will be followed by a new device, the music industry is continuously transformed. In 2009 it is possible for anyone, even one with the slightest bit of internet savvy, to have thousands of songs in their hard drive-all obtained free. Nothing is static in this technologically changing global economy and this includes the brick and mortar university.

Radical innovation has altered almost every facet of American life and cultures around the globe. In American, millions of manufacturing jobs, once considered safe, have been lost and the economy has been turned on its head by change. Consider the biggest supplier of clothes and toys to Wal-Mart and Target. It is Li & Fung, an outsourcing and trading company in China. In October 2009 it purchased Wear Me, a New York based design and manufacturing company. Wear Me holds licenses for brands like Calvin Klein, Timberland, Disney, Marvel and Nickelodeon. With the purchase of Wear Me, Li & Fung now had the capability to move into the business of designing, sourcing, licensing, marketing and selling of apparel and accessories.

We are witnessing the same phenomenon in newspaper industry as free online papers destroy traditional print journalism. Also the book publishing industry is being transformed and some predict that all books will eventually be free and digital. Today's students not only do not pay for music, they also do not pay for textbooks, and these publishers are scrambling in a feeble attempt to survive. They are busy creating platforms to supply learning materials on digital devices. The software is already in use in India, and it will be offered in other developing countries in Asia and Africa and of course it will be used by students in America. Just as a 10-year-old looked at a rotary telephone in an antique shop in 2008 and said "what's this, how do you work it?" years from now a teenager may look at a book and say the same thing.

We are witnessing a similar phenomenon with universities. Existing technology (often free) offers the ability to drive digital information (instruction, music, etc.) and distribution costs down to a fraction of traditional costs. Open source, open course, online synchronous and asynchronous delivery with facilitated group interaction through social media is already a nearly free educational tool. Anyone can sign on, read the same course materials, see and listen to the instructor and classmates at several campuses. Students can contribute, ask the professor questions or engage in group conversations with classmates online in real time, through video group chats. They can take the same tests and quizzes and collaborate with others through email, blogs, wikis, Facebook, YouTube, iPhone, iPad, shared docs, and video chats on Skype. In 2009, less the sheepskin, this is all available for free. We are beginning to witness the evolution of free universities.

Universities are struggling to keep up with the technology and they know that obsolescence means a fast end of business. The European School of Management and Technology (ESMT) offers the following:

* ESMT Open Lecture with Prof. Avinash Persaud

* New video series: ESMTcast "Learning for Leading" available on iTunes

* Up-to-date information presented on social networks Facebook, Twitter and YouTube

* Deutsche Welle TV's 4-part documentary on the ESMT MBA online

There is a model of education put forth by India, a country that sends 12 million young people into the labor force every year.

INDIA'S MODEL

Given the demand for secondary education (considered high school and junior college) India will need to increase the numbers to be educated from 17 million in 2008 to 57 million in 2017. In addition, India is attempting to achieve a university enrollment increase of 30 per cent by 2020. To meet these goals the traditional way (brick and mortar) would require the addition of 700 universities and 25,000 schools and junior colleges with an addition of more than a million teachers, 15,000 faculty with Ph.D.'s in management and over 30,000 Ph.D.'s in engineering (Pathak, 2011). They cannot and will not build institutions or hire thousands of professors that they do not have, instead they will use electronic means to deliver the needed education. As of July 2011 there were 3,500 MBA programs in India and their numbers are increasing at a rapid pace.

Consider one method they will use. NPTEL is a joint venture by Indian Institution of Technology and Indian Institute of Science established to deliver education in engineering throughout the country using curriculum-based video and web courses. This allows a single experienced professor to reach thousands of students. Each course contains materials that can be covered in depth in 40 or more lecture hours. In addition, 110 courses have been developed in video format, with each course comprising approximately 40 or more one-hour lectures. Students have access to 129 web courses in engineering/science and humanities, and these offerings will continue to grow.

India will also deliver distance education courses through so-called study centers where students go to take online and televised courses. If students do not have access to television or the Internet at home they walk to the local study center. Many of these centers are franchised operations owned by locals. The Indira Gandhi National Open University has over 2.4 million students with 3,000 study centers. Other players in distance education are: Punjab Technical University with 1,200 study centers; Sikkim Manipal University with 750 study centers and Maharishi Dayanand University with 759 centers. At present there are about 100 online universities, and the number will continue to grow. In addition these online institutions stream educational content through the third generation (3G) mobile telephony using the satellite-based Very Small Aperture Terminal (VSAT) Technology and Broadband. McGraw-Hill is developing a platform to teach English and test preparation on cell phones and of course they use YouTube and Facebook. NPTEL has around 4400 videos on YouTube contained in 120 courses and 2.6 million viewers. Indian corporations are also participating in higher education, especially in the areas of pharmacy, engineering and medicine. This is how India will educate its population and do it inexpensively.

No 6 to 12 hours a week studying for these students

No beer blasts that go from Thursday night to Sunday

No 110,000 students and alums at the football game

And

No $200,000 diploma

CELEBRITY PROFESSORS

We are also witnessing another phenomenon that will hasten the demise of the brick and mortar university. We are now seeing celebrity professors breaking away from the traditional university and offering their personal brand as an alternative to the expensive university brand. We have lecture and discussion networks called "open lecture series" initially sponsored by universities and later developed by celebrity professors in conjunction with television and internet news companies and moderated by celebrity news anchors. ESMT offers video platforms as well as the social networks Twitter and Facebook. The new ESMTcast format "Learning for Leading" aims to share business school research and expertise with a broad audience. The first videos include Professors Konstantin Korotov and Manfred Kets de Vries titled "Leadership and Coaching" and Professor Luc Wathieu on "Decision-making". The New York Times continuously advertises the "One Day University" offered by the Learning Annex. For $99, one can attend 17 lectures from "award-winning" professors from Harvard, Yale, and Princeton. Early in 2010 Bill Gates claimed: "Five years from now on the web for free you'll be able to find the best lectures in the world online." In the near future these lectures will have college credit attached. It may happen sooner than Gates predicted. In October 2010 the London School of Business and Finance (LSBF) announced it will offer MBA courses free online through Facebook, only charging tuition if you choose to take exams to gain formal credit towards the MBA. LSBF founder, Aaron Etingen said the free online MBA course material will include lectures online from its faculty and panel discussion groups including industry highflyers such as Partners at Accenture Management Consulting and Deloitte, the Head of Royal Navy Leadership Academy and the Director of Marketing at Viagogo (Olsen, 2010). It may very well be that these new education delivery models will adopt India's "study centers" where students can go to study and take examinations. Hey, we already have them. They are called "libraries."

NO NEED TO BRAND ONESELF

Besides offering goof times, the brick and mortar university bases its survival on branding. These brands are like clubs, where they establish networks and obtain sheepskins as the ticket to gain entry into a business or professional sector. The university screens and filters people into concentrates of similar socioeconomic status (SES), with a sprinkle of intentional diversity. Corporate recruiters go to these branded universities to obtain near clones, those that are considered "executive material" who can be molded into the culture of the company or profession. But this will change when the brick and mortar university ceases to exist. No longer will the university serve as an employment training feeder for the corporation, and we may see the end of what the university has become; a vocation technical institute. Perhaps we will witness a return to the universities' original mission. But only online. In addition, university customers no longer need to be branded. A recruiter for an MBA program told a student that the program would increase his contacts and networking only to be told by the student, "I've been on Facebook since the 10th grade and I have 1,100 friends and my 1,100 friends each have 1,100 friends, do the math. And you want me to spend how much to network and get branded?"

SCRAMBLING TO SURVIVE

As American students reject $50,000-per-year education and enrollment drops, college presidents have responded by going overseas and differentiating their degree offerings to keep the inputs flowing. This has left the colleges with increased administrative overhead and a faculty spread so thin that they often teach in areas they have little or no knowledge. It is common to have a tenured faculty member with a doctorate in electric engineering with no students to teach, to teach or administer a program far removed from his discipline. Deans are desperate, and they are forever looking for the new "cash cows" and a chance to move into or up the rankings in one of the many ranking magazines.

Will the brick and mortar university go down without a fight? Never.

Brick and mortar universities go to the state agencies, accrediting agencies, state boards of education and government, to keep online schools or schools with no boundaries out of their state. In particular they are going after the online doctoral programs by convincing state boards of education and other accrediting agencies not to recognize the degrees or credits. But this may be a losing battle. According to MBA Alliance (2006), two-thirds of all MBA's are now earned on-line. It is suggested that two thirds of all graduate degrees (masters and doctorates) in the next 10 years will be earned on-line. While colleges are fighting the online universities, especially the for-profits, they are scrambling to get into the online business themselves. In the 2006–07 academic year, 66 percent of the 4,160 two-year and four-year Title IV degree-granting postsecondary institutions in the nation offered college-level online courses. The overall percentage includes 97 percent of public two-year institutions, 18 percent of private for-profit two-year institutions, 89 percent of public four-year institutions, 53 percent of private not-for-profit institutions, and 70 percent of private for-profit four-year institutions (National education center for statistics, 2009).

Academic leaders know the laptop education is without boundaries and a New York resident can obtain an MBA from Duke University or Hikets School of Hotel and Hospitality Management in India or online certification in an array of specific business areas from Cornell, Boston University, Pennsylvania State University, University of California at Berkeley, University of Notre Dame, University of San Francisco, Tulane and Villanova. This phenomenon will continue to grow, making the brick and mortar institutions obsolete and with as much relevancy as summer camp. In 2009 there are 12,000 different degree offerings and hundreds of thousands of courses offered online in America, and we will witness continued growth. The demise of the brick and mortar university will also be expedited by a new generation of students, the first generation of students to have spent their entire lives in the new technological world; the Gen Y's.

ENTER THE GEN Y'S

Colleges and universities are addressing these new students in a variety of ways: by increasing the use of technology not only in the classroom but throughout the campus. Many are turning their campuses into a Google type office playgrounds, social media is pervasive and food courts and study/play centers that try to accommodate every student's need. Will it work? According to Symonds (2010), "Unless schools really understand the mind-set of the potential Gen Y ..., they risk looking at best like enthusiastic amateurs and at worst like the embarrassing "cool dad" attempting to engage with their teenage children about the latest release by Jay-Z or Lady Gaga."

Gen Y's are the first generation to reject sitting in class and later sitting in the cubicle. Why? Sitting in class means they cannot do other things, like being on their laptops, iPods, iPads, cell phones, TVs, etc., in most cases at the same time. In the process they have developed a unique method of cognitive functioning shaped by their always-on electronic communication. They demand to have lectures taped and they can watch them at their leisure while doing other things. Rejecting the classroom is the first giant step. Rejecting a $200,000 diploma will be the second. The Gen Y's will also question the value of another educational model, the for-profits. They have the capability to carefully assess these institutions and anyone with internet expertise will quickly discover their questionable quality and the outrage that exists in the cyberspace.

REJECTING THE EXPENSIVE DIPLOMA

Today's students, the Gen Ys, are clearly aware of the spiraling cost of higher education. Like their parents they are also more aware of their financial environment, much more so than prior generations. Being in deep debt at an early age contributes to considerable financial knowledge. They work hard to get out of debt and worry about their credit scores. Being in debt is one reason why so many, 50 percent to 60 percent move home after graduation and why they cram into urban apartments, and why they depend upon parents for financial help well into their late 20's. This also may explain why CEOs and managers maintain that all the Gen Y's care about is money. The 2007 the Society for Human Resource Management conducted a Job Satisfaction survey and found that for Gen Ys; compensation/pay was the number one factor in selecting a job, followed by benefits, job security, flexibility to balance work/life, and the ability to communicate effectively with management. In 2009 pay was replaced by job security with pay closely behind. It may be that the Gen Y's are more vociferous in their concern about pay not only because they are in deep debt but also given their electronic connections. They know the salary and perks that companies offer in every conceivable field and profession. According to Keeter (2006), 81 percent of 18 to 25-year-olds surveyed by the Pew Research Center for People and the Press said getting rich was their generation's most important or second-most-important life goal and 51 percent said the same about being rich and famous.

GenYs will not pursue the expensive degree option when they can ferret out alternative ways that will save them a bundle, have perhaps greater prestige, and have the education delivered in a manner they find appealing.

WHAT WILL SUCCEED? WHAT THE DIGITAL-GEN Y'S WANT

Is it possible for a student to get a degree taking classes taught by the world's best professors for one-tenth of $200,000? Of course: give lectures online by celebrity professors to thousands, have required work reviewed and assessed electronically, or give examinations using the SAT or GMAT exam model, or pay librarians a small fee to proctor examinations. It can be done electronically and the student can take a course anywhere. It's beginning to happen. New Jersey has its own exclusively online state college (Thomas Edison State) and New York will give a SUNY degree to students enrolled in its little known Empire State College where students can take classes at any of their 34 New York State locations, or work one-to-one with a faculty mentor, in small study groups and intensive residencies or take online courses from anywhere in the world that include access to faculty, fellow students, and other online resources. At $207 per credit for New York state residents, a degree costs a little over $26,000, and they will give credit for prior learning (credit for college-level learning gained from work and life experience, including employee training programs, professional certificates or licenses, and military training). At Washington Governors University, a not-for-profit school in Washington, students pay $3,000 for a six-month "all-you-can-eat" program where they can take as many credits as they wish. Even for-profits are getting involved by offering the cheap degree. Aspen University in Colorado is exclusively online, and it offers masters credits for $100 per credit. One can obtain an M.S. in Technology degree for $3,600. At that rate, one should be able to obtain a 128-credit B.A. for $12,800. But BYU-Idaho goes even better. Its online degree programs cost $65 per credit, or less than $10,000 for a degree. Will the Gen Y's flock to programs like this? Make it cheap and put it online-maybe. But if it's cheap, online, and prestigious, and if the student can offer "try before you buy," they will love it. As mentioned before, this is what the London School of Business and Finance is doing: Take classes online with the best faculty through an innovative and familiar delivery channel (Facebook) at no cost and then give the GenY's the *pièce de résistance*. Let them test the quality of the course before putting their money down. That is, take the course for free, and if one wants the credit then pay. They expect 500,000 to go online the first yearWhy will this work? GenY's do not like the concept of fixed time, they prefer to decide when things happen and they do not like to be told by some authority that they will be punished if they do not show up when expected. At the University of Florida students live in (summer camp) dorms and take their classes online. GenY's love to travel and live in a world with no boundaries, and they welcome alternative cultures. They avoid being stuck in one place for a period of time, no traffic jams on the way to class, no living in an uncivilized dorm rooms with strangers and no standing on line for showers, food, books, advisement, registration, etc. If students can afford it, they can do their degree in Mumbai, London, Costa Rica, etc. It's no longer "a year abroad," its four years abroad. If a student cannot afford it then it's off to work and to the community college for two years. The key is they want to be able to obtain their education their way; full time, part time and four years or 14 years. And they will avoid the one thing they hate: debt. Their goal is to obtain a viable degree (not necessarily an education) without debt.

TUITION DEBT BUBBLE

Because of the skyrocketing cost of a college education total education borrowing increased by 10 percent between 2009 and 2010, according to the CollegeBoard. At the most expensive schools, the elite private nonprofit institutions, 75 percent of students have a median debt of $21,100 dollars and at for-profit colleges 99 percent finished with an average debt load in excess of $43,000. The average (not median) student leaves college with a loan debt that varies from $28,000 to $39,000 and this type of debt is climbing fast.

Three out of four GenY's obtained their own credit cards while in college, often pushed by overzealous banks and loan companies. As a consequence, GenY's will leave college with between $3,000 and $7,500 in credit card debt. It is not surprising that 30 to 40 cents of every dollar earned after graduation will go to service their debt. This will get worse, not better, as one in nine high school students have credit cards co-signed by a parent. Chase bank actually will give a high school student $50 if they sign up for their debit card. However being in debt is no longer a process consumers are willing to accept and since the financial crisis of 2008 people are struggling to get back to living within their means. As long as one in four workers are either unemployed or under-employed, this trend will continue,

Most families in America are in a financial crisis, and this includes students and their parents and believe it or not colleges and universities. With unemployment soaring and now 43.6 million living in poverty sending a child to college is out of the question for millions of families. America is now in ninth place in college attainment in the world and dropping fast. But do college and university presidents care? Their business model encourages students and families to go into debt, and they have pushed for an increase in federal loans and grants to continue extraordinary growth: a 60 percent increase in two years, or $48 billion. The federal government heavily subsidizes colleges and universities. Parents fill out FAFSA forms and FAFSA produces a formula that determines how much they should pay. The difference is made up by a combination of Pell grants, state grants, private scholarships and loans, and of course the pervasive federally guaranteed loans. The need for awards of any type are so important to families that books and web sites have proliferated, promising shortcuts to navigate the morass of so-called "millions of dollars in scholarships" that go unclaimed every year. Unsuspecting families actually pay these hucksters in hope that their child will win something. Winning the lottery may be more realistic. However, if you want to get a good mailing list? Offer a $500 scholarship for an essay on "Being a Vegan" and you will get a list of thousands of emails and home addresses to sell your products.

Based on an analysis of the president's FY2011 budget, in FY2009 there were a total of $605.6 billion in federal education loans outstanding, comprised of $149.4 billion in the Direct Loan program and $456.2 billion in the FFEL program. The projected totals for FY2010 are $672.0 billion and for FY2011 are $745.5 billion. Each year more than $100 billion in federal education loans and $10 billion in private student loans are originated. At this rate the total student debt in America will approach a trillion dollars. In 2010 student loan debt exceeded total credit card debt. Consider this, if the projected default rate continues to grow by 2015 it could reach 56 percent for non-profit graduates and 70 to 90 percent of the for-profits. By the end of 2012 the amount of defaulted loans will be between $600 billion and $800 billion. Most of these defaulted loans are government backed, meaning the tax payers will pick up the tab. In 2010 gross public debt in America was $14 trillion, or over 95 percent of GDP. Over the next 10 years this public debt which includes student loans is expected to grow, adding another $10 trillion to outstanding federal debt. Therefore by 2020 debt will be $24 trillion.

Lenders love it when students and their families straddled with debt default. Why? Lenders like Sallie Mae spent millions lobbying congrees to pass the 1998 amendment to the Higher Education Act. This meant that if one defaulted on their college loans, guarantors could take a quarter from every dollar the borrowers eventually repaid, money that would not be applied to the principal and interest on the debts. All defaulted student loans, both government backed and private bank loans, allowed loan insurers and collection agencies (a major growth industry) to chase after students for years while piling on penalties and fees. Many students report that they pay 25 percent of their loan, it was all they could afford to pay, and the principle and interest is never reduced. In addition in 2005, the lenders, banks and collection agencies again got Congress to pass the Bankruptcy Abuse Prevention and Consumer Protection Act. Now all student loans became nondischargeable. This law would not forgive a loan or allow for bankruptcy. This meant that the student could have their pay garnished without a court order and when the student retired, if they still owed, collectors could take the debt from their Social Security benefits.

Even paying off a loan is no guarantee one is debt free. Almost all of these loans, like housing loans, were bundled and sold many times over, often as many as thirty times, leaving a bewildering trail of IOU's. Many students report that after paying off a loan to one collection agency another collection agency pops up demanding payment or the student discovers several banks and collection agencies are listed in their credit reports. It is common for a student who took out loans from several private banks and federal backed loan agencies to owe money to as many as 10 institutions. When the student tries to consolidate these loans they discover it is not possible.

FORGIVING LOANS: A BAILOUT FOR MAIN STREET

A similar situation existed in the 1960's when hippie/counterculture students failed to repay loans. When the late Bella Abzug a New York congresswoman suggested that the government should forgive the loans, the default rate in NYC and Boston jumped through the roof. But there may be another reason why government loan forgiveness may not be a bad idea.

Consider how this extraordinary default rate can damage the economy. In 2011 with the default rate climbing and credit scores or ratings for a majority of college graduates in the dumpster, it will have a profound impact on the economy, not only the outstanding debt, but the ability of these grads to buy condos, houses, cars, or even have a credit card. For the first time in American history, a significant portion of an entire generation, perhaps more than half will be considered a credit risk. In addition parents who signed or cosigned for these loans will have their credit ruined and those who have children planning to take out college loans in the future will be rejected. This will take its toll among all American colleges and universities that require loan backing to attract students. But more significantly, having a significant portion of a generation unable to secure credit will spell disaster for the entire economy.

There is also the psychological burden of being hopelessly in debt. Debt has ruined marriages, and leads to depression, drug and alcohol abuse. Those considered credit risks, with poor credit scores, find it difficult to function in any process that requires credit checks. People in this position, young and old, live with constant shame and worry, and a heightened sense of failure. Both signers and cosigners are constantly harassed at home and work by reckless debt collectors. For these debt-laden people, the American dream of going to college, getting a degree, home ownership, a nice car, a good job and the "good life" are remote.

France offers a more appealing model. It has 82 universities and 1.5 million students: tuition is free and undergraduate enrollment charges are a tiny €165 annually. No student debt, no lives ruined and no millionaire administrators and high-priced coaches. All employees are civil servants. This model is true for most European countries.

According Downie and Paulo, (2011), South American countries take a different tack. For example in 2012 Brazil will implement a program that awards 75,000 scholarships to attend the world's top universities. This will be available only to Brazilians studying subjects of strategic national importance like engineering. Chile will offer 30,000 scholarships, and Colombia and even El Salvador will offer study abroad programs. These countries want to emulate the Asian countries that send hundreds of thousands of students to the best schools to feed the growth of quality research and global expansion in Asia.

Meanwhile American universities and government agencies sit on their hands holding onto an educational model that enriches administrators, banks and loan agencies and does little to make the country competitive. How will colleges, universities and public officials respond when a significant proportion of the American population is priced out of higher education? They will continue the hopeless process of spiraling debt and tell young people to "Go to college, it does not matter if you cannot afford it there is plenty of money available." Recently, U.S. Secretary of Education Arne Duncan said just that. On a visit to a high school he spoke to students and encouraged them to load up on college loans: *"Please apply for our financial aid. We want to give you money. There's lots of money out there for you."* Snyder (2010) wonders where Arne Duncan will be when those students find themselves locked into decades of suffocating student loan debt repayments.

Like the housing bubble, when people were encouraged to take out mortgages they could not afford, we see the same thing with student loans. As the cost of obtaining a degree from these brick and mortar institutions rises faster than any institution or commodity in America, 18-year-olds are encouraged to keep them alive by going into major debt. This is outrageous and will hasten the demise of these institutions. Does anyone smell "bailout" here? We have to keep those games alive and they're too big to fail.

A neighbor who has an MBA read parts of this book, and said "Where's the solutions?" Here they are in the next chapter.

CHAPTER 14

Conclusion: What We Need

Tom Wolfe, in <u>The Bonfire of the Vanities,</u> *wrote of a financial wizard, "One fine day, in a fit of euphoria, after he picked up the telephone and taken an order for zero-coupon bonds that had brought him a $50,000 commission, just like that, this very phrase had bubbled up into his brain. On Wall Street he and a few others – how many? – three hundred, four hundred, five hundred – had become precisely that...Masters of the Universe. There was...no limit whatsoever." (1987)*

But then there are others who:"Load 16 tons and what do I get, another day older and deeper in debt. Saint Peter comes- a-calling but I can't go I owe my soul to the company store."

We have established that the enormous earnings gap between the CEO and the average employees (400 to 500 times) is uniquely an American phenomenon. This raises the following questions: Is there something about American culture that contributes to the CEO's behavior, or perhaps permits their behavior or even expects this behavior? Perhaps even encourages it?

This uniquely American phenomenon allows and even encourages corporate leaders to abandon any type of interest in accepting responsibility as an employee care taker. Corporations only see their care taker role as enrolling employees in a company stock-based pension system that is tied to profitability and even this is waning. The larger question we tried to answer is: How did this happen? We tied our answer to the phenomenon of CEO greed and identified the conditions under which this occurred. We also examined the type of thinking perpetuated by academics, business writers and business schools. We concluded that business schools were abysmal failures and contributed to the climate of greed, celebrity CEOs, and the production of alumni that would make Gordon Gekko smile. If we created some degree of sympathy for these defiled CEOs, we intended to do so. We do not consider these CEOs to be "bad people," we see them as caught in corporate cultures, and an executive world that demands displays of arrogant, self-confident, always right never wrong, "walk on water" behaviors. Some may have worked to create these cultures, but for most, these cultures evolved over the past 40 years. Newly minted CEOs, most with preparatory MBA training, are merely fulfilling the requirements and expectations of the CEO role. Could they have stepped back and chosen to demonstrate empathy, caution, self-doubt, and self-reflection? Of course-but at what price? To say they are guilty of trying to fit in would be a mistake. They gleefully contributed to the mess. They took the money as a way to justify their self-worth, or to hide inadequacies. Here is the psychoanalytic explanation that disturbs many. While overwhelmed with guilt they destroyed their workforce, companies and in many instances their lives (family, friends and loved ones). Some companies went bankrupt, some were saved by bailouts, some are shells of their former selves, and others were broken up, merged or purchased. The case we have tried to make is "guilt killed the beast." Of course this is a psychoanalytic position and some would find it far-fetched. However, if one takes the time to think about it, we know that guilt is a powerful motivator and it does strange things to people. Guilt forces people to work to alleviate powerful conscious and unconscious feelings. Engaging in reparations, relying on an array of defenses, punishing oneself or others, or destroying objects are just a few of the ways people try to escape feelings of guilt. It is a struggle that never goes away.

These greedy behaviors are actually expected and are embedded in the cultures of today's corporate executive constellations. Just as one who joins the military is expected to fight the enemy and perhaps kill, but then spends the rest of their life struggling with the guilt associated with the lives he/she destroyed. The same is true of these executives. They must live with the guilt associated with the lives they destroyed.

What's the lesson? Greed is not good. Even if one is a "full blown narcissist," guilt will eventually "do them in." As a prison psychologist reported; "They tell me they are all psychopaths and psychopaths do not feel guilt. However, it wasn't their psychopathology that motivated them to get caught and punished, it was their guilt."

While we have devoted our attention exclusively to understanding the "problem CEO," there are executives who are empathic and reluctantly participate in the pain of terminations. These CEOs appear to be the exception. They go against the grain and they seem to be able to stand firm in their convictions, despite working in a culture that suggests they do otherwise.

Let's recognize a few: In June 2008, Continental Airlines, under the crunch of soaring fuel prices, had to cut 3,000 jobs, or 7 percent of its work force. It's CEO, Lawrence Kellner, and President Jeff Smisek decided they would not take salaries or incentive pay for the rest of the year. Another CEO who demonstrates empathy is James Sinegal of Costco. He has kept his salary at $350,000 with a maximum bonus of $200,000. He works in an open office and his conference room contains six Formica tables (Machan, 2008). He answers his own phone and greets visitors to his office by himself. Costco's average hourly retail store associate earns $18.15, which is 68 percent more than the average pay at Wal-Mart. Sinegal puts his employees first and maintains an employee-customer-stockholder triangle. In 2006-07 Costco's stock increased 30 percent. In 2009 he took a 28 percent decrease in compensation as Costco's profits dropped 15 percent. But in 2010 as net profits rose 19 percent, Sinegal saw his compensation rise to $3.5 million. In September 2011 he announced he would retire, and they are not bringing some celebrity CEO who demands a wheelbarrow of cash. The COO of Costco will move up.

Jet Blue CEO Dave Barger was to take a 50 percent pay cut for the second half of 2008, and Air Tran's CEO, Bob Fornaro was to take a 15 percent pay cut starting in August 2008. In 2008 almost 26,000 jobs had been cut in the airline industry in the U.S. As the economic crisis snowballed in late 2008 the numbers of CEOs and their executives who had their pay reduced increased. The CEO of Japan Airlines has no limo or private jet. He takes the bus to work, flies coach on his own airline and has lunch every day in the employee cafeteria. He reduced his annual compensation to $90,000 because employees were laid off.

Maybe the ranks of these CEOs will increase. Maybe they will become the new celebrity CEOs and B-school professors will offer case studies on them. But this is unlikely. Despite the outrage against excessive compensation and payouts in a climate of massive layoffs and bailouts, American CEOs seem to care very little. According to the Economic Research Institute (2009) in the period from February 2008 to February 2009 at the height of the financial crisis, CEO compensation for publicly traded corporations dropped a paltry 7.4 percent, then shot back up again.

The question emerges: What is it about these CEOs who care and understand the consequences of greed and those described in this book? Another book!

WHAT WE NEED

Early on in his presidency Obama announced sweeping changes in the way the government monitors financial trading and executive compensation. This was an attempt to create transparency (the new corporate buzzword). Passing laws to get bankers and CEOs to behave will be just as effective as having MBAs take an oath. Instead we must understand these behaviors, and once this is accomplished the following eighteen fundamental changes are needed.

Let's begin with the most obvious and first of the 18 changes that must be made. These are broken corporate boards. Consider this. Despite the recession and falling profits, CEO compensation was up between 23 and 28 percent in 2010, and energy companies led the way. Wisconsin utility companies collectively paid out $44 million in bonuses to their top executives in 2010. The biggest bonus went to Gale Klappa, CEO, president and chairman of We Energies, who in addition to his $1.13 million salary received a $10.45 million bonus. Second on the list was Frederick Kuester, chief operating officer at We Energies, who collected about $5.5 million in bonuses. So how did these executives find a way to pay for these bonuses? They added a fuel surcharge to every customer's bill.

Top executives keep getting increases by using methods that have become common practice in Corporate America. They get their boards of directors to give and give and give. How do they do it?

The executive compensation committee of the board and/or the VP or director of executive compensation (a fast growing occupation) review market data of energy peers at the 25th, 50th and 75th percentile for annual cash compensation, bonuses, long-term incentive compensation, and perks. Of course, these boards and compensation executives also hire outside consultants, who are paid handsomely to help out by also benchmarking and conducting competitive assessments. So as one CEO's compensation goes up, other CEOs in the same industry demand that their compensation must go up, and then another and another. This is what has happened in the energy industry.

In many cases the CEO hires the compensation consultants and compensation executives who serve at the pleasure of the CEO so the deck is stacked in the CEOs favor. When the CEO also holds the title of chairman of the board, like Klappa of We Energies, the compensation game is completely tilted. It's a game of envy and "gimme more" that gets played out annually. And boards of directors go along for several reasons.

BOARDS OF DIRECTORS

Business in America has changed considerable over the years. Fifty years ago, businesses were primarily in manufacturing processes, and 25 years ago the primary business growth was in technology. Now it's in financial services. While the nature of business has shifted, the composition of boards have remained the same. Also the complexity of understanding the strategy and executive decision-making has significantly changed. Now CEOs surround themselves with CIOs, CFOs, IT officers, Six Sigma experts, "quants", and other "number-crunchers," who provide "bottom line" services. They also hire consultants who provide the mathematical models to assist CEOs in making their "bottom line" decisions. In addition, they hire coaches, consultants, and public relations professionals to help them engage in the work of self-promotion and self-confidence. Given the complexity of running a financial service business, most board directors sit in the dark. While Enron executives were cooking the books, Robert Jaedicke was chairman of the Enron Audit and Compliance Committee from 1985 to 2001. Jaedicke is dean emeritus of the Stanford Business School and a former accounting professor. Trying to understand the inner workings of a corporation is a daunting task for a part-time board director. Even an accounting professor could not get his arms around the complexities.

In addition, trying to be a responsible board director is especially problematic if one holds other positions or serves on several boards or even holds a full-time position. When Bob Nardelli served as the CEO of Home Depot, he also served on the Board of Directors of Pepsi.

To make matters worse, board directors use their position to feather their own bed. There is no better example of board incompetence and lack of responsibility and unethical behavior than the Enron board. CEO magazine selected Enron's board as one of the top five corporate boards in America. This was before the collapse and discovery that Enron's board, like most boards, engaged in little or no oversight. A U.S. Senate investigation found that the 13-member board of directors was intertwined with conflicts of interest and engaged in off-the-books financial arrangements. It was not only Enron's board that was asleep at the wheel but also the boards of scandalous corporations like WorldCom, Adelphia, Refco, Lehman, Tyco, ImClone, Martha Stewart Ominmedia, and HealthSouth. The ethical transgressions ranged from individual lapses of judgment to defective corporate cultures and involved embezzlement, insider trading and financial statement falsification (Fombrun & Foss, 2004; Smith & Walter, 2006).

People who serve on boards are supposed to be held responsible for overseeing their companies, but they are rarely accountable. Even if the company fails, board directors jump from board to board. The Senate commission to investigate the collapse of Enron concluded: "Board membership is no longer just a reward for 'making it' in corporate America; being a director today requires the appropriate attitude and capabilities, and it demands time and attention." This statement, made in 2002, has not been heeded, and boards are run the way they have always been. Directors are selected they way they have always been selected, from an interlocking corporate community of power elites. Take for example Thomas Gerrity, the former dean of Wharton Business School. He was a board director at Fannie Mae, the loan giant, when it took on enormous risks and accounting irregularities, was seized by the government in September 2009 and contributed to the financial crisis of 2008. But nothing has changed for Gerrity. He serves on several boards. According to Forbes (2011), Gerrity has served on the following boards: ICG since December 1998; PharMerica Corporation since 2007; Sunoco, from 1990 to 2010; Hercules, from 2003 to 2008; CVS Corporation from 1995 to 2007; Federal National Mortgage Association from 1991 to 2006; Knight-Ridder from 1998 to 2006.

Many corporate board directors see their job as an easy way to makes lots of money. This is certainly true for Gerrity. From 2006 to 2010 his total compensation for serving on boards was over $2 million. Directors may be given upwards of $100,000 to attend a board meeting and can receive in excess of $1 million in pay and stocks for serving. The median salary for these directors of corporate boards is $200,000 for a few hours of work per week. If one sits on several boards, one can easily earn from $500,000 to over $1 million. Many call it the world's best part-time gig, and retired CEOs and professors from elite MBA programs can live a comfortable life-style serving on a few boards.

Gross mismanagement on the part of the board occurs when the board allows a CEO to be the chair of the board. This has the potential of putting the fox in the hen house. Often this is done to allow board directors to do business with the company, creating massive conflicts of interests. When directors engage in questionable practices to enrich themselves, they contribute to creating a culture where greed is permissible and even encouraged. This creates a culture where executives see their main activity as the attainment of personal wealth.

In addition to holding directors accountable and making certain their careers suffer when they screw up, we must demand that they have greater involvement in the hiring of executives. When hiring, boards must look beyond the veneer of executive candidates and make certain stock-holders can obtain information on the candidate's experience, values, attitudes, and even mental health. Boards have the authority to carefully and deeply investigate the work of the CEO they appoint. The fact that the CEO functions at the service of the board must be taken seriously, and no CEO should be allowed to appoint a board member or fire a board member. This is especially true for members of the board's compensation committee. The practice must end where CEOs appoint compensation committee members who are high-salaried CEOs and / or have a history of maintaining that CEOs should be paid well. CEOs would love to have Ken Langone and Jack Welch, publicly stated believers that CEOs should be paid very well. If appointments to the board were the domain of stock-holders, Welch and Langone would never serve as directors.

CELEBRITY BOARD MEMBERS

Retired wealthy executives who have attained celebrity status in the business world are in hot demand to serve on boards. So are highly visible African-Americans: Vernon Jordan sat on six boards, and if you're an African-American ex-football player you are really in demand; Willie Davis sat on nine (Domhoff, 2005). Having a celebrity CEO on the board not only increases the likelihood the CEO will be well compensated, but also the CEO will become a celebrity themselves. CEOs also love to have deans from their alma maters on their board, especially business school deans. Boards have been known to have executive recruiters on their boards. These head hunters not only recruit executives but also board members. CEOs want friends, colleagues and those who will be agreeable, especially when it comes to compensation matters. Consider what Kathy Noland says. She is the vice president of the board of directors and CEO at B.E. Smith, a head hunter firm for hospital executives. She wants hospitals to guarantee high pay and large severance packages to let executives know they can make necessarily risky decisions without being penalized. She says: "The principle behind (high pay) is the board of directors wants the CEO to make prudent decisions for the mission and values of the organization." She goes on: "[The severance] package gives the CEO a confidence level to make those decisions. If for any reason they are terminated without cause, there is that extension of salary until they are engaged in their next employment" (Fields, 2011). What is she saying? Use big pay to encourage risk with no penalty, and big pay packages with big severance packages will encourage confidence, and if the CEO is fired and terminated, the CEO will be taken care of. Health care CEOs love this even though her comments can clearly be considered self serving. It is people like Noland who are responsible for excessive health care CEO salaries so are their board members. For example, in 2007, the top six health plan boards paid themselves a whopping $277,998,793 (Jodell, 2009).

Another problem with larger-than-life celebrities on the board is that they tend to dominate not only discussions, but the direction the company will move in including the choice of a CEO. Billionaire Ken Langone dominated the Home Depot board, and there is even a question as to whether he talked to the board before he offered the top spot to the problematic Bob Nardelli.

SHORT STAY AT THE TOP

The studies of the length of stay in the CEO position vary but they do offer a startling trend. According to Thompson (2010), 40 percent of CEOs last no more than two years at the top. The average CEO tenure dropped from 11.4 years in 1980 to 9.7 years in 1999 to 8.3 years in 2006, the most recent year for which statistics were compiled by consultants **Challenger Gray & Christmas**, **Crist Associates**, and **SpencerStuart**. However the New York Times (2008) put the trend at 8.6 years in 2000 and 3.2 years in 2007. Lubin (2010) found only 28 CEOs of companies in the Standard & Poor's 500 have held office more than 15 years, and she maintains that the average for S&P 500 CEO was about 6.6 years. While we see the length of stay drop significantly, so has the age. The CEO "class of 2004 was the youngest on record, with an average age of 57.8 years. With a young age and short stay, these CEOs have been called "the most prominent young temp workers" who retire at an early age. Where do they go after their term has ended? It is difficult to retread a CEO. The most difficult to retread are those with high compensation, bad press coming from either a scandal or grossly unhappy stockholders, and of course those who attained celebrity status. Not necessarily because no board wants to hire a celebrity CEO, but because once one attains such lofty, status they do not want to return to the trenches. They prefer to write books or give after-dinner speeches or appear on talk shows telling all who will listen "how they did it." They also become instant experts, giving advice and criticism on a wide variety of subjects. If one did research on "What are they doing now?" after a few years in the catbird seat, one would find that they join venture capital or some hedge fund firms, manage their money and/or sit on corporate or nonprofit boards or find some university post. Very few return to the corporate ranks, and most retire to the corporate CEO "graveyard," the golf course.

Some of the reasons for such a short stay at the top are attributed to burnout, retirements, resignations and forced terminations. With the average length of stay at 3.2 years, these CEOs barely have time to impact the corporation before they leave. What we have is instability at the top caused by this revolving door. The brief length of stay strongly suggests we have weakly committed CEOs, preoccupied with "filling their personal coffers," with little concern for their employees who they do not know or care about. Long gone are the days when a beloved CEO personally knew all their employees and symbolically "bled" when the company "bled"

Boards are clearly aware of this, and they know that in three or four years, at $10 million-plus a year and several thousand shares of vested stock, their "golden boy" will be gone. They typically set up a cue where the conga line of executives will grab the golden ring as they pass through. Does this encourage long term planning? Not a chance. It does encourage pumping up the stock, even if it means terminating thousands, outsourcing, off shoring and of course getting handsomely rewarded. While boards try to get a good CEO to stay by offering large retention bonuses, most CEOs have "golden parachutes" or "golden boots" written into their contracts. They are called severance agreements.

GROUP DYNAMICS IN THE BOARD ROOM

One needs to remember what it takes to make it to the top of a corporation. One needs to be: fiercely determined, relentlessly competitive, and have a demanding personality. These CEOs show up at compensation meetings with their expert compensation entourage, including attorneys, and scare the hell out of a group of board members who are old, retired and don't want the aggravation. All they want is to get to the golf course.

Pushing back against a demanding and aggressive CEO will often shorten a director's tenure. This creates an intimidating situation where the board becomes more aligned with the CEO than the corporation they are ultimately responsible to govern. Board dynamics can precipitate covert conflicts that can lead to one-off meetings and phone calls outside the conference room where a CEO can gather the support of board directors seen as trusting, protective, and on the same side. The CEO wants to discover the board's vulnerabilities that can be tapped as he/she maneuvers to obtain greater compensation. The issue of who is for and who is against the CEOs compensation package is information the CEO and his confederates will ferret out. Above all, the CEO wants members who are selected to serve on the compensation committee to be his best friends. In many cases the CEO, CFO and their compensation consultants, lawyers and others outnumber the board members on this committee. Meetings tend to be disorganized, and board members are swamped with data. The consultants and other experts present the compensation packages for each officer of the company, making certain "red flags" are not apparent, especially when "activist" stockholders are lurking. Most companies have a team consisting of several senior company officers including the CFO, general counsel, the director of investor relations and outside consultants who are experts responding to these pests.

Another issue that contributes to favorable compensation packages is the board's desire to create a chubby "good old boy" climate. Couple this desire for friendship with the prestige of the position, and there is a tendency to believe that they are more competent than they actually are and that their support of the CEO's strategy, decisions, and compensation is beyond reproach. They may actually collude in offering greater compensation to increase the climate of friendship and feelings of omnipotence. The rush to agreement and avoidance of conflict promote the feelings of cohesiveness and power. This type of group behavior is most apparent when board members are selected on the basis of personal friendships and networking.

These former executives possess a high degree of agreeableness in social situations and this most likely is due to their dependency on something that is foreign to them. They are out of the role of authority. The need for equality in social relationships and in the board room was not apparent when they were in the catbird seat. Observing these executives in the board room and at the country club the behavior was the same. They enjoy casual friendly talk and avoid discussions that hint of controversy. Keep it light and easy-going, and above all be agreeable.

What happens when you get a group of old and tired ex-CEOs in a room? Sounds like it could be a good question for a series of jokes. Working as a member of a team and facilitating discussions is something they rarely did when they were top executives. They are used to making the decisions, and in a group they are not familiar with equal give-and-take required for thorough discussion. Also, in thorough discussions, group conflict is bound to occur. As mention before, this type of discussion is avoided because it may rupture the friendly atmosphere.

Professors serving on the boards also present an issue. They are not trusted and struggle to fit in, primarily because they are viewed by ex-CEOs as intellectual eggheads writing books and cases about the company, who never worked in the trenches and do not play golf.

2. We must dramatically alter the way we admit young managers into training and educational programs, and we must rethink how we train and educate our corporate leaders and Wall Street titans. The first question we must ask is, what do these young people want out of life? Many corporations are beginning to shy away from the hard-driving business majors; the so-called elite MBAs. And the reasons are obvious. These young men and women seek and thrive on extrinsic rewards and

they want and need wealth, fame and power. They are preoccupied with their image, and they present what is typically called the "marketing" or "other directed" personality. They tend to be empty inside, and they have a need to fill up their emptiness with money, status and prestige. We are beginning to understand that leaders who have empathy are valued and loved by their employees, and they are intrinsically motivated. In college these potential leaders may be more enamored with liberal arts and may even reject the corporate life. But in the corporation they are valued by employees, except perhaps in hostile, aggressive corporate cultures. It is not a difficult process to select young managers who are motivated by solid and close relationships, and who are empathic with a strong sense of community. Wealth and power is not something they need. "Doing good" is better.

3. A review of 35 of the 38 top executives who made over $20 million in total comensation in 2010 held three titles: president, CEO and chair of the board. No CEO should be allowed to hold multiple positions. The more people share the top positions, the greater the possibility of critical analysis. Of course the board must make certain that executives hold differing and even conflicting points of view. It is the function of the board to not only eliminate conflicts of interest, but to create an executive constellation where their behavior and decisions are constantly questioned.

4. Transparency does not work if we have the equivalent of the Department of Defense revolving triangle, where Department of Defense employees become consultants and consultants go into industry and then back to the DOD. We do not want ex-Wall Street tycoons watching the chicken coop. What we need is radical transparency, which involves involvement from the bottom up. To think "Joe Six-pack" cannot comprehend the complexities of derivatives is elitist thinking. What these bankers and Wall Street traders do is intentionally

cloaked in such secrecy that even finance Ph.D.'s can be perplexed with the lack of information. But if this wheeling and dealing were open, and the public knew what these bankers, traders, and others do each day at work and how they do it, it would significantly reduce the hanky-panky. The public has the right to know everything that goes on in a publicly held corporation. The public owns these companies.

5. We estimate that one year after the government takes over health care, 29 million employees would quit their miserable, underpaid jobs that they keep for health benefits. Make health care free, and we will become a society of entrepreneurs, not a society of serfs sitting in cubicles or embarrassed adults wearing absurd vests with badges as they toil in some big-box or chain restaurant to get health insurance. Make it free and we will liberate the creative minds, end the fiscal crisis, and return to a society that makes stuff. We will see a new industrial revolution where people will be free to take risks and strike out on their own.

We now see a Wall Street strategy to maximize shareholder return. It's simple: first eliminate pensions and then health benefits. And it's happening. In 2011 in America, 50 million people have no health insurance. The graphs below suggest health benefits by industry in 2008.

No Health in Store

The retail industry lags behind other fields in the percentage of its employees covered by their companies' health benefits.

Industry	Workers covered by employers
State and local government	81%
Manufacturing	79
Finance	74
Service	63
Health care	61
Retail	45

Source: Kaiser Family Foundation

We knew retail was appallingly low, but to see 39% of all health care employees without health care coverage is astoundingly bad. It tells us something valuable about the lack of care and concern among our excessively paid healthcare executives, whose loyalties go in one direction: Wall Street. While millions of workers face rising health insurance costs and dwindling benefits in 2011, many CEOs will retain employer-paid medical plans and health benefits worth thousands of dollars. Hundreds of top corporate managers get medical benefits and supplemental coverage far beyond what's offered to rank-and-file employees. Benefits include "executive" physicals and reimbursements for out-of-pocket costs, deductibles and co-payments, according to corporate filings (Strauss, 2010). Between 2007 and 2009, HMO's and insurance companies have spent almost $800 million on federal lobbying to make certain the government does not take over health care putting them out of a job.

Meanwhile, total healthcare spending in US has increased from around 13 per cent of the GDP to around 17.3 per cent between 2000 and 2009. The growth in spending is estimated to grow from $2.3 trillion to $4.6 trillion by 2019 in America. As CEOs and the wealthy put more of this financial burden on the backs of working people, the numbers of uninsured will dramatically increase.

Employers are paying more, and employees are paying more, up 135 percent and 105 percent respectively between 2000 and 2011. Below is a graph of health insurance increases in Iowa. These figures are not unique to that state, suggesting that the present method of insuring American citizens is unsustainable, especially in the present economic climate.

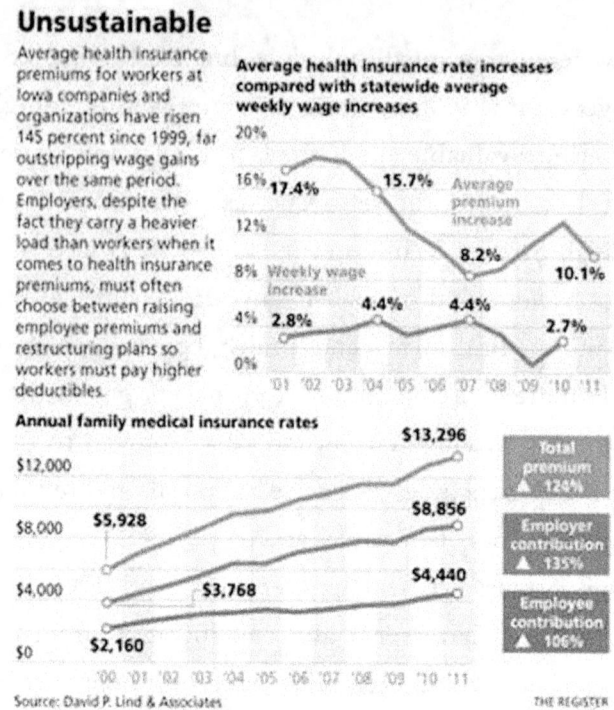

In 2009, after the financial crisis of 2008, the rich became less rich. However the poor were quickly getting poorer. Studies have determined that in countries where the income gap is great, the poor will suffer to a greater degree than in countries where the gap is small. This is certainly true in America, where in 2009, 39 million people lived below the poverty line. It is estimated that this population will increase annually by 12 percent. At this rate of growth, by 2014, 80.2 million people will be living below the poverty line in America. This puts the vast population of the poor in America in dire straits, where homelessness, and the lack of healthy food and medical care will mean they will be in poorer health and will die at a significantly younger age than their wealthy co-citizens.

6. If Obama and politicians want real pay for performance among corporate CEOs then this has to be clearly spelled out at the beginning of the year and posted on the web. This is radical transparency. In 2002, Congress enacted the Sarbanes-Oxley Act in response to a spate

of highly publicized business failures and corporate improprieties. This required corporations to make executive compensation public. It's not working, because we only get to know compensation and performance facts at the end of the corporation's fiscal year. For example, we know in 2009 what a CEO got in 2008. We need to know what CEOs will get at the beginning of the year and what he/she must do to get it. But there is a larger issue with CEO transparency.

7. We need a greater degree of vigilance on the part of journalists, business writers, scholars and politicians to come down hard on the Jack Welch's of the world, who destroy companies for profit and cause thousands to lose their jobs. We should not give these guys awards, put their pictures on magazine covers or call them the "Manager of the Century" as Forbes called Welch. America needs to know who these scoundrels are and how they will enrich themselves by terminating employees. Our "celebrity CEOs" should be the "good guys" who create jobs, sustain communities, and protect the environment. We must pay attention to Drucker (1974), who stated that; excessive compensation is designed to create status rather than income. "It can only lead to political measures that, while doing no one any good, can seriously harm society, economy, and the manager as well." Drucker (1996) later states; when a financial benefit accrues to a manager who terminates employees, "there is no excuse for it. No justification. This is morally and socially unforgivable, and we will pay a heavy price for it." Business writers, journalists, academics and others who do not heed Drucker's words are committing the same shameful acts as those who stood idly by as the propaganda machine convinced the American people it was justified to invade Iraq.

8. We need to look at the methods CEOs use to enrich themselves and their stockholders from an ecological perspective. We must understand the impact that outsourcing, closing factories, and agri-business

is having on American communities large and small. For example, no CEO has been held accountable for the destruction of Flint, Michigan which has gone from a flourishing city of 80,000 automobile workers to a destroyed town of poverty, drugs, and despair, with one-third of its homes abandoned and a government so broke that after terminating 66 police officers in 2010, the police department is closed on weekends. In addition, we must identify and stop CEOs who threaten and exploit the working poor in Asia, America and Eastern Europe. When the Agriculture Department reports in 2009 that 49 million Americans don't have enough food, up 13 million over 2008, we have to find out who is responsible and who is gaining as others loose. Main Street is so far removed and uninvolved that they even elect a president who cheats and enriches himself off their backs. According to Wessel (2011), American multinational corporations, which employ 20 percent of all U.S. workers, are increasingly hiring abroad while cutting back at home. Wessel (2011), using data from the U.S. Commerce Department, maintains these companies cut their work forces in the U.S. by 2.9 million during the 2000s while increasing employment overseas by 2.4 million.

Consider Jeffrey Immelt, the CEO of GE; in January 2011 Obama named Immelt to run his outside panel of economic advisers and chair a new Council on Jobs and Competitiveness. Obama said he wants the council to "focus its work on finding new ways to encourage the private sector to hire and invest in American competitiveness." Obama is either naive or dumb; to appoint Immelt is to appoint one of the chief proponents of increasing stockholder profitability by reducing the American payroll (called cost cutting) and going overseas. Between 2005 and 2010, GE terminated a whopping 28,000 employees in America. In 2000, 30 percent of GE's business was overseas; today, 60 percent is. In 2000, 46 percent of GE employees were overseas; today, 54 percent are (Wessel, 2011). Immelt would have Americans believe that he is going overseas because "that's where the customers are." He is lying. According to Samples (2011), in July 2011 it was discovered that Immelt was moving the headquarters of its 115 year old X-ray business to Beijing as part of his plan to invest about $2 billion across China over the next few years. He seems to forget that goods can be manufactured in America and sold overseas. He also forgets that that is what America use to do, and the country was prosperous, not just CEOs and stockholders. No politician has come forth and exposed this travesty. In 2010, General Electric earned $5.1 billion in America and more than $14 billion worldwide. It also received more than $3 billion in federal government tax credits while paying no U.S. income taxes in 2010 or 2009.

It's not only corporate leaders who do not care about jobs in America. The federal government has been complicit not only in destroying American jobs but in failing to create jobs. Since the 1990s the Department of Labor has been predicting job growth in America for programmers. While the feds were creating a rosy picture of job growth, these programming jobs actually went to India and China. America had zero growth in programmer jobs. To make matters worse, in 2010 the federal government, still interested in creating programmer jobs, decided to create jobs elsewhere. According to Bartlett and Steel (2011), in 2010, the State Department's Agency for International Development (USAID) put up $10 million to help Sri Lanka develop an outsourcing industry. The U.S. taxpayer dollars are aimed at training Sri Lankans in advanced IT skills such as Enterprise Java, as well as in business-process outsourcing and call-center support. The goal is to create 3,000 jobs. According to InformationWeek, a similar program is being funded by USAID in Armenia to train Armenians. In June 2011, 80 percent of the Fortune 500 companies outsourced their IT services. Also the National Law Journal reported that the top 250 law firms shed 1,409 jobs in 2010. Morrison and Forrester LLP, publicly stated it reduced its hiring by 30 percent in 2010. Law firms are closing down as the practice of law is increasingly outsourced to India (Moore, 2011).

Job loss increases each year in America. In Asia, job growth is meteoric. For example, Tata Consultancy Services, an Indian information-technology outsourcing firm hired, 70,000 employees in 2010 and plans to hire 60,000 in 2011. Meanwhile the number of Americans living in poverty in 2011 is 1 in 6, or 46.2 million people.

Indonesia is a country that corporate executives love. Labor laws are virtually non-existent, and the outsourcing of labor and contract-based recruitment practice is established by labor law. A national social security system (SJSN) was actually established in 2004 which requires the government to implement healthcare, occupational accident, old-age risk, pension, and death benefits programs. But the government has failed to establish an agency to implement the law. On May 1, thousands of workers took to the streets in protest against their government, which has been accused of collaborating with corporate executives to impoverish workers. The government police fired tear gas at the protesters who created congestion along major roads in Jakarta. This is a movement that will eventually play out, where American corporations will exploit the workers and if protests get too hot or wages climb too high they simply fold their tents and move onto another country to exploit the workers, harm the environment and pillage a culture. Globalization at its best.

Outsourcing may bring executives and their stockholders quick riches but the long term consequences are disastrous. Lets call them the unintended consequences associated with greed. For example, if a company has a product made in China, what is going to stop the Chinese from copying, making and selling the product themselves. Apple is terrified of this considering all their products are made in China. Also if all the American companies that manufactures the same product engage in outsourcing, where is the competitive advantage? And how does the supply chain costs, delays, etc., make going overseas cost efficient. And finally, having a product made outside America translates into fewer jobs for Americans and as the economy continues to sink, no one will have the cash to purchase these products. Hey, it's already occurring.

9. We have established that CEOs motivated by greed and business schools that offer training and education that focuses on the "bottom line" and share holder profits, are destroying the American corporation. We also know that the changing nature of the global marketplace and the inability of contemporary CEOs to think of the long term consequences of their actions have contributed to the financial crisis, and the loss of millions of jobs, (some suggest 65 million jobs lost) since 2007, with a significant portion of America resembling a Third World country. CEOs have not thought about the long term consequences of their off-shoring and outsourcing and get rich quick schemes. We now have a troubling fact that 50 percent of the MBA students in American colleges and 70 percent of the science graduate programs are made up of foreign students, and 40 to 60 percent of all goods sold in America are made overseas. When will the time occur when these students, who are educated in America and know the culture, decide to compete against and destroy Wal-Mart's and Home Depot's by setting up Indian and Chinese retail stores in America? And, of course, employ American's at $10 an hour. This process is already happening and with it the radical alteration of the American economy is in full swing. Soon the reverse will occur and China and other developed countries will look towards America as a Third World cheap labor country. It's already happening. IKEA now looks toward America as America once looked toward Latin America and Asian countries. Now companies look toward America as cheap labor, a [;ace with few if any rights or protection for workers and an easy way for executives to get rich. IKEA outsources its sweat shop manufacturing jobs to Danville, Va., and pay American workers $8 an hour (Sweden is $19 plus major benefits). In March 2011 the Swedish

krona hit a two-year high against the dollar and several Wall Street bankers, responding to the precipitous drop in the value of the dollar, suggested that the best place to invest in currency was in the Krona. I wonder what they would say if someone told these bankers that Sweden is a welfare state where the primary role of government is to protect and promote the economic and social well-being of its citizens by maintaining an equitable distribution of wealth. Sweden's generous benefits, emphasis on maximizing labor force participation, promotion of gender equality and a significant redistribution of wealth is the envy of Europe. Access to benefits are based on residency, not citizenship, and all residents in Sweden are entitled to nearly all the benefits available to Swedish citizens. The social security system is designed to ensure a minimum standard of living is based only on residence. Health care is accessible to all residents, and health and dental care is free for children under 18. Adults get vouchers. All workers are entitled to paid parental leave up to 480 days, 60 days for each parent with the rest divided up between them. Also, parents are free to take their days anytime until the child reaches the age of 8 or completes his or her first year of school. All children in Sweden are entitled to a tax-free child allowance which is paid, until 16. After 16 all children in full-time education are entitled to a study allowance, with a special large-family supplement paid to families with two or more children. All residents and citizens are guaranteed a pension, and Sweden invests more of its GDP to care for its elderly than any country in the world. And guess what? In September 2011, while many U.S. universities will be charging $50,000 per year, a university education in Sweden will be free. It's enough to make a "Tea Partite quiver." **And Wall Street says invest in the krona.** Meanwhile as the krona continues to climb and life gets good in Sweden, the union-less American workers toil in Sweden's sweatshops. And Wall Street, as usual, keeps on reaping the profits from their destruction, and the right wing seeks to destroy what little dignity seniors, the disabled, and the poor have left. By the way, in all studies that rank countries on "happiness" scales Sweden appears in the top 20 in everyone and the United States does not appear in the top 20 in any study.

On America, as millions lose their jobs and wages are stagnant or dropping, and employees fear terminations, loss of pensions and benefits, consumer spending is dropping. The middle class or the "consumer class" is not consuming, and a vicious circle results as more and more Americans are pushed out of the job market and putting food on the table or paying their mortgage becomes increasingly difficult. Depression and other mental health and health dysfunctions increase as many witness their largest asset, their homes, lose value. In response, the governments local, state, and federal, unlike the Swedes', engage in largescale contraction and budget cutting. If government took a close look at Sweden, they would discover the value of a social safety net, and free health care and education would strengthen, not weaken, America's economy.

10. In 2009, more women were in the workforce than men. Yet of the 237,843 firms established in the year 2004, only 19 percent were founded by women. and only 3 percent of the tech firms founded that year were women start-up executives (Peterson, 2010). While women now make up almost 60 percent of the undergraduate population in America, they make up less than 38 percent of MBA programs. Many of the so-called elite finance programs have an even smaller percentage. While women do very well in India, the opposite is true in America. According to Peterson (2010) Fidelity International in India was led by a woman, and so was the country's second-biggest bank, Icici Bank, and its third-largest, Axis Bank. Women also headed investment banking operations at Kotak Mahindra and JPMorgan Chase and the equities division of Icici and half of the deputy governors at the Reserve Bank of India are women. Why are American corporations bastions of

white male dominance? They have created a culture of exclusion based on aggressive, golf clubbing, beer drinking, bar hopping, machismo. Women are not mentored and they are strongly devalued by their male counterparts and undermined. In America, women who behave like the typical macho male at work are called bitches, if they display characteristics stereotyped as female they are called weak. Many have blamed this macho, risk-taking, boy's club mentality as largely responsible for the 2008 financial meltdown. This culture needs to change. We must change the type of culture where a woman who makes it to the executive suite, outnumbered by macho, competitive males, is brutalized and sent packing. The same situation exists in our most enlightened institutions, our universities. While we see significant changes in the numbers of women obtaining doctorate degrees, men still occupy the overwhelming majority of academic position at American universities. The doctorate was the last holdout for men among university degrees, but in 2009 for the first time the balanced shifted; 28,962 degrees went to women and 28,496 went to men.

In the future we will not only see the population of woman employees grow, but we will also witness a shift in the male employee population as Asians, African and Latino men join the women, leaving white American males in the minority. The critical question is: Will white males remain overrepresented in the executive constellations of corporate America, and will these executive suites remain bastions of white male dominance? We are beginning to see research suggesting that women are better than their male counterparts in supervisory roles that require observation; they make certain that rules are followed and foolish risks are not taken. Sally Krawcheck who was fired at Citi for not being a "team player," was hired in July 2009 to watch over 15,000 brokers at Bank of America's newly acquired Merrill Lynch. Most of these traders and brokers were white males, and they did not want to work for a woman. How long did she last? She was fired in September

2011 and given a $6 million "Golden Boot." It is clear that a shift away from these all white male fraternity clubs is necessary if we are to create fair and equitable corporations and society. Why? It was these white male fraternity clubs (boards and executive constellations as well as brokerage houses and venture capital firms) that fostered greed and entitlement and a culture of abuse that led to the financial crisis of '08. It is clear that a struggle exists between these white males and women and minorities. While we see women obtaining parity in medical schools, law and other professions, we have not seen similar changes in business schools in America. While corporations encourage their white male managers to obtain an MBA women report being discouraged. This is confirmed by The Economist (2010); their survey found, "Overall, women outnumber men by a third at American and European universities. But less than a third of MBA, students at the schools that *The Economist* surveyed were women. Sadly, that has barely changed since the ranking began almost a decade ago."

The GMAT reports that in America less than 38 percent of test takers in 2009 were women. Business schools, like executive suites remain the bastion of white males. Only 15 percent of B-school deans in America are women, and in the last decade the number of women faculty has increased a paltry 5 percent.

What happens when the males and females get their MBAs and enter into the job market? Females will start at $4,600 less than their male counterparts, and over the long course males are twice as likely to reach senior executive levels. In 2010 women remain stuck and over-represented in the lowers levels. However when we look at B-schools around the world we get a different picture. Quacquarelli Symonds (QS) study found that in 2010, 48 percent of MBA program hopefuls were women, up from 46 percent in 2009 and 35 percent in 2006. In Western Europe, women make up an even higher share of MBA program hopefuls, 54 percent, according to the survey (Schuetze, 2011). Will we witness a change in America? Maybe with the election of Obama in 2008, the appointment of Hillary Clinton as Secretary of State and the appointment of Sonia Sotomayor to the Supreme Court, change may be coming, and the days of the dominant and powerful white males may be over. We are not suggesting that putting African Americans, women or Latinos in positions of power and the world will be secure. We will never know until we have a thorough understanding of these white male executives and the cultures they create at work.

We now have attempts to stop executive greed and the damage they caused. We hear calls for new laws, stock holder intervention, watchdogs, and reformed compensation boards, etc., but very little concern about trying to understand these corporate cultures. These actions are similar to the sorry comment made by George W. Bush when he announced the first bailout. He said, " There will be ample opportunity to debate the origins of this problem later, now is the time to fix it." This is wrong, its like putting a bandaid on a cancer. If we fail to diagnosis and understand the origins of these financial problems it will be business as usual. We must answer the question, why greed and entitlement are so pervasive in these white male dominated executive suites? Trying to solve a problem without understanding its "root cause" is folly. Anyone who has studied high school science knows this. The just-get-it-fixed mentality does not work. In the case of the 2008 fiscal crisis, the fix-it mentality just kept those in positions of power secure and unthreatened.

11. We need to increase regulation and establish a genuine system capable of exposing those who cheat the system. It's impossible for government employees to regulate Wall Street tycoons who make at minimum 85 times the salary of the regulator. This is precisely the dilemma those who direct the Securities and Exchange Commission and the Fed-

eral Deposit Insurance Corporation face every day on the job. These two agencies lack the experienced and committed staff they need to protect average Americans from financial industry recklessness and greed. The Bernie Madoffs of the world go unchecked because those who are expected to check on them suffer from envy, low morale, and a desire to enter this world of the financial tycoons. They shun their responsibilities and in many cases look the other way in hope of obtaining a position in the world of high finance. According to Pizzagati (in Anderson, et al. (2009), "The lure of lucrative private sector jobs doesn't just siphon off talent from public service,... It also breeds corrosive and ever-present conflicts of interest: Why 'get tough,' as a regulator, on a firm that could be your future employer?" To "get tough" requires that regulatory agencies create an opportunity structure where their employees get rewards, salary increases, promotions, etc. when they discovered wrong-doing. A revolving door culture where government employees can join the regulated is a breeding ground for corruption. There is no better example of this relationship then Neel Kashkari, the government's bailout chief who went from Goldman Sachs to run the Troubled Asset Relief Program for banks (TARP) and then returned to finance at the Pacific Investment Management Company (PIMCO). Kashkari has been accused of doing this company's work even when he was employed by the government, as PIMCO benefited from various Treasury Department actions (Leonard, 2010).

This inability to regulate is not only a problem at the federal level, but also in state and local governments. The pension bubble has hit state and local governments hard, and coupled with the drying up of a tax base, it has forced the termination of hundreds of thousands of jobs. In 2011, New York State and City expect to terminate close to 20,000 employees, and in the State of Illinois, 8,100 teachers will lose their jobs. One factor that bleeds the government coffers is "double dipping." A school-teacher retires from one school district at 58 years old and then begins teaching at another school district knowing that after 10 years over the age of 55 she will get a second pension. In New York it is common for lawmakers to engage in "double dipping". Assemblyman Harvey Weisenberg retired in 2008 but he decided to stay on as a lawmaker. Consequently he earns $101,550 in salary and collects a pension of about $72,000. Rhonda Jacobs and John McEneny engage in the same practice, George Winner retired at 59 after his 2004 election to the New York State Senate. He now gets an $80,000 annual pension on top of his $80,000 salary, and he has a law practice on the side (Hakim, 2009). These guys manage to "double-dip: while staying in the same job, plus they cash their social security checks each month. The most common form of "double dipping" are among the uniformed civil servants who can retire after 20 years on the job with a pension close to 60 percent of the average of their last three years of employment. Often the salaries of the last three years before retirement are inflated with excess overtime, giving many public sector retirees a pension at 100 percent of their annual salary. What happens after they retire? In some cases, at 45 years old, they "double-dip" by beginning a new career. A young man joined the New York Fire Department at age 20. He worked in a firehouse for 20 years studying at NYU and obtaining his Ph.D. in English literature. At 45, he retired with an annual pension of $75,000 and joined a university as a full-time professor. He eventually retired at 65 with two pensions and social security. A high school principle was three years away from retirement when the district superintendent suddenly left. He announced he could do both jobs. For three years before retirement his salary doubled and he retired with $135,000 a year for life. He retired at 63 and died when he was 85. His pension cost the school district almost $3 million, plus he and his wife enjoyed excellent medical coverage for life costing the town an additional $100,000. According to the Chicago Tribune (2010) Roy McCampbell administrator for the village of Bellwood, had made $472,255 in 2009, more than any suburban municipal executive in Illinois. This included $128,940 in base salary; $115,101 for work performed as budget director, public safety CEO, human resources director, finance director, mayoral assistant and other posts; $66,000 for serving as corporation counsel; $126,214 for unused sick and vacation days and $36,000 he couldn't explain, but then neither could the Village Board. These bumps increased his pension from roughly $180,000 a year to more than $250,000, the highest in the state's municipal employee retirement fund. It seems this type of abuse is pervasive across America and there is no effective system of regulation to put an end to it. In Italy one is forbidden to collect two pensions and not allowed to work once retired. The assumption is "double-dipping" takes away a job from someone else.

Consider how President George W. Bush and his VP Dick Cheney enriched themselves in Texas before they decided to steal the election and ruin the country. How did they do it? Arthur Anderson LLP, formerly one of the "Big Five" international accounting firms was the accountant for Harken Energy, which was facing bankruptcy. Harken Energy bought Spectrum 7, run by Bush. Spectrum 7 was unprofitable and saddled with debt. The only thing the deal brought Harken was Bush's connections to his father who happened to be the president of the United States.

Harken extended generous stock options to Bush. Then the fancy accounting began: "it involved creating a dummy entity to serve as paper front to then purchase some of the firm's assets at unrealistically high prices, creating a phantom profit that inflated the stock price, allowing the executives to cash in their stock." According to Gutman (2002), Paul Krugman, writing in the New York Times, reported, "A group of insiders, using money borrowed from Harken itself, paid an exorbitant price for a Harken subsidiary, Aloha Petroleum. That created a $10 million phantom profit, which hid three-quarters of the company's losses in 1989." Once Harken's stock price was inflated by means of this maneuver (Arthur Anderson was the accounting firm, and Mr. Bush was on Harken's audit committee), Bush was able to sell his shares at a large profit shortly before Harken stock fell apart. To be specific, on June 22, 1990, Bush sold 212,140 shares for $4 a share, for a total of $848,000. Two months later, on August 20, Harken announced a loss of $23.2 million; on that day its share price dropped 20 percent to $2.375. It closed the year at $1 a share (Gutman, 2002). This was scandalous, and Americans elected a president who became wealthy by manipulating stocks. Despite cheating in school, manipulating stocks, using illegal drugs, avoiding Vietnam and admitting he was an alcoholic, he was forgiven. Why? He used one of the elite white male methods of redemption. He announced he was a "**born again Christian**." In case you want to know the other method, it's to enter a rehabilitation program to be cured of the dreaded disease that made him (they are all men) do it. (To read more about these energy CEOs, go to Appendix Y).

12. Put an end to corporate lobbyists. Banks and financial companies that contributed to the 2008 financial crisis and the loss of millions of homes and jobs in America want to make certain the status quo is maintained. Lobbyists make certain the banks and their superstar CEOs and economists get a seat at the government table. Politically connected banks received more federal largess than banks with less influence. A study by Denis Sosyura and Ran Duchin, looked at the possible connection between allotments of federal bailout money and banks' political donations and other factors, such as whether a board member sits on the board of a regional Federal Reserve Bank. They found that "A board seat at a Federal Reserve Bank is associated with a 31.3% increase in the likelihood of receiving [bailout] funds, while a bank's connection to a House member on key finance committees is associated with a 26.3% increase, controlling for other factors" (Cork-

ery, 2009). Main Street continues to be infuriated as banks that donate millions to lawmakers receive ample benefits. Banks, hedge funds, and Wall Street houses contributed almost half a billion dollars to buy politicians in 2009, the largest amount of any industry. Why? To avoid government controls and maintain a "free market" economy that allows the rich to get richer, while the numbers of poor increase and the gap between the rich and poor widens. What this lobbying has created is an elite group of CEOs, paid millions yearly to run banks and corporations that feed on Main Streets money given to them by politicians. These lobbyists wrote the fine print in laws that caused foreclosures and sent the middle class to the poor house saddled with mountains of debt. They destroyed home ownership for millions of American families as almost 1 in 4 homes, or 10.7 million homes, are underwater. In 2008 and 2009 the housing market lost an estimated $4.9 trillion. There are 50 million Americans in real poverty and tens of millions of Americans in a category called "near poverty." One in eight Americans – and one in four children – depend on food stamps to eat. No homes are being built, and in many areas unfinished homes are being torn down. In many industrial towns and cities, entire neighborhoods lie empty as nearly 6 million unemployed homeowners were forced to walk away from their homes. No one is held accountable, no corporation investigated or called to testify. It was the biggest theft in American history and the political gang in Washington does not care. Why? They lie in bed with Wall Street and the lobbyists.

13. Corporate leaders and bankers are increasingly obsessed with positive thinking, and as a result, delusional, high-risk behavior increases. Positive thinking is a way to avoid what is considered negativity. Just as "bottom line" thinking is a way to avoid diagnosis, positive thinking also avoids deep understanding. Positive thinking and the happiness gurus maintain, "If things go wrong it's because you are looking at it all wrong." They go on. "Change your vocabulary and use

only positive words." This type of thinking is connected to the wish to be omnipotent and the wish for perfection. Believing that one can "just do it" rejects the necessity of thoughtfulness and caution, processes that are vital for successful leadership in any industry. This "just do it" mentality has had significant power in the Wall Street banking culture where the accumulation of wealth is the measure of one's success, and in many cases one's manhood. This must change. As a Wall Street broker complained, "On a good day I make a million, on a bad day I lose a million." His good or bad day is based on money accumulation. So is a profitable quarter versus a unprofitable quarter or a good year versus a bad year. Why is this problematic? Employees and executives who work and live in a "black and white" world are under significant amount of pressure. Of course they want to avoid bad outcomes, a positive outlook is vital if one is to avoid vulnerability and fear. How is this positive outlook maintained? It is maintained through the process of splitting. Splitting as a central defense mechanism and it is used consciously and unconsciously as an attempt to stabilize one's sense of self positively in order to preserve self-esteem. A narcissisitic person would preserve their self-esteem by perceiving themself as purely upright or admirable and others who do not conform to his will or values as purely wicked or contemptible. Given the narcissist's perverse sense of entitlement and splitting he or she can move back and forth using black and white thinking to their complete benefit. If the object is over-idealized, the same object can be excessively devalued.

For many on Wall Street and in executive suite the senses are dulled and reality is distorted through the use of a combination of alcohol, drugs and positive thinking. They are necessary if the person wants to avoid the anxiety associated with negative ideation. Like an addicted gambler, when they lose it's a "bad run of luck" and they survive by a wishful delusion that luck is just around the corner and they will hit the jackpot. This is precisely why the military is using the positive thinking gurus. Think of the combat-weary soldier who is suffering from PTSD. The military does not want to know what caused it: that's negative thinking. Just cheer up and think positively and all will be good. No diagnosis allowed and no grey areas. You're the "good guy" and they are the "bad guys." Secondly, unlike the Wall Street broker and the gambler, they do not want their soldiers to believe their luck could run out. The phrase "There is a bullet out there with your name on it" means death is real, a time for negative ideation. Facing a depressing, worrisome and negative thought process, the military uses positive thinking to pump their troops up and avoid negativity. Now we see why anything related to negativity is forbidden. Negativity kills the wish that one will be a winner or perhaps survive.

This is delusional thinking and we must move away from the magical thinking being offered by these so-called happiness gurus and return to a state where it is acceptable to look at the depressing, negative and problematic consequences of our actions, like war, gambling and greed.

14. We must put an end to investment bankers who kill companies for profit. This is exemplified by the storied Oregon fruit company Harry & David (H&D). This story is ever so familiar in America where spreadsheet speculators buy a company and use whatever equity exists in the company to pay off the purchase price, then payoff investors and line their pockets by putting the company under crushing debt. This is precisely what happened to H & D.

In 1986 the family that founded Harry & David sold it to one of the champions of corporate flipping, RJR Nabisco, owned by the hedge fund firm of RJR. It changed hands a few more times before being purchased by buyout king Bruce Wasserstein in 2004 for $253.9 million. Wasserstein financed this deal by issuing $250 million in bonds and used some of the proceeds of the bonds and cash equity in the company to pay himself all the cash he had initially put up plus some handsome profits to himself and his investors. Of course he left the company strapped in debt.

It gets worse. Wasserstein appointed Steve Heyer CEO and Ross Klein marketing chief to run the company. Heyer had been fired by Starwood Hotels after facing allegations that he had sent inappropriate sexual emails. Klein had been accused in a lawsuit by Starwood of stealing corporate documents after he left the company. Neither of the men relocated to Medford, the home of H & D. Instead they ran the company out of their offices in Atlanta and Beverly Hills. H&D not only paid for these offices, they also gave Heyer a $9.4 million pay package, nearly seven times what he earned at Starwood.

Crippled by overwhelming debt, in March 2011 Harry & David filed for bankruptcy protection.

This Wall Street scenario has been played out over and over across America where once proud companies, often a center-piece of their community and often the biggest employer, like H&D were destroyed for profit. In the case of H&D their workforce was slashed by at least one-third, their local management team was terminated, and benefits, pensions, and salaries were cut. The ripple effects were felt everywhere in the small community of 77,000. Wasserstein, RJR and the plethora of investors did not see this. They never set foot in Medford. They made their profits, and for them, it's time to move on. They have already set their sights on the next company to loot, of course without Wasserstein, who died.

Another robbery to consider, in 1997, Josh Weston persuaded the founder of J.Crew to sell the company to TPG Capital. Then Weston headed a special board committee that approved TPG's offer to again buy the apparel retailer, (Weiss, 2011). Weston was also one of five outside J. Crew directors appointed by Chairman Millard Drexler or

TPG, which earned a more than fivefold return after taking the company public in 2006. Now Drexler was working with TPG Capital and Leonard Green & Partners LP to acquire J. Crew again, in a $3 billion deal. This is another example of the hedge fund boys flipping a company for profit, putting the company in extraordinary debt and screwing everyone. Of course this list goes on.

Much of manufacturing in America has been destroyed by these investors, whether it consists of buying a company and flipping it, or buying it and selling off its assets, or simply buying a company and killing it only to turn the factory building into co-ops or shopping malls. They continue their destruction of jobs without check, scrutiny, or a sense of morality.

Having destroyed most of the manufacturing industry in America these guys have their sights set on another industry, and hold onto your hats, or pockets, or health. In 2002 investors from Diageo PLC sold Burger King to a group of investors including TPG Capital, Bain Capital Partners (Mitt Romneys' company) and Goldman Sachs Funds for $1.5 billion. In 2006 it went public in an offering that valued the company at about $2.25 billion. In 2010, 3G Capital bought BK, the number two fast food giant with 12,200 restaurants in 73 countries, for $3.2 billion. True to form they began terminating hundreds of employees in America. In December 2010, 9 percent of the workforce was cut, and it is expected that 25 percent will soon be gone. In addition they stopped providing senior executives and dependents up to $100,000 a year for out-of-pocket health care costs. How will these hedge fund investors profit off this purchase? Rumor has it they are working on a synthetic Whopper. When these guys get into the food industry it will be ugly. But wait, they are in the food industry. (See Appendix W)

Americans now get fat on dollar meals and chips because they can no longer afford to eat healthy or buy stuff. In response to an America that no longer shops companies are moving abroad to countries that have economies that are doing well and have populations that can afford to buy their products. According to Lee (2011) multinational firms are adding droves of sales and marketing employees in countries such as China, India and Brazil — even as many cut back or hold the line on employment and other spending at home. He states that the Newell Rubbermaid Company, one of the biggest marketers of children's car seats, is expanding in Brazil. While young Americans are putting off having children, in part because of the poor economy, Brazil's middle class is growing, and many more young couples are starting families. American parents are making do with cheaper brands or hand-me-downs. The biggest growth industry in America consists of Goodwill and the Salvation Army and the second-hand shops which are booming. In many communities, church and yard sales, once the domain of Latin American immigrants, are now patronized by the unemployed and poor. It seems evident that CEOs, bankers and their MBA professors have destroyed the American economy and created this extraordinary gap between the rich and poor.

Let's see what some other hedge fund boys make. John Paulson, founder of New York-based Paulson & Co., was paid an estimated $3.7 billion in 2007. Other hedge-fund manager George Soros was paid about $2.9 billion, and James Simons made an estimated $2.8 billion. Philip Falcone of Harbinger Capital received $1.7 billion, Kenneth Griffin of Citadel Investment, $1.5 billion. According to Anderson (2008), the top 50 hedge-fund managers earned a combined $29 billion in 2007.

In 2007, the top 50 hedge and private equity fund managers averaged close to $600 million each, more than 19,000 times the average American worker. In 2008, while many hedge fund executives failed, James Simons made another $2.8 billion, John Paulson took a cut to

$2 billion, and George Soros had to get by with only $1.1 billion. In 2009 despite the recession the gravy train rolls on. David Tepper's hedge-fund company Appaloosa Management earned about $7 billion in profits and Tepper earned more than $2.5 billion.

15. Eliminate the bonus system. Mintzberg (2009) calls the culture of bonuses on Wall Street and public corporations a form of legalized corruption and largely responsible for the financial meltdown of 2008. According to Olive (2009), in public corporations "excessive CEO pay is the cancer eating away at sound corporate management. Excessive pay for top management distorts decision-making. It encourages reckless and short-term behavior that damages the enterprise and undermines the wider economy. He goes on, "Mostly this cursed phenomenon takes the form of CEOs betting the company for a quick windfall, hence the crisis in global finance that brought us to the brink of a second Great Depression." If one finds this hard to believe, consider the bonus system for the CEO at MicroStrategy. CEO Michael Saylor could make up to $4.8 million in cash off his company's diluted earnings per share (DEPS) for the fiscal year ending Dec. 31, 2011. He will get $400,000 per dollar of DEPS for the first dollar of DEPS, or $500,000 per dollar of DEPS for the second dollar of DEPS, or $600,000 per dollar of DEPS for each dollar of DEPS over $2. All Saylor has to do is enrich the stockholders and he gets a wheelbarrow of cash.

As we observe with the bonus system and compensation in general we can conclude that most executives operate with the belief that they are special, and how they are paid should have little relationship to reality. Consequently they have their special compensation systems structured by "compensation consultants" who guarantee a handsome bonus no matter what the company does. In addition these bonus systems only reward short-term goals and force greedy CEOs to terminate employees, outsource, offshore and reduce R&D and long-range objectives to fatten the bottom line for the big short-term bonus. While there is wide spread belief among academic researchers and business writers that CEO compensation should be aligned to corporate performance, the chief complaint is that current compensation practices tend to reward short-term profitability. Consequently, we find that current compensation practice results in short-term, bottom line results where CEOs push their employees to take short-term risks with little regard for the long-term effects. This practice became particularly visible during the crisis of 2008 and led to a movement by business writers, politicians and others to suggest that CEO compensation should be changed to consist of restricted stock and other forms of long-term compensation designed to avoid rewarding short-term performance. According to Cooper, Gulen and Rau (2009) this proposed system of compensation implies a positive relationship between long-term incentive pay and future firm performance. They disagree, and they have demonstrated that there is not only no positive relationship but in fact there is an inverse or negative relationship between CEO compensation and long-term shareholder wealth. In fact they discovered that the higher the CEO long-term compensation, the lower the shareholder returns. We now have significant evidence to suggest that overpaying executives will decrease shareholder wealth. Why? The answer is simple. Excessive pay is a disincentive to do well, but it is an incentive to "take the money and run." Since the crash of 2008 we have seen Wall Street bonuses come roaring back. In 2010 Wall Street will pay out $144 billion in bonuses. This would break a record for the second year in a row. This is clear evidence that Wall Street, the Washington politicians and the so-called regulators are all in bed together. The bailedout Wall Street gang is back in "business as usual" and the country is back on the road to disaster. Wright (2010) discovered that between 2005 and 2010 investment banks paid their staff about three times what their owners and shareholders made in profits. For example, Goldman Sachs paid its staff roughly 1.2 times what was left for shareholders; at Morgan Stanley's institutional securities division pay was about 3.3 times pre-tax profits; at Credit Suisse's investment bank it was 7.5 times. Wright could not calculate the number for the investment bank at UBS because it paid its staff about $34billion over the period, despite losses of more than $44 billion. This goes on despite research maintaining that bonus systems only create short-term wealth and encourages risk-taking behavior, and that this was responsible for the crash of 2008, the loss of millions of jobs and the financial mess the country is in. It's not just Wall Street. The Wall Street Journal and The Hay Group studied executive compensation at 50 major public companies and found that CEO bonuses increased 30.5 percent in 2010 (McIntyre, 2011).

Others argue that the real villain is the excessive stock options given to CEOs. In America upwards of 70 percent of CEOs total compensation is in stock options. In Germany it's between 20 and 30 percent. Some suggest that these excessive stock options cheat the company's stockholders and through creative tax accounting actually cheat American taxpayers to the tune of $20 billion annually (Mishra, 2011).

So what should be done? It is clear it would be foolish to mandate or corral CEO compensation or enforce stricter rules and regulations for the bonus systems for two reasons: (1) We do not have any clear understanding of the relationship between performance and reward. All we have is evidence that it does not work, and this is true for all employees. We have consistently suggested throughout this book that the entire performance review process should be canned. (2) Trying to control compensation and create stricter rules would encourage cheating and deception. Here is what can be done. We can demand that boards do a better job and that they hire and fire CEOs with a greater degree of involvement, with more care and concern, and that stockholders, politicians and journalists increase their watch over CEOs and scrutinize their decisions, especially decisions that include termination of employees, closing of companies, out-sourcing and destruction of the employee-employer compact. Journalists and business writers are key. They must cease celebrating these kingpins of greed and excess and dig deep to expose them for what they are. They must explain to Main Street how CEOs are stealing its money. And finally, B-school deans and professors must expose this behavior and refuse to accept their donations.

16. We must stop investment bankers from placing credit default swaps (CDS), collateralized debt obligations (CDO), or short selling and gaining wealth by betting against American companies and in some cases actually expediting failure. These are nothing but a bet that the company will fail and the motivation is to make certain the bottom drops, the stock tanks and the company files for bankruptcy. Billionaires were created who benefited from destruction. Wall Street hedge funds, private equity firms and the ever-larger banks got rich killing American manufacturing and they are riding the crest of a synthetic economy propped up by Chinese government dollars and American 401(k)'s and retirement funds.

In addition, they have discovered they could generate enormous profits out of small changes in the price of currency or through the securitization of assets, wrapped up in such a way that no one understood them. We have seen people who worked all their lives for a company only to see their retirement savings handed over to some investment bankers who bought company with a loan based on the companies assests and then bet it would fail while they stripped its assets and ran it into the ground. The poor employees loose their job and pension while the fat cats get fat. Only in America.

17. When will the American banking industry, already outsourcing thousands of jobs each month, become a former shell of it self as credit

dries up and disposable wealth drops? There are 18 states that require large companies to inform their employees and the state government 60 days before mass terminations or plant closings. We must hold these CEOs accountable, and every state and the federal government must hold investigative hearings before any corporation engages in mass terminations or decides to close a plant or offshore jobs.

Consider John Lechleiter, who became CEO of Lilly in April 2008. In 2009 Lechleiter continued Lilly's outsourcing policy and terminated 5,500 employees. And guess what? He received a compensation package valued at $16.4 million, a 54 percent increase from 2008. Leichleiter also received a salary as president and chairman, and this salary rose nearly 11 percent to $1.48 million. There is more. His performance-related cash bonus jumped 31 percent to $3.55 million. Since 2006 Lilly has been systematically reducing its workforce in America. In 2006, 20 percent of Lilly's chemistry research and production work was done in China for one-quarter the U.S. cost and helped fund a startup lab in Shanghai's Chem-Explorer Co., with 230 chemists. Lilly also slashed the costs of clinical trials on human patients by shifting this work to Brazil, Russia, China, and India (Engardio, Arndt, and Foust, 2006). It is difficult to know exactly how many Lilly jobs have been lost. For example, some suggest that by the end of 2011 another 7,500 American jobs will go. Lilly is not alone. It is just as difficult to know how many jobs in the country are lost each month through outsourcing and offshoring. There is a solution and this is perhaps one area where quick action by the government can put a stop to this "bottom line" mentality. Every time a company lays off or terminates an employee a report should be filed with Congress. Companies that terminate an excessive amount of employees like Lilly should appear in front of a commission and explain the motivations for such actions. This would provide scholars with a lot of data, and it would most likely stop this foolishness that is destroying America.

Consider what Whirlpool did in 2010; they closed their refrigerator manufacturing plant in Evansville, Ind., putting more than 1,100 people out of work. They will now manufacture refrigerators in Mexico, where weaker labor and environmental laws make them "cheaper." We did not hear a "peep" in the press, media or in Washington. This is especially outrageous because Whirlpool received $19 million in from the federal government as a part of the American Recovery and Reinvestment Act. We have a situation where federal economic recovery funds are being used to create jobs in Mexico at the expense of jobs in America and no one cares because those who occupy elitist positions; stockholders and money managers just see the money that is flowing into their pockets and remain insensitive to the plight of the American worker. While this was going on, Whirlpools CEO Jeff Fettig received an increase in compensation of more than 75 percent in 2009 to $10.8 million. This included a bonus of $5.9 million. Presumably this was his reward for terminating 5,000 employees. Fettig should be called to Washington to face Congress and explain himself and answer the question: How is this decision-making benefiting America, employees, and the communities? We need to shine the spotlight of public embarrassment, shame, and humiliation and force him and many others to think about changing and working to earn the respect of his workers, community and country. When a company engages in mass terminations nothing happens. Instead Fettig gets a 15 percent raise in total compensation in 2010 to $14.4 million. In July 2011 another 315 employees were terminated as Fettig continued to close plants in the Midwest.

18. Economists are pervasive in our government as regulators, among the managerial class, and in the financial sector of our economy. This is not to take an unfair jab at economists. However, whenever a profession becomes too powerful and too pervasive we will have a decision making process that is skewed and colored by arrogance. For many years complaints have been lodged against the fact that too many lawyers were

running government. We must have a system where all the professions and nonprofessionals are represented, and if we do this we will have a system that questions decision-making and promotes the possibility of critical thinking. Once a single profession dominates, there is a tendency to rely on that profession's theories and/or professional ideology. And this can precipitate a crisis. Laws drafted by lawyers cannot solve all problems, and neither can economists.

A FINAL WORD

It is incredible that we have gone from the Tech Bubble to the Enron's, and now the financial crisis, without any deep social and psychological understanding of how these problems evolve. We know what these executives did, and we have a plethora of economists and business writers and journalists describing what went on. But there is a huge difference between describing what happened and understanding how it happened. Unless we develop a full and deep understanding, another crisis will occur in a few years. This is guaranteed. It's like engaging in a repair of the office copy machine. The boss says get it fixed, and no one takes the time to diagnose why it's broken. Consequently, the machine breaks daily and the repairman becomes an office regular. CEOs, politicians and lawmakers, economists, business leaders, and educators have embraced this "fix-it" mentality. But here is the problem: They do not know what they are fixing because they do not know the depth of the problem. So they throw money at the problem and use phrases like, "too big to fail," and they appoint the very same economists and bankers who played roles in creating the financial mess. And these characters have one motto: "Let's get back to normal." One can question the education these economists obtained, because they spend so little time acquiring an understanding or developing a deep diagnosis of what caused this financial crisis. Maybe they do not want to know, because if they truly understood the cause of this crisis, it would require radical changes in the way banks and industries operated, and the decisions CEOs make to enrich themselves. They do not want change. Instead they want to return to normalcy, where they can continue acts of wealth accumulation for themselves and their cronies. If change does occur, you can bet they will undermine it because it has the potential of causing those who occupy positions of power and wealth the loss of social and economic status (SES).

Corporations and our banks provide fertile ground where decisions can be made to benefit some at the expense of others. The game of friendly fascism is played out daily in the Darwinian struggle for survival and power. If the corporate power game is identified and openly discussed and its systemic motivations are diagnosed and its problematic consequences understood, only then will corporate greed come to an end. As we have attempted to demonstrate greed behavior is a cultural phenomenon and it is a function of the interplay between the corporation, the larger culture and its institutions. The institutionalization of greed has dire consequences for society especially those in poverty. Poverty is the opposite of wealth. And those who professed the belief that wealth among the few is good because it would trickle down engage in self-serving optimism. The basic teachings of all religions maintain that greed is the cause of individual and collective sorrow and that generosity, compassion and love for one's neighbor, will eliminate poverty. The institutions established to sustain the obscene accumulation of wealth have created a culture without ethical and moral moorings and float adrift. It maybe the only thing that has "trickled down" is greed.

As America sinks under trillion's in debt that it will never repay, and stays afloat by frantically selling about $2 billion in Treasury bonds a day to the Chinese, Americans unable to find work give up and walk away from credit card debt, school debt and their homes. In 2010, 50 million Americans live in poverty and tens of millions of Americans live in "near poverty" and one in eight Americans (one in four children) depend on food stamps to eat. This group will grow as the tax base dries up and states and towns can no longer pay their employees or honor pension obligations. In 2010 school teachers, university professors, fire and police, along with other public servants were terminated by the thousands and many retirees no longer see a check in the mail. Who would have envisioned Michael Harrington's "The Other America," written in 1962, would become the opposite in 2010, where the "Other America" would be the elite and the middle class majority would vanish and the majority would be struggling poor? How did this happen? As we have try to point out, bankers, CEOs and their business school teachers lost their compassion for those who once made things, and in their pursuit of the almighty dollar and desire to get rich they sold out the country. The ripple effects of blatant greed are felt everywhere in America, as every day companies are forced to terminate millions or declare bankruptcy resulting in a reduced tax base for local governments, who respond by terminating millions of teachers, police, firemen and other public servants, which in turn makes it impossible for states to pay unemployment benefits for their increasing population of unemployed citizens leading about 30 states to borrow $41.5 billion from the federal government to pay for these benefits. As the country races towards the 2012 elections, politicians do nothing except bark about reducing government spending. They refuse to see how the elite are sucking billions from the government and destroying the middle class.

If every banker, hedge fund executive, CEO and business professor had taken a step back and pondered the fate of those American employees who lost their jobs to the Chinese, Indians or others overseas, America may not be in this mess.

And it's too late to fix it.

NOTES

1. Although there are different views and definitions of commitment in the literature, reviewing them is beyond the scope and the intent of this chapter. Interested readers, however, are referred to Ghemawat, 1991 (commitment as a form of persistence), Kaplan and Razin, 1981 (commitment as a strong attachment to an organization), Ingram, 1986 (commitment as a sense of intimacy).

   While all of these views enhance our understanding of the concept of commitment, that is, offer promise in creating a description of the phenomenon of commitment, they do not explain the depth of the relationship that is established when an employee becomes committed. For example what it is about the object that receives commitment, and what is it about the committed person and their relationship that provides a powerful sense of commitment? This is a major question asked by organizational theorists and managers alike as they attempt to promote and reap the benefits associated with commitment. On the other side, a critical question associated with the concept of commitment is what effect it has on employees. Does it provide for increased mental health, job satisfaction, and is it an ideal condition? Or is it nothing more than a form of psychic bondage in which employees are brainwashed into demonstrating the same selfless type of commitment that young adults demonstrate when they join a cult and sell flowers at an airport all day for a bowl of rice and praise from an over-idealized guru?

2. This is not to dismiss the significance of the employee's inner and earlier experiences and the notion that transference reactions are repetitions of earlier experiences. For example, some employees will tend to react negatively and show little response to the organization's desire to induce a positive transference reaction. In addition, the quality of the organization's psycho-social environment may be of little consequence in inducing a transference reaction because the organizational environment will attract personality types that will find the climate appealing. The key here is matching the personality of the recruits with the psycho-social environment. For example, research has suggested that if the personality of an employee is unable to fit into the desired personality type or culture of the organization, a result will be increased stress (Czander, 1993, Kets de Vries and Miller, 1984). An example of this type of stress was found with an automobile manufacturing employee who had to quit his job because of a mental breakdown. The courts ruled that the breakdown was the result of an incompatibility between his personality and the activities of his role and the culture of the factory. He was a parts inspector in the assembly line, and he suffered because the workers kept installing defective parts on the assembled autos. His personality demanded order, correctness, and cleanliness. He would be diagnosed as an obsessive compulsive personality. On the job he experienced dread. Working within a culture that permitted messiness and defects had a direct bearing on his mental health. In all cases where the employees demonstrate personality characteristics that do not fit in to the larger culture, this employee will be perceived as being out of step, as different, and will most likely experience stress. If the parts inspector were able to manifest and gratify his obsessional zeal, he might have been a contented and com-

mitted employee, and the organization as a whole may have benefited.

3. At West Point there is considerable diversity. They attempt to match the diversity in the military population. While the training is rigorous, a wide range of attitudes and cultures are acceptable. This is especially apparent as the military operates in such cultures as Iraq and Afghanistan where defeating the enemy requires winning over the population. What they want to avoid is all white male officers and a soldier population that is African American, homosexual, female and Hispanic.

4. All salary data without references were obtained from Security and Exchange Commission filings.

5. Textbooks also offer students advice about how to avoid being laid off. Consider this absurdity *"You are More Immune from Layoffs if…You have a good relationship with your boss. You have a midrange salary. You generate revenue for the company. You have expertise in your field. You have a willingness to work long hours when necessary. You are willing to relocate to another city or transfer to another position in the company"* (Greenberg, 2005). Several British students on internships for several major financial institutions were shocked at how much time these employees put in each week. They concluded it was just "face time" to reduce the possibility they would be fired.

6. "Indeed, organizations have been rapidly reducing the number of employees needed to operate effectively-a process known as downsizing. Typically, this involves more than just laying off people in a move to save money. It is directed at adjusting the number of employees needed to work in newly designed

organizations and is, therefore, also known as rightsizing. Whatever you call it, the bottom line is clear: Many organizations need fewer people to operate today than in the past-sometimes far fewer" (Greenberg, 2005, p. 13)

APPENDICES

Appendix A: The Compensation Problem

With CEO pay up sharply and the minimum wage falling farther and farther behind inflation, the average CEO's compensation outstripped minimum wage pay by a ratio of 821 to 1 in 2005 (Mishel, 2006). According to Mishel (2006) at the current minimum wage it would take a full 52-week year of work to earn what the average CEO earned before lunch on the first day of the year. Bob Nardelli, former Home Depot CEO broke the record, in 2002. His salary was 1,458 times that of the average hourly Home Depot employee. Then in 2008, Lee Scott, the CEO of Wal-Mart broke Nardelli's record by making more than 1,645 times what an average Wal-Mart worker earned in a year. But in 2011, amid outrage over these gross inequities in America, we had a new leader, and to make matters worse it was a health insurance company. CEO of UnitedHealth Group, Stephen Hemsley, received nearly $102 million, creating a ratio of CEO pay to median employee pay an outrageous 1,737-to-1. This means that Hemsley makes more in one hour of work than the median UnitiedHealth employee annual salary of $58,000.

The five highest-paid CEOs of publicly traded companies took home an astounding 9.8 percent of the aggregate earnings of those companies in 2005 (Sanford, 2006).

Consider this: If the average worker's salary had kept pace with the average CEO salary, the average worker's salary in 2006 would be $110,136 and the minimum wage would be $23 an hour (CRS, 2007). Clearly, average pay has not kept pace. In 1999 a full-time phone sales associate at Qantas earned about $30,500 a year. The Quantas CEO earned about $1.9 million. In 2006, the same employee earned about $38,000, while the CEO earned about $5.3 million. In 2011 the median salary (adjusted for inflation) for a typical midlevel worker was less than it was in 1969, and 90 percent of all workers have seen their salaries remain stagnant or drop.

In 2007 Stephen Schwarzman, CEO of the Blackstone Group, received $350.7 million in compensation. This was in addition to the $4.77 billion he received when his stake in the firm was converted into stock as part of the group's initial public offering. In 2008 Schwarzman gained the top spot again. Despite the deepening recession, he received close to $700 million. In 2007 Blackstone's stock dropped 40 percent. Meanwhile Blackstone paid President Tony James a $23.5 million bonus and Vice Chairman J. Tomilson Hill a bonus of $7.36 million and a stock award worth $8 million, not including $6.3 million in deferred compensation.

All of the executives have additional potential compensation tied up in Blackstone shares. Schwarzman, who earned $350,000 and no bonus in 2010, held vested shares worth $399.2 million at the end of 2010. He holds shares worth $544.7 million that haven't vested, according to the filing.

Hedge-fund managers made the most money in 2007 and continue to make top compensation as they continue to flip companies.

Second on the list for 2007, behind Schwarzman was Lawrence Ellison, CEO of Oracle, collecting a total of $556.9 million. Between 2006 to 2010 he made almost a trillion dollars, and Occidental Petroleum CEO Ray Irani came in third with a meager total compensation of 222.6 million dollars.

In 2007, 30 CEOs received total compensation increases of 1,000 percent or more, with the largest pay increase going to Richard Fairbank, CEO of Capital One, whose total compensation went up 46,574 percent.

In 2008 the highest paid CEO was Aubrey McClendon, Chesapeake Energy Corp., with $112.5 million. Between 2006 and 2010 he made over $300 million. (To Read More about energy CEO compensation go to Appendix Y). He was closely followed by India-born Sanjay Jha of Motorola, who was given $104 million while the company lost $4.2 billion and its stock plunged 75 percent, which wiped out $27.9 billion in stock market value. Another India-born CEO had the distinction of being the highest paid bailout CEO: Citigroup's Vikram Pandit, who was given $38.2 million in 2008 while the company lost $27.7 billion and its stock fell 78 percent destroying $124 billion in stock market value.

Despite complaints and public scrutiny of CEO salaries the gap continues to increase. According to a study by The Corporate Library, the median salary increase for CEOs at S & P 500 firms was 16 percent in 2007 for an average of 14.2 million. Compensation levels for private investment fund managers soared even further. In 2007 it is estimated that American CEOs received one-third of all wages paid out. Controversy over CEO compensation is not new. During the Great Depression in the 1930s Main Street was outraged over executive compensation when revelations of million-dollar-a-year pay packages brought forth calls for pay disclosure, litigation, punitive taxation and government imposed limits on pay (Wells, 2010).

As the fiscal crisis grew it was widely reported that CEO compensation fell in 2008. However, a careful reading of the largest 200 corporations suggests that this reporting of an average decline in CEO compensation in 2008 of 3 to 7 percent was in the area of stock and option awards, and their cash compensation actually increased. These CEOs knew their stocks were declining- 90 percent of CEO stock options are "under water"-so they compensated by getting more cash an average increase of 4.5 percent. In addition, four out of five CEOs received cash bonuses in 2008. Some suggest that while stock compensation declined 7 percent, cash allotments for perks increased 7 percent. In 2010 the median CEO salary increased almost 27 percent while millions of employees were terminated, hundreds of thousands of jobs outsourced and demands were so pervasive that employees work harder for less and their average compensation rose only 2.1 percent. As CEOs suspended their employees' pensions, reduced benefits, and forced their employees to take time off without pay, they still got more for themselves.

In 2009 the average compensation for S&P 500 CEOs was 263 times the average wage in the same S&P companies and in 2010 it climbed higher.

In 2008 the ten highest paid CEOs obtained $40.7 million while their companies lost $30 billion of their stock value. In 2009, the year of the federal bailouts of banks, and despite outcry over CEO greed the top five executives at each of the top 20 bailed-out banks received a combined increase in the value of their stock options of nearly $90 million (Anderson, Cavanagh, Collins and Pizzigati, 2009). Also according to Anderson, et. al. (2009) "From 2006 through 2008, the top five executives at the 20 banks that have accepted the most federal bailout dollars since the [2008] meltdown averaged $32 million each in personal compensation. One hundred average U.S. workers would have to labor over 1,000 years to make as much as these 100 executives made in three years. In addition, American workers lost an astounding $3.7 trillion in retirement benefits during the crash of 2008, meaning that the gap between the rich and poor dramatically increased. Now as boomers reach retirement age they have little money left in their accounts and are faced with conservative politicians pounding their drums against Social Security and Medicare."

The nation's biggest financial companies took $350 billion of bailout money from U.S. taxpayers in 2008-09, but that did not stop the greed. Executives of these bailed out companies saw their perks and benefits increase by an average of 4 percent. For example, GMAC Financial Services CEO Alvaro de Molina received $2.5 million from his company to help out with his personal tax bill. In November 2009 de Molina was fired. The chief executive of Comerica, Ralph W. Babb Jr., got more than $200,000 for country club expenses. Perks and benefits for CEOs at the 29 biggest financial companies rescued with taxpayer money averaged more than $380,000 in 2008 (Tse, 2009).

In 2008, the most notable executive in America's $1-a-year CEO club was Steve Jobs, CEO of Apple Computer. Jobs had been collecting $1 in annual salary since 1997. In 2009 his 5.5 million shares of Apple stock had a net worth of almost $2 billion. In 2006 Steve Jobs drew a nominal $1 salary but realized $647 million from vested restricted stock.

Lagging far behind Jobs is Ray Irani of Occidental Petroleum at $321 million and Barry Diller of IAC/InterActiveCorp and Expedia at $290 million. According to Aenlle (2011) *"In 2010, he racked up personal flights on company aircraft to the tune of $644,530 at IAC/InterActiveCorp. . . . Meantime, over at Expedia . . . Diller clocked another $605,786 of personal flights."* Following Diller was Oracle's CEO Larry Ellison, with

$192.9 million then William Foley of Fidelity National Financial $180 million, and Terry Semel of Yahoo at $174 million (Kirkland, 2006).

In 2007, these CEOs received the following: John A. Thain of Merrill Lynch, $83,785,021; Lawrence J. Ellison of Oracle $61,180,524; Lloyd C. Blankfein of Goldman Sachs $53,965,418; Kenneth I. Chenault of American Express $53,126,585; John J. Mack of Morgan Stanley $41,399,010; Ray R. Irani of Occidental $33,624,909; Miles D. White of Abbott Labs $28,955,662; Alan G. Lafley of Procter & Gamble $26,835,350; Edward Stack, Dick's Sporting Goods CEO, collected $61.8 million from salary, other payments and from cashing in stock options in 2007. The CEO of Halliburton, Dave Lesar, received $42,637,920 in 2007.

CEO of Gamco, a security firm, Mario Gabelli received $70.9 million in compensation for 2007. He beat Goldman Sachs CEO Lloyd Blankfein, who was paid $68.5 million. In 2009 Gabelli's total compensation was $43.6 million and in 2010 $56.7 million.

In 2007 BlackBerry founder Michael Lazaridis made $51.5 million and his co-CEO James Balsillie earned $32.05 million.

In 2008 Oracle Corp. founder and CEO Larry Ellison, worth more than $25 billion, received $84.6 million. In 2009 he was ranked number two with total compensation of $130,230,000.

In 2009 H. Lawrence Culp, CEO of Danaher, was ranked the number one in 2009 with total compensation of $141,360,000.

In 2010 Reed Hastings CEO of Netflix was expected to be close to $60 million in compensation making him the highest paid media mogul and passing CBS CEO Leslie Moonves. With ratings down and layoffs up (7 percent of the news staff cut) Moonves' total compensation in 2010 jumped to $57.7 million, up from $43 million in 2009 that's still below the huge $67.7 million payday he received in pre-recession 2007. Through the first eight months of the year, Hastings has pocketed $31 million through the little-noticed sales, according to data from The Washington Service, a firm which tracks insider stock trades.

Gregory Maffei, CEO of Liberty Media, made $87.5 million in 2009

Michael White, who just completed his first year as CEO of DirecTV, received a pay package valued at $32.7 million in 2010.

In 2010 executives running Real Estate Investment Trusts (REITs) quickly moved up the in the rankings of excessive pay. The average compensation for CEOs of top REITs increased by 83.6 percent in 2010, outpacing the sector's total shareholder return of 28.9 percent. Marc Holiday of SL Green, Manhattan's largest office landlord, took home $24.8 million in 2010, an increase of 117.6 percent compared to the previous year. SL Green's shareholder returns were 35.3% and David Simon of Simon Property Group received $24.5 million in 2010, up 430 percent from $4.6 million the year before.

Appendix B: The Stuff They Get

The new world of executive compensation started in 2007 when the public began to see the perks CEOs received. For example it was discovered that William Swanson, CEO of Raytheon, who received $17 million in 2009, enjoyed the following perks: personal use of the corporate jet for himself and his family; a company car and driver; reimbursement of club membership fees; and expenses paid for family-related travel, entertainment and gifts. Plus $31,000 to pay for the taxes incurred on the travel and gifts. In 2010 Raytheon's share price was down 10 percent and net income was down 4.9 percent and Swanson received total compensation of $7 million.

Stock and option awards also come to the fore in a flurry and every CEO not only wanted perks but also a plethora of stocks and options. The chairman and CEO of American Express Co. received compensation valued at $53.2 million in 2007, nearly double his pay in the previous year. The main driver of Kenneth Chenault's surge in pay was stock and options awards. He received $42.8 million in stock awards for performance in 2007 and a special incentive stock option grant. His base salary in 2007 grew by 13 percent in 2007 $1.24 million, plus he received $6.5 million in bonuses plus $126,992 for a home security system, $323,844 for personal use of the company plane, and $102,601 for personal use of company cars.

CEO of Goodyear Tire Robert Keegan received a base pay of $1.18 million in 2007, plus a bonus of $3.5 million, a performance-based bonus of $8.8 million, and stock awards and options that the Akron-based tire maker valued at $7.6 million. Perquisites totaled $82,323, including personal use of company aircraft and two sets of automobile tires a year.

Since 2002, Dwight Schar, CEO of homebuilding giant NVR has been compensated $625 million (Brunwasser, 2008).

The McKesson Corp. gave CEO John Hammergren $6.8 million in other pay, including $14,296 in financial planning services, $133,825 in private use of the company plane and $469 in "gifts." The company also reimbursed Hammergren $2,860 for legal fees he had incurred in renegotiating his employment agreement. (In other words, McKesson financed its CEO's efforts to extract a better pay package from the company.) (Kristof. 2008). In 2006, Hammergren earned $8.1 million and in 2007 negotiated full pension benefits in a lump sum of almost $76 million, if he quits. In 2007 he was 48 years old. In 2011 Hammergren received $150.7 million, an increase of 190 percent from 2010's $51.8 million. He got $32 million in salary, incentive pay and perks, including $17,000 for tax advice, $123,000 for home security and $100,000 for personal use of company aircraft and $112.1 million from exercising stock options

Liberty Media CEO John Malone received an "annual allowance" of $1 million for personal expenses in 2008. He also has use of the company apartment in New York and a car - along with a driver. The company also covers his "shipping and catering" costs (Paton, 2008). In 2007, Malone's compensation package jumped 80 percent to $6 million. This included $227,137 for use of a company jet, $745,832 in tax payments made on his behalf, and reimbursements for personal estate, planning and legal advice. He also received $214,323 in above-market returns on deferred compensation. Malone was replaced by Gregory Maffei, who made $87.5 million in 2009.

David M. Cote, CEO of Honeywell International Inc., received compensation valued at $19.9 million in 2007. Some $13.4 million came from stock and options, his base salary was $1.6 million, $4.2 million from an incentive plan, $158,739 for personal use of the company's aircraft, $62,000 in premiums for a $10 million executive life insurance policy, $64,731 in contributions to two savings plans, $50,000 for Cote to purchase benefits of his choosing, $6,126 for security protection and $1,942 for home security monitoring and $63,367 to cover taxes on a life insurance premium reimbursement. In 2009 Cote's compensation was $12.8 million as he locked out union workers for refusing to accept his proposal to eliminate retiree health care and pension plans for newly hired employees and increase workers' out-of-pocket health care to $8,500 a year. Good health care coverage for retirees is especially important to the company's uranium workers who suffer rates of cancer ten times higher than the general public due to their daily interaction with radioactive material.

In 2010 Ralph Lauren got a big pay day from the company he founded; $27.7 million. And $19.5 of it was a cash bonus, $1.25 million salary, stock and option awards worth $6.2 million, $558,376 for personal travel, not business travel, personal. But that's nothing compared to 2011 when he received compensation worth $75.2 million. That includes a $19.5 million bonus and $37.1 million from stock options gains. Again his Polo-paid perks include $200,000 for personal travel, nearly $70,000 in supplemental health medical expenses and over $60,000 for a car and driver

Comcast Corp. CEO Brian L. Roberts received about $27.8 million in compensation in 2006. In addition to his salary he received $8.4 million in incentive pay, stock options and awards, and nearly $3 million in perks that included insurance and use of the company aircraft for personal business. In 2008 he received $40.8 million in total pay, including more than $22 million from cashing out options and a $7.4

million bonus. But shareholders have lost more over the past five years than they would have by investing in the broader market, or a collection of cable companies. In 2006 his father, the company founder (It's good to be the son of the king) andcChair of the company's Finance Board, received $24.1 million. In 2010 Roberts (the son) receive total compensation of over $30 million.

The total compensation for departing Coca-Cola Co. chief executive Neville Isdell rose 4 percent in 2007 to $21.7 million. Isdell got a base salary of $1.6 million, $6.6 million from the non-equity incentive plan, $12.6 million in stock and option grants for the year and $817,066 in other compensation, which included $341,849 in personal use of the company aircraft.

In 2008 Ray Irani CEO of Occidental Petroleum was given $400,000 to cover the cost of financial planners in addition to $30 million in compensation. An Occidental spokesperson explained that this perk was beneficial to the corporation because it helped Irani "keep his complete attention on the company's business." Irani who is 75, made $97 million in 2009, plans to step down as chief executive officer at the 2011 annual meeting and become executive chairman before retiring in 2014 when he will be almost 80. In 2010 Irani ranked as the sixth-highest paid CEO in America received $76.1 million.

CEOs of financial institutions fear no public embarrassment when they accept government money to bailout their corporations while using corporate jets. For example, AIG received a bailout of $150 billion and still has seven jets, and Citigroup received $25 billion in TARP and $305 billion in loan guarantees and has four jets, and Bank of America received $25 billion has a whopping nine jets.

Let's not forget the CEO of the century, Jack Welch. He no longer works at GE and there is considerable confusion about what he receives.

Why? Possibly because GE has been secretive and has been under fire from shareholders, or because he gets so many perks it is difficult to keep track. This is what he most likely gets: A $9 million-a-year pension and every imaginable perk, including free toilet paper, New York Knicks tickets, flowers, dry cleaning, permanent access to a corporate jet, New York apartment, chauffeured limousine, a leased Mercedes-Benz, offices in New York and Connecticut, free consultations with estate-planning and tax advisers, personal assistant, fax, phone, and security systems at his four homes, bodyguards for his speaking engagements and book tours, access to VIP seats at sporting events broadcast by GE's NBC, cellular phones for five cars, satellite television in four homes, five computers, complete with technical support, and dues for three private golf clubs, including Augusta.

In his last year with GE, Welch earned $16.2 million. He also holds 22 million shares of GE (which, at $28 a share, in 2002 was worth $616,000,000). In March, 2009, GE's stock had lost 83 percent of its value. Poor Jack.

Appendix C: Women Join In

While the domain of CEO largess belongs to the white male, a few women are members. In 2007 Brenda C. Barnes, CEO of Sara Lee, received over $8 million and in 2009 over $10 million in total compensation. In August 2010 she resigned after having a stroke at age 57.

In 2007, Anne Mulch, CEO of XEROX received $13,459,450; Indri K. Noyil, CEO of PepsiCo, $11,790,552; Susan M. Ivey, CEO of Reynolds, $9,467,860; Christina A. Gold, CEO, Western Union, $9,411,000; Angela F. Bray, CEO of WellPoint, $9,094,271Carol Markowitz, CEO of TJX, made $8,629,084 in total compensation in 2007 and a whopping 30 percent increase in total compensation in 2011 to $19.3 million. Since 2007 she has more than doubled her compensation while terminating over 4,000 employees.

Also in 2007 Patricia A. Woertz, CEO of Archer Daniels Midland, received $7,637,295; Paula Rosput Reynolds, CEO of Safeco, $6,013,752; and Mary F. Sammons, CEO of Rite Aid, $4,270,966.

In 2007 Irene Rosenfeld CEO of Kraft made $11,299,535. In 2008 her compensation package rose about 50 percent to $17 million, as its shares fell 17 percent and its Standard & Poor's 500 SPX index fell 38.5 percent. In 2010 her total compensation rose to over $19 million.

CEO of TW Telecom Larissa Herda's base salary rose 6.25 percent in 2008, and her compensation was almost $5.3 million.

Appendix D:
The Wall Street Gang

In 2006 Morgan Stanley's John Mack found $40 million in his stocking and in 2009 the first time the company experienced a loss, its new CEO James Gorman only received only a $8.11 million bonus. In 2010 Mack and Gorman found themselves in court being sued by pension funds for "abdicating their responsibility" as they paid a total of $45 billion in compensation for 2006, 2007 and 2009 as shareholder value dropped to less than $30 per share from a high of $90 per share and they needed a government bailout. Gorman received a compensation package of $6.5 million for 2009 as Morgan reported losses and terminated over 2,000 employees. In 2010 Gorman's compensation rose to $15.2 million, which included a cash bonus of $3.9 million.

In 2006 Goldman Sach's Lloyd Blankfein got more than $53 million (Gettler, 2006). In 2007, Blankfein's holiday bonus was increased to $68 million and in 2007 Goldman distributed $12.1 billion in Christmas bonuses to its employees (up from $9.9 billion the year before). In 2009 despite accepting and quickly returning a government bailout Goldman gave out $22 billion in bonuses, which works out to an average of $700,000 per employee. Lehman Brothers had a 2007 Christmas bonus pool of $5.7 billion the year before it died. In January 2011, while unemployment continued and the recession deepened

Goldman Sachs top executives were to divide about $111.3 million worth of stock. Blankfein will receive about $24.3 million in January and Gary Cohn, Goldman Sachs president will get about $24 million. In January 2011 after three losing quarters in a row, Blankfein got a huge raise. The bank more than tripled the executive's base salary, to $2 million, while boosting his stock bonus 40 percent, which comes to an additional $3.6 million. Blankfein's total compensation, in 2010 was $13.2 million. In 2011 it is expected that around 1,700 traders will be terminated.

Bruce Wasserstein of Lazard had a 2008 pay package of $20.4 million. He died in October 2009. Forbes recently estimated his net worth at $2.2 billion.

In January 2011 BlackRock gave its CEO Laurence Fink a bonus valued at nearly $13 million in restricted stock and options perhaps the largest Wall Street bonus awards of the so-called "bonus season." Shareholder return was a minus 16 percent in 2010 and employees were terminated.

Appendix E:
The Health Care Gang

In 2009, American ranked number one in health care costs per person. At $7,960 per person the country that came closest to America was Norway at $5,352 per person. What accounts for the $2,508 that each Ameican pays over what Norway pays? Exective compensation and a return to stockholders accounts for a large portion this $2,508. The health care industry has come under considerable fire for compensation practices. In 2010 the fire got hotter as the median CEO pay in the health care industry reached $10 million, making these CEOs "the highest median pay of any industry," including consumer goods, telecom and oil and gas, according to a new Wall Street Journal CEO Compensation Study.

The spiraling costs are also attributed to hedge funds and venture capital firms that are busy buying up hospitals and creating giant health care systems to maximize profitability. For example, Vanguard Health Care Systems which owns 26 hospitals in five states, as well as three health insurance plans and two surgery centers in California is controlled by the infamous Blackstone Group and in June, 2011 they put forth an IPO, going public to raise $661 million. Out of this the so-called owners received $447 million. The hospitals are now deep in debt. Who then gets rich, the Blackstone boys, their investors and of course their hospital CEOs. In 2010 Mike Dugan CEO of the Detroit Medical Center, owned by Vanguard, was given $2.41 million in pay, bonuses and several years of stock options.

Health Care for America Now (2010), a coalition that fights for health reform maintains "that while America's families struggled with skyrocketing health insurance costs and the worst economy since the Great Depression, chief executives of the 10 largest for-profit health insurance companies collected total pay of $228.1 million, up from $85.5 million the year before." The CEOs of UnitedHealth Group, WellPoint, Aetna, CIGNA, Humana, Coventry Health Care, Health Net, Amerigroup, Centene and Universal American took almost a billion dollars in compensation from 2000 through 2009. In 2009 the average compensation for hospital CEOs in America was $1 million. In 2010 Aetna's CEOs total compensation package was $39 million and Cigna's was $30 million. These CEOs get perks and lots of them. In addition to stock options, bonuses and other benefits, they get to attend holiday parties and company gatherings in exotic places, company cars, severance and "golden" agreements and of course financial consulting.

In 2010 Americans were expected to spend $2.6 trillion on health, with 10 percent or $260 billion going for overhead. This accounts for an increase in health care costs of 72 percent between 2000 and 2009 and during the same period the health care industry overhead increased by 95 percent.

The jaw-dropping compensation for 2009 set new standards for the industry and for what CEOs will pay themselves in the future. The compensation for health-insurance CEOs was so enormous in 2009 that it could have paid for stress tests to check the heart health of up to 776,000 patients, or to pay for every resident of Philadelphia, Dallas and Minneapolis combined (3.2 million people) to go to their regular doctor for an office visit. Over the full decade covered in the report, average CEO pay has reached nearly $10 million a year per company. Consider this outrageousness, the CEO of Blue Cross Blue Shield of North Dakota Mike Unhjem received a 27 percent raise in March 2009 at the same time claiming that his company was in serious financial trouble, At the same time the insurer's top executives and 33 sales representatives and their guests took a trip to the Cayman Islands. A Blue Cross Blue Shield spokesperson said that the Cayman Islands trip is an annual event to reward the company's top salespeople.

BlueCross BlueShield of Tennessee doubled what it pays its directors and CEO in the past five years, boosting the salary for part-time board Chairman Lamar Partridge to $100,000 and raising the compensation package for CEO Vicky Gregg to more than $4.4 million in 2010 (Flessner,2011).

Northwestern Memorial HealthCare CEO Dean Harrison made approximately $9.7 million in total compensation in 2010, the highest of any Chicago hospital CEO. Harrison's 2010 compensation figure, which is nearly three times as much the $3.4 million he earned in 2009, includes a one-time retirement payment, a truly golden sendoff.

Want to get rich? Run a dialysis company. Kent Thiry CEO of Davita, made $14 million in compensation in 2011 and $36.8 million in the last three years. Most of the income Davita receives comes from the government.

Despite the fact that millions of Americans are losing their health coverage and insurance premiums skyrocketed in 2009, the executives at Blue Cross & Blue Shield of Illinois received big bonuses. CEO Patricia Hall saw her total compensation jump 62 percent in 2009, to $8.7 million. Her predecessor Ray McCaskey got a $15.7 million bonus as he walked out the door. Hall and McCaskey terminated 650 employees in 2009 and gave their top ten executives compensation increases of at least 48 percent.

Wellstar hired Reynold Jennings to be its new CEO in August 2011 and here is what he gets; an annual base salary of $975,000, and a bonus that could range from 35 to 65 percent of his annual salary. Jennings also gets: A month of paid vacation days, in addition to six holidays, payment for time lost from a serious health condition with proper medical certification, annual automobile allowance of $12,000, annual cell phone allowance of $2,400, annual physical exam allowance of $800, annual financial planning/tax preparation services of $3,000 and because Jennings has existing medical and dental coverage and does not need the Wellstar benefit plan so he gets and addition $12,000 allowance. He also gets life insurance, a retirement savings plan and long-term disability benefits.

Hoboken hospital, $50 million in debt, filed for bankruptcy in 2011 but somehow managed to pay its former CEO Spiros Hatiras $600,000 in compensation and offer full medical benefits for one year, even though the hospital does not have enough funds to pay its $1.9 million in city-related bills or the $1.45 million it owes to employees' pension and health funds.

In 2006, Michigan Blue Cross paid its president and CEO, the now-retired Richard Whitmer, a compensation package of $4,253,558. His replacement Dan Loepp received a 67 percent raise in 2007 to $1.6 million. Loepp's VP George Francis received an 83 percent raise in 2007, bringing his compensation to $1,380,322, and Kathy Elston, former vice president for employee services, with a 155 percent raise, from $383,453 to $979,434 in 2007. In 2008 before it announced a hiring freeze, the elimination of 1,000 jobs and losses of $144 million, Blue Cross Blue Shield of Michigan gave pay hikes to its nine top executives, including large retirement packages to five former senior vice presidents (Anstett, 2009). In 2010 Loepp got a 56 percent raise to $2.75 million in total compensation in 2010, up 56 percent from $1.76 million in 2009.

According to Anstett (2009) five Michigan Blue Cross executives leaving the company received large retirement packages. Departing Executive Vice President Les Viegas earned $3.46 million, the most of the top nine Blue Cross executives. Total compensations for the four other retiring Blue Cross executives were $2,069,782 for William Smith; $1,492,581 for John Austin; $1,338,316 for Jann Cantelon, and Dale Robertson, $1,000,554, all longtime workers for Blue Cross. Michigan Blue Cross is seeking a rate hike to cover what could amount to $1 billion by 2011 (Anstett, 2009).

BlueCross BlueShield of Oregon raised individual policy rates by 26 percent in 2008 and asked for another double-digit increase in 2009, while its CEO, Mark Ganz, received an 11 percent raise in 2008. His salary and bonus totaled $872,665 in 2008 while Ganz's company lost 32 percent (334,228) of its members, bringing its enrollment down to its lowest level in five years (776,647) and he got a bonus (Lund-Muzikant, 2009).

In 2008 Rand O'Donnell, CEO of Children's Mercy Hospitals and Clinics in Kansas City, Mo., received $5,987,194.

Express Scripts is terminating thousands of employees and pushing pthers to take wage cuts, and eliminate health care and pensions. In 2010 it plans to shut down its Bensalem, Pa. facility and lay off 950 workers while its CEO George Paz makes $10.6 million.

Joel Wernick CEO Phoebe Putney Memorial Hospital in Georgia received about $1.3 million in total compensation in 2010.

In 2008 Biogen CEO James Mullen sold $85 million in company stock and picked up $63 million in compensation in 2009 his total compensation was $11.3 million and included a cash bonus of $2.4 million. In June 2010 he retired and was replaced by George Scangos and in January, 2011 he terminated 192 employees in what was called the first round of layoffs. He will also terminate another 71 employees on March 31, 2011 and 64 more on June 30.

Between 2006 and 2010 CEO John Martin of Gilead Sciences made $204.2 million.

CEO Michael Israel of Westchester Medical Center received $1.2 million, which included a bonus while anticipating a $70 million loss in 2009 revenue, eliminating 400 jobs and closing a nursing home.

Former CEO Ralph de la Torre of Caritas Christi Health Care earned $2.2 million in 2009 almost doubling his compensation from 2008 ($1.2 million).

Fred Hassan of Schering-Plough was the highest paid pharmaceutical executive in 2009, thanks to a $33 million "golden handshake" when Merck bought the company for $41 billion, his total compensation came to $49.6 million. Schering-Plough executives received a total of $93 million in severance packages as they departed. Hassan then became chairman of Bausch & Lomb.

In 2009, George Halvorson, the CEO for Kaiser Foundation Health Plan & Kaiser Foundation Hospitals, received compensation of $6.7 million. Halvorson's package included a $1.2 million payment to his "supplemental non-qualified retirement plan." More than 40 other officers received payments to such retirement plans- several of them in the hundreds of thousands of dollars. At the same time Halvorson asked his employees to accept a more costly employee health insurance plan and reduce their retirement health benefits.

Michael Tarwater, CEO of Carolinas HealthCare System, was paid $3.5 million in total compensation in 2008. This includes base salary of $940,000, bonuses of $2 million, and other compensation, including retirement and health benefits, of $543,000.

Tom Breitenbach, CEO of MedAmerica Health Systems Corp. and Premier Health Partners, received total compensation $17 million during a six year period from 2002 to 2007. After exercising benefit cash out options of $3 million in 2007, Breitenbach made $4.1 million, or four times his 2002 earnings (Esrati, 2009).

CEO of Medco David Snow has all his bases covered. In 2009 he received compensation valued at nearly $13.4 million and he got an additional $17.1 million by exercising stock options. Snow's compensation included a salary of $1.3 million, stock awards of more than $1.8 million, more than $7 million in option awards and $3 million in non-equity incentive pay. He also received other compensation in the form of life insurance premiums, retirement contributions, financial planning and a car allowance. In addition to the options exercise, Snow realized more than $3.6 million in value from restricted stock awards that vested last year. At year end, Snow had 1.36 million shares of exercisable options, with exercise prices of $22.10 to $50.35, and nearly 1.16 million in unvested options. He also had nearly 141,000 shares of unvested stock awards valued at more than $9 million. Snow also had a deferred-compensation balance of more than $6.5 million. According to Brin (2010) should Snow lose his position because of a change in control at Medco, he would receive nearly $47.3 million in severance, long-term incentives and health-care coverage and he would receive $ 21.7 million for an involuntary termination not for cause or if he resigned for a good reason and $32.6 million if he left the company because of disability. It gets more absurd, if he died while in his current position, his heirs would receive more than $36.3 million, including his incentive awards and life insurance proceeds. Express Scripts, a Medco rival, is seeking to buy Medco for $29.1 billion and guess what Snow will get? A $39 million severance package.

The CEO of Boston Medical Center Elaine Ullian received a $3.5 million bonus in 2008 on top of her $1,348,504 salary and benefits as the hospital in dire financial straits may have to close.

Lifespan hospital in Rhode Island CEO George Vecchione's total compensation in 2007 was nearly $3 million, making him the highest paid hospital executive in New England. In addition, the 10 hospital CEOs in Rhode Island who have stayed in their jobs since 2000 saw their pay increase by an average of 87 percent, while the consumer price index climbed only 20 percent during the same time period (Brooks, 2009). In 2008-09 Vecchione made $9.5 million. In 2009-2010 he made $2.9 million and his nine executives made a total of $9.4 million.

Frank Perez, CEO, Kettering Adventist Healthcare, was paid $1.3 million in cash compensation and $1.7 million in total compensation in 2007, or about double from 2002. From 2002 to 2007, his total compensation — including retirement benefits and expense accounts — was $7.9 million (Esrati, 2009).

Paul Wiles, CEO of Novant Health in Charlotte, received $2 million in compensation in 2008. Wiles, based in Winston-Salem, received a salary of $900,000, a bonus of $829,000, and other income, including retirement and health benefits, of about $304,000 (Garloch, 2009).

In 2010, the head of New York-Presbyterian Hospital, Herbert Pardes, MD, received a bonus of $1.9 million, in addition to a $1.7 million salary and nearly $650,000 in "other" compensation.

Sam Wallace, 65, retired in March 2008 as CEO of Iowa Health System and he received $8 million in retirement income, in addition to $946,000 for three months' work.

Jeffrey Romoff, CEO of the University of Pittsburgh Medical Center, earned $3.95 million in 2007.

Tenet Healthcare Corp. gave CEO Trevor Fetter compensation valued at $9.7 million in 2008 which included a bonus of $2.3 million, as its stock plunged 77 percent. In 2010 his total compensation reached $12.2 million.

In 2006, Mike McCallister, CEO at Humana Inc., was paid $3,434,879 in total compensation, mostly in stock options, according to the company. Oxford Health Plans, CEO Norman C. Payson was paid $76 million plus unexercised stock options at $25.6 million. Aetna's CEO John Rowe, MD, $8.9 million in compensation plus $24.1 million in unexercised stock options of $24.1 million. Douglas Hawthorne, CEO of Texas Hospital Resources, received a compensation package of $1.4 million in 2006, and Baylor CEO Joel Allison had compensation of $1.5 million in 2006.

The CEO of Omnicare Joel Geminder more than doubled his compensation in 2008 to $13.7 million which included a $5.1 million cash bonus

This is the annual compensation given to health care CEOs over a five year period ending in 2005.

United Health Group CEO: William W McGuire 5-year: $342 million

Forest Labs CEO: Howard Solomon 5-year: $295 million

Caremark Rx CEO: Edwin M Crawford 5-year: $93.6 million

Abbott Lab CEO: Miles White 5-year: $25.8 million

Aetna CEO: John Rowe 5-year: $57.8 million

Amgen CEO: Kevin Sharer 5-year: $59.5 million

Bectin-Dickinson CEO: Edwin Ludwig 5-year: $18 million

Cardinal Health CEO: James Tobin 5-year: $33.5 million

Cigna CEO: H. Edward Hanway 5-year: $62.8 million

Genzyme CEO: Henri Termeer 5-year: $60.7 million

Humana CEO: Michael McAllister 5-year: $12.9 million

Johnson & Johnson CEO: William Weldon 5-year: $19.7 million

Laboratory Corp America CEO: Thomas MacMahon 5-year: $41.8 million

Eli Lilly CEO: Sidney Taurel 5-year: $37.9 million

McKesson CEO: John Hammergen 5-year: $31.2 million

Medtronic CEO: Arthur Collins 5-year: $39 million

Merck Raymond Gilmartin CEO: 5-year: $49.6 million

PacifiCare Health CEO: Howard Phanstiel 5-year: $8.5 million

Pfizer CEO: Henry McKinnell 5-year: $74 million

Well Choice CEO: Michael Stocker 5-year: $10.7 million

WellPoint CEO: Larry Glasscock 5-year: $46.8 million

Wyeth CEO: Robert Essner 5-year: $28.9 million

According to Jodell (2009), in 2005 Howard Solomon CEO of Forest Labs received $92.1 million, Richard Clark Merck's CEO $37.8 million, Edward Ludwig Becton-Dickinson's $10 million.

Below are the compensation packages of health care executives in 2007 from The AFL/CIO Executive Paywatch Database:

Miles White, CEO, Abbott Labs	$33.3 million
Ronald Williams, CEO, Aetna	$23 million
Daniel Amos, CEO, Aflac	$14.8 million
E. Edward Hanway, CEO, Cigna	$25.8 million
Michael McCallister, CEO, Humana	$10.3 million
William Weldon, CEO, Johnson & Johnson	$31.9 million
David Snow, CEO, Medco Health Solutions	$10.5 million
Richard Clark, CEO, Merck & Co.	$19.8 million
John Hammergren, CEO, McKeeson Corp	$39.9 million
Jeffrey Kindler, CEO, Pfizer	$ 9.5 million
Stephen Helmsley, CEO, UHC	$13.1 million

Massachusetts Blue Cross CEO Cliff Killingsworth received $3.6 million in 2007, including a $1.8 million performance bonus, since 2005 his total compensation has increased 38 percent. In 2008 he received another increase of 26 percent bringing his total compensation increase since 2005, 64 percent as its membership declined and net income fell 49 percent. Also, Killingsworth's Chief Physician executive Dr. John Fallon earned $1.2 million and between 2005 and 2007 his salary has doubled. In March 2010 Killingsworth resigned after receiving $8.6 million which included half of his $4 million in severance pay.

In 2008 Humana stock fell 50 percent, however CEO Michael McCallister received a raise and increases in various perks up 26 percent from 2008 but collected no incentive compensation and in 2010 they will terminate 2,500 employees as enrollment continues to decline.

After years of persuading employees to accept contract concessions and then filing for bankruptcy the Walter Pishkur CEO of Forum Health is retiring but will stay on as a consultant earning pay up to $9,000 a week for seven months earning $288,000. Nurses have accepted a frozen pension plan, elimination of a company match for a retirement savings plan, increases in what they pay for health-care premiums and a wage freeze.

From 2005 to 2008, CareSource more than doubled its total revenues — from $770 million to $1.8 billion becoming America's third largest nonprofit Medicaid HMO and their CEO Pamela Morris saw her compensation more than triple, from $877,000 in 2005 to $2.9 million in 2008.

Dan Loepp, Blue Cross president and CEO, received nearly $1.8 million in pay and bonuses, an 8.5 percent increase from $1,657,555 compensation in 2007 and nearly double his $990,351 in 2006.

CFO Mark Bartlett -- Blue Cross point man on many legislative and financial issues -- received $1,239,512, a 5.8 percent increase over his total compensation of $1,171,194 in 2007. He was paid $975,225 in 2006.

Linda Brady, CEO of Kingsbrook Jewish Medical Center in Brooklyn, N.Y., earned nearly $4 million in total compensation in 2009.

HCA CEO Richard Bracken in Tennessee received a 212 percent increase in 2010, totaling $38 million. Another Tennessee hospital Community Health Systems CEO Wayne Smith earned $21 million, and LifePoint Hospitals CEO William Carpenter earned $8 million.

Outgoing Boston Medical Center CEO Elaine Ullian is pocketing a nearly $3.5 million one-time bonus as she retires, at the same time the hospital she has run for 15 years is embroiled in a bitter lawsuit with the state as her hospital BMC fights for higher reimbursement rates.

Yale-New Haven Hospital CEO Marna Borgstrom made over $2 million in total compensation in 2008.

James Roosevelt, CEO at Tufts Health Care, received more than $1.6 million in 2007, a 110 percent jump over his $785,013 compensation in 2005, and Charlie Baker, President and CEO of Harvard Pilgrim, earned just under $1.4 million in 2007, a 26 percent hike since 2005 (Wu, 2009).

Health care researchers also receive significant compensation. David Silvers, clinical professor of dermatology at Columbia University received over $4 million in 2007. Following Silvers was Zev Rosenwaks of Cornell and Jeffrey Moses of Columbia received over $3 million.

Let's not forget the research professors. In the fall of 2008, for example, it was uncovered that Dr. Charles Nemeroff, Chair of Psychiatry Department at Emory University, made almost $3 million in consulting fees from the same drug companies whose products he was prescribing and evaluating. In November, it was discovered Harvard psychiatrist, Joseph Biederman, had received hundreds of thousands of dollars from Johnson & Johnson, which made medications that treated the same childhood psychiatric illnesses that he was suggesting that doctors use. Some call it a conflict of interest, but its greed.

Top Ten Health Care salaries in 2008

H. Edward Hanway - CIGNA - Total Compensation: $12,236,740.

Angela Braly - WellPoint - Total Compensation: $9,844,212.

Dale Wolf - Coventry Health Care - Total Compensation: $9,047,469.

Michael Neidorff - Centene - Total Compensation: $8,774,483.

James Carlson - AMERIGROUP - Total Compensation: $5,292,546. In 2010 his pay doubled to $10.5 million

Michael McCallister - Humana - Total Compensation: $4,764,309.

Jay Gellert - Health Net - Total Compensation: $4,425,355.

Richard Barasch - Universal American - Total Compensation: $3,503,702.

Stephen Hemsley - UnitedHealth Group - Total Compensation: $3,241,042.

In December 2009 Ron Williams CEO of Aetna announced that while his company made a profit in 2009 it was not high enough, therefore in 2010 Aetna will drop between 600,000 to 650,000 members from its insurance roles. They will do this by raising rates and forcing members off their rolls. Aetna's CEO like most health care CEOs are only concerned with the "Bottom Line" enriching their stockholders and themselves in the process. In November 2009 they terminated 1,250 employees. In 2009 Williams' $18 million compensation package was roughly 1.4 percent of his company's $1.28 billion net income, as reported in the company's 2009 annual report. In 2008 Williams earned a total compensation of $24,300,112. In November 2010 Williams retired and did he get a package. He got $20.7 million which included a $2.8 million cash bonus and he also exercised about $50 million in previously awarded stock options before he packed it in.

In 2009 Stephen Helmsley of UnitedHealth Group won the compensation top prize by taking home $106 million.

In 2010 Humana's CEO compensation was $6.1 million for Michael McCallister, this included nearly $600,000 in other compensation such as personal use of company aircraft, matching charitable contributions, financial planning assistance, club memberships and other benefits. In 2009 he made $6.51 million.

In 2009 for CEO of WellPoint Angela Braly got a 51 percent raise to $13.1 million. Other top WellPoint executives received similar percentage hikes, taking home between $4.5 million and $7.2 million. In 2010 Braly received a 3 percent increase in compensation last year, her total compensation was $13.4 million, this included a 83 percent increase in her bonus.

Horizon Blue Cross Blue Shield of New Jersey gave recently retired CEO William Marino a 59 percent pay boost in 2009, to $8.7 million, and its top 10 executives received an average 61 percent raise, totaling $24.3 million.

In 2010 the CEO of Blue Shield of California, Bruce Bodaken, made $4.6 million and in January 2011 they announced its third major increase in premiums in less than a year.

Appendix F: The Educators

According to Lewin, (2008) in 2007 David Roselle of the University of Delaware received a package of $2.4 million.

In 2007, Michael Johns, Executive VP of Health Affairs at Emory University made $3,753,759 and Arthur Rubenstein Executive VP and Dean of the School of Medicine at the University of Pennsylvania made $3,335,767 (Lewin, 2009).

The University of South Florida President Judy Genshaft received a $75,000 raise in 2011 plus a $500,000 incentive to stay for five years. Her salary for 2011 will be $470,000 plus a one-year performance stipend of $175,000. What's a performance stipend? While Genshaft is among the highest paid public university presidents the faculty at USF are among the lowest paid faculty in the country.

The University of Georgia President got a raise of $50,000 called an increase in deferred compensation. President Michael Adams will make $660,000 in 2012. While the increase is the result of a gift from the university's athletic association, a legal requirement mandates that that money go into the university's general fund while state money pays for the raise. Go figure that one out.

In 2011 Richard McCormick announced he will retire from the presidency of Rutgers University to return to teaching history. His contract states that he will be assured that his salary as a faculty member will be $335,000 because his salary cannot be "less" than the highest paid faculty member in the system.

University coaches also do well. Pete Carroll of USC was the highest paid coach receiving $4.4 million in 2007. In 2009 athletic director Mike Garrett, Carroll's boss took home more than $1 million, and Carroll made $4.1 million; Tim Floyd, the basketball coach, made $1.6 million; and Steve Sarkisian, Carroll's assistant made nearly $1.2 million. USC also paid its basketball coach $1.6 million (Sander, 2010).

The University of California at Berkeley announced 32 percent increase in tuition to more than $10,000 annually (a three-fold increase in the past ten years). The university also announced it will spend millions of dollars to renovate its football stadium and in 2009 they paid their football coach Jeff Ted for $2.8 million while facing a reduction of $150 million in state funding. While their football team gets more in 2010 they are laying off faculty and staff, cutting enrollment, slashing course offerings, degree programs and raising tuition again. They have their priorities straight. Also while the State of California deals with a major fiscal crisis, in 2010 the UC Chancellor Mark Yudof made $591,000 and got $11,500-a-month housing rental from the university. In 2011 while the university system suffers the University of California Regents gave UC Davis Medical Center CEO Ann Madden Rice a raise of nearly $259,000, bringing her compensation to $960,000 a year.

Charlie Weis of Notre Dame was paid $4.2 million in 2008 and then was fired. Bob Stoops of Oklahoma, and Les Miles of UCLA. Nick Saban of Alabama made $3.75 Million in 2008. After they won the national championship title Saban was given a contract in 2009 though 2018 paying him an average of $5.5 million a year. Meanwhile Alabama, in a major financial crisis had its professors take a salary reduction in 2009 of 1.5 percent. So while Saban makes his millions the faculty average about $80,000 annually.

According to Zimbalist (2010) more than 100 college football coaches had annual compensation packages that surpassed $1 million and more than a dozen of them exceed $3 million. At least 42 of the 119 Division I-A coaches earned $1 million or more in 2006 (Upton and Wieberg, 2006) and in 2008 the average pay of major college football coaches was more than $1 million a year. From 2007 to 2009, head football coaches' salaries rose 46 percent to an average of $1.36 million in the Football Bowl Subdivision of Division I. Some coaches earn five to 10 times what university presidents do (Zimbalist, 2010).

A recent report by the NCAA suggests that college sports lose money. Among the 119 schools with top Division I football teams, only 19 had athletic departments that generated a profit in 2006 (Winick, 2008). While the universities lose money there are plenty of affiliated groups that make a lot of money. For example the CEO of the New Orleans-based Sugar Bowl made $645,000 in 2009 and the CEO the Fiesta Bowl did well he made $600,000 plus $120,000 no-interest loan.

School superintendents, a job with the highest turnover rate in America, earn extraordinary compensation when compared to their teachers. In 2009 Philadelphia school superintendent Arlene Ackerman took home $338,000 in salary, plus a $65,000 performance bonus and if she stays through June 2010 a $100,000 retention bonus plus thousands in unused vacation days. Philadelphia has 163,000. She makes more than Joel Klein, her counterpart in the NYC system that contains 1.1 million students.

According to a 2008 survey by the Council for the Great City Schools, the average salary for a superintendent of a school district with more than 200,000 students was $286,000. The top salary was then

$327,500. Superintendents often make more than the governors in their states. For example, Steve Joel, has a contract worth $255,000 as superintendent of the Lincoln School District in Nebraska. That's more than twice the annual salary of Nebraska Gov. David Heineman, who makes $105,000, according to an Education Week news report.

The private for-profit schools top the list for the highest executive compensation. Apollo operates the for-profit University of Phoenix. Its founder and executive board chairman John Sperling's total compensation, excluding stock-option exercises, was $6.4 million in 2009. In 2010 Sperling's stock-option gains will total $38 million. This university claims to have the country's highest enrollment and in reality is the country's largest recipient of federal student aid. In 2008 it received $3.2 billion from the government. It has also received the highest number of federal lawsuits, in 2004 it paid nearly $10 million in enrollment abuse fines and in 2009 it announced it was putting aside $80 million to cover addition enrollment abuses. Abuses include tying recruiter's salaries to meeting enrollment numbers and using pressure tactics to enroll students which includes lies and false claims about classes, professors, transfer credits and financial aid. This problem is pervasive among the for-profit schools where strategy focuses on profits over education. Only 9 percent of students enrolled in Phoenix graduate within 6 years and student debt is the highest of all colleges and universities averaging $25,000 to $35,000 with the highest default rate and Kaplan another for-profit that gets billions from the government has an almost 70 percent dropout rate.

It is very clear the accreditation agencies are asleep at the wheel.

Appendix G: The Charities and the Chosen Ones

In 2006, the Rev. Dr. Daun McKee, CEO and president of Diakon Lutheran Social Ministries, received a package of over $1 million.

Angel Food Ministries, a charity that sells discount groceries in thousands of communities, paid nearly $2.5 million in compensation in 2006 to CEO Wesley Joseph Wingo its church pastor, his wife and two sons (Burke, 2009). In 2009 Wingo was paid $697,037, his son received $265,195 and Wingo's wife was paid $100,480. Under an FBI investigation the ministry closed down in September 2011 leaving the poor poorer.

According to Cline (2005), Bishop Eddie Long, pastor of the New Birth Missionary Church in Georgia accepted more than $3 million in salary and benefits, including a $1.4 million home and a $350,000 automobile from a now-defunct tax-exempt group called Bishop Eddie Long Ministries in 2005. The Washington Blade reported in September that Longs ministry received a $1 million faith-based grant from the U.S. Administration of Children & Families under George W. Bush's administration.

John Hagee the minister of the Corner Stone Church received over $800,000 in salary and over $400,000 in benefits in 2001. He also has a $2.1 million dollar, 7,969- acre ranch with five lodges, a manager's house, a gun locker, a smoke house, a skeet range and three barns (Gross, 2009).

Many in the congregation at Riverside Church in New York City were outraged that their new Pastor Brad Braxton received compensation in 2009 that exceeded $600,000. In June 2009 he resigned.

Other heads of non-profits received extraordinary compensation.

In 2008 Zarin Mehta CEO of the New York Philharmonic topped the list for charity compensation when he made $2,649,540.

Glenn Lowry president of the New York Museum of Modern Art, received $2,447,882 in 2008 and in 2007 he was taken to task for questionable reporting of his salary to the IRS and for his rent-free apartment paid for by the museum.

Reynold Levy the head of the Lincoln Center for the Performing Arts received nearly $2 million in total compensation in 2010.

Donald Johnson head of the Evans Scholars Foundation got $2,049,976 in 2008.

CEO Steven Sanderson, of the Wildlife Conservation Society made over $1.6 million in 2010.

These salaries are especially egregious considering the massive budget cuts from the government they are facing.

Leichman (2010) reports that Charity Navigator examined 3,005 mid-to large-size charities in 2009 and discovered the average salary for a CEO increased with education-related charities seeing the biggest boosts and religious charities seeing the smallest. On average, the salary for an education charity CEO was $272,645 (an increase of 5.9 percent from 2008) while the salary for a religious charity CEO was $90,000 (1 percent more than the year before). CEO pay includes salary, cash bonuses and expense accounts, but not contributions to benefit plans or deferred compensation that was allocated to be paid in later years or housing and other perks.

Appendix H The Long List-Performance Review for You, Not for Me (Incompetents Get Rewarded)

In a 2009 industry survey of hundreds of hedge fund managers and employees, in mostly privately held firms, showed a major disconnect between fund performance and compensation and that bonuses continue to rise despite 45 percent of respondents reporting fund losses. The average compensation of hedge fund employees was nearly $300,000 in 2008. In 2009, 28 percent expect increases of 15 percent or more in overall compensation and 9 percent of respondents expect their compensation to double over 2008 (Hedge Fund Jobs Digest, 2009).

LET'S EXAMINE HOW BANKS REWARD THEIR CEOS.

Citigroup demonstrates little relationship between performance and pay for their executives; shortly before losing nearly $10 billion in the fourth quarter of 2007, it purchased Old Lane Partners, a one year old hedge fund co-founded by Vikram Pandit. Citigroup paid $800 million for Old Lane to lure him to Citigroup, Pandit's share was $165.2

million (NY Times, 2007), for a total of $216 million. Citigroup then gave their departing CEO Charles Prince a $40 million payout from stock awards, a bonus and other benefits to leave, and then hired Pandit. In January, 2008 Pandit was awarded a "sign-on grant" worth over $48 million. Citigroup then approved a $1.95 million cash bonus, and $3.09 million in stock awards under the company's Capital Accumulation Program (CAP). Pandit's executive team also did well. $1.95 million in retention equity awards were given to Win Bischoff, who was named chairman of the company in December, 2007. His CFO, Gary Crittenden, received a cash bonus of $2.85 million, $4.59 million in stock awards under CAP, and $5.35 million in retention equity awards. His Global Wealth Management CEO, Sallie Krawcheck, received a $2.9 million bonus, bringing her pay to $12.5 million. In addition, $8.3 million in total awards were given to Citigroups Vice Chairman Lewis Kaden; and $10.25 million in total awards for Vice Chairman, Stephen Volk (NY Times, 2008). His Global Banking CEO, Michael Klein, received incentive and retention awards of $19.3 million. However, in July 2008 he resigned and in exchange for a non-compete agreement he will received a severance package of $34.3 million in cash and previously awarded shares worth $8.3 million. The non-compete agreement ends October, 2009. In 2011 the four top executives at Citi received $42.2 million in compensation and Pandit received more than $20 million "the good old days are back."

Retired CEOs from Citi are well cared for long into their retirement. Retired CEOs Prince, Klein and Weil are provided with offices and secretaries. Prince who retired in November, 2007, receives annual perks worth about $1.5 million a year, including an office, assistant, car and driver and any resulting income taxes. Those benefits last for five years or until he gets another full-time job (Keuon, 2009). Another retired CEO Sandy Weil, who retired in 2006, also received an office and secretary under his consulting agreement; he also receives a $1 million-a-year retirement pension, consulting fees of $3,846 a day for up to 45 days a year, a car and driver, private security, financial- planning fees and medical and dental coverage (Keuon, 2009). In December, 2008 amid the extraordinary looses, the New York Post, reported he used a Citigroup jet to take a family vacation to Mexico.

Another retired Citi CEO John Reed received a $5 million parting bonus in February 2000 and a $2 million annual "retirement benefit," he also received financal-planning services for up to five years, a car and driver, an office and secretarial support "for as long as you deem useful," according to Keuon, (2009).

Since January 2008, Citigroup has terminated 6,000 employees bringing total job loss since 2007, so far to 13,000. In response to Citigroup's loss of $20 billion, massive job losses and a 47 percent drop in shares Pandit has agreed to pay for his personal use of the bank's corporate jet (Economic Times, 2008).

On June 12, 2008, Citigroup announced the closing of Old Lane Partners and the termination of some of the 130 positions. Pandit is keeping the $165 million Citi paid him for his company (Dash, 2008a). In the second quarter, 2008, Pandit reported Citi lost another $2.8 billion. In September, he was still shaking up his executive staffing and Sallie Krawcheck was canned. In 2008 Citi received $45 billion in bailout money from the federal government in 2008. In 2009 the company terminated over 100,000 employees and in January 2010, announced a loss of $7.58 billion during the final three months of 2009. Despite these losses and bailout money Vice Chairman Edward Kelly got $8 million in 2009, including a **BONUS**. Also in 2009 Pandit paid investment- banking chief John Havens $9.5 million, Latin America regional chief Manuel Medina-Mora $9 million, CFO John Gerspach $5 million and the chief for Central and Eastern Europe Alberto Verme $7.43 million. In total Citigroup terminated 73,000 employees. In January

2011 Citigroup granted more than 18 million stock options to its top 15 senior executives as its top four executives received total compensation of $42.2 million. And in Dec. 2011, it was disclosed that Pandit will recieve a "retention bonus" of over $40 million.

There are more banks and their CEOs.

Kerry Killinger received more than $65 million in compensation from 2005 to 2008 as CEO of Washington Mutual (WaMu) and he had the distinction of residing over the largest bank failure in history. The FDIC is toying with the idea of suing him but Killinger's defendant says the government cannot sue for stupidity. The result was a "mortgage time bomb" that blew up in the face of families who couldn't pay their loans, shareholders of WaMu and the American economy. As it ticked, from 2003 to 2007, CEO Killinger was paid between $11 million and $20 million each year in cash, stock and stock options. Killinger was fired and paid $25 million, including $15 million in severance pay.

Employees and others protested outside Wells Fargo's offices in the SF Financial District in March, 2009. Wells Fargo received a $25 billion bailout from the federal government. Its CEO John Stumpf was paid $9 million in 2008 a 10 percent increase as its income dropped to $2.84 billion from $8.06 billion in 2007. His bank's tellers make a median wage of $10.20 per hour. These protests were against Stumpf and his executives in 33 states across America. Showing no shame, in January 2009, Stumpf announced that Fargo's four top executives will receive performance-based stock awards worth a combined $25 million. The company quickly repaid the $25 billion to the federal government so that it could avoid government controls on executive pay. In 2009 Fargo terminated hundreds of employees and in 2010 to reduce $5 billion in expenses it incurred with the purchase of Wachovia bank it terminated 2,800 employees and another 1,000 over the year. In 2009

Stumpf more than doubled his compensation to $21.3 million which included a $13 million bonus and his top five executives averaged more than $11 million each. In 2010 Stumpf received $17.6 million in total compensation that included a $1.6 million cash bonus. He'll show those whining protesters who want more than $10.20 an hour. Other executives also did well; when CFO Howard Atkins retires in August 2011 he will receive over $10 million as a going away present. In February 2011 Stumpf was awarded 24,432 restricted-share rights worth $766,676, this came on top of the 400,583 performance shares he received in June 2010, those shares were worth about $11 million. In March 2011 Stumpf announced that 1,900 employees would be terminated. Stumpf also sits on the board of Target and in 2010 made $332,110.

PrivateBancorp CEO Larry Richman saw his total compensation for 2010 triple to $2.68 million from $883,991. Richman's bank has not been able to repay the money it borrowed under the U.S. Treasury Department's Troubled Asset Relief Program, and had a net loss of $18.6 million, or 30 cents a share, for the fourth quarter 2009 and lost $12.1 million for the year compared to a net loss of $42.5 million, or $95 a share, in 2009.

The CEO of U.S. Bancorp Richard Davis received a pay package valued at $6.8 million in 2008, up 15 percent from 2007 while its stock dropped 72 percent in 2008. In 2010 Davis was paid $16.1 million a 143 percent increase in compensation and in January 2011 Davis terminated 64 workers in its Milwaukee office.

In 2007 Morgan Stanley, America's second largest securities firm, reported a decline in earnings of 60 percent and a $9.4 billion writedown in debt securities holdings for the fourth quarter. The same time, it announced an 18 percent rise in compensation packages to $16.6 billion. Its CEO John Mack will forgo his bonus in 2008, however, his annual compensation is $7.46 million and his stock ownership is more than $200 million.

In 2010 Goldman Sachs earnings dropped 38 percent but CEO Lloyd Blankfein's compensation almost doubled to $19 million.

Bear Stearns posted its first-ever quarterly loss and reduced earnings estimates by nearly $2 billion in 2007. In 2008, Bear Sterns was saved from bankruptcy, however, its CEO was paid $38 million in cash in 2007. In March, 2008 Bear Sterns collapsed and was purchased by JP Morgan. In 2007, CEO of Morgan Stanley, John Mack received compensation of $800,000, stock awards of $40.2 million, and $399,153 of other compensation (including $355,000 for personal use of the corporate jet). This was awarded in a year when the investment bank's profit plunged 57 percent. Mack did not receive a bonus in 2007 because his company Morgan Stanley lost $9.4 billion. In 2008 they terminated 20 percent of their employees in their Institutional Securities Group its largest business group.

UBS reported in April, 2009 that former CEO Marcel Rohner will remain on the payroll for one year after leaving in February 2009. UBS expects to terminate 9,000 jobs in 2009.

SunTrust CEO James Wells received 62 Percent Pay Increase in 2008 to $5.45 million as profit fell by more than half (Levy, 2009).

After terminating hundreds of employees and receiving a government bailout Henry Meyer CEO of KeyCorp will receive a compensation increase of $2.3 million in 2009.

First Merit received a $125 million federal bailout in January 2009 and CEO Paul Greig received a 22 percent increase in compensation. His executives received between 12 and 25 percent compensation increases, while his employees received between 0 and 1 percent increases and had their 401(k) matching contributions stopped after January 2009.

Albert Lord, CEO of Sallie Mae, received $4.7 million in total compensation in 2008, a 300 percent increase over 2007, while his company lost $213 million.

When banks lose billions, and terminate thousands, their CEOs take token compensation decreases. Wachovia Corp. CEO Ken Thompson's compensation fell 14 percent to $15.65 million, as the bank lost over $6 billion and terminated 4,000 employees.

After losing 28 percent of its stock value in 2007 Malon Wilkins, CEO of American Capital, earned $21.9 million in 2008 including $6.2 million in salary, bonus and incentive pay. Yes a bonus.

In 2009 T Rowe Price's assets fell and they terminated hundreds of employees but their top executives did well. Brian Rogers CIO received total compensation of $6.88 million in 2010, Edward Bernard, president, received $7 million, and James Kennedy CEO received $7.14 million.

LET'S LOOK AT SOME OTHERS.

From 2008 through 2010 U.S. Steel has terminated over 5,000 employees and in 2009 the company lost $1.4 billion and in 2010 it lost another $482 million and CEO John Surma got a $8.3 million, raise. Why? "Because of the steel manufacturer's improving business conditions" (Shore, 2011). What are improved conditions? The company lost less money. Suma got a total compensation package of $12.1 million in 2010 that paid him in a little more than 2 hours of what a pensioner made in an entire year. Pensioners make less than $1,000 a month on which 9,000 Hamilton retirees and widows survive (Srakococ, 2011).

According to Edwards (2009c) Howard Pien accomplished the following feats as CEO of Medarex in 2008:

- Revenues declined from $56.2 million to $52.3 million.

- Its net loss expanded from $27 million to $38.5 million.

- The company has not made a profit in the last five years. The deficit on its balance sheet grown to more than $1 billion.

- Its big melanoma cancer product, ipilimumab, a joint venture with Bristol-Myers Squibb, was rejected by the FDA.

- The stock started the year over $10, it ended at under $6.

- 2009's revenues will be below analysts estimates

So what did Pien get? A big reward. He was rewarded with a 91 percent compensation increase to $5.1 million and his executives obtained 10 percent raises.

In October 2009 the Supreme Court decided that Family Dollar Stores had to pay $35 million to 1,400 store managers who were denied overtime pay and in 2010 its CEO Howard Levine received a 10 percent compensation increase to $6.8 million which included a $1.6 million bonus.

Steelcase has been terminating employees and closing factories in America for a decade. In 2011 another 700 employees were terminated. Meanwhile CEO Jim Hackett received total compensation in 2010 of $2.2 million.

AL "Tom" Giannopoulos the CEO of Micros Systems has capped all salary increases at 4 percent. But Giannopoulos got a $5 million raise to $7.8 million for the fiscal year ending June 30, 2010, compared with $2.8 million for the previous fiscal year.

Abbott labs CEO Miles White earned close to $22 million in 2009 including a $3.9 million bonus and in 2010 he terminated 3,000 employees. In 2010 profits fell 19.48 percent and its stock fell 8.3 percent but White's compensation rose to $25.5 million

In 2008 Best Buy announced terminations of 53 employees at its headquarters while CEO Bradbury Anderson received a $1.2 million bonus. Also in 2008 its CIO Robert received $9.88 million in compensation.

Nestle CEO Paul Bulke made over $10 million in total compensation in 2010 as he closed plants in American and terminated workers.

In October 2010 Aon announced plans to terminate up to 1,800 employees over a three year period and they gave their CEO Gregory Case total compensation of $20,783,301

Ashland CEO Jim O'Brien's total compensation increased 22 percent in 2009 to $5.9 million, according to the company's recent proxy statement. O'Brien's company lost $119 million in the first quarter of 2009 and he terminated 9 percent of his employees or 1,300, he also froze employee wages, forced employees to take a two-week furlough, took away tuition assistance and slashed other benefits and in December 2010 that got an 85 percent raise in compensation. The chemical company blamed the loss in the first quarter on a severance charge, write-down and the acquisition of Hercules Inc. It said the work force cuts amount to about 9 percent of its work force and will be accomplished by the end of fiscal 2010.

Sales at Coach declined 2 percent in 2008 but its CEO Lew Frankfort more than doubled his compensation to $11.3.

In 2009 Toro terminated over 235 employees and CEO Michael Hoffman took a 10 percent pay cut to $2.1 million.

Union Pacific CEO Jim Young did not take a token decrease he received a compensation increase in 2008 of 20 percent, to nearly $12 million as he furloughed 3,150 employees.

In 2009 Emerson Electric terminated 14,000 employees and its CEO David Farr earned almost $6.9 million for the fiscal year that ended in September almost a 1 percent compensation increase.

CEO of Regis Corporation, Paul Finkelstein, received an 89 percent raise in 2009. He received $7.6 million in total compensation up from the $4 million he received in 2008, while his company reported a decline in revenue in fiscal 2009 from $2.48 billion to $2.43 billion. The company's net income also dropped to a loss of $124 million. In addition from July 1, 2008, to June 30, 2009, his company's stock dropped from $26.11 per share to $17.41 per share, a decline of 33.3 percent. And he gets an 89 percent raise?

LPL Investment Holdings lost $104 million in 2010 but CEO Mark Casady received $113.7 million total compensation.

Steve Malcolm, CEO of Williams Cos. Inc., received a 10 percent increase as its stock dropped 60 percent in 2008. His $8,939,581 compensation included a $2 million cash award. He then froze 2009 salaries for all of his officers.

CEO of International Paper John Farasci announced in Oct. 23, 2009, the closure of three plants and the termination of 1,600 employees. In December 2009 he terminated 270 employees in Albany, Oregon, and 230 employees in Pineville, Louisiana, without jobs. In the spring of 2010 he will close a mill in Franklin, Virginia, which will result in 1,100 terminations. In 2008 Farasci's compensation totaled

$13.03 million and in his five years as CEO he received $42.43 million. As he closes plants and destroys towns he gets rich. How? By offshoring jobs and building plants in Brazil and of course China. What did Faraci get in 2010? A 46.4 percent increase in total compensation to $17.85 million up from $12.19 million in 2009.

Mortimer Zuckerman CEO of Boston Properties, received total compensation of $22 million in 2010 as his company's net income was down 31 percent.

Michael Jeffries of Abercrombie & Fitch saw his pay climb 39 percent in 2008 to $72 million, even though the retailer's stock fell 72 percent and he terminated employees.

Estee Lauder CEO Fabrizio Freda received total compensation valued at $14.4 million in 2009 as second-quarter profit fell 30 percent and he terminated 2,000 employees.

The stock of Sirus XM dropped from $2 a share in 2008 to 46 cents in June 2009 and the company needed an infusion of $530 million to avoid bankruptcy but CEO Mel Karmazin got a contract renewal through 2010 and a pay increase of $250,000 a year and 120,000 options exercisable at 43 cents a share.

Foundation Coal Holdings nearly doubled CEO James F. Roberts' total compensation - to $3.8 million - in a year when the company's profits plummeted 65 percent and the stock lost three-quarters of its value.

Gregory Brown, co-CEO of Motorola, earned $21.6 million in 2008, his partner Sanjay Jha earned $104.4 million. In December, 2008 Motorola announced it would cancel most employees' raises, freeze its U.S. pension plan, suspend matching 401(k) contributions, and terminate 7,000 employees. In August 2011 Jha sold Motorola

Inc.'s ailing cellphone division to Google for $12.5 billion. Jha now works for Google and if he leaves within the next two years he could gain more than $62 million. Meanwhile it is estimated that 40 percent of Motorola's 16,000 employee workforce will be terminated. Jha is hoping he's one of them.

WHAT HAPPENS WHEN A COMPANY'S STOCK IS WORTHLESS?

The CEO merely shifts compensation from stocks to cash. This is the case with FairPoint Communications. CEO Eugene Johnson's cash based salary was increased 30 percent to $600,000. FairPoint's six other executives got raises averaging nearly 23 percent. The company's stock value has plummeted, falling from roughly $10 a share to just over $1 in April, 32009 and its board suspended quarterly dividend payments to investors, to conserve cash (Turkel, 2009).

Charter Communications, awarded its CEO, Neil Smit, a raise and gave him a new employment agreement through June 30, 2010. It calls for the company to boost Smit's base pay to $1.5 million from $1.2 million and makes him eligible for a $2.7 million bonus this year. Smit also gets a $2 million signing bonus. The agreement also calls for Smit's 2007 and 2008 incentive awards to be accelerated and to vest on June 30, 2010. Criteria for his target bonus may include revenue, and new product growth, but will not include the company's stock price, which had sunk below 80 cents a share in mid-morning trading on September 29, 2008 (Tomich, 2008). In 2008 Charter lost $2.45 billion and in June 2009 its stock was selling at $0.02, yes that's 2 cents.

Eugene Isenberg CEO of Nabors Industries received $59.8 million in 2008 a 73 percent raise 2008 as its shareholders saw losses for the third straight year. In 2008 returns fell more than 56 percent. Isenberg realizing Nabors stocks are not good got almost all of his compensation in cash.

Tofutti Brands earned $506,000 on sales of $18.6 million in fiscal year 2010while it's CEO David Mintz and CFO Steven Kass received a combined $1,086,000, more than twice the company's earnings. It is clear there is an inverse relationship between compensation and the company's performance.

Viacom's Chairman Sumner Redstone was awarded compensation valued at $12.1 million, in 2008 up from $8.3 million in 2007, and CEO Philippe Dauman earned $23 million, up nearly $3 million, while its stock lost half its value, (Flint, 2009). In December 2008 Dauman terminated 850 employees and in 2010 his compensation more than doubled from 2009. In 2010 Dauman was the highest paid CEO in the universe. His total compensation has more than tripled from $25.8 million in 2007 to $84.3 million in 2010.

ProLogis reported a compensation increase of 171 percent for CEO Walter Rakowich and 137.9 percent for outgoing CEO Jeffrey Schwartz as investors saw their holdings decline 78.1 percent in 2008.

Kforce's CEO David Dunkel received a 47 percent increase in compensation in 2008 to $7.2 million as its stock dropped 21 percent.

Omnicare CEO Joel Gemunder's pay doubled to $13.7 million in 2008 and in July 2009 he announced pay cuts up to 5 percent and layoffs.

Leucadia National lost $2,535,425,000 in 2008 and CEO Ian Cumming took a 5 percent cut in compensation.

Donald Felsinger, CEO of Sempra received a 6 percent pay reduction as his company's profit dropped more than 20 percent in 2007.

Amylin CEO Daniel Bradbury's total compensation increased 11 percent to $4.5 million in 2008 while the company lost 50 percent more in 2008 than it did in 2007. Amylin has not made a profit in 5 years.

David Lesar CEO of Halliburton Co., received a 4.4 percent compensation increase while his company posted earnings of $1.54 billion in 2008, down from $3.5 billion in 2007. The company also had to pay $559 million to settle corruption charges in 2008.

Real estate investment trust Kimco Realty Corp. gave its CEO Milton Cooper a 15 percent increase in compensation in 2007 as its shares fell 19 percent.

The CEO of the New York Times, Janet Robinson, received over a 100 percent pay increase in 2008, a $5.58 million pay package. In a financial crisis, the Times had to sell 21 of the 52 floors in their midtown Manhattan headquarters for $225 million, and suspended its dividend and secure a $250 million infusion from Mexican billionaire Carlos Slim Robertson. At the same time Robinson is seeking major wage concessions from Boston Globe employees and is threatening to close it down and is forcing all employees to take a 5 percent wage cut. On Oct. 21, 2009, the Times announced it would offer voluntary retirement (terminations) to 100 employees in its newsroom and if 100 did not volunteer then involuntary terminations would result. In 2010 as its stock dropped 21 percent Robinson's compensation dropped 8 percent from $4.86 million to $4.48 million but her bonus and salary increased. Also Chairman Arthur Sulzberger Jr. made $4.8 million in 2010.

CEO Keith Jackson of ON Semiconductor had his compensation increase 58 percent in 2008 as his company lost $398 million and he announced plans to close a plant terminating 350 jobs in 2010, and he is calling for a cut in his shift workers pay of 4.8 percent, and the elimination of their 401(k) matching funds, life insurance and bonuses.

In 2007 Black & Decker Corp. CEO Nolan D. Archibald earned a 7 percent increase though the company's stock price fell 13 percent (Smith, 2008a). In 2008 he earned $13.7 million in total compensation.

Stanley Black & Decker's CEO John Lundgren got a 253 percent pay increase to $32.6 million in 2010 after he announced plans to terminate 4,000 of its 38,000 employees.

Swiss drugmaker Roche saw sales and net income decline-and its stock drop by about one-third-in 2008, while CEO Severin Schwan got a pay boost of almost 50 percent (Staton, 2009).

Cardinal Health Inc. doubled CEO R. Kerry Clark's compensation in 2008 to $9.7 million. At the end of the fiscal year, June 2008, Cardinal Health's earnings fell to $1.31 billion, or $3.60 per share, compared with $1.93 billion, or $4.77 per share a year earlier. Cardinal Health shares fell 27 percent (Lee, 2008).

The Chairman of Donald R. Horton and his CEO Donald J. Tomnitz received a hefty raise of 56 percent in compensation in fiscal year 2009 as the company had a net loss of $5545.3 million and a revenue drop of 44 percent or $1 billion. The chairman is D.R. Horton. It's good to be the chairman of your own company.

Ronald A. Rittenmeyer CEO of Electronic Data Systems received a 10 percent salary increase bringing his compensation to nearly $14 million for 2007, even though its stock price fell by one-fourth.

In 2010 Constellation Brands lost its status as the world's biggest winemaker and CEO Robert Sands got a 25 percent raise in fiscal 2011. Sands' total compensation was valued at $8.43 million.

Compensation for Marijn Dekkers, the CEO of Thermo Fisher Scientific, went from $3.3 million in 2007 to $18.7 million in 2008 as shares fell 38 percent. In the spring of 2009, Thermo Fisher Scientific laid off 12 employees and forced employees to take voluntary layoffs in two-week increments until sales improved. In September 2010 the U.S. Department of Labor awarded $573,416 to Iowa Workforce Development through the National Emergency Grant program to help provide employment-related services to workers affected by layoffs at Thermo Fisher Scientific in Dubuque. Meanwhile Marc Casper who took over in October made $32.2 million in 2009. This is the way CEOs shake down the government to provide training that the company once provided. They fire the obsolete employees and get the feds to pay for necessary training that will benefit the company.

Fair Isaac terminated several hundred employees in 2009 but its CEO Mark Greene received $1,032,596 for the year ended Sept. 30, 2009. He got a salary of $625,000, non-equity income awards of $160,500, other compensation of: $22,738, value realized on vesting shares of $224,358. In addition, he received 401(k) matches, family and spousal travel and tax gross-ups, $1,208 for his membership at the Minneapolis Club. The company also booked expenses of $856,400 and $620,836, respectively, for stock and stock options awards authorized but not yet received by Greene. Fair Isaac's total return to their shareholders was minus 6.27 percent in 2009.

As profits dropped, JC Penney CEO Myron Ullman got a 48 percent raise in 2008 with compensation valued at $14.9 million. In February, 2009 its fourth-quarter profit dropped 51 percent. After failing to get the top position at Apple in June 2011, Ron Johnson replaced Ullman and was given $50 million in restricted stock to become CEO with a bonus of 125 percent of his annual salary of $1.5 million if he meets certain targets. While at Apple his total compensation was approximately $200 million.

Limited Brands CEO Leslie Wexner received a 32 percent increase in 2008 as its stock fell 59 percent and net income fell 69 percent. In 2009 he terminated 400 employees and in 2010 his compensation nearly doubled to $20.1 million, up from $10.4 million in 2009, because of a hefty increase in stock and option awards and a big bonus.

At Crown Holdings, sales rose 7.9 percent in 2007 to $7.7 billion, net income was up 71 percent and CEO John W. Conway's pay rose more than 300 percent.

LSI Corp. awarded Chief Executive Abhijit Talwalkar's compensation was valued at $6.2 million in 2008, an 82 percent increase from 2007 as its shares dropped 35 percent and its loss for the year was $622.3 million.

MetLife reported in January 2011 a fourth-quarter profit decline of 74 percent. Its net income fell to $82 million, or 5 cents a share, from $320 million, or 35 cents, a year earlier and they rewarded their CEO Robert Henrikson with a 39 percent compensation increase to $13.9 million in 2010. Terminations of employees will follow.

Caterpillar CEO James W. Owens received 2008 compensation valued at $14.6 million, a 1 percent compensation reduction from 2007. In April 2009, the company reported a first-quarter loss of $112. As of April 2009, 20,000 employees have been terminated, and between 2005 and 2010 its overseas workforce grew nearly 39 percent or 15,900 employees (Wassel, 2011). In 2010 Owens was replaced by Doug Oberhelman and they quadrupled his total compensation to $10.4 million. The retiring Owens' compensation more than tripled in 2010 to $22.5 million, mostly because Caterpillar's board gave him a stock grant worth $16 million to thank him for his leadership. In 2011 Oberhelman was invited to give the commencement address at Millikin University. One wonders how he will enlighten these graduates. In 2011 as profits increased 44 percent they were still terminating American employees.

The CEO of General Dynamics, Nicholas Chabraja. received a 15 percent increase in pay and compensation to $17.96 million during 2008, which included a $1 million bonus. In March, 2009 General Dynamics recently lowered its sales forecast, announced 1,200 terminations, and trimmed its earnings forecast for 2009. The company's share price has also plunged in the past year, dropping roughly 55 percent. He will step down in 2009 and under the retirement agreement outlined by the proxy statement Chabraja will receive roughly $24.5 million from the vesting of stock options and other benefits when he leaves. His company pension plans are also worth $24 million (Manning, 2009).

Executive pay at King Pharmaceuticals rose 12.3 percent in 2008 even though the company's stock — with which pay is supposed to be aligned — stayed flat. King pharmaceutical's CEO Brian Markison received an 8.9 percent compensation increase in 2008 as its revenues dropped 26 percent and the company posted a net loss of $333 million

Dell computer CEO Michael Dell's compensation package rose 5.7 percent in fiscal 2009 as the company's profit fell 63 percent. "Its good to be the founder." CEO Dell also received $1.1 million for personal security.

Ford Motor Co. CEO Alan Mulally, as well as several top executives, received bonuses and stock options in 2007 while the company lost $2.72 billion. Mulally's total compensation in 2007 was over $21 million which included bonus awards of $7 million. Ford's other executives also received bonuses: Don Leclair, CFO, obtained a $3 million bonus;

Mark Fields, VP, a $2.8 bonus; and VP's Lewis Booth and Mike Bannister each received a bonus of $2.25 million. In addition to the 2007 losses, in 2006 Ford lost $12.61 billion. Since 2005, 10,800 white-collar employees have been terminated and another 15 percent of salaried work force costs cuts have been announced in June, 2008 (NY Times, 2008). The company has also suspended tuition and scholarship programs and capped employee life insurance at $25,000. In November 2008 Ford announced an additional 2,600 jobs would be terminated. After losing more than $30 billion from 2006 to 2008 how does Mulally plan to return his company to profitability? By following the *Modus operandi* of Chainsaw Al and Neutron Jack and many others; he terminates employees. Mulally has slashed the North American workforce by 43 percent to 70,000 and closed 14 assembly and parts plants. So what did Mulally get in 2010 for the nard work of job cutting? A 48 percent increase in compensation from 2009 to $26.52 million. But wait that's not all. In March 2011 the board of directors awarded Mulally $56 million (before taxes) in Ford shares. Meanwhile Mulally got the AWU to agree to pay junior union employees half of what senior employees get, less than $15 per hour.

General Motors Corp. CEO Rick Wagoner received a 42 percent increase in compensation in 2007, to $6.6 million and added $4 million to his retirement plan, while his company lost $38.7 billion. GM President Fritz Henderson received a 44 percent raise, and Vice Chairman Bob Lutz a 36 percent raise in compensation for 2008. In 2007 Wagoner received a 64 percent increase in overall compensation at the same time the company lost $38.7 billion (Strieker, 2008). GM's stock is now the lowest it's been in 50 years. It once sold half of all cars in the US, now it sells 20 percent (Lowenstein, 2008). In addition, in July, 2008 GM announced the elimination of the dividends on common stock, all executive bonuses, and with the apparent approval of the United Auto Workers (UAW) union, health care coverage for salaried retirees over the age of 65. In addition, GM plans to launch a new wave of buyouts among its 32,000 salaried employees while freezing their salaries for the remainder of 2008 and 2009. Since 2000 GM has terminated 13,000 white-collar jobs and 40,000 union jobs (NY Times, 2008 a). In July, 2008 another 1,760 workers lost their jobs as GM closed two truck plants (Vlasic, 2008). In the second quarter of 2008 GM reported a loss of $15.5 billion this loss includes a $3.3 billion buyout of 19,000 hourly workers. Since 2000, 66,000 hourly employees have taken buyouts. Despite losing $30.9 billion in 2008 Wagoner made over $14.9 million, $3 million in cash and $11.9 million in stock and options that plummeted to $682,000 in value as of March, 2009. Since 2006 Wagoner's company has lost $82 billion. However, 8,000 white-collar employees get free GM cars and free gas estimated to cost $12 million annually.

In March 2009 President Obama asked Wagoner to submit a plan for GM's survival. He rejected the plan and asked Wagoner to resign. Wagoner expects to take $23 million as he leaves. The federal government appointed Fritz Henderson CEO and in December 2009 he was replaced by Edward Whitacre. You remember Ed: he spent 44 years at AT&T and retired as CEO in June 2007 (See his package below). Whitacre resigned as GM's CEO on Sept. 1, 2010, and Daniel Akerson took over. In October, a month after his resignation Whitacre was given shares worth $883,000. His total pay package for eight months' work as CEO was $6.4 million. Akerson's pay package was $9 million. In October 2010, 61 percent of GM wass still owned by the government and they allow this to happen. But it gets worse. In March 2011 GM announced it will give out $400 million in bonuses to employees while they still owe the government $27 billion of the $50 billion they borrowed to stay in business. While giving out bonuses in March 2011 they announced the temporary layoff of 3,900 employees.

Whitacre's compensation at AT&T for 2006 totaled $61 million, $17 million in 2005, and about $14 million in 2004.

In retirement from AT&T he is entitled to receive for life:

- Automobile benefits (estimated at $24,000 annually)

- Access to AT&T's corporate aircraft, up to 10 hours of usage per month (estimated incremental monthly cost of $20,000)

- Use of AT&T office facilities and support staff

- Home security (estimated at $6,500 annually)

- Payment of applicable taxes resulting from these benefits, except for use of the aircraft (estimated at $19,000 annually)

In addition, Whitacre has a three year consulting contract with AT&T, for which he will be paid about $1 million annually, and receive:

- Club memberships (estimated at $25,000 annually) and

- Payment of applicable taxes resulting from these benefits (estimated at $15,600 annually)

Whitacre's retirement package totaled $158 million. In 2008 AT&T terminated 12,000 employees and in 2010 they were still terminating employees 152 in October and 41 in December. It appears Obama's ideas about CEO greed have a very high threshold. In January 2009 it was discovered that GM's Board Director Stephen Girsky would receive compensation worth $900,000 per year plus expenses to act as Whitacre's special adviser. Why? Because Whitacre needs help. He has zero experience in the auto industry. In 2010 Whitacre will get a $9 million pay package. He also got another special advisor he rehired ex CEO Fritz Henderson as a $60,000-a-month consultant. But nine months after his ouster from GM, Henderson got recycled. He showed up at Sunoco. Sunoco's chairman said Henderson was "gifted."

In December, 2008 GM received a $15 billion bailout and Chrysler, $3 billion, from the federal government. In December, Chrysler closed all of its plants and GM announced that over the next year 16,000 employees would be terminated. In contrast Toyota, in the United States, experienced an equally significant decline in sales. However, their actions were very different from their American counterparts. In February 2009, they announced no layoffs but a voluntary exit program where they will pay employees who leave 10 weeks of pay plus two weeks of pay for every year employed by Toyota along with a $20,000 bonus. In addition, their executives will take between 20 to 25 percent reduction in total compensation.

In August 2007 Cerberus Capital purchased an 80.1 percent share of Chrysler taking the automaker private. No one knows the compensation of Bob Nardelli, Chrysler's CEO. However, occasionally some information is leaked. Documents obtained by Walsh and Higgin (2008) show that at least six Chrysler executives were to receive bonuses of more than $1 million apiece to stay through 2010. At the same time Nardelli terminated 1,000 salaried employees in September 2008 and 4,333 in October. He calls these terminations "voluntary retirements." August 2009 is the two-year anniversary mark of when private equity firm Cerberus Capital Management bought an 80.1 percent stake in Chrysler. Since early 2007, Chrysler will have cut 32,000 jobs (Bunkley and Vlasic,2008). In November Chrysler, along with GM and Ford asked the government for a bailout.

In November 2008, the big three automobile CEOs, Nardelli, Rick Wagoner and Ford CEO Alan Mulally, went to Washington and appeared in front of Congress to plead for a bailout. They promised Washington they would take only $1 in salary in 2008. However,

Mulally's total compensation over the past two years amounted to some $50 million. Since 2005, the big three auto makers have eliminated over 100,000 factory jobs (Bunkley and Vlasic, 2008).

They were publicly scolded for flying to the hearing to plead for money in their private corporate jets.

In April 2009, Chrysler filed for bankruptcy. Under the plan pushed by the government, Chrysler emerged from bankruptcy in June 2009 with a union retiree trust owning 55 percent, Fiat owning a 20 percent share that could eventually grow to 35 percent and the United States and Canadian governments holding minority stakes. GM also filed for bankruptcy and in June 2008 announced termination of about 4,000 salaried employees by October 2009 and 21,000 hourly employees. In August, the 53-year-old former CEO Wagoner will begin receiving his so-called pension, an annual salary of $74,030 for life and annual benefits of $1.6 million for five years, plus life insurance valued at $2.6 million. A nice reward for leading his company to the brink. In December 2010 GM new CEO Dan Akerson cannot pay back the feds for the bailout but he told members of the Economic Club of Washington that salary limits tied to the bailout make it difficult to attract and keep the right people. He wants more. These guys have no shame.

Does this list ever end?

Genzyme a biotech company lost $16.8 million in 2006, however, CEO Henri Termeer earned a 5 percent increase in 2007, bringing his total compensation to $14.6 million. This included a cash bonus of $2.1 million for the high performance levels he met for himself and the company. In 2010 Genzyme announced that 1,000 employees would be terminated.

The board of cash-strapped Grady Memorial Hospital fired CEO Otis Story after less than a year on the job. Mr. Story hired an attorney and demanded $2 million in severance pay.

CEO of CPI Corp. Renato Cataldo earned a 71 percent raise in 2010 as his company's sales and profit fell. He earned $921,068 with a salary unchanged at $475,000, and $316,000 in stock. Even though Cataldo failed to meet a bonus plan's earnings target he got a bonus anyway, a $105,000 bonus.

Alltel Corporation's CEO, Scott T. Ford received compensation of more than $141.8 million in 2007, including $107.7 million for taking the wireless company private. His package included a payment of $25.2 million for Ford's "change in control agreement" related to Alltel's $24.7 billion buyout by TPG Capital and GS Capital Partners and $30.8 million to cover Ford's income tax liability, and a $51.6 million lump sum payment of his accrued retirement benefits. Ford's base salary was $1.2 million, and he received $7.5 million in non-equity incentive plan compensation, among other payments. Ford also had stock and option awards that had an estimated value of $24.4 million. The cost of going private showed up in Alltel's fourth-quarter earnings as the company lost $525 million, attributed mainly to $619 million in takeover costs.

Henry Silverman, CEO of Cendant Corp., earned $61 million in 2007 by exercising stock options, even though his company's stock declined significantly.

James Stewart CEO of BJ Services received $34.6 million 2008, most of it from cashing out $30 million in stock options. Shareholders have not done so well. Its stock has lagged behind both its peers and the broader market significantly over the past five years.

BioMed's net income decreased from approximately $58.7 million to $38.8 million from 2009 to 2010 while its CEO's compensation rose from $4.07 million in 2009 to $5.03 million in 2010.

Curt Culver CEO of MGIC Investment got a 92 percent pay increase to $4.4 million even though his company lost $364 million in 2010.

Jeffrey Joerres CEO of Manpower, lost more than $263 million in 2010 and got a 63 percent raise to $8.7 million.

Royal & SunAlliance sold a division and terminated 228 employees in 1999. Just before doing so, it amended the division's pension plan to award larger benefits to eight departing officers and directors. One human resources executive got an additional $5,270 a month for life. But to do this and still pass the IRS's nondiscrimination tests, the company needed to give tiny pension increases to 100 lower-level workers, said the company's benefits consultant, PricewaterhouseCoopers. One got an increase of $1.92 a month (Schultz and Francis, 2008).

John Faraci CEO of International Paper saw his company's stock drop 63 percent in 2008, while he received $38.2 million in pay last year, his pay was bolstered by a $21 million pension payment. In 2010 Faraci received $12.3 million in total compensation, a 75 percent increase over his 2009 pay.

After failing miserably and leading Borders to the brink of bankruptcy, CEO Ron Marshall resigned in January 2010 and jumped to run A & P. And guess what? He lasted six months. Good CEOs are hard to find. He was replaced at Borders by its Chief Merchandising Officer Michael J. Edwards, who received a monthly supplemental payment of $29,167 in addition to his $400,000 salary. This is an 87 percent increase in pay and promotion after doing a mediocre job as a merchandiser. Marshall was replaced at A&P by former OfficeMax COO Sam Martin. You cannot keep up with these guys. In July 2008 OfficeMax terminated 2,700 employees and six months later it filed for Chapter 11. In 2010 CEO Sam Duncan retired with total compensation valued at $3.4 million, including his salary, roughly $1.5 million in non-equity incentives and more than $800,000 from the increase in value of his pension. The present value approaches $3 million. In addition he gets about $1 million worth of stock options that were vested ahead of schedule (Murphy, 2011).

Duncan was replaced by Ravi Saligram who was paid a $250,000 signing bonus, 125,000 shares of restricted stock, worth nearly $2.3 million at the end of its fiscal year and options to purchase 975,000 shares, valued at $9.2 million. Saligram's total compensation in 2010 was valued at nearly $12.1 million. To keep the recycling of executives of bankrupt companies ongoing, OfficeMax brought in the former CFO of bankrupted and out of business Circuit City to be its new CFO. That's not all. Now in Chapter 11, Borders has asked the court to approve $8.3 million for executive bonuses. This includes $1.7 million to new CEO Mike Edwards and a pay boost of between 90 and 150 percent of their base salaries for five other top executives. Meanwhile 11,000 employees lost their jobs and in July they began closing 399 remaining stores.

In December 2010 A&P filed for bankruptcy and in June 2011 demanded that its union employees take pay cuts, a five-year wage freeze, a reduction in paid vacations, pay an extra $5,000 annually for health care, take cutbacks in sick days, eliminate seniority rights and eliminate most job protections and grievance procedures. At the very same time workers were told it was their responsibility to save the company with givebacks, A&P's top six managers received $3.7 million in bonuses, including $1.2 million for the company's CEO Martin (Durso, 2011). Here is a quote from Martin when he took over as CEO in July 2010: "If (our employees) are not properly armed with the right information, they will give the wrong message – because they're going to give a message anyway. So getting the right message in the right hands quickly is important and essential to getting off on the right foot and having any chance of success in the outcome" (Bradt, 2011). One can only conclude the once great Atlantic and Pacific company is in deep trouble.

Indymac's CEO, Michael Perry received compensation of $15.92 million in 2007, and in July, 2008, the bank failed and was taken over by the government. Some 2,403 employees were terminated.

In 2007 Kenneth Chenault, CEO of American Express, received a pay package of $55.8 million. This is an increase of 141 percent over his $23.1 million in 2006. The company's total return in 2007 was a negative 13 percent. In 2008 he received a pay package worth nearly $43 million. American Express, facing soaring credit card defaults, has accepted capital from the government. In 2008, American Express shares fell 64 percent. Meanwhile, top executives received cash bonuses for 2008, Vice Chairman Edward Gilligan was paid a bonus of $3.5 million; President Alfred Kelly received $3 million; CFO Dan Henry received $2.1 million; and CIO Stephen Squeri received $1.65 million. In their SEC filing AMEX claimed its compensation committee "determined that the company's performance and the individual performance of the officers below CEO merited each of them a cash (annual incentive award) in respect of 2008 performance" (Read, 2009). In 2009 Chenault terminated 7,000 employees and he got a 60 percent increase in his base pay with total compensation of $16.9 million. In 2010 he took a pay cut with compensation worth only $16.3 million. Poor Chenault.

Forest Labs stock has dropped from almost $76 in February 2004 to $38 in June 2011. Plus the company had to pay $313 million as a settlement of charges it illegally marketed a drug. Meanwhile Forest's CEO Howard Solomon received almost $50 million in total compensation from 2004 to 2010; plus in 2007 Solomon sold $226 million in shares that were given to him by his admiring board. According to Edwards (2011) Solomon pocketed nearly $300 million in stock and compensation in a decade.

The Invitrogen Corporation had a good year in 2007 with a total return of 65 percent. However, CEO Gregory Lucier received the largest percentage increase in total pay of all CEOs in 2007, an increase of 522 percent.

According to Mutter (2008) Rupert Murdoch got a whopping total payout of $32.1 million in 2007. That was a 24 percent increase over the prior year, even though News Corp.'s shares lost about 8 percent. In 2010 his total compensation was $22.7 million and in 2011 rose to $33.3 million which included a $12.5 million bonus. His son James Murdoch, who is deputy COO, saw his compensation jump 73.8 percent from $10.3 million in the previous fiscal year to $17.9 million in 2011 fiscal year, which ended June 30. Shortly after News Corp. announced it will terminate around 110 employees at its newspapers.

CEO Mary Junck gained a 17.8 percent increase to her pay, to about $3.4 million, even though Lee's stock price was chopped in half during 2007.

Journal Register's former CEO Robert Jelenic enjoyed a 333.2 percent pay increase to $6.3 million, even though the company's shares shed three-fourths of their value. According to Mutter (2008), Jelenic left the company, but his pay included severance pay of $4.9 million.

Williams-Sonoma reported a loss of $35 million at the end of its first quarter in 2008 compared to 2007. CEO Howard Lester's total compensation was $4.5 million in 2007 and he decided to sell one of the company's two jets to get a smaller one. The smaller jet will cost $375,000 a month for a 36-month lease (Brown, 2008).

In 2002, Xerox stock dropped 66 percent and CEO Rick Thoman who led the company for 13 months was fired. However he will collect a lifetime salary of $800,000 a year. How does this happen? Anne Mulcahy took over and between 2003 and 2008 received over $35 million in compensation. In 2010 she terminated 2500 employees and in June 2011 she announced that 600 IT jobs would be outsourced to an Indian company.

Craig Dubow as CEO of Gannett Newspapers, received a $1.75 million bonus in 2007, despite the fact Gannett's stock lost 35 percent of its value in 2007. A bonus?

CIT Group paid CEO Jeffrey M. Peek $11 million in 2008, a 16 percent pay cut. CIT's stock lost more than half its value, $111 million. As of August 2009 CIT lost more than $5 billion, and in August 2009 alone it lost $1.62 billion. However it extended Peek's employment contract until September 2, 2010. One can only guess it was for doing "a hellava job." Peek is expected to resign in December 2009 as CIT teeters on bankruptcy. And who will replace Peek? None other than a refurbished John Thain, the former Merrill Lynch CEO, who will get $6 million pay package that includes a bonus, a car and a driver. No self respecting CEO in American would be caught dead without a car and driver. As a 10-year-old said, "I love to ride in a limo, it makes me feel special."

Sprint-Nextel reported an annual loss of $29.6 million, or $10.31 per share in 2007 and expected to lose 2 million customers in the first half of 2008. This caused CEO Gary Forsee to step down in October 2007. He received a pay package valued at $21.8 million in 2007 (a 47 percent increase over the previous year) and will also receive a retirement benefit of $84,325 a month for the rest of his life. His replacement Dan Hesse was paid a 2007 compensation package valued at $28.3 million while Sprint terminated 4,000 employees. In 2008 Hesse's compensation package was valued at $19.2 million which included a cash bonus of $2.65 million as the company continued to lose customers. In 2008 its shares dropped 86 percent. In the first quarter of 2009 Sprint reported a net loss of $600 million and an additional loss of 182,000 customers.

H.J. Heinz saw its net income increase 7.5 percent in 2007 and CEO William R. Johnson was rewarded in 2008 with a total compensation package increase of 51.4 percent. In 2009 the company's net income dropped 6.3 percent and hundreds of employees were terminated in several plants but Johnson got another raise as his compensation grew from $14 million to $19 million. In 2010 Johnson took a 2.6 percent cut, he received total compensation of $18.5 million last year. His salary of $1,245,111 remained the same, as did his stock awards

worth $1.5 million. His long-term performance award increased to $4.7 million from $3.8 million. But the value of his pension and deferred compensation declined to about $2.9 million from $4.1 million, and his annual incentive plan award declined to less than $4.3 million from about $4.8 million. In fiscal year ending April 2011 Heinz reported record profits as it terminated 1,000 employees.

Nike's net income rose 26 percent in 2007 and its CEO Mark Parker saw his total compensation more than double in 2008 (Associated Press, 2008a). Parker's compensation was $13,118,834 in 2009.

The Ryland Group a home builder, lost $334 million in 2007. As a result CEO R. Chad Dreier's cash and stock-based pay was slashed to $5.1 million from $20.9 million in 2006. But his other pay increased, he gained $4.7 million for his retirement plan, an $80,000 allowance for "personal health and services," $47,000 in life insurance premiums, $15,600 in personal flights on the company plane and $9,136 in medical reimbursements and more than $4 million in cash to offset the income tax Dreier owed on his perks. His "other pay" totaled $9.1 million (Kristof, 2008).

Another home builder, KB Home, lost almost $930 million in 2007. Its stock lost 60 percent of its value. Jeffrey Mezger, KB's CEO, not only made $24.4 million, he received a $6 million cash bonus for beating objectives his board set, such as improving performance on a customer satisfaction survey. Toll Brothers Corporation saw its stocks drop 30 percent in 2007. However, CEO Robert Toll received a $17.5 million bonus. Another home builder Hovnanian Enterprises saw its share value drop 76 percent in 2008, yet its CEO, the son of the founder Ara Hovnanian, received a 20 percent pay increase including an almost $1 million performance bonus (Ivry, 2009).

Aruba Networks terminated 46 employees in November 2008 to reduce costs. In June 2009 Aruba's CEO Dominic Orr got a 33 percent raise in salary.

Insurer XL Capital's profits eroded more than 80 percent last year, while its stock price slumped 30 percent. The company called its profits "unsatisfactory" in its proxy statement.. But CEO Brian O'Hara got a 23 percent raise to $7.5 million. He then announced his retirement and he was given 62,500 shares of restricted stock and 250,000 stock options the company said were to "reflect the importance of Mr. O'Hara's role in the CEO succession process."

Loews Corporation lost 40 percent of its value in 2008 but CEO J.S. Tisch's received a raise of 30 percent more than his 2007 compensation (Lee, 2009).

The CEO of the New York Stock Exchange parent NYSE Euronext Inc. said that Duncan Niederauer had been awarded total compensation of $7.1 million in 2008-his first full year in the job-including $4 million designated a "performance bonus." NYSE's posted a $738 million net loss, and the stock price fell 68 percent in 2008.

ValueClick suffered a loss of $256 million in the fourth quarter of 2008 however its five top executives received $19.8 million in compensation between them last year, a $14.2 million pay raise from 2007 (Edwards, 2009a).

Kenneth Lowe, the CEO of Scripps Networks Interactive Inc., received compensation of $5.4 million, in 2008 while its shares ended the year down 51 percent.

After a loss of $1.8 million in 2006, Tollgrade Communications lost $26.1 million in 2007. Its CEO Mark Peterson resigned in November 2007; he received $1.2 million, including a separation payment of $755,211.

Compensation, including cash awards based on performance, increased more than one-third for CEO David Swanson at R.H Donnelley in 2007, despite a 42 percent decline in the company's stock price. Swanson led Donnelley in and out of bankruptcy and the company changed its name to Dec One. In 2011 "the company sought new leadership" and Swanson left with a $17.8 million package including more than $6 million in severance related to "a termination not for Cause."

Sotheby, the auction house, reported a loss of 19 cents a share in the first quarter of 2008; however executive salaries and stock compensation increased 12 percent.

Sinclair Broadcast Group's share price dropped 22 percent last year, but CEO David D. Smith's compensation package nearly doubled, to about $2 million.

Under Armour founder and CEO Kevin Plank saw his compensation almost triple to $1.5 million as his company's stock price fell 13 percent.

Independent Health doubled the compensation of Dr. Michael Cropp to $1.7 million. Health- Now CEO Alphonso O'Neill-White's pay rose 75 percent to $2.24 million, and Excellus' David Klein took in $2.56 million, up 43 percent. The profits for these three nonprofit health insurers fell almost 37 percent in 2007 (Epstein, 2008).

Mark Pigott the Chairman and CEO of Paccar received 33 percent compensation increase to $9.2 million in 2007. Paccar's 2007 profit fell to $1.23 billion, and sales dropped 18 percent.

Sidney Taurel has been the CEO of Eli Lilly for 9 years and during his tenure the annualized 6 year total stock return was a minus $3.1. Taurel's nine year average compensation was $6.9 million and in 2007 he received a bonus and a 15 percent raise in salary.

CEO of the Kite Realty Group, John Kite's compensation increased 70.5 percent as its stock declined 65 percent.

CEO of Dow Chemical Andrew Liveris received $14.9 million in 2007, a 25 percent increase from the previous year, while Dow's profit fell 28 percent.

CEO of Travelers Insurance, Jay Fishman received $18.7 million in 2007, a 19 percent compensation increase when shares of its stocks remained stagnant. In 2009 Fishman's total compensation was valued at $20.6 million in 2009, a 42 percent jump from a year earlier. For years, Fishman has been dumping employees.

Norfolk Southern reported its profit down 1.2 percent in 2007 and a minor stock increase of 0.3 percent but its CEO Wick Moorman received a 20.9 percent raise in compensation.

Targeted Genetics, CEO H. Stewart Parker received an increase of 27 percent in compensation in 2007 while the company's stock dropped 72 percent in 2007.

SonoSite's CEO, Kevin Goodwin received a 60 percent increase in compensation in 2007, while the company's stock increased 7.5 percent.

Tyco CEO Ed Breen's compensation for fiscal year ending Sept. 30, 2007, was a package worth $33.3 million, a 100 percent increase from his 2006 salary. Tyco's total return in 2007 was 14 percentage points below the 16.4 percent return on the S&P 500, with a company net loss of $1.7 billion. Included in Breen's salary was a bonus of $3.2 million. The year 2008 was also a bad year for Tyco's stock. Since reaching a 52-week high of $47.95 in May 2008, the stock has lost more than 50 percent, closing at $23.18 on January 16, 2009. But Breen still gets rewarded his 2008 compensation was valued at $6.2 million. In January 2011 Tyco terminated 248 employees.

Sherwin-Williams CEO Christopher Commor received compensation of $5.8 million in 2008, with a base salary increase of 4.6 percent as profits declined 22 percent (Heher, 2009).

Allied Capital's stock lost about a third of its value in 2007, but its CEO William Walton, received $11 million; including a $1.5 million salary and a $5.3 million bonus.

Mylan CEO Robert Coury received a 12 percent compensation increase bringing his 2008 total compensation to $11.6 million. Included was a performance bonus of just under $3.8 million. In 2008, the company lost $320.3 million, or $1.05 per share, compared with a loss of $1.23 billion, or $4.91 per share, in 2007 (Associated Press, Forbes, 2009).In 2010 as revenues rose 7 percent Coury's compensation rose 41 percent from 2009 to $23 million. In 2010 he received $535,590 for his personal travel on a private jet for him and his family (total compensation in 2010 was $22.9 million). In 2008 his travel payments were $348,988 and in 2009, $433,387.

Illinois Tool Works CEO David Speer received compensation valued at $9.6 million in 2008, a 10 percent increase from 2007, while profit declined 19 percent.

Manulife Financial lost $1.9 billion in the last quarter of 2008 but CEO Dominic D'Alessandro received a compensation package in excess of $12.5 million for "extraordinary performance" in 2008, and another $12.5 million for working the five months until his retirement in May, 2009.

CEO of PerkinElmer Robert F. Friel received a 30 percent increase in compensation in 2008 while its stock fell 47 percent and profit fell 4 percent (Associated Press, Forbes, 2009a).

Boston Beer, the maker of Sam Adams beer saw a 24 percent drop in stock price and a 71 percent fall in its net income but still awarded more than $1 million in bonuses to its top executives and chairman in 2008.

There is no better example of a discord between how well a CEO performs, and the pay he receives upon exit, than Bob Nardelli of Home Depot. Nardelli took in $37,862,312 in total compensation in 2005, including stock option grants (Higgins, 2007). While Nardelli was getting rich, he gave his hourly workers salary increases that ranged between 35 and 75 cents an hour. When Nardelli left the company he was rewarded with $210 million. During his six year tenure the company's stock fell 7.9 percent, he experienced 100 percent turnover of 170 of his top executives and the stock of Home Depot's competitor Lowe's rose 188 percent (Mishel, 2006). After Nardelli left, Home Depot continued to slide. In 2007 profits fell 24 percent, however, his replacement Frank Blake, received a $500,000 bonus, in addition to $8.28 million in compensation. Under Blake, in January, 2008, Home Depot announced a 10 percent cut in employees at its headquarters in Atlanta. In April 2008 he announced another cut, the termination of 1,000 in-store human service managers, and the closing of 15 stores and another termination of 1,300 employees as its revenue decreased 7.8 percent, sales in its stores dropped 8.7 percent and profits dropped 34 percent. In January, 2009 he announced an additional termination of 7,000 employees and he closed Expo and HD Supply and more stores. Home Depot stock dropped 34 percent, and guess what? Blake gets a 29 percent increase in compensation. (You can read more about Nardelli and Home Depot in Chapter 9)

In 2008, MSCI CEO Henry Fernandez received a $3 million annual incentive payment even though the company's share price fell 44 percent and net income declined 16 percent.

Procter and Gamble spokesman Paul Fox announced "Quite simply we pay for performance and we didn't hit the targets we set." Yet CEO A.G. Lafley was awarded a compensation increase to $23.6 million in 2008. According to Fasig (2009) "In determining Lafley's pay, the compensation committee considered P&G's performance, the personal performance and individual leadership of Lafley and his focus on sustaining growth. It also measured his compensation against that of a 25-member peer group with a median revenue of $61 billion, including Wal-Mart, Coca-Cola and General Electric."

These compensation committees will find a way to give performance even if they have to make it up. To hell with performance targets. Lafley retired in July 2009. He was replaced by Bob McDonald who was paid $13.1 million in his first year that included a $2.67 million bonus. Ninety percent of McDonald's compensation was tied to performance. Unfortunately terminating P&G employees were not included in his performance equation as he terminated 7,747 employees. In 2011 they did it again. According to Ziobro (2011) P&G "struggled in fiscal 2011 through an environment of rising commodity costs and weak demand in developed markets." Yet McDonald received a 24 percent raise to $16.2 million in total compensation. CFO Jon Moeller also did well, his total compensation rose about 50 pwecwnr to about $5 million.

Morgenson (2011) calls these actions "moving the goal posts" on executive pay and in 2011 Wal-Mart did just that for their CEO

Michael Duke. In April 2011 Wal-Mart's compensation committee replaced a metric that was not showing their CEO's competence and they found a new metric that made certain Duke would get a handsome raise bringing his total compensation to $18.7 million of which $16 million was performance based. In January 2010 over 12,000 employees were terminated.

And, finally let's see how they do it in Disneyland. According to Sanders, (2009), Disney's CEO Robert Iger received $2 million salary and a $13.9 million bonus for fiscal 2008 and his overall compensation was up nearly 11 percent from 2007. Mr. Iger's total compensation for 2008 was valued at $30.6 million, which was up from the year before, when his total compensation was valued around $27.7 million. Disney's net income dipped by about 5.5 percent on weakness at the company's broadcast and movie studio units, as well as a softening at the theme parks division towards the end of the fiscal year. In 2008, he terminated 1,900 employees and Disney shares dropped 64 percent and he got a $13.9 million bonus? In 2009 things were equally bad for Disney, but not Iger. Disney's stock fell by 15 percent during fiscal 2009 and its revenue fell 4 percent to $36.1 billion and earnings dropped 25 percent to $3.3 billion but Iger got a $9.3 million performance bonus.

They also steal

Green Tree CEO Lawrence Coss was the highest paid CEO in 1995 ($65 million). As the market value of his firm grew from $330 million to $3.6 billion over five years, with earnings at a rate of 44 percent since 1990, like many other CEOs who oversaw meteoric growth, he was praised. Then came the bust. Coss was accused of violating the Securities Exchange Act by making false statements about Green Tree's profits so he could get rich. Coss left the company and it was sold in 1999. Coss was an early part of the growing movement that tied CEO compensation to shareholder wealth, which radically changed the way a corporation was to be managed and led to a climate of financial excess.

Countrywide Financial CEO, Angelo Mozilo, received a compensation package valued at more than $22.1 million in 2007, as his company lost over $700 million. Before the company's stock tumbled 80 percent, Mozilo cashed out $121.5 million in stock options. In June, 2009 he was charge by the Securities and Exchange Commission with lying to investors and reaping $140 million from insider trading. In October 2010 Mizilo was forced to pay the government $67 million in fines to settle fraud chargers.

Appendix I: Obscene Retirement Packages

AT&T Chairman and Chief Executive Edward E. Whitacre Jr. received total pay for 2006 valued at $60.7 million, a salary increase of over 100 percent. The Bedminster, N.J., telecommunications giant said in a filing with the Securities and Exchange Commission that Whitacre's total pay included a $2.1 million salary, $6.8 million in non-equity incentive plan compensation and stock awards valued at $47 million. On top of the salary, incentives and stock awards, Whitacre received $461,945 in "other" compensation, including $213,682 in life insurance premiums, $26,889 in auto benefits, and $38,214 for personal use of corporate aircraft and $24,505 for club membership. Whitacre retired in 2007 with a $158 million retirement package. In December 2008, he announced 12,000 employees would be laid off.

In January 2008 CEO Mike Eskew of UPS retired, and he left with a $12.8 million package.

Jeff Zucker resigned after Comcast closed its agreement to acquire a 51 percent stake in NBC the media giant from its current owners GE and Vivendi. His exit package is roughly $30 million to $40 million.

In the year before he retired in 2004 from Continental Airlines CEO Gordon Bethune's pay package reached $34.3 million, a golden sendoff.

Thomas Farrell CEO of Dominion Resources, the parent company of Dominion Virginia Power, received the largest pay raise among publicly traded electricity and gas utility companies in 2010. Farrell got a raise of $4.57 million bringing his total compensation to $14.95 million, about 44 percent more than in 2009.

Stephen Sanger retired as CEO of General Mills in May 2008. His performance ranked 148 out of 189 in the Forbes 2007 CEO performance rankings. In 2007, Sanger's compensation was $18.7 million in a combination of cash and stock. In the first five months of 2008, he received another $7.3 million, plus another $470,701 in other compensation including a $40,200 discount on the purchase of his company car and $17,298 for unused vacation days (Philips, 2008).

CEO of Omnicare Joel Gemunder retired on July 31, 2010 and will receive more than $130 million in severance, pension and departing payouts. This included a lump sum payment of more than $91 million (Bernard-Kuhn, 2010). The nation's largest provider of pharmaceuticals for the elderly will most likely pass the cost onto them. Over a five year period his compensation totaled close to $70 million. Just ahead of Gemunder on the big pension list is Thomas M. Ryan, president and CEO of CVS Caremark Corp., with $94.4 million at the end of 2009.

Ronald E. Logue, CEO of State Street, was to retire in March 2010 and he would receive a $6 million "transition award" for retiring and staying on as chairman until Jan. 1, 2011. Between 2008 and 2009 Logue terminated 2,000 employees as he received $29 million in 2008. He also has around $25 million in his pension (Healy, 2009).

Retired Target CEO Robert Ulrich retired and set up a new company Musical Instrument Museum which is set to open in 2010. Target gave him a $120,000 office space donation and free services of Target employees to aid in the project. His replacement was Gregg Steinhafel.

In 2008 the company failed to meet its annual financial goals and Steinhafel obtained $12.9 million which included a $447,680 bonus. In 2010 Steinhafel's compensation package increased 84 percent from 2009 to $24 million.

It's good to retire if you're an insurance executive. Cigna Health Insurance CEO H. Edward Hanway received compensation of $29.3 million in 2007. In January 2009 he announced he would cut 1,100 jobs, or about 4 percent of Cigna's workforce to lower costs. In January 2010 Hanway retired and he will receive a retirement package worth $110.9 million-which included $18.8 million in executive compensation for 2009, as well as a healthy pension plan, deferred compensation and stock options. The new CEO of managed-care company Cigna Corp. received a pay package worth more than $15 million last year. He was replaced by David Cordani, who took over as CEO at the start of 2010 and received $1 million salary, a performance-related bonus totaling more than $7.3 million and stock and option awards adding up to $6.7 million and a $48,000 home security system. In July 2011 Cigna announced that 500 more employees would be terminated.

William Jew was paid a severance package of $18 million CareFirst Blue Cross Blue Shield.

According to ALF-CIO Executive Paywatch (2007) these CEOs either receive or will receive the following annual retirement compensation (That's each year for the rest of their lives in addition to social security and Medicare.)

Edward Whitacre Jr. from ATT&T $5,494,107,

William McGuire from United Health Group $5,092,000,

Robert Nardelli, from Home Depot $4,612,500,

Samuel Palmisano from IBM $4,550,000,

Reuben Mark from Colgate Palmolive $3,700,000,

Brian Roberts from Comcast $3,600,000,

Richard Davidson, Union Pacific $2,700,000,

John Rowe, Exelon $2,600,000,

James Mulva, Conoco Philips $2,600,000,

Vance Coffman, Lockheed Martin $2,591,856,

Harold Messmer from Robert Half International $2,555,000,

F. Duane Ackerman, Bell South $2,512,300,

Patrick Stokes, Anheuser-Busch $2,500,000,

Robert Eckert, Mattel $2,500,000,

E. Neville Isdell, Coca Cola $2,500,000,

Arthur Ryan, Prudential Financial $2,456,000,

Lewis Hay, FPL Group $2,430,134,

Sidney Taurel, Eli Lilly $2,300,000,

Jeffrey Immelt, General Electric $2,300,000,

William E. Greehey, Valero Energy $2,236,000,

Angelo R. Mozilo, Countrywide Financial $2,171,358,

Steven S. Reinemund, PepsiCo $2,170,870 .

Appendix J: Parachutes, Handshakes, Sendoffs, and Hellos; They're all Golden

Top executives get rich coming and going and it doesn't matter how long they stay on the job or what they do while sitting in the catbird seat. Consider Paul Pressler an executive picking up a large sum on his way out the door. He is the former CEO of U.S. clothing retailer Gap Inc., who will receive about $14 million as part of his severance package, despite the company's decline in revenue and profit during his four years as chief executive (Business Week Online, 2006).

Gene Isenberg, former CEO of Nabors Industries, is now chairman and when he exits he will get $126 million.

CEO Michael Cherkasky was forced out for poor performance at Marsh and McLennan Cos and was given a lump sum $7.15 million in severance pay.

Office Depot has lost money in each of the past five quarters and is expected to lose $96 million in 2010, plus it is under investigation for overcharging state and local governments, however in 2008 its CEO Steve Odland made over $6 million and in 2009 he made $5.5 million. In October 2010 Odland left the company and to see him go away he was given a golden boot that included on top of his salary of $5.2 million: a severance package of $11.15 million and a $5 million retention award; and payment of the equivalent of two years of health and other benefits and part of his 2010 bonus. Now how can they give a retention award to someone who is leaving? And, who did they bring back for a second time? The 71- year-old Neil Austrian was appointed interim CEO and he will be paid $220,000 a month plus he was given 400,000 shares at an exercise price of $4.43.

Regis CEO Paul Finkelstein announced his retirement in September 2011 and his Golden Parachute had an estimated value of $33 million. This is occurring as the company makes millions in budget cuts. In a turn of fate the hedge fund boys that own part of Regis are angry and they are calling Finkelstein's package excessive. Hedge fund boys want all the toys and they do not like to share.

CEO, Robert Orlich, of Transatlatic holdings will retire at the end of 2011 and after making over $9 million in 2011, he will get a "golden sendoff" valued at as much as $15 million.

Jill Barad, chief executive of Mattel Inc. received $37 million when she resigned in 2000 after the company reported a loss.

In 2006 Jay S. Sidhu, chairman and chief executive of Sovereign Bancorp Inc., received a package worth $73.56 million when he resigned in 2006.

Sen. Ron Johnson CEO of Pacur in Wisconsin resigned in 2010 to run for US Senate and won in an election marred by accounts of voter fraud. As he left Pacur he gave himself a "golden sendoff" of $10 million, he owns the company.

Spiros Hatiras, the former CEO of Hoboken (N.J.) University Medical Center who stepped down July 2011, received a severance package of $600,000 in compensation and full medical benefits for a year three weeks before the hospital filed for bankruptcy.

While terminating over 600 employees over the years because of the lack of public funding a Salinas Valley Public Hospital District gave its CEO Samuel Downing $3.9 million in retirement payments and $947,594 in cash from a "special severance fund" set aside for his retirement, on top of his regular pension of $150,000 a year (Allen, 2011).

In June 2011 Matthew Rubel, CEO of Collective Brands, was given the Boot with a package of $15.8 million.

Equity Residential gave CEO David Neithercut a long-term compensation grant and retention award valued at $6.5 million in addition to his 2010 total compensation of $4.3 million.

Michael Dell, the founder of Dell Computers had to come out of retirement to rescue his company from CEO Kevin Rollins. Rollins left with a $5 million package (Higgins, 2007). In January 2009 executives left the company as its shares dropped 55 percent since the beginning of 2008. Mike Cannon, president of Dell's global operations left after less than two years with a severance package of $10 million. Chief marketing officer Mark Jarvis will receive a departure package worth $1.25 million (Crum and Batrash, 2009).

David West is leaving as CEO of Hershey and when he joins Del Monte Foods in 2011 he will receive a "Golden Hello" worth $12.5 million.

Martin Orlowsky retired as CEO of Lorillard in 2010 and he received a 91 percent increase in compensation from 2009, a "Golden Sendoff" of $18,820,303.

Stephen Elop was given a $6 million signing bonus to become CEO of Nokia in March 2011. And in April, one month later, Elop terminated 7,000 employees. What goes on when after a few weeks on the job a CEO decides to terminate 38 percent of a company's workforce? Where will most of those jobs go? Four thousand will be lost and 3,000 will be outsourced to Accenture and where will the jobs be located? Most likely to the Philippines. In November 2011, Nokia Siemens Networks, a joint venture with Siemens, announced plans to terminate 17,000 jobs worldwide.

MBIA lost $2.7 billion in 2008, after losing $1.9 billion in 2007, and CEO Gary Dunton lost his job. Upon exit he received a bonus of $960,000 and other compensation worth $3.61 million. The latter included $3.2 million in severance payments.

Thomas Ryan CEO of CVS will retire in 2011 and will receive total compensation of $29.2 million and another $50.4 million from stock-award vesting and the exercise of stock options. In addition he decided to take his pension benefit in a lump sum adding another $58.4 million. The golden sendoff is nearly $125 million. After retirement Ryan will continue as chairman.

Alfred Kelly president of American Express is leaving the company in April 2010. So what will he get? His boss Kenneth Chenault, will give him separation payments totaling $9.7 million along with a $4 million performance bonus and his regular salary of $765,000 per year through Dec. 31, 2010, and $850,000 per year from Jan. 1 until he departs in April. He is just leaving at the age of 51 to work somewhere else and he gets a "golden sendoff." What a boss.

When former Bank of America CEO Ken Lewis retired at the end of 2009, he took a package of stock and benefits valued at $83 million with him.

Gannett CEO Craig Dubow resigned in October 2011 and his golden sendoff was $37 million. During his six-year tenure he terminated nearly 40 percent of the company's workforce and its stock dropped 80 percent.

David Swanson, the CEO of Dex One, retired May 2010 and in his final year he received the gift of a 552 percent increase on total compensation of over $14 million. His "golden sendoff" included salary of $481,173; bonuses of $3,769,604; perks/other compensation $6,500,995; and stock option awards of $3,445,648.

State Street was sued for misleading town and cities about investments of their pension funds. CEO Ronald Logue retired at the end of 2009 and was awarded $5.4 million in incentive compensation. This comes on top of $6 million deferred cash "transition award" he was promised for agreeing to stay on as chairman until the end of the year.

Fred Hassan resigned as CEO of Schering Plough after Merck bought the company for $68 billion. Hassan left with a $17.7 million exit payment and pension benefits worth $13.2 million.

CEO of U.S. Music Lyor Cohen proceeded to negotiate a new contract, and his base pay went from $1.5 million to $3 million. His target bonus remained the same at $2.5 million but the minimum he could receive went from zero to $1.5 million and his golden handshake went from $4 million to $8.5 million. Cohen also received a $1.5 million bonus in 2007.

Adam Metz became CEO of General Growth in October 2008 and in April 2009 the company filed for bankruptcy. A month after it emerged in November 2010, Metz left and he was compensated according to a court-approved formula to the tune of over $49 million, which included a salary of $1,459,615, stock awards of $1,972,500 and a nonequity incentive of $46,258,678.

In the proxy for Mellon Financial, a list of perks for CEO Robert Kelly includes $194,000 use of a corporate jet to take him between

Pittsburgh and North Carolina, $94,000 on a car and driver, $66,000 for his country club membership and another $52,000 to provide him with financial planning services. In August 2011 Kelly was fired by the board and what did he get? According to Craig (2011) Kelly received severance of $2 million, plus he is eligible for up to $4 million based on the banks performance, $11.2 million for vested equity awards, and a pension valued at $16.6 million.

Lee Scott, CEO of Wal-Mart, retired on January 31 2009, and he earned $30.16 million in fiscal year 2009, however he was to be paid until Jan. 31, 2011.

Spectranetics CEO Emile Geisenheimer retired in November 2010 and he got an extra year lump sum payment, equal to a year of his previous salary, and vested his options to buy 140,279 of Spectranetics stock and half its current price. And in January 2011 they brought him back as a consultant being paid $15,500 through June 2011.

In April 2011, John Chidsey, the CEO of Burger King, got his golden boot, a severance package worth almost $20 million.

Baxter Phillips, the CEO of Massey Energy, got his "golden boot" a package worth over $34 million.

In 2007, his last year before retirement, George David CEO of United Technologies received $65 million of which $54.7 million was obtained when he exercised stock options, in 2006 he cashed in $28 million in options. In 2009, United Technologies Corp. will cut about 1,500 jobs said his replacement, CEO Louis Chênevert. In addition, in March 2009, United Technologies, Pratt & Whitney unit, will furlough workers for five days. United Technologies CEO Louis R. Chenevert earned $5.9 million in total compensation. In 2008 his company lost 30 percent of its stock value and cut thousands of jobs. In March 2009, Chenevert terminated 11,600 employees and in July

2010 another 1,500 and he received $19.5 million, a 9 percent raise which included a bonus that more than doubled.

Richard Grasso CEO of the New York Stock Exchange received a $139 million retirement package. He was sued by the NY Attorney General's office and after five years of litigation, he was allowed to keep the package. Guess who had the Stock Exchange give him such a sum, none other than Ken Langone.

Lee Raymond retired as the CEO of Exxon-Mobil in 2005 and received a package of $400 million including a $98 million lump-sum pension and of course use of a company jet

Stan O'Neal CEO of Merrill Lynch retired in 2007 with a $161.5 million package but no jet, also in that year Charles Prince of Citigroup packed it in with a paltry $42 million.

In 2011 Tim Hortons will give a golden sendoff of $6.5 million to CEO Don Schroeder $5,750,000 is severance pay and of course the rest is for consulting.

In April 2009, General Growth Properties filed Chapter 11 bankruptcy and emerged out of it in November 2010. A month later, CEO Adam Metz quit and he received $49.7 million.

Appendix K: The Golden Boot

What happens when you get fired? If you're a CEO only good things happen. Carly Fiorina CEO at Hewlett-Packard got the "golden boot" she was dismissed in February 2005 with a $21.4 million severance package. She also received $50,000 for financial counseling and was allowed to keep her computer equipment along with free tech support for three years. Should the company's stock improve, Fiorina will make millions more by exercising stock options.

Seneca Gaming Corp. fired Barry Brandon as its senior vice president in November 2008, but he will continue to collect his $700,000 a year base salary through the end of September 2009. He also continues to receive company-paid medical insurance benefits during that time. Likewise, E. Brian Hansberry got the boot in November 2008. He was Seneca Gaming's president and CEO, and he continued to receive his $360,000 annual salary through the end of September 2009, along with his health benefits.

St. Joe CEO Britt Greene got the "golden boot": he will receive $2.92 million in cash six months after his termination date, a pro rata $118,000 bonus, and another $1 million added to his retirement plan. Now how does one get fired and get a bonus?

Enmax, a city-owned utility, booted out CEO Gary Holden in January 2011 and the city will have to pay him over $5 million in a compensation package. Holden, who made $2.7 million dollars a year in salary and bonuses, left following allegations he accepted a trip to Monaco three years ago, paid for by a software company used by Enmax for billing.

Seven executives at Blue Cross Blue Shield of Delaware will be due a combined $6 million in severance pay if they get fired.

In June 2011, CEO Ian McCarthy got the "Golden Boot" after his company became a target of a federal investigation and had to pay $55 million in restitution. He was fired and he will get $5.2 million over three years, plus continuing medical coverage, $10,000 for legal fees and other compensation (Quinn, 2011). His total Boot package was $14.2 million.

Bob Nardelli had the distinction of receiving the highest golden boot when he got a "$210 million boot" from Home Depot. He was surpassed by Gianfranco Lanci of Acer, who got his boot in March 2011 to the tune of $300 million. Michael Ovitz had the distinction of getting the golden boot after the shortest stay. He was fired after 14 months as president of Walt Disney, and got a $140 million package. Let's see, that's $10 million a month.

It is hard to find a CEO who would disagree that the purpose of the bonus is to motivate an employee. But how does getting a bonus for getting fired fit into the equation? According to Associated Press (2008), Aquila's board of directors presented its CEO Richard Green with a $1 million departing gift for "superior performance," this was on top of his $3.5 million severance package. Over the past several years, Aquila's stock lost 90 percent of its value.

In 1996 Apple lost nearly $2 billion and some 3,600 employees lost their jobs. However, CEO Gilbert Amelio, who lasted 17 months on the job, received a golden parachute of $6.7 million plus other compensation.

Martin Sullivan was CEO of AIG when it lost 7.81 billion in the first quarter of 2008 and Sullivan was given a boot of $68 million (Morgenson, 2008). In the third quarter 2008, AIG reported that it lost another $25 billion and in November 2008 secured a new $150 billion government bailout package.

John Ferguson CEO of Hackensack University Medical Center, was given the golden boot and received a severance package of more than $5 million bringing his total compensation for 2009 to $7.7 million.

In January 2011, Beth Israel Deaconess Medical Center board gave CEO Paul Levy a "negotiated departure" which included $1.6 million in severance pay.

El Camino Hospital CEO Ken Graham got a "golden boot" in January 2011 with a nearly $1 million in severance package.

CEO Randy Talbot of Symetra Financial was canned in 2010 but three months before firing him the board gave him a $3.3 million performance bonus.

AOL fired its CEO in March 2009 but continued paying him $1 million salary and $7.5 million in bonuses through 2010. His replacement Tim Armstrong terminated at least 1,500 people in November and December of 2009. The question: What goes on in the executive suite when the CEO is fired and he gets a bonus?

Appendix L: The Benefits of Mergers/Acquisitions

CEO Dr. Ken Melani's insurance company Highmark merged with Independence Blue Cross. He would get a $1 million raise with incentives, bringing his total salary to $3.9 million (Pittsburgh Business Times, 2008). Other executives will benefit from the mergers; David O'Brien, executive vice president of government services, $1.55 million from $996,316; Dan Lebish, CEO of Highmark Life and Casualty, $1.08 million from $891,000; and Nanette DeTurk, executive vice president of finance and CFO, $1.7 million from $1.1 million.

CEO William "Jerry" Jurgensen of Nationwide Mutual Insurance agreed to buy 34 percent of its subsidiary, Nationwide Financial Services. The more Nationwide Insurance pays the more Jugensen receives, so they paid a lot and "Jerry" will receive $24 million from the deal (Mider, 2008).

El Paso Corp. was acquired by Kinder Morgan Inc. and CEO Douglas Foshee will receive a "golden sendoff" of $95 million if he leaves within two years of the acquisition.

CEO Bernard Poussot sold his company Wyeth to Pfizer and received a 69 percent compensation raise in 2008, to $21.3 million, in addition to a $24 million change-in-control bonus (Yes- A change-in-control bonus) for selling his company to Pfizer. Wyeth's top five executives — including Poussot — will share $64 million change-of-control bonus for saying yes to the Pfizer acquisition (Edwards, 2009b). These guys are creative geniuses when it comes to find ways to get more.

In September 2011 Temple-Inland CEO Doyle Simons will receive more than $61 million when the sale of the company to International Paper is finalized. It's his "golden parachute."

In 2011 Talecris Biotherapeutics was sold to Spain's Grifols for $4 billion and Talecris's CEO Larry Stern had a "change in control" agreement which means Stern could receive a payment of up to $8.1 million if he leaves after the Grifols deal, he also owns 5.36 million shares, including options and restricted stock, worth about $154 million before taxes, based on Talecris' closing price 5/31/11. In 2010 Stern received total pay, including base salary, options and other compensation of $3.87 million.

In April 2011, Johnson & Johnson agreed to purchase Synthes for $21.3 billion. If the deal goes through Michel Orsinger CEO of Synthes will get $51.9 million and if he stays for three years he will also get a stock package worth $17.2 million.

James O'Connor, CEO of Republic Services, almost doubled his compensation in 2008 as it merged with Allied Waste Industries. O'Conner's compensation went from $4.66 million to $8.39 million.

In November 2009, Sioux Falls, S.D.,Sanford Health and Merit-Care in Fargo, N.D., merged, and MeritCare CEO Roger Gilbertson, received a separation payment of $1 million.

NYSE Euronext is expected to merge with the NYSE and if CEO Duncan Niederauer loses his job he would walk away with $34.3 million in payouts.

AXA Asia Pacific will merge with AMP and AXA's CEO Andrew Penn will receive $17 million that will include $8 million in options payouts and a $9 million payout for being terminated.

The merger between Wilmington Trust and M&T Bank will bring about nearly $14 million in "golden parachute" payments to top managers should they lose their jobs. While 700 employees from Wilmington Trust were terminated because of the merger, newly appointed CEO Donald Foley could get a lump sum payment of $3.7 million. What a strategy: Merge your company watch your employees lose their jobs and you get rich.

Danversbank of Mass. was acquired by People's United Bank and Danversbank's top five executives will share more than $38 million in severance pay, bonuses, stock options, retirement plans, and tax and insurance payments as part of the deal. Danversbank CEO Kevin Bottomley, will serve on the board of People's United Bank, and his departure package is valued at $17.1 million.

Marshall & Ilsley Corp. CEO Mark Furlong negotiated the sale of Wisconsin's biggest bank to the parent of Chicago's Harris N.A. in December, 2010 and he eceived $24 million in cash payments in addition to the salary, bonus and equity awards when he signed a three-year contract to run the combined banks (Daniels, 2011). Furlong was due $18 million in severance pay under his "change-in-control" agreement with M&I and a $6-million "transition completion payment." You can't make this stuff up. In addition four other executives received payments of $4.1 million to $5.5 million apiece. Also there was $26.7 million for the remaining 12 banks officers to divide-up.

In March 2010 Black & Decker merged with Stanley and Black & Decker's biggest individual shareholder, Nolan Archibald, who had been CEO for 24 years owns roughly one percent of their stock. He could have a pay package worth $89 million after three years. This included a "cost synergy bonus" of $45 million. How will they accomplish cost savings? You guessed it. Terminations. In January 2009, Archibald terminated 1,500 employees. The he got the following perks in 2010: $526,391 of personal plane travel; $39,671 in reimbursed financial-planning costs; $9,522 for personal use of a company car; $16,200 as an additional car allowance; $4,528 in *"personal use of tickets to athletic and other entertainment events"*; $1,820 in club dues and $2,635 in free tools or other company merchandise (Aenlle, 2011).

Shortly after Oracle's purchase of Sun in January 2009, former CEO Jonathan Schwartz announced that 1,000 employees would not be included in the merger and would not be going to Oracle. Schwartz will not be going either but he will get a severance package of $12.8 million and health-insurance two years. What will the terminated employees get? Three months of pay and health insurance for two months. Oracle continues the process of terminating in American employees and hiring abroad. In 2000 it had more workers at home than abroad; at the end of 2010, 63 percent of its employees were overseas (Wessel, 2011).

Weeks before a merger agreement with Disney Marvel Entertainment, CEO Isaac "Ike" Perl-mutter was given 1.27 million stock options at almost half of what Disney agreed to pay landing Perl-mutter a quick $34 million for the deal.

Continental merged with United Airlines and CEO Jeff Smisek who promised in 2010 not to receive any salary until his company, Continental, made a profit. When it finally did turn a profit he made out. Smisek, who will be the CEO of the newly merged carrier called United Continental Holdings, received salary of $791,250 and $3.6 million in other incentives at year's end. What happened to Smisel's vow of no salary until a profit occurred? It was determined that Continental would have been profitable for the year had the merger not occurred so he was given $975,000. But this is nothing compared to what his counterparts from United received. Glenn Tilton former United CEO was given $16.8 million which included a $2.7 million bonus. Tilton also agreed to convert the cash severance he was eligible to receive by stepping down as United CEO into 207,157 restricted shares, with a grant date value of $5.1 million. The shares will vest at the end of next year, or earlier if he leaves his chairman's role due to death, disability or without "cause" (Johnsson, 2011). Three other United executives who were canned after the merger pocketed ample pay and severance packages. According to Johnsson (2011) former United president John Tague received $11.7 million in total compensation, including a $1.6 million bonus. Former chief financial officer Kathryn Mikells received $9.4 million, including a $1.3 million bonus; while Graham Atkinson, president of the carrier's Mileage Plus program, walked away with $6.9 million, including an $888,376 bonus. In addition to health and life insurance benefits, the departed United executives are also eligible for lifetime flight benefits, elite frequent-flier status and lifetime membership in the company's airport lounge clubs.

Mark Furlong, CEO of Marshall & Ilsley saw his compensation increase 205 percent in 2010 to $5.1 million while his company lost $617 million. Why so much? You guessed it, he will sell his company to the BMO Financial Group.

In 2010 Isadore Sharp announced his retirement from the company he founded, Four Seasons His company is in trouble, saddled with debt from a $3.37 billion buyout in 2007 with Saudi Prince Alwaleed Bin Talal and Cascade Investment LLC, an operation owned by Bill Gates. Sharp earned around $288 million from the buyout on top of retaining 10 percent equity in the company.

In December 2009 Comcast gained control of NBC Universal and as a result COO Steve Burke negotiated a new contract. Burke will continue to receive the same salary, $2.2 million annually, and a performance bonus for as much as 300 percent of that base. Burke will assume the added responsibility of overseeing the NBC Universal partnership once the deal closes in 2010 and he was eligible for two cash bonuses - each of $3 million - and two restricted stock grants - each having a value of $6 million. The new deal could potentially push Burke's total compensation to $28.8 million, assuming that he receives his full bonus (Farrell, 2009). In 2010 Comcast's CEO Brian Roberts made over $31 million in total compensation as they announced in 2011 that they needed to cut 100 positions.

Qwest CEO Ed Mueller sold his company to CenturyLink in 2010 and was paid $13.5 million. His COO Teresa Taylor received $10.7 million which included a base salary of $660,000, a cash bonus of $1.5 million and early severance pay of nearly $5 million. Other top executives were roughly $5 million for CAO Rich Baer, $4.7 million for CFO Joe Euteneuer and $3.1 million for EVP Dan Yost. In 2010 Qwest terminated 1,800 employees. The full merger will occur April 1, 2011 (Vuong, 2011). Once the merger is complete Mueller will receive $40 million.

According to Grant (2011) airline executives get rich when they merge; in Southwest Airlines' acquisition of AirTran, CEO of AirTran Robert Fornaro will receive $5.7 million, he will become a consultant and will get an estimated $1.2 million in consulting fees, $2.9 million in severance, $1.3 million in accelerated equity awards and a $290,000 merger-completion bonus. When Continental merged with United, CEO Jeff Smisek got a $4 million merger bonus and when Delta merged with Northwest in 2008 Northwest CEO Douglas Steenland received an $18.3 million payout.

In 1988 Kohlberg, Kravis, and Roberts (KKR) completed what was at the time the largest leveraged buyout (LBO) in history the debt-laden buyout of RJR Nabisco for $25.4 billion and its CEO F. Ross Johnson walked away with $52 million. Since the LBO about 9,000 jobs have been directly or indirectly eliminated.

In 2010 NewAlliance Bancshares merged with First Niagara Financial and New Alliance's CEO Peyton Patterson will receive a parachute totaling nearly $24 million when she leaves the bank.

Genzyme was sold to Sanofi-Aventis and Genzyme's CEO Henri Termeer will be out of a job but not out of money. He will get nearly $160 million and an additional $12.5 million in a "change of control" payment.

In May 2011 Teva announced its acquisition of Cephalon for $6.8 billion and Cepahlon CEO Kevin Buchi will be eligible for $14.6 million compensation, including $4.4 million in cash and the rest in shares. Four other Cepahlon executives will receive between $5.9 million and 7.9 million each (Habib-Valdhorn, 2011).

CenturyLink announced plans in April 2011 to acquire Savvis for $2.5 billion. Savvis CEO James Ousley would receive compensation and benefits worth an estimated $28.86 million if he is fired within one year of the merger "without cause" or he "voluntarily resigns for good reason." So guess what he will do? Is $28.86 million a good reason? Other senior Savvis executives will also get rich.

Appendix M: Terminate Employees and Get a Bonus

Warner Music Group's shares dropped 70 percent in 2007. However its CEO Edgar Bronfman Jr. received $1 million in salary and a $5.25 million bonus. Warner Music paid its five top executives more than $21 million in salary and bonuses in 2007, while terminating 1,600 jobs (Esra, 2008). In addition the Warner Music Group dropped 93 of the 193 artists signed to Warner Labels. In 2009 Warner Music paid its top five executives more than $21 million in salary and bonuses following the $2.6 billion acquisition of the US music group by a private equity consortium. Bronfman who led the buy-out received $1 million in salary and a $5.25 million bonus. Lyor Cohen, head of the US record music business, received $1 million and $5.24 million in salary and bonus, respectively. Paul Rene Albertini, head of Warner's international operations, was paid $1.25 million in salary and a $3.15 million bonus. Departing Warner/Chappell CEO, Les Bider, received a $2.44 million total payment. These payouts meant that Bronfman and his executives were paid more than three times Warner Music's $7 million operating income for the first 10 months of 2009. But that does not bother these thieves. They expected to recover $250 million by May 2010 when they would terminate 1,600 employees. While the record industry is in crisis with major label mergers, downsizing, the slashing of label rosters, and thousands of record company jobs being lost every year, along with the enormous change brought about by technology; what do we witness? An industry being led by executives who see their work as taking whatever money is left as they see the Titanic hitting the iceberg.

In November 2009 Michael Splinter CEO of Applied Materials announced that 10 to 15 percent of the company's workforce would be terminated and Splinter would take no bonus. But in 2010 he made up for that by receiving a $3.4 million bonus. DuPont Co. CEO Charles Holliday Jr., who retired in January 2009, received compensation valued at more than $10 million in 2008. This included a $1.7 million performance bonus. He terminated 2,500 employees in December 2008.

Cisco's net income rose 26 percent in 2009 and CEO John Chambers more than doubled his compensation to $18.9 million. How did he do it? He terminated 2000 employees. In May 2011 he announced another 4,000 would be terminated and two months later he revised that figure to 6,500 employees. In 2010 Chambers total compensation was $18.8 million, which included a bonus of $4.6 million.

In July 2011 RIMM announced that 2,000 employees would be terminated while the co-CEOs received base salaries of $1.2 million and were entitled to receive up to 128 percent of this salary in a year-end bonus.

In 2009 Freeport-McMoRan Copper & Gold announced that it would lay off at least 1,550 employees and in 2010 the company's chairman, James Moffett, received total compensation of $47.5 million. CEO Richard Adkerson received $43.8 million.

Paul Marciano, CEO of Guess received compensation worth $29.2 million in 2011, including $17 million from options — up 137 percent from 2010's $12.3 million. The company also paid nearly $40,000 for Marciano's auto expenses, including gas and insurance. Meanwhile he embarked on a cost cutting program and layoffs are looming.

In 2009 Union Pacific rail terminated 3,150 employees. In 2010 CEO Jim Young's bonus was increased to $3.7 million. Young's total compensation grew 6 percent to almost $12 million. About 1,500 Union Pacific employees remained furloughed at the end of 2010.

In 2009 about 175 employees at Brown Shoe Xpmpany took buy-outs, others were terminated and stores were closed. Their CEO Ronald Fromm nearly doubled his compensation in 2010 to $6.4 million, up from $3.2 million in 2009. This included a 175 percent increase in his bonus to $1.78 million.

In 2008 Motorola gave co-CEO Sanjay Jha a signing bonus of $100 million. In 2009 Jha and his partner in crime Co-CEO Greg Bown terminated 4,000 employees as Jha received a mere $3.77 million in annual pay. His pay included a guaranteed bonus of $1.2 million. Only in America can a CEO get a guaranteed bonus. Brown earned $8.46 million in 2009 and his bonus was $836,931.

In 2009 Albany International was closing plants and terminating employees but CEO Joseph Morone received a 47 percent increase in total compensation in 2010 to $2.9 million.

Former Milwaukee-based Aurora Health Care COO Donald Nestor received $8.2 million in salary, bonuses and other compensation after his retirement from the system in January 2009, a total that was disclosed two weeks after Aurora announced plans to eliminate 175 jobs by the end of 2010.

Since 2008 Royal Caribbean has been terminating hundreds of employees and in 2010 CEO Richard Fain received a 59 percent increase in compensation to $8.6 million, which included a bonus of nearly $4.1 million.

In July 2011 HSBC Holdings bank, announced it will be terminating 30,000 employees over the next decade, most of them Americans. In March 2011 their compensation committee awarded new CEO Stuart Gulliver a pay package of $22 million.

Raytheon has been terminating hundreds of employees and CEO Bill Swanson, in sympathy took an 8 percent decline in his cash bonus in 2010. In 2010 he received total compensation of $18.6 million and his bonus dropped to $2.8 million.

Lowes CEO Robert Niblock received a compensation increase of 11 percent in 2008, while its earnings declined 22 percent and employees were terminated. His compensation came to $6.6 million plus use of a private jet. In 2009 Lowe's CEO Robert Niblock received a raise in compensation to $11.7 million, which included a performance-based bonus of $2.8 million, up from $1.5 million in 2008. In 2010 he received a 3 percent raise to $12 million. In January 2011 he terminated 1,700 middle managers. In 2010 Niblock received a 3.3 percent raise from 2009 to over $12 million which included a bonus of $2.25 million. In January 2011 he told 1,700 middle managers they would be offered hourly positions to work in stores and if they refused they could leave. Technically they would be quitting and not entitled to unemployment benefits. Next Niblock followed the Home Depot trend and planed to hire 8,000 to 10,000 part timers. Niblock failed to study the absolute disaster it caused when Nardelli and other retailers tried part timers to save money. (See Chapter 11)

Since 2008, eBay has been terminating employees, and in 2011 CEO John Donahoe implemented the GE performance review system where the lowest performing 10 percent get the axe. Donahoe expects to axe the lowest 5 percent. Meanwhile in 2010, Donahoe's total compensation was $12.4 million and included a bonus of $736,538.

CSX has been terminating employees and putting thousands on furloughs and CEO Michael Ward received a raise and total compensation valued at $7.7 million in 2010. His increase was the result of a bonus that lumped 76 percent to $2.1 million.

Ameriprise Financial terminated 300 employees in January 2009 while it's CEO James Cracchiolo made $18.8 million in total compensation which included more than $9 million in "non-equity incentive pay." That's a fancy way of saying he got a cash bonus.

In 2010 State Street CEO Joseph Hooley received $12.9 million in total compensation, which included a $4 million bonus while announcing he planned to let go a total of 1,400 workers, or 5 percent of its global workforce, through 2011.

The CEO of Starwood Hotels & Resorts Worldwide Inc. received a pay package worth $9.5 million in 2010, up 7 percent from 2009, according to a regulatory filing. Since 2008 Starwood Hotels has been terminating employees and outsourcing their jobs and included in CEO Frits van Paasschen's pay package was a performance-based cash bonus of $3 million.

Robert Kelly, Bank of New York Mellon CEO, received a 38 percent increase in total compensation in 2010 to $19.4 million, compared with $14 million in 2009. In 2009 he terminated 1,800 employees. His 2010 compensation was $19.4 million, which included a $5.6 million bonus.

Since 2008 Coca-Cola has been laying off workers, and the cuts were to continue into 2011. Meanwhile in 2010 CEO Muhtar Kent received compensation valued at $19.2 million, 30 percent more than the year before. This included a 30 percent increase in his bonus to $6.5 million.

In May 2009, WellCare terminated 360 people companywide and then in February 2011 terminated 87 employees. Why? "To cut administrative costs." Then the compensation committee of the board of directors awarded CEO Alec Cunningham a $1 million cash bonus for 2010. In 2010 WellCare settled the claims with the U.S. Department of Justice for $137.5 million after it was accused of sending inflated medical bills to the federal government for reimbursement.

Fastenal terminated over 900 employees in 2009 and in 2010 CEO Willard Oberton's total compensation was $3,146,199 including a bonus of $2,661,199.

Schlumberger terminated 5,000 employees in March 2009 and in December 2009 its CEO Andrew Gould sold 550,000 shares of company stock for an average price of $65.55 a share. In 2010 his bonus increased 57 percent to $2.8 million from less than $1.8 million and his compensation rose 10.2 percent.

Barclays CEO Robert Diamond is expected to terminate between 7 and 10 percent of the workforce in early 2011. Bonuses were frozen but not for him. Diamond was expected to receive a 2010 bonus worth as much as $14.5 million.

Kimberly-Clark terminated 1,600 employees in 2009 and CEO Thomas Falk got a raise to nearly $9 million. This included a bonus of more than $2.8 million. In 2010 Falk again received $9 million.

Since 2009 Herman Miller had been terminating hundreds of employees and reducing the hours worked and eliminating 401(k) but in 2011 the five top executives nearly doubled their total compensation, rising 194 percent to $6.3 million from $3.2 million the year before.

CEO Brian Walker collected $2.7 million in total compensation, an 86 percent hike over the $1.45 million in compensation in 2010.

Since 2008 Whole Foods has be terminating employees. In July 2010, 59 were terminated. Meanwhile co-CEO Walter Robb received total compensation of $4.6 million in 2010, which included a $50,540 bonus plus a cash incentive bonus of $45,968. He got two bonuses.

Esco Technologies terminated 32 employees in 2009 and CEO Victor Richey got a salary and bonus increase in 2010. His total pay package of $2.56 million included a salary of $712,000, a bonus of $638,942 and stock worth $1.07 million. He also got $37,378 in perquisites, which included club dues, a car allowance and financial planning services, plus $9,660 to pay the taxes on his club dues.

While several baseball teams in 2011 are on the verge of bankruptcy and the gap between the rich teams and poor teams is increasing the President of Major League Baseball, Bub Selig is paid $18.35 million a year.

Deere CEO Samuel Allen received $4.28 million in fiscal 2009. Allen succeeded Robert Lane as CEO who took over as chairman in 2009. Lane received compensation of $14.02 million that included a salary of $1.51 million, non-equity incentives (bonus) totaling $4.86 million and stock and options valued at $7.49 million. Lane also received $127,309 in other compensation, including $91,509 for personal use of the company's aircraft (Connelly, 2009). In November, Deere said its fiscal 2009 profit fell 57 percent to $873 million, or $2.06 per share. The company lost $223 million in the fourth quarter due to big charges related in part to pension costs and job cuts. Its sales of farm and construction equipment fell 28 percent in the fourth quarter. In January 2009 Allen and Lane terminated 600 employees. In 2010 Allen's compensation almost tripled from the previous year to

$12.29 million, which included a $5.2 million bonus as he continued to terminate employees.

In 2009 Eastman Chemical terminated 300 employees and every U.S. employee took a 5 percent pay cut, but not CEO James Rogers. He received compensation valued at $3.5 million which included a $1 million cash bonus despite a 61 percent drop in earnings and 25 percent drop in sales.

Tyson Foods has been terminating jobs since 2008 and in 2010 terminated over 500 employees. But CEO Donnie Smith received compensation valued at nearly $8.7 million in his first year at the helm which included a performance-based cash bonus of nearly $3.8 million for the 2010 fiscal year.

In 2009 Donaldson Co. terminated 2,700 employees and William Cook, the chairman, president and CEO received $3.29 million in total compensation during the company's 2010 fiscal year, a raise of about 8 percent from the prior year. This included a bonus of $763,109 in 2010, up from $60,828 in the prior year.

In 2009, revenues at Affiliated Managers an asset management company fell for the second straight year. Affiliated did return to profitability in 2009 through terminations and reducing employee pay. But CEO Sean Healey had a blowout year. He was paid more than $18 million in 2009, 73 percent more than the previous year. His payday included a $5 million performance bonus and perks, such as use of the corporate jet (Wallack, 2010).

Microsoft terminated 5,000 employees in 2009 and in 2010 another 500 were shown the door while CEO Steve Ballmer got a 6 percent raise and $670,000 in cash incentives (a bonus) totaling $1.34 million in compensation. Ballmer owns 4.75 percent of outstanding Microsoft stock making him a billionaire. His highest paid executive was COO

Kevin Turner, who made $10.45 million during 2010. Next was Robbie Bach, the former president of the Entertainment and Devices Division, who made $7.65 million, and Peter Klein, CFO who got $3.21 million in direct compensation. In November 2010, Ballmer sold some of his 425 million shares for $1.3 billion. Now he only has 350 million left.

In April 2009 Apple terminated 1,200 fulltime Apple store employees and in 2010 COO Timothy Cook was amply rewarded. He received total compensation of $59.1 million for running operations during Steve Jobs medical leave, and this included a $5 million bonus. In 2009 Cook's total compensation was a meager $1.64 million. What a raise. In August 2011 Jobs decided his cancer would not allow him to function as CEO. He tragically passed away two months later. Cook, now CEO, was given a million shares of the stock that will vest over the next 10 years, worth an estimated $384 million. Jobs was given a similar grant in 2000 worth $600 million.

Tennessee Valley Authority (TVA) the government's largest supplier of electricity and established by President Franklyn D. Roosevelt to provide jobs during the Great Depression, decided to terminate jobs in 2010. It terminated 615 employees, but President Tom Kilgore could triple his pay- up to $3.6 million. In addition, Kilgore was eligible to more than quadruple his base pay of $850,000 with bonuses if TVA achieves the top level of performance standards for rates, reliability and reputation set by his board. FDR is turning over in his grave.

Dow Chemical CEO Andrew Liveris got a salary increase from over $12 million in 2008 to over $15 million in 2009. This included a $1.65 million base salary and the rest in performance awards and long-term incentives. In 2009 Liveris closed 20 plants and terminated over 5,000 employees. In 2010 as layoffs continued he received a performance-based bonus of $5 million and his salary increased to $1.69 million from $1.65 million. He also received stocks worth $5.68 million bringing his total compensation to $21.3 million.

In 2010 Blockbuster terminated 300 employees and began closing stores and was so strapped for cash it skipped a scheduled debt payment in July 2010. But CEO James Keyes got a performance bonus of $2.2 million and if he stayed til June 2010 he would get a $650,000 cash retention bonus. In September 2010 the company filed for bankruptcy. Keyes succeeded John Antioco who left in July 2007 after receiving $8 million in bonus and severance. It was reported that Antioco sold his blockbuster stocks and invested in its competitor Netflix.

Nike terminated 5 percent of its global workforce in March 2009 this included 500 employees at its headquarters in Oregon. And guess what CEO Mark Parker got? Parker got a 268 percent raise to more than $14.5 million in compensation, which included a bonus of $4.4 million.

No one knows exactly how many employees Master Card terminated since 2010 because they do it in small batches around the globe but in sympathy CEO Robert Selander took a .3 percent decrease in compensation to $10.3 million. Selander will retire July 1, 2010 and his replacement will be COO Ajay Banga who got a bonus of $2.1 million. Selander also got a bonus. As the new CEO Banga earned $11.9 million in 2010.

In 2009 Legg Mason paid CEO Mark Fetting $6.55 million for the fiscal year to March 31, a 39 percent increase as his company reported a net loss of $1.9 billion for the fiscal year. In 2010 he received a 12 percent increase in compensation as he terminated 350 employees and he got a bonus of $950,000.

While announcing the termination of 2,000 employees and the closing of several plants, Harley-Davidson's CEO Keith Wendell obtained a pay package valued at $6.4 million in 2010. The retiring CEO James Ziemer received a pay package valued at $2.9 million for four months of work which included a bonus of $455,144. In July 2010 they announced another 1,400 to 1,600 jobs would be terminated. Wall Street loves these guys: as sales decline profits go up because they know "cost cutting." That's the new word for terminations.

In 2009 Norfolk Southern revenues dropped $8 billion from $10.7 billion in 2008 and they terminated 150 employees, but CEO Charles Moorman suffered very little. His compensation was $10.9 million 9 percent less than 2008. This was because his bonus declined to $613,700 from nearly $1.8 million. His perks included $38,626 for the use of a corporate plane, $4,800 for a physical exam, $8,575 in contributions to an investment plan and $63,492 in charitable contributions.

Constellation Brands CEO Robert Sands received compensation of $6.77 million in fiscal 2010, a raise of 6.5 percent as he slashed the workforce from 8,200 in 2008 to 6,000. His compensation included a performance-based cash bonus of $1.27 million.

In 2010 Bristol-Myers Squibb hired a new CEO Lamberto Andreotti and gave him an annual base salary of $1.4 million, plus an "annual discretionary incentive payment" based on a target of 150% of his base salary, if he attains one or more pre-established performance goals. He will also receive a long-term performance award valued at $2.1 million, and a "market share unit award" valued at $1.4 million and if fired 2 times his base salary. Meanwhile Bristol-Meyers terminated 800 employees in 2009 and Andreotti terminated a whooping 4,300 employees in 2010, while he gets $11.8 million.

The executives at Westchester Medical Center really know how to kill morale. After a $70 million loss and termination of 400 employees in 2009, CEO Michael Israel and COO Gary Brudnicki reeled in

$456,360 in bonuses. Israel's pay was a record high of more than $1.2 million and Brudnicki's more than $720,000. In Dec. 2011, Isreal announced another 250 employees would be terminated.

In 2009 Corning CEO Wendell Weeks terminated 3,500 employees and his compensation was $7.82 million. In 2010 Weeks got a 19.6 percent increase in compensation to $9.35 million in 2010, this included a $2.2 million cash bonus. Also included was $429,114 in perks, including a retirement plan contribution totaling $178,715, $149,296 for home and personal security, and $85,241 for the personal use of company aircraft.

In 2009 CEO of UPS Scott Davis received total compensation valued at $5.5 million, a 6.2 percent increase from 2008: and this included a bonus of $130,523. In January 2010, Davis announced the termination of 1,800 employees and what did he get? Almost a hundred percent increase in compensation, to $10.7 million.

Goodyear terminated 5,000 employees and froze salaries in 2009 but not for CEO Robert Keegan. He got a 40 percent increase in compensation. This included a doubling of his bonus up to $9.5 million from a paltry $4.6 million in 2008. In April 2010 Keegan retired and Richard Kramer took over: he terminated another 2,000 employees as the company lost $216 million. Kramer is such a talented manager that his compensation increased 69 percent to $8.5 million (Durbin, 2011).

In 2007, Lockheed Martin CEO Robert Stevens obtained nearly $20 million in stock options while government auditors were accusing the aerospace firm of more than $8 billion in cost overruns. In 2009 and early 2010 he terminated over 3,000 employees and he took 10 percent pay cut in 2009 to $20.6 million. In actuality his salary edged up, but his bonus dropped to $1.8 million and incentive pay dropped to $5.2 million. In November 2010 Stevens announced it would close a Minnesota facility by 2013 and transfer work to two other facilities, terminating about 1,500 employees. He sought voluntary buy-outs for another 6,500 in July 2011. The buy-out offer is two weeks salary and one additional week salary for every year worked up to 26 years. Why would employees take such a pittance of a buy-out? Because they know terminations are the next step and they could receive a pink slip any day. Meanwhile the CEO's total compensation in 2010 was $21.9 million.

Another defense contractor Northrop Grumman offered 23,000 employees voluntary terminations in 2011 while in 2010 CEO Wesley Bush doubled his total compensation to over $22 million. Then they announced 800 job cuts will occur in January 2012. This is how they pressure employees to take the voluntary termination with some benefits by creating fear that if they try to hang onto their job they will be fired with nothing.In November 2008, La-Z-Boy terminated 240 employees, CEO Kurt Darrow received a $202,000 bonus for fiscal year 2008. In 2007 he received a $150,000 bonus.

In 2003 employees at American Airlines took pay cuts of up to 50 percent in an effort to save the carrier from bankruptcy. But not CEO Gerard Arpey of American's parent company, AMR. Arpey had his base salary rise every year since 2005, except 2009. Meanwhile the airline's pilot's wages have been stuck in a wage-adjusted base, which means they are being compensated for the same amount they were paid in 1992. At the same time the airline's executives have received $330 million in stock grants and option awards since 2005. At the end of 2009, the airline will have terminated as many as 1,600 workers while giving over 1,000 executive's bonuses. The union is outrageously upset at the bonuses. Their bosses get more and more while employees have not recovered from the pay cuts they took in 2003. This fight continues into 2010 in what has become an annual protest by the Association of Professional Flight Attendants against AMR on the day each year bonuses are given out to executives. In 2009 AMR awarded about $3 million in stock bonuses to about 1,000 top executives and managers as part of its annual incentive program and the top five executives also received $12.5 million in total compensation that year, including CEO Gerard Arpey's $4.7 million, most of which was stock grants and options. In 2010, AMR lost $471 million, the only major airline to lose money and what did Arpey get? A raise of 11 percent to $5.2 million in total compensation. Plus Arpey's newly appointed President Tom Horton who was promoted in 2010 from CFO got a 45 percent increase in total compensation. In November 2011, AMR filed for bankruptcy and Arpey retired at age 53 and Horton took over with compensation in excess of $9 million. AMR has demanded more concessions from employees.

Alcoa's CEO Klaus Kleinfeld received compensation valued at $9.7 million in 2008. He has threatened to curtail production and terminate 275 workers at a smelter in Canada if workers there did not agree to a 15 percent pay cut by April 30, 2008. In 2009 he earned $11.2 million while he terminated 13,500 employees. His compensation included a doubling of his PERFORMANCE BONUS of $3.8 million. In 2010 his compensation increased about 21 percent to $12.3 million but his bonus dropped to $2.6.

In 2009 International Game Technology (IGT) terminated 55 employees after forcing hundreds into early retirement in 2008. However it's CEO Patti Hart received $6.3 million in 2009 including a $400,000 bonus. Hart expects to cut $100 million in 2010, more heads will roll.

DuPont CEO Ellen Kullman got a salary increase and bonus in 2009 after she terminated 2,000 employees. She was also awarded a bonus of $1.5 million for 2009 and was given a target bonus of about $2 million for 2010. They did not say how many employees she had to terminate to obtain that bonus. These were called "short term bonuses": she also was granted a long-term incentive award (bonus) valued at $6.5 million. In 2008 she terminated 2,500 full-time employees and 4,000 contractors. In 2009 and 2010 she continued the outsourcing process and terminating American workers. In 2010 she received a 36 percent increase from 2009 with compensation valued at $11.3 million.

While this is not actually a bonus it is a hefty windfall for two executives at CAE. The company will give two executives $1 million each if they do not get the CEO position when Robert Brown retires in 2009. This is a million each for not getting promoted. Jeff Roberts got his million but Marc Parent did not because he got the promotion. In addition to receiving $17.3 million 2008, the newly retired Brown will collect $768,764 a year. Oh, by the way, CAE laid off 700 of its employees in 2009.

Cincinnati Bell terminated 130 employees and offered a buyout plan to about 900 of its 1,200 union workers and ended contributions to its employee's 401(k) retirement plan. But CEO Jack Cassidy does not need to worry. He was rewarded with a $2.1 million retention bonus and a $1.9 million performance bonus and his total compensation increased 72 percent over his 2009 pay package to $8.6 million in 2010. Cassidy expects to continue outsourcing and terminating jobs in America. Cassidy gets his raise despite reporting a loss of $61.8 million in net income and an 18.8 percent negative annual return for investors. Also Cassidy's partners CFO Gary Wojtaszek and General Counsel Christopher Wilson received raises of 80.3 percent and 54.3 percent, respectively.

Appendix N: Fail and Get a Bonus

American International Group (AIG) and Wall Street banks have caused a furor by giving bonuses to the very same executives who got them into their financial mess. Let's look at the AIG disaster. CEO Martin Sullivan resigned in June 2008 after his company posted two quarters of record losses. He was given a $47 million severance package. In September, the federal government saved AIG from bankruptcy by taking it over and presenting it with an $85 billion loan. A month after receiving the $80 billion loan, AIG sent 70 of their top performers to a California resort where they spent $440,000 for rooms, meals and spa fees. AIG recently fired its President of Financial Products, who had earned $280 million during his stay with the company. When he was let go he kept his $34 million bonus and is now being paid $1 million a month as a consultant to AIG (Ahrens, 2008). A celebrity CEO was installed to head AIG, Edward M. Liddy, a former CEO of Allstate who lasted less than a year. In August 2009 he was replaced by Robert Benmosche former MetLife CEO who receives more than $98,000 a month in his retirement package. AIG will pay him $7 million annually. Talk about double dipping. Almost immediately after taking the position Benmosche took off for vacation to his 12 bathroom villa in Croatia. In the company jet?

In October 2008 the Federal Reserve Board gave AIG $37.8 billion in addition to the $480 billion bailout AIG obtained from the government. In March 2009 AIG reported another loss, the largest quarterly loss in corporate history, $61 billion. At the same time they gave out bonuses totaling $165 million. The highest bonus given was $6.5 million and seven executives from the unit that brought down the company will each got over $3 million. Then AIG obtained an additional $31 billion bailout and sought to split up and sold off, as if anyone would buy this toxic dump. Maurice Greenberg, CEO from 1967 to 2005, brought his former company to court claiming the management team's deception had cost him $2 billion. In August 2010 a federal judge awarded Greenberg and former CFO Howard Smith $60 million from the company's insurers to cover legal and other costs as part of a proposed settlement of investor lawsuits.

Another example is Sprint. In 2007 Sprint won the title as the worst pay-for-performance rating among the Standard and Poor's 500 index of corporations. Sprint executives were awarded pay valued at nearly $74 million as the company lost $29 billion (Graybow, 2008a). In the second quarter of 2008 the company lost close to a million customers and $344 million. In January 2009 Sprint announced approximately 8,000 layoffs, a suspension of its employee 401(k) match for 2009, an extension of a 2008 salary freeze for nonexecutives through 2009, and an end to its tuition reimbursement program. Things were bad for everyone at Sprint except for Dan Hesse, its CEO. He was awarded a base salary of $1.2 million in 2008 along with a $2.7 million cash signing bonus, plus a bonus potential targeted at 170 percent of his base salary, or $2 million, with maximum bonus potential of $4 million. With his participation in the company's long-term incentive compensation plan, he was given the opportunity to gain equity, cash based awards and restricted shares valued at $10 million, along with options for 3.275 million shares of Sprint common stock.

In December, 2008 Brian Tierney CEO of Philadelphia Media Holdings (PMH) received a Bonus increasing his pay 40 percent. In February

2009 PMH filed for bankruptcy. The bonus was awarded two months after the company's unions voted to postpone $25-a-week raises for each of its members at the request of Tierney. Tierney also terminated 71 employees in January 2007, 68 employees in February 2008, and 35 employees in December, 2008 as he received his bonus (Hilzoy, 2009.) The Philadelphia Daily News sought a $10 million bailout from the state of Pennsylvania after it filed for bankruptcy in February, 2009 while its CEO Brian Tierney received $1.175 million in compensation. This included a $350,000 bonus.

Another newspaper chain the Tribune, owner of the Baltimore Sun, the Los Angeles Times, the Chicago Tribune and the Chicago Cubs baseball team, filed for bankruptcy in December, 2008. But that did not stop the company from paying millions in performance bonuses in 2009. Under the bonus plan Tribune's top ten executives would get about $2 million each, while 29 additional "key" executives would split $15.6 million. In January 2010 the bankruptcy judge ruled that these executives could keep their $45.6 million bonus money. Then these executives devised another great payday plan. This plan would pay its top 43 executives a severance package of cash and benefits if they were fired by the board after the company emerged from bankruptcy. Oh yes, over 3,000 employees have lost their jobs and what did they get, you guessed it, nothing, in addition the shares that about 10,000 nonunion employees received in the ESOP [employee stock ownership plan] deal are now worthless as a result of the bankruptcy. Between May 2009 and February 2010 executives have earned a total of $57.3 million in bonuses. In November 2011, the company agreed to pay former CEO Randy Michaels (a former radio disk jockey) up to $725,000 to settle a dispute over his bonus.

In 2008 Hovnanian Enterprises saw its stock drop 62 percent, revenue fall 31 percent and the company posted a $1.1 billion loss in the fiscal year ended Oct. 31, 2008, but CEO Ara Hovnanian got a bonus of $1.5 million in cash and stock.

Allied Capital's stock lost about a third of its value in 2007, but its CEO William Walton, received $11 million; including a $1.5 million salary and a $5.3 million bonus

In 2008, Euronext CEO Duncan Niederauer got a $4 million bonus despite a net loss of $738 million and a stock decline of 69 percent.

Hologic's posted a $2.2 million loss in 2009 but CEO John W. Cumming, a $1.5 million "retention payment" (Bonus) as part of his $10.5 million pay package. He then resigned and became chairman.

A bonus of $5.4 million went to outgoing State Street CEO Ronald Logue. The financial services firm posted a $1.8 billion loss in 2009. State Street said that Logue would receive the $5.4 million over two years (Wallack, 2010).

Campell Soup CEO Douglas Conant received $10.1 million in the fiscal year that ended Aug. 1st, down from $11.59 million in fiscal 2009. Conant terminated over 3,000 employees in 2010 but he still got his bonus, incentives and perks.

In July, 2006 Cedar Fair acquired Paramount Parks and incurred huge debt and in 2010 its share price has dropped 48 percent and its annual dividends fell 90 percent but the base pay of CEO Dick Kinzel rose 23 percent to $1.3 million. In October, 2010 Cedar Fair's stock price dropped to $13.62 from $26.05 before the acquisition but Kinzel still got a bonus of $1.2 (Vellequette, 2011).

Novell lost money in 2007, 2008 and 2009 but CEO Ronald Hovsepian received a $1.3 million performance award.

Eaton Vance Corporation gave its CEO Thomas Faust a $2.7 million bonus as profits slipped 34 percent.

Fraser Papers stock tumbled in 2008 and in mid-2009 it filed for bankruptcy. But its six top executives received bonuses. Its CEO Peter Gordon received a $162,500 cash bonus atop his $325,000 base salary, stock option awards of $637,500, another $15,750 in pension value and $3,126 in "other compensation." His take in 2008 was $1.14 million (Sambides, 2010).

Occidental's CEO Ray Irani received $31.4 million in total compensation in 2009, a 39.4 percent increase over the previous year as its earnings dropped 57.5 percent and revenues dropped 36.4 percent from 2008. His compensation included a $3.75 million cash bonus.

CEO Mickey Arison of Carnival received a 51 percent compensation increase in 2009 as his company's profits fell nearly 22 percent. His base salary was only $880,000 but his performance-based bonus was $2.2 million, and his restricted stock awards were $3.6 million on the day they were granted. Arison got other compensation totaling $496,513, including personal use of the company aircraft, personal use of sporting event tickets, health insurance costs and premiums, automobile leases and a driver and security.

Fidelity National Information Services CEO, Lee Kennedy, received a 1 percent increase in compensation in 2008, valued at almost $10 million, which included a performance based cash bonus of $2.3 million as the corporation's net income fell 62 percent and its shares lost nearly 30 percent.

Assurant awarded its CEO Robert Pollock a 53 percent compensation increase in 2008 valued at $5.4 million. This included a 100 percent increase in his performance bonus as his company's profit fell

31 percent and stock fell 55 percent. A performance bonus? Since 2004 Assurant has been quietly terminating hundreds jobs.

Boston Scientifics' CEO J. Raymond Elliott began work in June 2009 and received a $1.5 million bonus. Boston Scientific posted a $1 billion loss in 2009 however Elliott received compensation totaling $33.4 million. In 2010 Elliott received only $4.9 million and decided to leave the company. In July 2011 they terminated 1,300 employees. In September, 2011 Michael Mahoney was given the top spot and he was given a sign-on bonus of $1.5 million plus an additional sign-on bonus of $750,000 if he stays 30 days plus a base salary of $900,000 and stock grants and options benefits worth $16.7 million. Let's not forget his perks. He gets a $100,000 corporate aircraft perk, a $69,230 supplementary cash payment related to his hire date perk and $90,000 to reimburse Mahoney for legal costs tied to his employment negotiations. Are you kidding!

At Southwest Airlines, CEO Gary Kelly received a raise in compensation of $1.7 million up from $1.3 million in 2007. As the company reported a $91 million loss in the first quarter of 2009 his pay included a $462,000 bonus. However, as of April 1st 2009 he will reduce his pay by 10 percent until profitability returns.

Howard Schultz CEO of Starbucks terminated 19 percent of its workforce in 2009 and he got a pay increase of 25 percent in 2009 including a $1 million bonus. The number of terminated employees is difficult to determine because he does them in small batches with no public announcement. Estimates suggest he has terminated between 14,000 to 45,000 employees in 2009. In 2010 Schultz got a 42 percent increase in compensation to $22 million.

In 2008 Michael Szymanczyk CEO of the Altria Group had his compensation increase 29 percent from 2007, when Szymanczyk's total compensation was about $9 million. This included a performance bonus of $2.8 million. Altria's profit for 2008 fell 50 percent. Net income dropped to $4.93 billion, or $2.36 per share, from $9.79 billion, or $4.62 per share.

AK Steel will temporarily idle some of the 2,100 employees over the next six-to-seven weeks or more in the spring of 2008 and 130 employees were terminated. However, CEO Jim Wainscott got a 3 percent increase in overall compensation, making $9.5 million in 2008. This included $4.5 million in bonus pay for great performance.

According to Singer (2007), General Electric (GE) CEO Jeffrey Immelt received about $17.86 million in total compensation in 2006 as calculated by the company; including a $5 million bonus. Immelt's pay included a $3.3 million salary, $7.4 million in stock awards, and $574,322 in option awards. Included in Immelt's 2006 compensation, was $219,533 for the use of aircraft, and $76,614 for other benefits such as financial counseling, tax preparation, leased car and annual physical exam. In 2008, GE stock lost half its value and in the first quarter of 2009 the stock fell another 33 percent. Immelt then announced he will forgo his $11.7 million bonus and performance award. **BONUS and PERFORMANCE REWARD?** In June 2009, GE came under investigation for accounting manipulations going as far back as 2003. In 2010 Immelt got a raise in total compensation to $15.2 million which once again included a bonus of $4 million meanwhile his company not only did not pay any federal taxes but instead received $3.3 billion refund.

In 2008 CUNA, a credit union, saw its net assets declined $7.9 million and its pretax income drop to $887,173 from $3.2 million in 2007. CUNA also experienced severe losses in its defined benefit plan. Those and other losses caused CUNA to lay off 26 employees in 2009 and freeze salaries of senior staff and institute mandatory five-day furloughs. But CUNA's CEO Dan Mica did not suffer, he had a good year.

Mica received a 12 percent increase in compensation with a bonus of $667,393. **A bonus!** In addition to his bonus he received a base salary and fringe benefits totaling $810,528; a car allowance of $26,617; and deferred compensation of $349,039.

Windstream Corp., CEO Jeffery Gardner received a compensation package valued at $6.4 million in 2008, a 51 percent increase from the prior year and his performance-based bonus payment increased by more than a million dollars to $1.79 million, from $774,474. In 2007 Windstream's earnings for the year dropped 55 percent. (AP, 2009).

In spite of the financial meltdown and the anger over bonuses and executive compensation, PNC Financial Services Group's top five executives received in 2008 bonuses valued at about $7 million. In the fall of 2008 PNC received a $7.6 billion bailout from the government and terminated 5,800 employees (Lepro, 2009). In February 2011 they terminated another 5,300 and at the same time they gave their CEO James Rohr a 20 percent for 2011 raising his annual salary to $1.2 million.

Vertex CEO Matthew Emmens, took over five months into 2010 and he received $2.8 million performance award as the company lost $642 million (Wallack, 2010).

Hercules Offshore lost $145 million and shareholders received a negative 27 percent return in 2010 but CEO John Rynd got a 90 percent pay boost to $2.5 million. His VP James Noe got 107 percent hike to $1.2 million; his CFO Stephen Butz's pay nearly tripled, he got a 189 percent raise to $963,000; Chief Accounting Officer Troy Carson's pay jumped 159 percent to $829,000; VP Terrell Carr got a 149 percent raise to $1 million; and HRVP Lisa Rodriguez only received a 40 percent raise to $959,000 (Langford, 2011).

Employees at Channel 10 in Rhode Island were forced to take 15 unpaid days off between June and December of 2011 while their boss CEO Marshall Morton, received a $.6 million increase in 2010. His total compensation was under $2 million in 2010.

Appendix O: Kill the Unions and Get Rich

In April 2009, The New York Times owner of the Boston Globe threatened to close it down unless the newspaper's unions agreed to $20 million in concessions. But no concessions were required from Times CEO Janet L. Robinson who made $5,578,451 in compensation for 2008. This includes $1,552,603 in restricted stock awards, as well as a salary of $1 million.

AT&T CEO Randall Stephenson, who made $15 million in 2008, asked his union employees to take a 40 percent cut in pay and announced the company could no longer afford to pay employee health benefits. He wants the 110,000 employees to pay between $3,300 to $4,500 a year toward their own health care coverage. Stephenson terminated over 2,500 employees in 2009 and expects to terminate thousands more and what did he get, a 35 percent increase in compensation to $20.3 million. This included a $5.85 million cash bonus. His board determined he had earned this money "in light of the economic environment and the workforce reductions." This is one of the few times a board of directors stated in their proxy statement that a CEO was rewarded for terminating employees. This is a direct affront to AT&T's unions. In 2010 he was at it again, terminating union employees while receiving $27.3 million in total compensation, which included $5.1 million bonus. His 2010 perks included: $77,182 for personal use of company aircraft; $28,991 for auto benefits; $15,174 for club memberships; $14,000 for financial counseling, including tax preparation and estate planning; $11,256 for supplemental health insurance premiums; and $2,714 in communications expenses. Stephenson also received $164,189 in company-paid premiums on supplemental life insurance; $73,400 for matching 401(k) contributions and $30,504 for home security (Bednarz, 2011).

In 2010 Larry Young CEO of Mott/Snapple/Dr. Pepper demanded his union employees take wage and benefit cuts including a $1.50/hour wage reduction, a freeze in pension benefits, a 20 percent reduction of the employer match to the 401(k) plan, and other negative changes to the employees' health insurance plan. Meanwhile Young made $6.5 million in compensation a 113 percent increase from three years ago.

Frontier Communications will terminate 3 percent of its work force in Pennsylvania and blamed the unions. In West Virginia Frontier purchased Verizon's land line and the union wants Frontier (legacy) employees who make $6 per hour less than Verizon employees to have parity. While CEO Maggie Wilderotter seeks to destroy the unions, her total compensation jumped from $4.8 million to $8.6 million in 2010. The Communications Workers of America claim that Frontier is rewarding its top executives -- to the tune of $2 million in bonuses -- but snubbing rank-and-file employees (Eyre, 2011).

In the five fiscal years through 2006, CEO of Verizon Ivan Seidenberg received over $114 million in compensation, while total shareholder return was a negative 5 percent. In 2008 he received $20.2 million, as Verizon's stock fell 20 percent. Verizon's second-quarter profit fell 21 percent and the company terminated more than 8,000 employee and contractor jobs in July 2009 and another 8,000 in December 2009. In

2010 Seidenberg terminated another 13,000 employees (Ellis, 2010). He received compensation in fiscal 2009 valued at $17.5 million as its net profit fell 18 percent to $10.36 billion, or $1.29 per share. He is so hated by his union employees that they call him "Ivan the Terrible." Forbes ranks http://current.com/1crit4c Seidenberg's efficiency at 184 on their pay/performance score, and the worse a CEO can get is 189. So what did he get in 2010? A 4 percent raise to $18.1 million which included a 33 percent increase in his bonus to $3.9 million. In August 2011, Seidenberg resigned a very rich man. He was replaced by Lowell McAdam, former chief of Verizon Wireless and current president of Verizon. Seidenberg will remain as chairman. Of course he will. In 2010 Verizon earned $11.9 billion in pre-tax profits in the United States and received a $705 million federal tax refund. Despite a $6.89 billion in profit the first six months of 2011, in August the company demanded that its union employees give up compensation of up to $20,000 per year per employee and the right to outsource even more jobs overseas, having already sent 25,000 out of the country. Meanwhile, the company's top executives collected $258 million in salaries and bonuses in the last four years (Durso, 2011).

Appendix P: Pay Me More

FedEx has classified its drivers as "independent contractors" so it does not have to provide benefits such as overtime pay or workplace protections like those guaranteed under the Americans with Disability Act or the Family and Medical Leave Act. However, its executives have a "Management Retention Agreement" that ensures them they have a job up to three years after a merger or acquisition. As they closed facilities and terminated thousands of employees in 2009 and 2010, CEO Fred Smith's compensation fell 2 percent in 2011 to $7.3 million, mostly because his perks were worth less than in 2010. But his performance-based cash bonus fell 6 percent to $375,000, and his other compensation slid 37 percent to $428,061. His perks already had dropped almost by half between 2009 and 2010. His perks included: a bonus, retirement plan contributions, tax reimbursements, jet travel, use of a company car, security services, tax preparation services, financial counseling and insurance premiums.

In 2011 Simon Property Group gave their CEO David Simon shares worth $120 million to stick around until 2019. In 2010 he was paid $7.1 million in salary, bonus, long-term incentives and an additional $17 million in equity awarded.

Appendix Q: The Airline Industry

In September 2005, Northwest and Delta airlines filed for Chapter 11 bankruptcy and defaulted on their pension payments to employees. Since 2000, Delta lost $10 billion, cut 23,000 jobs and obtained pay cuts for pilots, and managers. In the meantime, Delta spent more than $44 million setting up trusts to protect executives' pension benefits from creditors, saying it was needed to retain executives in hard times. In early 2011 Delta offered "buyouts" and got 2,000 employees who jumped on it. Then in September they said the buyouts did not reduce enough operating expenses and they terminated 200 managers and administrators. It's take the buyout or you're going to be fired.

The airline industry may be experiencing turbulence, but not their CEOs. When Glenn Tilton joined United Airlines as CEO in 2002, he was given a $4.5 million pension trust, plus a starting salary of $950,000, a $3 million signing bonus and 100,000 shares in UAL Corp. Like Northwest and Delta, three months after he was hired, Tilton led United into Chapter 11 bankruptcy proceedings. In 2005, he terminated United's four employee pension plans, covering about 120,000 active and retired workers. It was the largest pension default in U.S. history, dumping about $5 billion in obligations on the government-run Pension Benefit Guaranty Corp. In 2006, when United emerged from bankruptcy, Tilton's total compensation was valued at almost $24 million (Lazarus, 2008). The union representing pilots at

United had urged CEO Tilton to resign, accusing him of steering the carrier down a path of poor morale, customer service and financial performance. In 2008, United Airlines has lost more money than nearly all other U.S. competitors combined. But Tilton was drawing $10.3 million. In 2008, United's stock price had fallen from $50 a share to $10 a share.

Retiring Delta CEO Leo Mullin was paid $13 million in compensation in 2001, and was given 22 years of instant seniority—although he worked for Delta for only five-and-half years—boosting his retirement package to $16 million. Former Delta CEO Ronald Allen, who was fired in 1997, continued to draw $500,000 a year from Delta for consulting services up until 2005. Allen's exit package also included a $4.5 million cash severance payment and a $765,000-a-year pension. He also got 10 years' worth of perks, such as a $91,099 for a 2,090-square-foot office and secretary and $408,776 to design build and furnish the office. Delta also paid $25,565 for his home security system and $210,000 in legal fees to work up his retirement agreement. Only a CEO could be fired and given such treatment.

Union workers at Northwest had a pension plan based on years of service. In 2004 they went on strike against Northwest's demands for the elimination of more than half their jobs and the replacement of traditional guaranteed pensions with 401(k) plans that offered them $85 a month for every year they work. According to the Aircraft Mechanics Fraternal Association (AMFA), a mechanic who retires at 65, after 40 years at Northwest, will collect about $40,000 a year (Isaacs, 2005). However, when Northwest Airlines CEO Richard Anderson left the company in 2004, he received his pension in a lump-sum payment of $3,028,700. In September 2007 Anderson returned, this to time to run the merged Northwest and Delta Air Lines. In 2008 Delta lost $8.9 billion, but Anderson was awarded an almost 80 percent compensation increase to over $17 million, and Deltas President Ed Bastian did very well as his total compensation went from $4.6 million in 2007 to $8.7 million in 2008.

The company's four retired executives—Steenland and executive vice presidents Tim Griffin, Phillip Haan and Andrew Roberts—will receive a total of $2,476,100 in annual pension benefits. This is enough to fund the pensions of 90 flight attendants with comparable years of service (Isaacs, 2005).

In addition to their pension benefits, Northwest's top five executives (the above-mentioned, plus Executive Vice President and General Counsel Barry Simon) have taken in $32 million in compensation since 2002, not including other perks such as lifetime health-care coverage and travel benefits. The five also sold more than $1 million worth of stock in the months leading up to the bankruptcy announcement, as did big investors, like professional financier and former NWA Board of Directors member Al Checchi, who sold 1,650,240 shares from April 23 to May 3, raking in $8,439,884 (Isaacs, 2005).

The *New York Times* reported that the timing of Northwest's bankruptcy filing allowed the company to protect its assets while executives reneged on a payment of $65 million into the employee pension fund, which is already under funded by $3.8 billion. If Northwest skipped the payment before filing for bankruptcy, it would have been in violation of federal pension laws, and the government-run Pension Benefit Guaranty Corporation (PBGC) could have placed a lien on the airline's assets, giving itself a better chance of recovering some of the money (Isaacs, 2005).

Instead, the newspaper noted, "[S]ince Northwest filed for bankruptcy first then skipped the pension contribution, the government has no legal power to place a lien on its assets. It makes the pension guarantor—and the employees and retirees whose interests the government represents—into unsecured creditors for the $65 million. Unsecured creditors generally fare poorly in bankruptcy recovering just pennies for every dollar they are owed."

If the PBGC takes over Northwest's pension plans, pilots would suffer the loss of half or more of their pensions because the PBGC caps payments at $45,613 a year for plans canceled in 2005. Other unionized workers could also see drastic reductions.

After 20 months of restructuring Northwest Airlines came out of bankruptcy in May 2007. Doug Steenland its CEO cut $1.4 billion in labor expenses, with pilots and flight attendants having their wages cut between 20 and 40 percent. However, CEO Steenland received a bonus of $516,384 dollars, and he will get a total compensation package of more than $26.6 million in stock ($5.8 million in stock options and $20.8 million worth of restricted stocks that will vest over the next four years.).

When USAirways emerged from bankruptcy in 2005, CEO Doug Parker was awarded an almost $6 million package — employees got pay cuts of up to 53 percent. USAirways pilots lost their pensions completely. In 2008, 2009 and 2010 as hundreds of employees were terminated Parker got a 6.5 percent increase in compensation in 2010 to $2.8 million, which included an incentive bonus of almost $1 million.

Delta's pension funds are in even worse shape. If the company defaults on its obligations it would set a record, surpassing the size of the United Airlines pension collapse and further staggering the overburdened pension guarantee board. According to board officials, Delta's pension plan has promised benefits worth $17.5 billion, but it only has $6.9 billion in assets. With its bankruptcy filing the company is expected to press for even more drastic cuts than it outlined in its corporate restructuring plan last year, when it announced plans to cut $5 billion and 7,000 jobs by 2006 (Issaacs, 2005). Delta has terminated its pilots pensions.

After two and a half years of negotiation the pilots of Hawaiian Airlines made significant concessions in their pension agreements to help Hawaiian out of its 2005 bankruptcy. At the same time CEO Mark Dunkerley obtained a 42 percent compensation increase in 2008 to $3.2 million.

This problem is not unique to the airlines. We are seeing a growing number of CEOs denying pensions to their retirees. This means that the government-run PBGC will need to pay out billions of dollars to hundreds of thousands of retirees. The annual deficit of PBGC nearly doubled to $22 billion in fiscal 2009 from $11.2 billion in fiscal 2008 (Dixon, Kerber & Krasny, 2009).

Estimates suggest that 30 to 44 million employees in America are at risk of not being paid the pensions they are owed, and the PBGC owes more than $11.2 billion to employees in failed pensions programs than it has available to pay them, suggesting that a crisis is at hand.

An employee can work a life-time and will be denied a pension, but not their CEOs: they can work a few years and walk away with multimillion dollar pensions. The Government Accountability Office reported in November 2009 that ten large U.S. companies paid senior executives a total of $350 million in five years prior to dropping retirement plans for their employees.

Appendix R: Terminate Employees and Get a Raise

CEO of Lenovo William Amelio got a 54 percent increase in compensation in fiscal 2009. He earned $17.6 million as he resigned in March 2009. His compensation included $3.25 for "loss of office." In fiscal 2009 he terminated 2,500 employees and Lenovo lost $226.4 million.

Walgreen purchased Drugs.Com and CEO Dawn Lepore received $9.1 million in stock and options when the deal was completed, this is in addition to $6.2 million in salary, bonuses and the sale of stock she accumulated between 2004 and 2009. In 2009 Walgreen terminated 1,000 salaried jobs as part of a plan to save $1 billion in annual expenses by 2011. And in fiscal 2011 Walgreen CEO Gregory Wasson was amply rewared as his total compensation jumped 51 percent to $12.1 million.

Constellation Brands lost $301.4 million in fiscal 2009 and $613.3 million 2008 and in March 2009 terminated 5 percent of its work force of 8,000. However CEO Robert Sand received a 2 percent raise in compensation valued at $6.36 million.

Hormel terminated over 300 employees in April 2010 but CEO Jeffrey Ettinger took home total compensation of $10.45 million for the year, a 44 percent increase from the previous year.

Joe Robles CEO of USAA, saw his total compensation jump from $1.49 million in 2008 to $4.31 million in 2009 and then to $6.79 million in 2010. Meanwhile he terminated 109 employees in 2010.

In 2009 American Equity Investment Life Holding Company closed offices and terminated employees. CEO Wendy Waugaman got a big raise valued at $1.4 million in 2010, compared with $697,021 in 2009. Also American Equity's profits were down 37 percent for the year.

Life Technologies CEO Gregory Lucier terminated 150 employees in 2010 and got a 457 percent raise in total compensation to $33.7 million, with $29.5 million of the total coming from the vesting of restricted stock grant.

In 2009 Smithfield Foods terminated over 1,800 employees, and compensation for CEO C. Larry Pope almost doubled to $20.2 million in fiscal 2011. His EVP CFO Robert W. "Bo" Manly IV more than doubled his, to $8.5 million.

Lions Gate terminated 41 employees in 2008, in 2009: 45 were axed and in 2011, 13 were gone. But CEO Jon Feltheimer's total compensation grew from $3.6 million to $7.9 million in 2011, which included a $1.9 cash bonus..

Since 2008 Yum Brands has been terminating employees and closing stores. In 2010 CEO David Novak received a 31 percent increase in compensation worth nearly $12.6 million.

Home Shopping Network (HSN) had been terminating employees since 2008, but in 2010 CEO Mindy Grossman received a 298 percent increase in compensation to $12.1 million.

As profits dropped 38 percent and thousands of employees were terminated (3,200 in 2008 and 1,800 in 2011). Goldman Sachs' CEO pay package almost doubled in 2010. Lloyd Blankfein, who once stated his firm does "God's work," received stock share awards of $12.6 million on top of a $5.4 million performance-related cash bonus, and a salary of $600,000. He also received additional perks worth $464,000.

In 2008 after four quarters in a row of net losses, and months before terminating hundreds of employees, co-founder and CEO of Marvell Technologies Sehat Sutardja received a $100,000 pay raise, lifting his annual salary to $657,000, a stock-based bonus and new option grants good for 415,800 shares. In March 2009 he terminated 850 employees and in 2011 his total compensation was $10.8 million, up from $1.6 million in 2010.

Terex terminated 5,000 employees in 2009 and in the fourth quarter lost $421.5 million, and in 2010 CEO Ron Defeo's Compensation increased 76 percent to $5.99 million compared to 2009.

Since April 2008, Kennametal has cut its work force by about 1,600 through layoffs, plant closings and selling off businesses. About 800 job cuts were announced in January — including about 90 from its headquarters and another 20 from its Carbidie plant. In 2010 it asked managers to take a 10 percent cut and all others to take a 5 percent cut in pay, and in 2011 CEO Carlos Cardoso saw a 34 percent increase in his total compensation (Spencer, 2011).

In 2008 Polyone closed six plants and in January 2011 terminated 20 employees and in 2009 froze salaries, but in 2011 CEO Stephen Newlin received total pay of $6.9 million with a salary of $860,000, NEIP (Non Equity Incentive Plan) payouts of $3 million, stock awards of $967,589 and options of $850,590.

In December 2008 Stephen Angel, CEO of Praxair terminated 1,600 employees and his total compensation in 2009 was $10.18 million and in 2010 it increased to $15.33 million.

In January 2011 J.C. Penney announced it will close 47 stores and cut nearly 5,500 jobs in an effort to return to profitability. In 2010 CEO Myron Ullman received about a 50 percent increase in total compensation for 2010, to $13 million. Ullman will retire in early 2012 and his "golden sendoff" is valued at over $30 million, which includes a $10 million cash payout.

Alan Joyce, CEO of Quantas had his total remuneration package raised 71 per cent to $5.1 million for 2010/11 and announced 1,000 employees would be terminated.

Real Estate Investment Trusts (REITs) have been terminating hundreds of employees since 2008. In 2010 the top 20 highest-paid CEOs in the industry received a total of $192 million, for an average of $9.6 million per executive. That's up from $104.7 million, or $5.2 million per CEO, in 2009.

After terminating and "offering" early retirement to 800 employees in 2009, Tiffany CEO Michael Kowalski got a 13 percent raise in 2010 to $7.1 million, which included a bonus of nearly $1.6 million.

From 2007 through 2009 Discovery Communications has been engaged in restructuring (another word for terminating employees), and in 2010, CEO David Zaslav's received a 265 percent increase in total compensation from 2009. Zaslav was paid a total of $42.6 million in 2010 with more than 80 percent of that in stock and option awards. Since 2006 Zaslav's compensation has increased 440 percent.

Altria's CEO Michael Szymanczyk terminated over a thousand employees in 2009 and in 2010 his pay nearly doubled from $12.4 in 2009 to $24 million in 2010.

In July 2008 IBM Tivoli, in Research Triangle Park, terminated 100 people while CEO Sam Palmisano received $21 million in compensation, an 11 percent increase from 2007. In contrast, most employees did not receive any pay raise. In January 2009 IBM announced an additional 16,000 terminations. IBM makes it difficult to accurately know how many employees are being terminated; they never make announcements. Palmisano claims he wants his company to be "lean," and in 2009 he promised additional terminations of employees through 2010 as he follows his offshoring strategy. Palmisano is doing such a great job terminating American employees' jobs that he awarded himself a raise in 2009 and a $4.75 million bonus. In November 2010 he terminated another 299 employees. IBM calls these terminations "resource actions" and what is a resource action? It's nothing more than outsourcing and offshoring, where IBM terminates American employees and sends their jobs overseas to their Global Delivery Framework Centers (DGF's). So what did Palmisano get for destroying American jobs? In 2010 Palmisano saw the total value of his compensation rise 30 percent to $31.7 million, and this included an almost doubling of his incentive (bonus) pay to $9 million. IBM is so proud of its outsourcing that in 2010 they ranked number five in the top 100 global outsourcers by the International Association of Outsourcing Providers or IAOP. As an outsource provider it uses employees primarily in Asian countries. So what does Palmisano get for destroying American jobs? Lots of awards. In 2010 Columbia University's B-school gave him the Edward Deming Cup (Deming is turning over in his grave) and in 2011 he gets the "CEO of the Year" award given by Webster University's George Herbert Walker (Greatgrandfather of George W. Bush) School of Business & Technology. Now there's a B-school that has its priorities straight. Palmisano, will retire in January 2012, and his "golden sendoff" is valued at $170 million.

Bucyrus International terminated an unspecified number of employees (they would not say how many) in 2009 but its CEO Timothy Sullivan did not suffer. His compensation rose 23.3 percent: this included a bonus (they called it a "performance based incentive") of $1.86 million.

Since 2009 Halliburton has been terminating hundreds of employees, but in 2010 its CEO David Lesar received a 20 percent increase in compensation from 2009 worth $14.9 million.

The University of Massachusetts Medical School terminated 63 employees in April 2011, citing financial concerns over potential reductions in state and federal funding in coming years. The layoffs came less than two months after the medical school chancellor Dr. Michael F. Collins got a 12 percent raise, from $524,300 to $585,290 a year.

Amgen has been reducing its workforce since 2007 through outsourcing, and in 2010 CEO Kevin Sharer received a 38 percent increase in compensation valued at about $21.1 million, which included perks such as a company plane, personal use of a car and driver, personal financial planning services, and $17,939 for guests who travel with him on business. Meanwhile he terminated 2,700 employees. In June 2011 he continued to terminate employees by axing 134 and another 380 R&D employees in October.

Robert Eckert, CEO of Mattel received compensation valued at $10.8 million in 2010, up 20 percent from 2009. In 2009 he terminated 86 employees. He announced that he will reitre in Dec. 2012 and COO Bryan Stockton will take over the top job.

Dominion energy's CEO Thomas Farrell received a 40 percent raise in 2010 in total compensation. His stock awards, options and performance bonus brings his annual compensation to almost $15 million. Dominion has been terminating employees since 2009.

Xerox terminated 2500 employees in 2010 and plans additional layoffs in 2011, while CEO Ursula Burns gets a raise. She got an increase in total compensation to $13.2 million in 2010, up 18 percent from the previous year.

PulteGroup has been terminating employees and closing plants but in 2010 CEO Richard Dugas received a raise of 13 percent, to $6.6 million.

In 2009 ConocoPhillips announced it would terminate 4 percent of its 32,000 employee workforce while CEO Jim Mulva got a 25 percent compensation increase in 2010 to $17.9 million, which included a performance-based cash bonus to $4.3 million from $1.3 million bonus in 2009. In 2010 Mulva received about $17.9 million in total compensation in 2010, a 25 percent increase from the previous year, and in 2009 he terminated 1,300 employees. Mulva made $15 million in 2007, including a $3.4 million bonus. He also had at least $234 million worth of unvested performance stock, thanks to an increase in the company's stock price to $90 a share from $68 during 2007. When Mulva retires he will receive at least $2.6 million annual pension (Brunwasser, 2008). In 2008, while Mulva was cutting the workforce and two months later the company announced that Mulva had earned $29 million in 2008, on top of nearly $100 million he had made in the two prior years.

Eaton Corp. terminated 5,200 employees in 2009 and in 2010 CEO Alexander Cutler got a raise in compensation of about 50 percent to $8.5 million.

Since 2008 Boeing has been terminating thousands of employees. In January 2009, 4,500 were terminated and in January 2011, 1,100 were gone but CEO James McNerney did not suffer. In 2010 he got a raise of 1.5 percent and his compensation was valued at $19.7 million. In July 2011 an additional 510 employees will be terminated. Meanwhile

Boeing paid only $13 million in federal taxes and spent $20.8 million on lobbying in 2011.

AutoNation began terminating personnel before the recession officially began in December 2007 and shed 9,000 jobs nationwide between the end of 2006 and March 2011. Since 2008, 5,000 employees have been terminated (Mann, 2011). In 2010 CEO Mike Jackson received a 31 percent raise in total compensation for 2010 valued at $6.8 million.

Hershey has been terminating hundreds of employees and has plans to move its factories from America to Latin American while CEO David West got a nearly 3 percent raise in 2009 to $6.4 million and a bonus that doubled. In June 2010 he terminated up to 600 employees and he got a 16 percent increase in total compensation to $7.4 million.

Since 2008 Johnson Controls has been terminating hundreds of employees. In 2009 it closed 10 plants, but in the year ending September 2010 its CEO Stephen Roell's compensation doubled from $6.5 million to $15.2 million. In 2011 plant closings and hundreds of terminations continued in America as Roell moved production to Mexico to take advantage of cheap labor. For contributing to the destruction of the American economy got a nice raise, $22.34 million in fiscal 2011, up from $17.56 million the prior year. Also, members of his board of directors got raises, a 9 percent increase, to $240,000 in 2011, up from $220,000.

In April 2009 Apache Corporation terminated 6 percent of its workforce or 200 employees and in 2010 CEO G. Steven Farris more than doubled his compensation to $19.3 million. In 2008, those awards were valued at $36.4 million, while the next year the Houston company said they were worth about $1.8 million. In 2010, Farris saw stock awards worth about $9.8 million, according to the filing. Farris also had his $3.25 million cash bonus paid in Apache shares.

In July, 2010 Valspar terminated 19 employees and in October CEO William Mansfield got a 46 percent raise bringing his total compensation to over $4.5 million

In April 2010 more than 70 Ameritrade workers, including an undisclosed number in Omaha were terminated as the company announced they were outsourcing terminated employees work to India and CEO Fred Tomczyk received a 23 percent raise to nearly $6 million. TD Ameritrade shareholders are suffering, but the firm's chief executive officer is not thanks to the generosity of the discount brokerage firm's board. And in 2011 sharkholders took a beating as the stock dropped. And guess what Tomczyk got? A 40 percent increase in his base compensation, and and increase in his bonus target by $100,000 to $5.6 million.

In 2009 Disney terminated 1,900 employees. In January 2011, 250 Disney employees lost their jobs at the same time it was announced that CEO Bob Iger got a 30 percent raise in 2010 valued at $28 million and this included a $13.5 million dollar bonus.

From December 2008 to November 2009 Adobe terminated 17 percent of its workforce: 1,280 employees got pink slips and what did the CEO get? In 2010 Shantanu Narayen, the CEO, received compensation valued at $12.2 million, up from $5 million a year earlier. The CEO gets over 120 percent increase for "cutting costs," that is terminating employees.

In 2010 Steve Wynn, the billionaire owner of Wynn Resorts, raised his base salary to $4 million per year excluding bonus and perks while terminating 260 employees.

In 2008 Fair Isaac terminated 420 employees and in 2009 another 250 and in 2010 CEO Mark Greene received a 16 percent increase in compensation to $1.8 million.

Navistar International terminated 340 employees in July 2010 and in October another 250 and CEO Daniel Ustian got a 27 percent total compensation raise.

Emerson CEO David Farr more than doubled his total compensation in fiscal 2010 to $24.8 million from 2009 thanks to a $16 million performance-related stock award. In 2009 Emerson terminated 14,000 employees and in 2010 he terminated 250 employees.

Siemens has been terminating thousands but its CEO Peter Loescher received a 26 percent salary increase in 2010 to $11.8 million. In July 2008 he terminated 17,000 employees, in March 2010 6,300 and in September, 2010 4,200 employees.

Charleston Area Medical Center (CAMC) will be reducing jobs, leaving open positions unfilled and cutting hours and overtime to trim $15 million from its budget by the end of 2011 while its top 16 executives received about $4.89 million in combined salaries in 2009, a 3 percent increase.

William Marino, CEO of Horizon Blue Cross Blue Shield of New Jersey, received $8.7 million in compensation in 2009 while terminating 200 employees and demanding that they take a three-year contract with an average annual increase of 2.5 percent. As a gesture of gratitude, they were allowed to wear jeans and sneakers on Friday.

Since 2008 Western Digital has been offshoring and terminating thousands of employees, but in 2010 CEO John Coyne got a 2.6 percent compensation increase to $7.03 million.

The Psychology of Greed and Destructiveness among CEOs and Bankers

From April 2002 to February 2010, Compuware terminated hundreds of employees, but CEO Peter Karmanos saw his compensation double in the company's fiscal year that ended March 31, 2010. His salary, bonus, stock awards and incentive payments jumped to $8,592,364 from $4,155,941.

After posting two years of losses, Sony terminated 450 employees in February 2010 while it's Welsh-born CEO Howard Stringer received about $8.8 million in compensation. His compensation caused an outrage in Japan because an average Japanese male university graduate makes 300 million yen ($3.3 million) during his entire lifetime, and a female university graduate 260 million yen ($2.86 million). The "ugly" Welshman.

Qwest's CEO has been terminating hundreds of employees; the company will not divulge the numbers. Estimates are that 2,800 employees were terminated in 2009. However, Qwest could not hide their CEO's compensation. Edward Mueller received a 5 percent increase in 2009 to $12 million, and in 2010 his stock awards totaled $57 million.

Duke Realty terminated 4 percent of its workforce and closed offices yet its CEO Dennis D. Oklak, 56, earned total compensation of $3.4 million in 2009, or 4.1 percent more than in 2008.

Peabody Energy Corp., one of the world's biggest coal producers, is closing mines and terminating hundreds of employees but its CEO Gregory Boyce received total compensation of $11.4 million in 2009, a 52 percent increase. Boyce's salary has tripled since 2006.

In 2009 Anne Chenoa, CEO of Florida Blood Centers terminated 42 employees and then got a 13 percent compensation increase to over $600,000.

Since 2008 KeyCorp has terminated 1,000 employees but CEO Henry Meyers saw his compensation rise 15 percent in 2009. He got a pay package worth about $5.1 million. Meyer's base salary rose to $1.6 million from $1 million. His stock and option awards were $3.4 million as of the date they were granted, up from $3.3 million in 2008. Meyer got perks and other compensation worth $83,300. That included $61,200 in retirement contributions, $12,500 for financial planning services, and $3,000 for disability insurance and $3,500 for club dues.

Texas Instruments saw its revenue drop 17 percent and income drop 22 percent and in January 2009 it terminated over 3,400 employees, but CEO Rich Templeton's compensation grew 2 percent from 2008 up to $9.8 million. In 2010 Templeton saw the total value of his compensation rise 23 percent to $11.9 million and this included a 74 percent increase in his bonus.

In 2008 3M terminated 3,500 employees and in 2009 1,200. CEO George Buckley promised more terminations in 2010, but he managed to receive compensation valued at nearly $14 million in 2009, a 14 percent raise higher than the year before. In 2010 Buckley's compensation increased 41 percent to $19.7 million.

As Valero Energy lost $2 billion and terminated 550 employees in 2009, its CEO, president and Chairman Bill Kleese got a 64 percent raise from 2008 to $10.9 million. In 2009 Kleese terminated hundreds of employees and idled several major processing plants and began hiring contract workers with no benefits, and in 2010 his compensation was $11 million.

ECOLAB terminated 1,000 employees in 2009 but that did not bother CEO Douglas Baker. He received a raise to nearly $8.8 million in total compensation, up from about $7.2 million in 2008.

In 2009 the CEO of M&T Bank, Robert Wilmers received a compensation increase of almost 300 percent while he terminated over 1,000 employees. Included in Wilmers compensation was $65,222, to cover his life insurance premiums, retirement plan contribution, club membership dues and expenses, parking and meals and expenses related to his apartment in Buffalo, N.Y., where the bank is based. He was not allowed to receive a cash bonus due to federal restrictions placed on the bank in connection with the $600 million in TARP funds it received in late 2008. In 2009 Wilmers received total compensation of $2.1 million and in 2010 he got a raise to $2.4 million as he continued employee terminations. In Feburary 2011 M&T Bank announced the acquisition of Wilmington Trust for $351 million and the merger will result in more than 721 Wilmington terminations.

Three months after Talbots terminated 370 workers and announced suspension of its quarterly dividend and a freeze of its employees pension plans, CEO Trudy Sullivan was to receive an extra $1.2 million to offset the recent reductions in her retirement benefits. Also its legal executive Richard O'Connell will receive a 23 percent raise. In January 2009 Talbot announced it lost $560.7 million. Since she became CEO in 2007 Talbots has not reported an annual profit but she does well. In 2009 her base salary remained at $1 million, but she also got an extra $1.4 million to cover perks like paid commuting expenses between her home in New York and Talbots' headquarters in Massachusetts, as well as a housing allowance and more reimbursement for the loss of retirement benefits that still remain frozen for all employees. In addition she continued to terminate employees and reduced surviving employees' benefits. Has anyone suggested to Ms. Sullivan that she has significantly lowered morale throughout the company and this is poison for a retailer that needs quality customer service in order to survive?

Time Warner Inc. CEO Jeffrey Bewkes was to get a pay raise of 33 percent, potentially worth an extra $3.25 million, for 2010 and his annual discretionary cash bonus was increased by $1.5 million to $10 million, and his long-term annual incentive compensation increased by $1.5 million to $10 million. Bewkes planned to cut 400 to 500 positions, including 280 by the end of January 2010.

Furniture Brands International extended the contract of CEO Ralph Scozzafava by three years in February 2010. Significant changes in it include the following: A change in severance pay from three times base salary plus the average bonus paid over the three years before termination, to twice base salary plus the target bonus for the year of termination. Plus an additional right to receive a prorated annual bonus as if he had remained an employee throughout the period. Elimination of a prorated cash long-term incentive payment unless at least 18 months of the three-year performance period has lapsed. Elimination of the tax gross-up on health, dental and vision benefits Elimination of the excise tax gross-up on change in control benefits, effective Dec. 31, 2011. An increase in the non-compete period from 12 months to 24 months after termination. A new clawback provision that would let the company recoup the after-tax portion of any performance-based pay that would not have been earned based on restated financial results, if the amount was paid no more than three years before restating the results. Furniture Brands also said it will reimburse Scozzafava for up to $20,000 in attorney's fees in connection with the amended agreement. In 2008, Scozzafava received total compensation of $4.8 million, according to the company's proxy statement. Hundreds of employees were terminated in 2009 and since 2001 the company has terminated thousands as it has moved in the direction of importing its furniture. In addition, in 2009 the company lost $4.2 million with a sales decline of 35.9 percent.

Fortune Brands terminated 260 employees in 2009 but its CEO Bruce Carbonari received nearly $9.9 million in compensation, a 19 percent increase from the previous year.

David Nelms, CEO of Discover Financial Services, terminated employees and got a government bailout and then got a 79 percent increase in compensation in fiscal 2009. Under the rules set by the U.S. Treasury for companies that received bailout funds, he received no bonus. Discover Financial got $1.2 billion in March through Treasury's capital purchase program and has yet to pay back the government. In 2009 Nelms terminated 500 employees. But that's not all, in fiscal 2010 Nelms compensation almost doubled to about $8.5 million, which included a $1.7 million bonus.

Consider Hank McKinnell, CEO of Pfizer. In 2005 he received nearly $200 million in severance and retirement while his company's stock fell 40 percent during his five year tenure. Later Pfizer terminated 10,000 employees. McKinnell was replaced by Jeffrey Kindler, a lawyer with no management experience, who received $11.4 million in 2006 and 2007 as Pfizer's earnings plunged to $8.3 billion (or $1.20 per share), from $19.34 billion, or $2.66 per share. In 2006 he received a 10 percent increase in his pay package. They had a "good" compensation committee. In April 2010 Kindler received another salary increase of 12.5 percent. Since 2005 Pfizer has terminated 26,000 employees and by 2012 they expect the total numbers of employees terminated to reach 30,900. In 2009 Kindler had to suffer when his total compensation dropped almost 4 percent to $14.9 million and this included $3.5 million bonus. In November 2010 Pfizer, continuing its cost-reduction initiatives was expected to terminate up to 11,700 more employees in connection with its buyout in 2009 of Wyeth Pharmaceuticals. In December 2010 Kindler announced he would step down, and his going away package is at least $16.5 million plus an equity package that is

$24.7 million. Why is he stepping down "To spend more time with his family." This is typically said when an executive is fired. Kindler was immediately replaced by Ian Read who will have a base salary of $1.7 million plus a $2.6 million bonus for 2011. Only CEOs get to know their bonus before the year begins.

Merck, another pharmaceutical giant terminated 17,500 in 2010 while its CEO got a 65 percent increase in total compensation compared to 2009 to $17.9 million. CEO Clarke then retired and became chairman. In September 2011, Merck announced plans to terminate another 12,000 to 13,000 jobs by the end of 2015.

The total number of drug company terminations reached 50,000 in 2010, and this will continue as they offshore to India and China. Pfizer announced 1,100 employees would be terminated in 2011.

Rockwell Collins will cut 500 full time jobs and 100 workers who are now employed on a temporary, contract basis and will freeze all salaries. But not for CEO Clay Jones who received $7.9 million in fiscal 2009, a nearly 22 percent increase from the year before.

Energizer Holdings paid its CEO bonus in stock instead of cash this year, and that skewed pay comparisons from 2008 to 2009. Did CEO Ward Klein's total compensation really drop from $7.1 million in 2008 to $4.2 million in 2009? No his pay actually doubled. He received stock-based incentives with a total fair value of $8.3 million. Meanwhile he terminated 170 employees.

GE is working hard to eliminate American jobs and go overseas. For example, the biggest demand in the world for locomotives is India and China. GE is building factories in India and it is expected that GE Transportation will move all its factories to India. In addition, in 2009 CEO Jeffrey Immelt terminated over 1,500 employees in its transportation division, 1,000 from Aviation, more than 75 from GE Capital, and 250 from its call center, you know where those jobs went. In 2009, GE's earnings dropped 38 percent and revenue dropped 14 percent from in 2008. Immelt announced he would receive no bonus in 2009, but he gave his executives bonuses that totaled more than $10 million. Immelt's total compensation increased to $9.885 million, up from $9.28 million in 2008. **He got a raise**. In 2010 he got a giant raise, to $21.43 million. In January 2011 Obama named Immelt to run his outside panel of economic advisers and chair a new Council on Jobs and Competitiveness. Obama said he wants the council to "focus its work on finding new ways to encourage the private sector to hire and invest in American competitiveness." Immelt's claim to fame as the CEO of GE is to increase profitability by reducing the payroll and going overseas. When Immelt traveled with Obama to India in November 2010, the White House announced a string of business deals between India and American companies, including a $750 million order from India's Reliance Power Ltd. for steam turbines manufactured by General Electric. But who and where will they be built? Immelt is a prime example of the type of CEO that the unemployed on Main Street blame for the destruction of manufacturing in America. You may also want to know that Immelt and GE got a $140 billion bailout in 2008 but unlike other major lenders who got bailouts GE had never been subject to the Fed's stress tests or its rules for limiting risk. Also unlike corporations that have received bailout money in the Troubled Assets Relief Program, or TARP, GE was never subject to restrictions such as limits on executive compensation. In 2010 Immelt's compensation nearly tripled to $15.2 million, but for the first time shareholders protested and Immelt had to accept new performance conditions on 2 million stock options he was awarded. He was given options valued at $7.4 million on the day they were granted and all he had to do was stay with the company and he would have seen half vest after three years and the other half after five years. The stockholders demanded that this be change, and performance targets were added.

The CEO of EMC Corp., Joseph Tucci, received 2008 compensation valued at $11.7 million, more than twice the value of his package in 2007 As its profit fell 19 percent in 2009, Tucci terminated 2,400 employees, or 7 percent of the work force, as the company's stock declined 43 percent, continuing a slump that began in the fall of 2007. In 2010 Tucci got a 37 percent raise to 12.4 million, which included a bonus. Tucci has three vacation homes on Cape Cod, the Jersey shore and Florida keys and over a four year period he used the corporate jet to make 393 trips, The Wall Street Journal reported.

Sycamore Networks saw its sales drop 42 percent in 2009 and it terminated nearly a third of its employees, but CEO Daniel Smith made out well as his salary increased over 100 percent.

Wesley Card, CEO of Jones Apparel Group Inc., received a raise in compensation of 68 percent to $5.4 million in 2008, but voluntarily elected not to accept an $810,000 cash performance bonus, because he felt it may negatively impact his employee's. What a CEO. In February 2008, Jones Apparel Group posted a significant fourth-quarter loss and Card will terminate 185 positions. In Dec. 2008 shares were down 63 percent.

After freezing executive salaries and eliminating life insurance and tax reimbursements, and after reporting a loss of $54 million for three months ended February 2009, and after terminating 7,000 employees, CEO of Home Depot Frank Blake's 2008 total compensation increased 3.6 percent. He then promoted his son. In 2009, as he continued layoffs and profitability dropped, Blake received compensation valued at $9.9 million, up 7 percent from a year ago. This included a performance bonus of $2.1 million. In January 2010 he terminated an additional 1,000 employees and what did Blake get? A 5 percent increase in compensation up from 2009 to nearly $10.5 million, which included a performance-based bonus of nearly $2.2 million.

CEO of Beth Israel Deaconess Medical Center Paul Levy was paid $1,007,841, according to the medical center's 2008 filing, which included a $231,000 bonus, $79,000 in benefits, $618 for his cell phone and $1,414 for parking , while he was terminating 70 employees.

Medtronic's CEO Bill Hawkins received a 26 percent increase in total compensation in fiscal 2009 to $8.9 million. This included a $2.2 million performance-based bonus. This comes after he terminated 1,800 employees after its fiscal fourth-quarter plunged 69 percent on slipping sales. Medtronic has been quietly terminating American-based employees and outsourcing and offshoring. In 2010 Hawkins' compensation rose 6 percent. His pay included $9,038 to install a home security system. In December 2010 Hawkins announced his retirement and he got a cash separation payment of over $3.8 million. But that's not all. After Hawkins retires he was to stay on as a "consultant" for a year, drawing a salary of $104,167 a month, plus benefits and bonuses. Now how does a consultant get benefits and a bonus? In February 2011 it was announced that another 1,500 to 2,000 employees would be terminated. Hawkins was replaced by Omar Ishrakin who received a signing bonus of $650,000, plus $40,000 for "business allowances" and $50,000 to cover attorney fees spent in negotiating his contract with Medtronic, plus more than a million in his base salary and lots of bonuses.

In 2009 while most CEOs received increases in compensation and their perks grew and became increasingly complex they found an array of creative ways to cut costs by taking perks away from their employees, and making them suffer. One new trend found in 2009 was making employees take pay cuts. Challenger, Gray and Christmas polled 100 HR managers and discovered the following cost cutting activities were prevalent in corporate America.

How companies are reducing costs	
Cost cutting move	%
Reduced Travel Expenses	66.7%
Hiring Freeze/Reduction	57.8%
Permanent Layoffs	55.6%
Cancelled Employee Holiday Party	32.0%
Other	31.0%
Reduced Or Eliminated Other Perks	29.0%
Salary Freeze/Reduction	27.2%
Reduced Year-End Bonus	26.7%
Cut Workers' Hours	24.4%
Eliminated Year-End Bonus	22.2%
Temporary Layoffs	15.6%
Cancelled Customer Holiday Party	11.0%
Cutback Tuition Reimbursement	10.8%
Reduced Or Eliminated Matching Contributions To Employees' 401(k) Plans	11.0%
Forced Vacation	8.9%
Four-Day Work Weeks	7.0%
Instituted Furlough Program	6.7%
Cut Office Space Through Increased Telecommuting	6.7%

Retrieved 5/21/11 from: http://economy.ocregister.com/files/2009/01/challenger-correct-cost-survey.pdf

Appendix S: Terminate Employees and Run for Cover

As CEOs grab higher paychecks, while they offshore, outsource, take away benefits, eliminate pensions, and terminate thousands they find themselves objects of hate. They become justifiably paranoid and as a consequence they seek greater security systems and become more physically isolated from their employees, customers and community. Things are so bad that 10 percent of all CEO live more than 100 miles from their companies. According to Jones (2009), "The median spending on personal and home security for CEOs at the 100 largest publicly traded companies was $65,348 in 2008, up 123 percent from $29,291 in 2007. Ten companies alone spent a total of $4.6 million on CEO security in 2008, 40 percent more than the 10 biggest spenders of 2007." CEOs live in gated communities and country clubs and have high priced security consultants at their disposal, use only corporate jets, have several limos at their disposal so no one knows what car they are in, go off to unannounced vacation spots, and are rarely seen in public or corporate events without security guards. The buildings they work in become armed fortresses, and often their own private elevator is the only one that stops at their office floor. In many cases the CEO enters the corporate office though the parking garage to their private elevator, which carries them to their floor where they spend the day locked inside their office, with their private dining room and chef, leaving in the evening the way they entered. Gone are the days when the benevolent CEO knew his employees and could walk freely among them and was loved and when they retired tears were shed.

The 12 Fortune 100 companies that spent the most in 2008 on the CEO's home and personal security are:

Company	CEO	Personal security
1. Dell	Michael Dell	**$1.2 million**
2. Disney	Robert Iger	$645,368
3. FedEx	Fred Smith	$595,875
4. Occidental Petroleum	Ray Irani	$575,407
5. McKesson	John Hammergren	$401,706
6. General Motors	Rick Wagoner	$270,450
7. Hewlett-Packard	Mark Hurd	$255,872
8. American Express	Kenneth Chenault	$246,627
9. Lockheed Martin	Robert Stevens	$234,262
10. ExxonMobil	Rex Tillerson	$222,985
11. Abbott Laboratories	Miles White	$180,467

| 12. Ford Motor | Alan Mulally | $112,114 |

Source: Equilar

After Starbucks CEO Howard Schultz terminated employees his company spent $511,079 in 2008 on the personal and home security.

After FedEx's CEO Fred Smith ceased matching his employee's 401(k) contributions and made his drivers independent contractors and took away their benefits, his company had to spend $595,875 on security for him in 2009.

Richard Fairbank, CEO of Capital One, received over $48,000 for personal security and a driver.

Affiliated Computer Services spent more than $1.7 million from 2004 through 2007 for security systems, advice and equipment along with "personal protection services" for CEO and founder Darwin Deason.

In June, 2011 the New York Times reported that moguls were paying $40,000 to $50,000 for guard dogs and up to $320,000 for the protective creatures (Tierney, 2011). They are called "executive protection dogs" to protect executives from what? Not autograph hunters, or infatuated star-gazers: perhaps angry ex-employees seeking revenge. But the startling thing is these expensive pure breed killer dogs have become status symbols. The need to display ostentatious status symbols; homes, trophy wives, cars, jets, artwork, country clubs, etc., now includes animals used to protect executives.

Appendix T:
(Get a Bailout and Get a Raise)

The 116 banks that received $186 billion in TARP bailout money paid a total of $1.6 billion in compensation and benefits to their top executives in 2009. This money was paid to 600 executives and included: salary, bonuses, use of company jets for personal purposes, personal chauffeurs, health insurance, pension payments, home-security services, country-club memberships and professional-wealth-management services.

The Hartford Financial Services Group received $3.4 billion from the government's TARP program in May 2008 and also received a $2.5 billion investment by European insurer Allianz in October 2008. Its new CEO Liam McGee, hired in October 2009, could get as much as $8.2 million.

AIG one of the "too big to fail" losers that needed a massive bailout, is paying its new CEO Robert Benmosche a $10.5 million annual pay package that was formally approved in 2009 by Obama administration's pay czar Kenneth Feinberg. In 2010, still unable to pay back the government bailout, Benmosche received $8.4 million in compensation.

Sun Trust bank received $4.85 billion bailout in TARP money and on January 1 2009, its President William Rogers received an 11 percent raise.

The 116 banks that received $188 billion bailout money that was supposed to be used to bolster these institutions paid out $1.6 billion in compensation and benefits to their top 600 executives in 2009. It is expected that many of these executives will return to Washington for more bailout money.

Appendix U: The Boy Scouts and Other Do-Good Agencies: The Charities

In 2010, senators questioned the high salaries and expensive travel bills for executives at the Boys & Girls Clubs of America. The CEO Roxanne Spillett, who has been closing local clubs for lack of funding, was compensated nearly $1 million in 2008, and officials spent $4.3 million on travel for their executives, $1.6 million on conferences, conventions and meetings, and $544,000 in lobbying fees.

Clark Baker, top executive of the YMCA of Greater Houston, was paid nearly $700,000 in 2010.

Bob Mazzuca, chief Scout executive of the Boy Scouts of America, was paid $1,046,415 in 2010.

In 2008, the Jewish Federation of Cleveland paid its CEO Stephen Hoffman $687,043, more than any other Jewish federation head in North America and in July 2009 he terminated 25 employees, or 21 percent of the federation's workforce.

A small nonprofit United Way located in Central Carolina (UWCC), paid CEO Gloria Pace King more than $1.2 million in 2008, following the addition of $822,507 to her retirement plan. In 2010 she was given $700,000 to go away.

Michael Kaiser, the CEO of The John F. Kennedy Center for the Performing Arts, made $1,091,444 in 2008.

Thomas Krens, CEO of the Guggenheim Foundation, made $1,716,343 in 2008.

Glenn Lowry, CEO of the Museum of Modern Art, made $2,447,882 in 2008.

New York Philharmonic's president, Zarin Mehta, made $2,649,540 in 2008

Donald Johnson, the CEO of the Evans Scholars Foundation, made $2,049,976 in 2008. This foundation was created in 1930 to support golf caddies who wanted to go to college. Johnson collected more than $2 million in 2008. However his salary in 2007 was only $195,000. Such a huge difference must be due to deferred salary or a retirement bonus, as Johnson left the organization at the end of 2009.

In 2010, Chamber of Commerce CEO Tom Donohue recieved $4.7 million which included a $3.7 million bonus. Donohue is on record deploring the "high" compensation and pensions given to public sector workers.

In December 2010, Sunrise Senior Living gave its CEO Mark Ordan a base salary of $650,000 and target bonus of $975,000 (with a maximum bonus of $1.95 million) and a whopping $3 million cash signing bonus (He has been with the company for 2 years). He also got 1 million shares at a Dec. 2010 closing price of $3.94 a share that will vest over the next three years. One can now get rich taking care of grandma and grandpa and there are a lot more boomers coming.

Appendix V: The Golden Coffins

Omnicom CEO John Wren will get a $41 million "coffin" when he dies.

Abercrombie & Fitch's CEO Michael Jefferies is given a $6 million "stay bonus" to keep him running the successful fashion clothing retailer, and if Jefferies dies, the bonus stays and is paid out, along with $10 million from a company-purchased life insurance policy, to his estate. The retailer would also pay some of his incentive compensation, bringing the golden coffin's value to more than $17 million.

If General Dynamics CEO Nicholas Chabraja died at the end of 2008 (He didn't), his estate would have received almost $30 million which included a lump-sum cash payment of $8.56 million in lieu of his use of corporate aircraft and reimbursement for office space, administrative support and moving expenses. It also included the cost of paying taxes on those benefits- known as gross ups.

Should Omnicom CEO John Wren die in office, his family will collect $41 million in posthumous benefits, including equity awards, incentives and life insurance. He's not alone; numerous companies have special clauses embedded in their executive compensation contracts to provide massive payouts in the event of a death. Talk about pay for performance.

Ivan Seidenberg CEO of Verizon is entitled to nearly $50 million upon death.

Appendix W: The Reason Food Prices are Climbing- The Myth of a Shortage

What's the reason global food prices keep rising?

We witness a plethora of reasons for the rise of food commodities. Some have blamed transportation costs, others claim it's the money exchange rate, and there are even some who say its bio-fuels. And of course the Chinese are on the blame list (they get blamed for almost everything). And, now the Middle East is being blamed.

Eric Pooley and Philip Revzin (2011) maintain that the rising food prices were the result of turbulent weather around the world. They state:

"The hunger that has roiled the Middle East was not caused by the whims of autocrats and cops. It began last year with crippling drought in Russia and later Argentina, and torrential rains in Australia and Canada. The deluges in Saskatchewan were so sustained and intense that farmers couldn't plant some 10 million acres of wheat, according to the Canadian Wheat Board. "What is typically the driest province was never wetter," said the governmental agency Environment Canada. Shrunken wheat harvests in those countries, along with cool, wet summer weather in the American Midwest that delayed the U.S. har-

vest, helped drive wheat prices at the Chicago Board of Trade up by 74 percent in the past year. Corn traded in Chicago rose by 87 percent during the same period. More recently, grain prices have spiked even higher because of yet another drought, this one threatening China's wheat crop, the world's largest. In that country's eight major wheat-producing provinces, some 42 percent of winter wheat cropland has been hurt by a dry spell, according to Agriculture Minister Han Changfu."

In their article they briefly mention that the rising price of food may also be a result of corporations making extraordinary profits by pushing the price of basic seed and fertilizer high. But this does not surprise me considering their article appeared in Bloomberg Business Week where executives and their corporations are treated with "kid gloves."

Several have claimed that rising food prices are the result of rapidly growing consumption of food. They claim the industrial growth in China and India has increased consumption. They say there is not enough food to go around and we have a fertilizer shortage brought about by the need to increase food production. However a UN report debunks this theory by claiming by 2011-12 the supply of fertilizer will increase by 21.2 percent while total demand will only increase 11 percent (UN, 2008). The fact is we have is an oversupply of fertilizer and still the price continues to grow. What about basic foods? Despite claims of bad weather the New York Times maintains there is no worldwide wheat shortage (Bowley and Martin, 2011). This is confirmed by reports from the UN and others suggesting there is no worldwide shortage, but in fact an oversupply. What one learns in Eco 101 is if there is an oversupply of a commodity the price goes down. Not true with these commodities. Despite an oversupply the price goes up.

So what's causing the price to rise?

Perhaps the answer is not **what** but **who** is causing the price to rise.

Let me suggest that it's not the bad weather or all these other factors that is causing food prices to go through the roof. It's the greed of corporate executives and commodity traders. I am suggesting there is a direct link between CEO greed and the pain and suffering food prices are causing around the world. Much has been made of CEOs who engage in mass firings, who outsource and offshore, who steal billions from retirement funds, who flip companies with LBO's and engage in what has become the new America way to manage called "take the money and run." We now have yet another way these marvels of creative investing found to obtain riches. They have entered the food industry with gusto and reaped extraordinary profits by engaging in food price inflation and in the process leaving the poor, the fastest growing segment of the world's population, unable to feed themselves. Many commentators and analysts have suggested that part of the reason people are taking to the streets in Egypt, Ethiopia, Yehman, Tajikistan, Tunisia, Libya, Morocco, Jordan and other Middle East countries is in response to the rising cost of food. They have joined the poor from West Africa, Mauritania, Burkina Faso and Cameroon, along with Haiti and Bangladesh to protest because they are no longer able to feed their families. We also witnessed food riots and protests in parts of China, India, Bangladesh, Khartoum, Sri Lanka, and even Hungary.

The crisis is particularly egregious in Egypt, where wheat sold for 2.5 Egyptian pounds per kilogram in January 2011 and in May 2011 is 3.5 Egyptian pounds, the same for tomatoes at 2 pounds per kilogram then, and in May 2011, 4 Egyptian pounds. This is a disaster for a country where 40 percent of its 80 million people live on less than $2 a day with an unemployment rate estimated by some to be as high as 20 percent. So they protest in the street and vent their collective rage by burning some Christian churches.

According to Brasher, (2011), some 44 million people have been driven into extreme poverty since June 2010 because of higher food costs, and another 10 percent increase in food costs would put 10 million more people into that category. Another 30 percent increase would lead to 34 million more poor. Extreme poverty is defined as living on less than $1.25 a day. Under these conditions the poor will not only engage in protests but also in waves of crime and gang violence to feed their families.

I maintain it is not the shortage or scarcity of fertilizer that is contributing to the high cost of basic foods around the world. It is the blatant greed of executives, bankers, and the hedge fund guys. Let's look at fertilizer.

FERTILIZER

Let's begin by taking a look at the Potash Corporation in Saskatchewan, Canada. In August 2010 this company was on the auction block and was offered $38.6 billion from BHP Billiton the world's largest mining company. Also the Chinese want a piece of Potash and so do other mining companies and of course the hedge fund managers. The stumbling block seems to be the Canadian government. Why so much interest? According to Murray Fulton, an economist at the University of Saskatchewan "What you have in the potash industry are a set of players that are able to control supply and price." (Austen and de la Merced, 2010).

Whoever buys the company for this outrageous price will incur heavy debt, and how will this debt be paid? By increasing the price of fertilizer and this is easily done when one is one of the "big players" who can "corner" the fertilizer market. These spreadsheet executives along with their hedge fund supporters will simply raise prices. Maybe that's why the Canadian government is resisting the sale.

Why is the Potash Corporation valued so high and worth more than $38 billion to these executives and hedge fund managers? The money that can be made is alluring. The CEO of Potash, William Doyle, has stock options worth $600 million, up from a meager $7 million at the end of 2003. Doyle's windfall reflects soaring potash fertilizer prices, up from $100 to $600 per ton. On October 23, 2008, Potash reported that it earned more in its third quarter of 2008 ($1.24 billion) than it did in the entire record setting year of 2007 ($1.1 billion). Doyle's total compensation in 2007 was $17,188,621 (up from $8,943,757 in 2006), including a $2.19-million bonus based on the company's performance. This works out to $47,092.11 a day. According to Ebner (2008) "The soaring price of potash has made the top three executives who run Potash ... fantastically wealthy, with stock options worth a total of $846-million." To make this even more absurd if Potash is taken over by another company Doyle will get a $400 million golden parachute and Potash will pay his taxes. These executives actually run the company from their offices in Chicago. There job is simple; pay miners peanuts to take the Potash out of Saskatchewan, put a price on it and ship it around the world and they get paid millions for this.

The actions of Doyle and his executives have contributed to the mounting worldwide food crisis by keeping fertilizer expensive. The higher prices for all Potash Corp products, including potash, nitrogen and phosphate fertilizers, have contributed to the massive increase of some the most basic international food commodities. For example, consider the international market price of wheat: Between February 2007 and February 2008 the price of a bushel of wheat doubled hitting a record high of over $10 a bushel and according to the Labor Dept.

between October 10 and January 1 of 2011 a bushel of wheat rose 15 percent. In July 2010 a metric ton of wheat cost $190 and over a period of six months that same ton cost $327.

Another contributor to the high price of food is MOSAIC. It is a publically traded arm of Cargill the world's largest privately held company. Because it is privately held Cargill's profits and how they are obtained are not public but it's safe to say that Cargill controls much of the world's potash and phosphate two of the main ingredients of chemical fertilizer. Associated Press (2011) reported that Cargill's net earnings in the first quarter of 2011 was up 23 percent from a year ago and the company is on a buying spree and is planning to sell its shares of the highly profitable MOSAIC. Sitting on MOSAIC's board is former Cargill CFO Robert Lumpkins, who received $344,229 in 2010. In December 2011, Cargill announced that 2,000 employees would be terminated.

MOSAIC's CEO Jim Prokopanko earned $3,263,890 for the fiscal year ending May 31, 2008. In 2008 Prokopanko got a non-equity incentive bump 96 percent higher than in fiscal 2007 (Kennedy, 2008). In 2009 Prokopanko received a 40 percent increase in compensation. In January, 2010 Prokopanko sold 52,000 shares of MOSAIC for almost $4 million. In 2010 Prokopanko earned $6.26 million in salary, stock and other compensation. MOSAIC has quickly become the darling of Wall Street.

MOSIAC like the Potash Company is largely responsible for the tremendous spike in the price of basic foods. In April 2008, the joint offshore trading arm for Mosaic and Potash hiked the price of its potash by 40 percent for buyers from Southeast Asia and by 85 percent for those from Latin American. India had to pay 130 percent more than the year before and China was up an astounding 227 percent. (Patridge and Hoffman, 2008).

SEEDS

It's not only the cost of fertilizer that is contributing to the high cost of basic foods, it's also the rising price of seeds. Consider agricultural biotech giant Monsanto. They expect to see their profits double by 2012. Monsanto has been buying agriculture companies expecting a so-called worldwide food shortage to continue. But in fact they are planning to profit off soaring prices (Hiralal, 2008). Monsanto is another darling of Wall Street and in 2010 "Chief Executive Magazine" named CEO Hugh Grant the "Chief Executive of the Year" (Donlon, 2011). Chief Executive Magazine seems to have lost its ethical moorings. Monsanto makes its profits selling genetically engineered seeds to farming industries and farmers around the world. Many worry that genetically engineered food will wind up destroying natural or organic foods and some consider it potentially the most harmful invention since the atom bomb. It is the cost of Monsanto's seed that has contributed to the growing price of food. Farmers know that these engineered seeds of corn, wheat, cotton and soybeans stand a better chance of maintaining profitability because they tend to produce more crops per acre and survive under the most difficult weather conditions including drought. So they need these seeds to stay in business. Monsanto refuses to allow farmers to reuse the seed so every year they must purchase new seeds. This plays havoc with farmers in Third World countries and significantly contributes to the price of food (Donlon, 2011). Monsanto is also developing genetically engineered animals: their pigs will soon be in the supermarket and its weed killer "Round Up" is known to kill 44 varieties of plants. They have some business model: Sell the seed, allow the plants to grow, sell the herbicide to kill weeds and insects but also kill what is to be harvested. One major side effect, it causes birth defects. And he gets CEO of the year! From 1935 to 1985 DuPont had TV ads that said "GE Better Living through Chemistry." DuPont no longer exists but its negative impact on the environment will last for generations. Monsanto is on the road to becoming the DuPont of the 21st century.

Other darlings of Wall Street are Archer Daniels Midland and Bunge. Their stocks are soaring as the worldwide demand for food grows and the price of grain prices continues to remain high.

THE REAL REASON THE PRICE OF BASIC FOOD IS RISING

We have already established that the price of fertilizer and seeds are major contributors, but what about hoarding? There is widespread belief that hoarding of wheat, corn, grain and other commodities is occurring but who is doing the hoarding? Again we need to look at the villains of Main Street and the poor. Of course hoarding is just another method executives, hedge fund operatives and their Wall Street colleagues use to benefit, and you can bet their doing it. While it is difficult to actually catch investors actually hoarding, the question is raised because investment funds are pouring billions into food commodity markets. The capacity to make millions is clearly an incentive to bet, but to ensure they do not lose requires them to engage in price control. This is clearly not the first time investment managers have tried to control the price of a commodity and make a killing. These investors would like federal regulators to believe that they are speculators and they merely invest in price movement of a commodity and they do not buy or sell a physical commodity. But they do not disclose how they influence price and how they are guaranteed they will make that killing. The truth of the matter is contrary to their claims: they do control the physical commodity. It's called "hoarding."

How does one hoard? It's surprisingly easy. Get a silo, purchase a commodity before it is seeded. Then at harvest fill the silo with several million tons. If that does not work, then load millions of tons of the food commodity onto a giant tanker ship and leave it anchored in a local harbor, keep it there until the price climbs and sell for a major profit. Take some of your profits and build two or three more silos or rent more tankers and do it over again. Of course they do not call it hoarding it's called "controlled inventories." If enough do this, they effectively control the price and the price moves in one direction. How much is being taken off the market and hoarded is unknown without federal oversight. This terrifies commodity hoarders, so to keep the Feds off their tail they make certain the price for food in the U.S. rises in small increments and Main Street is kept quiet with stories of drought, bio-fuel, population growth and other fabrications.

WHY IS HOARDING OCCURRING? LOOK TO THE WALL STREET BANKERS

Commodity speculation is a rapidly growing investment field and hedge fund managers disillusioned with the Wall Street market have flocked to trading commodity futures. According to Steward and Waldie (2008) "hedge funds and other sources of hot money are pouring billions of dollars into commodities to escape sliding stock markets and the credit crunch, putting food stocks further out of poor people's reach." Sinclair and Waldies, (2008a) maintain that investment funds now control 50–60 percent of the wheat traded in the world commodity markets and that the amount of speculative money in commodities futures like rice or wheat has ballooned from $5 billion in 2000 to $175 billion to 2007 (Stewart and Waldie, 2008). At this rate by 2014, $350 million will be bet on prices of food commodities.

However we may be at that figure in 2011. According to Olivier De Schutter, a UN reporter, commodity index funds rose from $13 billion in 2003 to $317 billion by 2008 (Inman, 2011).

Food has become a commodity treated by speculators the same as gold and precious metals where hoarding is increasingly common.

The financialization of food as a commodity is far greater in the EU than America. According to Inman (2011) in April 2011 the World Development Movement blamed Barclays Capital, the UK's giant food commodity trader, for driving up prices. Inman (2011) maintains that "Using these new derivative products, pension funds, especially in the U.S., have invested large slices of their overall portfolio in commodities as it has become more difficult to generate above average returns from more traditional sources of income, such as stock and bond markets."

As we have witnessed with precious metals hoarding; price inflation results and the investors get rich but this sets off a vicious cycle. Consider copper: If you walk around the Bronx you will notice that anything made of copper has disappeared: Drain pipes, gutters, siding, decorations, cupola's, doors, and even wiring. In some areas of the country rising copper prices have prompted thieves to climb poles and cut down live telephone and electrical lines for the valuable copper inside. Throughout the Midwest abandoned homes are gutted of copper pipe, not by addicts but by people trying to feed their families. Furthermore we see ample evidence of destruction around the world as antiquities made of precious metals are destroyed. In Egypt men have raided museums looking for metal to melt so they can buy food for their families. We also witness food reaching the level of a precious commodity: thieves are stealing food. According to Neuman (2011) in April 2011 a gang of thieves stole six tractor-loads of tomatoes, one truck of cucumbers and a truckload of frozen meat. Total value: about $300,000.

ETHICAL QUESTION

This raises the question: Should governments allow food be treated as a commodity? Should speculators be allowed to engage in making money off the price movement of food? Given the absence of transparency it is impossible to know the quantity of food harvested or needed in the global marketplace. We do not know who is producing what, and how it is being shipped, stored, priced or consumed. What we do know is millions are starving and suffering has increased throughout the world. And, we do know that commodity speculators, hedge fund managers and executives and their stockholders are in the game and getting rich. And, we know that Goldman Sachs is right in the middle of this (Kaufman, 2011). It's one thing to get rich closing U.S. factories, sending jobs overseas, fudging derivatives and getting bailed out, but it's quite another to get rich making food so expensive hundreds of millions of adults and their children no longer have adequate food.

France may the first country to establish tough new regulations on commodity speculation at the first ever summit of agriculture ministers of the G20 group of top economies in June 2011

Of course fund managers do not want any form of regulation and they maintain that the 40 percent rise in global food prices in 2010 was driven by short supplies, burgeoning demand, the Middle East, and of course the weather-not speculation.

Appendix X: Want to Get Rich? Open Up a For-Profit School, But You Better Do it Soon

There is no better example of educational institutions that have grossly misplaced priorities than the publically traded for-profits. They are corporations in business and their objective is to enrich stockholders and their executives. These so-called colleges spend less than a third of the money they get on educating students than public universities do, even though for-profit schools cost nearly twice as much as public institutions. These for-profits have created a stink that has permeated all educational institutions by engaging in practices that prey on minorities and the poor; not to lift them up educationally but to exploit and put them in debt and ruin their lives all in the name of profit. There are approximately 3,000 for-profit schools now operating in America and while enrollment rates are approaching 2 million, almost three-fifths of those enrolled drop out within a year with debt they cannot repay. These schools are criminal, and they survive by using aggressive recruiters to lie to naive recruits and by paying off politicians. They are the most powerful educational lobbying group among all universities and colleges and in 2011, when federal and state governments began to investigate and demand accountability, their lobbyists were all over the place touting bogus research and singing their praises. When the

University of Phoenix wanted to move into Connecticut, universities and colleges banded together to keep them out of their state. Like most states, they failed. Federal and state governments have investigated them for years and investigative journalists have exposed them to little or no avail.

According to Hechinger and Lauerman (2010), Strayer Education Inc., a chain of for-profit colleges that receives three-quarters of its revenue from U.S. taxpayers, paid CEO Robert Silberman $41.9 million in 2009. That's 26 times the compensation of the highest-paid president of a traditional university. Right behind him was Andrew Clark, CEO of Bridgepoint education, at $20 million. K12, a company that offers online precollege education, almost doubled its CEO Ron Packard's total compensation to $5 million in 2011. Now that's a niche, your child can avoid going to school from kindergarden through grade 12 and perhaps beyond.

Kevin Modany of ITT only made $7.6 million in 2010 but he also received a $1.2 million retention bonus in December 2010 if he stays for 6 months. From 2003 to 2010, top executives at the top 15 U.S. publicly traded for-profit colleges received $2 billion from the proceeds of selling company stock (Hechinger and Lauerman, 2010). At the same time, these schools had the worst loan-default and four-year-college dropout rates in U.S. higher education history. Since 2003, nine for-profit college insiders sold more than $45 million of stock, each while receiving 90 percent of their revenues from government grants and loans.

Apollo is the largest and most notorious of these for-profits and operates the for-profit University of Phoenix, which claims an enrollment of over 400,000, a number many claim is grossly inflated. Its founder and executive board chairman John Sperling's total compensation, excluding stock-option exercises, was $6.4 million in 2009. In 2010

Sperling's stock-option gains will total $38 million. Phoenix claims to have the country's highest enrollment and is the country's largest recipient of federal student aid. In 2008 it received $3.2 billion from the government. In the year ending August 2010 Phoenix spent over $1.1 billion on sales, promotion and recruiting. There is no record of how many admission recruiters work for Phoenix but ITT Educational Services a for-profit one-fifth the size of Phoenix employs 1,700 recruiters (Lauerman, 2010). Why so many? It takes a lot of convincing to get a teenager or young adult to pay $1,000 for a course that can be taken at the local community college for $80. In response to losing their civilian student population they now want to get their grubby hands on the soldiers and the GI bill that funds college education for veterans. So the for-profit schools like Capella, DeVry, ITT Tech, Kaplan, and the University of Phoenix hire marketing firms to go after returning vets. Spending on military education benefits was at $10 billion in 2010 and these for-profits want it and their Wall Street backers are salivating as their take has gone up 600 percent since 2006.

Phoenix's enrollment practices have received the highest number of federal lawsuits than any university in the country; in 2004 it paid nearly $10 million in enrollment abuse fines and in 2009 it announced it was putting aside $80 million to cover additional enrollment abuses. Abuses include tying recruiters' salaries to meeting enrollment numbers and using pressure tactics to enroll students which includes lies and false claims about classes, professors, transfer credits, credit for "life experience" and financial aid. This was confirmed by a 2010 report by the U.S. Government Accountability Office. They found that recruiters from Apollo and other for-profit companies misled students about the cost and quality of courses.

According to Coutts (2009) about 50 percent of University of Phoenix students default on their student loans, three times the percentage at private, nonprofit colleges. This problem is pervasive among these for-profit schools where strategy focuses on profits over education. If anyone doubts this consider the fact that since he founded Apollo, Sperling has collected over half a billion dollars. In 2009 Apollo Group paid its co-CEOs Charles Edelstein $11.3 million and Greg Cappelli $7.3 and its president and chief operating officer Joe D'Amico $6.5 million, Meanwhile most of the faculty are poorly paid adjuncts without doctorates (they spend 28 cents out of every dollar for instruction). While these executives get rich (32 cents out of every dollar goes to administrative costs) their students do not get an education but instead become saddled with debt. The graduation rate is a paltry 6 percent and the median debt over $30,000 (Kiley, 2010). The default rate hovers at between 70 and 90 percent. The for-profit doctoral programs are even worse with over 90 percent of those enrolled failing to get their doctorate after six years and instead they become burdened with enormous debt. Even if one managed to obtain a doctorate from one of these institutions most academics would consider it worthless and in some cases public school districts do not recognize the credits or degree as an entitlement for a salary increase or upgrade. Capella offers an online Ph.D. specialization in Addiction Psychology. Who is on the faculty? They do not say. Could this be approved by the American Psychological Association? No way. In addition they are experts in coming up with degree offerings that have titles to purposely appeal to some hot vocational employment. For example Capella offers an online Master of Science in Homeland Security.

These for-profits use deception and false promises to hook potential students while the executives who run these mills get rich. According to Hechinger and Lauerman, (2010) Robert Huntson retired CEO of Pittsburgh-based Education Management, which claims to be the second- largest for-profit college chain by enrollment, got $132.4 million and Dennis Keller and Ronald Taylor, former co-CEOs of another for-profit, DeVry

Inc., together collected $110.4 million in stock proceeds. And Keller named DeVry's MBA school after himself, the Keller Graduate School of Management. For almost $40,000 one can get a degree from a company with no full time faculty and a college catalogue that lists no faculty.

For-profits increasingly claim they are serving the disadvantaged population that would never attend college if it were not for them. They use this as a justification for their existence. This may be far from the truth. A study by Fox, Garrity, Garrison, and Fiedler (2008) finds that the for-profits use the category "unknown" to slot white students and this increases the percentage of the non-white population. They identify a study in California suggesting that white students are the most likely to be categorized as "unknown" (Smith, Moreno, Clayton-Pedersen, Parker, & Teraguchi, 2005). They state, "Should this be the general case, it would challenge for-profits' claims about serving minorities." But even if it turns out that for-profits do serve the poor, civil rights groups and organizations want them to stop, and have expressed concern that these for-profits take advantage of low-income and minority students, putting them hopelessly in debt.

It seems likely that the day of the for-profits will come to a close as federal and state regulators close in on them and reject their model of "enrollment equals success." Success must be linked to graduation and jobs after graduation and it is clear that if the for-profits use this as an indicator of success they will come up woefully short. Furthermore, it is an outrage that these institutions, which claim to serve the disadvantaged, actually offer little to the student and a lot to their executives and stockholders. Fortunately, the for-profit stocks have begun to tank. New federal rules in 2011 would limit their access to federal financial aid if their students debt and default levels are too high and they must now prove that their programs prepare students for "gainful employment."

According to Blumenstyk (2011), in 2011 colleges are barred from federal student-aid programs if their two-year default rate is 25 percent or higher for three successive years, or above 40 percent in a single year. Under a law that will take full effect after September 30, 2014, the default rate will be measured for three years and colleges with three-year rates of 30 percent or higher for three successive years, or above 40 percent in any single year, will be barred. In addition, in 2011 the Justice Department along with several state attorney generals (at least ten states) are bringing lawsuits against for-profit recruiters who defrauded thousands of unsuspecting students. In 2009 the Apollo Group paid $78.5 million to settle one suit and in May 2011 EDMC, which is owned by Goldman Sachs (40 percent ownership), will end up in court defending itself against the False Claims Act (Lewin, 2011). EDMC owns Argosy U, the Art Institute, Brown Mackie College, and South University. Why so many schools? They play a shell game where if one school receives bad press they have their recruiters push another school. EDMC is accused of practices that were barred by the feds. They recruit by using "boiler room" operations in which so-called recruiters, who get paid by head count, engage in borderline harassment and outright lies to enroll students. The phrase "don't worry it wouldn't cost you a cent" is commonly used.

Will the Department of Education's so-called "gainful employment" rule, under which the for-profits will have to identify the employment incomes of their graduates, put these for-profits out of business? And what will these for-profits do when the feds come looking for data? They will do what any solid American corporation will do, they will "cook the books." It's already happening. Teachers at these institutions are told to alter their attendance records and change failing grades and if they protest they are immediately fired. Administrators also doctor attendance, grades, employment records and enrollment numbers. An administrator was actually caught. Career Education Corp. CEO Gary

McCullough resigned in Nov. 2011 after an investigation revealed the company was inflating job placement rates. What does he get? A Golden Boot worth more than $5 million which includes $2.4 million for two years of his average bonuses and $1 million for his prorated 2011 bonus (Perez, 2011).

The feds will never close these so-called schools down. The for-profit lobbyists are "loaded for bear" and will line the pockets of politicians. But it's not only the feds these so-called schools will battle. Many states are introducing legislation to control spending on such institutions. State-level bills, which enjoy bipartisan support, are designed to limit state spending on for-profit colleges, increase oversight, and require more information about for-profit college finances. "The idea behind this is that the money that would normally go to the for-profits would be redirected to the community colleges and the public and private universities in this state," said Edward Maloney, an Illinois state senator who is pushing the movement (Montano, 2011).

The real killer of the for-profits will be the next generation of students. It is apparent that as more GenY's enter college age, they will question the value of these for-profit degrees. They will not be duped by untruthful or misleading advertisements (these schools spend upwards of 40 percent of their revenue advertising). The Gen Y's will rely on their large network of friends and web based information before deciding. In the long run it may not be the government that shuts the for-profits down but this new generation. And we are beginning to their enrollment dropping precipitously. Phoenix reported a 40 percent drop in enrollment in November 2010 and Capella saw its enrollment drop 35 percent in January 2011. They started terminating employees, and of course their stock is dropping. Strayer reported student enrollments fell 21 percent in the second quarter 2011, the fourth straight quarterly decline. In July 2011 it was reported that John Sperling, founder of the University of Phoenix, dumped more than $59 million in company stock and Donald Graham dumped $12.5 million in Washington Post Company stock. (The company owns Kaplan University.)

Of course in an attempt to survive they are passing on these losses to their consumers. Argosy LA raised its tuition 88 percent and DeVry NJ 82 percent in 2008-09. In August 2011 DeVry reported a 26 percent drop in enrollment sending its stock spiraling downward.

If you wanted to set up a for-profit school and get rich, you are too late.

End note: The author of this book graduated from City College of New York, CCNY, in 1971. The tuition was $27 a semester, and when they raised it to $35 the students and faculty gathered for a mass protest. The school was founded by Townsend Harris, who said: *"Open the doors to all. Let the children of the rich and poor take their seats together and know of no distinction save that of industry, good conduct, and intellect."*

Appendix Y: The Energy Boys

If you want to get a raise and makes lots of money no matter what your company does become an energy CEO. In 2008 the highest paid CEO was Aubrey McClendon of Chesapeake Energy Corp., who earned $112.5 million (between 2006 and 2010 he made over $300 million). Oil and gas producer Devon Energy Corp. gave its CEO J. Larry Nichols CEO a 5.5 percent increase in compensation in 2008 to $16.7 million. This included a 15 percent increase in his bonus as Devon lost $2.15 billion, or $4.85 per share.

CEO compensation was up between 23 and 28 percent in 2010, and energy companies led the way. Wisconsin utility companies collectively paid out $44 million in bonuses to their top executives in 2010. The biggest bonus went to Gale Klappa, CEO, president and chairman of We Energies, who in addition to his $1.13 million salary received $10.45 million bonus. Second on the list was Frederick Kuester, chief operating officer at We Energies, who collected about $5.5 million in bonuses. So how do these executives find a way to pay for these bonuses? They added a fuel surcharge to every customer's bill.

Pacific Gas & Electric Corp. CEO Peter Darbee announced in April 2011 he would retire after a year that included the death of eight people and injury of dozens more when one of its natural-gas pipelines exploded, and the subsequent downward trajectory of its stock price. Because Darbee is retiring, rather than resigning or being fired, he is entitled to an estimated $35 million retirement package (Worth, 2011). He was replaced by Anthony Earley who will be paid a $1.25 million salary, and receive a $1.5 million signing bonus, along with $6 million in stock awards.

Why does energy CEO compensation keep on rising? They use methods that have become common practice in Corporate America. The executive compensation committees review market data of energy peers at the 25th, 50th and 75th percentile for annual cash compensation, bonuses, and long-term incentive compensation. Of course these committees and the CEO hire outside consultants, who are paid handsomely to help out by benchmarking and conducting competitive assessments of the energy industry. So one CEO's compensation goes up and the other CEO needs to go up and then another and another. It's a game of envy and "gimme more" that gets played out annually.

Approximately 165 employees of Pittsburgh-based PPG sued the company stating they were forced to work 60-hour and 70-hour weeks with no overtime. In addition CEO Charles Bunch terminated 2,500 employees in March 2009. In 2008 Bunch made $7.3 million in 2008. PPG has a reputation as America's greatest air polluter.

In 2010 Constellation Energy CEO Mayo Shattuck made $15.7 million in total compensation, a 44 percent annual increase in a year when the company he manages posted a nearly billion-dollar loss. In 2009, Shattuck's compensation was valued at $10.9 million. Company officials said his compensation package is based in part on **future performance** (Cho, 2011).

In 2011, Exco CEO Douglas Miller, had a plan to take his natural-gas company private. He failed miserably, loosing some $2 billion. So what did he get? Cash and stock awards with a current value of $3.26 million. This included a cash bonus of $500,000.

J. Brett Harvey of Consol Energy received $20.1 million in total compensation in 2010.

Anthony Earley earned nearly $8.5 million in total compensation for the DTE corp. in 2010. In September 2011 he moved over to become CEO of PG&E. With incentives, his pay between September and December could reach $10 million.

Marcus Rowland CEO of Frac Tech a company that specializes in the environmental disaster known as fracking, earned a whopping $24.4 million in 2010.

Michael Hsing CEO of Monolithic Power Systems, saw his total compensation increase from $3.29 million in 2009 to $11.33 million in 2010, which included a pay increase of more than $4.6 million.

Con Edison of New York CEO Kevin Burke obtained a compensation package of about $7.3 million in 2008, up from $5.5 million in 2007. Burke's compensation package includes $1.1 million in base pay-about a 5 percent increase over his 2007 salary-a performance-based cash bonus of nearly $1.1 million, and restricted stock that was valued by the company at $3.2 million as of January 2008. His pension benefits totaled about $2.7 million, and he also received compensation of $103,256, which included $2,168 for personal use of a company car, $7,470 for driver costs, $10,150 in legal fees and $46,709 for life insurance. Apart from his 2008 compensation, Burke realized about $488,789 from exercising option awards and $987,943 from vesting stock awards from previous years. The largest increase in Burke's compensation package was in his pension plan, which was about $2.7 million in 2008 compared to $1.7 million in 2007 (Padnani, 2009). In 2009 he announced that New York residents woulf see an average $6 per household increase in their Con Ed bill.

CEO Steven Malcolm of Williams Cos. received total compensation of $7,259,272 in 2010, down from $8,080,038 in 2009 and $8,939,581 in 2008. He retired at the end of 2010.

Paul Evanson CEO of Allegheny Energy, received total compensation of $12.6 million in 2010.

In 2002 the CEO of Westar Energy Davis Wittig, was fired amid allegations and an investigation by federal authorities that he was looting the utility for personal gain. After years of trials he was awarded approximately $39.1 million as part of a settlement.

John Gibson, CEO of ONEOK received total compensation of $5,514,750 in 2010.

CEO Larry Pinkston of Unit Corp., received an increase of 159 percent in 2010 from $1,074,7115 in 2009 to $2,784,715 in 2010.

Duke Energy is planning to buy Progress Energy for $13.7 billion and Progress CEO Bill Johnson will be given the following for three years: $1.1 million per year in base salary and up to $1.38 million in short-term incentives, as well as up to $5.5 million in long-term incentives (paid in shares). If Progress backs out of the deal it could owe Duke a $400 million break-up fee and up to $30 million in merger-effort costs. If Duke pulls out, it could owe Progress $675 million and up to $30 million in merger costs. Duke Energy's CEO will stay on as chairman, he and his wife own about $34 million in Duke shares. In 2010 Dukes CEO James Rogers compensation rose 29 percent to $8.8 million. Almost all his compensation was in stocks and options. Why so much in stocks and options? To increase their value all one has to do is raise the price of energy. And they are doing just that. In July 2011 they announced they will raise their energy prices 17 percent, bringing in an additional $646 million. Those stocks will soar.

As the price of gas rises, so does the industry's executive salaries. In 2007 Chevron's CEO, David O'Reilly's compensation increased over 400 percent from 2006, from $8.8 million to $31 million in 2007. He also holds stock options worth more than $34 million. In 2007 O'Reilly received close to $16 million in compensation and $29.1 million from exercising options and stock awards. In 2008 he received a compensation package worth $15.7 million for the year, including a $1.7 million salary, $10.2 million of stock and option awards and $3.6 million of incentive awards. There was an additional $255,251 in other compensation as well. In February 2009 O'Reilly was replaced by John Watson. In 2010 Watson received about $16.3 million in total compensation an 85 percent increase from 2009. Exxon Mobile CEO Rex Tillerson, made more than $21.7 million in salary and bonus in 2007, up from $13.16 million in 2006. Tillerson's pay included a bonus of $3.36 million. In addition, he has about $77.9 million worth of unvested incentive stock, thanks to an increase in ExxonMobil's stock price last year to $95 a share from $63. But what happens when profits plunge? He still gets a raise. The year 2009 was a bad year, in the third quarter, profits fell 68 percent but Tillerson will get a 7 percent increase in salary in 2010 to $21.5 million. In 2010 as the gas industry received $4 billion in tax breaks from the U.S, government, profits soared as prices at the pump went through the roof.

XTO, an energy corporation, saw its profit decline 9.1 percent in 2007, but CEO Bob Simpson obtained a cash bonus of $35 million. The shares fell $2.56, or 9.3 percent, to $24.91 in New York Stock Exchange composite trading. The stock has lost half of its value in 2007.

The son of the founder of Hess Oil made over $200 million between 2006 and 2010. Michael Watford CEO, of Ultra Petroleum. also made over $200 million during the same period. Americans will pay for this compensation at the pump, where the price of gas has increased 25 percent in 2010 and is going higher.

Massey Energy had a stock decline of 30 percent in 2006. However, its CEO Don Blankenship earned roughly $27 million in pay and perks. In 2009 with demand for energy dropping he asked his employees to take a 6 percent cut in pay and Blankenship received just under $1 million in salary with an increase in the size of his performance bonuses. His cash bonus was increased from $900,000 to $1.5 million in 2009 and 2010 also he now has numerous opportunities to earn Massey stock. For instance, he can receive the right to 81,500 shares for hitting one set of performance targets this year and 32,250 more for achieving another set. Blankenship's targets include financial results, sales volumes, costs, safety performance and reducing environmental violations, according to the filing. His stock compensation totaled $19.7 million in 2008 — a 17 percent decrease from the year before as Massey's stock fell 61 percent (Huber, 2009). In April, 2010 an explosion at the Massey Energy coal mine in Raleigh County West Virginia. took the lives of 29 miners, workers. According to Kolhoff (2010) in the month prior to the deaths, Massey Energy incurred 57 safety violations at the Upper Branch mine where the explosion occurred, including violations related specifically to inadequate ventilation, the cause of the explosion. In 2009 alone, the Mine Safety and Health Administration cited the Upper Branch mine with 495 separate violations and almost $1 million in fines. Paying the fines (at their leisure) was cheaper than making the safety repairs. In 2009 Massey Energy made a profit of $104 million, double what they made in 2008, and this was specifically through cutting jobs (over 700) and cutting safety costs (Kolhoff,2010). Wall Street loves this shit. In November 2010 Blankenship left and incoming CEO Baxter Phillips doubled his compensation to $8 million. Why? In the event the company is sold or merged.

DynaMotive Energy Systems lost $14.7 million in 2007 raising its cumulative losses to $87.3 million. However, in 2007, CEO Andrew Kingston received a 23 percent increase in salary and cash bonuses.

Aubrey McClendon, the CEO of Chesapeake Energy, saw the company's profit drop by almost 50 percent in 2008 and its stock price drop 59 percent. McClendon lost 95 percent of his stake in Chesapeake, once valued at $2 billion (Schnurman, 2009). But the board replenished McClendon's wealth by awarding him a $77 million bonus for superior performance as investors saw their stock and 401(k) drop by half. This amounted to $100 million a 500, percent increase. McClendon's compensation rose more than fivefold from $18.8 million in 2007, the company said in a filing with the Securities and Exchange Commission. In 2009 shareholder's sued claiming the company paid him too much and sought a return of compensation. They claimed McClendon was granted a $77 million bonus in 2008 while the company's stock price fell 60 percent. In February 2010 a judge threw out the lawsuit on a technicality. In 2011, with shareholders up in arms over McClendon's compensation, the board of directors promised to place some "objective" performance assessment criteria in his annual review. In the past the board used criteria such as "clear and insightful decision making," "attitude" and "demonstrated commitment to the company" (Koppenheffer, 2011).

Philip Ackerman, who retired last June as National Fuel Gas Co.'s chief executive, still is the Amhers- based energy company's chairman under a deal that pays him $400,000 a year and also requires him to be available for up to 50 days annually to act as an adviser and consultant for the company's management. T. Rudgers, who will retire in June as executive vice president, will be paid $75,000 a year for the next 10 years, plus $50,000 a year for the next two years to act as a consultant. Ronald Miller, CFO, will take early retirement in March 2010 and be paid $66,000 a year for the next 10 years.

Lynn Elsenhans, the CEO of Sunoco, was paid $11.7 million in 2010 while cutting the pension benefits of her employees.

Southern Union a gas pipeline, was purchased in June 2011 by Energy Transfer Equity for $4.2 billion or $33 a share. Many believed Southern Union could have gotten a better price but CEO George Lindemann was willing to take an undervalued offer. It seems Lindeman will get an array of perks from Energy Transfer including consulting and noncompete agreements that will pay an additional $10 million per year for five years, plus club memberships, insurance coverage, company jet usage and other goodies.

In April 2011 Constellation Energy announced a merger with Exelon and Mayo Shattuck CEO of Constellation would become the new company's chairman. In 2010 his total compensation was $15.72 million.

And, finally, Marathon Oil's CEO, Clarence Cazalot, saw his total compensation rise 53 percent to $13.1 million in 2007, a year in which the company's earnings fell 24 percent. In 2010 his compensation jumped 34 percent to $8.8 million as the company's revenue rose 36 percent. It seems it's better to fail.

And you wonder why the price of fuel is so high. These guys have created a perfect world. Every year is a success all they need to do is jack up the price of energy and pass it on to their unsuspecting and financially strapped customers. Also consider another aspect of their immoral perfect world. They are the biggest environmental polluters. They are largely responsible for global climate change, which makes the summer stifling hot and winters very cold, thereby increasing energy usage.

Appendix Z: Madness at HP

The meteoric growth of HP, recognized as the symbolic founder of Silicon Valley, has been well documented with over 15 books and as many cases. Founded by Bill Hewlett and Dave Packard, both electrical engineers from Stanford, they created their company in Packard's garage in 1939.

After Dave and then Bill stepped down in 1978 John Young, who had been with the company for 20 years took over as CEO, a position he occupied for another 14 years. He was followed by another HP lifer, Lew Platt. These top executives loved the company, and they were all engineers.

Often when the founders leave the company, their replacements suffer as does the company, but this did not happen. Both Young and Platt were in tune with the company's mission and were able to keep the company on a steady course.

ENTER FIORINA

In 1999 the Board of Directors made a major mistake. They hired and outsider, and the decline of this once proud and successful company began. Carly Fiorina was appointed president, CEO and chairwoman of the board (Another major mistake) and HP had its first top executive from the outside the company and their first non-engineer and first professional manager (an MBA from U of Maryland). At the age of 45, this inexperienced manager was going to run HP her way, and she immediately chipped away at the company's culture. HP ranked tenth on *Fortune's* "100 Best Companies to Work" list and five years later was completely removed from the list. It was also removed from "The Most Innovative Companies" list. How did she manage to destroy a company in less than five years at the helm? She called it a restructuring, but it was nothing more terminating 18,000 employees and offshoring their jobs to Asia. She also brought in professional managers. Gone were the engineers who worked their way up the ladder. Now the executive ranks were filled with MBA managers brought in from outside the company. The managerial focus was no longer on innovation and creativity, it was on managing the bottom line and squeezing the cost lemon and of course paying the top executives very well. In 2002 Fiorina's total compensation was $10.7 million. Employees who remained were beset with fear, and they hated what Fiorina was doing to their beloved company. With limited understanding and perhaps fear of the culture Dave and Bill created, she had to destroy it.

WHAT DID FIORINA FEAR?

The old HP culture would strike fear in the heart of any MBAer. Consider Bill and Dave's collegial, team-oriented, non-hierarchical culture comprised of nerdy engineers with a focus on being creative and smart with a brand and reputation that many considered stronger than IBM's. Integrity in relations with employees and customers was valued. It was a culture where management knew the technology and the technological core was valued above all else. Fiorina and her professional managers were not engineers, and the technological core frightenws them. She responded the way many executives respond when faced with a core they do not understand and cannot communicate with, something that creates feelings of both humiliation and envy. They typically respond by creating situations where they can project their feelings of envy and humiliation into those engineers and technicians within the technological core. They may have varied styles, but top executives brought into a company from the outside with limited knowledge of the work with the technological core will unconsciously engage in decision-making that destroys it and this is precisely what Fiorino did. She replaced the old HP culture of bottom-up, engineering driven design and attention to details and customer needs with a top-down, marketing driven regime with a bottom line mentality that will drop a product in a heartbeat, regardless what loyal customers want. She needed to destroy the culture of collegiality and replaced it with a performance review management system that intimidated and instilled fear in employees. Now managers were the evaluators and judges of employee behavior and productivity. The collegial atmosphere was gone.

She took the core and killed I,t and in the process HP became just another outsourced-offshore shifter of boxes with plastic nameplates slapped on generic innards.

She was so bad that *Conde Nast Portfiolo* listed her among the "20 Worst CEOs of All Time."

ENTER HURD

In January 2005 the board gave Fiorino the "Golden Boot" a severance package reported to be worth between $22 million to $45 million and gave their newly hired CEO Mark Hurd a "Golden Hello" worth $20 million. This act infuriated HP employees, who saw their retirement stocks dropping 50 percent during Fiorino's stay, and now giving Hurd such largess was considered obscene. Hurd was doomed from the day he took the job. HP employees were out for blood. Hurd was given the title of president and CEO and a year later chairman. Like Fiorina, Hurd was a professional manager. After receiving his degree in business he joined NCR as a junior salesman and stayed with them for 25 years.

Like Fiorina and many professional managers, Hurd engaged in aggressive cost-cutting. Shortly after his arrival the terminations began. He reduced the IT department from 19,000 to 8,000, and the number of software applications that HP uses from 6,000 to 1,500, and consolidated HP's 85 data centers to 6. He then imposed a 5 percent pay cut on all employees and removed many benefits. Hurd then took a pay cut of 20 percent in his base salary and then increased his bonus by the same amount. All the while Hurd was unaware of the resentment among present and past HPers who plotted to get him out.

To make matters worse, in September 2008, HP announced it would eliminate 24,600 jobs. Meanwhile Hurd's total compensation in 2008 rose 73 percent to about $33 million as HP's stock fell 29 percent. His compensation included a base salary of $1,450,000, stock award of $7,907,660, cash bonus of $23,931,882, and $662,695 in perquisites and other compensation. It was the largest bonus of any CEO in 2008, and he then implemented a wage freeze on the employees. In addition, HP paid $7,472 for travel expenses related to Mark Hurd's family accompanying him to business meetings. His expenses for security service roughly doubled to $256,000 and he did need security. Hurd's senior staff also did well; CIO Randy Mott's total compensation went up 400 percent in 2008 to $28 million, EVP VJ Joshi's total compensation jumped 83 percent to $22 million, EVP Todd Bradley's total compensation jumped 263 percent to $21 million, EVP Ann Livermore enjoyed a 31 percent bump in total compensation to $21 million, and CFO Catherine Lesjak got a 49 percent increase in total compensation to $6 million. They also received $18,000 for financial advice. One can guess they were told to stay away from HP stock. What a team, they are pulling for another major stock decline in 2009. For all his good effort Hurd got an extra $6.6 million in restricted stock awards in 2009.

While the executives were filling their coffers a year after HP acquired EDS in August 2009, they imposed huge salary cuts. EDS employees reported that under HP they experienced salary cuts of between 10 percent and 47 percent. At HP Hurd's management team had one management philosophy: "Less for you and more for me."

Needless to say Hurd and his gang have taken a company that once was considered among the "best" to work for in America and destroyed it while enriching themselves. The following was written on a blog by a current Hewlett-Packard Software Engineer IV:

"Pros

Very capable and smart people to work with. Peers provide the only support and motivation to stick around.

Cons

It will not be the competition or climate changes or business conditions what will bring this once a great company down, but the greed of those that run this company. The CEO running this company has only one thing on his mind and is to increase his net-worth. It will be another case study in future MBA courses in how not to run a company.

How is it possible that while employees are losing their lively-hoods and those of us so called "survivors" instead of being motivated to create great products and satisfy our customers all we do is motivated by fear of losing our jobs?

There used to be a time when I did not mind putting in 10 to 16 hours a day working for HP, there was a sense of ownership and satisfaction and we always knew that we would be compensated fairly, today I find it difficult to do that, however does not I don't do it because if I don't on my next review I might be flagged as not a team player and be ranked as a P-.

How is it possible that on a year of record profits we saw our incomes decreased by almost an 18% (this includes salary cuts, 401K contributions, stock purchase plans, vacations restrictions, low morale, etc) all while Mark Hurd and his minions are giving themselves record bonuses? I can't hardly wait until the SEC filings for this year during the next few days to see what kind of obscene bonuses are paid to the CEO and the executive council.

They don't care there is discontent in the ranks they can always replace all of us with people in India, China and now from I hear even Africa and at the "end of the day" (Hurd's favorite cliche) after the company is in shambles Mark Hurd will still walk away a multi millionaire.

In May 2010, Hurd announced another cut and he will terminate 6,000 more employees. The total terminations at HP for 2010 reached 9,000.

During the summer of 2010, stories filled media outlets accusing Hurd of inappropriate conduct in a claim of sexual harassment made by former reality TV and soft porn actress Jodie Fisher. She worked as a contractor with HP's marketing division from 2007 to 2009. It was reported that she earned up to $5,000 per event to greet people and make introductions among executives attending HP events that she helped organize." She filed a very well publicized sex harassment suit against Hurd. In August 2010 Hurd resigned amid stories of sexual harassment and troubling expense reports. Stories circulated that employees were so angry they went after him.

In exchange for releasing HP from future litigation, Hurd received a $12.2 million "Golden Boot" plus vested options and restricted stock for an estimated total of $34.6 million and he reached a settlement with Ms. Fisher. So where does Hurd end up? Larry Ellison of Oracle immediately hired him and made him a co-president and gave him a compensation package bigger than Ellison's. Hurd got a pay package valued at $78.4 million for fiscal year 2011 which ended May 31 and Ellison only got $77.6 million.

ENTER APOTHEKER

Hurd was replaced by Leo Apotheker, who was not even interviewed by board members. They gave him a salary of $1.2 million, a $4 million "Golden Hello" and $4.6 million in relocation costs and reimbursement for non-compete payments from his former employer and restricted stock worth nearly $38 million the day it was granted in September 2010. And what did Apotheker do? His background was in software development, therefore he decided HP will no longer make hardware and will enter the software and consulting business like IBM. In September 2011, 525 employees were terminated at HP's webOS division. In September 2011, employees pressured the board to get Apotheker out and the board immediately appointed former eBay CEO and Republican candidate for Governor Meg Whitman their new chief. She will take $1 dollar in compensation. Billionaires do that. But then she will receive a "boat-load" of stock options and a bonus of at least $2.4 million and reaching as high as $6 million.

What did Apotheker get for his 11 months on the job? He got what most CEOs get the "Golden Boot." He is receiving a severance payment worth $7.2 million, accelerated vesting of shares worth $3.56 million, 424,000 of the 728,000 performance-based restricted stock units awarded to him under the terms of his employment agreement and a performance bonus worth $2.4 million. (How does one get a performance bonus after being fired?) It gets better. He will also receive relocation expenses and air travel for him and his wife to return to

France or Belgium, and up to $300,000 to compensate for any loss on the sale of his California residence, and he and his dependents will receive medical and dental care for 18 months. Not bad for 11 months of work. One wonders what Whitman's "Golden Boot" is worth.

ENTER WHITMAN

Whitman was a member of HP's dysfunctional board for 8 months before they gave her the position. Her claim to fame was running an auction house, eBay. Now how does running an online auction prepared one to run HP? You guessed it. She will auction-off HP.

If one wants to gain an idea of where such dysfunctional leadership comes from, it always pays to look at the board of directors. Half the board's members at HP came from venture capital firms which gives a clue about the people they chose to lead the company. These venture people don't make things, except for money. They buy, sell, flip, breakup and destroy industries. And they make money in ways that would make most people scratch their heads in disbelief. Take board member John Hammergren, his full-time job is functioning as the CEO of McKesson. In 2009 he received an 11 percent compensation increase to more than $29.7 million, as the company's stock fell 33 percent and overall profit declined 17 percent. Included in his package was a $12 million performance bonus.

It's been widely reported that Whitman will only receive $1 in salary annually. This brings forth the response: If you believe this I have a bridge I want to sell you. What will she really get?

- $2.4 million target bonus, with $6.0 million maximum bonus

- 1.9 million stock options that carry an 8-year term and a $23.59 exercise price, and vest upon meeting the following conditions:

- 300,000 that vest ratably over 3 years contingent upon Whitman's continued employment

- 800,000 that vest upon one year of service and achieving a closing stock price of 120 percent of the option exercise price (i.e., $28.31) for 20 consecutive trading days

- 800,000 that vest upon two years of service and achieving a closing stock price of 140 percent of the option exercise price (i.e., $33.03) for 20 consecutive trading days

- A severance benefit equal to 1.5 times the sum of base salary and the average actual bonus for the preceding three years, upon involuntary termination without cause

According to Ferracone (2011) the target value of this total direct compensation package sums to approximately $16.5 million.

Appendix CZ: Government Employees Become Multimillionaires

In 2007, Richard Syron CEO of Freddie Mac, earned $14.5 million, including a $2.2 million performance bonus. A company spokesman said the $2.2 million was only 66 percent of his targeted bonus of $3.34 million, showing that the board of directors held Syron accountable for the rough sledding at Freddie Mac. In 2007 Freddie Mac's stock dropped by 50 percent destroying billions in shareholder value. Since 2003 Syron has made $38 million, even though Freddie Mac lost billions of dollars in 2008 and was taken over by the government.

His counterpart, Daniel Mudd, CEO of Fannie Mae, received a 15 percent cut in compensation in 2007. Still Mudd received $14.2 million, including a $10 million direct stock award. The drop in the Fannie Mae share price has resulted in a paper loss of nearly 66 percent.

According to Utt (2005): *"Fannie Mae's management team appears to be the chief beneficiary of the federal privileges and the accounting irregularities over the years. For example, in 2003, 749 members of Fannie Mae's management team received a staggering $65.1 million in bonuses, a portion of which was attributable to the overstated earnings that followed from the accounting* *irregularities. Over the past five years, the top 20 Fannie Mae executives reportedly received combined bonuses of $245 million.*

Although management's unearned bonuses have generated most of the headlines, the real cost to the nation is not the tawdry looting of the company by its top management team. The real problem is the concentration of risk in the hands of two massive and privileged companies that dominates America's housing finance markets."

In September 2008 the federal government bailed out Fannie and Freddie and both CEOs were officially terminated, but allowed to stay on "during the transition."

Paying for bad performance is nothing new at Fannie Mae. In 2004 CEO Franklin Raines was paid $30 million after he was fired for manipulating accounting procedures so he could reach projected profit targets. Regulators forced him to pay back almost $25 million, allowing him to keep $5 million. However, between 1998 and 2004, Raines received about $90 million. During the same period J. Timothy Howard, the CFO, received about $30.8 million. In Mudds first four years, he received $10 million (Duhigg, 2008).

It is unclear how much the bailout of Fannie and Freddie will cost U.S. taxpayers but estimates suggest the total for both could be in the range of $100 billion. However, it does appear that their CEOs will walk away wealthy. Richard Syron could receive an exit package of as much as $15 million and Daniel Mudd could receive $14 million (Duffy, 2008). In September 2009 a new CFO was appointed, and to show the world the gravy train had not ended, they gave him a $2 million signing bonus and a salary of $2.3 million. And what about their replacements? In 2009 the Federal Housing Finance Agency approved compensation plans for Fannie CEO Michael Williams and Freddie CEO Charles Haldeman to receive packages in a range of $4 million to $6 million. Slip ahead to 2010: Freddie and Fannie companies saw their shares de-listed from the New York Stock Exchange, posted $28 billion in losses through three quarters and ran their tab to the U.S. taxpayers to a startling $150 billion. But Fannie CEO Michael Williams and Freddie chief Charles Haldeman each stand to make some $6 million and under the guise of "we can't have top talent leave." Their top lieutenants could make between $2 million and $3 million each (Barr, 2010). In 2010 Williams and Haldeman each received a $2 million bonus.

REFERENCES

ABC Australia online (2008). Quantas engineers awaiting pay rise response. Retrieved from: www.abc.net.au/news/ May, 29, 2008.

Aenlle de, C. (2011) Executive Pay: Some Perks of the Job Are Better Than Others. Retrieved from: http://moneywatch.bnet.com/investing/blog/against-grain/executive-pay-some-perks-of-the-job-are-better-than-others/1154/#ixzz1RRazWwq8

Adler, A. (1956). The Individual Psychology of Alfred Adler. H. L. Ansbacher and R. R. Ansbacher (Eds.). New York: Harper Torchbooks.

Ahrens, F. (2008). Joe Cassano: The Man Who Brought Down AIG? 10/7/08. Retrieved from: http://voices.washingtonpost.com/livecoverage/2008/10/joe_cassano_the_man_who_brough.html?hpid=topnews

AFLCIO Executive Paywatch (2007). Retrieved from AFLCIO executive paywatch 4/3/07 http://www.aflcio.org/corporatewatch/paywatch/retirementsecurity/index.cfm

Alic, M. (2007) Robert L Nardelli. Answers.Com. Retrieved from: http://www.answers.com/topic/robert-nardelli

Allen, S. (2011) Public hospital official got nearly $1 million in severance on top of $3.9-million retirement payout. LA Times. Retrieved 5/18/11 from: http://latimesblogs.latimes.com/lanow/2011/05/

public-hospital-official-got-nearly-1-million-in-severance-on-top-of-39-million-retirement-payout.html

American Housing Survey (2001) United States Census Bureau. Retrieved from: http://www.census.gov/hhes/www/housing/ahs/ahs01/ahs01.html

Anderson, J. (2008). Wall Street Winner Hit a New Jackpot: Billion-Dollar Paydays New York Times 4/18/08.

Anderson, J. and Story, L. (2008), Fortunes reverse for a bank and its leader. N.Y. Times, C1, 6/10/2008.

Anderson, L. M. and Bateman, T. (1997). Cynicism in the workplace: some causes and effects Journal of Organizational Behavior, 18, 449-466.

Anderson, S. (2004) CEO's and Outsourcing. Retrieved from: money.cnn.com/2004/08/31/news/economy/**outsourcing**_pay/index.htm - 46k-

Anderson. S, Cavanagh, J., Collins, C. and Pizzigati, S. (2009) America's Bailout Barons. The 16th annual Institute for Policy Studies "Executive Excess" report exposes this year's windfalls for top financial bailout recipients Retrieved from: http://www.ips-dc.org/reports/executive_excess_2009 Anstett, P. (2009) Blue Cross raised execs' pay in 2008

Hikes came year before job cuts, hiring freeze. March 9, 2009. Freep.com. Retereived from: http://www.freep.com/article/20090310/BUSINESS06/903100309

Aquinas, T. (1991) Summa Theologiae of Thomas Aquinas:Timothy McDermott (Editor), Christian Classics Arango, T. & Creswell, J.

(2008). Goodbye to All That. New York Times, Sunday Business, October 5, 2008, p. 1.

Ariely, D. (2008). What's the Value of a Big Bonus? New York Times, Op Ed. November 19, 2008 . Retrieved from: http://www.nytimes.com/2008/11/20/opinion/20ariely.html?_r=1&bl&ex=1227330000&en=cb254b577ccf4790&ei=5087%0A

Arum, R. and Roksa, J. (2011) Academically Adrift: Limited Learning on College Campuses. University of Chicago Press.

Asimov, A. (2011) UC regents hand out incentive pay a day after cuts. Retrieved 1/21/11 from:http://www.sfgate.com/cgi-bin/article.cgi?f=%2Fc%2Fa%2F2011%2F01%2F20%2FMN0O1HC6RT.DTL

Association to Advance Collegiate Schools of Business (2008). Largest single B School donations from a single source. Retrieved from: http://www.aacsb.edu/members/communities/interestgrps/donors.asp

Associated Press, (3/27/07) CEOs who outsource got the biggest payday. Retrieved 3/28 from Swopblogger http://sfgate.com/cgi-bin/article.cgi?f=/n/a/2007/03/27/financial/f095731D17.DTL

Associated Press, (03.23.09) Windstream CEO compensation rises 51 percent Retreived from Forbse .com http://www.forbes.com/feeds/ap/2009/03/23/ap6202261.html

Associate Press (2008) Aquila board gives CEO Green $1 million bonus. Associated Press 07.16.08, 11:39 AM ET KANSAS CITY, MO. –

Associated Press (2008a) Nike CEO received $7.6M in 2008. In: CNNmmoney.com, August 08, 2008.

Associated Press (2008b) Grown over 150 years, Lehman end came swiftly. September 16, 2008. Retrieved from: http://www.iht.com/articles/ap/2008/09/15/business/NA-US-Lehman-Brothers-Profile.php?page=1

Associated Press (2009) Mylan CEO gets $11.6 million in 2008 compensation. In Forbes.Com 03.10.09, Retreived from: http://www.forbes.com/feeds/ap/2009/03/10/ap6147642.html

Associated Press, Forbes (2009a) PerkinElmer CEO compensation rises 30 percent 03.20.09, Reteived from: http://www.forbes.com/feeds/ap/2009/03/20/ap6193869.html

Associated Press (2011) Cargill profits rise amid food-price swings. Retrieved 4/13/11 from:http://www.businessweek.com/ap/financialnews/D9MISJJG2.htm

Auletta, K. (1986). Greed and Glory on Wall Street. NY: Warner Books

Austen, I. and de la Merced, M.J. (2010) Potash Producer Rejects Bid by BHP Billiton NY Times Business day. Retrieved from: http://www.nytimes.com/2010/08/18/business/18potash.html

Babiak, P. and Hare, R.D. (2006). Snakes in Suits. N.Y.: HarperCollins.

Bakija, A; Cole, A.; Heim, B.T. (2010) Jobs and Income Growth of Top Earners and the Causes of Changing Income Inequality: Evidence from U.S. Tax Return Data. Retrieved from: http://web.williams.edu/Economics/wp/BakijaColeHeimJobsIncomeGrowthTopEarners.pdf

Banjor, J. (2004) "Medical Errors and Medical Narcissism" Sudbury, Mass. :Jones & Bartlett Publishers, Inc.

Barnard, J.W. (2008) Narcissism, Over-Optimism, Fear, Anger and Depression: The Interior Lives of Corporate Leaders. Working Paper Series. Retrieved from: http://papers.ssrn.com/sol3/papers.cfm?abstract_id=1136888

Barr, C. (2010) More big paydays at Fannie, Freddie, CNN Money. Retrieved from: http://finance.fortune.cnn.com/2010/12/31/more-big-paydays-at-fannie-freddie/

Berenson, A. (2003) The Number-How the drive for quarterly earnings corrupted Wall Street and Corporate America. New York: Random House.

Bernard-Kuhn, L. (2010) $130M payout for ex-Omnicare CEO. Retrieved from: lbernard@enquirer.com August 6, 2010

Barnes, A.H. (2008) Narcissistic Entitlement Syndrome. Retrieved from: http://www.bcgsearch.com/crc/nes.html

Bartlett, D.L. and Steele, J.B. (2008) The Broken Promise, Time Magazine, Sunday, Oct. 23, 2005

Bartlett, D.L. and Steele, J.B. (2011) Offshoring stole many U.S. programming jobs. Retrieved 5/1/11 from: http://www.philly.com/philly/opinion/inquirer/121042084.html

Bartlett, T. (2010) Are Narcissistic Students More Likely to Cheat? The Chronicle of Higher Education. 12/6/10. Retrieved from: http://chronicle.com/blogs/percolator/are-narcissists-more-likely-to-cheat/27543#comment-694

Batson. D. et al (1978)., "Buying kindness: Effect of an extrinsic Incentive for Helping on Perceived Altruism," Personality and Social Psychology Bulletin, vol. 4, p. 90

Bauerlein, M. and Jaffery, C. (2011) All Work and No Pay: The Great Speedup. Mother Jones July/August 2011 issue Retrieved from: http://motherjones.com/politics/2011/06/speed-up-american-workers-long-hours?page=2

Bebchuk, L, Cremer M. and Peyer, U.(2006) Pay Distribution in the Top Exsecutive Team. Harvard Law and Economic Discussion Paper, # 574

Bebchuck, L. and Fried, J. (2006) Pay Without Performance. Boston: Harvard University Press.

Bednarz,A.(2011) AT&T CEO's compensation slips 6% to $27.3 million Declines in Randall Stephenson's bonus and perks were offset by a slight salary bump and greater equity awards, Network World Retrieved March 11, 2011 from http://www.networkworld.com/news/2011/031111-att-stephenson-compensation.html

Bennis, W.G. and O'Toole, J. (2005) How Business schools have lost their way. Harvard Business Review, May.

Bensman, T. (2009). Scouting Can Pay Off Big for Groups Executives. My SA Press, 2/1/09. Retrieved from: http://www.mysanantonio.com/news/38761372.html

Berkowitz, S. and Upton, J. (2011), Rutgers athletic department needs fees, funds to stay afloat. USA Today. Retrieved 2/27/11 from: http://www.usatoday.com/sports/college/2011-06-28-rutgers-athletic-department-subsidies_n.htm

Bhagat. S, Bolton, B. and Subramanian, A, (2010) CEO Education, CEO Turnover, and Firm Performance August 3, 2010 Retrieved from: http://www.unh.edu/news/docs/bolton_CEOEducation.pdf

Bion, W. 1970. Attention and interpretation. New York: Basic Books.

Bloomberg News (2010) Top-Earning U.S. Households Averaged $345 Million in '07. 2/18/10. New York Times Business, B11.

Blumenstyk, G. (2011) Default Rate on Federal Student Loans Jumps to 8.9%, a Nearly 2-Point Rise. Retrieved 5.20/11 from: http://chronicle.com/article/Default-Rate-on-Federal/127602/?sid=at&utm_source=at&utm_medium=en

Bollas, C. (1987) Normonic illness. In The Shadow of the Object: Psychoanalysis of the Unthought Known. London: Free Association Books.

Bollas, C. (1989) Forces of Destiny. Psychoanalysis and Human Idiom. London: Free Association Books

Bookman, J. (2010) Show me the money? Here it is October 8, 2010, Retrieved from: Jayhttp://blogs.ajc.com/jay-bookman-blog/2010/10/08/show-me-the-money-here-it-is/

Boswell, J (2008). The wisdom of enough. Maui Weekly, August, 7, 2008. Retrieved from: http://www.mauiweekly.com/search.aspx?term=wisdom

Bowley, G. and Martin, A. (2010) No Wheat Shortage, but Prices May Rise. Published: August 6, 2010 NY Times.

Bowman. J. (2010) The Success of Failure: The Paradox of Performance Pay *Review of Public Personnel Administration* 2010; 75,10 Retrieved from: http://rop.sagepub.com July 19, 2010

Bradt, G. (2011) How CEO Sam Martin is Driving the Imperative to Overhaul A&P. Forbes. Retrieved from: http://www.forbes.com/sites/georgebradt/2011/03/16/how-ceo-sam-martin-is-driving-the-imperative-to-overhaul-ap/

Brasher, P. (2011) Food prices pushing world to poverty's 'danger zone'. Retrievedfrom:http://www.desmoinesregister.com/article/20110415/BUSINESS01/104150347/0/prep_insider/?odyssey=nav|head

Braverman, H. 1974. Labor and Monopoly Capital. New York: Monthly Review Press

Brewster, D. (2006). Survey: Numbers of Millionaires hits new Record. Wealthy households boosted by overseas markets, alternative investments. Financial Times.com. April. 19, 2006 Retrieved from: http://www.msnbc.msn.com/id/12393877/

Brin, D. Wisenberg (2010) Medco CEO '09 Compensation Was $13.4 Million; Saw $17.1 Million From Options DOW JONES NEWSWIRES. Retrieved from: http://www.nasdaq.com/aspx/stock-market-news-story.aspx?storyid=201003111111dowjonesdjonline000612&title=medco-ceo-09-compensation-was-134-millionsaw-171-million-from-options

Brooks, R. (2009). Do Hospital CEOs Make Too Much Money. February, 23, 2009. Retrieved from: http://unapchat.blogspot.com/2009/02/do-hospital-ceos-make-too-much-money.html

Brown, S.E.F. (2008) Williams Sonoma sell one jet, rents another. 6/4/08 Retrieved from: http://sanfrancisco.bizjournals.com/san-francisco/stories/2005/11/07/story4.html

Bunkley, N. (2008) Auto parts workers approve a contact. New York Times, 5/23, section C2.

Bunkley, N. and Vlasic, B. (2008). Latest Chrysler Buyout Offer Lures Quarter of Salaried Staff. New York Times, Business Day B1, November, 29, 2008.

Burke, M.N., (2009). Charity Paid Leaders $2.5 Million. York Daily Record, 1/25/09. Retrieved from: http://ydr.inyork.com/ci_11545409

Burns, J.M., (1978). Leadership. New York: Harper and Row.

Burger, K., (2007). Study compares big 10 faculty pay. Online at http://www.collegian.psu.edu/archive/1993/11/11-10-93tdc/11-10-93dnews-5.asp

Bursten, B. (1973).Some Narcissistic Personality Types. International Journal of Psycho-Analysis, 54:287-300

Business Week Online, 2006. Executive Compensation Scoreboard. McGraw Hill. Also see. USA Today (2006). Executive Compensation.

Business Week (1998) How Al Dunlap Self Destructed, 7/6/98.

Retrieved from: http://www.businessweek.com/1998/27/b3585090.htm

Cameron, K.S., S.J. Freeman & Mishra, S.J. (1993) Downsizing and redesigning organizations. In: Organizational Change and Redesign. (eds.) G.P. Huber & W.H. Glick. N.Y. Oxford University Press

Campbell, W., Bush, C.P., Brunell, A.B. and Shelton, J (2005). Understand the social costs of narcissism: The case of the tragedy of the commons. Personality and Psychology Bulletin, 31, 10, 1358-1368

Carr, D. (20110) Furloughs, But Paydays for the Brass. New York Times, Business Day. B1, April, 11, 2011.

Cassidy, J. (2002). Greed Cycle: How The Financial System Encouraged Corporations to go Crazy. The New Yorker September 23, 2002

Centre for Corporate Governance at the University of Technology (2008), Failures Show the Executive salary defense is based on a lie. Retrieved from: *business.smh.com.au/business/*

Chapman, P. (2010). The Last of the Imperious Rich: Lehman Brothers 1844-2008. NY: Penguin

Chasseguet-Smirgel, J. (1986). Sexuality and mind : the role of the father and the mother in the psyche New York : New York University Press

Chasseguet-Smirgel, J. (1985) The ego ideal : a psychoanalytic essay on the malady of the ideal. New York : W.W. Norton.

Chicago Tribune (2010) Culture of Greed/ Retrieved 9/7/10 from: www.chicagotribune.com/news/opinion/editorials/ct-edit-highland-20100907,0,5717856.story

Cerny, M., MCKinnon, M.A.W., Capwell, J.R. and Hellmuth, K.L.,(2010). New Scrutiny of College and University Executive Compensation and Unrelated Business Activity. Journal of College and University Law, 37,1, 95-152. Retrieved from: http://www.mcguirewoods.com/news-resources/publications/Scrutiny-College-University.pdf

Christie, R. (1970). Studies in Machiavellianism. New York: Academic Press.

Clark, S. (2009) Postmaster General Gets Pay Bonus as Agency Falters 2/16/09. Retrieved from: http://www.foxnews.com/politics/2009/02/18/postmaster-general-gets-pay-bonus-agency-falters/

Clark, R. (2010) To what shrinking extent do the rich any longer need the rest of us? Retrieved November 10, 2010 from: http://www.

opednews.com/articles/To-what-shrinking-extent-d-by-Richard-Clark-101110-280.html

Cline, A. (2005) Pastor Supported Faith-Based Plans, Investigated for Outrageous Salary Friday November 11, 2005 http://atheism.about.com/b/2005/11/11/pastor-supported-faith-based-plans-investigated-for-outrageous-salary.htm

Cho, H. (2011) Constellation CEO's total compensation up 44%: Mayo A. Shattuck's pay valued at $15.7 million in 2010. Baltimore Sun. Retreieved April 15, 2011 from: http://articles.baltimoresun.com/2011-04-15/business/bs-bz-constellation-exec-comp-20110415_1_edf-nuclear-development-venture-compensation-package

Collegiate Employee Research Institute CERI (2007)

Conference Board (2008), CEO Pay Shifts Toward Stock. Retrieved from: http://www.bizjournals.com/gen/company.html?gcode=3AC7BECD8C8C49F8BFD14845468B276A

Connelly, E.A.J. (2009) Deere CEO Allen gets $4.28M in fiscal 2009 pay. Associated Press, 12/4/09. Retreived from: http://www.google.com/hostednews/ap/article/ALeqM5jpwyPjMTvcYkJ4DxEk8xrx-o4AZngD9CCPVJ80

Congressional Research Service (CRS) (2007) Excessive CEO Pay. Order Code RS22604, February 13, 2007. Retrieved from: http://wordpress.com/tag/capitalism/

Conyon, M. (2008) Wishing Upon a Star: Hiring a CEO from Inside the Company Vs. Going Outside. April 06, 2005 in Knowledge@Wharton. Retrieved from: http://knowledge.wharton.upenn.edu/article.cfm?articleid=1175

Cooper, M.J.; Gulen, I.T. and Rau, P.R. (2009) Performance for pay? The relationship between CEO incentive compensation and future stock price performance. Retreived from: http://online.wsj.com/public/resources/documents/CEOperformance122509.pdf

Corkery, M. (2009) Did the Banks' Political Connections Drive TARP? Wall Street Journal Blog. 12/23/09 Retrieved from: http://blogs.wsj.com/deals/2009/12/23/did-the-banks-political-connections-drive-tarp/

Corporate Library (2006) Pay for Failure. Retrieved from: http://thecorporatelibrary.blogspot.com/2006/04/pay-for-failure.html

Cossin, D. (2011) Financial models create a false sense of security. Financial Times. Retrieved from: http://www.ft.com/intl/cms/s/2/af6d86de-d57a-11e0-9133-00144feab49a.html#axzz1X5ercmnR

Coutts. S. (2009) Real Student Default Rates Much Higher Than Previously Known. Retrieved 12/19/09 from: http://www.propublica.org/article/real-student-default-rates-much-higher-than-previously-known-1216

Cowherd, D.M. and Levine, D. I. (1992). Product quality and pay equity between lower-level employees and top management. Administrative Science Quarterly, 37, 302-320.

Craig, S. (2011) Severance of $2 million for Departing Bank Chief. NY Times, 0/3/11. Section B.,p.2.

Crainer, S. and Dearlove, D. (1999). Gravy Training: Inside the business of business schools. San Francisco: Jossey Bass.

Creswell, J. (2009) Profits for Buyout Firms as Company Debt Soared.,10/4/09. Retrieved from: http://www.nytimes.

com/2009/10/05/business/economy/05simmons.html?_r=1&pagewanted=all

Crosby, F. (1984). Relative deprivation in organizational settings. In: B.M.Shaw and L.L. Cummings (eds.) Research in Organizational Behavior (Vol. 6. pp. 51-93) Greenwich, Ct.: JAI.

Crum, R. and Bartash, J. (2000) Outgoing Dell Executives To Cash In With 8-Figure Severances. CNNMONEY.COM, Retrieved from: http://money.cnn.com/news/newsfeeds/articles/djf500/200901091356DOWJONESDJONLINE000759_FORTUNE5.htm

Czander, W. M. (1993) The Psychodynamics of Work and Organization., N.Y.: Guilford Press

Czander, W.M, (1996). The sick building syndrome: A psychoanalytic perspective, Forum in Psychoanalysis, 12, 28-39.

Czander. W. (2010) CEOs and Their Need for Money: A Psychoanalysts View of Greed. Opednews Part one, two and three. Retrieved from: http://www.opednews.com/articles/5/CEOs-and-Their-Need-for-Mo-by-william-czander-100921-70.html

Daniels, S. (2011) Merger pays off for incoming Harris N.A. CEO. Retrieved 2/22/2011 from: http://www.chicagobusiness.com/article/20110222/NEWS01/110229977/merger-pays-off-for-incoming-harris-n-a-ceo#axzz1EoFnGTYH

Daily Planet (2007) Twin Cities Community Newswire. Minneapolis, Mn, May 27 Retrieved from: info@tcdailyplanet.net

Davenport, T. H., Prusak, L. & Wilson, J. H. (2003, June 23). Reengineering Revisited. Computerworld, 25, 48-50. Retrieved January 25, 2004 from EBSCO Academic Search Elite.

Davis, J. (2009) Just before defaulting on debt, Spansion gives new CEO 4-month salary advance February 20th, 2009 at 6:46 pm. Retrieved from: http://www.siliconbeat.com/2009/02/20/just-before-defaulting-on-debt-spansion-gives-new-ceo-4-month-salary-advance/

|Dash, E. (2008). All Told, the Price Tag for Citigroup.s New Chief is $216 Million, New York Times, 3/14/08, C4.

Dash, E. (2008a). Bye, Old Lane, New York Times, 6/13/2008, C4

Davis, C. and Wilcock, E. (2008)Teaching Materials Using Case Studies Retrieved from: http://www.materials.ac.uk/guides/casestudies.asp

DeFeo, J. (2010) 10 Highest-Paid CEOs in 2009. The Street. Retrieved from: http://www.thestreet.com/story/10806956/11/10-highest-paid-ceos-in-2009.html 07/16/1

DeMarco, T. and Lester, T. (1999). Peopleware: Productive Projects and Teams (2nd Ed.) N.Y.: Dorset.

Dial, J. and Murphy, K.J. (1995) Incentives, downsizing, and value creation at general dynamics. Journal of Financial Economics. 37, 3, 261-314

DiCello, N. (2008) Former Allstate CEO to Run AIG - Yikes!

September 19, 2008 Retrieved from: http://cleveland.injuryboard.com/miscellaneous/former-allstate-ceo-to-run-aig-yikes.aspx?googleid=247858

Diamond, M.A.,(1998). The Symbiotic Lure: Organizations As Defective Containers, Administrative Theory & Praxis, Vol.20, No.3, September 315-325.

Dietsch, P. (2006) Show me the money: the case for income transparency. Journal of Social Philosophy. 37, 2, 197-213

Domhoff, G.W. (2005) Interlocking Directorates in the Corporate Community. Retrieved from: http://sociology.ucsc.edu/whorulesamerica/power/corporate_community.html

Donlon, J.P. (2011) Monsanto's Hugh Grant, CEO of the Year 2010. Chief Executive Magazine. Retrieved from: http://chiefexecutive.net/ME2/Audiences/dirmod.asp?sid=&nm=&type=Publishing&mod=Publications::Article&mid=8F3A7027421841978F18BE895F87F791&tier=4&id=7EA0D0757ECB49E895AC5EFE2948BE77&AudID=F242408EE36A4B18AABCEB1289960A07

Dow Jones Newswire (2008) Motorola offers hefty compensation package to co-CEO, August 29, 2008. Retrieved from: http://www.chicagotribune.com/business/chicago-motorola-ceo-pay-mot-aug29,0,5988248.story

Downie, A. and Paulo, S. (2011).How Brazil Is Sending 75,000 Students to the World's Best Colleges. Retrieved Wednesday, Sept. 21, 2011from: http://www.time.com/time/world/article/0,8599,2094119,00.html#ixzz1YmdXUvC9

Drezner, D.W. (2004). The Outsourcing Bogeyman, Foreign Affairs, May/June 2004. Retrieved from: http://www.foreignaffairs.org/20040501faessay83301-p0/daniel-w-drezner/the-outsourcing-bogeyman.html

Drucker, P. (1974) Management: tasks, responsibilities, practices. N.Y.: Harper Row

Drucker, P. (1996) The Executive in Action: Managing for Results, Innovation and Entrepreneurship, the Effective Executive. New York: Harper Business.

Duffy, P. (2008) Scary Times. Retrieved 9/7/08 from: http://www.housingchronicles.com/

Duhigg, C. (2008) Pressured to Take More Risk, Fannie Reached Tipping Point. New York Times, October 5, 2008. p. 1.

Durkin, H. (1964). The group in depth. New York: International University Press.

Durbin, D. (2011) Goodyear Tire and Rubber Co.'s top executive saw his compensation rise 69 percent in 2010. Manufacturing Business Technology. Retrieved 3/9/11 from: http://www.mbtmag.com/Content.aspx?id=2180

Durson, J. (2011) CEOs are winning and labor is losing, these are dark days for working people. Daily News. Retrieved from: http://www.nydailynews.com/opinions/2011/09/05/2011-09-05_dark_days_for_working_people.html#ixzz1X6yRZYqP

Dvorak, P. (2008) Companies Cut Holes in CEO's Golden Parachutes. Wall Street Journal. 9/15/08 Retrieved from: http://online.wsj.com/article/SB122142930977433861.html?mod=googlenews_wsj

Eagle, M. 1981. Interests as object relations. Psychoanalysis and Contemporary Thought, 4(4), 527- 565.

Ebner, B. (2008) "Saskatchewan: A lot more than wheat" *Globe and Mail*, Toronto, 11 April 200Eckholm E. reported in NY Times (2008) 2/20/08 P. A14. Study says education gap could further limit poor

Economic Research Institute (2009). Study: Top executive pay falls 7.4%, Charlotte Business Journal. 2/20/09 Retrieved from: http://

www.bizjournals.com/charlotte/stories/2009/02/16/daily55.html?t=printable

Economic Times (2008). Pandet to Pay for Personal use of Citi Corporate Jet. March 16, 2008

Edwards, J. (2009) Merck Executive Pay: $36 million, Use of Private Jet, Cash Bonuses Despite Failures. March 6th, 2009, Retreived from: http://industry.bnet.com/pharma/10001287/merck-executive-pay-36-million-use-of-private-jet-cash-bonuses/

Edwards, J. (2009a) ValueClick Execs Got $14.2 Million Pay Raise Despite Missing Performance Targets. March 10. 2009. Retreived from: http://industry.bnet.com/advertising/10001190/valueclick-execs-got-142-million-pay-raise-despite-missing-performance-targets/

Edwards, J. (2009b) Wyeth CEO Got 69% Pay Raise; Was "Required" to Use Helicopter; Plus $24 Million Pfizer Sale Bonus. March 30th, 2009. Retreived from: http://industry.bnet.com/pharma/10001519/wyeth-ceo-got-69-pay-raise-was-required-to-use-a-helicopter-plus-24-million-pfizer-sales-bonus/

Edwards, J (2009c) Medarex CEO Got 91% Pay Raise Despite Delivering Nothing April 9th, 2009. Retreived from: http://industry.bnet.com/pharma/10001643/medarex-ceo-got-91-pay-raise-despite-delivering-nothing/

Edwards, J. (2011) Carl Icahn vs. Forest Labs: CEO Took $300M While Stock Fell. Retreived June 21, 201 from: http://www.bnet.com/blog/drug-business/carl-icahn-vs-forest-labs-ceo-took-300m-while-stock-fell/8807#ixzz1PwTRXL4T

Ehrenreich, B. (2008). The Power of Negative Thinking. New York Time Op Ed 9/24/08, p. A27.

Ellin, A. (2006). Was Earning That Harvard M.B.A. Worth It?, New York Times, June 11, 2006 http://industry.bnet.com/pharma/10001643/medarex-ceo-got-91-pay-raise-despite-delivering-nothing

Ellis, B. (2010) Verizon to cut 13,000 jobs CNNMoney 1/26/2010 Retreived from: http://money.cnn.com/2010/01/26/news/companies/verizon_layoffs/

Emmons, R. (2007) How the New Science of Gratitude Can Make You Happy, NJ: Houghton, Mifflin, Harcourt

Engardio, P., Arndt, M., and Foust, D. (2006) The Future of Outsourcing. Business Week 1/30/06 Retrieved from: http://www.businessweek.com/magazine/content/06_05/b3969401.htm

Equilar, Executive Compensation Trends 12/20/07 Retrieved from: www.equilar.com

Equilar, 2004. Executive Compensation. Human Resource Executive. Retrieved from: http://equilar.com/NewsArticles/070004_HumanResourceExecutive.pdf

Epstein, J.D. (2008). Health insurance executives earn healthy pay. The Buffalo News, Business Today, June 15, 2008

Esra, R. (2008) Warner Music Executive Payments. Retrieved from: http://ezinearticles.com/?Warner-Music-Executive-Payments&id=19712

Esrat, D. (2009) If you are wondering why health care costs are high, look to CEO pay. February 22, 2009. Retrieved from: http://esrati.com/?p=1879

Execunet (2008). The Whole Package. New York Times. Business Section, page 2, 8/10/2008.

Eyre, W. (2011) Union assails Frontier CEO's $8.6M pay package Execs make out big while workers ignored, CWA leadership says Retrieved 8/12/11 from: http://sundaygazettemail.com/News/Business/201108122650

Fain, P. (2010) Airplanes of the Southeastern Conference. The Chronicle of Higher Education Retrieved from: http://chronicle.com/article/Airplanes-of-the-SEC/125362/

Fairbairn, R. (1954). An object-relations theory of the personality. New York: Basic Books.

Farber, L. 1976. Lying, despair, jealously, envy, sex, suicide, drugs, and the good life. New York: Basic Books.

Farrell, M. (2009) Comcast's Burke, Angelakis Ink New Pay Deals: Base Salaries Frozen, Added Incentives. Multichannel News, 12/23/2009. Retrieved from: http://www.multichannel.com/article/441590-Comcast_s_Burke_Angelakis_Ink_New_Pay_Deals.php

Fasig. L. (2009) P&G's Lafley collects slight pay increase at $23.6M. 8/28/09 Business Courier. Retrieved from: http://www.bizjournals.com/cincinnati/stories/2009/08/24/daily57.html

Fenichel, O. (1938). The drive to amass wealth. Psychoanalytic Quarterly, 7, 69-95.

Ferracone. R. (2011) Will Hewlett-Packard's Shareholders Finally Get an ROI on Their CEO? Forbes. 11/2 Retrieved from: http://www.forbes.com/sites/robinferracone/2011/11/02/will-hewlett-packards-shareholders-finally-get-an-roi-on-their-ceo/

Fields, R. (2011) 5 Common Hospital Executive Compensation Practices Retrieved 1/19/11 from: http://www.beckershospitalreview.

com/compensation-issues/5-common-hospital-executive-compensation-practices.html

Fishman. S. (2008). Burning Down this House: Is Lehman CEO Dick Fuld the true villain in the collapse of Wall Street, or is he being sacrificed for the sins of his peers? Published Nov 30, 2008 Retrieved from: http://nymag.com/news/business/52603/

Fitza, M., Hayward, M., and Larsen, K. (2008). Claims to fortune: Linking availability of CEO press attention to CEO discretionary compensation. (Under review: Administration Science Quarterly.)

Flanigan, J. (2008) Makeover for MBA Programs. L.A. Times. June 25, 2005. *in print edition C-1*

Flessner, D. (2011) Greenbacks for Blue Cross. Retrieved 5/15/11 from: http://timesfreepress.com/news/2011/may/15/greenbacks-bluecross/

Flint, J. (2009) Viacom executives got pay raises in 2008 although stock fell. LA Times Business, April 18, 2009. Retreived from: http://www.latimes.com/business/la-fi-ct-viacom18-2009apr18,0,5459000.story

Foley, Brian , 2007. Comments about Executive Pay. Retrieved from: http://www.sec.gov/rules/proposed/s70306/btfoley4083.pdf

Forbes (2011) Profile of Thomas Gerrity. Retrieved from: http://people.forbes.com/profile/thomas-p-gerrity/44869

Foster, J.D. and Campbell, W.K. Are there such things as "narcissists" in social psychology? A taxometric analysis of the Narcissistic Personality. Personality and Differences, 43, 1321-1332.

Foust, D. & Grow, B. (2003). What Worked at GE Isn't Working at Home Depot, *Business Week*, January 27, 2003, p. 40.

Fox Garrity, B.K., Garrison, M.J., and Fiedler, R.C. (2008) Access for Whom, Access to What? The Role of the "Disadvantaged Student"Market in the Rise of For-profit Higher Education in the United States. *Journal for Critical Education Policy Studies,* vol.8. no.1. Retrieved from: http://www.jceps.com/PDFs/08-1-08.pdf

Frank, R.H. (2009), Should Congress Limit Executive Pay?. New York Times. Sunday Money, January 4, page 5.

Freud, S. (1917) Mourning and melancholia. *SE*, 14: 243-258. London: Hogarth Press Freud, S. (1917). Mourning and Melancholia. The Standard Edition of the Complete Psychological Works of Sigmund Freud, Volume XIV (1914-1916): On the History of the Psycho-Analytic Movement, Papers on Metapsychology and Other Works, 237-258

Freud, S. (1921) Group Psychology and the Analysis of the Ego. SE, 18:67-143. London: Hogarth Press

Freud, S. (1914) On narcissism: An introduction. SE, 14. London: Hogarth Press.

Freud, S. 1958/1912. The dynamics of transference. In J. Strachey (Ed. and Trans.). The Standard Edition of the Complete Psychological Works of Sigmund Freud (Vol.12, pp.97-108). London: Hogarth Press. (Original Work published 1912).

Freud,S. 1955/1921. Group psychology and the analysis of the ego. In J. Strachey (Ed. And Trans.) The Standard Edition of the Complete Psychological Works of Sigmund Freud. (Vol.18, pp.67-143). London: Hogarth Press. (Original work published 1921).

Fromm, E. (1955) The sane society. N.Y.: Holt, Reinhart and Winston

Fromm, E., (1970). Thoughts on Bureaucracy. Management Science, 16(12), B699-B705.

Frydman, C. and Molloy, R.S. (2011) Does Tax Policy Affect Executive Compensation? Evidence from Postwar Tax Reforms NBER Working Paper 16812 Retrieved from: http://www.nber.org/papers/w16812.pdf

Gabriel, T. (2010) Pressed to show progress, educators tamper with test scored. June, 11, 2010. New York Times. P. 1

Gabriel, Y. (1998). Psychoanalytic Contributions to the Study of Emotional Life in Organizations. Administration and Society, 30, 292.

Gardner, J. (2011)/ New Study reveals objective decision making on promotions a sham. http://hereisthecity.com/2011/08/29/new-study-reveals-objective-decision-making-on-promotions-a-sham/#

Garloch, K. (2009) Carolinas HealthCare discloses its top pay packages: For first time in nearly a decade, Carolinas HealthCare System reveals executives' pay. Charlotte observe, 1/14/09. Retrieved from: http://www.charlotteobserver.com/597/story/470957.html

Garone, E. (2010) No Experience Necessary. WSJ.com Retrieved from: SEPTEMBER 30, 2010 http://online.wsj.com/article/SB10001424052748703946504575469840650190572.htm

Galinsky, E. et. al. (2004). Overwork in America. Family and Work Institute. Retrieved from: http://www.familiesandwork.org/summary/overwork2005.pdf

Gettler, Leon. (2006). Christmas bonus time for Wall Street bosses. Sox First: Management and Compliance, Dec. 22.

Ghemawat, P. 1991. Commitment: The dynamics of strategy. New York: The Free Press.

Ghoshal, S. (2005) Are business schools bad for business? In a forthcoming article published posthumously in *Academy of* Management Learning & Education. *2/17/05*

Giannone, J.A. (2009) Merrill paid bonuses early as BofA deal closed- FT, Reuters-UK 1/22/09. Retrieved from: http://uk.reuters.com/article/marketsNewsUS/idUKN2150757420090122

Gill, J. (2008) Scholars raise concerns over business school 'theory fetish' in Times Higher Education. Retrieved from http://www.timeshighereducation.co.uk/story.asp?storyCode=400232&sectioncode=26

Glader, P. (2009) The Jack Welch MBA Coming to the Web, Wall Street Journal 6/22/09/ Retreived from : http://online.wsj.com/article/SB124562232014535347.html

Glassdoor.com (2009) Hewlett-Packard – "Another example of how damaging greed can be." Dec 20, 2009. Retrieved from : http://www.glassdoor.com/Reviews/Employee-Review-Hewlett-Packard-RVW346966.htm

Glowinski. K. D. (2008). Narcissistic Personality Disorder. Washington: Booksurge

Gopal, P (2008) Which College Grads Earn the Most?, A new study ranks the earning potential of graduates from the top colleges in the U.S.. Business Week 8/7/2008

Goffman, E. (1957) Presentation of Self in Everyday life. N.Y.: Doubleday.

Goldin, C. and Katz, L. (1999). Human Capital and Social Capital. Journal of Interdisciplinary History, Spring, 29, 4, 683-724.

Grant, A. (2011) Airline executives get millions of dollars in mergers. The Plain Dealer. Retrieved Saturday, March 05, 2011, from: http://www.cleveland.com/business/index.ssf/2011/03/airline_executives_get_millions_of_dollars_in_mergers.html

Graybow, M. (2008). Merrill CEO stands to collect $9.7 ml payout. Mon Sep 15, 2008. Retrieved from: http://www.reuters.com/article/rbssFinancialServicesAndRealEstateNews/idUSN1532885520080915?sp=true

Graybow, M. (2008a) Sprint Nextel executives top list of most overpaid Wed Oct 8, 2008 Retrieved from: http://www.reuters.com/article/newsOne/idUSTRE497AU420081008

Green, C. (2008). Too Big to Trust or too Trustworthy to Scale. 3/15/10. Retrieved from: http://www.thecustomercollective.com/TCC/52364

Greenberg, J. (1990). Reacting to procedural injustice in payment distributions. Journal of Applied Psychology, 72, 55-67.

Greenberg, J. (2005) Managing Behavior in Organizations. N.J. Prentice Hall

Greenberg, J.R. & Mitchell, S.A. 1983. Object relations in psychoanalytic theory. Cambridge, MA.: Harvard University Press.

Greenhouse, S. (2010). More Workers Face Pay Cuts, Not Furloughs. The New York Times., P.1., 8/4/10.

Greenson, R. 1967. The technique and practice of psychoanalysis. New York: International Universities Press. Guntrip, H. 1969. Schizoid phenomena, object relations and the self. New York: International Universities Press.

Gross, J. (2009). John Hagee Corner Stone Ministry. Retrieved from: http://www.blog.joelx.com/pastor-john-hagee-cornerstone-church-ministry-heresy-divorce-dirty-deeds/910/

Grow, B. (2006) Home Depot: Last Among Shoppers. Business Week. June 6, 2006. Retrieved from: http://www.businessweek.com/magazine/content/06_25/b3989044.htm

Gunbaum, R. (2008). Seattle biotech rewards execs after stock dropped 99 percent. The Seattle Times, Sunday Buzz. Retrieved from: http://seattletimes.nwsource.com/html/sundaybuzz/2008613921_sundaybuzz11.html

Guntrip, H. (1969) Schizoid Phenomena, Object Relations and the Self., N.Y.: International Universities Press.

Gutman, H. (2002) Dishonesty, Greed and Hypocrisy in Corporate America. Retrieved from: http://www.commondreams.org/views02/0712-02.htm

Habib-Valdhorn, S, (2011) Teva to pay Cephalon execs golden parachutes: Cepahlon CEO Kevin Buchi will be eligible for $14.6 million compensation. Retrieved 2 June 11 From: http://www.globes.co.il/serveen/globes/docview.asp?did=1000651387&fid=1725

Haefner R. (2007) In: CIO (10/31/2007). Employers Change Corporate HR Policies to Cater to Generation Y, Survey Finds. M. Levinson .

Hakim, D. (2009) Some New York Lawmakers Collect Pensions on Top of their Pay New York Times page 1 8/18/09

Halpern, J. & Halpern, I. (1983). Projections. New York: Seaview/Putnam Press.

Hammer, Michael & Champy, James (1993). Reengineering the Corporation: A Manifesto for Business. New York, NY: HarperCollins Publishers, Inc.

Harris, G. (2009). Drug Making's Move Abroad Stirs Concerns. New York Times, Science Times 1/20/09, D1.

Hartmann, H. 1958. Ego psychology and the problem of adaptation. International Universities Press.

Hartmann, H. 1984, Essays on ego psychology. New York: International Universities Press.

Hartung, A. (2009).Harvard Business Review: The Decade's top Performing CEOs - Apple, Cisco, Amazon, eBay, Google 12/31/09. Retreived from: http://nycbiznetworking.typepad.com/my_weblog/2009/12/harvard-business-review-the-decades-top-performing-ceos-apple-cisco-amazon-ebay-google.html

Harvey, J. (1988). The Abilene paradox and other meditations on management. Lexington, MA: Lexington Press

Healy, B. (2009) Logue's parting gift set at $6m. Boston Globe. Retreived: http://www.boston.com/business/articles/2009/11/25/logues_parting_gift_at_state_street_corp_set_at_6m/

Health Care for America Now (2010) CEOs From 10 Health Insurers Took Nearly $1 Billion in Compensation, Stock Options in Last Decade Aug 11, 2010. Retrieved from: http://yubanet.com/usa/CEOs-From-10-Health-Insurers-Took-Nearly-1-Billion-in-Compensation-Stock-Options-in-Last-Decade.php

Hechinger, J. and Lauerman, J (2010) Executives Collect $2 Billion Running U.S. For-Profit Colleges. Retrieved Nov 10, 2010 from http://www.bloomberg.com/news/print/2010-11-10/executives-collect-2-billion-running-for-profit-colleges-on-taxpayer-dime. html

Hedge Funds Job Digest (2009). Hedge Fund Compensation Survey. 12/13/06. Reteived from: http://hedgefundcompensationreport.com/

Hefner, R.W. (Ed.) 1998. Market Cultures. New York: Westview Press, Columbia Institute of Southeast Asian Studies.

Heher, A. (2009) Sherwin-Williams CEO earns $5.8 million. Forbes.com, 03.05.09, Retreived from" http://www.forbes.com/feeds/ap/2009/03/05/ap6131704.html

Helft, M. (2009). Yahoo to Trim 700 More Workers. New York Times, Business, B3, 4/22/2009.

Heller, R. (2005) Managements Pay: Are Managers Hugh Salaries Justifiable? Retrieved from: http://www.thinkingmanagers.com/management/management-pay.php

Hemsworth, D, (2010). Ivory Tower Grudge Match, THE HAMILTON SPECTATOR (Mar 27, 2010) Retrieved from: http://www.thespec.com/News/Local/article/743582

Hendrik, I. 1943. Work and the pleasure principle. Psychoanalytic quarterly, 12, 311-329.

Herscher, P. (2009) Carol Bartz Will Turn Yahoo Around. Market Mine, 1/14/09 Retrieved from: http://pennyherscher.blogspot.com/2009/01/carol-bartz-will-turn-yahoo-around.html

Hickok, T.A. (2008). Downsizing and Organizational Culture. Retrieved from: http://humanresources.about.com/gi/dynamic/offsite.htm?zi=1/XJ/Ya&sdn=humanresources&cdn=money&tm=

35&f=00&tt=14&bt=1&bts=1&zu=http%3A//www.pamij.com/hickok.html

Higgins, Tim. (2007) CEO pay, Free Press Business Writer, Februrary.

Hightower, J. (2009). Top 10 Earners Made $209 Million in 2008 as Firm Foundered March 4, 2009. Wall Street Journal

Hilzoy,(2009). Populist Anger Made Simple. Washington, Monthly, 3/29/09. Retreived from: http://www.washingtonmonthly.com/archives/individual/2009_03/017498.php

Hiralal, B. (2008) Monsanto raises CEO pat: Expects huge Profits Retrieved from http://www.thedeal.com/corporatedealmaker/2008/12/monsanto_raises_ceo_pay_predic.php

Hirschhorn, L. 1988. The workplace within. Cambridge, MA.: MIT Press. Narcissists at Work: How to Deal with Arrogant, Controlling, Manipulative Bullies

Hoffman, T. (2008). Narcissistic employees—yes, IT has its fair share—can wreak havoc in the office and put your own job at risk. June 11, 2008 Computerworld, CIO. Retrieved from: http://www.cio.com/article/447071/Narcissists_at_Work_How_to_Deal_with_Arrogant_Controlling_Manipulative_Bullies

Hoover, E, (2007) Researchers Challenge View of "Millennial Students" Chronicle of Higher Education, 00095982, 11/9/2007, Vol. 54, Issue 14

Horney, K. (1950) Neurosis and Human Growth. N.Y. Norton.

Hotchkiss, S. (2002) Saving yourself from the narcissists in your Life, N.Y.: Free Press

HR.BIR.com (2006) 1/3 of U.S. workers leave…and lose…vacation time. Retrieved from: http://hr.blr.com/news.aspx?id=18429

Huber, T. (2009) Coal producer Massey Energy Co. increases potential payout for CEO Don Blankenship. January 7, 2010 The Associated Press. Retrieved from: http://abcnews.go.com/Business/wireStory?id=9502489

Hudson, J. (2008) Chrysler's Secret Weapon: Military Talent: Bob Nardelli built success at GE and The Home Depot by hiring military. As CEO of Chrysler, he now plans to use that same winning formula. GI Jobs. Retrieved from: http://www.gijobs.net/magazine.cfm?issueId=84&id=1075

Hudson, J. (2008) Bob Nardelli built success at GE and The Home Depot by hiring military. As CEO of Chrysler, he now plans to use that same winning formula. Retrieved from: http://www.gijobs.net/magazine.cfm?issueId=84&id=1075

Hughes, W. G. (2010) CSUSB business school earns top ranking Island Valley Daily Bulletin. Retrieved from: Created: 11/23/2010 From: http://www.dailybulletin.com/ci_16696080

Ingber, D. 1981 Computer addicts. Science Digest, July, 114-121.

Ingram, D.H. 1986. Remarks on intimacy and the fear of commitment. American Journal of Psychoanalysis, 46(1), 76-79.

Inman, P. (2011) UN report calls for regulation to curb speculators pushing up food prices. Retrieved 6/6/11 from: http://www.guardian.co.uk/business/2011/jun/05/commodities-food-security

Institute for Policy Studies (2010) Executive Excess 2010: CEO Pay and the Great Recession (S. Anderson, C. Collins, S. Pizzigati, K.

Shih). Retrieved from: http://www.ips-dc.org/reports/executive_excess_2010

Iosco, B.R. (2009) Corporate greed is a horrendous business. 2/1/09, Free Lance Star Retrieved from: http://fredericksburg.com/News/FLS/2009/032009/03012009/448251

Isaacs, J. (2005), Northwestern and Delta Executives Make Millions From Bankruptcies, Retrieved from: http://www.wsws.org/articles/2005/sep2005/nwa-s19.shtml

IU News Room (2009) New leaders take the reins of Kelley School's MBA and undergraduate programs 8/31/09 Retreievd From: *http://newsinfo.iu.edu/news/page/normal/11670.html*

Ivry, B. (2009), Hovnanian CEO Gets Bonus as Company Value Drops 76% (Update2) . Bloomberg Press, 2/6/09. Retrieved from: http://www.bloomberg.com/apps/news?pid=20601087&sid=ad5a0nJfglXQ&refer=home

Jarrad, H. and Kai, Li (2007) Decoupling CEO Wealth and Firm Performance: The Case of Acquiring CEOs. Journal of Finance, Volume 62: Issue 2.

Jodell, J. (2009). Why American Health Care Costs So Much. January 14, 2009.Retireved from: http://jackjodell.blogspot.com/2009/01/why-american-health-care-costs-so-much.html

Johnsson, J. (2011) United CEOs reaped rich rewards for 2010 merger. Chicago Tribune. Retrieved 4/22/11 from: http://www.chicagotribune.com/business/breaking/chibrknews-united-ceos-reaped-rich-rewards-for-2010-merger-20110422,0,7914812.story

Jones, D. (2009) Spending on personal security perk for CEOs is skyrocketing. USAToday 9/11/09 Retrieved from: http://www.usatoday.

com/money/companies/management/2009-09-07-CEO-security-spending_N.htm

Junco, R and Mastrodicasa,J. (2007),*Connecting to the Net.Generation*: *What Higher Education Professionals Need to Know About* Today's Students. NASPA; First Edition (March 29).

Kanter, R.M. 1968, Commitment and social organization: A study of commitment mechanisms in utopian communities. American Sociological Review, 33, 499-517.

Kanter R.M. 1983. The change masters. New York: Simon and Schuster.

Kaplan, J. (2008). Poor performance often linked to excessive executive pay. Retrieved from: http://www.researchrecap.com/index.php/2008/12/09/poor-performance-often-linked-to-excessive-executive-pay/

Kaplan, S.R. & Razin, A.M. (1981). Psychosocial dynamics of group cohesion. In H. Kellerman (Ed.)Group Cohesion. New York: Grune & Stratten.

Kaslow. F.W. (ed.) (1996) Hankbook of Relational Diagnosis and Dysfunctional Family Patterns (Wiley Series in Couples and Family Dynamics and Treatment. NY: Wiley

Kaufman, F. (2011) How Goldman Sachs Created the Food Crisis retrieved from agriculture corner. Retrieved from: http://www.agricorner.com/how-goldman-sachs-created-the-food-crisis/#comment-293

Kellerman, H.J. (1981) The Deep Structures of Group Cohesion. In: Group Cohesion: Theoretical and Clinical Perspectives. N.Y.: Grune & Stratton pp. 3-21.

Kennedy, P. (2008) . CEO Paywatch: Mosaic's Prokopanko, $3.26 million. StarTribune. 8/25/08. Retrieved from: http://www.startribune.com/business/27410754.html?elr=KArks:DCiU1OiP:DiiUiD3aPc: Yyc:aUU

Keeter, S. (2006). Politics and the "DotNet" Generation. Survey conducted by Pew Research Center for People and the Press. May, 30, 2006.

Kenworthy, J. (2008) Styles of Leadership and Golf, MBA Association. 4/21/2008. Retrieved from: http://www.mbaassociation.org/Leadership/stylesofleadershipandgolf.html

Keoun, B. (2009) Citi Cost-Cutters Skip Offices, Staff for Ex-CEOs Prince, Reed. Bloomberg.com, 2/18/09. Retrieved from: http://www.bloomberg.com/apps/news?pid=20601103&sid=a.MJ0tBKx67w&refer=news

Kernberg, O. (1975) Borderline conditions and pathological narcissism. NY: Aronson.

Kets de Vries, M.F.R. (1989) Alexithymia in Organizational Life: The Organization Man Revisited. Human Relations, Vol. 42, No. 12, 1079-1093

Kets de Vries, M.F.R. & Miller, D. 1984. The neurotic organization. San Francisco: Jossey Bass

Kiley, K. (2011) Never a Good Time. Retrieved July, 19 from: http://www.insidehighered.com/news/2011/07/19/san_diego_state_president_s_pay_hike_highlights_politics_of_such_decisions

Kiley, K. (2010) Report Faults For-Profit Colleges as Providers of 'Subprime Opportunity'. Chronical of Higher Education. Retrieved

11/23/10 from: http://chronicle.com/article/Report-Faults-For-Profit/125486/?sid=at&utm_source=at&utm_medium=en

Kim, D., Kerber, R. & Krasny, R. Companies drop pensions, pay execs $350 million: watchdog. 11/19/09. Retreived from: http://www.reuters.com/article/ousivMolt/idUSTRE5AI4DY20091119?pageNumber=1&virtualBrandChannel=0

King, G. (2007). Narcissistic Leaders & Effective Crisis Management: A Review of Potential Problems and Pitfalls. Journal of Contingencies and Crises Management, 15, 4, 183-193.

King, R. (2009) The 5 Most Highly-Paid CIOs. Business Week, June 11 http://www.businessweek.com/technology/technology_at_work/archives/2009/06/the_5_most_high.html?chan=technology_technology+index+page_top+stories

Kirkland, R., (2006). The real CEO pay problem. Fortune, June 30.

Klass P. (2009) Texting, Surfing, Studying? New York Time Section D5, 10/13/09

Kochan, T.A. (2006). The American Worker: Disposable or Disposable. Work and Occupations, 33, 4, 377-381.

Kohn, A. (1993). Why Incentives Plans Cannot Work. Harvard Business Review, September/October.

Kohut, H. 1971. The Analysis of Self. New York: International Universities Press.

Kolhoff, M. (2010 The Price of Coal: Greed and Corruption Kills 29 Miners. Ideas and Actions Retrieved from :http://news.infoshop.org/article.php?story=20100611014900668

Komaki, J.L., Coombs, T. & Schepman, S. 1996. Motivational implications of reinforcement theory. In: Motivation and Leadership at Work 6th ed. Eds: R.M. Steers, L.W. Porter and G.A. Bigley. 35-52

Konigsberg, E. (2008) Challenges of $600-a-session patients. New York Times. Monday, July 7, B1

Koppenheffer, M. (2011) It's the Same Old Story at Chesapeake. Retrieved 6/13/11 from: http://www.msnbc.msn.com/id/43379017/ns/business-motley_fool/

Krangel, E. (2008) Gannett CEO: Sorry For The Layoffs, I'll Take A 3% Pay Cut. November 4, 2008. Retrieved from: http://www.alleyinsider.com/2008/11/gannett-ceo-sorry-for-the-layoffs-i-ll-take-a-3-pay-cut

Krantz, J & Gilmore, T. (1990) The Splitting of Leadership and Management as a Social Defense. Human Relations, Vol. 43, No. 2, 183-204

Kristof, K. (2008) More firms are cutting perks, LA Times, 5/25/08 kathy.kristof@latimes.com

Krystal, H. (1988) Integration and Self-Healing: Affect, Trauma, Alexithymia: Henry Krystal, M.D. Analytic Press, Hillsdale, NJ

Lachkar, J. (1992). The Narcissistic/Borderline Couple. N.Y.: Brunner/Mazel.

Labi, A. (2011) University Mergers Sweep Across Europe Leaders hope larger, more-diverse institutions will improve research. Retrieved from: http://chronicle.com/article/University-Mergers-Sweep/125781/?sid=at&utm_source=at&utm_medium=en

Lambert, C. (2011). Our Unpaind, Extra Shadow Work. New York Times, Sunday Review. 10/30/11, P. 12

Lang, J.A. (1984). Notes toward a psychology of a feminine self. In: P.E. Stepansky and A. Goldberg (Eds.) Kohut's Legacy. Hillsdale, N.J.: Analytic Press.

Lang, J.M. (2003) Shameless self promotion. Chronicle of Higher Education, September. Retrieved from: http://chronicle.com/jobs/news/2003/09/2003090901c.htm

Langford, C. (2011) Shareholders Sue Over Gusher of Bonuses. Retrieved 6/13/11 from: http://www.courthousenews.com/2011/06/13/37303.htm

Lauerman, J. (2010). For-Profit Colleges Charging More While Doing Less for Poorest. Bloomberg. Retrieved from: http://www.bloomberg.com/news/2010-12-31/for-profit-colleges-charging-more-while-doing-less-for-low-income-families.html

Lawler, E.E. (2002).The Folly of Forced Ranking. Retrieved from: http://www.strategy-business.com/press/16635507/20290

Louis Lavelle, L. (2010) Business schools: Hotbed of Narcissism. August 12, 2010 Retrieved from: H*ttp://www.businessweek.com/bschools/blogs/mba_admissions/archives/2010/08/business_school_hotbed_of_narcissism.html*

Lazarus.D (2008). Fair is fair-but pensions for executives often aren't. Los Angeles Times, Business Section, 5/25/08.

Lee, D. (2011) As U.S. stumbles, companies invest in consumer growth overseas. Many begin to give up on the ailing American shopper and make plans to chase growing demand in Asia and Latin America. Retrieved 8/8/11 from: http://www.latimes.com/business/la-fi-consumers-overseas-20110808,0,6537651.story

Lee, G. L., (1981) Who gets to the top: a sociological analysis. England: Aldershot.

Lee, M. (2008) Cardinal Health CEO compensation more than doubles. Business Week. 9/29/2008 Retrieved from: http://www.business-week.com/ap/financialnews/D93GMQA00.htm

Lee, Hecht and Harrison (2007) Survey of Gen Y's. Retrieved from: http://www.usatoday.com/money/workplace/2005-11-06-gen-y_x.htm

Lee, K.A. (2009) Loews CEO receives $5.5M in 2008 compensation. Forbes.Com. Retrieved from: http://www.forbes.com/feeds/ap/2009/02/23/ap6085574.html

Lee, P. (2009) Looking beyond the bottom line 9/21/09. Retrieved from: http://www.businesstimes.com.sg/sub/campus/story/0,4574,351077,00.html

Leichman, A. (2010) Charity Navigator Study: Non-Profit CEOs See Boosts in Salaries http://www.christianpost.com/article/20100823/study-non-profit-ceos-see-boosts-in-salaries/

Leonard, D. (2010). After a year of Tumult at Treasury, Former Bailout Chief Took a Quite Path to Pimco. 1/1/10. New York Times Section B1.

Leonard, A. (2011) Ikea's Third World outsourcing adventure -- in the U.S. Retrieved 4/11/11 from: http://www.salon.com/technology/how_the_world_works/2011/04/11/ikea_s_third_world_outsourcing_adventure_in_the_united_states

Leonard, W. (2010) Trucking company donates to University of Utah business school. 2/9/10 Retrieved from: http://www.deseretnews.

com/article/print/700008390/Trucking-company-donates-to-University-of-Utah-business-school.html

Leondar-Wright, B. and Canvanagh, J. (1997), "Executive Excess: CEOs Gain from Massive Downsizing," Institute for Policy Studies. Retrieved from: http://www.faireconomy.org/press room/1998/executive excess 98 ceos reap millions from massive lay offs

Lepro, S. (2009) PNC Financial to pay CEO $3 million stock bonus. AP 02.17.09 Retrieved from: http://www.forbes.com/feeds/ap/2009/02/17/ap6062196.html

Lesting, J. (2009)Carol Bartz: Liberating Yahoo From Its 'Rocks' 12/3/09 Retreived from:http://online.wsj.com/article/BT-CO-20091203-706222.html

Levy P.E. and William, J.R. (2005) The social context of performance appraisal: A review and framework for the future. Journal of Management 30 (6) 881-905

Levine, D.P. (2000). The attachment of greed to self interests. Psychoanalytic Studies, 2,2, 131-140.

Levinson, D. J. and Astrachan, B. (1970) Organizational boundaries: Entry into the mental health center. Journal of administration and policy in mental health, 2, 1

Levinson D.J. & Gallagher, E.B. (1965) Patienthood in the mental hospital. Boston: Houghton Mufflin, Boston

Levitz, J. (2009) CEO's Pay Rose as Stock Sank. WSJ, 3/16/09 Reteived from: http://online.wsj.com/article/SB123716165812835623.html?mod=rss whats news us

Levy, A. (2009) SunTrust CEO Wells Received 62 Percent Pay Increase in 2008. Bloomberg.Com. 2/24/09. Retrieved from: http://www.bloomberg.com/apps/news?pid=20601087&sid=a6ioAY4hkl0A&refer=home

Lewin, T. (2008) Presidents' Pay Rises Faster at Public Universities Than Private Ones, Survey Find, NY Times, November 17, 2008. Retrieved from: http://www.nytimes.com/2008/11/17/education/17college.html?_r=1&ref=education

Lewin, T. (2009). Many Specialists at Private Universities Earn More Than Presidents. February 23, 2009. New York Times Page A17.

Lewin,T. (2010) College May Become Unaffordable for Most in U.S. NY Times Retrieved 12/3/10 from: http://www.nytimes.com/2008/12/03/education/03college.html

Lewis, H. B. (1971) Shame and Guilt in Neurosis N.Y. International Universities Press.

Lifton,R.J. (1968 Winter) Protean man. Partisan Review. Pp. 13-27

Liston, M. (2007) Valpaks Blog. Retrieved from: http://valpakmark.blogspot.com/2007/11/cbss-report-on-millennials-fan-or-foe.html Lovallo. D. & Kahneman, D. (2003)Delusions of Success: How Optimism Undermines Executives' Decisions," Harvard Business Review, Vol. 81, No. 7, July 2003.

Lowenstein, R. (2008). Siphoning G.M.'s Future. NY Times OP-ED , July 10, Page A21.

Lund-Muzikaut, D. (2009) Health care CEOs owe us. Oregon live.com. April 18, 2009, Retrieved from: http://www.oregonlive.com/opinion/index.ssf/2009/04/health_care_ceos_owe_us.html

Lubin, J. (2010). CEO Tenure, Stock Gains Often Go Hand in Hand. Wall Street Journal, July 6, 2010. Retrieved from: http://online.wsj.com/article/SB10001424052748703900004575325172681419254.html?mod=googlenews_wsj

Lubit, R.H. (2004) Toxic managers, subordinated and other difficult people, NJ: FT Press

Lynd, Helen M., (1961). On Shame and the Search for Identity. New York: Science Editions. Maccoby, M. (2000). Narcissistic Leaders: The Incredible Pros, the Inevitable Cons. Harvard Business Review January-February

Maccoby, M. (2002). Toward a Science of Social Character. *International Forum of Psychoanalysis* 11: (33-44)

Maher, J (2011) UT athletic directors DeLoss Dodds, Chris Plonsky getting pay raises, contract extensions. AMERICAN-STATESMAN. Retrieved Sunday, Feb. 13, 2011: http://www.statesman.com/sports/longhorns/ut-athletic-directors-deloss-dodds-chris-plonsky-getting-1250368.html

Mahler, M. 1972. Rapprochement sub-phase of the separation-individuation process. Psychoanalytic Quarterly, 41, 487-506.

Mahler, M., Pine, F. & Bergman, A. 1975. The psychological birth of the human infant. New York: Basic Books.

Manning, S. (2009) General Dynamics CEO compensation up 15 percent Associated Press, Forbes, 03.20.09. Reteived from: http://www.forbes.com/feeds/ap/2009/03/20/ap6195035.html

Marks, J. (2009) The Quotable Bob Nardelli: What His Appointment Means For Chrysler August 06, 2009. Retrieved from: http://

seekingalpha.com/article/43622-the-quotable-bob-nardelli-what-his-appointment-means-for-chrysler

Marlow, I. (2009) Ex-Nortel staff slam executive bonuses: Payment in leaked file to keep bosses on board. The Star.com. 12/2/09 Retrieved from: http://www.thestar.com/business/companies/nortel/article/731961--ex-nortel-staff-slam-executive-bonuses

Martin, A. (2009). Give Him Liberty, but Not a Bailout. New York Time, Sunday Business. 8/2/09

Maslow, A. 1954. Motivation and personality. New York: Harper and Row.

Martin, C.A. and Tulgan, B. (2007) Managing the Gen Y at Work.

Melborne, E. (1999). We are going to own this generation. Retrieved from: Business Week Online http://www.businessweek.com/dated-toc/1999/9907.htm

Meindl, J.R., Ehrlich, S.B. & Dukerich, J.M. 1985. The Romance of Leadership, Administration Science Quarterly, 30, 78-102.

Maslach, C., Jackson, S. E., & Leiter, M. P. (1996). The Maslach Burn-out Inventory (3rd ed.). Palo Alto, CA: Consulting Psychologists Press, January 21, 2010

Marchand, A. (2010) Cost of College Is a Big Worry of Freshmen in National Survey. The Chronicle of Higher Education. Retrieved 1/21/10 from http://chronicle.com/article/Cost-of-College-Is-a-Big-Worry/63671/

Maremont, M. (2008). Companies Promise CEOs Lavish Posthumous Paydays. **Options Vest, Insurance Flows; Even Salaries May Continue. Wall Street Journal.** June 10, 2008; Page A1

Machan, D. (2008). CEO Interview: Costco's James Sinegal. *Smart Money Magazine,* March 27, 2008

Mann, J. (2010) Value of Auto Nation's CEO compensation rose 31 percent in 2010. Wall Street Journal. Retireved 3/24/11 from: http://online.wsj.com/article/BT-CO-20110323-713252.html

Marks, J. (2007) The Quotable Bob Nardelli: What His Appointment Means For Chrysler. August 06, 2007. Retrieved from: http://seekingalpha.com/article/43622-the-quotable-bob-nardelli-what-his-appointment-means-for-chrysler

Masterson, J. (1981) The Narcissistic and borderline disorder. NY: Brunner/Mazel

MBA Alliance (2007). The Online MBA Comes of Age. Retrieved From: http://www.online-education.net/business/articles/mba-comes-of-age.html

McDonald, L.G. (2009) A Colossal Failure of Common Sense. NY: Crown Business

McLean, B and Elkind, P. (2003). The Smartest Guys in the Room: The amazing rise and scandalous fall of Enron. London: Penguin Books

McLean Parks, J. , R. C. and A. Carpenter Taylor (2010). Give & Take: Incentive Framing in Compensation Contracts. Retrieved from: http://www.1888pressrelease.com/olin-award-winning-research-examines-compensation-and-fraudu-pr-216096.html

McIlvaine, A.R. (2003) Retooling HR .*HR Executive of the Year Dennis Donovan is helping Home Depot better manage its enormous size while preparing for an increasingly competitive environment.* 10/3/03. Retrieved from: http://www.hrexecutive.com/HRE/story.jsp?storyId=4222054

Mider, Z (2008) Nationwide CEO to Get $24 Million as Customers Pay (Update2) . Bloomberg.com, Retrieved from: http://www.bloomberg.com/apps/news?pid=20601087&sid=asCQzPSMMM_g&refer=home

Mintzberg, H (2004) Managers Not MBA's: A Hard Look at the Soft Practice of Managing and Management Development CA: Berrett-Koehler.

Mintzberg, H. (1975). The Manager's Job Folklore and Fact. Harvard Business Review, July-August.

Mintzberg, H. (1989) Mintzberg on Management. New York: Free Press.

Mishel, L. (2006). CEO to worker pay imbalance grows. Economic Policy Institute, June 21.

Mishra, P. (2009) JPMorgan Chase to Increase India Outsourcing 25% Business Week India. Retrieved from: http://www.businessweek.com/print/globalbiz/content/mar2009/gb2009039_431274.htm

Mishra. C. (2011) Excessive CEO stock compensation steals money from shareholders, doesn't align their interests. Sun Sentinel. Retreived 4/22/11 from: http://www.sun-sentinel.com/news/opinion/fl-cmcol-ceo-pay-stock-options-mishra20110421,0,2654825.story

Mitchell, T, George-Falvy, J. & Crandall, S.R. (1993). Business students justifications of exceptionally high salaries, Group and Organizational Management, 18, 500-521

Moore, B. (2011) Outsourcing the law to India. Retrieved June 14, 2011 from: http://www.pbs.org/wnet/need-to-know/voices/outsourcing-the-law-to-india/9803/

Morgan, G. (1988) Images of organization. CA: Sage

Morgenson, G. (2008). How Big a Payday for the Pay Consultants? New York Times, June 22, 2008, Sunday Business. P.1

Morgenson, G. (2008a) If the Pay Fix Is in, Good Luck Finding It. New York Times, September 7, 2008, Sunday Business. P.1..

Morgenson, G. (2009b). Gimme Back Your Paycheck. New York Times. February 22, 2009. Sunday Business. Page 1.

Morgenson, G. (2009a). What Iceberg Just glide to the Next Boardroom. New York Times. 12/16/09. Retrieved from: http://www.nytimes.com/2009/12/27/business/economy/27gret.html?_r=1

Morgenson, G. (2011). Moving the Goal Posts on Pay. NY Times. Sunday Business. Page 1.

Montano, A. (2011) States Move to Limit Spending on For-Profit Colleges While Tightening Oversight. Retrieved July 16, from: http://chronicle.com/article/States-Move-to-Limit-Spending/128241/

Mowday, R.T. Equity theory predictions of behaviour. In: Motivation and Leadership at Work 6th ed. Eds: R.M Steers, L.W. Porter and G.A.Bigley. 53-72

Mutter, A. (2008), Newspaper shares -35% CEO pay -11%. Retrieved from: newsosaur.blogspot.com/2008/05/newspaper-shares-35-ceo-pay-11.html - 32k –

Murphy, K.J. and Sandino, T. (2008). Executive Pay and 'Independent' Compensation Consultants . Retrieved from: http://papers.ssrn.com/sol3/papers.cfm?abstract_id=1148991

Murphy, M. (2011) New OfficeMax CEO Got Modest 2010 Salary, Large Stock Awards. Dow Jones, Retrieved March 4, 2011 from:

http://www.automatedtrader.net/real-time-dow-jones/50893/new-officemax-ceo-got-modest-2010-salary--large-stock-awards

McIntyre, D.A. (2011) American Executives get the Pay Raises They Deserve. Retrieved March 18, 2011 from: http://247wallst.com/2011/03/18/america-executives-get-the-pay-raise-they-deserve/

National Center for Educational Statistics (2009) Retrieved from:http://nces.ed.gov/fastfacts/display.asp?id=80

Neidhart, E. (2005) Reengineering. Retrieved from **http://edweb.sdsu.edu/people/ARossett/pie/Interventions/reengineering_2.htm**

Neuman, J. H., & Baron, R. A. (1998). Workplace violence and workplace aggression: Evidence concerning specific forms, potential causes, and preferred targets. Journal of Management, 24, 391-419.

Neuman,W. (2011) Price of tomatoes has a lot to do with these thefts. Retrieved from: http://www.nytimes.com/2011/04/15/business/15bandits.html?_r=2&hp

New York Times (2008). All Told, the Price Tag for Citigroup's New Chief is $216 Million, Eric Dash, 3/14/08, C4.

New York Times (2008). Ford to cut white collar jobs. Section C, Page 5. June 6, 2008.

New York Times (2008a) General Motors is Expected to Announce More Cuts July 15, 2008, C1

New York Times (2008b) For Executives Pay is Good But Time is Short., Sunday Business, Page 2, 8/10/2008.

Nijhawan, A. (2011) Run the UC as a university, not a corporation: To improve as an educational system, UC should focus more on students and less on executives. Retrieved 1/31/2011 from: http://www.dailybruin.com/index.php/article/2011/01/run_the_uc_as_a_university_not_a_corporation

Nocera, J. (2009) First Lets Fix The Bonuses, New York Times, February, 21, 2009. Business Day B1.

Nunberg, H. (1934). The Feeling of Guilt. Psychoanalytic Quarterly., 3:589-604.

Oliva. D.,(2009) Bonus culture called destructive: Beyond repair. SPON, Dec 03 2009 Retreived from: http://www.thestar.com/business/article/733856--bonus-culture-called-des...

Olive, D. (2011) Widening income gap hurts us all Retrieved 7/23/11 from: http://www.thestar.com/business/article/1029399--olive-widening-income-gap-hurts-us-all

Olsen, D, (2010) MBA course offered through Facebook – for free. Retrieved 29 October 2010 from: http://www.dynamicbusiness.com.au/articles/articles-hr-and-staff/facebook-free-mba-courses-2164.html

Onaran, Y., (2006). Bonus pay for Wall Street big 5 surges, Bloomberg News.

Onaran, Y., (2007). Lehman's Fuld Gets $35 Million in 2007 Stock Award (Update1) December 11, 2007 Bloomberg News. Retrieved from: http://www.bloomberg.com/apps/news?pid=newsarchive&sid=aTOtapLMUPL0&refer=us

Onaran, Y. and Helyar, J. (2008). Fuld Sought Buffett Offer He Refused as Lehman Sank (Update1). Bloomberg. Com, November 24, 2008.

Retrieved from: http://www.bloomberg.com/apps/news?pid=20601109&refer=home&sid=aZ1syPZH.RzY#

O'Reilly, C.A., B.G. Main, and G.S. Crystal. 1988. CEO Compensation as Tournament and Social Comparison: A Tale of Two Theories. Administrative Science Quarterly. 33: 257-274.

Ouchi, W. G. 1981. How American business can meet the Japanese challenge. Reading,MA: Addison-Wesley.

Padnani, A. (2009) Rate hike jolts Con Ed customers :Second increase in a year comes as the CEO enjoys a significant pay hike. Staten Iskand Advance. Thursday, April 23, 2009 Retreived from: http://www.silive.com/news/advance/index.ssf?/base/news/1240488934304000.xml&coll=1

Palmatier, R.A. and Ray, H.L. (1989).Sports Talk: A Dictionary of Sports Metaphors. Ct.: Greenwood Press

Parramore, L. (2010) The Upside: A Better Way for B-Schools. Retrieved April 22, 2010 from: http://www.recessionwire.com/2010/04/22/the-upside-a-better-way-for-b-schools/

Partridge, J. and Hoffman, A. (2008) "China deal sends Potash soaring" *Globe and Mail*, Toronto, 17 April 2008.

Pascal, A. M. (2001), "Tidying Up at Home Depot," *Business Week*, November, p. 102.

Pathak , K. (2011) ISB to start doctoral programme. Business Standard. Retrieved, January 31, 2011from:http://www.business-standard.com/india/news/isb-to-start-doctoral-programme/423455/

Paton, J. (2008). The executive perks? Gas, greens, planes and ski lessons. Rocky Mountain News, June 6, 2008.

Pellet, J., (2001), Mr. Fix-It Steps In, *Chief Executive*, October, pp. 44–47.

Perez, E. (2011) For-profit college firm to pay $5M to ex-CEO. Retrieved 12/6/11 from: http://www.signonsandiego.com/news/2011/dec/05/for-profit-college-firm-to-pay-5m-to-ex-ceo/

Perrone, M. (2011) J&J raises executive's salary, but cuts bonus. Retrieved 2/27/11 from: http://www.sunherald.com/2011/02/25/2895316/jj-raises-executives-salary-but.html#ixzz1F5zuIiL7

Personnel Today (2005) Home Improvement. HR Australia. Retrieved from: http://www.humanresourcesmagazine.com.au/articles/49/0C030049.asp?Type=60&Category=875

Peters, T.J. & Waterman, R.H. 1982. In Search of Excellence. New York: Harper & Row.

Peters, T. 1992. Liberation Management. New York: Fawcet Columbine.

Peterson, L. (2010) If there were more female executives, we would have a different business world. 2/5/10 retrieved from: http://jezebel.com/5464950/if-there-were-more-female-executives-we-would-have-a-different-business-world

Peterson, P.G. (2009) Why I'm giving away $1 billion. Retrieved from: http://www.newsweek.com/2009/05/29/why-i-m-giving-away-1-billion.html#

Perez-Pena, R. (2009). Gannett Plans to Furlough Employees. 1/15/09, New York Times, Business Section, B12.

Pfau, B, and Kay, I (2002) Does 360-degree feedback negatively affect company performance? Studies show that 360-degree feedback may do more harm than good. What's the problem? - Performance

Management - Statistical Data Included. HR Magazine, June. Retrieved from: http://findarticles.com/p/articles/mi_m3495/is_6_47/ai_87461017/pg_1?tag=artBody;col1

Pfeffer, J. and Fong C.T. (2002). The End of Business Schools? Less Success Than Meets the Eye. *Academy of Management Learning & Education*, Volume 1, Number 1, September 2002

Philips, D. (2008) No Reforms in CEO Pay at General Mills. Retrieved from: http://blogs.bnet.com/secdocuments/

Piekara, E. (2008). Culture of Greed. 9/23/08 Retrieved from: http://theulot.wordpress.com/

Piers, P.O. & Singer, M.B. (1952). Shame and Guilt. Springfield, Ill.: Thomas.

Pittsburgh Business Times (2008). Highmark Blue Cross merger would bring pay raises for some company execs.

8/13/2008

Pizzigati, S. & Anderson. S. (2008). Workers need added clout to close the pay gap with CEOs. Monday, September 01, 2008, Star-ledger Perspective. Nj.com. Retrieved from: http://www.nj.com/opinion/ledger/perspective/index.ssf?/base/news-1/1220243752111960.xml&coll=1

Pollack, A. (2008). Genentech to Pay Retention Bonuses

Published: August 21, 2008 New York Times, Business.

Pooley, E. and Revzin, P. (2011) World Feeding Itself Spurs Search for Answers. Retrieved from: http://www.bloomberg.com/news/2011-02-17/world-feeding-itself-spurs-search-for-answers-eric-pooley-and-phil-revzin.html

Post, J.M. (1993). Current concepts of the narcissistic personality: implications for political psychology. Political Psychology, 14, 1, 99-121.

Pressley. J. (2010) Fuld's Lehman 'Peddled Junk,' Betrayed Firm's Founders. September 1, Retrieved: http://www.bloomberg.com/news/2010-09-01/fuld-s-lehman-peddled-junk-betrayed-founders-principles-book-review.html

Quinn, C. (2011) Beazer's fired CEO gets multi-million dollar payday. Retrieved 6/15/11 from: http://www.ajc.com/business/beazers-fired-ceo-gets-977828.html?printArticle=y

Read. M. (2009) AmEx CEO Kenneth I. Chenault declines 2008 bonus. AP, 3/11/09. Retrieved from: http://www.google.com/hostednews/ap/article/ALeqM5hFZsXqZID_HWW1qRLHBbQat_IGYQD96RF8RO0

Real, T. (1999). I Don't Want To Talk About It. N.Y.: Simon and Schuster.

Rennie, C, (2006). Layoffs and CEO Compensation, Daily Headlines, Oct. 30. Retrieved from: http://dailyheadlines.uark.edu/9365.htm

Reich, A. (1960). Pathological forms of self-esteem regulation. Psychoanalytic Study of The Child, 15, 215-231.

Reich, W. (1928). On character analysis. In : R. Fliess (Ed.), The Psychoanalytic Reader. (Pages 121-147). New York: International University Press.

Reider, N. 1953. A type of transference to an institution. Bulletin of the Menninger Clinic, 7, 58-63.

Reider, N. 1957. Transference Psychosis. Journal of Hillside Hospital, 6, 131-149.

Reiss, S. (2010) BP's Cheating not about greed. June 11, 2010, Retrieved from: http://www.psychologytoday.com/blog/who-we-are/201006/bps-cheating-not-about-greed

Robertson, J. (2008). Sun Microsystems CEO gets $11M 2008 pay package. Associated Press. September 24, 2008. Retrieved from: http://ap.google.com/article/ALeqM5gpoU-NOX6RIINqO1hd-JTk6j9Bi5wD93DCTU00

Romzek, B. 1989. Personal consequences of employee commitment. Academy of Management Review, 32, 649- 661.

Root, J. (2009) Higher tuition, higher pay for top UT execs. Associated Press Feb. 14, 2009, 8:27AM Retrieved from: http://www.chron.com/disp/story.mpl/ap/tx/6263541.html

Rothstein, A. 1980. The narcissistic pursuit of perfection. New York: International University Press.

Riesman, D. Glazer, D, and Denney, R. (1950). The lonely crowd. New Haven: Ct., Yale University Press

Ring, N. H. (2001, July 19) American Express to cut 5,000 more jobs. American Banker, (166) 138. Retrieved February 1, 2004 from RDS Business & Industry Database.

Robertson, J. (2007). Associated Press, 3/27/07 Retrieved 3/28 from Swopblogger. Retrieved from: http://sfgate.com/cgi-bin/article.cgi?f=/n/a/2007/03/27/financial/f095731D17.DTL

Robertson, J. (2009) New York Times CEO got $4.4M package in 2008. AP 3/17/09 Business Week

Rogers (2006). Pink Slip Retrieved from: http://pinkslipblog.blogspot.com/2006/09/we-regret-to-inform.html

Rosales, C. (2010) UT tuition hike necessary, committee says. Retrieved 1/20/10 from: http://www.statesman.com/news/local/ut-tuition-hike-necessary-committee-says-188259.html

Rosenfeld, A. and Wise, N. (2000). The over-Scheduled Child: Avoiding the Hyper Parenting Trap. St. Martin, NY

Rummell, N., (2008). CEO wallets not dented by class-action suits, study finds Compensation tends to go up after litigation, the Corporate Library says; pay policies not reviewed either. Financial Week, 8/20/08.

Sacks, H. (1996). The NY Times, Sunday, 10/27/1996, Connecticut Section. Retrieved from: http://www.ctvip.org/web2b.html

Sambides, N. (2010). Fraser execs got bonuses as company sought bankruptcy. 2/16/10. Retrieved from: http://www.bangordailynews.com/detail/136976.html

Sampels, S. (2011) GE CEO Jeffrey Immelt, The Head Of Obama's Jobs Council, Is Moving Jobs And Economic Infrastructure To China At A Bliste Retrieved 8/1/11 from: http://www.opednews.com/Quicklink/GE-CEO-Jeffrey-Immelt-The-in-General_News-110730-890.html

Sander. L. (2010) Performance Pay?, Chronicle of Higher Education, June 30, 2010. Retrieved from: https://chronicle.com/blogPost/Performance-Pay-/25233/

Sander, L. (2011) 22 Elite College Sports Programs Turned a Profit in 2010, but Gaps Remain, NCAA Reports Says. Retrieved 6/15/11 from: http://chronicle.com/article/22-Elite-College-Sports/127921/?sid=at&utm_source=at&utm_medium=en

Sander, L. & Fuller, A. (2011) In Athletics, Ambitions Compete With Costs:Median budget deficit at less-elite programs tops $9-million. Retrieved 6/26/11 from: http://chronicle.com/article/In-Athletics-Ambitions/128033/?sid=at&utm_source=at&utm_medium=en

Sanders, P. (2009). Disney CEO Receives $13.9 Million Bonus for 2008. Wall Street Journal. 1/16/09. Retrieved from: http://online.wsj.com/article/SB123214722152391805.html

Sanford, J. (2006). Canadian Business Online. April 3

Satow, J. (2009) Ceo Bonus Pay Rises Despite Poor Performance. Wall Street Journal, 3/18/09

Saulny, S. and Brown, R. (2009).. On a Furlough, but Never Leaving the Cubicle. New York Times , June 15, P.1

Scelfo, J. (2007) Men and Depression: Facing darkness Newsweek 2/26/07

Schultz, E. and Francis, T. (2008) Corporations "STEAL" Workers' Pensions To Fund CEO Pensions. Wall Street Journal, August 5, 2008.

Schnurman, M. (2009) Chesapeake CEO is a winner either way Retreived from: http://www.star-telegram.com/business/story/1338868.html

Schuetze, C. (2011) Women Gaining on Men in M.B.A. Aspirations THE INTERNATIONAL HERALD TRIBUNE. Retrieved: February 27, 2011 from:http://www.nytimes.com/2011/02/28/education/28educBriefs.html?_r=1

Schurr, S. (2002) The Good CEO: Endangered but Not Extinct. 10/15/02. Retrieved from: http://www.thestreet.com/print/story/10047126.html

Schwartz, H. S. (1990). Narcissistic process and corporate decay: The theory of the organizational ideal. N.Y.: NYU Press.

Sellers, P. (2001), Exit the Builder, Enter the Repairman: Home Depot's Arthur Blank Is Out. New CEO Bob Nardelli Is In. His Job: To Tackle the Company's Renovation after Two Decades of Nonstop Expansion, *Fortune*, March 19, 2001, pp. 86–88.

Sellers, P.(2002), Something to Prove: Bob Nardelli Was Stunned When Jack Welch Told Him He'd Never Run GE. 'I Want an Autopsy!,' He Demanded. *Fortune*, June 24, 2002, pp. 88–94.

Schockey, K. (2005), Management Hack Two Retrieved from: http://www.oreillynet.com/onlamp/blog/2005/01/management_hack_2_understandin.html

Shefelman, D. (2008). Personal communication

Sheridan, J. H. (1997, June 9) Going for Growth. Industry Week, 246 (11). Retrieved February 1, 2004 from RDS Business & Industry Database.

Shepardson, D. (2007) Welch: he will bring in the right people. Car and Driver. August 7, 2007. Retrieved from: http://74.125.45.132/search?q=cache:itVjFpJ7nTEJ:www.waycar.net/news/welch-he-will-bring-the-right-people-in.html+raymond+nardelli+bobs+father&hl=en&ct=clnk&cd=16&gl=us&client=firefox-a

Shore, S. (2011) Pay Package Totals $8.3M for US Steel's CEO. US Steel CEO earns $8.3M in 2010 total compensation after stock awards, full salary reinstated Retrieved 3/21/11 from: http://abcnews.go.com/Business/wireStory?id=13194890

Sievers, B. (1990) Zombies or people- What is the product of work? In B.A. Turner (Ed.). Organizational Symbolism (pp. 83-94). New York: de Gruyter.

Simeon, D., & Abugel, J. (2006). Feeling Unreal : Depersonalization Disorder and the Loss of the Self. NY: Oxford University Press.

Sinclair, S. and Waldie, P. (2008) "U.S. food producers, speculators square off", *Globe and Mail*, Toronto, 23 April 2008,

Sinclair, S. and Waldie, P. (2008a) "Why grocery prices are set to soar", *Globe and Mail*, Toronto, 24 April 2008a,

Singer, S., (2007). GE CEO made more than 15 million in 2006. Lancaster Online. Feb. 27. Also in Reuters, 2007, General Electric Co., Fortune, Feb., 2007

Smith, J. (2008 a). Top Paid Executives. Baltimore Sun. 8/17/08. Retrieved from: http://www.baltimoresun.com/business/bal-te.bz.compensation17aug17,0,7516253.story?page=1

Smith, R. (2008). Rewarding Performance Management. August 8, 2008. Retrieved from: http://www.callcentercafe.com/2008/08/08/rewarding-performance-management/

Snyder, M. (2010) 16 Shocking Facts About Student Debt And The Great College Education Scam. Business Insider. Retrieved from: http://www.businessinsider.com/facts-about-student-loan-debt-2010-12##ixzz19i75eZhV

Society for HR Managers (2007) Job Satisfaction Survey at http://www.shrm.org/surveys/

Solomon, H.M. (2004). Self creation and the limitless void of dissociation: the 'as if' personality. Journal of Analytical Psychology, 49, 635-656.

Sonnefeld, J. (2007) Bob Nardelli's comeback, or comeuppance? Atlanta Business Chronicle, 2/2/07 Retrieved from: http://www.bizjournals.com/atlanta/stories/2007/02/05/editorial3.html

Spencer, M. (2011) Kennametal CEO pay up. Retrieved from: http://www.bizjournals.com/pittsburgh/news/2011/09/13/kennametal-ceo-pay-up-company-plans.htm

Spolsky, J. (2000). Incentive Pay Considered Harmful. Monday, April 03, 2000. Retrieved from: http://www.joelonsoftware.com/articles/fog0000000070.html

Srakocic, K. (2011) U.S. Steel's Surma earned as much in two hours as pensioner did the entire year. Retreived 4/18/11 from: http://www.thespec.com/news/business/article/518182--ceo-pay-packages-companies-aren-t-in-the-business-of-morality

Staton, T. 2009. Roche CEO pay rises as profits fall, Fierce Pharma. February 5, 2009 . Retrieved from: http://www.fiercepharma.com/story/roche-ceo-pay-rises-profits-fall/2009-02-05

Stone, L. (2006), The O'Reilly Emerging Media Technology Conference| Download MP3 | Recorded Address Recorded 7/6/06

Story, L. (2008). As Wall Street Stumbles.... New York Times. Business Day C1, 8/12/08.

Story., L. (2010) Income Inequality and the Financial Crisis. 8/21/2010 NY Times Retrieved from: http://www.nytimes.com/2010/08/22/weekinreview/22story.html?_r=1

Stein, M. (2007). Toxicity and the Unconscious Experience of Body at the Employee-Customer Interface. Organizational Studies, 28, 1223.

Steinberg, D. (2008), Pay and performance: The view from the top: The Philadelphia area outpaced the nation in CEO raises last year. Here's a look at companies' pay criteria. Thursday, Jun. 26, 2008, THE INQUIRER

Stieker, A. (2008) GM shareholders complain about high executive pay. Motor Trend, June 4. Retrieved from: http://wot.motortrend.com/6254841/industry-news/gm-shareholders-complain-about-high-executive-pay/index.html

Stillman, J. (2011) Is College a Bad Deal? More Than Half of Americans Say Yes. Retrieved 5/18/11 from: http://www.bnet.com/blog/entry-level/is-college-a-bad-deal-more-than-half-of-americans-say-yes/4768

Strauss, G. (2010) Executives keep health perks while workers' benefits are cut. USA Today. Retrieved from: http://www.usatoday.com/news/washington/2010-12-10-rw_ceohealthplan10_ST_N.htm

Sullivan, H.S. (1931). Socio-psychiatric research. American Journal of Psychiatry, 87, 972-991

Symonds, M. (2010) Business Schools Beware: Gen Y is at the Door. 1/21/10. Retrieved from: http://www.businessweek.com/bschools/content/jan2010/bs20100121_624849.htm

Taibbi, M. (2010) The Great American Bubble Machine, April. Rolling Stone.

Taylor, F.W. (1911). Principles of Scientific Management. New York: Harper Row

Taylor, M.C. (2010) Academic Bankruptcy. Published: August 14, 2010 retrieved from: http://www.nytimes.com/2010/08/15/opinion/15taylor.html

Tomich, J. (2008) Stock sagging, Charter CEO Smit gets a raise. St. Louis Post-Dispatch, 9/30/08. Retrieved from: http://www.stltoday.com/blogzone/business-news/biz-buzz/2008/09/stock-sagging-charter-ceo-smit-gets-a-raise/

Thomas, R. (2010) So Long and Farewell, Lon – You're Simply Part of the CEO Trend. Retrieved from:http://www.tlnt.com/2010/07/28/so-long-and-farewell-lon-youre-simply-part-of-the-ceo-trend/

Thomas, K. (2011) Facing Title IX pressure, Cal May Restore the Teams it Cut. NY Times, B4, 2/9/11

Thomas, K. (2011a) Fiesta Bowl's Spending Attracts Scrutiny. New York Times. B11, 3/30/11.

Thomson Financial News (2008). US home foreclosures climb again in August. 9/12.08, Retrieved from: http://www.forbes.com/afxnewslimited/feeds/afx/2008/09/12/afx5416431.html

Tibman. J. (2009). The murder of lehman brothers: An insiders look at the global meltdown. NY: Brick Tower Press.

Tierney, J. (2011) For the Executive with Everything, a $230,000 Dog to Protect It. New York Times, page 1, June 12, 2011.

Times of London (2008) Exposed: Dick Fuld, the man who brought the world to its knees. December 14. Retreived from: http://business.timesonline.co.uk/tol/business/industry_sectors/banking_and_finance/article5336179.ece

Timmons, H. (2008). ...India's Role is Growing. New York Times, Business Day, C1, 8/12/08.

Timmons, H. (2010). Due Diligence From Afar. New York Times, Business Day, B1, 8/5/10

Tong, V. (2008) CEO Richard Fuld to Leave Lehman USA Today. 11/5/08. Retrieved from: http://www.usatoday.com/money/economy/2008-11-05-3175882139_x.htm

Tracer, Z. (2010). Business school applications sputter. 8/12/10 Retrieved from: http://www.businessweek.com/bschools/content/aug2010/bs20100812_392560.htm

Tse, T.M. (2009) At rescued banks, perks keep rolling. BOSSES BENEFIT AFTER BAILOUT, Washington Post, 10/20/09

Tyler, I. (2007) From 'The Me Decade' to 'The Me Millennium' The cultural history of narcissism. *International Journal of Cultural Studies, vol. 10, no.3, 343-363.*

Tuckett, D. and Taffler, R. (2008). Phantastic objects and the financial market's sense of reality: A psychoanalytic contribution to the understanding of stock market instability.

The International Journal of Psychoanalysis, Volume 89 Issue 2 Page 389-412, April 2008

Turner, J. (2009) Gannett CEO gives up $18,690, still has $968.040 in base salary coming, plus bonus, benefits. 1/14/09 Retrieved from: http://rturner229.blogspot.com/2009/01/gannett-ceo-gives-up-18690-still-has.html

Turkel, T. (2009) FairPoint CEO's base pay rises 30 percent. Portland Press Herald, May 5, 2009, Retrieved from: http://pressherald.mainetoday.com/story.php?id=254570&ac=PHbiz

Uchitelle, L., (2006), The disposable American: layoffs and their consequences. NY:Knopf

UN Report (2008) FOOD AND AGRICULTURE ORGANIZATION OF THE UNITED NATIONS Current world fertilizer trends and outlook to 2011/12 Rome, 2008 ftp://ftp.fao.org/agl/agll/docs/cwfto11.pdf

Upton, J. and Wieberg. S., (2006) Contracts for college coaches cover more than salaries

USA TODAY

U.S. Department of Commerce (1996) "Population Projections of the United States by Age, Sex, Race, and Hispanic Origin: 1995-2050" (P25-1130), 3/14/96

Utt, R.D. (2005), Time to Reform Fannie Mae and Freddie Mac, June 20,2005, Retrieved from: http://www.heritage.org/Research/GovernmentReform/bg1861.cfm

Van Gelder, T. (2003). Teaching critical thinking. College Teacher, 45, 1 Retrieved from: http://www.philosophy.unimelb.edu.au/reason/papers/Teaching_CT_Lessons.pdf

Van Valkenburg M. (2011) At Harvard Business School, Nitin Nohria Pushes Reforms on a Bankrupt Culture. Published 7/18/11 on *The Nation* (http://www.thenation.com)

Vellequette, L. (2011) Ads slam Cedar Fair executive's pay Investment fund's letter cites compensation, return on stock. Toledo Blade. Retrieved from: http://toledoblade.com/article/20101231/BUSINESS03/101239963/-1/BUSINESS06

Verneulen, F. (2008) Pay inequality – good or bad for team performance. October, 21, 2008. Retrieved from:http://freekvermeulen.blogspot.com/2008/10/pay-inequality-good-or-bad-for-team.html

Villanova, P, Bernardin, H.J., Dahmus, S.A. & Sims, R.L. (1993) Rater leniency and performance appraisal discomfort. Educational and Psychological Measurement, 53(3): 879-799.

Vlasic, B. (2008), GM Cuts Jobs as Part of a Production Curb. N.Y. Times, C4, July 29, 2008.

Vuong, A. (2011) Amid job cuts, Qwest CEO receives 11 percent pay bump. *The Denver Post.* Retrieved: 03/25/2011 from: http://www.denverpost.com/breakingnews/ci_17700264

Wachtel, P. (2003), Full Pockets, Empty Lives: A Psychoanalytic exploration of the contemporary culture of greed. American Journal of Psychoanalysis, 63, 2, 103-122

Wallace, H.M., Baumeister R.F. (2002). The Performance of Narcissists Rises and Falls With Perceived Opportunity for Glory. Journal of Personality and Social Psychology, 82, 5, 819-834. Wallack, T. (2010) Executive Share. Boston .com, 10/2/10 Retrieved from: http://www.boston.com/business/articles/2010/10/03/executive_share/?page=2

Walsh, T and Higgins, T. (2008). Chrysler leaders get millions: Automaker defends payouts amid looming bailout talks. Free Press Business Writers • November 13, 2008. Retrieved from: http://www.freep.com/article/20081113/BUSINESS01/311130002/1002/BUSINESS

Walsh, M.W. (2008) With Fed's $85 Billion Loan, A.I.G. Starts to Calculate a Measured Sell-Off. September 17, 2008. New York Times.

Walsh, M.W. (2011) Sanford Sigoloff, 80, Expert at Turnarounds. February, 25, 2011 New York Times, B14.

Welch, J. (2001). Jack: Straight from the Gut. NY: Warner Business Books.

Ward. V. (2010) Lehman's Desperate Housewives. April 2010. Retrieved from: http://www.vanityfair.com/business/features/2010/04/lehman-wives-201004?currentPage=all

Ward. V. (2010) The Devils Casino. NY: Wiley

Weiss, M. (2011) J. Crew Board Ties to TPG, CEO Drexler May Pose Conflicts in Second Buyout Retrieved 1/13/11 from: http://www.bloomberg.com/news/2011-01-13/j-crew-board-ties-to-tpg-ceo-drexler-may-pose-conflicts-in-second-buyout.html

Weinstein, N.O. Z (1980). Unrealistic optimism about susceptibility to health problems, Journal of Behavioral Medicine, 10, 5, 481-500

Wells, H. (2010) 'No Man can be Worth $1,000,000 a Year': The Fight Over Executive Compensation in 1930s America. *University of Richmond Law Review, Vol. 44, p. 689, January 2010* *Temple University Legal Studies Research Paper No. 2009-36*

Wessel, D. (2011) Big US Firms Shifting Hiring Abroad. Wall Street Journal. Retreived 4/21/11 from: http://online.wsj.com/article/SB10001424052748704821704576270783611823972.html

Wharton, (2007). CEO Richard Fuld on Lehman Brothers' Evolution from Internal Turmoil to Teamwork. Published: January 10, 2007 in Knowledge@Wharton http://knowledge.wharton.upenn.edu/article.cfm?articleid=1631 Recorded Jan. 10, 2007. Wharton School of Business. CD.

White, B. (2009). What Red Ink? Wall St. Paid Hefty Bonuses. New York Times, January, 29, 2009. P. 1.

Whyte, W.H. (1956). The Organizational Man. N.Y.: Doubleday.

Wiles, J.G. (2008). Former Sovereign Exec May Get Third Golden Parachute In Three Years, The Bulletin. 10/1/08. Retrieved from: http://

www.thebulletin.us/site/printerFriendly.cfm?brd=2737&dept_id=576361&newsid=20144777

Wilmott, P. (2008). For Wall Street, Greed Wasn't Good Enough. Op-Ed, New York Times, 9/18/08.

Winer, L. (2008) Chapter 7. HBS Case Method Deprives Students Of An Authentic Learning Experience Retrieved from: http://mbatoolbox.org/stories/storyReader$11

Winik, L (2008) Are College Coaches Overpaid. Parade Magazine, 7/20/08. Retrieved from: http://www.parade.com/articles/editions/2008/edition_07-20-2008/Intelligence_Report

Winnicott, D.W. 1958. Through pediatrics to psychoanalysis. London: Hogarth Press.

Winnicott, D.W. 1965. Ego distortions in terms of true and false self. In D.W. Winnicott (Ed.) Maturational processes and the facilitating environment (pp.140- 154). New York: International Universities Press.

Winnicott, D. W. (1960). "Ego Distortion in Terms of True and False Self," In: The Maturational Process and the Facilitating Environment: Studies in the Theory of Emotional Development. New York: International UP Inc., 1965, pp. 140-152

Winnicott, D.W. (1965) The maturational process and the facilitating environment. London: Hogarth

Witzel, M. (2000), How to get an MBA. U.K.:Routledge Press.

Wolberg, A. 1975. The leader and society. In Z. Liff (ed.), The Leader in the Group (pp.247-250). New York: Aronson

Wolfe T (1987). The bonfire of the vanities. *London: Picador.*

Worth, K. (2011), PG&E shareholders, not customers, to pay ex-CEO's $35M severance. Retreived 4/25/11 from: http://www.sfexaminer.com/local/bay-area/2011/04/pge-shareholders-pay-ex-ceo-s-35-million

Willers, Rob (2007) The Airline Hub Retrieved 3/28/07 from http://www.theairlinehub.com/2007/03/unions at united airlines are.html

Wright, F.; O'Leary, J. and Balkin, J. (1989). Shame, Guilt, Narcissism and Depression. Psychoanalytic Psychology, 6:217-230

Wright, W. (2010) The Inconvenient True about Bank Bonuses. Financial News. Retrieved from: http://www.efinancialnews.com/story/2010-12-13/inconvenient-truth-bank-bonuses

Wu, J. (2009). Health Insurance Executives Get Big Raises. WCVBTV/DT. Retrieved from: http://www.thebostonchannel.com/news/18449413/detail.html

Yao, D. (2007). Under New Deal, Comcast Founder Ralph Roberts' Salary Will Go to Beneficiaries After Death. AP News. Dec 29.

Young. L. (2007). Soft Landing for CEOs. Business Week 11/15/07

Zalesnik, A. (1977). May-June. Managers and Leaders: Are They Different? Harvard Business Review. 47-60

Zimbalist, A. (2010) Executive Briefing. Dallas News 9/26/10 Retrieved from: http://www.dallasnews.com/sharedcontent/dws/bus/stories/DN-harvard_26bus.ART.State.Edition1.249962b.html

Zimmerman, J.L. (2001). Can American Business Schools Survive? Retrieved from: http://www.olin.wustl.edu/faculty/macdonald/zimmerman.pdf

Ziobro, P. (2011) Procter & Gamble CEO to get $16.2 mln compensation. Retrieved from: http://www.marketwatch.com/story/procter-gamble-ceo-to-get-162-mln-compensation-2011-08-26

Key words: Psychoanalysis, CEO, psychodynamic, entitlement, depersonalization, narcissism, corporate greed, CEO compensation, CEO salary, wall street, business school, mba, performance review, executives, executive bonus, bottom line, corporate board, Executive salary, greed, CEO salary, layoffs, terminations, main street, tarp, government bailouts, golden boot, golden handshake, food shortage, Home Depot, Nardelli, executive compensation, Gen Y, ethics, money

www.ingramcontent.com/pod-product-compliance
Lightning Source LLC
Chambersburg PA
CBHW071147230426
43668CB00009B/867